THE PLAYS OF ERNST TOLLER

Contemporary Theatre Studies

A series of books edited by Franc Chamberlain, Nene College, UK

Volume 1
Playing the Market: Ten Years of the Market Theatre, Johannesburg, 1976–1986
Anne Fuchs

Volume 2
Theandric: Julian Beck's Last Notebooks
Edited by Erica Bilder, with notes by Judith Malina

Volume 3
Luigi Pirandello in the Theatre: A Documentary Record
Edited by Susan Bassnett and Jennifer Lorch

Volume 4
Who Calls the Shots on the New York Stages?
Kalina Stefanova-Peteva

Volume 5
Edward Bond Letters: Volume I
Selected and edited by Ian Stuart

Volume 6
Adolphe Appia: Artist and Visionary of the Modern Theatre
Richard C. Beacham

Volume 7
James Joyce and the Israelites and Dialogues in Exile
Seamus Finnegan

Volume 8
It's All Blarney.
Four Plays: Wild Grass, Mary Maginn, It's All Blarney, Comrade Brennan
Seamus Finnegan

Volume 9
Prince Tandi of Cumba or The New Menoza, by J. M. R. Lenz
Translated and edited by David Hill and Michael Butler, and a stage adaptation by Theresa Heskins

Please see back of this book for the other titles in the Contemporary Theatre Studies series.

THE PLAYS OF ERNST TOLLER

A REVALUATION

Cecil Davies

LONDON AND NEW YORK

First published 1996 by Harwood Academic Publishers

This edition published 2013 by Routledge
2 Park Square, Milton Park, Abingdon, Oxon OX14 4RN
711 Third Avenue, New York, NY 10017

Routledge is an imprint of the Taylor & Francis Group, an informa business

---

British Library Cataloguing in Publication Data
Davies, Cecil W.
Plays of Ernst Toller: Revaluation. –
(Contemporary Theatre Studies, ISSN
1049-6513; Vol. 10)
I. Title II. Series
832.912

ISBN 3-7186-5614-0 (hardback)
ISBN 3-7186-5615-9 (softback)

Cover design: Neppach's poster advertising Karl-Heinz Martin's production of *Die Wandlung*. Reproduced by kind permission of the Staatliche Museen zu Berlin, Kunstbibliothek, and the Bildarchiv Preußischer Kulturbesitz(bpk), Berlin.

CONTENTS

INTRODUCTION TO THE SERIES

Contemporary Theatre Studies is a book series of special interest to everyone involved in theatre. It consists of monographs on influential figures, studies of movements and ideas in theatre, as well as primary material consisting of theatre-related documents, performing editions of plays in English, and English translations of plays from various vital theatre traditions worldwide.

Franc Chamberlain

Portrait of Toller by Eugen Spiro, 1930.

LIST OF PLATES

(Between pp. 263–264)

ACKNOWLEDGEMENTS

This book could not have been written without the active help of many individuals and institutions. To all of these I wish to extend my thanks, and in particular to: Professor Dr Walter Huder and his staff at the archives and library of the Akademie der Künste, Berlin; Dr Noltenius and his staff at the Fritz-Hüser-Institut für deutsche und ausländische Arbeiterliteratur, Dortmund; Professor Wolfgang Frühwald, Institut für Deutsche Philologie, University of Munich (especially for his having let me have a tape-recording of Toller's voice); Dr Roswitha Flatz and her staff at the Theatermuseum des Instituts für Theaterwissenschaft der Universität Köln (Schloß Wahn); Dr Werner Volke, Margit Berger and the staff of the Schiller-Nationalmuseum Deutsches Literaturarchiv, Marbach am Neckar; Leela Meinertas at the Theatre Museum, Victoria and Albert Museum, London; the staff of the Central Reference Library, City of Manchester and the John Rylands University Library, Manchester (especially the Inter-Library Lending Department); to the staff of the Goethe Institut, Manchester, and especially to its Librarian, Jean Walker, for her unfailing help in obtaining books from Germany, her assistant Gabriele Reinsch who helped me to decipher Toller's *Sütterlinschrift*, and to Elke Dehmel from whom I have gained innumerable insights over the years into the nature of German Literature. I am particularly grateful to the Librarian of the University of Birmingham for allowing me to examine in Manchester that library's copy of the Second Edition of *Die Maschinestürmer*. My thanks are also due to the German Academic Exchange Service (DAAD) and to Inter Nationes for making possible some of my study-visits to Germany.

Among individuals who have helped me I must mention especially Gerda Redlich and Stephen Wardale, both of whom allowed me to tape-record their personal recollections of Toller, and Ian Hyslop, who kindly translated the Bandello *Novella* into English for me. I also received useful information from the late Lord (Fenner) Brockway and the late Professor Walther G. Oschilewski. The *New Statesman* kindly provided photocopies of contributions by Toller to the *New Statesman and Nation*, and the Religious Society of Friends let me have a photocopy of Toller's talk, *Masses and Man: the problem of non-violence and peace.*

Professor Kenneth Richards and Vivien Gardner of the Department of Drama, University of Manchester, have been most supportive throughout.

I am grateful to Edward Mendelson, Literary Executor of The Estate of W. H. Auden, for granting non-exclusive permission to reproduce the lyrics from *No More Peace* included in Appendix G. These lyrics are copyright by the Estate of W. H. Auden. I have been unable to trace the executor of Herbert Murrill, composer of the settings of the lyrics.

Eugen Spiro's portrait is reproduced by kind permission of Peter Spiro with the agreement of the Galerie von Abercron, Munich, and of the Schiller-Nationalmuseum, Marbach am Neckar, where it is Item 241 in the Catalogue *Das 20. Jahrhundert.*

The skeletons scene from Karl-Heinz Martin's production of *Die Wandlung* is reproduced by kind permission of the Deutsches Theatermuseum, Munich.

If I have omitted anyone, I hope they will forgive me. But I must add to this list my wife, Marian, who has cheerfully tolerated my absorption in this work during years when she had every right to expect me to be virtually free of academic study.

I

INTRODUCTION

INTRODUCTION

It is now over half a century since the death of Ernst Toller, and 1993 has seen the centenary of his birth (1). It is an appropriate time to attempt to assess afresh his stature as man and writer. The present book has the more limited objective of re-examining his achievement as a dramatist, though such a re-examination must of course be carried out against the background of his life, his political opinions and activities, and of his non-dramatic writings. In particular this study aims to show that Toller's works transcend many of the limitations which a too facile tendency to attach labels to them and to their author has imposed on critical judgements and evaluations.

In his lifetime Toller "was undoubtedly the best-known German dramatist of his generation" (2). At first his reputation depended almost as much upon his personal notoriety as a political prisoner as upon the quality of his writing for the theatre. As early as 1919 Rowohlt published a pamphlet by Stefan Großmann, written within a few days of Toller's trial, which not only defends Toller against his accusers, but uses *Die Wandlung,* his only play then written, as evidence of his character and motivation (3). Großmann thinks that the key words in the play are the italicised:

> *wartet bis zum Mittag.*
> *(wait till midday)* (4).

By midday in the play's final scene, when the members of the crowd realise their own basic humanity, the time for revolution is ripe. But in Munich that time never came:

> He had never urged the mob to actions for which he did not find them inwardly ripe. In the hour of apparent victory in Munich, when Leviné and Lewien were drunk with the most dangerous applause, the most bitter doubt came into his mind (5).

Großmann's argument indeed smacks of special pleading, but he was writing within the stream of contemporary events. For him *Die Wandlung* was primarily evidence — evidence not admitted in the trial — of its author's motivations and political aims.

Only three years later Toller was considered a sufficiently important dramatist to be included in a series of Theatre Guides (6). This little book, *Ernst Toller and his Works for the Stage*, by Fritz Droop, was the first actual book about Toller. From prison Toller contributed some — censored — autobiographical notes, and his letter to Landauer was also included. Droop, who considered that on the whole the current mode of disowning the inner experience of the war was as suspect as the enthusiastic rhapsodies in support of war which had inflamed everyone in 1914, wrote of *Die Wandlung*:

> But Toller's literary work is the confession of a man who struggled with himself in an impassioned fight, and who is leading us out of a dying century into a new age (7).

Droop also interpreted *Masse Mensch* in terms of Toller's political aims:

> His dream is the ideal anarchy which Dehmel's prophetic spirit promised us (8).

At the same time he perceived both plays' intrinsic depth. Of *Die Wandlung* he wrote:

> Toller's imagination is grounded in pain (9).

And of *Masse Mensch*:

> *Masse Mensch* is not one of those works which depend upon theatrical action. The drama is rooted entirely in thought, and it is difficult to indicate in a sketch of the content the profound ethos which gives it its impact (10).

Droop comments on *Die Maschinenstürmer* that it is not a propaganda piece (11) and that its message is that

> what is mechanical on earth must be subordinated to what is spiritual (12).

Droop was conscious of parallels between these plays and Toller's choral works and lyric poems (13); and he regarded *Die Rache des verhöhnten Liebhabers* as an exceptional breaking out from "the iron ring of his [Toller's] serious creativity" (14). *Hinkemann,* though he had seen it only in manuscript, he described as mature and moving — the most moving play to appear for several decades.

The work of this perceptive critic shows how early in his career as a dramatist Toller earned the high reputation that he retained until his death (15).

After the Second World War his celebrity suffered eclipse, especially in the light of Brecht's growing international reputation.

A doctoral thesis presented in the University of Iowa in 1940 by W.A. Willibrand, only a year after Toller's death, was the first comprehensive scholarly treatment of Toller (16). A condensation was published in 1945 (17). Willibrand's was a pioneering work written long before any detailed bibliographical research had been carried out and at a time when much material was totally inaccessible. Partly perhaps because of the limited material available, Willibrand's thesis as published is very clear and uncluttered. Inevitably some of his judgements can be seen now to be at fault, but taken as a whole the thesis was an auspicious foundation for post-war Toller scholarship.

However, it was not followed up for over a decade, and the next comprehensive studies were those of Martin Reso (1957) and Hans Marnette (1963) (18). Both these unpublished theses were in German, Reso's being the first broadly-based one in Toller's native language, limited, however, by the fact that some of the plays were not available to him. Marnette's thesis does not take productions into consideration. It is written from a strictly orthodox Marxist viewpoint, and opens:

> In its research our Marxist literary study originates from the needs of building up socialism in our Republic [viz. G.D.R.], and consequently directs its work in accordance with the recommendations of the leading force in this process, the German Communist Party (19).

In spite of the rigidity of the restricted approach, Marnette's thesis embodies a great deal of valuable research and many interesting insights.

Reso's thesis, though less dogmatically ideological than Marnette's, nevertheless approaches Toller from a broadly Marxist angle and sees him as a transitional writer between bourgeois and socialist literature. It is a work of keen intelligence based on wide knowledge and close research. Partly because of this, Reso's judgements are frequently better founded than those of Willibrand, with whom he often disagrees.

These two theses, particularly Reso's, exerted strong influence on subsequent work. This was in part due to their thoroughness and good scholarship, and in part to their comparative isolation between the work of Willibrand and the crucial work of John Spalek. A consequence of this has been that many students of Toller have repeated as objectively true, statements and judgements actually based on Marxist analysis and Communist ideology.

The turning-point in Toller studies came in the second half of the 1960s, primarily through the scholarship of John M. Spalek. In November 1966 Spalek published an important article, *Ernst Toller: the Need for a New Estimate* (20). This was based on Spalek' s own findings during the preparation, by then nearly complete, of his monumental bibliography, *Ernst Toller and his Critics* (21), which he published in 1968. This at once became, and still remains, an indispensable tool for all serious students of Toller. The 1966 article is in itself the germ of a "new estimate". From the enormous knowledge acquired in preparing the bibliography Spalek was in a position to survey all previous criticism, including that from both extremes of the political spectrum, and to suggest the lines along which a truer evaluation of the man and his works should be sought:

> . . . Toller's socialism was an ethical creed. He expressed it through his sympathy for the poor and the oppressed by identifying himself actively with the cause of the working class. His criticism of the capitalist system, quite radical during his early years, stemmed from the same source . . .
> . . . a man who, despite his participation in the revolution and his sharp criticism of the *status quo,* subscribes to the traditional values of humanistic culture . . .
> . . . not just a *Gefühlsmensch* . . .
> . . . a rational person able to judge himself and his environment objectively. On a number of occasions we see him as a person who is painfully aware of his limitations and skeptical about his achievements as a person and an artist . . . (22)

With Spalek's bibliography as groundwork and his seminal article as inspiration, Toller scholarship flourished for the next ten years, with ten or more major theses on various aspects of his work: his use of dramatic form, his prose, his political drama, his tragedy as a revolutionary, his position in the Weimar Republic, and many more.

A further and more popular impetus to renewed interest in Toller also came in 1968 with Tankred Dorst's play *Toller* (23). It is written with knowledge and sympathy. Dorst told the present writer he had been attracted to write on Toller because he felt an affinity with him (24).

Then, exactly ten years after the publication of the bibliography, Spalek and Frühwald brought out in 1978 Toller's *Gesammelte Werke* (25) in five volumes, followed by a companion volume, *Der Fall Toller*, in 1979. In the latter year there also appeared a comprehensive study of Toller by Malcolm Pittock in the series *Twayne's World Authors* (26). Even this book, however, did not wholly succeed in re-establishing Toller's position as a dramatist of major stature. In particular it still remained necessary to follow two lines of enquiry and to bring them together: to re-examine all the texts of the plays in a deeper historical perspective, and to re-create imaginatively their major stage productions. Fortunately there exists much primary and secondary material on these productions, as they have aroused critical and scholarly interest in themselves among students of theatre history. On the basis of these two lines of enquiry Toller's own work can be disentangled from that of his theatrical interpreters, and his independent qualities assessed anew.

In 1986 a major study of Toller's work by Richard Dove (27), had as its aims,

> to examine Toller's philosophy of revolutionary socialism and trace its development between 1917 and 1939, to place this development in its contemporary political context, and to examine the reflection of his political consciousness in his work (28).

Thus, while Dove in his very thoroughly researched thesis, often reaches conclusions in areas of common interest, which are in harmony with those of the present study, he does not attempt to see the plays in a deeper historical context or to examine in detail their principal stage productions.

In the following chapters each of Toller's plays is examined in its literary, theatrical, political and biographical contexts. Particular attention is paid to the historical position of each play in the traditions of German drama and indeed in the broader European traditions. Critical judgement of Toller's plays has been strongly influenced by their initial productions, especially those of Karl-Heinz Martin, Jürgen

Fehling and Erwin Piscator. These and other productions are examined in detail and an attempt made to reach evaluations of the plays which are not dependent upon these particular productions. It is argued that the great and lasting value of the plays resides fundamentally in Toller's language, an element too often neglected amidst the excitements of their theatrical and political aspects. A central chapter, placed between his plays written principally in verse and those wholly in prose, is devoted to Toller's use of language. In it his dramatic use of language is related to his non-dramatic, both in poetry and prose.

> Every author wants to push into his first work everything he knows, everything he has ever experienced. I did that too (29).

Thus Toller wrote in 1930 about *Die Wandlung*, and the study of the text reveals this to be true not only of what he called the private, lyrical elements (30), but also of his reading, even in boyhood, his awareness of cultural traditions, of German political theatre from Schiller onwards, of Judaeo-Christian religious mythology and its dramatic expression, of the influence upon him of modern left-wing thinkers like Landauer, and of German and Scandinavian dramatic literature from Goethe's *Faust* to Strindberg. In style the play is Expressionist, for, as Toller himself wrote, Expressionism was at that time an essential artistic form (31); nor was it, for him, merely a mode, it was an attempt to refashion the environment in its very essence, to change it and give it a juster, brighter face (32).

The tendency for *Die Wandlung* to be regarded as confessional rather than political was the result of the cuts and rearrangements made by Rudolf Leonhard in the text as produced by Karl-Heinz Martin. Brilliant though that production was in itself, it was in no way a definitive production of the play Toller wrote, but even so, contemporary critics realised that the vital element was speech — the speaking of Toller's language. At the same time critical opinion recognised that this play's production was momentous in the history of the theatre: it was seen as a turning point and as a new beginning. Both author and director had significant futures.

In his first play Toller revealed roots that reached back to the Middle Ages, but those of his second, *Masse Mensch*, reach even further — to Greek tragedy, while its central problem, the compatability or incompatability of non-violence and social revolution, has proved to be a major question of the twentieth century, with such figures as Mahatma Gandhi and Martin Luther King embodying one answer, and such as Augusto César Sandino and Nelson Mandela another.

This play's second production, by Jürgen Fehling, was the important one, and unlike Karl-Heinz Martin's production of *Die Wandlung,* this was totally in harmony with the author's text and intentions. It was also highly influential, and not only on later productions of *Masse Mensch.*

Die Maschinenstürmer is in a real sense "Shakespearean" in form and style, but at the same time it anticipates some of Brecht's methods and techniques, particularly that of juxtaposition or Montage: indeed it may fairly be classed as an Epic Drama in the Brechtian sense. The character of its first production, again by Karl-Heinz Martin, was primarily determined by the vastness of Reinhardt's Großes Schauspielhaus, which made a mass spectacle inevitable. Linguistic subtlety, finesse of characterisation and constructional detail were unavoidably lost, so that once again one of Toller's plays has to be extricated from a powerfully striking but fundamentally inappropriate production before its own merits can be fairly assessed.

In view of Toller's imprisonment and political notoriety it was certain that the first productions of his plays should become entangled in immediate contemporary events, with the result that they tended to appear to be political ephemera rather than lasting works of art belonging to mainstream traditions. Thus the first night and early performances of *Die Maschinenstürmer* were dominated by the recent murder of Walther Rathenau, and although there had been six productions of *Hinkemann* before the "theatre scandal" at Dresden, those riots greatly influenced subsequent criticism, although in fact the play was merely a pawn in the Weimar Republic's internal conflicts. *Hinkemann* can now be recognised as a tragedy of universal validity, a tragedy of the insolubility of the insoluble which makes most other socialist drama appear shallow and facile in comparison.

After *Hinkemann,* nearly all Toller's plays were based on historical and political fact (33), but he still imparted to his material a universality that transcended particularities.

Der entfesselte Wotan is not primarily based on Hitler. It cannot therefore be fairly accused of trivialising the Nazi threat. It is based on the impracticable emigration plans of a fellow-prisoner of Toller's, and it is really remarkable that while Toller does actually anticipate Hitler's story in some minor particulars, many critics, even after the publication of *Mein Kampf (Vol I)* and the Beerhall Putsch, saw the play as outdated, not prophetic: Toller's political imagination, even when filtered through the medium of comedy, was truer than that of his critics.

Feuer aus den Kesseln anticipates by two decades the genre of post-World War II documentary. *Die blinde Göttin*, though based on a special and by no means straightforward case, in which Toller had taken a practical and humanitarian interest, does not lose its topicality, and its sad image of human shortcomings continues to ring true. His last play of all, *Pastor Hall*, is only weakened by the fact that, though well-informed, Toller had not lived in post-1933 Germany.

Most famous of these later plays and most difficult to detach from its celebrated Berlin production directed by Piscator, is *Hoppla, wir leben!* By examining on the one hand in detail Piscator's production as planned and recorded in his working prompt-copy, and on the other hand the extant versions of Toller's text, we can both reassess the theatrical and ideological qualities of Piscator's remarkable stage achievement and rediscover the independent meaning and values of Toller's play.

To look again at plays ignored or denigrated in most studies of Toller, *Die Rache des verhöhnten Liebhabers* and *Nie wieder Friede*, is to make interesting discoveries and raise our estimate of their author's powers. In its original German, now made readily available in the *Gesammelte Werke*, the latter, though still Toller's weakest play, is far superior to the published and acted English version. Toller must be held responsible for the way in which he revised the text and allowed it to be changed, but in his German typescript is to be found a far better written work than the translation would suggest, and one whose very faults can be seen, at least in part, as products of Toller's inner conflicts between his pacifist convictions and his belief that Nazism must be fought — by war if necessary. It was, in a new context, the dilemma propounded in *Masse Mensch*, and it was destined to destroy him.

Die Rache des verhöhnten Liebhabers on the other hand is well-wrought in every respect, — in structure, language, verse, and in the ways in which it improves, immeasurably in some respects, on its Italian source; but politically orientated critics have dismissed it as trivial and others have recoiled from its amoral sexuality. From the perspective it offers, however, we see afresh the importance of sexuality in all Toller's works. A sensual and passionate man, he made some aspect of sex or sexual relationships the key or climax to virtually everything he wrote, whether he was writing of the nesting swallows, the castrated ex-soldier, the body of the raped girl hanging on the barbed wire, or the adulterous lovers accused of murder. In the puppet-play itself Toller can be seen to have transformed a light and perhaps trivial Italian novella into a vehicle for conveying through a delicately conventionalised form of drama certain quite profound insights into the nature of the basic instincts of self-preservation and that of the human species.

From this detailed and close textual, theatrical and contextual study of his plays Toller emerges as a dramatist of considerable stature and versatility. His plays represented and made noteworthy contributions to the developing styles of the period between the wars. At first he adopted Expressionism as being an established mode, but still a growing-point of contemporary style. He soon both enriched this and assimilated it into his own far more diversely and historically based dramatic art, fusing it with elements derived from Shakespeare and the Greeks as well as with the central German traditions stemming from Goethe and Schiller. At the same time he anticipated in practice some of the essential characteristics of epic drama as written and theoretically expounded by Brecht. He adapted himself to the requirements of the new wave of naturalism of the later 1920s and early 1930s without losing his ability as a poet to charge his language with more meaning than could a mere prose dramatist. In his creative dramatisation of documentary material he anticipated the documentary plays of the post-1945 period. After 1933 the loss of a German-speaking theatre audience deprived him of the stimulus to put his best creative energies into drama and diverted them to what proved to be his best non-dramatic prose works and his more directly political use of language.

A revaluation of his dramatic oeuvre thus not only reveals the individual plays as better written, more artistically constructed and both subtler and more profound in content, themes and characterisation than has usually been thought, but also sets their author firmly as a leading figure in the main stream of German and European drama during his two decades of activity and creativity.

II

THE PLAYS
DIE WANDLUNG TO *DIE MASCHINENSTÜRMER*

DIE WANDLUNG *(TRANSFORMATION)*

In a study which proposes to set Ernst Toller's dramatic work in its literary, theatrical and political perspectives, *Die Wandlung* must be considered comprehensively in every respect. It is not only his first play, but it stands alone among his plays. Even as recently as 1980 Michael Ossar could write:

> . . . the seriously distorted view that has dominated Toller research to date and led to the common view that he was a man ruled by his emotions and out of touch with the realities of Weimar Germany is largely the result of an unjustified generalisation of the attitudes of *Die Wandlung* to all his other works. *Die Wandlung* is uniquely optimistic among Toller's works — it is the only one of his plays written before his experiences in the Munich Revolution. (1)

Not only, however, is this play the beginning of the author's personal development as a dramatist, but it is also a culmination of a number of lines of growth in German dramatic traditions, some having their roots as far back as the eighteenth century and some of recent origin. Indeed its structure as a "station" drama reaches right back to the religious drama of the Middle Ages. We must therefore not only set the play in its proper place in the Expressionist movement but in the longer traditions of German drama back to Goethe and Schiller. Within the Expressionist context we must examine its style, themes and content. We must therefore consider it autobiographically and confessionally (the two are not precisely identical), as reaction against the war, and as bearing on the strife between the generations (2). As it is also an overtly propagandist piece we must relate it to the long and rich tradition of plays of political and social propaganda, and to the continuous thread in the history of German drama and of the theatre considered as a moral institution. At the same time we must examine the immediate and specific political influences upon the play. After this we must analyse Karl-Heinz Martin's original production in detail, especially as this production, which involved important alterations in the text, had enormous influence on subsequent assessments of the play and hence on wider judgements of Toller's oeuvre.

> In 1917 the play [viz. *Die Wandlung*] was for me a political pamphlet (3).

That was Toller's firm, and in fact italicised, opinion concerning his initial attitude to this play when he wrote some notes upon it from the fortress-prison at Eichstatt in October 1919. He defined his conception of 'political pamphlet' with some care:

> If 'political pamphlet' signifies a signpost or "guidebook" born from the necessity of outward reality, moral dilemma, and wealth of inner strength, then *Die Wandlung* may confidently be counted as 'pamphlet'. (4)

When Toller states that in 1917 the play was for him a political pamphlet, the implication is that by October 1919 it had become for him something else or something more. In the meantime it had been completed — during his first period of imprisonment (5) — and had been produced upon the stage (30. 9. 1919), while Toller himself had undergone the experiences of the Munich Revolution and was writing his first post-Munich play, *Masse Mensch*.

Ten years later, in 1929, re-assessing Expressionism as a wartime and post-war phenomenon, he wrote concerning that period:

> Never since Schiller's *The Robbers*, since *Cabal and Love*, had the theatre been such a tribunal for contemporary events, so washed around by the strife and conflict of public opinion (6).

Chronologically therefore it is reasonable to consider the play in the first instance as a 'political pamphlet'. Like a pamphlet, it was written to be read, elther aloud to a group, or privately. The dust-cover of the First Edition (7) justified its being printed as continuous prose with the words:

> Drama is the spiritual and intellectual expression of our time. Contemporary people read drama as yesterday they read a tale, an ordinary, gripping book (8).

It is impossible to date precisely the writing of the first draft. Toller simply tells us,

> This work came into being in its first draft in 1917, in the third year of world-slaughter (9).

Obviously it was before his hasty departure from Heidelberg on 21 December of that year because he tells us (10) that he read scenes from it to a circle of young people in Heidelberg before his flight to Berlin. We can also relate the date of the first draft to that of his first reading Gustav Landauer's *Aufruf zum Sozialismus*. On 20 December he received a letter from Landauer which he answered (11) in a letter which endorses many of Landauer's own ideas. He had by now read the *Aufruf*, but as Rosemarie Altenhofer has pointed out (12), the influence of Landauer on ideas and language in *Die Wandlung* begins only after Scene 7, 4th Station, where the play ceases to be in any sense autobiographical (though remaining 'confessional') and begins to present a "programme". She therefore concludes that the first seven scenes were written in Heidelberg *before* Toller had read the *Aufruf*. Once Toller had read this, however, it became an immediate political influence upon him, and the letter of 20 December not only reflects Landauer's own ideas but contains verbal similarities with the later scenes of *Die Wandlung*. This division of the play is of immense importance. It means that quite apart from the uniqueness of the whole play, as preceding Toller's Munich experiences, the first seven scenes have their own uniqueness in being his only dramatic work written before Landauer began to influence him: and Landauer was the most important single political influence in Toller's thought.

Landauer and his writings came into Toller's life at the very moment when Toller first became politically active. His first 'political' publication, written in Heidelberg, distributed as a leaflet and published in a Munich newspaper, the *Münchener Zeitung*, on 10 November 1917, was an appeal for academic freedom of speech in support of a Munich professor, Friedrich Wilhelm Foerster, a wholehearted pacifist who was convinced of Germany's war-guilt. The "Foerster Case" originated in an article by the professor published in Switzerland in May 1916 under the title *Bismarcks Werk im Lichte der großdeutschen Kritik (Bismarck's Work in the Light of Pan-German Criticism)*. When he returned to resume his lectures in Munich at the end of October 1917 students representing the newly-formed *Deutsche Vaterlandspartei (German Fatherland Party)* would have beaten him out of the lecture-theatre had he not been defended by his own students. Toller's appeal, signed by 135 students of Heidelberg university, asked for no more than the freedom of academics to express their personal opinions outside the classroom and the university.

> *Outside the University* teachers *and* students must be entitled to unrestricted freedom in political movements (13).

Thus Toller first entered the political field as a pacifist and civil libertarian, without as yet any socialist or other ideological framework to support his direct personal response to his war experience. It must have been just at this moment that Toller, with his intense inner need to find a coherent framework for the totally new attitudes he had been driven to adopt, read Landauer's *Aufruf zum Sozialismus*, for the documents from his hand that immediately follow the Foerster Appeal are permeated with Landauer's ideas and words.

The Foerster Appeal was linked with a more ambitious attempt to combat the Deutsche Vaterlandspartei and to work for peace, namely, the founding of *Der Kulturpolitische Bund der Jugend in Deutschland (The League of German Youth for Culture and Politics)*. There is little or no evidence that this body had any real existence outside the University of Heidelberg, where the original group was formed and Toller at once elected Chairman (24 November 1917). However, an appeal for membership and for the forming of other groups was hectographed and sent to all German universities and to a large number of well-known persons in public and political life, some of whom expressed their agreement with it, including F. W. Foerster, Walter Hasenclever, Carl Hauptmann, Karl Henckell, Heinrich Mann, Walter von Golo and Alfred Wolfenstein. The covering-letter sent with the Appeal explained that this was only a first step and freely admitted that it did not present a programme:

> We know that it does not present a programme. That is not our intention (14).

Rather it was a statement of principles. These were founded on a Schilleresque call to be a person and to treat others as persons:

> Let each, radiating soul and spirit, act as person to person (15).

The preamble to the specific principles ends, significantly:

> The community for which we strive can only grow out of the inner transformation of individuals *[Mensch-Wandlung]* (16).

The specific aims mentioned are obvious enough. For example: peaceful solution of international problems; the abolition of poverty through 'a form of economy which brings about sensible production and just distribution of material goods'; separation of church and state; abolition of capital punishment; lowering of the age of franchise; and so on. The League opposed what it called the `militarisation of youth, of eroticism, of school, university, leisure and physical education. ' It favoured comprehensive schools and wanted to publish cheap editions of such writers as Tolstoy, Carl Hauptmann, Henri Barbusse etc. The document ended:

> We demand the revolutionising of fundamental attitudes! (17).

While many prominent figures, including Heinrich Mann, supported the appeal, a public controversy developed in the press. The appeal was described by one newspaper (18) as the work of "muddle-headed people without historical or political education". Of course the appeal's anti-war views provoked the inevitable crop of sadistic anonymous letters. More practically serious was the attack mounted by the authorities and the Army High Command. Some Austrian women students who were members of the League had to leave the country within twenty-four hours. All male members were summoned to the District Command headquarters, where even those previously declared unfit were suddenly found fit for service and sent to barracks.

Fortunately for Toller (it was the first of several similar fortunate chances in the course of his life) he was in hospital with influenza and a high temperature on the day his flat was visited and searched, and he was warned by a fellow-student, a girl, that he must leave Heidelberg or face arrest. On 20 December, the day before he left, he received the letter from Landauer already referred to. Despite his illness and peril, he replied at once. His letter, though betraying his feverish condition, or perhaps *because* of it, is an exceptionally revealing document, not touched, as is so much of Toller's 'autobiographical' writing, by afterthought or artistic manipulation.

In the letter he tried to explain his own motives for being

involved in the peace movement, and these are expressed in highly subjective terms:

> What I do, I do not *only* because of distress, not *only* because of suffering at the *ugliness* of everyday life, not *only* because of indignation over the political and economic order — all these are causes, but not the only ones. I fight because of my own abundance of life . . . I'm not a religious ecstatic who sees only himself and God — not people; I'm not an opportunist, who sees nothing but the external conditions (19).

Toller makes big demands on would-be followers, who must be prepared to stake their whole lives — spiritually, intellectually and physically — for the cause. At the heart of the letter lies an existentialist concept of commitment and choice:

> In order to arrive at a conviction, as I understand it, one must do so through distress, through suffering in all its fullness; one must believe oneself to have been "uprooted", must have played with life and danced with death, must have suffered in the intellect and overcome it through the spirit — one must *have struggled with the human being* (20).

"One must have *struggled with the human being*": "Man . . . muß *mit dem Menschen gerungen haben*". The letter here echoes the sub-title of *Die Wandlung: Das Ringen eines Menschen*. This struggle with and within oneself is ultimately fought in isolation:

> In the *last* spiritual things we must experience our isolation — that is to say, our being alone with God, — not "tragically", but *joyfully* (21).

After referring to the need to fight war, poverty and the state, and to establish a community based upon peaceful barter, Toller resumes the subjective rôle:

> Finally there is only this: that I feel a peace in my innermost core which *is* freedom and which *gives me* freedom; that I can live in the greatest restlessness, can fight passionately and excitedly against dirt and narrow lack of judgement, and still this innermost peace remains with me (22).

In this letter Toller is expressing many ideas (particularly that of the inwardly free person) which he knew to be Landauer's own.

Gustav Landauer had translated Kropotkin's *Mutual Aid* into German in 1904, re-issued in 1908 (23), and in 1911 he published his own *Aufruf zum Sozialismus (Call to Socialism)* which, as its brief Preface states, is to be read as a speech, with all that implies (24). Landauer's debt to Kropotkin is considerable, and it seems certain that Toller read Kropotkin in Landauer's translation, at any rate before the writing of *Die Maschinenstürmer*; but at this point it was Landauer himself whom Toller read and absorbed. Landauer strikes his characteristic keynote on the opening page:

> Socialism is the endeavour to bring a new reality into being with the help of an ideal (25).

The roots of socialism were therefore to be found within the individual:

> . . . no kind of progress, technique or virtuosity will bring us salvation and blessing; only out of the spirit (*Geist*), only out of the depths of our inner distress and our inner wealth will the great change come which we today call socialism (26).

Such a view was strongly antagonistic both to Marxism and to Darwinism. The true teaching of Marx, says Landauer, is that when capitalism has triumphed completely over the remnants of the Middle Ages, progress is assured and socialism as good as there. Not for nothing is the Bible of Marxism called *Das Kapital*! Marxism, indeed, is the plague of our time and the curse of the socialist movement. (Die Pest unserer Zeit und der Fluch der sozialistischen Bewegung) (27). Marxism and Darwinism see human history as consisting of anonymous processes and the accumulation of many tiny mass events. For the socialist in Landauer's sense, history is carried forward by persons, and therefore responsibility and guilt exist. For the Marxist, the true Philistine, nothing is more important than technology and progress. Asked to choose between a new type of locomotive and Jesus on the Cross, the Marxist will choose the locomotive.

> The father of Marxism is not the study of history, nor is it Hegel, it is neither [Adam] Smith nor Ricardo, . . . nor is it any revolutionary-democratic situation in time, still less is it the will and desire for civilisation and beauty among people. *The father of Marxism is steam.*
> Old wives prophesy out of coffee-grounds, Karl Marx prophesied out of steam (28).

Marxism, in this view, is associated with centralisation, but, says Landauer, it is not the centralisation of capital (which could still operate economically with village and home industries) but the centralisation of industry, brought about by mechanisation (primarily through the steam-engine) which demands barrack-like factories and the subsequent barrack-like blocks of workers' flats. (In German these had long been called *Mietskaserne: barracks to let*). These two forms of centralisation are associated with each other, but there is another, independent of the other two, which flourishes in our time: the centralisation of the state, of bureaucracy, of the armed forces. These lead to two further types of 'barracks', for the army and for the civil service, while prisons and brothels are simply two more species of 'barracks' in the centralised state. It is not surprising that opposition to Marxism was growing in England and the Mediterranean countries and that the ideology was flourishing in the countries of the drill-sergeant and the civil servant: in Prussia and Russia. Landauer sees no hope in the kind of socialism that merely takes over the various forms of economic, industrial and political centralisation developed under capitalism. On the contrary, he prophesies all too clearly the road that Marxist socialism did in fact take in Eastern Europe, namely state capitalism. He foresees a time when a Marxist World Production Authority will poke its nose into everybody's affairs (in jedes Töpfchen gucken) and enter up in its books the exact amount of lubricating oil to be used on every machine.

Turning away from a centralised, technological socialism. Landauer emphasises the importance of land and agriculture.

> Hunger, hands and the soil are there, all three are there by nature, and apart from them mankind needs nothing except to order sensibly what goes *between* them (29).
> We must have the soil again. The communities of socialism must share out the ground anew. The earth is nobody's property. Let the earth not be private property: only then are the people free . . . *And the abolition of property will also be essentially a transformation of our Geist . . .*
> The *Geist* will create forms for itself; forms of movement, not of rigidity . . .
> So — Land and *Geist* — that is socialism's solution.
> *Socialism's fight is a fight for the soil; the social question is an agrarian question* (30).

Against this background we now examine the play itself *as a political pamphlet*. In the first instance this means the first seven scenes, and of these especially the two scenes (3rd Station, Scenes 5 & 6) which Toller selected for distribution as a pamphlet in Munich in January 1918.

Following the regular pattern of the first four Stations, the 3rd Station consists of a realistic scene (forestage) and a dream scene (rear stage). Toller ran the risk that some details of the scenes taken thus in isolation might not be comprehensible to his readers.

In the first, Friedrich, the 'Toller' persona, sole survivor of a tiny volunteer party, lies in hospital. As a Jew (like Toller), constantly relating himself to the Wandering Jew, Ahasuerus, he has felt himself to be an outsider.

> FRIEDRICH (*in his fever*): Where are you others? Oh, the drifting desert sand . . . gritty fog . . . do not rest . . . further . . . don't know you . . . who are you . . . . Ahasuerus . . . . miserable man . . . go away back . . . . into towns gasping in nightmares, you'll not find caves here . . . I'm not journeying with you . . . no . . . (*cries out*) no . . . . (31).

We are not yet concerned with the autobiographical aspect of this, but Toller clearly believes that the Jew's sense of being an 'outsider' in German society will strike a chord with many of his contemporaries — not only Jews. In this assumption he was fully justified. Roy Pascal has demonstrated with detailed clarity the importance and distinctive features of German (and Austrian) anti-semitism in the latter part of the nineteenth century and the first two decades of the twentieth (32). Although that anti-semitism "still fed on a primitive fear and hatred of a people of alien beliefs and manners" (33), the granting of civil rights to Jews added "resentment against a community whose liberation symbolised bourgeois liberalism . . . to the older hostility" (34). Jews were still barred "by custom if not by law" (35) from some professions, and were relatively more numerous in 'free professions' as private practitioners.

In the 1890s (that is, in the period of Toller's childhood) the traditional meaning of "Jew" as a believer in the Jewish religion and member of the Jewish community with its complex of distinctive ritualistic practices, who, when converted to Christianity ceased to be a Jew, was being replaced by the racialist anti-semitism later exploited by Hitler to supply what Pascal calls "the chief emotional drive" (36) of National Socialism.

Toller, by basing Friedrich's alienation from society upon his Jewishness, is using material readily and universally understood in

Germany and Austria. Pascal quotes Schnitzler, himself an Austrian Jew, as saying,

> It was not possible for a Jew, especially a Jew in public life, to ignore the fact that he was a Jew; nobody was doing so, not the Gentiles, and even less the Jews (37).

In this fictional, colonial war, Friedrich, the outsider, wins his civil rights through his military valour. An officer comes to him:

> The Fatherland knows how to value your services. Through me it sends you the [Iron] Cross. You were a stranger to our people. Now you have won your civil rights (38).

But no sooner has Friedrich rejoiced in his 'belonging', than he learns that his action has led to the deaths of ten thousand of the enemy, and the news shatters his joy:

> ... Through ten thousand dead I belong to them. Why don't I burst out laughing? Is that liberation? Is that the Great Time? Are these the great people? (*His eyes stare rigidly out*) Now I belong to them (*Blackout*) (39).

Out of the context of the play the scene makes one, simple, anti-war, pacifist point: that the Iron Cross is won and its winner earns his place in society not simply through courage, but through causing the deaths of ten thousand human beings.

The second scene used in the pamphlet is a 'dream' scene on the rear stage, conceived so as to present in the theatre an overwhelming visual effect, with the immense, low room, the skull-headed doctor and the war cripples, who consist of torsos with mechanical limbs, like Otto Dix's card-playing *Crippled War Veterans* (1920) or the actual parodies of humanity whose photographs were later displayed in the International Anti-war Museum (Berlin, Parochialstraße 29, closed down and converted into an SA-Hostel in March 1933). Clearly, when the scene was read as a pamphlet the visual effect would be minimised: even the fact that two of the characters have Friedrich's face could not make its full impact; and one must consider primarily the verbal content to judge the effectiveness of the scene as a political pamphlet.

The key lines are spoken by the medical professor, once near the beginning and once at the very end of the scene:

> /We could call ourselves the positive branch,/The negative is the armaments industry./In other words: We are the representatives of synthesis,/The armaments industry proceeds analytically (40).

The satirical effect is very similar to that of Brecht's *Legende vom Toten Soldaten.*

> Es zog die Ärtzliche Kommission
> Zum Gottesacker hinaus
> Und grub mit geweihtem Spaten den
> Gefallnen Soldaten aus.
>
> Der Doktor besah den Soldaten genau
> Oder was von ihm noch da war
> Und der Doktor fand, der Soldat war k. v.
> Und er drückte sich vor der Gefahr.
>
> (The medical commission marched out to the churchyard and dug up the fallen soldier with a consecrated spade. The doctor examined the soldier meticulously (or what still remained of him) and the doctor found that the soldier was fit for active service and was shirking danger) (41).

Brecht's *Legend,* written in the same year as the early scenes of *Die Wandlung,* was his direct reaction to the realities of the Augsburg Military Hospital where he served as a medical orderly. He too evidently regarded his creation as 'pamphleteering', for he, like Toller, read it aloud in public. He sang the *Legend* (for he also composed its music) before an audience of war veterans in a Munich public-house, presumably anticipating a sympathetic reaction from them. But it is reported that, misunderstanding at whom the attack was aimed, they went for him with beer glasses (42).

Both Brecht's *Legend* and Toller's *Cripples* Scene can justly be described as 'political pamphlets, in that they are, each in its own *genre* and idiom, polemical writings aimed at influencing public opinion through satirical attacks on the misuse of medical knowledge and skills in the service of war.

The scene emphasises that within the war context even normally beneficent activities become evil. In performance, the Doctor's skull-head incorporates the image of the life-giver becoming the death-giver. Although the impact of their both having Friedrich's face is partly lost on the mere reader, the figures of the student attending the professor and of the padre are ironic comment on the Friedrich of the previous scene. The Friedrich-student faints at the climax of the Doctor's exposition, when he declares that 'the possibility of reproduction has now been achieved; the joys of marriage, too, await these men. ' With a patronising smile the professor remarks:

> Faint, young man, at the work of love?/How would it have been, then, out there on the field of battle? (43)

The reader takes the point that the same man who could faint at this parody of "the work of love", could win the Iron Cross. The Friedrich-padre who comes with the clichés and commonplaces of religious comfort, when he actually sees the cripples as they are, breaks his cross into pieces, crying that he cannot deceive these men with pious words. The scene highlights the passages in the realistic scene in which the Sister tells Friedrich:

> They found you tied to a tree. The sole survivor.
> FRIEDRICH: Not to a cross . . . The sole survivor . . . (44)

The two-scene pamphlet was thus purely anti-war, with a powerful emotional appeal and no ideological basis or constructive alternative. It was a direct appeal to the humanity of the reader.

This is also true of the rest of the first four Stations. (When Toller read from *Die Wandlung* in Heidelberg and in Munich, we do not know what parts he selected, or how much).

The *Prologue* ("which can also be thought of as an Epilogue", we are told) is called *Die Totenkaserne (The Barracks of the Dead)* and represents a broad graveyard by night, the only characters being *Der Kriegstod (Death In War), Der Friedenstod (Death in Peace),* and . . . skeletons. The conception of the scene seems to owe something to the last scene of Wedekind's *Frühlings Erwachen (Spring's Awakening)* in which Melchior, escaping from the reformatory, gets into the graveyard where Wendla and Moritz are buried. Melchior becomes involved in a life-and-death discussion between the dead Moritz, who appears with his head (which he blew off when he shot himself) under his arm, and *Der vermummter Herr (The Masked Man),* who represents the call to life, with all its unknowns and uncertainties. Wedekind himself played the Masked Man in the first production (11. 12. 1906), in a top-hat (45). In Toller's play *Death in Peace* wears a top-hat on his skull-head, and the scene is in effect a debate between the two *Deaths,* as that in Wedekind is between Moritz (Death) and The Masked Man

(Life). Both scenes, also, are written with irony and grim humour. But whereas the conclusion of Wedekind's scene (which is without question an *Epilogue*) is that Melchior should 'Choose Life!' (46), the conclusion of Toller's is that *Death in War* has in fact been defeated: he is subordinate to War and the War Machine. He is scorned by *Death in Peace.*

> You little death! / You swanking hypocrite with your puffed-up empty military phrases. / Commend me to your boss, the war system (47).

After the *Prologue* the first two Stations (4 scenes) contribute to the pamphlet-character of the play almost entirely in expanding and making explicit the events leading up to the Third Station. The Fourth Station (which consists of a single, realistic, scene) shows Friedrich's personal transformation after the shock administered in the Third Station. Therefore in choosing the Third Station to be printed as a political pamphlet Toller deliberately selected that part of the play then written in which the political element, rather than the personal and religious elements, predominated.

Thus the first four Stations of the play constitute (insofar as they form a complete entity) a *Flugblatt* against war, making an appeal to individuals as individuals to destroy in themselves the dream of *The Victory of the Fatherland* as Friedrich destroys his statue of that name, and to set out on the *Way* that leads,

> To God, who is *Geist* and love and strength,
> To God, who lives in humanity (48).

The structure of the play now changes. The following three scenes form a unity; they contain in dream images the process by which Friedrich becomes "human" (49).

In these three dream scenes Friedrich identifies himself in turn with a *Schlafbursche*, a prisoner and a *Wanderer*. A *Schlafbursche* is a man who cannot afford to rent a room, but only a bed (50). The Prisoner is in effect the Crucified One, and the Wanderer the Resurrected One:

> As if I had rolled away a heavy gravestone and rise again (51).

The three scenes lead to the *Volksversammlung (People's Assembly)* with Friedrich's first public political speech, and (with the intervention of the *Mountaineers* scene, in which Friedrich's *persona* determines to climb ever higher) to the Square in front of the Church, with Friedrich's second and larger political speech.

The implied pattern by which social change takes place is that an unusually gifted individual undergoes some kind of personal "conversion" which he then transmits to the masses. This concept belongs entirely to the second half of the play and it derives directly from Toller's reading of Landauer. Hans Marnette, an acute critic of the play, though, as a Marxist deeply antagonistic to Landauer's ideas, writes:

> The essential ideological roots for the message of *Die Wandlung* lie in Toller's taking over particular ideas from Gustav Landauer. We are speaking deliberately not of learning from or making use of Landauer's ideas, but of taking them over directly (52).

Such an immediate adoption of another person's ideas naturally implies that in Landauer's writing Toller found the expression of what he himself was seeking, of thoughts so closely in harmony with his own that the second half of the play follows as naturally from the first as if it had been part of the original intention. Nevertheless, not only the content but the form of the latter part of the play is determined by Toller's reading of Landauer and is relevant to its "political message". Whereas Friedrich's conversion in the first four Stations is brought about through a series of external pressures and influences (mother, sister, friend, war experience, the ten thousand dead, and finally the meeting with his old wartime comrade as a beggar with a hurdy gurdy and his syphilitic wife) and is externalised in his smashing of the statue, while the related dream scenes are intensifications of real experiences, the first three scenes of Station Five show us instead Friedrich imaginatively projecting himself into human situations outside his personal experience, and by thus achieving empathy with the poor and the oppressed (the *Schlafbursche* and the Prisoner) learning the way he must go:

> I know the way to the place of work,
> Now I know it (53).

There is rich ambiguity in the word *Arbeitsstätte (place of work)*: it is both the place where the workers are to be found and the place where Friedrich must do *his* appointed work, that is, give his message.

Thus the play actually presents two versions of Friedrich's *Wandlung*, though in first reading or in performance the second will probably be taken simply as an internalisation of the first in greater depth. In fact this second version of the transformation is conceived in terms of Landauer's *Aufruf*: the need for the individual to discover and remake his own humanity. This process is an inward one, achieved in loneliness and isolation. In Landauer's opinion no truly humane society can come into being,

> so long as we have not discovered and newly created humanity in ourselves as individuals. Everything begins from the individual; and upon the individual everything is laid (54).

This is exactly what Friedrich is achieving in this sequence of dream scenes. In bed with the Daughter, the *Schlafbursche* with Friedrich's face learns (not merely cerebrally but in his feelings) the sufferings of the poor:

> Since the news came one day that the big hammer had crushed him, she groans every night; the eleventh child, which she was still carrying, she lost — of course it was dead — a great piece of luck (55).

Friedrich, the middle-class artist, is experiencing imaginatively the condition of the people, a far deeper and more certain way of "assimilation" than the heroic deed on the field of battle.

Next, he experiences the identity of Factory and Prison:

> THE NIGHT-VISITOR: . . . At first glance you think joyfully*, oho — there's a prison in store for somebody here. Strain your eyes! We've arrived already! Do you see the sign-board? You're trembling — let me read it — I'm not deceiving you: *The Big Factory!* (56)
>
> *Presumably because the *Schlafbursche*, being innocent of any crime, has nothing to fear from a prison.

The dream-identification of factory and prison derives immediately from Landauer's *Aufruf* where each is simply another kind of "barracks".

As we have already seen, Landauer associated Marxism with the centralisation not of capital but of industry and the state, and used the concept of "barracks" to typify both capitalist and Marxist industrialised societies. The relevant passages in the *Aufruf* refer to:

> Factory-barracks, barracks-to-let, bureaucrats' barracks, soldiers' barracks, and "the further barracks": work-houses, prisons and penitentiaries, "and the brothels ('sex-houses') in which prostitutes are quartered in barracks" (57).

Landauer saw the steam-engine as the cause of industrial, and therefore of social, centralisation:

> . . . the steam-engine, which must have the working machinery and the working people near it, the centre of power, and has therefore created big factory concerns and highly specialised division of labour . . . So it was the technical necessities of the steam-engine that have produced the big factory-barracks and the barracks-to-let (58).

Toller creates an exact theatrical correlative of this statement. Friedrich has just left the *Mietskaserne* and stands before the building whose sign says *Die große Fabrik (= Fabrikskaserne)*. In the blackout that follows the Night Visitor's reading this notice, the audience hears the sounds of a steam-industrialised society:

> For several minutes the roar of pounding pistons, the boom of whirling wheels, the hiss of streams of white-hot molten metal (59).

When the lights go on again after "several minutes" (a long time in a blacked-out theatre) they reveal not the anticipated "Big Factory", but "the groundfloor of a prison". Factory is prison and prison is factory and both are "barracks" demanded by the centralisation of power in the steam-engine and the state. The sequence is a classic example of the translation of discursive intellectual content into the immediacy of pure theatre.

Landuer believes that the individuals who undergo the inward process of finding their humanity are essentially solitary.

> *Geist* withdraws into the individual . . . now it lives in individuals, geniuses . . . . . who are without *Volk*: lonely thinkers, poets and artists, who, without security, as if uprooted, stand almost in the air (60).

Such Toller creates Friedrich. He is an artist, a sculptor, from the start of the play. In this second part he becomes more and more isolated. At the conclusion of the sequence of three dream scenes he is the lonely Wanderer in thick mist, who gets up out of the ditch by a country road; while in Scene 12, *The Mountaineers,* he leaves his last companion (a persona of the Friend) behind on the mountain in order to retain his solitary integrity:

> 2nd MOUNTAINEER: You have gone too far already. Think of yourself. I'm afraid for you.
> 1st MOUNTAINEER: Because I will not abandon myself, I am abandoning you . . .
> Farewell! . . . (61)

One is reminded of Rilke's great poem, written under the impact of the outbreak of World War 1, *Ausgesetzt auf den Bergen des Herzens (Exposed on the mountains of the heart).* Toller's Friedrich, like Rilke, must reach the peak of solitariness.

> –Aber
> ungeborgen, hier auf den Bergen des Herzens (62).

Where, asks Landauer, are the Columbus-like natures who prefer to sail away on the high seas in a frail ship into the unknown rather than wait for things to develop?

> . . . wo sind die Kolumbusnaturen, die lieber auf gebrechlichem Schiff und aufs Ungewisse hin aufs hohe Meer gehen als auf die Entwicklung zu warten (63).

But neither for Landauer's 'lonely thinker, poet or artist', nor — in the latter part of the play — for Toller's Friedrich, is the voyage of inner discovery an end in itself. For Landauer it is through these lonely individuals that socialism will come into being. These individuals

> speak out of the *Geist* to the people and of the people to come (64).

For these few isolated spirits are actually like the isolated people who make up the masses.

> And to these few isolated persons into whom the *Geist* has fled . . . correspond those who are isolated from each other, the many atomised persons for whom nothing remains except emptiness, inanity and misery: the masses, who are called the People, but who are only a heap of beings torn from their place and abandoned . . . the masses into whom the *Geist* must stream again (65).

Marnette rightly points out that all those characters who represents the People in this play do correspond with this characterisation of the masses: the Student (Scene 11) who laments, "What good is education to us when the *Geist* is tormented?" (66), the Lady, the Sick Man, the Girl Student.

Friedrich's political speeches in Scenes 11 and 13 are expressions of Landauer's political philosophy.

In his very first address to the people in Scene 11 Friedrich echoes the passage just quoted. He says he knows all about the people's misery (*Elend*) and says of the communist speaker (*Kommis des Tages*),

> But for him "people" is "mass". For he knows nothing of the people (67).

Friedrich understands that the Masses ("a heap of beings torn from their place and abandoned") are potentially the People, if the *Geist* can only stream into them again. For the communist the masses remain masses. (Here at the end of Toller's first play, the central conflict of his second, *Masse Mensch,* is already adumbrated). Friedrich attacks the Communist on precisely the same grounds that Landauer attacks Marxism: his god is the machine.

> The People is God! . . . God is a machine. Therefore the People is a machine. Nevertheless he will rejoice in the swinging levers, whirling wheels and pounding pistons (68).

The words are virtually identical with the stage direction between scenes 8 and 9. The Communist will actually rejoice in those very objects which created the necessity for the existence of the factory-prison. He is offering not freedom but slavery. Like Landauer, Friedrich is attacking in one breath and one image both the fact that Marxism is derived from industrial centralisation brought about by mechanisation, and the essentially mechanical operation of Marxist dialectical materialism which sees the advent of socialism as the historically inevitable consequence of the rise of capitalism.

Landauer says that because all men and women, however alienated and abandoned, carry their humanity imperishably within them, they respond to the call of the gifted individual into whom the *Geist* has fled.

> *Geist* is something that dwells in the same way in the hearts and souls of individuals; something that with natural compulsion breaks out of everyone as a binding quality and leads everyone into a common bond (69).

Friedrich wants his hearers to feel the inner need for this *Geist*:

> I wanted you to feel spiritual need (70).

He goes on:

> I want you to be (spiritually) rich, people filled with life (71).

Both these sentences echo Landauer in thought and expression:

> . . . Only out of the *Geist*, out of the depths of our inner need and our inner wealth will the great change come which we call socialism (72).

In Friedrich's closing speech in Scene 13 one of the most striking Landauerisms is Friedrich's attitude to the wealthy, and his appeal to the people on their behalf.

> I know . . . about you, you wealthy man, who heaps up money and despises everyone, the others and yourself (73).
>
> Go to the wealthy and show them your heart, which was becoming a heap of rubbish. But be good to them, for they also are poor people who have gone astray (74).

The attitude expressed here comes straight from Landauer:

> The worker too knows far too little what fearful, unworthy and overwhelming troubles the capitalist has, what quite unnecessary, completely unproductive torment and destruc-

> tion is laid upon him, and the workers heed far too little this similarity between themselves and the capitalists (75).

Finally Friedrich cries to the crowd:

> O, if you were persons — absolute, free persons (76).
> O, wenn ihr Menschen wäret, — unbedingte, freie Menschen.

Toller significantly uses the adjective *unbedingt* — unconditional, free of constrictions and limitations. For the Marxist, mankind's fate is ultimately *conditioned, determined* by the forces of dialectical materialism; for Toller as for Landauer, mankind can be unconditionally independent, the individual person can be a genuinely free agent. He or she can become *Mensch,* and when the *Menschen* who constitute the people (*Volk*) realise this, then comes the revolution.

The response to Friedrich's cry is in fact that very realisation. First the voice of a single youth, then those of a few women and girls, and then (notice the sequence: Youth, Women, All) the voices of all cry out:

> We are persons after all (77).
> Wir sind doch Menschen.

And after a moment's silence in which, in the theatre, the meaning sinks into the consciousness of characters and audience alike. Friedrich calls upon the people to "*March!*". This is the sequence by which, in Landauer's view, revolution comes about:

> The isolation of the individual.
> The renewal of the person through the renewal of *Geist* in the individual.
> The bearing of this *Geist* into the masses by the individual.
> The enlightenment of the masses through the *Geist*.
> Outbreak of revolution (78).

That which is the turning-point according to Landauer is what is chosen by Toller for the climax and conclusion of his play, namely:

> Puppets become Persons (79).
> Puppen werden zu Menschen.

The text of the play as published is preceded by what Spalek rightly describes as an *Author's preface in free verse* (80), presumably written, as prefaces normally are, after the completion of the play. As Marnette points out, this falls into three sections, clearly distinguished from each other typographically and in tone (81). In the first section is portrayed the twilit dream-world of pre-war youthful days, filled with imagination and the sense of wonder. The mood evoked recalls that of the opening stanzas of Hölderlin's *An die Natur*, with their descriptions of *goldne Kinderträume (childhood's golden dreams)* (82). Hölderlin's poem represents the beginning of the poet's recovery from his sense of alienation from Nature:

> In the lament for what has been lost apparently beyond recall, he becomes aware of its value (83).

For Hölderlin the dreams of youth were shattered by his philosophy studies under the influence of Fichte; for Toller they were shattered by his war experiences:

> *Da! mordend krochen ekle Tiere*
> *Flammenspritzend auf der Erde! (84).*

Italicised by the poet, these lines break into the dream:

> Wir blickten traumschwer blinzend auf
> Und hörten neben uns den Menschen schreien! (85).

In the third section, the Brother, the Wise Poet who bears within himself both the great knowledge (*Wissen*) and the great Will (*Willen*), will show the Way to build *enraptured temples of exalted joy* and to *open wide the gates to exalted suffering.*

> Ein Bruder, der den großen Willen in sich trug,
> Verzückte Tempel hoher Freude zu erbauen
> Und hohem Leid die Tore weit zu öffnen (86).

These lines recall two passages from the Bible:

> Jesus antwortete, und sprach zu ihnen: Brechet diesen Tempel, und am dritten Tag will ich ihn aufrichten.
> Da sprachen die Juden: Dieser Tempel ist in sechs und vierzig Jahren erbauet; und Du willst ihn in dreien aufrichten.

> Machet die Thore weit und die Thüren in der Welt hoch, daß der König der Ehren einziehe (87).

(Notice the actual verbal echoes: *Tempel . . . erbauen. Tore . . . weit zu öffnen*).

Though neither of these passages actually occurs in the Passion story, both are normally associated with it. The first occurs only in St John's Gospel, where it is placed with the story of Christ's driving the money-changers out of the Temple at the very beginning of his ministry. In the synoptic Gospels, however, the cleansing of the Temple occurs immediately after the Palm Sunday entry into Jerusalem and in popular tradition the declaration about the re-building of the Temple occurs then, as, for example, in the Oberammergau Passionspiele:

> *Christus*: Fort mit euch! Ich will daß diese entweihte Stätte der Anbetung des Vaters wiedergegeben werde!
> *Sadock*: Mit welcher Vollmacht tust du das?
> *Einige*: Durch welche Wunderzeichen kannst du beweisen, daß du Macht dazu hast?
> *Christus*: Ihr verlangt Wunderzeichen? Ja, eines kann ich euch geben: Zerstört diesen Tempel hier, und in drei Tagen werde ich ihn wieder aufbauen!
> *Ezechiel*: Sechsundvierzig Jahre hat man an diesem Tempel gebaut, und du willst ihn in drei Tagen wieder aufbauen? (88).

Similarly the passage from Psalm 24, a Psalm of David, is often interpreted as a prophecy of the entry of Christ, the Son of David, into Jerusalem. The entry into Jerusalem is, of course, an entry into *exalted suffering (hohem Leid)* — the Passion itself.

For those born into the European-Christian tradition Jesus Christ is an obvious archetype of Landauer's gifted individual who retreats into loneliness (as Christ into the desert), is filled with the Spirit (as at the Baptism by John) and then preaches his message to the multitudes. We have seen how in Scenes 9 and 10 Toller identifies Friedrich/ Prisoner and Friedrich/Wanderer with the Crucified One and the Resurrected One. Here too, as the gates are opened wide to exalted suffering, the Brother is given a 'Christ' dimension.

Toller has not written here a private or purely lyric poem. Its title, *Aufrüttelung (Arousal)*, makes clear that it is to be read as part of the 'political pamphlet': the Brother who shows the way is identified with the Wise Poet. The question remains: what is the Way?

Marnette says (89) that the theme of the poem is that one person must show the way, *even though it is not clear which way it leads*. In fact Toller does make clear what is the way and where it leads. Jesus Christ said, "I am the Way" (Ich bin der Weg. Joh. 14. 6). and we might think that Toller's Poet/Brother, with 'Christ' associations, might be making the same claim. However, the verse Preface is preceded by a *Motto* (as Spalek calls it; but perhaps *dedication to the reader* would be more accurate) which reads:

> You are the way.
> (Ihr seid der Weg) (90).

Addressing his readers in the familiar second person plural, Toller tells them (us) in advance that they (we) are the Way. It is the readers' realisation — taught by the poet, the solitary — that they, like the poet, are free human beings that makes them (that is 'us', the readers) the Way to the revolution that ends the play. Thus from its very dedication the play addresses itself to the bringing about of social change. *Die Wandlung* (the title) is not merely *Das Ringen eines Menschen* (sub-title), as it was when only the first four Stations were written. In the play as completed the Transformation is not simply one man's struggle but the prelude to the Transformation of the Volk and from this the transformation of society: that is, revolution.

It thus becomes evident that Toller was wholly justified in regarding his play, in the revolutionary times during which it was completed, as a *Flugblatt*, a political pamphlet. And if it is to be seen as a political pamphlet it must be seen as a revolutionary one. This view, however, has not gone unchallenged. Towards the conclusion of his analysis of the play Marnette roundly declares:

> Toller's *Wandlung* is not a revolutionary drama (91).

This opinion is perfectly logical in Marxist terms. Toller neither portrays nor accepts the Marxist analysis of historical processes. He proceeds, like Landauer, from the renewal of the individual, not from the victory of the working-class. Marnette says truly of the play:

> The working-class is not given any form at all (92).

He knows that his Marxist readers will draw the immediate conclusion that this cannot be a revolutionary play.

The generalised and emotive criticism of the war is also taken to task:

> The criticism of war remains abstract and slips into irrationality (93).

The 'renewal of the person' is merely an 'idealist Utopia' — where 'idealist' as opposed to 'materialist' is chosen to evoke an automatically hostile response. It is fundamentally Toller's 'voluntaristic view of the world' (Die voluntaristische Weltsicht Tollers) that impairs both the realistic content and the structure of Toller's play (94).

The literary-critical conflict expressed here between Marnette the Marxist scholar and Toller the idealistic socialist was to be lived out in real terms in the struggles between Toller and Leviné in Munich even before *Die Wandlung* appeared on the stage or in print, for in Munich in the early months of 1919 Toller was working with Landauer, until the latter's murder on 2nd May, in opposition to the doctrinaire Marxists led by Levien and Leviné (95).

In fact *Die Wandlung* is both revolutionary and anti-marxist (96).

In re-emphasising that the play is designed as an *Arousal,* to use the title of its preface, we place it in a strong and honourable tradition of German political pamphleteering. The Brechtian *Lehrstück* is not the only possible kind of dramatic *Flugblatt*. Büchner's *Woyzeck* is another kind and his *Dantons Tod* yet another. Not for nothing has Toller been described as *A German Danton* (97). A political pamphlet may make a primarily emotional appeal, as does Büchner's own pamphlet *Der hessische Landbote* (*The Hessian Courier*), 1834. Though very different in tone from Toller's play, Büchner's pamphlet also is a primarily emotional *Arousal,* and draws, as does *Die Wandlung,* on the language and imagery of the Christian tradition:

> In the year 1834 it looks as if the lie were given to the Bible. It looks as if God had created the peasants and manual workers on the fifth day and the princes and aristocracy on the sixth, and as if the Lord had said to the latter: "Have dominion over every creature that creepeth upon the earth", and had regarded the peasants and town-dwellers as worms.
>
> Things look now in Germany as the Prophet Micah writes, Chap. 7, v. 3 & 4: " . . . the great man he uttereth his mischievous desire, and so they wrap it up. The best of them is as a briar; the most upright is sharper than a thorn hedge".

> You built the strongholds, then overthrow them and build the house of freedom. Then you can baptise your children freely with the water of life and . . . be on guard and arm yourselves in the spirit and pray yourselves and teach your children to pray:"Lord, break the sticks of those who drive us and let thy kingdom come unto us — the Kingdom of Righteousness. Amen" (98).

There are, of course, many hard facts and figures in Büchner's pamphlet, but the passages he emphasises typographically are written in the style here illustrated. They are an arousal to action through feeling, and they draw much of their emotional strength from their appeal to traditional and deeply rooted religious images and phrases. Familiarity with Luther's Bible is assumed, and Büchner uses direct quotation (Micah), close paraphrase (Genesis) and stylistic similarity (e. g. such phrases as *Wasser des Lebens.* cf. *Offenbarung S. Johannis* Chap. 22. v. 17.) in order to associate his political message with the traditional religious one. This, as we have seen, Toller does also.

This leads us to consider *Die Wandlung* in the German tradition of Political Drama.

Political drama, as illustrated in *Die Wandlung,* has a strong ethical element in it. The scenes used by Toller as a pamphlet primarily appeal to the reader's moral revulsion from war. This is a very different branch of the political tradition in drama from that which may be exemplified by Shakespeare's History Plays and Brecht's *Mutter Courage.* Whereas Shakespeare's history plays and Brecht's history play operate through the principle Brecht christened *Verfremdung,* and aim at the maximum degree of detachment of the audience from the stage, the maximum objective consideration of the political (including ethical) problems presented, Toller's scenes make a direct assault on the reader's emotions, inviting rather than discouraging the reader to identify with Friedrich. (The word "reader" is used deliberately here because the scenes are also being thought of as a printed pamphlet).

The close relationship between the ethical and the political is deeply rooted in the German tradition of drama. Schiller's 'political' plays are largely concerned with ethical questions. His own most celebrated and explicit statement on this theme is his lecture; *Was kann eine gute stehende Schaubühne eigentlich wirken? (What can a good permanent theatre really achieve?)* (99). Within the context of the undemocratic German states of his day, Schiller sees the first and most direct political effect of the theatre to be upon the rulers themselves and particularly that of influencing them in the direction of humanity and toleration.

> Humanity and toleration are beginning to become the ruling spirit of our time; their beams have penetrated into the halls of justice, and even further, — into the hearts of our princes. How much share in this divine work belongs to our theatres? Is it not they which gave humanity knowledge of itself and laid bare the secret mechanism according to which that divine work operates? (100).

When one bears in mind that virtually all theatres were Court Theatres, their importance as a politico-ethical influence is obvious.

> A noteworthy class of people has cause to be more grateful to the stage than all others. Here the great ones of the world hear what they never or seldom hear: truth. What they never or seldom see, they see here: the human person (101).

It may seem a long road from influencing the absolutist princeling to influencing the working-class of Munich, but the connection is real.

> The theatre is the common channel into which the light of wisdom streams down from the thinking, better part of the people and from there and in more gentle beams spreads through the whole state (102).

It was in this Schilleresque spirit that Toller acted when he first became involved in public politics, in the anti-war strike-movement in Munich.

> I go to strike-meetings, I would like to help, to do something, anything. I distribute war-poems among the women, the Military-Hospital and Cripple scenes from my play *Die Wandlung*, because I believe that these verses, born from the horror of war, strike at it and accuse it (103).

Friedrich himself is, if remotely, a descendant of the Schilleresque hero, the exceptional person, the idealist. Apart from the heroes he himself created, Schiller remarks how the example of August, offering the hand of friendship to the traitor Cinna, or Franz von Sickingen on his way to punish a prince and to fight for the rights of others, turning and seeing the smoke rising from his fortress where his hapless wife and child remain, but pressing on *to keep his word* can inspire us to similar noble deeds (104).

Friedrich is of the middle-class, like Toller himself. When he wrote the first four Stations Toller had never, he says, had contact with real, socialist, working people.

> I went to Eisner's meetings in which workers, women and young people were looking for the way which brings peace and saves the people. In these meetings I saw the figures of workers which I had not encountered until then, men of sober understanding, social insight, great knowledge of life, hardened will, socialists who served the cause in which they believed, without considering any immediate advantage (105).

Between Schiller and *Die Wandlung* lies the entire history of nineteenth century German drama, culminating in the Naturalist movement of the 1890s, as well as the twentieth century movement from Naturalism to Expressionism.

For our present purpose we shall refer only to one dramatist before the inception of the Naturalist movement, Friedrich Hebbel (1813–1863) who, "alone among the dramatists of the nineteenth century formulated a tragic philosophy of life which was also an intellectual system. In thus wanting his tragedy to have intellectual justification he was related to Schiller" (106).

He bridges the gap between the older dramatists who wrote high tragedy in monumental style, seeking to create myth in dramatic form, and the Naturalists. He points forward to Ibsen, especially in his radical yet tragic viewpoint, in his narrative realism, in his psychological understanding of lonely individuals alienated from God, and in his social criticism.

The fullest exposition of Hebbel's philosophy of drama is to be found in his essay of 1843, *Mein Wort über das Drama*. The very first sentence of this establishes the fact that Hebbel's views are completely remote from those of *l' art pour l'art* and that he takes as his starting-point the relationship of art to life:

> Art has to do with life, both inner and outer, and I suppose it can be said that it portrays both at the same time — its purest form and its highest content (107).

Moreover art must depict life both as Being and Becoming (*als Sein und als Werden*). In particular, drama represents the process of life in itself (*Das Drama stellt den Lebens prozess an sich dar*) (108). It is this ability of drama to represent the actual process of being and becoming that makes Hebbel declare elsewhere that drama is *die Spitze aller Kunst (the peak of all art)* (109). But drama does not present life in all its breadth, as epic poetry does. Instead it is concerned with one particular and fundamental process of life, namely:

> . . that it represents for us the questionable relationship in which the Individual, released from the original nexus faces the Whole, of which, in spite of his (her) incomprehensible freedom, he (she) still always has remained a part (110).

In these phrases Hebbel epitomises a whole tragic philosophy embracing the eternal tragic problems of Freedom and Necessity, Free Will and Causation, and of the tragic situation of the human being, both part of and separate from the universe. The words have not only a cosmic application, but also a social one: the individual is both part of and separate from the fabric of society, an aspect of tragedy to which Hebbel gave expression, particularly in *Maria Magdalena.* It is the aspect that most interested the Naturalists from Ibsen through the nineties and has been re-expressed in the mid-twentieth century by Arthur Miller in his important essay *On Social Plays,* which he printed as an introduction to *A View from the Bridge,* where he writes:

> The tragic figure must have certain innate powers which he uses to pass over the boundaries of the known social law — the accepted mores of his people — in order to test and discover necessity (111).

With whatever aspect of the *Whole* the Individual is in the *Questionable Relationship,* be it physical, metaphysical or social, the individual acquires Guilt (Schuld), but this guilt, says Hebbel, is quite unlike the Christian Original Sin (Erbsünde). Drama must never weary of repeating the eternal truth that life, as a process of individuation which knows no limit, does not produce guilt by chance but necessarily and essentially includes it and causes it. Christian guilt arises from the way the human Will is directed, whereas dramatic 'guilt' arises directly from the Will itself, from the expansion of the Ego, which occurs intransigently and without any outer authority. It is therefore a matter of complete indifference whether the hero comes to grief through a splendid endeavour or a reprehensible one (112).

Hebbel's profound account of the tragic predicament applies equally well to Greek tragedy, Shakespearean tragedy or modern existentialist tragedy as exemplified in the plays of Sartre.

Obviously, as drama must portray both Being and Becoming, it must show not static characters but characters in the process of formation, and that process is in the conflict between the individual Will and what Hebbel calls *der allgemeine Weltwillen (the universal world-will)*. The concept is not easy, but appears to be very similar to that of Thomas Hardy's *Immanent Will* (though for Hardy the tragedy is of a different nature, mankind being victims of the blind Will).

Hebbel goes on to consider more closely the relationship of the factual material out of which drama is created and the drama itself. He asks, for example, how far, in the relationship of drama to history, drama must be historically correct. Certainly, he says, drama must provide the atmosphere of the period, but in the last resort naive questions about naturalism are irrelevant, because nothing in art is 'real', nothing in drama is 'real'. Ultimately not only the drama as a whole, but every one of its elements, is symbolic.

> ... it has been recognised that drama, not simply in its totality, which goes without saying, but in every one of its pre-existing elements, is symbolic and must be regarded as symbolic, just as the painter does not distil from real human blood the colours with which he gives his figures red cheeks and blue eyes but uses vermilion and indigo quietly and without fuss (113).

This leads Hebbel to consider also the artificiality of Form. Art uses the material of life,

> But the content of life is inexhaustible and the medium of art is limited (114).

The threads of life are continuous and lead to infinity, but in art the threads must be worked into a circle.

> . . . and this is the point which Goethe alone could have in mind when he declared that all her Forms (i. e. the Forms of Art) bring with them something inauthentic (115).

Hebbel next demonstrates that the German drama of that time was developing in three directions: social, historical and philosophical. He, however, aims at transcending these categories:

> Now a fourth [sc. category] is still possible, a drama which unites in itself the trends characterised here and for that very reason does not allow any single one to predominate dis-

> tinctly. This drama is the goal of my own efforts, and if I have not made clear what I mean through my own actual experiments in writing drama, through *Judith* and *Genoveva*, which is to appear some time soon, it would be foolish to try to help by developing it in the abstract (116).

In the following year (1844) Hebbel developed his theories further in his *Vorwort* to his play *Maria Magdalena*.

"Drama", he says, " as the peak of all art, should illustrate the *state of the world and of mankind* of each period in its *relationship to the Idea.* " In a complex parenthesis Hebbel seeks to explain what he means by *the Idea* in this context. It is the *moral centre* which is the precondition of everything, a moral centre whose existence in the world-organism we must assume, simply because it is necessary for its self-preservation.

The highest form of drama, epoch-making drama, is therefore only even possible when a decisive change is taking place in *the state of the world and of mankind*. Hebbel appears here to be arguing that only in certain periods of history — namely those when distinct changes are taking place in the state of the world and of mankind, periods, one assumes, like the Renaissance, the French Revolution or the First World War — can the greatest drama be written. Drama is therefore, he says, a product of the age, but only in the sense that such an age is itself the product of all preceding ages and is in fact the link which joins a chain of centuries just ending to another just beginning.

According to Hebbel, Shakespeare had put the conflict within the Ego, the individual, the person, but Goethe had laid the foundation-stone for a new kind of drama by putting the dialectic, the conflict, in the *Idea* itself, that is, in that 'moral centre' already referred to, round which the ego must move. This Goethe had done, he says, in *Faust* and in the novel *Wahlverwandtschaften (Elective Affinities)* which he claims to be 'dramatic'.

What Hebbel appears to be saying here is that whereas the earlier dramatists, including Shakespeare, assumed a stable moral centre upon or around which the conflict within the ego took place, Goethe has, so to speak, de-stabilized that moral centre by portraying conflicts within it. This is consistent with Hebbel's view expressed in *Mein Wort* that life does not produce guilt by chance or merely by misdirection of the Will, but necessarily and essentially. Such a view is also basically modern and can be applied to the plays of Toller: not so much to the fundamentally optimistic *Wandlung* as to the later plays of ideological conflict and ineluctable tragedy.

With all this Hebbel believed that the kind of drama he was advocating and attempting to write had an historical-political-social purpose and function:

> . . . dramatic art should help to fulfil the world-historical process which is taking place in our days and which intends not to overthrow existing institutions, political, religious and moral, of the human race, but to establish them more deeply and thus secure them against overthrow (117).

Art is thus seen as having a real historical function to fulfil: it is seen as able to produce, or at least contribute to, the production of definite historical consequences. In Hebbel's view these consequences, however revolutionary they may appear to be, are actually conservative and conserving in their effects.

Toller, too, when in prison, discovered what he called *conservative elements* in himself and wondered whether he had only become a revolutionary *out of a utopian conservatism* (118). In his last play, *Pastor Hall,* written when the Hitler régime was destroying the best elements in German conservatism, he presented in the character of General von Grotjahn a positive image of that conservatism.

There is not the least suggestion that Hebbel saw drama as anything so immediate, or indeed ephemeral, as a 'political pamphlet', but he clearly saw it as reinforcing the great, underlying processes of historical change and development. It did this, in effect, by giving philosophy artistic form and thus bringing it from the realm of the abstract to that of the concrete.

> . . . art . . . is philosophy made real, as the world is the idea made real (119).

Although Hebbel appears superficially to be standing Plato on his head (Plato's Ideas being more real than his Appearances), he is effectively using a Platonic image to explain what he sees as the nature of drama. Behind the concrete appearance (reality) of the world lies the abstract idea, the logos. But the world is simply the totality of brute fact. Philosophy gives meaningful form to the world, to this totality of brute fact, but only in the abstract; art, by imposing an intellectually determined order upon a representation of brute facts, gives abstract philosophy concrete, tangible appearance.

Thus Hebbel is restating in terms of the nineteenth century and in terms of the deeper philosophical scepticism of his own age and in terms of his own artistic philosophy of the inevitability of tragedy, what Sir Philip Sidney had stated in terms of the sixteenth century in *An Apologie for Poetry*:

> The Philosopher therefore and the Historian are they which would win the gole, the one by precept, the other by example. But both not having both, doe both halte. . . . Nowe doth the Peerelesse Poet performe both: for whatsoever the Philosopher sayth shoulde be doone, hee giveth a perfect picture of it in some one, by whom hee presupposeth it was doone. So as hee coupleth the generall notion with the particular example. A perfect picture I say, for hee yeeldeth to the powers of the minde an image of that whereof the Philosopher bestoweth but a woordish description: which dooth neyther strike, pierce, nor possesse the sight of the soule so much as that, other dooth (120).

We turn now to the play to which this celebrated *Vorwort* was written, bearing in mind that the *Vorwort* was both conceived and written after the completion of the play. While not a political play in the narrow sense, *Maria Magdalena* is based upon an implied criticism of bourgeois society of the *Vormärz* period, namely that its limited code of morality could not accommodate powerfully sexual natures. In the *Vorwort* Hebbel described the play as *ein bürgerliches Trauerspiel (a bourgeois tragedy) (121)* and claimed that in it he had raised that *genre* to universal significance. The class of society in which tragedy was set, he said, was unimportant.

> It is really a matter of indifference whether the hand of a clock is made of gold or brass (122).

Tragedy must go beyond concern for the fate of an individual arbitrarily selected by the author, to a fate common to all human beings (*ein allgemein menschliches*), even if this is depicted in an extreme form; also, tragedy must depend upon *insoluble* problems (as Toller later showed in *Hinkemann*). Indeed, Hebbel's tragic view, as we have seen, is that the universal human problems are indeed insoluble.

Considering his importance as a theoretician of drama who was also a practising playwright, Hebbel's drama had, and has, little popular appeal, and his plays are not often seen on the German stage. In Berlin, East and West, between 1945 and 1970, for example, there were only seven productions of plays by Hebbel, of which three were of *Maria Magdalena*. For comparison, there were in that period in Berlin,

14 productions of Kleist, 21 of Ibsen, 41 of Goethe and 52 of Schiller (123). In academic circles on the other hand his plays have generated a vast body of secondary literature on account of the interesting aesthetic and critical problems they present. Yet, Hebbel, through Ibsen, did exercise an important influence on the German Naturalists.

> . . . Ibsen once expressed surprise that he should be hailed as a pioneer in the country that had nurtured Hebbel. In *A Doll's House, The Lady of [sic] the Sea, John Gabriel Borkman*, the central thesis is, as so often in Hebbel, the rights of the individual. Hebbel's influence on the succeeding generation of Realists thus came through the intermediary of a foreign dramatist rather than direct (124).

Both Hebbel and Ibsen wrote tragedies based on the conflict between the sexual drive and the social mores of nineteenth century society (*Maria Magdalena* and *Ghosts*), but neither thought of his plays as being in the more limited sense, 'political'.

It was the German working class which 'adopted' the originally middle-class naturalistic drama as its own. Darwinism and *Milieu-Theorie* were major elements in the intellectual framework of working-class clubs, debates and discussions.

> The working class associated its theatre with the new art of Naturalism. An art which professed to portray life as it really is might well seem suitable to be associated with revolutionary politics which want to change reality (125).

Thus Heinrich Braulich, writing from a strictly Marxist viewpoint, introduces the contrast between a tragic viewpoint (which he dubs 'pessimistic') and the basic optimism of dialectical materialism. Nevertheless, –

> The revolutionary workers used the critical elements of the naturalistic plays as an opportunity to confirm their class war with the bourgeoisie. They politicised the naturalistic theatre (126).

Even if Braulich's dogmatically Marxist approach is discounted, his last sentence expresses a truth: it was in the theatre, and above all through the new working-class audience that the middle-class naturalistic drama of social criticism became political.

The marriage was brief. By the mid-nineties Ibsen had moved and Hauptmann was moving away from Naturalism, the one towards symbolism, the other towards poetic fantasy, and the political theatre was left without a school of dramatists developing in and with it. The production lists of the Freie Volksbühne and the Neue Freie Volksbühne (the two great working-class theatre-audience organisations) from the mid-nineties until the end of the First World War (127), where we might reasonably expect to find plays representing growing-points of political drama, show increasing dependence upon the plays of the Naturalist *Blütezeit*, the later plays of the former Naturalists, the classics and lighter works. Wedekind and Shaw are the only two significant names that appear on these lists in the realm of socially critical drama until Kaiser's *Gas* (8. 2. '19).

The figure bridging this apparent gap between the socio-political drama of the Naturalists and that of the Expressionists is that of Strindberg. His *Preface* to the 'naturalistic tragedy' *Miss Julie* is in many respects a direct successor to Hebbel's *Vorwort* to *Maria Magdalena*. To take only two important examples:

Just as Hebbel insisted that drama must show both Being and Becoming, so also Strindberg eschews the 'middle-class conception of the immobility of the soul' (128).

As Hebbel distinguishes between original sin (which is a religious conception and is thought of as arising from the misdirection of the Will) and guilt (which he sees as inherent in the nature and existence of Will) so Strindberg treats of 'guilt' as the inevitable consequence of "a whole series of motives . . . "which he then lists, adding with irony, "I have not even preached a moral sermon; in the absence of a priest I leave this to the cook. " (129). Later he says:

> The Naturalist has abolished guilt with God, but the consequences of the action. . . . he cannot abolish (130).

It is true, of course, that Strindberg's naturalistic plays are not political or even social in the way that Ibsen's are (or the way Ibsen's may be taken) but they are Darwinian and thus closely related to the political thought of their period.

> *Miss Julia* is the tragedy of the Darwinian ethos. The concepts in it are through and through Darwinian, but the tragic interpretation is itself a critique of Darwinism (131).

Strindberg, however, is the bridge or link because he was not only a supreme practitioner of Naturalism, but also the major predecessor, both in techniques and in subject-matter, of Expressionism.

> Strindberg came to regard Naturalism as something he had outgrown . . . A moral difference separates his "Naturalist" from his later "Expressionist" plays. In the former the fantastic element is merely a demonic force which wrecks lives; in the latter it is also the creative fancy and imagination which are associated with religion: in them the irrationality of life leads not to the frightening joy in living of *Miss Julia* but to religious resignation. Naturalism and Expressionism, the twin poles of the Strindbergian mind, are two answers to the challenge of a Darwinian world. They are not philosophies. They are the two archetypal patterns of defeat in the modern world: defeat at the hands of naturalistic nihilism and defeat at the hands of a compensatory supernaturalism (132).

Later in his seminal book *The Modern Theatre,* Eric Bentley says, — seriously, but with a wry and critical smile:

> Dramatic Expressionism has three roots: Strindberg, adolescent despair, and electric light (133).

Adolescent despair in the period of the First World War was inextricably involved in youth's reaction against the war and against the social system which had engendered the war. Both the causes of this despair and its consequences were in part political. Toller's frail optimism, as seen in Friedrich's recovery from despair, is expressed in political terms. Thus through Expressionism, Strindberg, Ibsen and the German Naturalists, and Hebbel, we can trace the political aspect of *Die Wandlung* straight back to Schiller's concept of the theatre as a moral institution, whose moral nature has political effects.

While some of Toller's later work is directly related to the traditions of the working-class amateur dramatic movement, with its Speaking Choirs and propagandist *tableaux vivants,* in this play the middle-class poet is offering in Friedrich an idealised persona of himself as a leader of the masses. Out of Toller's attempt to put such leadership into practice during the hectic weeks of the Munich *Räterepublik* grew the deeper understanding of the problems of politics, the inner conflicts and the sense of tragedy that give the best of his work from then on its claim to greatness. *Die Wandlung* is his only optimistic play. If this play looks back to Schiller through the lens of

Expressionism, he was soon to be drawing strength from the 'other' dramas of the nineteenth century, from Büchner, Lassalle and the named and anonymous dramatists of the working-class, social-democratic clubs and societies between 1848 and his own times.

Die Wandlung does not, however, belong only to the tradition of political drama. Toller's division of the play into *Stations* places it also in the tradition of religious drama. In many religious dramas of the later middle-ages throughout Europe various Stations were simultaneously presented and the action focused on each in turn; in other places the multi-storeyed waggons visited various Stations in the city to perform the various stages or stations of biblical story.

The oldest and most fundamental 'Station' series is that of *The Stations of the Cross*, the fourteen episodes from the condemnation of Christ to death, to the Deposition in the Sepulchre, that were and are placed around the walls of a church to be visited in turn with appropriate prayers. Thus the figure of Christ is inextricably associated with the concept of Station Drama. As Michel Bataillon reminds us, one does not define Station Drama simply as a linear succession of scenes. It is a dramatic *genre* which must not be confused with Epic dramaturgy, despite profound analogies. In the first place, he points out, there is in Station Drama "hypertrophy of the function of the hero" (134) linked with a schematisation of the world with which he is confronted. In the best of Station Drama there is a progress, at once physical and mental of the central individual figure. This is true in the case of the Stations of the Cross, which Bataillon sees as to some extent the prototype of the *genre*. In varying degrees Christ's earthly progress is a kind of thread running through these plays. He suggests that this is true of Strindberg's *To Damascus* as well as of *Die Wandlung*, in which the hero is also a 'younger brother' of Ahasuerus, the Wandering Jew.

Thus the genealogy of *Die Wandlung* can be traced right back to the late medieval passion plays such as the *Osterspiel von Muri* (Aargau, mid-13th Century), the so-called *Wiener Passionsspiel* (c. 1315), the *Frankfurter Passionsspiel* (about 1350) and even the still-running *Oberammergau Passionsspiele*.

As a passion play that is still a living part of twentieth century theatre, this last merits somewhat closer examination in this context. For the original play of 1634 a text was provided by the neighbouring monastery at Ettal. This underwent many changes and by the latter part of the eighteenth century the text in use (*Passio Nova* by P. Ferdinand Rosner) was thoroughly Baroque in character. The play was rewritten in 1810/1811 by a Benedictine Father, Othmar Weis, with music composed (also in 1810) by the remarkable local composer and teacher, Rochus Dedler. This is in effect the text used today (1984 production), with important modernisations in 1850/1860 by the priest of that period, Jos. Alois Daisenberger. The most recent modifications, made in 1983 for the 1984 production (350th anniversary), included striking out what remained of passages which could be regarded as anti-semitic. Dedler's music, which had suffered during the nineteenth century from inappropriate orchestral accretions, was also restored to its pristine simplicity in 1950, by Prof. Eugen Papst (135).

The structure of Weis's play is by no means that of a simple chronicle of events. The stage that has been built to meet its requirements embodies and reflects its complexity. It is a very wide, relatively shallow open stage, recalling the Greek theatre, and will accommodate enormous crowd scenes. In the centre of the stage-buildings which form the permanent backing to this open stage, and raised a little above it by a couple of shallow steps, is a proscenium-arched inner or rear stage which can he artificially lit and where pictorial scenery can be prepared and displayed. Each side of this are large arched entrances wide enough for rapid mass entrances and exits, and leading to hints of further "streets" off-stage. Beyond these entrances, left and right, are pillared 'houses' (in the sense of the medieval stage) led up to by broad, slightly convexly curved flights of some eight or nine steps. These can represent specific locations, that on the actors' left normally serving as the Temple and that on the right as the seat of Roman power. Finally, at extreme right and left are downstage entrances primarily used by the chorus.

The play consists of a Prologue, two Parts (*Abteilungen*) and a closing 'Station' (*Schlußvorstellung*). The first Part runs for two-and-a-half hours, the second for two-and-three-quarter hours. The Parts are divided into sections each of which is called a *Vorstellung* (literally Performance). In effect each *Vorstellung* is a Station in the play. Each Station contains several elements. Not every Station contains every element, but the typical, fully developed Station has this, or a very similar, pattern:

1. *Prologue*. The mixed Chorus of 48 enters very formally from right and left and the Prologue speaks from centre Stage. The Prologues are written in Classical Lyric Metres (e.g. Sapphics), their language is clear and forceful, but quite complex, and their matter is the theological content of the Station and often refers to Old Testament parallels to or foreshadowings of the passion story. Here, as an example, are two stanzas from the Prologue to the Fifth Station:

The Traitor. After two stanzas referring to Judas, the Prologue continues:

> Gleicher Sinn verhärtete Jakobs Söhne,
> Daß sie unbarmherzig den eig'nen Bruder
> Um erbärmlichen Preis in der fremden Wuch'rer
> Hände verkauften.
>
> Wo das Herz dem Götzen des Geldes huldigt,
> Da ist jeder edlere Sinn geschwunden;
> Ehre wird verkäuflich und Manneswert,
> Liebe und Freundschaft. (136)

The fine rhetorical speaking of the complex rhythms and language of these Prologues is one of the most impressive features of the whole performance.

2. The rest of the *Vorstellung* normally falls into two sections, marked *A* and *B* in the printed text.
   A is the *Vorbild*, the *Example*, that is, the Old Testament parallel or foreshadowing. This usually consists of:
   i) a sung chorus.
   ii) The Chorus swings back from the centre, and the rear stage opens for a *tableau vivant* of the Old Testament incident. (e. g. in the Fifth *Vorstellung*, the sale of Joseph by his brethren for twenty pieces of silver: Judas' price was thirty).
   iii) The rear stage closes and the Chorus leaves very formally by the side entrances.

The words of the sung choruses are in traditional hymn-like metres, the language much simpler than that of the spoken Prologue, while Dedler's settings of these choruses often recall traditional Chorales, though in general his music has a Haydnesque flavour.

> Rochus Dedler was a child of his time. Haydn and Mozart exercised great influence upon his compositions. His music is popularly traditional and rooted in his native soil, and rises in many places to thrilling beauty and massive dimensions (137).

B is the *Handlung*, the *Action*. This is the actual passion story written in simple naturalistic prose, with many echoes, naturally, of the biblical text. In performance even this is not presented as simple naturalism: for example, when crowds or groups speak or shout they do so *in unison*, as they would in an oratorio or musical Passion and not at random as in a naturalistic play. Certain scenes, too, are presented in heightened style. For example, while Christ distributes the Bread and Wine at the Last Supper a hidden chorus sings a chorale, so that the impact resembles that of a sung Mass, and the ritual connection between the Mass and the original Supper is brought home to the audience in theatrical terms and by theatrical means.

The *Handlung* in any one *Vorstellung* may consist of several Scenes (*Auftritte*).

Although there is no question of Toller's owing a direct debt to the Oberammergau play, the parallels between this nineteenth century Station Drama and *Die Wandlung* are close enough to be of interest. The conception of a "Station" (*Vorstellung*) as a unit in the play, containing not only part of the action, but also other elements with the functions of intensification, internalisation and parallelism (e.g. *The Mountaineers*) is shared by the two plays, though the structure of the Stations in *Die Wandlung* is much simpler than that of the *Vorstellungen* in the Passion Play. In particular the use of the rear stage for the Old Testament *tableaux vivants* which intensify and at the same time universalise the significance of the Action scenes on the front stage, anticipates and has much in common with Toller's use of the rear stage and different style for his Dream Scenes. Each play has a *Vorspiel* (*Prologue* — the same word is used) in non-naturalistic style, not part of the actual story but introducing its essential theme. In the Oberammergau play the double origin of the play is shown: 1) the Expulsion of Adam and Eve from Paradise; 2) the Oath taken by the people of Oberammergau in the churchyard in 1633 (138).

Although the example of the *Passionsspiele Oberammergau* shows that religious Station Drama was, as it still is, a living *stage* tradition in German, and not merely a literary inheritance, it was certainly not directly from these station-dramas that Toller derived the form of *Die Wandlung*, but from Strindberg. As we have already seen, Strindberg is the link between the socio-political drama of the Naturalists and the socio-political drama of the Expressionists. He is also the link between traditional religious Station-drama and Station-drama as practised by the Expressionists, and as Eric Bentley (139) pointed out, it was when Strindberg expressed "creative fancy and imagination . . . associated with religion" that he wrote his "expressionist" plays, of which that which concerns us in this context is the Station-drama *To Damascus*, whose very title alludes to the conversion (or 'transformation', *Wandlung*) of St Paul on the Road to Damascus. Thus through Strindberg's 'religious' plays Station Drama re-emerged in the modern theatre.

Die Wandlung has many important analogies with *To Damascus*, and Toller almost certainly owes a direct debt to this play through his reading, even as a schoolboy.

> I love the books which the school forbids: Hauptmann and Ibsen, Strindberg and Wedekind (140).

As Bataillon suggests, Toller's play in its completed form owes a structural debt to Strindberg's.

Part I of *To Damascus* consists of seventeen scenes cyclically arranged around Scene 9 (9 is the Square of the Trinity), thus:

Sc. 1	Street Corner	Sc. 17
Sc. 2	Doctor's House	Sc. 16
Sc. 3	Room in an Hotel	Sc. 15
Sc. 4	By the Sea	Sc. 14
Sc. 5	On the Road	Sc. 13
Sc. 6	In a Ravine	Sc. 12
Sc. 7	In a Kitchen	Sc. 11
Sc. 8	The 'Rose' Room	Sc. 10
	Sc. 9 Convent	

(141)

Toller also uses an uneven number of scenes — 13 — with number seven (another 'holy' number, especially in Jewish traditions (142) as the 'hinge' of the whole work. The 'realistic' and 'dream' scenes (6 of each) are balanced, though less regularly than in the Strindberg scheme, before and after this scene, which is the only single-scene Station:

Stn. 1:	Realistic . . . . Dream
Stn. 2	Realistic . . . . Dream
Stn. 3	Realistic . . . . Dream
	Station 4: Realistic.
Stn. 5	Dream . . . . Dream . . . . Dream . . . . Realistic
Stn. 6	Dream . . . . Realistic

(143)

Bataillon suggests that the dream scenes change in function in the second part (after Sc. 7), and that as Toller gives no directions as to whether Scene 7 (Station 4) is to be played on the fore-stage or the rear-stage, it is probable that he intends the whole stage to be used for this key scene. In view of the big break (in terms of experience even more than of time) between the writing of the first and second parts (Stns 1–4 & Stns 5 & 6), one must exercise caution in ascribing too careful authorial intention to Toller. A case can be made for regarding Stations 1–4 as originally conceived to be a complete entity, beginning with Christmas and ending with the transformation of the protagonist — a sunrise scene contrasting with the evening scene at the opening. But the decision to extend the play resulted in changes. Ahasuerus, the Wandering Jew, disappears as a symbol of the protagonist's fate, and Christ takes his place. This occurs in the sequence of three Dream Scenes (Stn 5, Scs 8, 9 & 10) which follow Stn. 4, Sc. 7. In this second part of the play dream scenes precede realistic scenes and show the psychological processes which lead to those realistic scenes: a totally different function from the dream scenes of the early part, which show the psychological *consequences* of what has occurred in the realistic scenes. The sequence of three scenes certainly breaks the neat schematisation established in the early part; but it also gives scope for the 'new' Friedrich to be developed before he reappears to make his two long public speeches.

The first scene in the second part (Stn 5, Sc. 8) marks a new departure in the use of dream figures with Friedrich's face. In scenes 2, 4 & 6 the dream figures are in situations (the military transport train, No-Man's-Land, and the Military Hospital) which Toller himself had experienced (not, of course, as a padre). In Stn. 5, Sc. 8, however, the Friedrich figure is a *Schlafbursche* (a man who cannot rent a room but only a bed or part of a bed, and often only for the night *or* for the day). The scene thus represents Friedrich's mental and spiritual efforts to identify with the working class. We see him sharing the bed with the young woman forced into prostitution and then see him taken from his bed by the Night-Visitor, who takes him from the *Mietskaserne* to that other 'barrack', the factory-prison. The dream-shift from *Die große Fabrik (The Big Factory)* to the ground-floor of the prison is, as already noted, made during blackout to the accompaniment of factory noises.

Although Friedrich in Sc. 8 is not identified with Christ, the audience will recall, when that identification does come in Sc. 9, that Jesus was criticised for his association with sinners, including prostitutes (144). For the reader (and the play's director) Sc. 9 is clearly headed *Tod und Auferstehung (Death and Resurrection)*, and as the lights come on, the dying prisoner (with Friedrich's face) is lying on the concrete floor with his head thrown back and his arms outstretched "*as if he were crucified*". It must be emphasised that this is the first time in the play that any identification of Friedrich with Christ has been suggested. It is impossible to know whether it had been in the author's mind from the start (Stn. 1, Sc. 1 is Christmas) or whether he now saw the way forward in this light. In any event this scene continually emphasises the Christian aspect:

> The Christian command of the Church
> He has twice transgressed in sin (145).
> It was not Romans who nailed him to the cross: /
> He crucified himself (146).

In this scene, too, the relationship between a Station-Drama and the Stations of the Cross is made explicit:

> We ourselves go through painful Stations
> And send out children
> To their own crucifixion (147).

Or later:

> Helpless, we watch the *via dolorosa* (148).

The prisoner himself dies, but in his dying words he prophesies that his unborn child may be able to redeem himself through crucifixion:

> Perhaps, crucified, he can redeem himself
> Rise again to great freedom (149).

At the end of the scene the child is actually born and the mother holds it out bathed in joyful light to the awe-stricken prisoners, while the ceiling arches up to the infinite skies.

Immediately afterwards appears the Wanderer, with Friedrich's face, not this time the Wandering Jew, but the Risen Christ:

> I feel as if I was awakening today for the first time,
> As if I had rolled away a heavy gravestone
> And rise again (150).

In a final touch, the Wanderer refers to the judges and the accused each putting aside their dignity or their ignominy like *crowns of thorn*. This is the end of the close Friedrich-Christ identification, and the final words of the scene lead back to the world of reality:

> I know the way to the work-place,
> Now I know it (151).

So the last (reality) scene of the Fifth Station presents a public (evening) meeting in which Friedrich, entering upon his role as a public figure, joins in a public debate. An old soldier with his military decorations, a university professor and a priest all speak for the 'establishment' and are answered by an advocate of violent revolution. Friedrich intervenes, putting his Landaueresque answer to socialism through violence. With apparently little dramatic justification he asks the people to wait until midday (?symbolically) the next day, when he will put his case to them in the market-place outside the Church. The scene has a curious coda in which Friedrich resists two temptations:

1) to become a personal *Führer* (that is the word used), and
2) to accept the love of a girl-student who wants to bear his child.

After this comes a further post-script in which an anonymous man with his coat collar turned up high, tells Friedrich he hates him and that he ought to turn monk.

The first (dream) scene, Sc. 12, of the final Station (6) is called *Die Bergsteiger (The Mountaineers)*. In this two mountaineers have the faces of Friedrich and his Friend from Sc. 1 and Sc. 7. The Friedrich figure must push on to the heights, while the Friend figure gives up. The Mountaineer figures are a completely new element in the dream sequences and are unrelated to any of the earlier dream figures. While the image of the dauntless mountaineer (e.g. the 'Excelsior' figure) is common enough, there could well be a direct link between this scene and Rilke's poem, already referred to, *Ausgesetzt auf den Bergen des Herzens* (152). Certainly no apparent link between Toller and Rilke can be ignored.

In the last scene Friedrich first has to recapitulate the 'stations' by which he has reached his final position. The Friend has already been disposed of in Sc. 12. He has to encounter his Mother, the Uncle referred to in Sc. 1, the Doctor of the Military Hospital, and a sick man with shifty eyes, who seems to be related to the war invalid of Sc. 7, after meeting whom Friedrich had nearly killed himself, but was prevented by the hospital sister. The sick man with shifty eyes wants to persuade *Mankind* to commit suicide, not through war, but voluntarily. He advocates building "hygienic places for self-annihilation", a curiously horrible prophecy of the Nazi gas-chambers which Jews entered having been told they were baths. Here, at the very beginning of

Toller's career as a writer we find his persona having to battle with the temptation of suicide.

After a short scene with a woman who equates love with lust (*Liebe peitscht Leiber: Love whips bodies (153)*) the Sister comes again, as in Sc. 7 to give Friedrich final encouragement.

The scene and the play then end with Friedrich's impassioned speech calling for bloodless revolution and with the positive reaction of the crowd. The sacrifices that seemed to threaten the Friedrich figure as Mountaineer are not demanded of him in the course of this play, even though the final scenes were in fact written in prison: but Toller had not yet experienced extremities of conflict between his pacifist and his socialist ideals.

Even at the end of the play the quasi-religious character of Toller's and Landauer's revolutionary ideals are kept in sight, partly through biblical allusion:

> Go to the soldiers, they should beat their swords into ploughshares (154).
>
> (155)

There is another entirely different thread that links *Die Wandlung*, though less directly, with the station-dramas of the late Middle Ages, and that is through the medium of Goethe's *Faust*.

One critic of the first production (see below, note 227) remarked that the sub-title of the play suggested to him: *My Golgotha, Via Dolorosa*, and *Faust*. As the influence of Goethe's *Faust* on subsequent German literature and drama has been all-pervasive, seminal and inescapable, a mere generalised suggestion of a *Faust/Wandlung* connection would be facile. The real interest lies in the specific and particular way in which Toller's play is linked with Goethe's.

Goethe's knowledge of the Faust legend came to him from two sources: a late eighteenth century publication of the 1725 version of the *Faust-Book*, and a *Faust* puppet-play he saw when a boy. The eighteenth century *Faust-Book* gave him many motifs of the Faust tale, but in this version there was virtually nothing left of the "stormy, scholarly mind" (156) which was still vitally alive in the original 1587 *Faust-Book*. That original 1587 *Faust-Book* had soon made itself felt in England, and before his early death in 1593 Christopher Marlowe had used it as the basis for his *Tragicall History of Doctor Faustus*.

Marlowe's play was probably first taken to Germany in 1592 by Robert Browne (157) and in some form, probably prose, was in the repertory of the *Englische Komödianten* who toured Germany at least until 1659 and exercised such enormous influence there. The play continued to be toured and adapted in Germany throughout the seventeenth century and into the eighteenth, though the earliest surviving German version dates from about 1800 (158). In this the comic Hanswurst rôle is much developed and Faust himself, while he has lost much of the Titanism of Marlowe's creation, retains his thirst for knowledge. With the rise in popularity of marionette theatres in the later seventeenth century, the Faust play entered their repertoire. There were many versions, some perpetuated in oral family traditions and some in written texts. After the publication of Goethe's *Faust Fragment* in 1790 and especially after the publication of *Faust I* in 1808 the interest these aroused led to the collection of some of the marionette versions. It is not known which version the young Goethe saw. Nor, as we learn from his diary, did he read Marlowe's play until 1818 (159). The essential point for our argument, however, is that the puppet-play which he saw with enthusiasm as a boy and recalled in detail throughout his life, was derived ultimately from Marlowe.

It is accepted that Marlowe's *Faustus* owes many features of its form to morality plays. The Good and Evil Angels, for example, occur in the morality play *The Castle of Perseverance* (160), as do the Deadly Sins. The morality plays, like the mystery plays, often were in effect 'station' dramas. Instead of the Stations being stages in the development of the biblical story (often associated in performance with specific physical 'stations' grouped and presented as a multiple, simultaneous setting), in the morality plays they took the form of stages in the testing and development of one protagonist called, for example, *Mankind* or *Everyman*. Thus there is one character running through the play and the connecting thread is not an external objective conflict, but the internal, subjective conflict resulting in the protagonist's moral development as he encounters personifications of various vices and virtues at each stage. The Stations thus become (as indeed they are in *Die Wandlung*) not stages in a *story* but in a *moral process.*

This form Marlowe adopts with the modification that (except at the very beginning and end of the play) Faust is accompanied by Mephistophilis: even so this on-stage conflict between Faustus and Mephistophilis is purely an externalisation of Faustus' own inner moral processes. Faustus passes through a series of 'Stations'. As Erich Trunz has said, Marlowe's grasp seizes upon what he calls "die großen Situationen" (the great situations) (161): the opening monologue in which Faust examines all branches of learning and turns to magic; the conjuration; the pact; intervention in high politics; the conjuration of the spirit of Helen of Troy; and finally repentance, and the longing, all too late, to burn the books of magic; and his midnight damnation. Marlowe's play can thus fairly be described as a tragic station-drama, a Station Tragedy.

Goethe's *Faust I* is similarly constructed. Goethe had originally no overall plan for it, as he had for *Faust II*, but built it up out of individual scenes, each the product of passionate inner vision. The scene-headings themselves suggest the idea of 'Stations': *Nacht, Vor dem Tor, Studierzimmer, Auerbachs Keller, Hexenküche, Straße etc (Night, Outside the Gate, Study, Auerbach's Cellar, Witches' Kitchen, Street, etc),* locations connected only by the figure of Faust and serving in the process of his moral downfall. Seen thus *Faust I* is very close to Bataillon's definition of Station-Drama. As in morality plays and in Marlowe, the conflict is within the soul of the protagonist and the real action subjective. ("Zwei Seelen wohnen, ach! in meiner Brust, ": Alas, two souls dwell within my breast. *Faust I*. 1112.) Goethe himself fully understood that the drama of *Faust I* was the subjective, inner drama of the individual:

> The First Part is almost entirely subjective. It all stems from one diffident, passionate individual (162).

Faust II was seen by its author in a very different light:

> In the Second Part, however, there is practically nothing subjective; there appears here a higher, broader, brighter, more dispassionate world (163).

So far we have adduced nothing that could not be explained by regarding *Faust I* and *Die Wandlung* as totally separate developments from religious and moral station-drama. But there is a remarkable parallel between the beginning and ending of the "*Ur-Wandlung*" (Stations 1–4 regarded as originally complete in themselves) and Goethe's *Faust*, a parallel close enough for it to be argued that in writing the *Ur-Wandlung*, Toller was influenced (whether consciously or unconsciously is not the issue) by Goethe.

Die Wandlung begins with Christmas and evening, and ends, (in Stn. 4) with the transformation of the protagonist, and sunrise. The stage direction at the beginning of Stn. 1, Sc. 1 reads:

> Fore-stage. A room in a town correspondingly disfigured. In the twilight forms and colours are blurred and wavering. In the houses on the other side of the street the candles on the Christmas Trees are lit. Friedrich leans at the window (164).

The room is 'disfigured' in urban style. The implication is that taste is poor or corrupt, furniture and decoration lack form or beauty. In addition the twilight blurs colours and forms so that they seem infirm and wavering. Friedrich feels himself a part of this uncertainty and corrupt ambiguity, for he refers to himself in the first few moments as *Ekler Zwitter* (165) (*a loathsome hermaphrodite, a disgusting hybrid*), a being of uncertain shape, like the setting in which we see him.

The opening of *Faust,* too, is full of darkness, semi-darkness and ambiguous forms. The *Dedication,* the first words a reader of the work meets, begins:

> Once more you approach, you hovering forms,
> Who at one time, early, showed yourselves to my clouded sight . . .
> You crowd near me! good, then, — you may prevail,
> As you rise around me out of haze and fog (166).

The first scene, simply headed *Night,* is full of similar images of visual uncertainty:

> It is becoming cloudy above me,
> The moon hides its light
> The lamp is extinguished!
> It grows misty — red beams flutter around my head
> A horror drifts down from the vault and seizes me (167).

In the second scene also, the visual uncertainties persist as Faust sees the approaching poodle streaming a trail of fire. Wagner says:

> You are probably suffering from an optical illusion (168).

The openings of the two works are also parallel in that each takes place in the context of a major feast of the Christian Year, though these are used by the two dramatists for very different purposes. *Die Wandlung* begins on Christmas Eve, with the candles on the Christmas Trees emphasising for Friedrich his exclusion as a Jew from the sense of belonging to German-Christian society. *Faust* begins on Easter Eve and it is the sound of Easter bells and the choral song, *Christ ist erstanden! (Christ is risen)*, that prevents Faust from drinking the goblet of poison already at his lips.

From these common beginnings — a Feast of the Church; blurred and cloudy uncertainties — each protagonist sets out on his false route out of the impasse in which he finds himself. Faust chooses the false route of magic through his pact with Mephistopheles, and Friedrich sets out on *his* false route of volunteering for the colonial war.

These resemblances between the opening of *Die Wandlung* and that of *Faust* would not be so remarkable were it not for the fact that the conclusion of the *Ur-Wandlung* (the end of Stn. 4, Sc. 7) also has striking resemblances to the scene in which Faust begins his long journey to redemption, *Faust II*, Act 1, Sc. 1, *Anmutige Gegend (Pleasant Landscape)*. This scene is the beginning of Faust's own *Wandlung*. Healed through the hours of the night by the ministrations of Nature, through Ariel and the Chorus of Spirits, he arises from restless half-slumber as a tremendous tumult announces the approach of the sun (169). He feels the pulses of life freshly awakened as the sunrise approaches

> Look up! The gigantic mountain summits
> Already announce the most solemn hour (170).

The sun rises and Faust, blinded by its direct light, turns his back upon it and sees instead the rainbow colours in the foam and spray of cataracts: the light of the sun, refracted, is what creates life:

> So let the sun always remain behind me!
> The cataract, thundering through the cleft in the rock,
> I look at it with growing joy . . .
> But how magnificent, springing out of this storm,
> Curves the coloured rainbow in all its continual changes . . .
> We have Life in the coloured reflection (171).

Station 4 of *Die Wandlung* begins in early morning (*Morgenfrühe*). During the scene the sun rises and sunbeams fall on Friedrich's monstrous statue of *Sieg des Vaterlands (Victory of the Fatherland)*. Then follows Friedrich's encounter with the woman and the war invalid, his old comrade, after which he smashes his statue and takes a revolver from the drawer of his desk in order to end his life (like Faust at the beginning of *Faust I*). But at this moment the Sister comes, urging him to take the way

To God, who lives in humanity (172).

Friedrich buries his face in his hands. Then he stands up, staggers, and stretches himself:

FRIEDRICH:
Sun flows around me,
Freedom streams through me,
My eyes see the way.
I will travel along it, Sister,
Alone, and yet with you,
Alone, and yet with all,
Knowing about mankind.
(He strides ecstatically out to the door) (173).

The first scene of *Faust II* was evidently conceived as a hinge, an opening door, a fresh start for Faust, who, instead of being consumed and destroyed by remorse, sets out on his new pilgrimage. Station 4 of *Die Wandlung* could well have been conceived by Toller in the first instance as an end, a conclusion. But just as *Faust* strides out towards the rainbow colours of life in the morning sunshine at the beginning of *Faust II,* so could this scene of *Die Wandlung* serve the author as a central hinge, a new beginning, as Friedrich in the final scenes of the play, goes out, as does Faust, into a life of more public service.

Thus *Die Wandlung* has in its structure and conception, clear links with Goethe's *Faust* and through the Faust plays of Goethe and Marlowe, with the Station-dramas of the later Middle Ages.

It is patently obvious that apart from its roots in older dramatic traditions, the basis of the play is in some sense autobiographical.

> Dans l'approche de l'oeuvre c'est la charactéristique la plus extérieure, la plus évidente, la plus banale aussi (174).

Yet the point is worth pursuing both to investigate just *how* Toller has adapted his own experience and to observe the place of an autobiographical play in the Expressionist movement.

For knowledge of Toller's own early experiences and how they affected him our primary source is his autobiography *Eine Jugend in*

Deutschland, published in 1933, and this autobiography is itself considerably stylised and dramatised, as examination of those sections that can be paralleled in other of his works (e. g. *Justiz: Erlebnisse; Briefe aus dem Gefängnis*) shows. Toller, inveterate self-dramatiser, saw his own life as 'exemplary', as the indefinite article in his title indicates, so that in comparing the play and the autobiography we are in fact comparing two highly wrought versions of the underlying factual history. With this caution we proceed with the comparison.

Station 1, Scene 1 begins with Friedrich the young Jew looking longingly at the Christmas Tree candles lighting the rooms of his Christian neighbours and feeling his own exclusion. This vivid image, though it may well have a basis in fact, is not paralleled in *Eine Jugend in Deutschland*. In the first chapter of this, *Kindheit (Childhood)*, he describes, as if it is his earliest childhood memory (he says he was still wearing a frock) how a little girl, Ilse, who was holding his hand, was called away from him by her nursemaid because he was a Jew. But he adds immediately the fact that although the Polish son of the night-watchman is his friend, he, as a German, shouts "Polack" at him when the others do. This is more complex than the play: Toller, the Jew, is a minority among the Germans, but Toller the German is in the ruling majority in relation to the Poles. The very first dramatic image of the play is thus both a fictionalisation and a simplification of autobiographical fact, in so far as that can be ascertained. Friedrich is not given the majority / persecutor rôle that Toller himself played alongside his minority / persecuted one.

The use of the Christian Christmas Tree celebrating Christ's birth is an excellently chosen opening to a play in which the Jew (and Jesus was a Jew) experiences (in a dream scene) *Tod und Auferstehung (Death and Resurrection)* (Sc. 9). Among the images through which Friedrich introduces himself is that of the *Stehaufclown* (the *Kellyman* toy which always stands up again when knocked down), a comic resurrection figure. At the same time the sense that Friedrich has of being patronised by the Christians (175) reflects Toller's childhood experience of being accepted and then snubbed by an evangelical group, the *True Christians* (176).

The rest of the first scene, introduced by Friedrich's soliloquy, consists of two dialogues: one between Friedrich and his mother, the other between Friedrich and his friend. The former is closely autobiographical. Friedrich's father, who is dead, was a good businessman: Toller's father, Max, was a shopkeeper. He had died in 1910. As a father-surrogate the mother cites 'Uncle Richard'. When young Ernst, just before he went to Grenoble, got into a scrape with an actor's girl-friend, it was 'My Uncle, the Lawyer' who lightly took the matter in hand and bought off the actor for 75 Marks (177). So the family situation is closely paralleled. That Toller's mother's care and hard work, like Friedrich's mother's, enabled him to continue his studies must also be factual. But both the parental and the avuncular care seem to Friedrich to be oppressive:

> Good father . . . he obstructed my youth!
> . . . yes, my economic progress is assured.
> But what did you do for my *soul*? (178).

The mother, supported by the dead father and living uncle, becomes the epitome of a repressive and narrow-minded society. Although the German Christians "only tolerate us. They despise us", she conforms and attends church service and wants Friedrich to do the same, for social rather than religious reasons, while at the same time she teaches him to hate the Gentiles. In the last speech of the scene Friedrich cries:

> I called you mother, because you bore me. Can I still call you mother today, when you exposed my soul, as stupid mothers expose their naked child? (179).

Friedrich's denial of his mother echoes almost literally Toller's own as expressed in his earliest surviving poem, *Der Ringende* (*The Striver*: and cf: *Das Ringen eines Menschen*) written in 1912:

> Mutter, Mutter,
> Warum bist Dus nicht?
>
> Kann ich nicht jene Frau,
> Die mir mit ihrem Blute
> In dunklen Nächten Herzschlag lieh,
> Aus frommen Herzen Mutter nennen,
> So will ich weite Wege wandern (180).

The parallel is even clearer when we recall that at the opening of the dialogue Friedrich has told his mother he has been *Auf der Wanderschaft (on his travels)*, like Ahasuerus, the Wandering Jew (181).

In thus establishing what today we call the 'generation gap' as symbol of youth's alienation from a traditional society, Toller is placing his play firmly in the Expressionist series. In the pre-history of the

Expressionist movement Wedekind's *Frühlings Erwachen (Spring's Awakening)* made the *Kindertragödie (Tragedy of Childhood)*, as he called his first play, the vehicle for a devastating critique of repressive, conformist society. The family play with its conflict of generations became typical of Expressionist drama even before the outbreak of the First World War. F. N. Mennemeier in his study of modern German drama refers to

> the typical expressionist reduction of the topic of revolution, a pressing one at that time, to the pattern of a middle-class family drama (182).

In this connection he mentions particularly Fritz von Unruh's *Ein Geschlecht (A Generation)* and Walter Hasenclever's *Der Sohn (The Son)*, remarking of the latter:

> Hasenclever's drama *The Son*, too, treats of the theme of revolution from the restricted viewpoint of the generation-conflict (183).

Von Unruh's play was written during the war (1915–16) and printed in 1917, achieving immediate success (28th thousand by 1922), while Hasenclever's was written as early as 1913 and also published in 1917.

Of earlier Expressionist plays it is *Der Sohn* which has the closest affinities with the 'family' element in *Die Wandlung*. In view of Toller's later collaborations with Hasenclever in *Bourgeois bleibt Bourgeois* and *Menschen hinter Gittern* (the German-language version of *Big House*) it is not surprising to find Toller evidently modelling some of his dramatic patterns on those of his slightly (but, considering their youth, significantly) older contemporary. (Hasenclever was three years the elder). Hasenclever in *Der Sohn* drew heavily on his own home life. The fact that in his play the mother does not appear and is never mentioned, so that the Son appears to belong, like Friedrich, to a one-parent family, is paralleled by the real-life fact that Hasenclever never mentioned his mother and had no relationship with her other than a negative one, described by the family doctor simply as *Mangel jeglicher Liebe (Lack of any love)* (184). At the time he wrote the play he did not know that during her pregnancy his mother had suffered from a pregnancy-related psychosis which had caused her to be sent to an asylum for some months: consequently she had always hated her son. How far the father's treatment of the son in the play (the sadistic nightly beatings with a riding-whip, the testing of homework before he left for school and so on) was a literal transcript of the author's boyhood, even his friend Kurt Pinthus is not certain. The son's governess certainly derives from real life, as does the strict censorship of his reading and his being denied going to the theatre. Like Toller, Hasenclever nevertheless read the modern literature disapproved of by his elders.

There is no parallel in Toller's childhood with the severity of Hasenclever's. Toller tells us little about his father except that his dying words declared the family, and Ernst specifically, to be "guilty":

> Ihr seid schuld, stöhnte er, Du bist schuld (185).

It was a fearful and negative memory to carry through life. The father had in fact died of cancer. Like Friedrich's mother, Ernst's had worked very hard, even in her husband's lifetime, for the sake of her family (186). Her desire to exercise power over her son, however, must have been strong. After his imprisonment for three months from February 1918 in the Leonrodstraße on a charge of treason, during which the later scenes of his play formed themselves in his mind, she contrived to have her son sent to a lunatic asylum (*Irrenanstalt*: Toller uses the now dated word).

> My mother could not grasp that her son was accused of treason; the accusation seemed fearful to her, as did the threatened punishment; she did not understand how a person of middle-class family could devote himself to the workers' struggle; he must be ill, she thought, I want to help him; she alerts the resident doctors, she sends certificates to the Court to the effect that I had been nervous even as a child. The result was this psychiatric examination (187).

Toller's charitably understanding account of his mother's motives is in harmony with the gentleness of the parent-son relationship in this play, when compared with Hasenclever's.

This opening scene suggests that Toller's play is going to follow the "typical expressionist reduction" of revolution to family drama in the manner of Hasenclever, and as the Tribüne's only previous production had been two of the latter's short plays, *Der Bettler* and *Die Entscheidung*, only ten days earlier, it was natural when the play was produced that Toller should be compared with Hasenclever, — though the comparison was to Toller's advantage (188). It will therefore be appropriate to notice here the second dialogue of the first scene, that with the Friend, although this is not autobiographical, for the idea of using a "Friend" figure would seem to be adopted directly from *Der Sohn*. Hasenclever's 'Friend' seems to be intended to serve three purposes: he is the means of the Son's escape; he is a parallel figure to the Son, but by no means identical, being more emancipated; and Hasenclever seems also to try to use him as a *raisonneur*; expressing the author's viewpoint (189). Toller's "Friend" serves the same functional purposes as Hasenclever's in that he brings the news of the outbreak of colonial war that gives Friedrich his opening to escape from the house and prove his identity with society, but there the likeness ends. Friedrich's Friend is not more but less emancipated than Friedrich himself. To the very end of *Die Wandlung* the Friend lags behind Friedrich, a relationship vividly theatricalised in Scene 12, *The Mountaineers*. If Hasenclever's "Friend" is something of a *raisonneur*, Toller's rather resembles a classical *confidant*.

The first scene of Toller's play thus clearly shows the author as following in the steps of Hasenclever, though the *Prologue* should already have prepared the reader (the first *audience* was not shown it) for wider development. This development begins immediately with the *Transport Train*, the *Water-Hole in the Desert*, and the *Barbed-Wire Entanglements*. It is a development both stylistic (Scenes 2 and 4 are Dream Scenes) and autobiographical (190). The Military Transport Train and the scene between the barbed-wire entanglements are both nightmarish transformations of Toller's own wartime experiences. *Eine Jugend in Deutschland* contains three accounts of military train journeys: on Toller's arrival in Lindau at the very outbreak of war he was forced to travel in a goods train, each waggon marked *16 Men or 8 Horses* (191); then comes the heady journey over the Rhine (192); and last, the brief but densely described journey to the Front (193). Only the last of these has anything approaching the evocative quality of language achieved in the very short scene in the play, a strongly rhythmic poem, its lines divided among seven speakers, while the two most important figures (that with the face of Friedrich and that with a skull-head) remain silent. If this is to be called autobiographical it is the autobiography of the inner, not the outer life. It is confessional rather than autobiographical. Toller has here broken through to a new non-naturalistic mode of portraying reality. Even the verse, irregular though it is, has purposeful shape, most lines having four stresses, which imitate the endless rhythm of a railway train in the days when the sound of the bogies on the regularly placed gaps between the lengths of rail was the predominant sound of a train. At the same time the 4-stress rhythm links the verse with that of the oldest Germanic poems such as the *Hildebrandslied* (c. 800 AD):

> Wie lánge ráttert schón der Zúg,
> O díese éwige knírschende Stámpfen
>
> Stínkend verfáulendes Ménschenfléisch . . .
> Zíellos írren wir, fúrchtsame Kínder

> Hádubrant gimahálta,/Híltibrantes súnu
> (194)

In the third scene, at the Water-hole in the desert, Toller uses a setting outside his own experience to bring together the essence of two crucial points in his own life: his first sight of casualties and his decision to volunteer for front-line service. In fact he first saw wounded men on a railway station in August, soon after volunteering (195), and Friedrich's volunteering for the dangerous reconnaissance mission is Toller's fictional version of his own sudden decision to volunteer for action on the Western Front in order to escape the inactivity and endless, soulless drill of Alsace-Lorraine. Here Toller, still retaining the sequence of his own experiences, has changed not only the setting and external details, but even the inner motivation, — for Friedrich's motive is to earn his civil rights (*Bürgerrechte*) through the closest conceivable co-operation with the non-Jewish Germans who, he feels, still want to reject him:

> CORPORAL: . . . Who of you here is volunteering?
> FRIEDRICH: I am. *I will, in spite of you* (196).

By now it is evident that if we call *Die Wandlung*, even in its first four Stations, 'autobiographical', it must be in a strictly qualified sense. Yet the next scene (Sc. 4 *Between the Barbed-Wire Entanglements*) complicates matters further, for in this scene, which must be designed to portray, in 'Dream' form, the essence of Friedrich's mission in the fictional colonial war, we are presented with an archetypal image of the Western Front of World War I, where skeletons of bodies which have been sprayed with lime hang on two lines of barbed-wire entanglement between which the earth is churned up with shell-holes. Such a scene would be improbable in a colonial war, and though the author tries to remind us of his 'colonial' intention with occasional phrases (197), the scene, which seems to have made the strongest impression of all on the critics, remains primarily an expression of Toller's experience in the Priesterwald rather than of Friedrich's in the African desert. It is significant, therefore, that there is no "Friedrich" figure in this scene.

What has been largely ignored by critics is the fact that the 'key' skeleton is that of a 13-year-old girl who died after multiple rape. It is the moral corruption of war and the sexual violence it brings in its train that Toller makes the centre of his No-Man's-Land scene. Like the Jew, the girl is without a fatherland (198). The introduction of the girl's skeleton among those of the front-line soldiers emphasises how far this dream scene is from being merely a stylisation of front-line reality.

The Military Hospital (*Lazarett*) scene which follows provides a fascinating example of what Carel ter Haar calls the *fusion* (*Zerschmelzung*) of Toller's life and works (199). C. ter Haar quotes Walter von Molo as saying in a book published in 1957:

> He told me what had radicalised him, the wartime volunteer, so utterly:
> He was lying in the military hospital when his Iron Cross arrived. The Regimental Doctor, or else someone or other who had to say something, handed him the decoration with the words: 'Look, the stigma of your origin is made up for now!'. Because of that he had been furious, and since that time he had been against Germany. How well I understood him (200).

Von Molo met Toller at Lauenstein in 1917, but had little later contact with him. There is no evidence that Toller ever received a decoration for war service, but in this scene of *Die Wandlung* the officer bringing Friedrich his Iron Cross says:

> You were a stranger to our people: now you have won your civil rights (201).

Von Molo is no doubt unwittingly transferring the incident in this scene to Toller's own life (though it is the fact that his 'civil rights' have cost the lives of ten thousand men that most affects Friedrich). But the very fact that von Molo could make this mistake, obviously in good faith, a vivid evidence of how Toller transformed autobiographical material into fiction, while retaining its essence.

Toller wrote these early scenes before he had experienced the real horror of a military hospital in the summer of 1918 (202), but after he had been treated in a Franciscan monastery in 1916:

> I am sent to a military hospital in Strasbourg, a quiet Franciscan monastery. Quiet, kindly monks look after me (203).

Therefore the hospital scene on the fore-stage (Sc. 5), although it satirises the pompous and pedantic attitude of the doctor, represents the Red Cross Nurse as genuinely kindly, associated in Friedrich's mind with Mary, the Mother of God, and working under the sign of the crucifix. The hospital in the play is thus derived from Toller's own experience of the kindly Franciscans. Had it been written after the summer of 1918 it might well have been very different! As it is, the satirical dream scene (Sc. 6 *The Cripples*) which follows, attacks not the degradation and nauseousness of a military hospital but, taking up the theme of the scientifically inclined doctor of Scene 5, exposes the way in which the context of war perverts even the art of healing, and subordinates it to the ends of destruction. This scene is not in any meaningful sense autobiographical, though it is confessional, being a powerful expression of the author's thoughts and feelings about an objective situation.

Thus, too, Scene 7, usually described as the last of the autobiographical scenes, is autobiographical only in that it provides an objective correlative for Toller's own 'conversion' from pro- to anti-war. It may be called obliquely confessional. None of its content bears any relation to Toller's own life; indeed the closest parallel to it is the incident in Gerard Hauptmann's life when a similar monstrous sculpture he had constructed fell about his ears (204). Toller may well have known of this.

To summarise: the basis of the early part of the play is autobiographical, but the autobiography is fully fictionalised. The use of the family drama, with parent/son and son/friend relationships as a paradigm of social revolution probably results from the influence of Hasenclever's newly published play, *Der Sohn*. Toller quickly breaks through this framework which, although borrowed, corresponded with aspects of his own experience. Even his representation of his own front-line experience is not merely a stylisation of fact. The description 'confessional' is more appropriate than 'autobiographical', and such a scene as *The Cripples* is a theatrical embodiment of thought and feeling, not a stylisation of recollected fact. The sculpture scene also is only autobiographical or confessional inasmuch as the author had undergone a similar change of heart in very different circumstances. The relationship of the play to Hasenclever shows that in its initial use of a 'family' situation to express a 'political' theme, it owes at least as much to the Expressionist movement as to the author's private life. Thus although there is a clear break between the two parts of the play, the break is by no means absolute. The first part as well as the second is to a considerable extent a dramatisation of the author's *ideas* rather than of his life and experience.

THE PLAY ON STAGE

The first production of *Die Wandlung* opened on 30 September 1919 at *Die Tribüne*, Berlin-Charlottenburg, under the direction of Karl-Heinz Martin, with designs by Robert Neppach and music by Werner R. Hagemann, and with Fritz Kortner as Friedrich. The text was edited by Rudolf Leonhard. The production ran for 115 Performances (205).

In his article *Bühne und Expressionismus (Theatre and Expressionism)* (206) written in 1918 when he was *Oberspielleiter (principal regisseur)* at the Thalia Theatre in Hamburg, Karl-Heinz Martin, then thirty-two years old, set out fully his thoughts in relation to Expressionism on the stage. For him Expressionism was no mere artistic school or movement but "A new view of the relationships between the universe, the world and the ego" (Eine neue Anschauung der Beziehungen von All, Welt und Ich). He wishes to relate the catchword "Expressionism" and its contrary "Impressionism" to the "eternally latent problem of the art of the theatre", namely "the dual rôle of this art as an end in itself and as mediator for another art — poetry", while bearing in mind that both words had the limitations and advantages of being "catchwords" (*Schlagwörter*). Impressionism, he says, proceeds from outer appearances to the inner being, so that the inner being, the soul, emerges from the *impression*.

> Expressionism, passionately and without consideration for the natural conception of the world, seizes possession of the inner being, the soul of nature, the world-soul, and only when it is able to *express* this passionately, as it has experienced it, does this experience becomes a creation. It feels the cosmic centre of the world in every Ego and records and defines it in every work rightly founded upon the Ego (207).

It follows that expressionistic creation can give no imitation of nature or illusion of nature, but is true, original creation, the fashioning and creating of forms. (Meanwhile one must not deny the valid ideals of Impressionism and Realism. Realism remains the one great choice for art as well as thought; idealism or classicism the other).

From his position as artistic leader of one of the big traditional theatres Martin claims that for the Expressionist movement no compromise with the large, mechanised, proscenium-arched theatres, which divide the performers from the "secret members of the cast, the audience", is possible.

> For the theatre is neither a literary institution, nor a place of amusement, nor a booth for technical spectacles, but solely and only the place of an artistic experience (208).

This experience is created on an invisible stage between the soul of the author and the soul of the audience. The actor, using all his humanity, has to create this through the words of the author,

> For the word, the rhythmically vibrant word, the intellectually structured word, the word experienced in action, is the bridge to the mental and the spiritual, to the metaphysical (209).

Realising this, the new theatre must look closely at the problem of style. At the centre of Expressionism is the depiction of the person (*Darstellung des Menschen*). For the person is no longer the passive object of psychological interpretation but the inspired bearer of the active idea, the source from which stream the fires of all passions, the symbol of the world.

> In the Person is the drama of the world (210).
> The new theatre can again become an essential manifestation of Expressionism: a pulpit for its new ecstasy, a lecturer's desk for its new logic, a Tribüne for its new pathos (211).

In 1919 Karl-Heinz Martin went to Berlin with the actor Fritz Kortner in order to found a new theatre. He obtained a room in the Victoria-Studienhaus in Charlottenburg, which he redesigned as a simple but revolutionary theatre, with 296 seats, a flat platform with no division between stage and auditorium, and simple lighting over the front rows. He called it, significantly, the Tribüne. It was to be a modern theatre for finding new solutions on expressionistic lines. Important though it is in the history of workers' theatre, the Tribüne was in no way a poor man's stage. One could become a patron for 300, 400, or 500 Marks, and the season tickets (which worked out at half the box office price) were 75, 90 or 120 Marks for ten performances.

The theatre opened on 20 September 1919 with Karl-Heinz Martin's production of two short plays by Hasenclever (*Der Bettler* and *Die Entscheidung*). Eight days later there was a matinee of readings of political poetry led by Rudolf Leonhard, and on 30 September Martin's production of Toller's *Die Wandlung* opened. These two were Martin's *only* productions at the Tribüne between September and December 1919, and, despite all he achieved later in a long and distinguished career, *Die Wandlung* was his most famous and influential production. It brought *scenic* Expressionism in Berlin to a peak which up till then had only been reached by *literary* Expressionism (212).

Rudolf Leonhard, who had heard Toller reading scenes from the play, prepared the text for the theatre with considerable omissions and rearrangements about which Toller, who was in prison, could not be consulted. Schematically shown, the changes were:

TOLLER'S TEXT	*LEONHARD'S ADAPTATION*
Prologue	Omitted
Station 1	*Station 1*
Scene 1	Scene 1
Scene 2	Scene 2
Station 2	*Station 2*
Scene 3	Scene 3
Scene 4	Scene 4
Station 3	*Station 3*
Scene 5	Scene 5
Scene 6	Scene 6
Station 4	*Station 4*
Scene 7	Scene 7
Station 5	*Station 5*
Scene 8	Scene 8. First part only.
Scene 9	Omitted here. See below.

Scene 10	Omitted
Scene 11	Scene 11
Station 6	*Station 6*
Scene 12	Omitted.
Scene 13	Scene 13. With no final *Aufruf.*
	Scene 9, altered.

Thus what Leonhard did was to present (minus the Prologue) the play as Toller had written it in Heidelberg and from which he had heard scenes read, butchering the latter part so as to provide a conclusion which minimised the activist, political 'Landauer' side of the play and kept Friedrich's individual fate always in the foreground. In this way Toller's subtitle *Das Ringen eines Menschen (A Man's Struggle)* acquired new importance and the production was brought into harmony with Karl-Heinz Martin's emphasis on the *Darstellung des Menschen ('In the Person is the drama of the world').*

To look more closely at Leonhard's alterations: the omission of the Prologue meant that instead of the play opening with emphasis on war, on death in war and on the lordship of the war-system, after which Friedrich's personal struggle would inevitably be seen in the light of the Prologue, the keynote first struck was that of the individual, the Jew, alienated from the society in which he lived. Then followed the seven scenes of the first four Stations, scenes which evidently constituted the essentials of the play for Leonhard, for what he did include of the later scenes he used only to extend and conclude the drama of the first seven. He so arranged and cut the scenes as to broaden the canvas to include *some* of the 'political' material and then narrow the focus once more upon the protagonist. The broadening process begins with the Dream Scene of the *Schlafbursche,* but the latter part of that scene (The Night-Visitor) is omitted, because this exists in order to lead into Scene 9 (*Death and Resurrection*) in the prison, which Leonhard wished to make the climax and conclusion of the whole play. He also had to omit Scene 10, for this scene exists in order to show the resurrected Friedrich, as the Wanderer, moving towards the workers, the people, in order to deliver the message which was *Toller's* climax and conclusion.

Leonhard then goes from the *Schlafbursche* scene (which now must have fitted rather awkwardly into the play's pattern) straight to the public meeting (Scene 11), which he apparently played complete. Omitting the Mountaineers (Scene 12), which is only meaningful if between Scenes 11 and 13 Friedrich really advances in the direction of becoming a public political figure, he went straight on to the recapitulations of the early part of Scene 13, apparently omitting Friedrich's final speech altogether, and then returning to Scene 9 as his conclusion. Thus he imposed his own interpretation upon the play as a whole.

Moreover, he did not leave Scene 9 unaltered. The Friedrich figure was no longer a Prisoner with the face of Friedrich, but Friedrich himself, so that the scene was no longer a Dream Scene, but actuality. Friedrich, instead of dying, throws off his chains and gains his freedom, which he finally sees in the new-born child, before whom all the prisoners kneel, as the shepherds knelt before Jesus. The political colour Toller gave to the concept of Freedom is thus largely lost and a more personal, metaphysical tone given to the idea.

As it was through this production, and its reviews, that Toller as dramatist first made his public mark, the tendency for him from then on to be labelled as a 'confessional', rather than as a 'political' dramatist must be to a great extent laid at Leonhard's door.

The staging by Robert Neppach was extremely simple. There was no 'front stage' for 'real', and 'rear stage' for 'dream' scenes. This made it easier for Martin to ignore the difference when he chose and to turn the *Death and Resurrection* scene from a 'dream' to a 'reality' scene.

The action took place in front of a dark curtain. The scenery consisted of a screen about two metres square, with sketches of essentials for each scene. For the Transport Train: in front of the dark curtain there stood a piece of wall of medium height and breadth, with barred windows. For the Military Camp in the desert, there was a painted camp-fire (213). For the *barbed wire* scene (Sc. 4) there were two wooden frames with barbed wire and skeletons. The Military Hospital (Sc. 5) had three beds, their feet towards the audience, in front of a distempered wall. The *Schlafbursche* scene (Sc. 8) had a sort of bed or *Lager*. In some scenes bright colours were used, though no details are available as to what colours, and the black-and-white photographs are no help. The scenes were 'harshly bright', an anticipation of Brechtian lighting. The existing photographs (214) show that the scenes were like rough pencil sketches, the idea being, apparently, to let the audience see the scenes as the protagonist saw them, — as he might, so to speak have "sketched" them through his "psychological spectacles". Only a small area of the stage was lit, the dream scenes being darker and lit only from above. Using a very small company, Martin created crowd effects by letting a few people appear at the edge of the pool of light, so that they seemed to be a few of a much larger number. Within this highly stylised, if simple, framework, costumes were realistic, and Friedrich changed his costume appropriately for the different scenes. Make-up also (skeletons excepted) was naturalistic, though the criticism was advanced that the cripples were all too obviously made-up (*Überdeutlich geschminkt*). For the skeletons (Sc. 4) actors wore black tricots with skeletons painted on them, while their heads were made up as skulls.

In all this Karl-Heinz Martin was true to carrying out his theoretical view of the Expressionist Theatre as given in the article written in Hamburg the year before: an absence of machinery, the simplicity of staging, the breaking of the barrier between stage and audience, the avoidance (apart from the realistic costumes) of naturalistic or impressionistic imitation of nature. But above all he carried out faithfully his belief in the supremacy of the word — the author's word — in creating the invisible stage and building the bridge to the intellectual, spiritual and metaphysical reality. Speech predominated. In the lead Kortner used sharp accentuation, speaking rhythmically under Martin's direction, while the secondary characters, the Mother, the Friend, spoke quietly and gently. All the critics agreed that it was the speech, and through the speech Toller's writing, that dominated. Gesture and movement were secondary to, and influenced by the speech and its rhythms. Thus at the start Kortner's gestures and movements were very simple and spare and as naturalistic as those of the Mother and Friend, but they gradually became bigger and more excitable until, as Jhering wrote in his critique the next day,

> He reached beyond the boundaries of the stage and burst the spatial limits (215).

As Jhering remarked,

> Kortner did not act transformation, but indignation and rebellion (216).

Everything was derived from the rhythms of the text. Naturally, with the scenes taking place in a pool of light on an already small stage there was not a lot of movement in the sense of moving about, and characters were usually 'discovered' when the stage lights came on; but in compensation gesture was strong and often over-stepped the bounds of naturalism. Sudden changes in tempo were also employed. This is well illustrated in the Barbed-wire scene. At the start the skeletons were motionless and then moved more and more. Critics refer to their "ecstatic twitching": their movements were sudden, angular and jerky, strongly rhythmic, accompanied by the sound of clattering bones. The effect was that of a fantastically macabre Dance of Death firmly situated in the traditions of German art from medieval times. Critics also referred to the *tollgespenstische Unwirklichtkeit (wildly ghostly unreality)* of this scene.

In the Military Hospital the suffering was expressed in the *Tonfall* or intonation. At the end all broke out into a cry which was deeply effective. Although in this scene the emphasis was strongly upon the word, as the patients were lying in bed, this comparative lack of movement led to more in the following scene, The Cripples. Evidently the gestures and movements of the cripples were clearly distinguished from and in sharp contrast with those of the skeletons. They got up from bed simultaneously and stood in a row. Their painful getting up had, it seems, a horrible effect, as did their standing stiffly, continuously trembling; while their attempts to exercise simultaneously were horribly conditioned by their varying disabilities. Noteworthily we are told that the emotions aroused by this scene were of horror and anger, not of pity.

It was in his 9th scene (Scene 11 of the text) that Martin chiefly used the trick of conveying the sense of a crowd by means of figures at the end of the pool of light. Individual figures came into the light to speak and instead of a 'mass' of people, he suggested groups. Roma Bahn as the girl-student was particularly noticed by the critics.

In Martin's last scene (Toller's Sc. 9) the rhythmically moved groups of people, the prisoners, no longer seemed like a group in their own right. Their choric lines echo those of the Friedrich-prisoner, and so also their movements were made to reflect his, so that they appeared as his comrades in suffering, sharing his fate. They acted as he did, they tore at their chains when he did, cried to the audience for freedom, and so on. In front of them, facing the audience, the young woman collapsed and eventually brought forth her child. (It is not clear how this was done. Presumably she was masked by the group of prisoners). And the prisoners kneeled before the child. Critics said that in this production Karl-Heinz Martin had not tried to improve on or alter older forms of production, but had shown a new principle of theatre-playing and given Expressionism a decisive push on to the stage. At the same time it was emphasised that he had actually not used any "forms" which he had not previously employed, but had rather used a new way of interpreting the text, putting his hero and his fate into the very middle.

It is fortunate that thanks to Karl-Heinz Martin's already considerable reputation as a director, and Kortner's as an actor, together with the notoriety of the fact that the author was in prison for a political offence, the Berlin critics turned up in force to the first night; these included critics of the calibre of Herbert Jhering, already quoted, and Alfred Kerr. Spalek lists nearly fifty reviews, notices and comments on the production. Of the eleven critiques in the press-cutting collection at the Theatermuseum, Köln, not one is lukewarm.

> The production . . . was an event in the history of the theatre (217).
>
> That was an evening that will remain in the memory (218).
>
> The incomprehensible tragedy of the World War burnt itself into the consciousness in impassioned symbolism (219).

The new Tribüne Theatre is also praised:

> With this production of Toller's *Wandlung* the Tribüne has shown its mission in the history of the theatre (220).

Another critic, Karl Strecker, having dismissed Hasenclever as overvalued and as being one of the most wretched representatives of contemporary drama, goes on, having mentioned Toller's political imprisonment,

> One can be a runaway political visionary and yet be a great artist. And it must be admitted that in the last point (which for us is the first) Toller towers above Hasenclever to the extent that we never want to see *his* work again (221).

Apart from general enthusiasm, two threads run through the critiques: that of the humanity of the play and its author, and that of his poetic power. *M.M.*, the critic of the *Neue Zürchner Zeitung*, says it was the personal experience expressed that impressed him. In this play he considers that Toller is not yet a dramatist, though he is *perhaps* a poet. *M.M.* thinks, however, that Toller 'ought' to see the beauty in ugliness, using the curiously striking image of the ivory teeth of a dead dog on a muck-heap (222). This view palpably fails to understand the nature of art. In the language, the images, the forms, Toller *creates* beauty in his art out of the appalling ugliness of his material. As Schiller says at the end of the Prologue to *Wallenstein*:

> Ernst ist das Leben, heiter ist die Kunst.
> (Life is earnest, art is bright)
> (*Wallenstein. Prolog.* 1. 138)

Another critic, E.H., also emphasises the human element:

> Man faces man, naked . . . .
> Ernst Toller's humanity has something of the humanity of the first days of creation. It is very strong and pure (223).

Other critics as well as *M.M.* doubted Toller's dramatic ability, but none his poetic. Dr Kober, admitting that as a 'bourgeois' he finds it difficult to write about Toller's success, goes on to pronounce very categorically:

> Toller is a poet (224).

Emil Faktor, giving his first impressions, writes:

> This beautifully shaped work of poetry, shot through with the power of dreams and the warmth of emotion, cannot be judged as drama (225).

A similar judgement is implied by *E.H.* who, after saying that in the dream scenes Toller's individual characteristics come to the fore with a kind of flickering genius, goes on to say that the realistic scenes are much weaker, and that Toller, primarily a lyric poet, does not show himself especially good at characterisation. Even of the protagonist Friedrich, the man who struggles, all we learn is that he is a Jew and that he suffers (226). The personal and poetic aspects are sensitively brought into close relationship by the Berlin Correspondent of a Viennese journal (227). He sees the play (in its 5-station form, of course) as a *Way of the Cross (Passionsweg), My Golgotha (Mein Golgotha)* or even as a *Faust*, these ideas being suggested to him by the sub-title.

> In truth this piece ends with the birth of Toller, the artist (228).

He adds,

> In truth he isn't a socialist at all and even in this piece he burlesques agitators of the type of Liebknecht and Leviné (229).

No sentence in contemporary criticism of the production brings out more clearly than this the radical change wrought in the play's meaning by Martin's omissions and transpositions. Toller does indeed present a critical image of the Marxist Communist. This is the Marxist as seen through Landauer's *Aufruf zum Sozialismus*. Toller was not burlesquing Liebknecht (to whose memory he later dedicated *Der Tag des Proletariats*) or Leviné, whom he had not yet encountered when he wrote the play. The view that Toller 'isn't a socialist at all' is only made possible because his Landauer-style final speech is cut out.

Alfred Kerr, in a typically idiosyncratic critique, draws together some of these views (230). He recalls a conversation with a young Bavarian girl about the brief communist period in Munich, a conversation in which he had held up Toller, in contrast to Leviné, as humane and disinterested. She had answered precociously, "Aber unreif. So a junger Kerl, net viel über zwanzig. " (But immature. Such a young fellow, not much over twenty). He was presumptuous, she added. Kerr took her words as his text. Yes, he says, the play is immature and presumptuous, like the young buds on the vines in April. In similarly ironical vein he leads to his main point:

> The hero of Toller's 'five Stations' is so stupid. So shattering. So surrounded by light. So immature. So presumptuous. So ignorant. So completely with a beginner's outlook. So wonderful. So saintly. And he shall be blessed, for ever and ever, today and for evermore (231).

Strangely enough Kerr here (about one third of the way through his article) remarks that there is not much more to say: obviously for him, as for others, the humanity, the innocent, primal humanity, of the hero, is the kernel of the play. He does, however, say a great deal more. He emphasises the fact that the Jew is a symbol for something wider, for all who experience injustice; and perhaps also an embodiment of the race who for three thousand years have possessed the most highly developed moral law in the world. The play does not attack war, but a *Weltanschauung*. It recalls the *Sturm und Drang* period, and Büchner. Kerr saw how Toller had escaped in this play from the 'wailing tone' (*Lamento*) of his predecessors in Expressionism and instead brought the most terrible aspects of war on to the boards with massive striking-power. He is no demagogue. (Perhaps the omission of the final speech of Scene 13 helped Kerr to this conclusion).

Finally, Kerr refers briefly to the production, — briefly, but succinctly. The Theatre of Suggestion, the Theatre of Hints (*Andeutungsbühne*) had won a victory this evening. Neppach's sketchy lines were as strong in their effect as a whole theatre of fantastic spectacle. The single violin which, he tells us, played between scenes, did as much as an orchestra would have done. (He questioned whether the skeleton effect 'came off' for the very front rows). Karl-Heinz Martin had taken a step forward in the history of the theatre, helped above all by Fritz Kortner with his massive speech welded with emotion. (Da ist Sprachwucht; verschweißt mit Gefühl).

Evocative though Alfred Kerr's critique is, that of Herbert Jhering is the most informative, as well as having been the most influential. Although perhaps so carried away by enthusiasm as to fail to see *any* shortcomings in play or production, he described and understood both far more clearly than any other critic. He understood the importance of the production and of the new playwright. Revolutionary poetry had become mere 'literature' and declamation. "Radical change in the spirit" had become a mere radical change in style; revolutionising the heart meant merely revolutionising the form; exalting the soul meant merely exalting the metaphor; but

> Here for the first time there is again a poet who is nothing other than a person. Whose artistic genius signifies nothing other than intensity of the personal (232).

But although based on Toller's own experience, this, says Jhering, is not a play of self-justification or self-defence. Nor is Toller interested in the outward appearances of a degenerate world.

> What rouses him are the demons that stand behind appearances (233).

Jhering thus sees the depth of the play. He realises that it is not a Morality but, in spite of the final resurrection (in Martin's version), of the nature of tragedy.

> The play is not the philistine, petty-bourgeois play of guilt and expiation. It is the play of tragic necessity: the contemporary Dance of Death. And the music which strikes up to the round-dance of ghosts, is belief in resurrection (234).

Only by comparison with the earlier Expressionist plays can we now share Jhering's opinion of the *simplicity* of the play and its language. To the modern reader or theatre-goer, the rhetoric inevitably belongs to its period, but *within that period* Toller could be heard and seen as bringing, even here, something of a new sobriety into language and style.

> The most daring thing is simple, the most gruesome is plain. Toller scorns originality. His language has no great gestures, his thoughts are not showers of sparks (235).

Jhering notices with approval Toller's ability to combine the grotesque with the solemn, the emotional with the droll. Constantly emphasising the humanity of the work, Jhering startlingly calls it a 'folk play' (*Volksstück*), primitive and sparse even where it goes astray. Moreover it is in his view too, a great break-through of Expressionism into the theatre, — a break-through to which Neppach's scenes make an important contribution. As for Martin:

> He has achieved the demonising of the factual (236).

At this point in his argument Jhering claims that because Martin had unloosed the inner strength of the play, it did not matter that he had changed the order of the final scenes so that the Hero's 'work-place' was no longer the revolution, but surmounting revolution (*die Überwindung der Revolution*, a curious phrase in this context). Had Jhering said that the changed play was *as good as the original in its own way*, he would have had an arguable case; but to say it is no longer crucial (*nicht mehr entscheidend*) that the changes were made, cannot be sustained.

Finally Jhering has most interesting observations on Kortner's performance. Kortner, he says, gifted though he is, cannot play parts which have not yet been detached from the author. Therefore at the start he was not free and was dependent on imitative intonations (not fully felt). In Jhering's opinion he then rebelled against both the play and the direction. It is a curious view, and one cannot prove now that it may well have been both play and direction that became freer and more expressive in the later scenes.

One other critique needs to be mentioned, as it suggests the very way forward as a dramatist that Toller in fact followed. Carl Rahmer (237) addresses himself directly to Toller, as one young man to another. He asks by what right Toller, having been involved in the violence of the Munich Revolution, has to 'hammer into our souls' the phrase "be humane". He reminds Toller of the hundreds of deaths in Munich, just for the sake of an idea — an idea which Toller shared.

> You have killed people through an idea. Toller, can you accept responsibility for that? (238).

Rahmer pleads that love be set in the place of violence.

> Let us be convinced by the thought that man is born for love . . .
> Toller's transformation (*Wandlung*) from violence to love, to the Word, let that be his next work (239).

It is a prophecy of the theme of *Masse Mensch.*

Although no later production had the weight and influence of the première, *Die Wandlung* was produced several times in Germany during the 1920s, notably at the Hamburg Kammerspiele (1920), where it was given thirty-five performances, and Leipzig (1924) (240). The latter production, which was directed by Alwin Kronacher and designed by Thiersch, was put on as part of a Socialist Week of Culture, of which it was regarded as the high point (241). Toller, only recently released from prison, spoke the prologue and was given an enthusiastic reception (242). It was the first time, also, that the *Vorspiel, Die Totenkaserne,* had not been omitted in production (243). The play was also produced at Stuttgart (Spring 1920) (244), and its last recorded production was by the amateur *Sprechchor* of Nuremberg, a single performance on 6 December 1926, directed by Magner. A reviewer called the play "too significant to be performed by amateurs" and gave several examples of inadequate performance and staging (245).

The play continued to lend itself to recitation. In 1922 there was a reading in Leipzig (246) which was unfavourably reviewed, as the speaker, Ernst Friedrich, was not thought adequate for Toller. At the Volksbühne Celebration to welcome Toller's release from prison the author read some of his own poems and a part of *Die Wandlung*:

> A frail figure moved like a ghost across the stage: the Poet before the People (247).

The play has been translated into seven languages (248), but there is no record of any non-German production (249).

Despite the comparative paucity of productions the play was regarded as dangerous by the extreme right. On 25 November 1931, the Education Committee of the Prussian State Parliament passed a motion proposed by the Deutsche Volkspartei banning *Die Wandlung* from school libraries and from use in schools, on the grounds that it undermined morality, religious faith and social traditions (250).
A newspaper report reads:

TOLLER'S *WANDLUNG* IMMORAL
PROHIBITED IN SCHOOL LIBRARIES

Toller's revolutionary play, *Die Wandlung,* is to be removed from all school libraries, following a motion of the Deutsche Volkspartei, which was passed today by the Education Committee of the State Parliament. The motion was justified on the grounds that in many of the things it portrays the book grossly offends the *moral* feelings, especially of the young (251).

Thus Toller's first play became a victim of political repression even before 1933.

MASSE MENSCH *(MASSES AND MAN)*

INTRODUCTION

In this chapter it will be argued that *Masse Mensch* is a classical tragedy, not an imitation of one, but a re-creation in contemporary terms of Greek tragedy, and that it is a play of high calibre in that *genre*. Its central conflict, as Toller regards and treats it, will be seen as both particular and universal. The political aspects of that conflict will be examined and it will be argued that in this play many diverse elements — personal, political, literary, theatrical, traditional and modern — are brought together and combined into a major unified work of art, a tragedy at once classical and contemporary.

Behind Toller's first play lay the first major experience of his adult life, — the Western Front and its effect upon him. Between the first and second plays lies the second major experience, that of the Munich Revolution and all that this implies for Toller, including the early days of his subsequent imprisonment. This second experience, or more properly, series of experiences, developed and matured Toller's character and outlook, and in so far as *Masse Mensch,* like its predecessor, has an important 'confessional' element, it is linked to *Die Wandlung* through similarities and differences. In particular, the politico-moral teachings of Landauer uncritically proclaimed in the later scenes of *Die Wandlung* are now the principal ideological material of the central dramatic conflict.

Moreover there *is* in this play a central dramatic conflict (despite the arguments of Hans Marnette, to be examined later), which was lacking in *Die Wandlung,* and this dramatic conflict is expressed both externally / objectively and internally / subjectively, in the outer conflict between Sonia and *The Nameless,* and the inner debate between Sonja and her so-called *Begleiter*. It is thus clear from the start that *Masse Mensch* is fundamentally dramatic in a way that *Die Wandlung* was not. It has a unity arising from its having been conceived and drafted in one intense wave of inspiration:

> The drama *Masses* and Man is a visionary presentation which really 'broke out of me' in two and a half days (1).

At the same time it has the artistic polish and finish given by a year's careful work in the solitude of a prison cell:

> The arduous (but blessedly arduous) work of remoulding and polishing lasted a year (2).

Its pattern (for instance, the pattern of dream and other scenes), instead of being broken in the middle like that of *Die Wandlung,* is carried consistently through the play and the stages in the development of the conflict internally and externally follow this pattern closely: that is to say, form and content are integrated. It is therefore incorrect to say, even at this early point in the argument, that it is an "artistically weaker play" (3) than *Die Wandlung*: the contrary is true and our thesis is that artistically the play is masterly.

The first task will be to establish its formal structure.

FORMAL SCHEME OF "MASSE MENSCH"

I.
Back Room of a Working-Class Inn
Plan for Strike
Sonja and her Husband
Personal love/political disagreement

II.
Stock Exchange
Husband as Clerk
Sonja and Companion
War and Prostitution

III.
Large Hall
Chorus
Sonja and *The Nameless*
Sonja gives way to 'Mass' view

IV.
Courtyard surrounded by high walls.
Sentries. The Nameless.
Sonja and Companion
Drama of the Prisoner with Husband's face.
Prisoner with Husband's face becomes a sentry.

V.
Large Hall
Strike has become violent
Sonja/The Nameless
Sonja arrested

VI.
Boundless Space
The Fettered Woman (Sonja) in cage.
The Warder (Companion).
"You are healed."

VII.
Prison Cell
Sonja and her Husband
Sonja and *The Nameless*
The Priest
The Officer
Two Female Prisoners.

THE PATTERN OF PLAYERS IN "MASSE MENSCH"

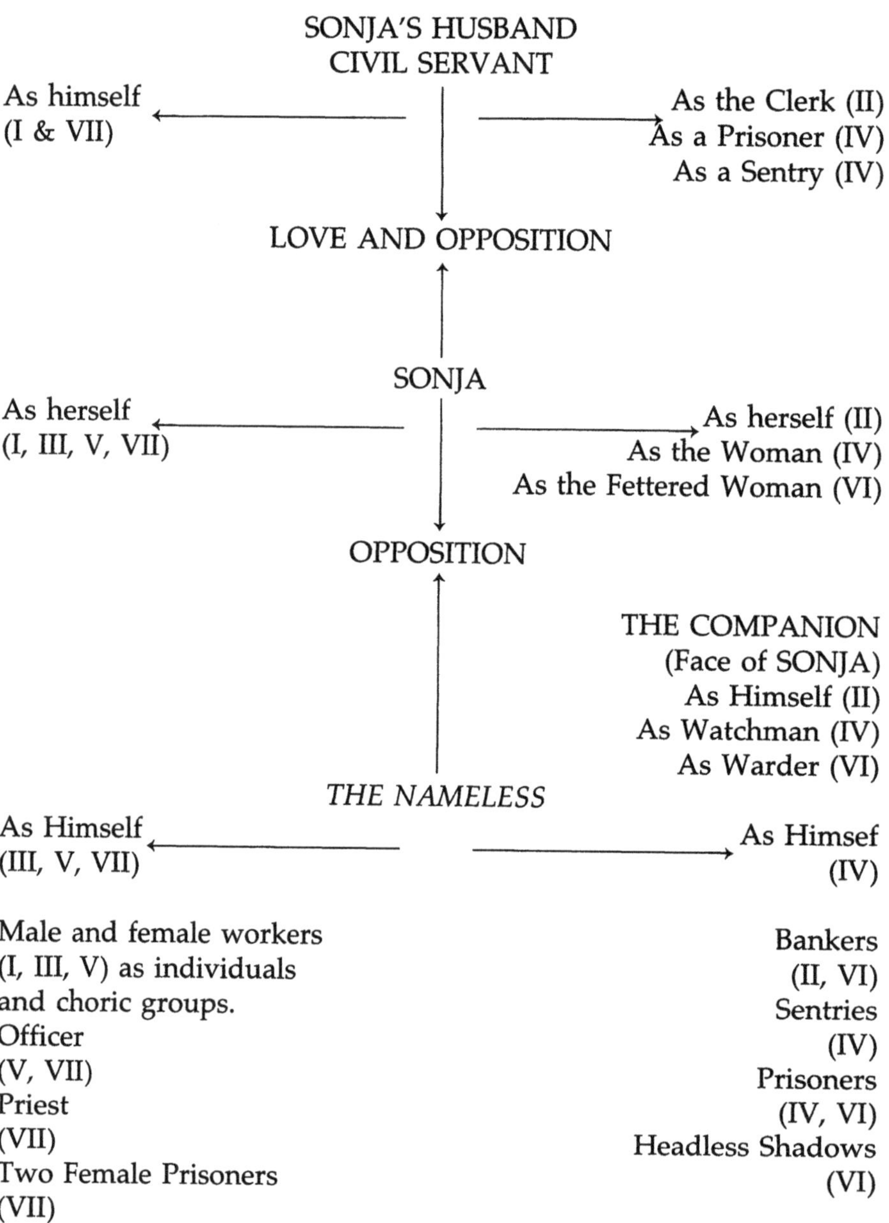

BASIC STRUCTURE (See preceding diagrams)

The title *Masse Mensch* epitomises the dramatic and moral conflicts embodied in the play (4). It is the antithesis between human beings considered collectively 'in the mass', and individually as persons. Neither word translates straightforwardly into English. *Masse* in this context has to be translated by the plural, *Masses*, thus losing the singularity and unity implied in the German. *Mensch* presents its usual problems; expressions such as *person, human being*, are flat and colourless, yet the translation *Man* is particularly unhappy in view of the fact that the *Mensch*-figure in the play is a woman. However, the normal English translation, *Masses and Man*, first used by Vera Mendel in her translation of the play (5), is a fair compromise between accuracy and inelegance.

Toller may have originally intended that the external conflict should be represented as that between *The Woman, Sonja*, on the one hand, and a *Chorus of the Masses* on the other, for this is the impression given by the opening of Scene III. Had he done so he would have created an interesting link between the play and Pre-Aeschylean Greek Tragedy which, we know, "was enacted by one actor and chorus" (6) If so, however, he quickly abandoned the idea. As soon as he broke his mass-chorus into sub-groups (Young Working Women, Young Workers, Farm Labourers) he made it impossible for the chorus to represent the undifferentiated abstract *Mass* or *Class* of the proletariat required by that side of the debate. In fact the smaller groups are soon expressing ideas and aspirations taken from Landauer. This is strikingly seen in the group of agricultural workers (*Landarbeiter*) who appear to be putting the view of peasant small-holders dispossessed of their land by wealthy capitalists who buy up the land, prostitute it, and force the country-dwellers into the town where they wither and decay (7). This is pure Landauer:

> We must have the earth again . . . The earth is no-one's property. Let the earth belong to no-one; only then are the people free . . . The struggle of socialism is a struggle for the soil; the social problem is an agrarian problem (8).

Obviously the Chorus used thus could not be *The Masses* as understood by Marxists, and it is interesting to notice that even the first *Chorus of the Masses* is in fact *Choruses of the Masses (Massenchöre)*, a point lost in Mendel's translation. Clearly Toller was aware by the time the play was fully worked up, that the Chorus was to be made up of a number of sub-choruses. Once the Mass Chorus has acquired plurality it is debarred from taking on the dramatic function of *The Masses* (viz. *The Proletariat*) as a singular concept. Toller's Chorus is not monolithic; the Marxist proletariat is.

Toller therefore, about half way through the scene introduces as the Woman's antagonist the character of *Der Namenlose (The Nameless [One]),* who "hastens out of the *Masses* in the Hall on to the platform" (9). . Hurrying thus *out* of the *Masses, Der Namenlose* seems to represent them, to speak *for* them. It is vital to realise that he speaks for them only in so far as they accept the role of impersonality which *Der Namenlose* assigns to them, and do not assert their individual humanity, or even, like the farm-labourers, their group individuality.

This point has been clearly argued and stressed by R. A. J. Altenhofer, who states firmly that *Der Namenlose* is not the voice of the Masses, *as most critics say,* but the voice of the Communist Party, which *claims* to speak in the name of the Masses (10). It is a name (i. e. a proper noun) which individualises a member of a group who otherwise remains faceless and unidentifiable, able to be replaced by any other member of the same group. We should therefore treat with great caution Wolfgang Rothe's assertion that by *Der Namenlose* Eugen Leviné was intended (11). Leviné was for Toller a person, known individually in all his complexity. *Der Namenlose* is not an individual at all. *Die namenlose Masse* is a common expression in German, and the language's ability to use adjectives as substantives makes this embodiment of the Mass in a single *nameless* figure easy. The need which may be felt in English to say *The Nameless One,* as in Mendel's translation, rather weakens the effectiveness of the device.

Apart from Sonja and The Nameless, there are only two other principal parts:

1) *Der Mann (Der Beamte).* This is Sonja's husband. The word *Mann* means both *husband* and *adult male human being,* so once more something is lost in translating it, as we must do, either as *The Man* or *The (or Her) Husband.* It is also difficult to convey in English the full significance of the description of him as *Der Beamte.* A *Beamter* is usually translated as *official* or *civil servant,* but the word covers a far wider range of posts and professions in the government service than the English words imply. Sonja's husband might have been a Professor: the original Sonja Lerch's husband was a *Privatdozent,* a non-established university lecturer, paid by the hour (12), though Toller himself describes him as a University Professor (13).

2) *Der Begleiter*. Unsatisfactorily translated by Mendel as *The Guide*, this word means *Companion. (begleiten=to accompany)*. In appropriate contexts it can mean escort or courier. This figure, with Sonja's face, is a kind of *Doppelgänger* or second-self through which Toller can give Sonja's internal conflict external expression in dialogue. He appears only in Scenes II, IV, and VI, the *Dream* scenes, and so has no 'real life' existence.

The diagram preceding this section shows the pattern of relationships between the figures in the play, and presents graphically how the moral and political conflicts are represented as *dramatic* conflicts within this pattern (14). The cast-list of *Die Wandlung* was headed *Personen (Persons, or Personae)*. Here Toller provides two headings: *Spieler (Players)* in the 'real' scenes, and *Gestalten (Figures)* in the Dream Scenes. *Der Begleiter* is thus purely a *Figure*. These two headings both suggest, though in different ways, the *distancing* from everyday reality he refers to in his published *Letter* to Jürgen Fehling in the Second Edition (15).

Central to the structure is Sonja, involved in conflict with two external antagonists: the Husband she loves, and the Nameless to whom she is opposed in political morality. Her conflicts with the beloved Husband occur in the first and last scenes of the play (I & VII), and take on dream forms in the first two dream scenes (II & IV). Her internal, subjective conflicts, represented in dialogue between herself and the Companion, are seen in all three dream scenes, thus:

II. *Sonja* (herself).	*Companion* (himself) + *Husband* (Clerk)
IV. *Sonja* (Woman).	*Companion* (Watchman) + *Husband* (Prisoner/Sentry) & *Nameless*
VI. *Sonja* (Fettered Woman)	*Companion* (Warder)

Thus Scene IV, the exact centre of the play, is the one scene in which all four principal figures appear (in dream form), and Scene VI the one scene in which the only principals are Sonja and her other self and in which the subjective conflict is finally resolved.

The shape of the story and its conflicts — a symmetrical rainbow curve — is built thus into the seven scenes (16):

I. Sonja will lead the workers in a strike, but she must break with the husband she still loves.

II. She realises fully her husband's involvement in capitalism, and hence in war and sexual corruption.

III. Sonja, in conflict with the Nameless, gives way to his view of the need for violence.

IV. The Companion shows her her husband condemned to death because she has accepted violence — but shows her, too, that her husband, who also accepts violence, could equally well be the executioner.

V. The strike has developed into violent revolution. Sonja sees that her original, non-violent, view was right. But it is too late. She is arrested.

VI. In prison she comes to terms with the innocent guilt and guilty innocence of the human situation.

VII. Sonja has a final moral struggle with her husband, loving him still. But he leaves, and she is alone.
In a final test, the Nameless offers her freedom, at the price of the life of one of the guards.
She will not accept.

Two 'epilogues' follow:

1. Sonja's dialogue with the Priest, in which she denies the orthodox Christian view of man's innate depravity.
2. The officer comes, and Sonja is taken away to be shot: the moment of her death touches the consciences of two female prisoners about to steal her bread and mirror.

The formal perfection of the basic structure of the play which has now been demonstrated must be borne in mind throughout all that follows, for it is the foundation upon which the whole is built. If two and a half days of initial inspiration gave the play its power, it was a year of devoted craftsmanship that wrought it into an artistic masterpiece.

MASSE MENSCH AS TRAGEDY

That *Masse Mensch* has more than merely formal links with ancient drama was first noted by Rosemarie Altenhofer in a thesis of 1976 (17), a hint which she developed in her *Nachwort* to the Reclam edition of the play in 1979 (18). The relevant section comprises only the last seven paragraphs of a twenty-page essay in which the play is discussed fully and with penetration: it is probably the best single paper yet written on the play. Even so, it raises this issue almost as a matter of secondary importance. In this section, after examining Altenhofer's arguments, we shall approach the same matter from a rather different viewpoint.

Altenhofer says that alongside what she refers to as the "epically-alienating tendencies of the dream-scene technique, " the dramatist falls back very noticeably on the form of Greek tragedy. She sees the function of the dream scenes as corresponding with that of the classical chorus, though working indirectly through visions instead of directly through words. She also notes that in Scene III, for example, the Chorus is integrated into the dramatic action, but also points out that the emergence of The Nameless deprives the Chorus of its dramatic function. (We have already seen in our analysis that the relationship of The Nameless to the Chorus is more complex than she suggests).

Developing the hint in the earlier thesis, Altenhofer goes on to show that the dependence on ancient drama is not merely formal but enables Toller to introduce the classical idea of Fate, not, of course, in a metaphysical sense, but in a socio-economic one. This "Fate" is to the masses as impenetrable as the ancient form of Fate, and therefore results in powerless revolt against the mere manifestations of socio-economic forces (mass-production, machines), not their fundamental causes. But this modern "Fate" differs from the ancient in that a knowledge and understanding of its causes makes it possible for human intervention to change it, as the compulsions are no longer divinely ordained but merely human. She suggests that both Sonja and The Nameless do possess this knowledge and simply differ over the function and effects of violence in bringing about change: the former seeing the problem in terms of individual responsibility and tragic entanglement, while the latter, because of his fixed and dogmatic perspective, which regards revolutionary violence as the necessary pre-condition of effective political action (revolution), excludes from the outset the experience of tragic conflict.

Altenhofer's conclusions are carefully measured, but it will be argued later that despite her detailed and penetrating analysis even she finally undervalues *Masse Mensch* as tragedy.

Her conclusions, in summary, are as follows:

1. Toller has only partially taken over the ancient, metaphysical conception of Fate and has done so from "functional points of view" (unter funktionalen Gesichtspunkten). I take it she means that the conception is introduced as a tool rather than as a reality which he accepts.
2. He has done this in order to show that mass-consciousness has not developed in step with technical developments.
3. This lack of understanding of the forces governing modern society has led to a regression in which these forces are regarded by the masses in the same way as the mythical relationships in the ancient world, as presented in classical tragedy.
4. Toller does not always succeed in bringing his intellectual conception and his realisation of it in language into complete harmony.
5. Toller has too imprecisely worked out the relationship between modern and ancient 'speech-gestures' for the tension between archaic problems and those of contemporary society to find adequate expression.
6. The language only sporadically achieves the elevation of the intellectual problems.
7. Toller's intellectual and emotional commitment too often runs into rhetoric at once exaggerated and antiquated.
8. This produces in the present-day reader (NOTE that she says *Reader,* not *Audience,* thus betraying an academic, non-theatrical approach to the play) an effect of displeasure (*Befremdung*) rather than of calculated alienation (*Verfremdung* – Brecht's word) and tends to distort the educational and illuminating (she uses the word *aufklärerisch,* with its overtones of the Eighteenth Century Enlightenment) intention of the drama (19).

Bearing in mind this earlier examination of the relationship between *Masse Mensch* and ancient Greek drama, we now proceed to our own analysis of the play from this point of view.

In *Masse Mensch* Toller used the particularities of the major inner conflict of his own life (a conflict that persisted until that life's tragic end) as the material for a fully realised classical tragedy of universal and timeless significance; but it took him a whole decade to come to an understanding of the magnitude of his achievement.

Naturally enough, his earliest comments, written in prison within months of its composition, emphasise the intensely private and personal element:

> After experiences whose brunt a human being can perhaps bear only once without breaking down, *Masses and Man* was liberation from psychological distress, liberation which did not self-deceptively banish the disunity from the world through some form of words or other, but accepted the existence of the disunity and recognised it to be one's destiny (20).

Even in this earliest formulation of his ideas about the play, however, Toller recognised that his personal disunity was a universal one, for he continues:

> The individual can wish for death. The masses must wish for life. And as we are individuals and masses in one, we choose death and life (21).

About the same time (1920) he emphasised that, at least in a political sense, the problem was not only his private one:

> I have attempted to give form to one of the most serious conflicts of our revolutionary age, one which keeps on confronting anyone who has recognised the necessity of ploughing things up (22).

(A note of warning must be added here. Where the originals of the letters in *Briefe aus dem Gefängnis* (1935) do survive, they reveal heavy editing and re-working on Toller's part. It is therefore more than possible that these letters, too, have been modified in the light of his later thought, formulated in *Quer Durch* and *Eine Jugend in Deutschland*).

A similar emphasis on the intensely personal nature of the material is found in the version of Toller's letter to Jürgen Fehling printed as a preface to the Second Edition of the play (1922). The letter is there dated 'October 1921', which makes sense, as Fehling's Volksbühne production opened on 29 September 1921. The considerably altered version in *Briefe aus dem Gefängnis* (1935) is placed among the letters of 1920, which is nonsense.

In the 1922 version the following passage occurs:

> Today I can regard the play critically. I have recognised the conditional nature of the form, which stemmed — in spite of

> everything — from an inner inhibition of those days, from a human embarrassment which shyly avoided the issue of giving artistic form to personal experience and to naked confession, and which could not yet summon up the will to objectify it purely artistically (23).

This somewhat inelegant translation attempts to render something near the meaning of the original. Toller is evidently struggling to express very complex thoughts and feelings. Mendel translates very freely and loses in the process Toller's strivings after honesty.

The passage implies (if one may so simplify it) that in Toller's opinion in 1921 'personal experience and naked confession' were the substance of the play, and that the play only partially succeeded in creating an 'objective correlative' for that experience. He was still too near both the experiences themselves and the writing of the play to view either of these dispassionately and detachedly.

His clearest and fullest statement about the play was written and published in 1930 (24). He concludes his comments on *Die Wandlung* thus:

> Every author wants to push into his first work everything he knows and has experienced. I did that, too. And so it is not to be wondered at that the private and lyrical elements thrust themselves forward more strongly than the dramatic structure might allow (25).

After this interesting admission, he continues:

> The form is purer even in the next play, *Masse Mensch*. It was very curious: after the piece had been put on, some said it was counter-revolutionary because it rejected all force, others that it was Bolshevik, because the representative of non-violence was destroyed, and although the masses were admittedly defeated for the moment, they remained victors in the long run. Only a few recognised that the struggle between individual and masses does not only take place outwardly, and that each one is at the same time individual and masses at heart. As an individual, he acts according to the moral idea he recognises as right. He wants to serve that even if the world is destroyed. As one of the masses, he is driven by social impulses and situations; he wants to reach the goal, even if he has to give up the moral idea. The contradiction is still insoluble for anyone active in politics today, and it was just its insolubility that I wanted to show (26).

Three years later (1933) Toller restated much of this in appropriately more personal terms in *Eine Jugend in Deutschland*. Recalling his feelings in prison, he writes:

> I had failed; I had believed that the socialist who despised violence might never employ violence: I myself have used violence and called for violence. I hated bloodshed and have shed blood (27).

He adds that he had turned down an opportunity to escape from the Stadelheim Prison because it would have cost a warder his life. He asks himself whether Max Weber, whom he had met at Diedrich's seminar at Lauenstein Castle in September 1917 (28), was not perhaps right after all and that the pacifist could only live like St Francis of Assisi and leave practical politics alone. He goes on to ask what is probably the central question of the tragic vision of the human condition:

> Must one who acts become guilty, for ever and ever! Or if one is not willing to become guilty, be destroyed? (29).

He continues, re-phrasing the problem of the motivation of the masses:

> Do moral ideas drive the masses, or do not rather poverty and hunger drive them? (30).

One recalls Brecht:

> Grub first, then morality (31).

Toller then restates, almost word for word, the passage quoted from *Arbeiten*, and concludes:

> The sensuousness and richness of the experiences were so strong that I could only master them through abstraction, through clarifying dramatically the lines which determine the causes of things (32).

In these passages Toller restates in twentieth century terms some of the basic elements of tragedy, though we must not expect a complete, or even necessarily a wholly consistent philosophy of tragedy. Toller is not a professional philosopher, nor is he promulgating a 'theory of drama': he is simply commenting on one of his own plays.

First then, in the (possibly revised) published version of his earliest statement on the play, Toller states that through the play he was able to come to terms with an inner division (*Zwiespalt*), not by banishing it through verbal sleight of hand but by accepting it ("saying 'yes'") and recognising it as fate or destiny (*Schicksal*). The inner division, the splitting of the personality, he understands to be universal, even though his own experiences in Munich's revolutionary politics caused him to be acutely aware of it: it is the inward division into *Mensch* and *Masse*. As *Mensch* the individual can wish for death, as *Masse* he is compelled to wish for life. (For example, the individual is capable of deliberate self-sacrifice; the mass is not. Admittedly some people today would regard the mass as capable of a collective death-wish, and the possibility of the masses acting like lemmings is often canvassed, — for instance in relation to the nuclear threat — but Toller's reading of Marx and other socialists would have prevented his adopting this idea.) Because he is both *Mensch* and *Masse* the individual chooses both death and life.

The exact nature of this inward disunity is not made clear in this letter, but the liberation from psychological stress through conscious acceptance of it as the human fate, *is* clear, and strikingly recalls Agamemnon in Aeschylus' play of that name.

Agamemnon makes the conscious decision to sacrifice Iphigenia rather than give up the expedition upon which he has embarked.

> Then he put on the yoke-strap of necessity (33).

Or as Philip Vellacott glosses it in his translation:

> So he put on, of his own will,
> The harness of Necessity (34).

While one must not exaggerate the closeness of the parallel, *Schicksal*, Toller's word, is a fair translation of the Greek *ananke* (35).

The irreconcilability of apparent free-will and apparent necessity, the heart of the tragic vision, was expressed by Aeschylus in religious and mythological terms. It is expressed by Toller in psychological and sociological terms: on the one hand the freedom of the individual to act according to the moral idea he recognises to be right, whatever the consequences; and on the other hand the fact that the same individual is driven by social impulses and situations. Like Agamemnon, "he wants to reach the goal, even if he has to give up the moral idea" (cf. Note 26).

Toller's concept of *die als recht erkannte moralische Idee* (the moral idea recognised to be right) is derived ultimately from Kant's concept of the "categorical imperative" (*kategorische Imperativ*), "which says that a certain kind of action is objectively necessary, without regard to any end" (36). Toller's concept is firmly rooted in the ground of German Idealism (37). As Toller expresses it, the "moral idea recognised to be right" is so recognised in a purely subjective way. There is no objective criterion by which its 'rightness' is asserted or proved. This inadequacy in the concept is also rooted in Kant. As Albert Schweitzer convincingly argued (38), the greatness of Kant was in the raising of ethics from the plane of utilitarianism to that of immediate and sovereign duty, but his weakness was his failure to give this duty content.

> In powerful language he proves . . . that ethics is a volition which raises us above ourselves, frees us from the natural order of the world of the senses, and attaches us to a higher world-order. That is his great discovery.
> In the development of it, however, he falls short of success. Whoever asserts the absoluteness of moral duty, must also give the moral an absolute and completely universal content. He must specify a principle of conduct, which shows itself as absolutely binding, and as lying at the foundations of the most varied ethical duties. If he does not succeed in doing this, his work is only a fragment (39).

Toller's contrary concept of the individual driven by social impulses and situations (*getrieben von sozialen Impulsen und Situationen*) is derived from the *Milieu-Theorie* wide-spread in the Social Democratic movement during the preceding decades, which emphasised the part played by environment in determining human behaviour. In *Eine Jugend in Deutschland* Toller gives the 'necessity' of the masses concrete form when he says that far from being morally motivated, the masses are driven by need (*Not*) and hunger. The concept is also derived from the Marxist doctrine of the inevitability of certain socio-political changes:

> . . . dialectic . . . while supplying a positive understanding of the existing state of things, . . . at the same time furnishes an understanding of the negation of that state of things, and enables us to recognise that that state of things will *inevitably* break up . . . (My italics. CWD) (40).

Marxism also maintains that:

> Man is conditioned but not determined by social structure and the stage of economic development. An airman is most strictly conditioned by the laws of flight and his machine, by the changing atmosphere and his supplies of petrol and electricity; but he is free in so far as he accepts, understands and utilizes these conditions. Freedom is the knowledge of necessity (41).

So The Nameless persuades Sonja in Scene III that she must abandon her idealistic morality (her awareness of the categorical imperative) and submit to necessity as embodied in the masses:

> *Masse* ist Schicksal
> (The *Masses* are destiny) (42).

He advances the Communist doctrine of the necessity of the final class war between proletariat and bourgeoisie:

> Doch vorher letzten, rucksichtslosen Kampf!
> (But before that, the last, ruthless struggle) (43).

Against this Sonja opposes her moral sense:

> Gefühl zwangt mich in Dunkel,
> Doch mein Gewissen schreit mir: Nein.
> (Feeling forces me into darkness,
> Yet my conscience cries "No" to me) (44).

And it is, in the play, through emotional rhetoric with its appeal of 'feeling', rather than by dialectical logic, that The Nameless persuades Sonja:

> Krieg ist Notwendigkeit fur uns
> (War is for us Necessity) (45).

She "puts on the harness of Necessity" of her own will, agreeing to support violence in order to win the struggle, – just as Agememnon agreed to sacrifice his daughter in order, finally, to win the Trojan War.

Having decided upon immoral action in order to comply with 'necessity', Agamemnon learns the next tragic fact expressed in Aeschylean tragedy: that action inevitably leads to suffering. As the Chorus puts it much later in the play:

> The doer must suffer (46).

This is restated interrogatively by Toller in his comments in *Eine Jugend in Deutschland*:

> Muß der Handelnde schuldig werden?
> (Must he who acts become guilty?) (47).

Aeschylus implies that the suffering arises from guilt; Toller, too, that the guilt leads to suffering. And Sonja does suffer. She suffers in her mind in Scene IV, and she suffers death, even though she has by then returned to her moral stance. She is a tragic heroine in the most ancient traditions.

There is another parallel with Aeschylean tragedy implicit in the play, but not explicit in Toller's own comments upon it. According to Aeschylus, Zeus has ordained that wisdom comes through suffering, that man grows wise against his will.

> We notice that Zeus is not called the god of Wisdom and Justice, rather the god of learning through experience, hard experience; at least, what Aeschylus says about him is that he brought a new law, Learn by suffering. How was this new? We cannot imagine that under his predecessors men learned without suffering; Aeschylus did not believe in a past Golden Age. The only interpretation is that under the earlier gods man suffered but did not learn; nothing came of hard experience. This is what the poet commemorates here; under the reign of Zeus, learning, progress, becomes possible (48).

Sonja learns wisdom through the mental suffering she experiences in Scene IV; and the play implies, too, in the brief Epilogue of the two female prisoners, that through one person's suffering it is possible for a trace of moral wisdom to develop in others.

In a passage quoted earlier (49) Toller says that his own experiences were so sensuous and rich that artistically he could master them only through a process of abstraction, thinning and clarifying the lines of causation. In other words he had to give them artistic form, and we are going to suggest that (although there was almost certainly no *conscious* imitation involved) the structure of *Masse Mensch*, as shown on the diagram, owes much to the structure of Greek Tragedy: indeed there is no other type of play it resembles more closely.

Greek Tragedies, of course vary greatly in formal detail; but certain generalisations are possible (50):
Many begin with a *PROLOGOS* which is introductory in character.
This is followed by the first Chorus, called the *PARADOS*.
A series of *EPISODES* follows.
Between each Episode and the next is a Chorus known as a *STASIMON*.
At the end there is an *EXODOS*, or final section.

The *Prologue* introduces the story; the *Episodes* continue it. The Choruses do not normally advance the outward story, but develop its inner significance. It is perfectly reasonable to describe *Masse-Mensch* in these terms:

SCENE I	PROLOGOS
SCENE II (dream)	PARADOS (Chorus)
SCENE III	EPISODE
SCENE IV (dream)	STASIMON (Chorus)
SCENE V	EPISODE
SCENE VI (dream)	STASIMON (Chorus)
SCENE VII	EXODUS

The dream scenes thus not only perform the function of the Greek Chorus in developing and deepening the meaning and significance of the play rather than advancing the action (as Altenhofer has already pointed out) but they do this within a structural pattern which itself closely corresponds with the basic pattern of a Greek Tragedy.

This reduction of the complexities of 'real life' experience to the austere paradigm of the earliest great tragedies is what Toller is evidently referring to when he speaks of mastering the events through "abstraction, through clarifying dramatically the lines which determine the causes of things" (51).

We are now in a position to argue that *Masse Mensch* actually does belong to the *genre* of classical tragedy and to assess its calibre in this field.

To begin on the formal level: as we have just seen, the sequence of scenes ('real' and 'dream') follows the pattern of an ancient Greek tragedy far more exactly than even Altenhofer has suggested, and if we refer back to the diagram, *Formal Scheme of "Masse Mensch"*, we shall see that in content as well as in form, the scene-sequence is a modern counterpart of ancient dramatic movement. If we add to this the further aspects discussed in the section *Basic Structure* (especially the 'rainbow curve' and the extraordinary symmetry shown in the diagram *Pattern of Players*) and re-affirm the "formal perfection of the scheme of the play" in the light of the comparisons we have made with the form of classical tragedy, we are bound to be led to the conclusion that in terms of structure (that is, both the externals of formal structure and the structuring of the treatment of the content) the play stands very high among modern emulations of classical tragedy.

It does not, like Grillparzer's *The Golden Fleece (Das goldene Vlies, 1821)*, Hauptmann's Atrides tetralogy (1941–1948) or Sartre's *Les Mouches*, seek to represent a classical legend in the light of modern thought; nor, like O'Neill's *Mourning Becomes Electra* (1931) or T. S. Eliot's *The Family Reunion* (1939), try to impose on a modern story the strict outline of a classical myth. Pre-dating all the twentieth-century examples mentioned, its use of the classical tragedy form is both more original and more subtle than any of these, in that it takes a contemporary story and a contemporary mode of tragic dilemma and presents these in what is not an imitation (e. g. using primarily verbal choric comment) but a modern re-creation of classical tragedy using techniques and conventions drawn largely from the dominant contemporary style: Expressionism.

The central tragic dilemma, moreover, is not, as Altenhofer appears to suggest, simply a problem of what are the correct means to achieve a certain end (the modern socio-economic version of "Fate" being merely an illusion born of ignorance among the masses and able to be liquidated by the rational approach of intellects of the calibre of Sonja and The Nameless), but the more profound and universal dilemma that no human action can be free of guilt ("The doer must suffer": Aeschylus; "Must he who acts become guilty?": Toller).

Toller's is a truly tragic *Weltanschauung*: he understands that the tragedy of the human predicament is that life inevitably contains within it *insoluble* problems (52). The inner and outward forms of *Masse Mensch* are thus congruent and worthy of each other in every way.

The final question to be answered in this connection is whether in this play Toller achieves a linguistic medium capable of carrying his exalted theme and of fleshing out and breathing life into the bare paradigm of structural perfection, or whether, as Altenhofer claims, he falls far short of this.

That he does succeed in the matter of language will be argued in a later chapter (53).

MASSE MENSCH ON STAGE

Masse Mensch, even before publication, had a stormy introduction to the stage when, rather surprisingly, the authorities did not forbid a series of closed performances arranged by and for trades unionists in the Nürnberg Stadttheater. The theatre's Intendant, Stuhlfeld, was, according to a police report, known to belong to the radical left, while his deputy, Urban, was a "self-confessed communist" (1).

In the opinion of the author of the police report the play simply gave its proletarian audience an opportunity to be convinced of Toller's "psychopathic predisposition". The style of the play was said to be so fantastic that, apart from a few places where the actual content could have a provocative effect, it had no effect on the audience and there was no applause until the end. Even this applause was rather in appreciation of Toller as a "Hero of the Revolution" than as author. Another source (2) informs us that a huge laurel wreath with a red ribbon flew on to the stage at the end of the play, but simply lay there, as the author, for whom it was intended, was in prison. The authorities therefore regarded themselves as having been justified in allowing the performances: the play, in their opinion, would soon have been forgotten and would only have had the effect of depriving the writer of his "halo".

The first performance was on 15 November 1920. For the fourth performance on 26 November 1920, about 100 entrance tickets, which the management had been unable to sell to trades unionists, were offered at the door to outsiders, provided they simply signed a list. Apparently some at least of these were bought by members of the strongly anti-semitic *Deutschvölkischer Schutz- und Trutzbund (The Alliance for the Unity and Protection of the German People)* who deliberately staged disturbances during the performance: catcalls led to scuffles, and forty-three people were forcibly ejected by the theatre personnel and members of the audience. The police report regretted the free publicity given to the play and thought the demonstration had back-fired!

In spite of these events, reported the next day (27. 11. '20) by the Northern Bavarian police, two further closed performances were given in the Stadttheater at Fürth. Meanwhile the matter was taken up by the Bavarian government and, according to Minister Zetlmeier, speaking in parliament on 17. 12. '20, the police had been instructed not to allow any more performances, even if 'closed'. Several interesting points arise in this statement (3). One is the admission that as the play was not yet in print it was not possible to know its content in detail, and further, that as the Nürnberg theatre-management had made considerable cuts and re-arrangements in the text, it was possible that the production and the author's text did not agree. Interestingly enough, too, in view of Toller's own comments that criticisms came both from right and left, they came not only from the anti-semitic rowdies but also from the *Verband der Staatsbürger jüdischen Glaubens (The Association of Citizens of the Jewish Faith)* which objected to the Stock Exchange scene!

Also noteworthy in the minister's statement was the fact that, as he pointed out, under Article 118 of the Constitution of the German Reich of 11. 8. 1919, theatre censorship was no longer permitted. A ban on performances must be based on the breaking of specific laws. In this case the duty of the police to maintain law and order justified the ban in view of the disturbances of 26 November.

Obviously neither a police report nor a ministerial statement is the ideal source for an objective comment on the play or its production. I have seen only two newspaper critiques of this production (4). Neither gives any clear idea of the production, though one or two hints can be picked up. One of the critics, signing himself "k", says that the seven scenes are really nothing but a lyrical monologue and adds that he does not think the verse is very good. He thinks the play could be effective if individualised and realistic: though whether he thinks this could be achieved simply in production or only by re-writing is not clear. The implications of his critique are that the choruses were presented statically and were inadequately choreographed, and that the dialogues were not sharply dramatised. A production that was in effect a recitation would naturally not do justice to dramatic poetry: but the critic himself is evidently unsympathetic to the piece.

The other critique, by Karl Bröger, is far more understanding and his summary shows that he understands much of the play's basic theme. He concentrates on political aspects of the play, remarking,

> Shadows from the Munich Soviet Republic run through the scenes (5).

He considers that Nürnberg was not the ideal place for the production of this play, its political aspects being so strong. He also tells us (which the police report failed to do) that the 'closed' arrangements for the performances were actually the result of advance protests from the *Deutschvölkischer Bund*, the very people who disrupted the fourth performance.

Bröger thinks this play inferior to *Die Wandlung*. He appreciates at a perhaps rather superficial level that Sonja's moral problem is Toller's own; but he sees in the unresolved dilemma a weakness in the play, not tragic strength:

> His heart is with the person, his conviction and will, apparently, with the masses. Does his road to Damascus go via Moscow? (6).

Perceptively and sympathetically Bröger comments that although Toller will be pleased that working people were present for the first performance of his play, the fact that the middle-class members of the *Bund* were not prepared to experience a play about conflict taking place in the breast of a middle-class woman was a sign of how the middle-class mind shirks the conflicts that concern no one more than the middle-class itself.

Bröger gives us no idea of the production in detail. He says it was careful and removed all difficulties. He concludes:

> The outstanding achievement of the director Friedrich Neumann in scenic expression, together with the performances of Marg. Hannen and Fischer-Streitmann left nothing to be desired (7).

Some photographs of the production exist. One picture appears to show Scene III (8). In front of a dark and indefinite background (apparently heavy drapes) Sonja in a dark dress on a dais or rostrum stands facing the camera and is appealing directly to the crowd. The crowd *appears* to be entirely male, certainly all clearly visible figures are male. Over thirty figures can be counted and the number may well be nearly double that. All wear the ordinary outdoor dress of the period, including hats. On the rostrum six other figures, all male, form a group leaning towards Sonja and apparently not in agreement with her, but this is uncertain.

The rostrum figures are clearly spotlit, while the crowd is lit only from one side (Stage L., P. S.) so that heads only are strongly lit and the lower parts of the men largely in shadow. The crowd stands naturalistically with no stylised grouping. The rostrum group forms a natural pyramid topped by the faces of Sonja and, presumably, The Nameless. The picture suggests a naturalistically presented, unchoreographed crowd, and platform rhetoric. But the dramatic side-lighting interestingly anticipates Hans Strohbach's designs for the Berlin Volksbühne and reminds us of the critic Bröger's strong praise for Director Friedrich Neumann's outstanding achievement in scenic expression.

Another picture shows the Stock Exchange, Scene II (9). This also seems to tend to Naturalism. The hatless Clerk sits at a quite ordinary desk on a rostrum three steps above stage level, backed by dark drapes. The top-hatted speculators, (twelve can be seen) crowd around or stand at one side in irregular groupings. The impression is of a simplified but not stylised Stock Exchange.

The amateur performance put on by the Municipal Committee for Adult Education (*Städtischer Volksbildungsausschuß*) at Chemnitz, 27 February 1921, was a production of selected scenes only (10).

We move on to firmer ground with the second professional production, Jürgen Fehling's at the Berlin Volksbühne, 29 September 1921 (11). This celebrated production was seminal and in effect definitive. We must examine the production itself, contemporary criticism of it, its place in theatre history and its influence.

Jürgen Fehling had been 'discovered' as an actor in a touring company [the Märkisches Wandertheater] by Adolf Edgar Licho, who gave him his first Berlin engagement in the 1910/11 season at the Neues Volkstheater, the re-named Theater in der Köpenicker Straße rented in 1910 for the exclusive use of the Neue Freie Volksbühne. From 1913 to 1918 he played at the Volksbühne in Vienna and then became a member of Friedrich Kayssler's company at the Volksbühne's Theater am Bülowplatz.

Fehling really wanted to direct plays, and as Kayssler, though theatre-director, was his own principal actor, he eventually gave Fehling the opportunity to direct Gogol's comedy *Marriage* in March 1919. This production was highly praised by the critic Herbert Ihering, who had been dramaturge at the Vienna Volksbühne and therefore already knew Fehling well as an actor. Ihering in fact saw Fehling as a rising director primarily of comedy, and indeed in the 1920/21 season he did direct three more comedies, *The Comedy of Errors* (Shakespeare) (1920), *Captain Brassbound's Conversion* (Shaw) (Feb. 1921), and *Der Bauer als Millionär* (Raimund) (May 1921). But he nevertheless seems to have made the biggest impression on the critics with his first production of tragedy, Sophocles' *Antigone* (April 1921).

This production proved to be in a very real and concrete sense a highly significant prelude to the historic production of *Masse Mensch* in September 1921, some five months later. It will therefore be appropriate to examine it closely, as it throws a great deal of light on Fehling's aims in the Toller production. For both plays Fehling had the same production team, Hans Strohbach as designer and Heinz Thiessen as composer, and the same leading lady, Mary Dietrich.

The critic Paul Fechter gives a clear description of the set, one which also shows us, with hindsight, how many characteristics of the *Masse Mensch* set were foreshadowed in it.

> The set by Hans Strohbach shows the usual structure of steps with a slight platform in the middle; above in the background a brown wall with a central archway as entrance to the palace; to its left a solitary stylised flowering tree in front of a plain, dark bluish-purple sky. The relationship of the size of the human figures to the high, entirely open setting produced a very fine effect. Invisible Fate was made perceptible here simply through the silent effect of space (12).

It is not clear whether Fechter refers to the steps as being "usual" (*üblich*) for a classical play, or for an Expressionist, Jeßner-influenced production. (Alfred Kerr in his critique of *Masse Mensch* says in his customary telegraphese:

> Natürlich die Treppe der Expressionisten.
> (The Expressionist Stairs — of course) (13))

In any case the steps are, as we shall see, a link between *Masse Mensch* and this classical tragedy, quite apart from current modes.

Broadly, Fechter sees this as *Theatre of Space* in which space itself has a dramatic function. (Further, the coloured cyclorama not only contributes to space but, through its colour, to Expressionist symbolism, a function developed more fully in the production of *Masse Mensch.*)

In front of this stillness of coloured space the chorus on the forestage was nearly in darkness, at times even the faces were barely seen. In this uncertain light were costumes of contrasting colours. Their voluminousness was striking and seemed to drag and hinder the rhythmic movement of the arms (14). Following the example of the ancients Fehling made the Chorus (in this case consisting of fifteen Old Men) the very cornerstone (*Grund- und Eckpfeiler*) of the whole performance (15). He did not divide the chorus mechanically into *Chorus I* and *Chorus 11,* says Wiegler, but divided the words between the speakers so that the effect was not systematic. He used, says Fechter, pretty well all the methods tried recently to solve the problem of the chorus: unison-speaking in the mass (with or without musical accompaniment), semi-choruses, single strophes given to single members of the chorus; but he avoided the 'fugal' speaking used by Reinhardt.

Fechter nevertheless complains of a certain uniformity in the choruses, but he blames this on Walter Amelung's translation. He says this worked well in dialogue, but in the choruses had too simplifying and reductive an effect, being very regular rhymed verse which deprived the Director of many opportunities for variety, and became tedious.

In view of the important influence of Hölderlin on Toller's poetry (which we shall demonstrate elsewhere) it is interesting that Fechter brings Hölderlin into his argument:

> It is indeed not necessary to imitate the complicated verse structure of the ancients slavishly (although that can be done successfully, too, as a reading of Hölderlin's translation shows) (16).

If Fechter found a certain monotony in the chorus-work, Franz Servaes emphatically did not (17). He speaks of the rich and dynamic shading from a whisper to a voice of thunder, of the resounding unisons in contrast with single voices. Back-stage music came in at the most striking moments and frequently accompanied the choric recitations. Fechter was particularly impressed by the glory and solemnity of the trombones accompanying the Hymn to Eros (18), while Servaes heard in their sound at the beginning and end of the play the penetrating cries of Fate.

The paean of praise was somewhat tempered by the voice of Herbert Ihering, who was obviously not eager to admit the inadequacy of his view of Fehling as a director of comedy. He accused Fehling of too often giving us *Theatre Music* instead of psychological reverberations. He said the speech was not rhythmically heightened [cf Fechter's criticism] sufficiently to justify the use of music, which thus tended to be either melodramatic or sentimental in effect. Ihering cannot deny the thoroughness of the production or the discipline of the chorus, but he seems determined to deny Fehling the power to cope with the psychology of tragedy.

Both Ihering and Fechter praise Fehling's success in directing Mary Dietrich as Antigone, the former admitting that the director had made her free herself from several mannerisms, the latter pointing out that he had brought her tendency to emotiveness (Ger: *Pathos*) under control.

Thus despite Ihering's critical attempt to stereotype him as a director of comedies, Fehling through his *Antigone* established himself as a director of classical tragedy, — and as we have already seen, *Masse Mensch* is, as Fehling evidently understood, a modern counterpart of this *genre*. It is also particularly closely related to *Antigone*. In both plays a woman, driven by duty and conscience, is involved in and becomes victim of a political situation of conflict and violence.

From the sources available we are able to reconstruct much of the production of *Masse Mensch*, to know Fehling's intentions and Toller's own response to what he, in prison, could learn about the performance. In addition, of course, there are many contemporary reviews, including the memorable and influential ones by Alfred Kerr and Herbert Ihering.

Because Fehling and his designer Hans Strohbach obviously worked in complete harmony we need not try to distinguish between their individual contributions to the production.

In the first place, no attempt was made to present the non-dream scenes more naturalistically than the dream scenes. Fehling wrote:

> The scene and action are universal and free from local detail, so that, in my opinion, not only the second, fourth and sixth acts, which the author designates as "dream pictures", but the whole play should be staged without realism (19).

Toller concurred:

> There are critics who find fault with the fact that, although the dream-scenes wear the faces of dreams, you have given the "realistic scenes" visionary faces and have thus softened the boundaries between reality and dream. I would like to tell you specifically that you have done as I would have wished. These "realistic scenes" are not scenes of naturalistic environment; the figures (apart from that of Sonja) are not markedly individualised. *What can be realistic in a drama like "Masse Mensch"? Only the breath [=life, CWD] of the mind and spirit (20).*

Nevertheless, as Michael Patterson has emphasised (21) the Fehling/Strohbach production did make a visual distinction between the two types of scene, using heavy, dark drapes for the "realistic", and a cyclorama for the "dream" scenes, thus:

I. (The back room of a working-class inn)
Drapes. A rough table and chairs.

II. (Dream) (Stock Exchange)
Drapes drawn back to show triangle of cyclorama. Colour changes (symbolic) during scene. Clerk on 'impossibly high stool', writing on an 'impossibly high desk, almost in silhouette' (22).

III. (Meeting in Hall)
Drapes. Broad steps facing front. Chorus of 24 on steps. Lighting from sides and above. Hard-focussed spots.

IV. (Dream) (Prison Yard)
Towering walls leaning inward.

V. (The Hall)
Drapes. Broad steps diagonally or off-centre (see below) leading up to stage left (P. S.). At end, after machine-gun effect, drapes partly open stage R. (O. P.) to reveal soldiers against yellow cyclorama. Faint smoke haze.

VI. (Dream) (Boundless space)
Cyclorama with threatening moving shadows. Sonja in scarlet bird-cage.

VII. (Prison Cell)
Drapes. Minimal furniture.

This outline provides a framework within which to examine the production in greater depth and to consider the assessments made of it. It has on the one hand been described as,

> the hour of birth of stage-expressionism and light-production (23).

and on the other hand as,

> one of the last examples of truly expressionist staging . . . a remarkable synthesis of abstractionism and primitivism (24).

Which of these apparently mutually exclusive judgements is the nearer to the truth is one of the questions that must be addressed, though that truth is certainly more complex than either of them!

Fehling's approach to the production was in the strictest sense 'expressionist', although he does not use the term:

> (*Masse Mensch*) has proved one of the most conspicuous theatrical events of recent years, because its latent dramatic force and truth, revealed by an imaginative producer using the resources of modern stage-craft, gives concrete form to a passionately moved and moving spiritual experience (25).

For him, evidently, Sonja as *The Woman* was less individualised than she was in Toller's imagination, for Fehling says that she,

> creator and preserver of life, represents the human soul (26).

And he sees this soul "urged on by dreams . . . groping through darkness and despair to the hills of vision (27). It is this "twilight of the soul" that Fehling says he has attempted to convey through "an elusive blending of the limelight rays" (28) — at the same time taking a firm stance for the supremacy of the spoken word, as against some aspects of the movement represented by Edward Gordon Craig and some of his successors such as Terence Gray, in affirming,

> that unless the theatre is to become a laboratory for sensory stimuli, the spoken word must, as always, dominate all scenic effects (29).

Whether he was wholly successful in maintaining the domination of the spoken word is a question we must bear in mind as we proceed. One critic, at least, found that the production rather than the words provided the climax:

> The climax, as the masses sing their battle-song [viz. The Internationale, CWD] in opposition to the chatter of machine-gun fire — boldly, rapturously, fanatically, inflamed, driven into ecstasy, works up to a white heat. People tremble. The author asks: Without any credit to me? Yes — for we don't understand one syllable, we don't need to . . . (30).

But who, indeed, needs to hear the *words* of the Internationale? And who but the author juxtaposed the song and the sound of machine-guns?

Fehling himself conveys in general terms the character and intentions of the settings. They were, he tells us, "severely architectonic, composed of light and space" (31). In this Fehling was following in the foot-steps of Adolph Appia, particularly his sketches for *Rhythmic Spaces* (1909), and of course in those of Craig.

The lighting of the production had, however, another dimension in addition to those already mentioned (viz: light as architectonic, and light as 'twilight of the soul'), namely, light as significant colour (32).

In the revolt against the naturalism of Impressionist painting at the turn of the century, colour, freed from the necessities of representation, acquired new freedoms and an independent power of communication. Thus colours became "the true medium of the new artistic reality" (33). Picasso, for example, in his earliest paintings "dramatised misery with powerful colours" (34), later concentrating this emotional violence on the single colour, blue.

Colour symbolism also became important in German painting. When, for instance, Kandinsky and Marc broke from the New Artists' Association in 1911, they called their exhibitions and almanach *Der blaue Reiter (The blue Horseman)*, and the meaning of Marc's work in particular is largely governed by his colour symbolism, — witness his *Blue Horse* (1911) and *Tower of Blue Horses* (1913) and the ever-popular *Red Horses*. Yellow in Marc's paintings is a threatening colour, for example in his tawny-yellow *Tiger* (1912); and red, for him, as for other expressionist painters, symbolises storm and stress (e. g. Marc *Struggling Forms*, 1914; Macke, *The Storm*, 1911).

Colour symbolism has also a strong literary tradition in German. Since Novalis (1772-1801) used the image of the blue flower, *Die blaue Blume*, blue has been associated in German literature with endless longing

> for the mysterious, radiant source of reality which unites everything (35).

It is but a small step from such longing to a death-wish, another 'blue' association.

Both in visual art and poetry colour also became, for Expressionists, a medium for synaesthesia. Thus redness suggests noise and clamour, as in George Grosz's unnamed painting of crowds in a street, dedicated to Oskar Panizza, (1917/18) (36). Among Expressionist poets Georg Trakl makes the boldest use for symbolism and synaesthesia of the colour-freedom released by the Expressionist painters and the revolt against naturalism. Some examples of his poetry will illustrate this.

Die Sonne

Täglich kommt die *gelbe* Sonne über den Hügel.
Schön ist der Wald, das *dunkle* Tier,
Der Mensch; Jäger oder Hirt.

Rötlich steigt im *grünen* Weiher der Fisch.
Unter dem runden Himmel
Fährt der Fischer leise im *blauen* Kahn.

. . . .

The Sun

Every day the *yellow* sun comes over the hill.
The forest is beautiful, the *dark* animal,
The man; hunter or herdsman.

Reddish, the fish rises in the *green* pond.
Under the round sky
The fisher moves softly in the little *blue* boat

. . . .

Gesang einer gefangenen Amsel

Dunkler Odem im *grünen* Gezweig.
Blaue Blümchen umschweben das Antlitz
Des Einsamen, den *goldnen* Schritt
Ersterbend unter dem Ölbaum . . . .

Song of a Captured Blackbird

Dark breath in the *green* branches.
Little *blue flowers* hover about the face
Of the solitary one, the *golden* step
Dying under the olive-tree . . .

An einen Frühverstorbenen

O, der *schwarze* Engel, der leise aus dem Innern des Baums trat,
Da wir sanfte Gespielen am Abend waren,
Am Rand des *bläulichen* Brunnens.
Ruhig war unser Schritt, die runden Augen in der *braunen* Kühle des Herbstes,
O, die *purpurne* Süße der Sterne . . . .

To one who died early

O, the *black* angel, who stepped softly out of the inside of the tree,
Where we gentle playmates were in the evening
At the side of the *bluish* fountain.
Our walk was quiet, the round eyes in the *brown* coolness of autumn,
O, the *crimson* sweetness of the stars . . . .

(The emphasis given to colour-words is mine. CWD) (37)

These random examples from Trakl's poetry give some idea of expressionist use of colour. The *yellow sun* is ambiguous as the colour yellow imparts a threatening dimension to the life-giving sun (cf. Marc's *Tiger*). The *yellow* is to be contrasted with the *golden step* of the blackbird, whose bright and vividly moving legs are seen as images of life. The fisherman's boat that threatens death to the fish is *blue,* and even the normally life-giving fountain becomes *bluish* in the presence of the *black* angel of death. The dying blackbird is surrounded by *little blue flowers*, symbols at once of death and of the longings of the dying bird. The symbolism of *dark* and *black* is plain, and the *Dunkler Odem (dark breath)* conveys the idea of 'dying breath' through synaesthesia. In the first two examples *green* retains its traditional symbolism of hope and life, though both the green pond and the green branches, in themselves living and hopeful, are only contexts of death, whether of fish or bird. The *reddish* fish will struggle against the fisherman and death in the little blue boat. In the third example the *crimson (i. e. purplish-red)* ascribed not to the stars themselves but to their *sweetness* synaesthetically associates that sweetness with both conflict (red) and death (blue).

We are now justified in anticipating that Fehling's use of coloured light is more than merely decorative, as well as being emphatically non-naturalistic.

It is evident that colour was used *only* on the cyclorama, for R. E. Jones' description refers to it only there, while Fehling's own reference to "an elusive blending of limelight rays" suggests that the rest of his lighting was white, like Brecht's, but for very different ends. Moreover, Fehling says that everything on stage was draped, curtained or carpeted in uniform black, so he clearly did not envisage colour-effects on the acting area.

The first scene, then, would have no colour. In the second, according to R. E. Jones, the clerk on his impossibly high stool, writing on his impossibly high desk, was almost in silhouette against the revealed triangle of cyclorama dome. He tells us that this was lighted yellow, in expressionist colour-language threatening and ominous. Another observer, however, (38) says that in this scene the cyclorama was initially blue, "a beautiful yet sulphurous and sinister illumination". This does not sound like the *blue flower* symbolism, and indeed the word 'sulphurous' brings to mind the yellow of the substance as well as the livid blue flame it emits. Is there some confusion or failure of memory here? Or were both colours used early in the scene?

At all events, as the bankers speculated in war and sexual exploitation the cyclorama turned fiery red (violence and lust), eventually, on Sonja's entrance, turning to the green of life and hope.

In Scene IV the cyclorama is described as "greenish almost submarine". It is difficult to imagine precisely how this looked and which of the two primary colours which together constitute green (yellow and blue) predominated. Was it threatening yellow or death-longing blue? The adjective 'submarine' does not suggest the green of hope seen in Scene II.

Scene V is the one 'realistic' scene in which the cyclorama was used, and to see how it was used demands a careful examination of how the scene was staged.

Patterson says that the scene "again employed steps before the back curtain, the steps this time at an angle to the front, leading on a diagonal up to the dark emptiness of the black drapes" (39). He himself, however, prints pictures of the scene which plainly contradict this description: Hans Strohbach's design, a production photograph and Robert Edmond Jones' impression (40). Yet another illustration of the scene is reproduced in the First English Edition of the play (1923). This is captioned: FIFTH PICTURE. *Design by Hans Strohbach. Photograph by*

Lisi Jessen (41). All four pictures show the same moment in the scene: the tableau immediately after the entrance of the soldiers almost at the end of the scene. All show the soldiers stage right (OP) with Sonja isolated centrally and the chorus cowering towards the top of the steps at stage left (PS).

The two 'design' pictures are so different in style that it is difficult to believe that they are by the same artist. Neither design shows the actual steps but the disposition of the figures suggests that Strohbach may have intended them to run diagonally, as Patterson says. But in both the production photograph and R. E. Jones' sketch of his impression of the scene, which, as Patterson rightly remarks, is "Perhaps the most reliable visual evidence", the steps squarely face front but are disposed centre and left of centre.

The Strohbach design reproduced by Patterson (Plate 24) shows a horizontal beam of light from stage right lighting the chorus, and an almost vertical beam lighting Sonja, standing at stage centre. The group of soldiers, like her apparently standing at stage level, I took at first to be lit by another, brighter and wider beam from above (German *Lichtkegel — light-cone* — best expresses this form of lighting), and I believed that Fehling must have developed the idea of drawing aside the drapes in the course of production, for they certainly are drawn aside, both in the production photograph and in R. E. Jones' sketch. However, the very different 'design' picture reproduced in the English edition of 1923 does *not* indicate the light sources faintly illuminating the Chorus and Sonja, but shows the soldiers (again at stage level) in a vividly white triangle that clearly seems to indicate the cyclorama revealed rather than a cone of light from above. It seems fair to assume that this is the way to interpret the other version of the design.

The production photograph, for which at that period flat, overall lighting had to be used, shows the chorus cowering up the steps, stage left, the soldiers grouped on the steps (the leading officer high and dominating the scene) against the partially revealed cyclorama, and Sonja sitting rather stiffly on the third or fourth step: but this may well have been a pose taken simply for the composition of the photograph.

R. E. Jones' sketch shows the horizontal light from stage right illuminating the cowering chorus left, Sonja standing just right of centre, lit from above, and the soldiers silhouetted (no detail or faces) against a triangle of cyclorama. One is high at the edge of the steps, dominating the scene, the others lower and further right. Only this sketch shows the curved line of the drawn-back drapes in contrast with the straight edges of the cones of light.

We are told that the cyclorama is yellow and that the soldiers were enveloped in a thin haze of smoke, suggesting the smoke of the machine-guns fired immediately before the drapes were drawn apart. Evidently Fehling and Strohbach developed this effect from Toller's rather naturalistic stage direction that doors at the rear and sides of the stage are burst open by the entering soldiers. Instead of a realistic, violent entrance, Fehling and Strohbach presented a sudden revelation. The ominous, yellow cyclorama and the silhouetted figures suddenly revealed were not only more in harmony with the scale of the production as a whole, but also more theatrically effective than a 'busy' entrance.

Most importantly of all from the point of view being advanced here, though Fehling himself does not refer in his *Note on the Production* to the close derivation of the play from Greek tragedy, the revelatory effect just described has much in common with the use of the Greek *eccyclema* for the presentation of dramatic tableaux. The way in which this moment in the play is dealt with visually — the sudden revelation of a tableau, plus the non-naturalistic use of colour — is a most interesting fusion of the classical and the expressionistic.

In Scene VI, the only other scene in which the cyclorama was used, we are not told its colour, only that it was "luminescent" (42), but the bird-cage in which Sonja is spiritually imprisoned was scarlet — symbolic of her inward struggles in this scene.

There are certain other respects, apart from the lighting, in which this production belongs to the current expressionist mode. This is particularly true of Scene IV, with its towering walls leaning inward, well seen in the design photograph in the English edition (43). These recall innumerable expressionist theatre designs such as, for example, Otto Reigbert's designs for *Der Sohn* (Hasenclever) (1919) and for *Trommeln in der Nacht* (Brecht) (1922), Ludwig Sievert's for the *Great Highway* (Strindberg) (1923) or Robert Wiene's film *Das Kabinett des Dr Caligari* (44).

The vast, angular, distorted shadows on the cyclorama in Scene VI (45) owe their existence to Craig (cf. the huge shadow in the famous and influential *Electra* design) and their form to Expressionism.

The Expressionist characteristics are, however, ephemeral and belong to a passing, though extremely important, fashion. Far more important was the fundamentally classical simplicity of the setting, embodied principally in the use of space and the use of steps. We have already quoted Fehling's own comment that the settings were "severely architectonic, composed of light and space" and have examined the use of light. Space was either deliberately confined by the dark drapes (Scenes I, III, V, VII) or vast and open through the use of the cyclorama (Scenes II, IV, VI), the most striking spatial contrast, for which the *author* has the initial credit, being that between the last two scenes: Scene VI, *Unbegrenzter Raum (Boundless Space)* — containing the basic symbol of confinement (especially of a woman), a bird-cage; and Scene VII, *Gefängniszelle (Prison Cell)*. Toller's authorial scenic direction *Boundless Space* may be regarded as the seed from which Fehling's spatial production grew.

This concept of the *Spatial Stage* is the most precise way of defining both this production and Fehling's personal contribution to the art of the theatre.

Michael Patterson classifies the production as:

> Abstractionist and primitivist theatre: an attempt at a synthesis (46),

where his example of Abstractionist Theatre is Kaiser's *Von morgens bis mitternachts (From Morning till Midnight)* (1917), and his example of Primitivist Theatre Toller's own play *Die Wandlung* in Karl-Heinz Martin's production of 1919. This backward-looking classification leaves it in a kind of No-Man's-Land as

> one of the last examples of truly Expressionist staging (47)

apparently without any creative future, for Patterson sees primitivism after 1922 becoming a cliché of distortion, and angularity and abstractionism giving way to

> the striking but largely empty products of Constructivism, where set design became almost independent of the works for which it was created (48).

If instead of emphasising his debts to and links with other strains of contemporary stage design we stress Fehling's peculiar contribution to staging, the Spatial Stage, (while recognising, of course, his general debts to Appia and Craig, and more immediate ones to Jeßner and Pirchan) we arrive at a much more positive position and one which looks forward to Fehling's own future work and to his influence.

Günther Rühle has rightly pointed out that "movements" in the theatre take place through changes in the scenic material, and that every change creates for itself its own form of theatre. He offers the following "schematic classification" of twentieth century German Directors who have made seminal contributions to theatre style, and the scenic techniques and materials associated with them:

Reinhardt:	Revolving Stage (*Drehbühne*)
Jeßner:	Step Stage (*Stufenbühne*)
Brecht:	Demonstration (Curtain) Stage (*Demonstrations (Gardinen) bühne*)
Piscator:	Scaffolding- and Practicable Stage (*Gerüst-und Praktikabelbühne*)
Fehling:	Spatial Stage (*Raumbühne*) (49)

This classification, relating artistic aims and effects to the specific material techniques characterising the work of each director, enables Fehling's importance to be made manifest, and with it, of course, the importance of this, the most celebrated of his early productions.

Spatial Theatre became Fehling's trade-mark. Frühwald and Spalek are all too obviously making an untenable assertion in declaring the production to be the *birth* of stage Expressionism and of light-production, but it is true to regard it (with *Antigone* as its prelude) as the initiation of Fehling's contribution to theatre styles: Spatial Theatre.

When he left the Volksbühne Company Fehling joined Leopold Jeßner at the Staatliches Schauspielhaus, Berlin, where he became in effect Jeßner's partner and where his influence grew as Jeßner's declined:

> Jeßner's theatre was, and became ever more clearly, Jürgen Fehling's theatre (50).

And there, as in *Masse Mensch*, Fehling used space to release the power of language.

> Fehling used cold, large space in which he could give speech its dominant effect and translate it into the actor's bodily tensions (51).

Fehling thus brought to Jeßner's theatre what he had first created at the Volksbühne in *Masse Mensch*.

Nevertheless, in this production he already owes his own debt to Jeßner and Jeßner's designer Pirchan. Jeßner became director of the Staatstheater in 1919 at the age of 41 and invited Emil Pirchan, six years his junior, to join him. A conscious opponent of Reinhardt's psychological and romantic approach to theatre, Jeßner sought to discover and emphasise in production the fundamental theme of a play. *Grundprinzip (fundamental principle)* and *Grundidee (fundamental idea)* were two key words in his theatrical vocabulary. This approach eschewed impressionism and naturalistic detail and aimed at very economical and simple means of expression, — always with the associated dangers of over-simplification and stridency. Pirchan's contribution towards the realisation of Jeßner's ideas developed from the ideas and theories of Craig and Appia. He sought in his designs to create "acting areas" which were dramatically and spatially related, and his particular contribution was to relate these acting areas three-dimensionally, that is, to place them on various levels, a method he called the *Terrassierung des Terrains (dividing the ground into terraces)*. Putting this into practice led directly to the *Stufenbühne* which we now associate with Jeßner's name.

Pirchan's design for Jeßner's first production in his new post, Schiller's *Wilhelm Tell* (1919) is a clear forerunner of Fehling / Strohbach's *Masse Mensch*. Here are the same broad flight of steps, the same heavy drapes and the trapezium of cyclorama revealed between them (52). As Denis Bablet says,

> Jeßner's famous steps do not link, they separate, isolate, create a dramatic distance between one group and another (53).

It was almost inevitable in the context of Jeßner's aims that such a spatial structure should lead to its symbolic application with 'up' and 'down' symbolising the power-relationships of the characters or groups. Jeßner did in fact apply it in this way in his next outstanding production, *Richard III*, in which, as Kortner, who played Richard, says,

> Richard's fortune and end were played out on the Up and Down of the stairs (54).

Jeßner's dynamic symbolism here was very elementary, not to say crude, as was his colour-symbolism, which used the primaries black, white and red in what today would seem an excessively simplistic manner. Fehling's colour-symbolism in *Masse Mensch* was much more subtle, as was his use of the *Stufenbühne*.

Alfred Kerr, after his rather dismissive reference to "the Expressionist stairs — of course", continues:

> Symbolically the steps produced the wrong effect. The people of the lower depths really ought by rights climb out of the depths, while here they far more gravitate from above to below (55).

This is too simple. Fehling's production was less crude, as befitted the greater moral subtlety of the political problems in *Masse Mensch* in comparison with Shakespeare's blatantly propagandist play on behalf of the Tudors. For example, in the final tableau of the scene (Scene V) whose staging we have studied most closely, the Officer is *up* but also standing prominently silhouetted against the yellow cyclorama — the commanding figure on stage; Sonja is *down* — appropriately, as this is the moment of her arrest; and the Chorus is in retreat *up* the steps *but* regressively into the dark, unlit upstage corner. The inverted triangle with Sonja at the 'apex' is excellently symbolic of the relationships at that moment:

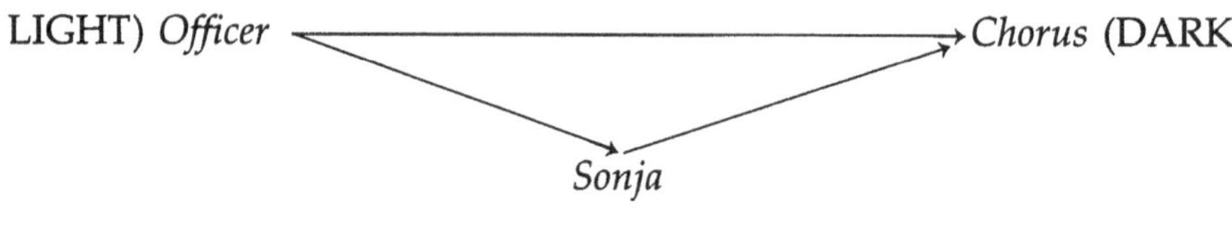

(*LIT FROM ABOVE*)

When considering two contemporary directors as powerful, original and as closely related in style and Jeßner and Fehling one is dealing with mutual influences rather than, so to speak genealogical ones.

In his use and disposition of the steps Fehling is not only being "Expressionist" but is also seeking for a method of deploying and choreographing his Chorus which will be a proscenium-stage equivalent of the Greek Orchestra. For Jeßner, what he called the *Grundprinzip* was ultimately more important than the particularities of the author's text — hence the broadness and unsubtlety of his use of symbolic space and colour. For Fehling, on the other hand, the author's *words* were supreme. (That he was prepared to lose some of the familiar words of The Internationale in a moment of stage drama in no way invalidates that).

We thus conclude that though Fehling's production owes a debt to Jeßner, and though it makes effective symbolic use of forms and colours associated with Expressionism in literature and art as well as in the theatre, and though it belongs to the theatre of space and light initiated by Appia and Craig, it makes a fundamentally new contribution to theatre style by employing space as the catalyst for *the release of meaningful speech* and as a twentieth century equivalent of the means at the disposal of the Classical Greek Theatre to body forth upon the stage a play which itself, as already argued, is a modern re-creation of classical tragedy.

Having now arrived at a description of Fehling's production as seen from the perspective of over sixty years, we turn to contemporary criticism of it, to which passing reference has already been made. Contrary to the view later disseminated, contemporary criticism was by no means nearly unanimous in praising the production at the expense of the play. Thirteen contemporary critiques listed and summarised by Spalek (56) distribute praise and adverse criticism remarkably evenly. Expressed in crude terms of + & –:

Toller +,	Fehling +	:	4
Toller –,	Fehling –	:	1
Toller +,	Fehling –	:	2
Toller –,	Fehling +	:	2
Toller +,	–	:	2
– ,	Fehling +	:	1
Toller –,	–	:	1
			13

There is no doubt of the success of the production. Says one anonymous critic:

> Go to the Volksbühne, if you can grab a seat still for the performances: they are sold out, — and see the production of Toller's *Masse Mensch* for yourself (57).

Herbert Ihering wrote:

> The production of *Masse-Mensch* was the best production of this short season (58).

It is not unreasonable that to one critic, Karl Strecker (59) the play was *Part II* of *Die Wandlung*: but he also saw it as in itself a "Wandlung" (i. e. change) in the direction of shallower theatricality! — and this despite the fact that he recognised the intelligence underlying the play's fundamental tendency and Toller's "astonishing ability" to conjure up strong theatrical effects. Strecker, however, decided that the whole thing was really a hollow sham, a *Regiekunststück* — a mere trick of production, *ein Heerwurm von Phrasen* — a long procession of empty words. "Nichts fehlt — als das Drama" (Nothing is lacking — except drama.) On the other hand Alfred Klaar (60) said there were plenty of conflicts — except that everything was in "dream" form. But, he says, "the worlds (sc. those in conflict) do not engage with each other, they float confusedly in the air. " He is less dismissive of the author than is Strecker:

> Certainly Ernst Toller is a talent to be taken seriously (ernst). (with a pun on his first name).

Another critic, Ernst Heilborn (61), spoke of the play's poetic strength, saying that Toller united the ecstasy of the lyric poet with the controlling will of the dramatist, but he undercut the praise by adding "without at present being a dramatist". Heilborn also compared the play with a symphony, thus showing his appreciation of its structure, and suggested that the choice of a woman protagonist was a move on Toller's part towards greater objectivity than in *Die Wandlung*.

It was Michael Charol (62) who, among others, criticised Fehling (wrongly in Toller's opinion, as we know) for not distinguishing between realistic and dream scenes. And yet another critic, presumably a left-winger dissatisfied with Volksbühne policies and signing himself "Lg" (63), remarked that although in this play the Volksbühne has got away from what he alleges to be the bourgeois tradition governing its repertoire, it also, ironically, returns to it, because the play's pacifist ideology is itself "bourgeois" — presumably because it conflicts with orthodox Marxism (64).

Perhaps the oddest comment of all came from Strecker, who thought the name "Sonja" (which was in fact that of the character's prototype, Sarah Sonja Lersch) was derived from Dostoievsky's prostitute (65) because, as he rather sarcastically comments, some literary groups pray to her as the modern guardian saint.

Another critic to give what he calls the lion's share of the credit for the play's success to Fehling, whom he calls a Mount Ararat rising out of the Flood of Berlin's 'experimentalists', was Hermann Kienzl (66). He says that Fehling's Expressionism fits " this completely lyrical stage poetry and really is a lesson to those who misuse its methods". With reference to the subject matter, this critic questions whether the enthusiastic audience realised that Toller rejected "the bloody sacrifices of revolution" with his whole soul, just as much as he rejected war.

Unlike Charol, Siegfried Jacobsohn (67) realised that the similarity of realistic and dream scenes was rightly interpreted by Fehling, though he accounts this a fault in the writing. He considered that Toller's essentially "good" nature had not produced a "good" play, that Toller's voice and gesture were inhibited by his "political armour", that he had failed to give literary form to his own best characteristics of liberality, warmth, honesty, magnanimity, pain at the unjust distribution of the good things of life and longing for a brighter future. He evidently thought the audience found the evening a bore, and for this he blames them, as petty bourgeois, and the author: but not Fehling! It has already been noted that he gave the author credit for the climax in Scene V.

The two critiques that merit closest attention are those of Herbert Ihering and Alfred Kerr, not only because these were the two most influential theatre critics of the time, but also because their *judgements* were very influential. Herbert Ihering's critique (68) must be read in full awareness of its author's rigidly left-wing viewpoint: it was Ihering who later wrote a bitter attack on Volksbühne policies in his leaflet, *The Betrayal of the Volksbühne* (69).

In Ihering's view the play was justified because of its author's life-history, not in itself. He thought Toller's symbolism weak, the intellectual content banal, albeit honest, warm and fanatical. The play contained no creative ideas or symbols. Its author was an idealist who had given up (!). The play was strong in its visual aspect, linguistically weak. It lacked lyricism, reverberation, even though Toller aspired to stillness and spiritual melody. Fehling used Thiessen's music in an attempt to restore the lyricism: he gives Fehling the whole credit for *any* lyricism. Ihering interestingly suggests that Fehling was consciously avoiding anything that might seem imitative of Karl-Heinz Martin's production of *Die Wandlung*. The critique, in effect, is in praise of Fehling, and concludes:

> In Fehling lies the future of the Volksbühne (70).

Historically, things worked out differently, with Fehling joining forces with Jeßner; but the connection continued in some senses and even as late as 1947 Fehling, described by Siegfried Nestriepke as *Berlins angesehnster Regisseur* (Berlin's most respected director), read a short essay by Julius Bab at the ceremony re-establishing the Volksbühne organisation (71). Soon afterwards (January 1948) the Volksbühne members went to his 'impressive' production of Sartre's *The Flies* at the Hebbel Theater (72). Twice in his book on the post-World War II Volksbühne, Nestriepke says he would have liked Fehling's services — first, as Director of the Open-Air Theatre (73); and again, in the 1951 season, when Fehling was under contract at the Residenz-Theater in Munich, he wanted him to direct a festival week (74).

When Ihering said that *Masse-Mensch* was the best *production* of the season, he avoided saying whether or not it was the best new play!

Kerr wrote the play up twice. The first notice, signed "K. .r" is so brief that it may usefully be quoted in full:

> Everyone followed these seven scenes with an unusual feeling of inward emotion. The seriousness [*Ernst*] of a poet, not his fate, seized upon the conscience of the audience.
> Even to those to whom, as to me, this doctrine of peace seemed too passive.
> In any case it was the strongest of all impressions of the present winter arts season — and a triumph for the Volksbühne.
> The successful director Jürgen Fehling, promised the always newly grateful crowds that he would send a greeting to Ernst Toller.
> More later on the work and performance.
>
> K. . r (75).

In contrast both with Ihering and with the critic Karl Bröger at Nürnberg, Kerr sees the impact of Toller on his audience as being that of the poet, not that of the political prisoner.

This, indeed is the heart of his immediate comment. The promised fuller treatment of the play and production appeared in the *Berliner Tageblatt* (76).

Kerr devotes the core of his full critique (three of his eight numbered sections) to arguing the falsity of Sonja's doctrine that there is no distinction to be drawn between violence as an instrument of political oppression and violence in the service of liberation from that oppression. Both George Fox and Mahatma Gandhi, archetypal pacifists and prophets of non-violence though they were, would have agreed here with Kerr: but Kerr fails to appreciate Toller's profound realisation of the tragic dilemma the play propounds, and sees it instead as simplistic pacifist propaganda. Nevertheless Kerr, unlike the other critics so far quoted, sees that it is the quality of Toller's writing that moves us so deeply:

> And if nevertheless [i. e. in spite of the doctrine. CWD] we are deeply moved, if an almost religious mood comes over people; if political discussion, weighing of arguments, exchange of opinions almost becomes an oratorio, no other reason can be ascertained except that a man with an unascertainable aura, that is, a poet, created it (77).

Referring to the most moving moments of the play, he says they are the kind never forgotten:

> That is no longer theatre. It is poetry. (Even if a politican stands behind it who became a political sacrifice as young as twenty-four) (78).

Indignant at how Toller has been treated, he adds:

> A strange feeling, when you compare the worth of this poet with that of the thugs who oppose him . . . And he preaches gentleness! (79).

Kerr sees the Volksbühne as realising itself in this production and Fehling as *helping*. He sees how Fehling's method of making characters "appear", often in pools of light, is an interpretation of Toller's "entrances" which improves upon the author: he co-operates creatively with the author — which is the best thing you can say about one of his profession.

Kerr also appreciates the qualities Fehling can derive from space:

> In his production distance acquires a quality of sound, so to speak (80).

More than any other critic, Kerr understood both the genius of the author and the contribution of the director.

We now look briefly at the play's subsequent stage history, with special reference to certain historically important productions.

Between Fehling's production in 1921 and the end of 1939 it was produced twenty-six times in many countries, though the most significant productions were in England and the USA.

The very first production after Fehling's was in Estonia (81), but the first of major importance was Meyerhold's at the Teatr Revoliûtŝii in Moscow (82). This Constructivist production was very interestingly reviewed. Predictably most critics attacked the play's ideology, some even saying that The Nameless was the potential hero if the play were differently presented (83). Apparently the play was performed without a break (84) and the commentator says that the action on various levels was not without danger to the actors!

The most thorough review was by V. Tikhonovich (85). This reviewer, who had clearly studied the play very carefully, did not think that Meyerhold had successfully integrated the style of acting with his constructivist setting (86). He saw the play as being constructed on the contrasts between the three leading characters (a perceptive idea), and did not think Meyerhold had taken adequate advantage of this. Of course, he thinks that The Woman is presented too sympathetically, but this is to be expected in a Soviet review.

In the following year (1924) came two of the most important productions, especially for English-speaking students of the play: Lee Simonson's production for the New York Theatre Guild at the Garrick Theatre, New York, which opened on 14 April and had about forty performances; and Lewis Casson's in London for the Stage Society at the New Theatre, which, sadly, had only four performances and which opened just a month later on 18 May (87).

Lee Simonson's production is extremely well documented: there are pictures, reviews in plenty, and comments by Lee Simonson himself. We shall concentrate on certain aspects that bear on our general theses concerning the play and its place in dramatic history.

Simonson seems to have been the first Director of the play — and indeed the first commentator on it — *formally* to compare *Masse-Mensch* with a *Greek* Tragedy. His production was doubtless influenced by this realisation. For example, he was criticised by some reviewers for using too few actors in his 'crowd' scenes (some twenty-five or thirty can be seen in production photographs); but if, as seems reasonable, he regarded these not as 'crowd scenes' but as a Greek Chorus, it would be natural for him to use a smaller number, — though in fact more than were used in the classical period in Athens. The photographs of the production, especially the one captioned *Revolution* (88), suggest choreographic treatment of the group as a choric entity, with virtually identical, somewhat stylised gestures.

Simonson's original intention had been to copy faithfully Fehling's production, of which he had written two years earlier:

> It seemed to me the greatest piece of stage craft I had ever seen (89).

But during the course of his work he departed from this idea and created a production of his own. Nevertheless, as the photographs show (90), his production still owed a vast debt to Fehling: here again are the *Jeßner Steps*, the heavy, dark drapes, the great cyclorama with its threatening shadows, and a grouping for the entrance of the soldiers that is plainly derivative from Fehling — the drapes partly open, the soldiers high on the rostrum, stage right, against the light, the Woman centre and the Chorus cowering on the steps towards darkness, stage left.

In spite of Simonson's claim to have created a completely new production, what he *did* produce still had its basis in the Berlin production.

The first English production, which opened only a month and a few days after that in New York, cannot have been influenced by Simonson, but was an independent emulation of Fehling (91). It was originally intended to be performed only twice, on 18 & 19 May, 1924, but because of the interest aroused, two additional matinees were arranged, on 30 May & 3 June. The Stage Society's team reads impressively:

Translation	Louis Untermeyer
Production	Lewis Casson
1st Workman	Raymond Massey
The Woman	Sybil Thorndike
Husband	Milton Rosmer
Guide	Lewis T. Casson
Nameless One	George Hayes
Setting	Aubrey Hammond
Costumes	Bruce Winston
Music	J. H. Foulds
Dances (arr.)	Penelope Spencer
	(92)

A German critic, Paul Christoph, London correspondent of the *Leipziger Volkszeitung,* who had expected to be disappointed in the production, said that (except for two scenes) it was the equal of the Volksbühne production in Berlin (93). This statement sets a standard by which to judge other critiques.

The two most distinguished London critics of the time, James Agate and Ivor Brown, both praised play and production highly, the former defending Toller against misunderstandings, the latter calling it the most important piece of work attempted by the Stage Society. Brown appreciated the play's lyricism and abstract qualities, and he realised that the use of the Chorus was a return to the origins of tragedy. Himself waxing somewhat lyrical, he called the play,

> a kind of ecstatic battering against the closed doors of eternal problems which Toller does not seek to answer but restates from the abysses of his own despair (94).

The *Daily Telegraph* was unstinting in its praise for Sybil Thorndike as The Woman (95). She was playing this part immediately after her success as Saint Joan, and one critic actually says:

> She conceived the part in the spirit of St. Joan (96).

He does, however, criticise her for the fact that "she chanted most of her words", and he questions whether a simpler form of speech would not have created greater effect. He says that it was a "fine creation" but that it was "sometimes monotonous like a litany". The comment reminds one that Sybil Thorndike had already played Euripides' *Hecuba* and *Medea,* (the former several times) in Gilbert Murray's somewhat 'romantic' translations (97). It is surely reasonable to suggest that the style of delivery was in recognition of the close relationship of Toller's play to Greek tragedy. The same critic — obviously a perceptive one — notices also the echoes of Schiller in the text. He tells us that George Hayes (The Nameless One) was,

> all flame and hell-fire and brimstone: the incarnation of revolt. The masses were wonderfully attuned in rhythm and movements.

Once more, specially composed music evidently added an important dimension to the production. It was by John Herbert Foulds, a Mancunian, son of a member of Manchester's Hallé Orchestra, and himself initially a cellist in that same orchestra. He was both prolific and experimental, but one critic, while commenting favourably upon the music, admits to having no knowledge of the composer. "E. A. B. " in the *Daily News* said of the music that it was,

> important, connecting the pictures with a remarkable feeling for the character of the play, and although his style is quite modern, he has not thrown aside the power of melody (98).

"J. T. G. " in *The Sketch* said that,

> in the sombre, ominous, aching music there was real tragedy. The music and the vivid stage pictures, in which the individuals as well as the masses were entities, not mere automata manoeuvred at will, were far more eloquent than the words (99).

Yet in spite of his references to "scenes of intense poignancy" and "utterances that proclaim the naked truth with the awe-inspiring sonority of the tocsin, " this critic is prepared to give the author credit neither for construction nor for dramatic language. He says that,

> Prison . . . explains the spasmodic, disjointed, unbalanced nature of the incidents and impressions,

and, so to speak, 'excuses' the author by referring to the "mental vagaries of the prisoner in his cell" in Galsworthy's *Justice*.

> As a drama (he says) it leaves no other impression than that of fevered lucubration. It is like a flood gushing the waters wildly over meadows and fields, creating devastation endless, and for what purpose?

Other critics, too, were impressed by the poetic qualities of the play and production: passionate poetry (100); a kind of free verse; a cry of workers . . . poignant in its thrilling passion; great intensity and unflagging inspiration (101).

A picture (102) of the 'cage' shows The Guide in a black robe and head-scarf, and the Woman in a plain dress. The Cage itself is stylised, a trapezium-shaped object with straight, almost vertical bars.

It does not suggest a bird-cage, as did Fehling's, but rather a sort of abstraction derived from the bars of a prison cell.

The two 1924 productions, one on each side of the Atlantic, established the play in the English-speaking world as not merely an interesting example of German Expressionism, but as a modern tragedy in its own right.

Perhaps the comments of later critics sympathetic to the play may be summed up in Spalek's précis of I. W. P.'s critique in the *Liverpool Echo* of the amateur performance on 4 December 1925 at the Sandon Studios in Liverpool:

> A very favourable view of the amateur performance. The same is said about the play itself, which is called *a tragedy as complete as any conceived by the Greek Masters*. (My italics. CWD). The reviewer considers this play as "the quintessence of modern expressionist drama wherein words and not action, thoughts and deed, count" (103).

DIE RACHE DES VERHÖHNTEN LIEBHABERS (THE SCORNED LOVER'S REVENGE)

As this play is not reprinted in GW or PBDG, as copies are not readily accessible in German or English, a brief description of it follows.

THE SCORNED LOVER'S REVENGE

The play is in two acts and is written in rhymed verse. Apart from the opening lines of Act I, where the author seems unsure of his rhyme-scheme, it is written throughout in rhymed couplets (apart from two little songs in Italian). The lines are basically iambic, with anything from three to eight feet in a line. The action takes place in Venice about 1550.

Elena is married to Giuseppe, an elderly and impotent councillor. In Act I she is visited in her husband's absence by Lorenzo, who forces his way in despite the efforts of the maid, Rosa. During his vigorous but unsuccessful attempt to win Elena's favours Giuseppe returns from the Council. Elena hides Lorenzo behind a curtain and then provokes her husband into demonstrating his duelling skill, getting him to 'fight' with the curtain behind which Lorenzo is hiding. Giuseppe departs and Lorenzo emerges, furious, and leaves, promising revenge.

Act II takes place in Lorenzo's palace. Lorenzo has got Giulia, his sister, to invite Elena to come to watch a festival from his window — Lorenzo being allegedly ill. Giulia soon makes an excuse to leave Elena alone. Lorenzo comes, locks the doors, and carries Elena into a room at the back of the stage. Soft violin music is heard: this continues to the end of the play. Rosa and Lorenzo's servant, Pietro, knock at the doors but go away.

When Lorenzo emerges from the inner room he is carrying Elena's clothes, which he hides in a chest. He locks the inner room and opens the other doors. Dancers and guests arrive, including Giuseppe. Lorenzo explains that he has been cured of his 'illness' by a magic medicine. Having aroused his guests' curiosity he takes them to the inner room, where Elena lies under a white silk coverlet. (N.B. A stage direction says that they 'block the door'. It is not certain whether what follows is actually seen by the audience). Lorenzo gradually removes the coverlet, beginning at the feet and, with a wealth of artificially poetic compliments to the beauty he is revealing, slowly pulls the coverlet up until the whole of Elena's naked body is revealed — but not her face.

The guests, including Giuseppe (who has been outspokenly appreciative of the spectacle) leave. Lorenzo gets the clothes from the chest and takes them into the inner room. Giuseppe knocks and is admitted to the outer room. He seeks to learn the name of the woman, but Lorenzo pretends to have taken a solemn oath not to reveal it. Strangely enough, this seems not to displease Giuseppe, who leaves, laughing. Elena emerges, dressed. She seems shamed and angry, but her attitude quickly changes, revealing her real feelings. She tells Lorenzo that in his haste he has failed to notice a distinguishing mark, a tiny mole on her left breast: the implication is that Giuseppe must have seen it. Lorenzo begs to take further 'revenge' in future — which Elena grants! They embrace tenderly and exeunt severally. After a brief interlude of the servants, Giuseppe returns yet again. He is alone on the stage, and his final speech is ambiguous:

> Ich muß doch nachschaun . . . ha . . . das Pärchen ausgeflogen,
> Ich irr mich nicht, heut hat ein Weibchen ihren Mann betrogen.
> Da lobe ich mir Elena. Sie wird zur Abendmesse gehn
> Und Gottes reichen Segen auf unser Eheglück erflehn.
> Vielleicht erhört Er sie und schenkt uns einen Sohn . . .
>
> (Still, I must have a look . . . ah . . . the birds have flown.
> I'm not mistaken, a wife has betrayed her husband today.
> That's what I like about Elena. She'll go to evening Mass
> And beg for God's rich blessing on our marriage.
> Perhaps he will grant her prayer and give us a son . . .)

Die Rache des verhöhnten Liebhabers was finished in January 1920 in prison at Eichstatt, after Toller had written the initial draft of *Masse Mensch* (October 1919) and while he was engaged in the long work of polishing and revising that play.

Nearly all critics and scholars of Toller either ignore the play entirely or dismiss it in a sentence or two as unworthy of their notice.

Only Malcolm Pittock in his very full study of Toller (1) treats it seriously or at all fully. Even he, however, relegates it to the very end of a chapter headed *Other Plays*, where he considers it unchronologically and virtually without relation to the rest of Toller's plays. He says it is "something of a sport", and declares:

> It has no obvious connection with any other play of Toller in subject matter or style (2).

Although Pittock's two-page account of the play contains some keenly suggestive critical insights and recognises the psychological pressures that evidently motivated its composition, his isolating this play from the context of Toller's oeuvre as a whole, and particularly from *Masse Mensch*, with which his mind was also occupied at the time, greatly weakens the impact of his very intelligent comments and deprives him of the opportunity of allowing this play to throw light upon Toller's other writings — except for his perceptively relating *Die Rache* to *Hinkemann*. Nor does Pittock make any comments whatsoever upon the fact that this is described as a puppet play (the only play of Toller's to be so described), nor that nevertheless its first production by the Freie Volksbühne at Jena, 8.5.1923 (3) was clearly not by puppets.

Here we shall work on the assumption that very frequently it is the writing that appears untypical of an author ("a sport") that provides important material for understanding the so-called "typical".

The first version of the play, which "differs radically from the book version" (4), was published in a periodical in 1920 (5) and according to Spalek was produced "several times" before its publication as a book in 1925 (6). The 1925 edition was "arty" in format and style. It was bound in green with a 'sword and horns' motif in gold. It was illustrated with nine etchings by Hans Meid; the whole play was printed in *italic* (this in Germany in 1925!), presumably in harmony with the story's Italian origin and subject matter. The etchings lightly suggest theatrical design sketches, and the frontispiece is a stage (?puppet-stage) proscenium. 120 copies of the edition were also produced in luxury format, evidently as a collectors' item, using hand-made paper, the etchings done on a hand press and signed by the artist. The one copy of this known to Spalek is bound in brown leather, with gold-stamped lettering. Toller had, of course, finished his prison sentence a year before this publication and was in a position to revise the play and to benefit from the profits of such an edition.

This mode of publication reflects an important aspect of Toller's character. He liked the good things of the senses, such as staying in good hotels, and he enjoyed luxury whenever possible. Doubtless he appreciated the edition (especially the limited edition) as a piece of expensive craftsmanship. The publication symbolised the sybaritic side of his character, and subsidised it as well.

What is true of the physical production of the book in relation to its author is also true of the play itself. Of course Pittock is right in describing the play on one level as "a masturbation fantasy"(7). This appears to shock Pittock, who seems to be apologising for the play's nature, and who refers rather smugly to "the impure feelings that inspired the play" (8). But it is *also* a consciously *artificial* as well as *artistic* piece of writing. There seems no reason to suppose that Toller "disguised" something "essentially pornographic" as "a work of culture and taste", as Pittock affirms, implying, indeed, a certain lack of artistic integrity in the author:

> The stylization of the language, so exaggerated as to be self-mocking in its sensuousness and sensuality, seems to indicate that Toller was both indulging his imagination and yet protecting himself at the same time against a full awareness of what he was doing (9).

It could also be that Pittock, who finds parts at least of the play "very obvious, very coy and rather corrupt" (10), is protecting *himself* from accepting that a play he obviously finds distasteful could be written with conscious artistic integrity by an author he admires.

Practically every principal work of Toller's (including his major prose and poetry) is experimental in one way or another. *Die Rache* is no exception. Its very artificiality and remoteness from everyday life can be seen as Toller's attempt to find a purely artistic, conventionalised form through which to sublimate the tremendous psychological pressures of sexual frustration.

In describing his artistic development at this time Toller wrote, in connection with intense personal experience and the writing of *Masse Mensch*:

> The sensuousness and richness of the experiences were so strong that I could only master them through abstraction, through dramatically clarifying (thinning) the lines which determined the causes of things (11).

He also referred in 1922 to,

> the human embarrassment which shyly avoided the issue of giving artistic form to personal experience, and to naked confession, and which could not yet summon up the will to objectify it purely artistically (12).

In the problem of the frustration of his sexuality in prison Toller faced 'personal experience' more embarrassing, less easy to confess nakedly, more difficult to objectify than the problems he has in mind in relation to *Masse Mensch*. Is it not reasonable to suggest that while working on *Masse Mensch* Toller did find in Bandello's Novella an artistic correlative for his own almost intolerable sexual frustration — a sexual frustration which, as Pittock also notes, was exceptionally strong at Eichstatt, where there were women prisoners as well as men? In thus basing his play on a Bandello Novella Toller was once more placing himself (despite his experimentalism) in a main stream of dramatic tradition, for Bandello's *Novelliere* (214 stories in all: Parts I-III, 1554; Part IV, 1573) has been a 'source book' for drama since the sixteenth century, when Bandello was used by the English Elizabethan dramatists, including Shakespeare, as a source for plots (13).

A desire and a tendency to fictionalise his observation and experience of sex-life in prison is also found in Toller's prose writings on the subject. The clearest and most completely unromanticised account he wrote was in a remarkable introductory essay to Joseph Fishman's *Sex Life in Prison* (London, 1935). In this he describes how men prisoners sent women prisoners samples of their semen in matchboxes, while the latter responded with pubic hairs. In the same essay he describes how one woman prisoner, who worked at a window facing the men's cells, used to expose herself while the men masturbated. The account is unadorned in its banal details and brings out the complete *impersonality* of these *ersatz* sexual relationships.

In *Briefe aus dem Gefängnis* (1935) he prints a letter dated from Stadelheim, 1919. It claims to be one of the letters confiscated by the authorities (and presumably returned to its writer when he left). This gives another version of the 'exposure' story, although chronologically Toller's imprisonment in Eichstatt (where there were women) *followed* that in Stadelheim. So in editing the letters Toller has obviously falsified something: the simplest explanation, and the most creditable to him, would be that he erroneously and carelessly added the address *Stadelheim* to a letter with no date line actually written from Eichstatt.

(There are no letters dated from Eichstatt in the collection.) Whatever the explanation, the letter was obviously written after or during the Eichstatt period of imprisonment. In this version, the men prisoners, in some way that Toller says would be too complicated to describe (is this because it was actually imaginary, and Toller could not be bothered to invent the details?) establish a correspondence with a girl who regularly works by an open window in a little scullery, visible from the men's cells. She is a child-murderer sentenced to eight years' imprisonment, but having served five years is to be released in a few weeks' time. The exchange of secret messages develops:

> Playful and innocuous at first, then feverish, passionate, confused. Everything that had accumulated in isolation, dreams, wishes and fantasies, forced its way towards this woman (14).

Then one day she indicated that they should all stand at their windows at a specified time. They did so, and saw the girl with her dress unfastened, naked at the window. She was seized and led away. Afterwards they learned that she had lost her remission as a consequence.

Thus a story of habitual sexual exposure and masturbation has been romanticised into one heroic gesture. Toller claims to have been deeply moved that this imprisoned girl, in order to make the men happy for a few seconds and in a very questionable manner, accepted three more years' imprisonment. He even introduces the subject matter of the letter (which is, significantly enough, addressed to a woman, Frau L.) by referring to the romantic story of Charlotte Stieglitz, the poet's wife, who committed suicide in the belief that the shock would awaken her husband from lethargy and enable him to recover his creative power! For our present argument the closing sentences of the letter are of particular interest. He says he often ('often' over what period of time? one asks) wanted to portray this experience in a Novella, adding, "Ich empfand Scheu" (I felt inhibited)(15), thus echoing what he wrote to Fehling about the writing of *Masse Mensch*. Yet what he wrote in this letter was already nearer to being material for a Novella than the de-personalised sexual relief described in the essay, and as if admitting to himself something of what he is doing, he adds finally:

> You, my dear friend, will understand that [viz. the inhibition, CWD]. You said once that the most refined and delicate private experiences have a touch which distinguishes them from the banal only by the minutest nuances (16).

The most highly romanticised version of the story is that in Chapter XVI of *Eine Jugend in Deutschland* (17). Toller introduces this version by stressing the men's sexual frustrations, — how they talked, thought and dreamed of women, pressing their heads into their pillows at night; and how they thumbed through the illustrated periodicals, gazing at pictures of naked women, naked breasts and naked legs. He describes (as in the later essay) how not only notes, but curls, handkerchiefs and pubic hair were lowered on threads through the drainpipes by the women on the floor above. This time the girl in the wash-house across the yard gazes at the cell windows in the hope of identifying the man with whom she has already corresponded for weeks. He recognises her and overcomes her doubts as to his own identity by pointing to his hair, nose, and a scar which he has evidently described in his letters. She stretches out her arms, in vain, longing to embrace him; then, overcome by her emotions, she fumbles with her rough, grey dress, unbuttons it and shows him her body, her firm little breasts and sturdy, well-rounded legs; she laughs and weeps for joy at being thus able to show to the man she loves that she would indeed give herself to him, were that possible. Again, the wardress has observed the scene; again the girl loses her remission. This time the romanticisation is complete: not only does the girl strip on *one* occasion only, as in the version in the letter, but she strips for *one man*, and not out of sexual generosity, but as a love-symbol. It would only have been necessary for Toller to fill out the story in detail for it to have become the Novella he felt impelled to write.

He never did write that Novella, but instead he dramatised this one by Bandello. To fictionalise the raw prison history of exposure and masturbation in order to make it palatable for a lady correspondent (or for the general public for whom the collection of letters and the autobiography were intended) Toller was constrained to romanticise and personalise the facts. In doing this he inevitably lost something of the sheer harsh sexuality of the experience he had apparently shared with his fellow-prisoners. The Bandello story, on the other hand, whose theatrical climax is not the off-stage rape, but the deliberate, gradual stripping of a woman's body on stage, is unromantic to the point of inhumanity. The headless, faceless body has the impersonality of sexual fantasy, an impersonality similar to that of the stripped woman-prisoner's body watched by the men from their cells. This voyeuristic climax is particularly appropriate in that the most Toller and the other prisoners could hope for was to see — never to touch — the body of a woman whose name they did not even know.

The male prisoner in his isolation feels impotent, like the elderly husband, Giuseppe (whose impotence is one of Toller's own inventions), but at the same time envies, and wishes to identify himself with the sexual experience of the rapist Lorenzo. Yet (as the romanticised version of the prison incident shows) male pride demands that the woman *enjoys* the rape, which is then followed by further, mutually desired intercourse. Another factor that makes the Bandello Novella peculiarly appropriate for Toller's purpose is that it (like those of Boccaccio) springs from an aristocratic society hemmed in (metaphorically "imprisoned") by an elaborate code of social conventions, a society that found an outlet for its own inhibitions in the bawdy Novella and the fabliau. In its own context the Novella, like Toller's play, was a fantasy outlet for readers normally deprived of genuinely individual freedom of expression in sexual behaviour.

This highly stylised play can now be seen as a genuine transformation of sexual frustration born of imprisonment into a light play, not to be taken too seriously *in itself*. That is to say, it is artistically inappropriate and irrelevant to discuss its treatment of rape or impotence (18) in naturalistic terms.

Toller dedicates the play as a *Spiel einer heiteren Laune (A play of a merry mood)* (19) to his friend E.K. in exile, as a greeting. "E.K." is Dr Erich Katzenstein, a doctor, born in Hanover in 1893. He was married to Nanette (Nettie), born in Munich in 1889. She is the *Tessa* to whom many of Toller's letters from prison are addressed. Toller had been friendly with the Katzensteins since 1917 and their house in the Herzog-Heinrich-Straße had been above all a meeting place for Toller's 'party' during the revolution. In 1919 Dr Katzenstein escaped to Switzerland (20). That he dedicates the play to a close friend who also supported him politically and with whose wife he also had a deep and lasting friendship confirms the view that it must not be dismissed as an irrelevance when assessing Toller's work.

Sexuality in its numberless manifestations was for Toller frequently the focus for his most serious dramatic statements on life and politics. This play is isolated only in that it is concerned with sexuality and (virtually) nothing else.

In his other plays Toller uses sexuality as the material for almost every major climax and many major and subsidiary motifs. In *Die Wandlung* the skeleton of the multi-raped thirteen-year-old girl hangs on the barbed wire entanglements with those of the soldiers (2nd Station, 4th Picture); in *Masse Mensch* Sonja in the Stock Exchange scene (Scene II) realises her beloved husband's involvement in sexual corruption, through his involvement in capitalism. A central climax (Act III Scene 4) in *Die Maschinenstürmer* is the women's attack on Mary Wible as she leaves Henry Cobbett's house. *Hinkemann* is a tragedy of emasculation, of shattered sexuality. A sexual-marital motif pervades *Der entfesselte Wotan,* finding particular expression in the *Dance of the Virgins before Wotan* (*Andante* GW2 p 271) and in Wotan's rejection of his wife (GW2 p 287ff). Sexual relationships punctuate *Hoppla, wir leben!*: that of Karl Thomas and Eva Berg on the positive side; that of Graf Lande and the corrupt, lesbian drug-taker Lotte Kilman on the negative. In the almost entirely male cast of *Feuer aus den Kesseln* the bar-girl Lucie makes a big impression in her scenes with Reichpietsch. Mary Baker Eddy's sexual affairs play an important rôle in *Wunder in Amerika* [with Hermann Kesten]. *Die blinde Göttin* is wholly based upon an adulterous relationship. Even in *Nie wieder Friede,* Rahel [Rachel] is the focal point at which several men's characters are tested and defined, and the plot of *Pastor Hall* is set in motion through Fritz Gerte's desire for Christine.

Thus *Die Rache des verhöhnten Liebhabers,* is seen, through its sexual theme and material, to be related in greater or lesser degree to every one of Toller's other plays.

THE PLAY IN RELATION TO ITS SOURCE

Toller's play is not a close dramatisation of the Bandello Novella, but is, as the title-page says, "freely based" on it (1). The degree of freedom assumed by the dramatist is considerable. The differences between the play and its source suggest that Toller had not got the book in front of him but was working from memory, while new elements introduced by him reveal, as a careful comparison of Novella and Play shows, a high proportion of original creativity by the dramatist. The very title shifts the centre of gravity from a 'jest' and the way the tables are turned on it, to the lover's 'revenge', a word which acquires ironic overtones by the end of the play, (2) while the sub-title suggests a nice balance of the masculine and feminine modes of cunning ('List').

Bandello's novella takes place in an unnamed 'city of Lombardy', but is transferred by Toller to Venice, a specific place and one not only quickly visualised by a North European audience but also rich for such an audience in literary associations including Shakespearean drama, and in overtones of Renaissance amorality. Even if this change occurred purely through lapse of memory, the city chosen by Toller is more effective dramatically than any city of Lombardy could be.

Bandello calls his Lady, Eleanora, which he pretends is a pseudonym. Toller's 'Elena' may well be 'Eleanora' imperfectly recollected, but it is also a name traditionally associated with great beauty and sexual scandal. (If Toller did in fact remember the name 'Eleanora' he may well have deliberately rejected it, for it would have for him and for a German audience, very different associations — with Beethoven's *Fidelio*.)

Eleanora is introduced, though not yet by name, in the very first sentence of the novella, as being "of a more capricious and wayward nature than became a woman of gravity" (3). Her haughty and malicious character is fully described in the following paragraphs with emphasis on her way of amusing herself "by teasing everyone and ridiculing them." This character is united with "angelic" beauty.

Toller's Elena is, of course, not described but dramatically revealed. Left alone a mere twelve lines from the play's beginning, she sings to herself a little Italian Cradle Song: so our first important impression is of a woman longing for a baby, a woman whose maternal instincts are frustrated. Nothing of Eleanora's whimsical and capricious hauteur is to be seen. Indeed, the character of Elena owes virtually nothing to that of Eleanora: her motivations are entirely Toller's conception.

In Bandello the first scene between Eleanora and Pompeio is not only introduced in a leisurely manner but itself moves smoothly with a minimum of dramatic confrontation:

> He, entering the house and meeting nobody, went directly to the hall, and here saw the lady before he was seen by her, and entered in her direction . . . etc (see Note 3)

There is minimal dialogue, followed, when the husband is heard outside, by the rather undignified hiding of Pompeio under a heap of clothes. The corresponding scene in Toller, which is analysed in detail later (see *An Examination of the Text*) opens abruptly, even violently, is conducted on Lorenzo's (Pompeio's) side in a spate of vigorous language, highly charged with sexual imagery, and *involves and introduces* the husband, Signor Giuseppe, even before he appears. Lorenzo hides behind a curtain which only incidentally conceals clothes belonging to Elena.

The husband in Bandello is a shadowy figure, barely characterised and nameless. Signor Giuseppe on the contrary, is vividly seen ("He shoves his paunch into the room.")(4), while his impotence provides a central pivot for the plot and the motivations of the other two principals — a fulcrum missing from Bandello's less tightly organised narrative structure.

The whole matter of the purchase and heroic, crusading history of the sword and the circumstantial way this is related to Giuseppe's activity in Venetian political life, is far more convincing in Toller's version.

As he has altered the nature of Lorenzo's (Pompeio's) hiding-place, so, of course, does Toller alter the mechanics of the fright Elena (Eleanora) engineers for her lover. In doing so he gains in immediate theatrical effectiveness, for a 'duel' with a curtain behind which — shades of Polonius! — the audience knows a man to be hidden, can be projected visually with more impact than the slow teasing indulged in by Bandello's Eleanora while her husband apparently stands there inactive.

On the other hand, by abandoning Bandello's chest full of clothes Toller has sacrificed perhaps the one feature of the novella which is subtler and more elegant than its dramatic equivalent, namely, the parallel between the woman's trick and the man's in the gradual, titillating progress from the victim's legs to neck (5).

In the second half of the story, Act II of the play, Toller's freedom and originality are shown to even greater advantage. The clumsy device by which Eleanora and Barbara (Giulia in Toller's play) leave a dinner party on getting Pompeio's (Lorenzo's) message is avoided, and instead, Elena goes to Lorenzo's palace at Giulia's invitation to witness a festival, having been assured that Lorenzo is too ill to appear.

Instead of the Volpone-like scene of Pompeio's leaping out at Eleanora from his supposed bed of sickness (6), Giulia leaves Elena on the excuse of domestic duties. Left alone, Elena begins to sing to herself — a habit of hers for which we have been prepared by the Cradle Song in the corresponding position early in Act I. This time, however, the stanza she sings is answered by Lorenzo with the second stanza as he enters from the bedroom upstage, and she — a parallel with his hiding-place in Act I — slips behind the window-curtain.

Using the traditional stage with entrances left, right and upstage centre, Toller makes Elena herself (the side doors having been locked by Lorenzo) throw open the upstage door to reveal the bed: and this same bed is used for the 'revelation' scene later, whereas Bandello, very awkwardly, has the lover take Eleanora (without any explanation) into another bedroom, which is described at inordinate length, for the 'revelation' scene.

During the actual seduction, behind the closed door of the inner room, Elena's maid-servant, Rosa, and Lorenzo's man-servant, Pietro speak outside the locked doors to the accompaniment of violin music which continues to the end of the scene.

The 'revelation' is similar to Bandello's — though Toller makes no mention of 'hiding that which dwelt between her legs'; indeed, Lorenzo describes it fully, though in poetic imagery (7). But the vital, essential, difference between Bandello's and Toller's versions is that whereas in the novella the husband has gone to Rome, in the play he is one of the guests watching his wife's body being stripped.

Thus instead of the tamely-written ending and the trite 'moral' of Bandello, Toller gives the closing speech to Giuseppe, with beautifully ironic ambiguities which bring the play to full circle in the probable conception of the baby Elena has longed for from the beginning.

Just as the play owes to Bandello almost nothing with regard to characterisation and only the barest skeleton of plot, so, too, it owes nothing to him as regards style.

Bandello writes an ornate and complex prose style (8) but reserves actual decorativeness for his elaborate description of the second bedroom, where the 'revelation' takes place, and of its furnishings. Speeches, even when passionate, do not use imagery, and even Eleanora's body is described in prosaic detail, with the addition only of the conventional clichés of ivory toes, nails resembling pearls and breasts of alabaster.

In total contrast Toller, writing in verse, has devised a linguistic manner that evokes for the modern audience the flavour of Renaissance and Elizabethan sonneteering. Lorenzo's speeches especially, as we shall see in the detailed examination of the text, are carefully cultivated gardens of sexual imagery, while *his* description of Elena's body exploits every kind of traditional image from the *Song of Solomon* onwards.

Yet, like the best of the Renaissance sonneteers, Toller can so control this *pastiche* – for *pastiche* it is, in no derogatory sense, a deliberate re-creation of a sixteenth century poetic style — that he can move easily from the decorative to the passionate and from the passionate to the ironic.

This irony (and especially the ambiguities and double meanings that play primarily around the figure of Giuseppe) has no place at all in Bandello, who accepts unquestioningly the sexual *mores* of the society about which he writes and, unlike Toller, provides no insights into the psychology of sex, of adulterous adventure and cuckoldry.

In Toller's play, it is not only Lorenzo who gets what he really wants by deviousness, but also Elena and Giuseppe, though their deviousness may not be wholly conscious and is in any case *post factum* — as far as we can judge!

This examination of the play in relation to its 'source' has thus shown it to be a genuinely original work, as independent of, and as superior to, its 'original' as, for example, the plays of Shakespeare and his most gifted contemporaries are independent of and superior to the *novelle* of Bandello and others upon whom they drew for their material.

A PUPPET PLAY

That Toller wrote *Die Rache* as a puppet play was no mere eccentricity. In doing so he associated himself and his work with an old and important tradition which was at that time experiencing a renaissance, — a renaissance which itself was related to the more general reaction against naturalism which Toller shared and to which he had already, in *Die Wandlung* and *Masse Mensch*, made a significant contribution.

To realise the importance of the puppet theatre in Germany we need go no earlier than the mid-eighteenth century (1). As their Christmas present from their grandmother in 1753 Goethe and his sister received the puppet theatre over which he enthuses in his autobiographical and semi-autobiographical works. He also wrote plays for fair-ground puppets (2). We have already noted the puppet play in relation to Goethe's *Faust*. Goethe's interest obviously lends prestige to this kind of theatre. On the other hand the puppet theatre in Germany, as in England and France, came in for much criticism in the seventeenth and eighteenth centuries. In June 1794, for example, it was laid upon provincial German governments to get rid of all unlicensed marionette operators, "because low tramps try to get applause through suggestive *doubles entendres*" (3). But opposition only strengthened the puppet theatres, so that everything shut out from the legitimate theatre — the character of Hanswurst, for example, and other 'folk' material — fled to the puppet stage. So many puppet operators were there in Germany in the eighteenth century that they assumed the character of a Trade Guild, with its own rules, such as, for instance, that the texts of plays must not be written down, but learnt by heart, stage-directions and all, presumably as a protection against piracy (4).

Parallel with the folky, fairground aspect of the puppet theatre ran the interest of educated writers and composers. Goethe's interest was typical, not exceptional. Prince Esterhazy had a puppet theatre at Eisenstadt for which Joseph Haydn wrote five operettas between 1773 and 1780. The puppet ensemble was so successful that it was also seen at Schonbrunn at the invitation of Maria Theresia (5). Many celebrated writers such as Brentano and Achim von Arnim had puppet plays in their houses. Above all, E.T.A. Hoffmann, the grotesqueries of whose writings often hovered on the boundaries of the purely human, wrote much for marionettes, though nothing has survived (6). Hoffmann also made brilliant use of a puppet play of *David and Goliath* in his great novel *Die Elixiere des Teufels (The Devil's Elixirs) (7).*

During the nineteenth century the repertoire of the German puppet theatre was very wide indeed and by no means limited to folkpieces, nor even to folk versions of *Faust* and *Don Juan,* popular though these were. There were a host of "thrillers" with such titles as *The Passing Bell at Midnight, The London Grave-robbers* or *The Murder in the Wine-Cellar,* and also such dramatisations as Jules Verne's *Round the World in Eighty Days* (in which no doubt the balloon played a spectacular part) and even Kleist's *Das Käthchen von Heilbronn* (8).

Not only did the puppet theatre adopt what the legitimate theatre rejected; it also presented what the legitimate theatre could not stage. In the eighteenth century, for example, *The Public Execution of Fräulein Dorothea* was very popular (9). The victim's head was chopped off, and when applause came was popped back on and once more chopped off. Clearly the puppet stage lends itself also to scenes, like the stripping scene in *Die Rache,* which might be considered indecent if played by humans, and in 1862 a puppet theatre was founded in Paris under the title *Théâtre érotique de la Rue de la Santé*. It apparently had little success despite the fact that, as Boehn rather smugly comments," it was indecent enough for Parisian taste" (10). If, as would seem reasonable, Toller chose the puppet medium partly because of the stripping scene, he had plenty of precedents for so doing, though, as will appear later, there could be profounder reasons than those of public decency for presenting this material through puppets. (But the 'public decency' explanation is well founded: even in the emancipated 1960s a review of the production at the Forum-Theater, Berlin (11) comments unfavourably on the fact that in this production "Toller's play was embellished by a 'strip tease'" (12).)

The first quarter of the twentieth century saw a real "Renaissance of the Marionette": the phrase is Boehn's (13). The reasons for it were many, but the core was the reaction against the Naturalism of the live theatre of the nineties and the search for new modes and conventions, including Expressionism.

> Schnitzler and Hugo von Hofmannsthal, too, found the human material of the theatres which played their pieces, too coarse and wilful, and they flirted with the puppet theatre (14).

Eleonora Duse wrote to Vittorio Podrecca, who ran the Teatro dei Piccoli puppet theatre in Rome:

> I envy you. I'd like to be the leader of a marionette troupe, too. Your actors don't speak, and they obey. Mine speak and don't obey (15).

Bernard Shaw also wrote to Podrecca in similar vein (16).

An unexpected factor in the renewal of interest in puppetry was the war. The trenches saw an extraordinary flowering of puppets. Soldiers bored by the long and tedious hours in the trenches carved figures from any available materials for puppet theatres. The Bavarian Army Museum in Munich has limestone figures carved in the trenches of the Vosges, while in Leipzig there are puppets carved from roots by German soldiers in Russian trenches. In POW camps also, soldiers made puppets and puppet theatres. A picture even exists of 'backstage' during the performance of a puppet play given by members of the 2nd Bavarian Territorial Army Infantry Regiment on the Eastern Front (17). Toller does not mention puppetry in his autobiographical account of his army experiences, but it is by no means unlikely that he saw or heard something of this kind of activity.

However, the central figure of the renewed interest was the Englishman, Edward Gordon Craig, whose indirect contribution to Fehling's *Masse Mensch* production has already been noted.

Two aspects of Craig's work are especially relevant here: his actorless miniature theatre, *Scene for the Poetic Drama,* and his essay *The Actor and the Über-Marionette*. Both these date from the period immediately following "the establishment of his renown in Europe" (18) in 1905, the year of the publication of the original version of *The Art of the Theatre* (first published in *German* (19)) and of his designs for *Venice Preserved* at the Lessing Theatre, and of his wonderful but unused *Electra* designs commissioned by Eleonora Duse. The etchings of *Scene,* based on the miniature theatre, belong to 1906–7, and the essay, *The Actor and the Über-Marionette* to 1907. The miniature theatre, whose working has been vividly described by Filiberto Scarpelli (20), demonstrated two principles above all:

1. That size is irrelevant to the impressiveness of theatrical effect:

> A ray of electric light comes to strike between those simple rectangles of cardboard, and the miracle is accomplished: you behold a majestic scene; the sense of the small disappears absolutely; you forget the dimensions of the theatre (21).

2. That the actor is only one element, and possibly an expendable one, in the total theatrical effect.

> . . . Craig made an extraordinary discovery . . . This was that there was a dramatic principle in nature — something akin to music or architecture. To demonstrate this he built a working model of screens which changed and unfolded before the eyes of the spectators, a Scene which was dramatic *in itself* (22).

It was not in his native England that Craig's ideas fell on fruitful soil, but in Germany, where *The Art of the Theatre* was first published. In July 1903 Craig visited Otto Brahm at the Lessing Theatre and during 1904 prepared his designs for *Venice Preserved,* which were used in 1905 at that theatre. When Craig's booklet appeared, Brahm's pupil Reinhardt, who had left Brahm in 1902 (at the cost of a 14,000 Mark fine for breach of contract (23)) to manage the Berlin Kleines Theater, had taken over the Deutsches Theater from Brahm. Ever eclectic and constantly on the lookout for new ideas, Reinhardt immediately made Craig's ideas his own. His success was enormous.

> From Reinhardt it [viz. the movement initiated by Craig] was ultimately to spread to the whole German-speaking stage, so that a *Craigische Vorstellung* became an accepted expression for a performance on the lines advocated by Craig, and added a new adjective to the German language (24).

In parallel with the poetic non-naturalism of his light-and-space concept of stage settings Craig advocated a form of supra-natural acting which was derived from, but not restricted to the acting of marionettes. He used for the expression of his idea the word *Übermarionette,* which would easily find its place and meaning in a language that had inherited from Goethe the word *Übermensch,* recently given new currency by Nietzsche. Craig argued that,

> in order to make any work of art . . . we may only work in those materials with which we can calculate;

adding,

> Man is not one of those materials;

because,

> the whole nature of man tends towards freedom,

therefore man

> carries the proof in his own person that as *material* for the theatre he is useless (25).

He argues against the concept of acting as an imitation or impersonation of living externals, in favour of its being a reflection of spiritual essence:

> Rather should life reflect the likeness of the spirit, for it was the spirit which first chose the artist to chronicle its beauty (26).

And as a footnote to this Craig quotes William Blake, to whom the book is dedicated:

> All forms are perfect in the poet's mind: but these are not abstracted or compounded from Nature; they are from the Imagination (27).

Thus Craig sees the marionette as a means towards a more *artistic* theatre. In the Preface to the 1924 edition he found it necessary to clarify what he meant, and to answer critics who had misunderstood him:

> The Übermarionette is the actor plus fire, minus egoism: the fire of the gods and demons, without the smoke and steam of mortality (28).

Craig thus declares that the actor can learn from the marionette a more artistic approach to his work, and further, that what he learns from the purely material, sub-human marionette can make him super-human, godlike, with "the fire of the gods and demons".

These ideas were not new in Germany but constitute a restatement of what the dramatist Kleist had written in his essay *Über das Marionettentheater (Concerning the Marionette Theatre)* (1810). Like Craig's original 1905 *The Art of the Theatre,* Kleist's essay is cast, though less formally and with much indirect speech, in dialogue form, — the ideal form, surely, for writings on drama. (Brecht evidently shared this view when he wrote his *Dialoge aus dem Messingkauf.*) Kleist's dialogue purports to be between himself and a certain "Herr C.", the principal dancer at the opera, whom he finds enjoying the performance of a marionette theatre in the public gardens. Kleist at first professes himself surprised that this talented and cultured person should derive pleasure from this popular entertainment. The dancer replies that he, as a dancer, has much to learn from the marionettes. The body of the essay develops this statement. In brief outline, these are the stages in the argument, which begins on a disarmingly simple mechanical basis and ends at a level closely related to William Blake.

1. The marionette operator does not have to think about every thread to every limb of the marionette all the time. It is only necessary to control the centre of gravity within the figure and guide this along the principal line of the movement. The limbs are mere pendulums which follow appropriately without further assistance, mechanically.
2. The achievement of this result, however, is far from being mechanical, but on the contrary is very mysterious. The line followed by the centre of gravity is nothing less than *The Way of the Dancer's Soul.* To discover this the operator must "transplant himself into the marionette's centre of gravity, that is, in other words — dance" (29).
3. The three principal requirements of a good dancer are: Elegance of proportion, mobility and ease. The marionette has advantages over the live dancer in all these respects.
4. Further, the marionette never adds airs and graces to essential, expressive movement, as living dancers all too often do. The living dancer lacks paradisal innocence.
5. The marionette has the further advantage of being weightless [*antigrav*]: the force which lifts it into the air is greater than that

which fetters it to the earth. The puppet need only brush the ground and need never rest upon it.

6. The argument then becomes more metaphysical, Herr C. arguing that only a God is comparable with matter in this field, and that this is the point "where the two ends of the ring-like world seize upon each other" (30). It is the ancient image of the serpent with its tail in its mouth. Only someone who has read carefully the third chapter of the Book of Genesis can justifiably discuss later stages of human education. After eating the fruit of the Tree of Knowledge of Good and Evil, Adam and Eve become self-conscious and are no longer able to sustain natural unselfconsciousness when naked. Selfconsciousness is the root of all lack of grace. (Kleist here interpolates an anecdote of a graceful adolescent who loses his innocent grace by seeing himself in a mirror in a naturally artistic pose when drying himself after a bathe, and then trying unsuccessfully to repeat the pose deliberately. In that moment he lost his innocence and with it the loveliness (Lieblichkeit) he had formerly possessed. Kleist's interlocutor caps this with the story of how a bear, though chained to a post, had proved that its instinctive, unselfconscious movements were more than a match for those of a skilful fencer.)
7. The final sentences must be quoted in full.

> We see that, in the organic world, grace emerges ever more radiantly and dominantly in proportion that reflection* becomes less clear and weaker. Yet just as the intersection of two lines on one side of a point, after passing through infinity suddenly arrives on the other side, or the image in a concave mirror, after it has retreated to infinity, suddenly comes close to us again, so, too, when cognition has passed so to speak through infinity, grace suddenly comes again. Thus it appears in its purest form in the human shape that either has no consciousness or infinite consciousness: that is to say, in the articulated model, or in God.
> So, said I, a little absently, we must eat from the Tree of Knowledge again, in order to recover the state of innocence. Of course, he agreed; that is the last chapter in the history of the world.
>
> (31)
>
> *(Note. *Reflection*. In philosophy: The mode, operation or faculty by which the mind has knowledge of its own operations, or by which it deals with the ideas received from sensation and perception.
>
> [Shorter OED])

Thus both for Kleist and Craig the sub-human marionette becomes the image of the super-human, the godlike. Both see in the marionette an artistic purity unachievable by human actors or dancers; and Kleist sees also in the marionette an image both of pre-lapsarian innocence and of the godlike innocence that lies beyond experience: as in William Blake's language, the synthesis of Single Vision (Innocence) and Two-fold Vision (Experience) leads to Three-fold Vision (Beulah). Kleist's marionette philosophy is therefore one which lays great stress on the sexual innocence and unselfconsciousness of the marionette.

This view provides a much profounder justification for Toller's choosing the puppet medium for this play. By doing so he is endowing it not only with artistic detachment from ordinary life, including prison life, but also endowing a risqué tale with a kind of primal innocence. Thus, as in Kleist's essay, extremes meet, and the impersonal, psycho-physical sexual frustration of the prisoner, his need for the basic physical and psychological organic relief of masturbation, is given expression through a non-organic, sub-human medium whose innocence and purity unconscious matter shares only with the super-human infinite consciousness, God (32).

AN EXAMINATION OF THE TEXT

To begin at the beginning: the play's title tells us its subject matter, while the sub-title, *Frauenlist und Männerlist (Female Cunning and Male Cunning),* which is abstract and generalised, tells us its theme. Although it is true that a number of celebrated naturalistic plays (e.g. many of Galsworthy's in English) have abstract and generalised titles (e.g. *Justice, Loyalties*) the material of such plays is usually a single example of the workings of that theme. Actually to give dramatic expression to an abstract title (or to an abstract theme not necessarily expressed in the title) some other dramatic convention is called for. It will be argued that in this verse play for marionettes Toller found, or devised, such a convention and that the play, despite its apparent triviality, is a real contribution to the development of non-naturalistic theatre in line with the ideas of Craig and bearing out the marionette theory of Kleist.

By way of introduction, let us consider another mode of comedy which serves similar ends: farce. In farce at its best, in Feydeau's plays, for example, immediately recognisable types of persons are presented in a manner so distanced from "real life" that our laughter at the situations in which they become entangled is not inhibited by empathy, and events which would border on the tragic if they were seen to affect the deeper layers of the characters' personalities provoke at the time only laughter. Yet this apparently facile and superficial representation of human affairs can, through the re-creation of life in purely artistic terms, abstracted from the painful inner process of learning associated with tragedy from Aeschylus onward, invite and stimulate its laughing audience to keen and often profound questioning of universal human problems and values. Thus John Mortimer:

> Farce is a form of drama which seems to me often more true to the facts of life as we know them than many great tragedies (1).

Note that he says farce is 'true to the facts of life' and not that it actually represents them.

The power of puppetry to produce distancing and abstraction is not unlike that of farce. The Bandello story is not the material of farce, and another medium was called for if it were to be dramatised. Puppetry was an obvious solution. As Joe Orton, himself a master of the art of provoking laughter at material also calculated to shock, has said:

> . . . farce originally was very close to tragedy, and differed only in the treatment of its themes, like rape, bastardy, prostitution. But you can't have farce about rape any longer (2).

As Orton also pointed out, adultery was the limit to which sexual material could be carried for purposes of laughter in nineteenth century French farce, while by the time of Ben Travers it was only *suspected* adultery. So in the early 1920s, rape (if indeed that *is* what occurs in the play) would have been unacceptable farce material.

Puppetry, however, has the potential for distancing its artistic product even further from "real life" than is possible for farce, and for this tale of apparent rape, Toller used puppetry. The subtitle, however, makes it clear that while the material of the play is the single story of *The Scorned Lover's Revenge*, the theme is not that of lovers' revenges, with this story as an example, but that of male and female cunning — a theme far more universal. And as we have already seen, one of the things that Craig emphasised about the marionette theatre was its ability to present life in its essentials (its universals) uncluttered by detailed realism.

> . . . the purpose of art . . . is not to reflect the actual facts of this life (3).

We turn to the opening of the play. Immediately we perceive the paring-down to absolute essentials: action — Lorenzo's violent entrance — begins after only sixteen lines of exposition (six speeches and a stanza or song).

> ROSA: As you ordered, I sent away the visitors who had come.
>
> *(Situational facts; hint of Elena's character; mistress/servant relationship established.)*
>
> But one gentleman out there persists all the time: he wants to speak to you.
>
> *(Plot)*
>
> Says if the gate had a thousand bolts he'd smash them and force his way to you.
>
> *(Lorenzo's use of heightened language)*
>
> – and, I confess, he's handsome.
>
> *(Lorenzo's attractiveness; Maid's susceptibility.)*
>
> ELENA: Tell your gentleman, I don't want to see anyone.
>
> *(Elena's mood)*
>
> ROSA: If the answer doesn't satisfy him?
>
> *(Anticipation of next action)*
>
> ELENA: Evidently you like him.
>
> *(Ironic. Ambiguous. Does it imply her possible interest? or even jealousy?)*
>
> ROSA: As I said — he's handsome.
>
> *(So naturally I like him!)*
>
> ELENA: You bore me.
>
> *(Why? More ambiguity. Evasion?)*

Tell him to get along.

(Plot)

(ROSA leaves the room.
ELENA sings a four-line cradle-song in Italian.)

(Elena longs for a child. What is her situation: single? married? virgin? barren?..)

(LORENZO bursts in followed by ROSA)

(4).

In these few words a certain situation and certain character-aspects are exposed: the bored, childless, frustrated woman, shutting herself away from society, perhaps even jealous of her maid's vulgar sexuality; the maid, carrying out her orders, but evidently not really wanting to send this handsome, aggressive man, with his persuasive tongue, about his business; the man, even before he is seen, revealed as handsome, persistent and very articulate.

The costumes and decor will tell us this is sixteenth century Italy, and the language of the cradle song confirms this. But the exposition is loaded with unanswered questions, as the annotations here added to the translation show.

In prose, however, as this flat translation shows, all this is banal, and *because* it is in prose and therefore apparently naturalistic in intention, unconvincing, a dead skeleton, neither living organism nor wrought artifact; it belongs neither to the 'mackerel-crowded seas' nor to such forms 'as Grecian goldsmiths make'. To achieve the latter, as art and abstraction demand, Toller uses verse, rhymed verse remote from naturalistic speech, and after a hesitation already noted over the rhyme scheme in lines three to seven, rhymed verse in that most overtly conventionalised form of dramatic verse: rhyming couplets. In verse inessential details can be omitted, naturalistic 'empty' words are not required, ambiguities are given edge, and the rhyme and rhythm automatically remove the speakers away from the world of natural appearances, so that an expression of essential reality becomes a possibility, depending upon the intentions and skill of the writing.

Cunning (List) implies ambiguity. Thus the ambiguities inherent in the opening lines are wholly appropriate to the theme, while the first clear example of *Frauenlist* is to be found in Rosa's words of 'apology' as she follows Lorenzo in:

I was helpless, Mistress, zealous (5).

Does she mean helpless before the strength of the man although zealous in her duty to her mistress? Or was she psychologically helpless before the man? Or was she helpless because of her sense of duty to the man? Or was she zealous to serve some unconscious wish of her mistress? Grammatically, the line leaves much open to doubt. Moreover (and this is important) it is impossible to tell whether the ambiguity arises from conscious cunning or whether the speaker herself is unaware of the ambiguity.

Significantly, Lorenzo's opening words are *Mein Wort*: it is through words that Lorenzo operates and effects his ends. Words are his first medium of cunning. His wooing of Elena in this scene is verbal, a flood of couplets which expand themselves from the predominating pentameter into longer lines, Alexandrines and even lines of up to eight feet. In a torrent of imagery he 'savours the aroma of her eyes'(!), he drinks them greedily, he sinks into them as into a hyacinthine night in June. Through every extravagance of synaesthesia he pours out his flood of erotically charged rhetoric: a stream of red torch-flames storms through his blood; Elena is a goblet in which the restless pilgrim finds rest; his will is a sword. This blatantly sexual symbolism is succeeded by religious allusion: he is the flowers at the foot of Our Lady. This in turn is finally succeeded by the whimsy of himself as the trembling, fugitive cloud in the blue sky of midday! (6).

Words, the play of words and the power of words, words as fantastically artificial as are to be found in any sixteenth century love-poetry, overstepping indeed the strict bounds which convention and rigid form normally imposed upon such poetry: these are the first manifestation of *Männerlist*.

Image succeeds image in prodigal profusion: he wants to be the wing-beats of the doves of St Mark's, the sweet breath of a jasmin arbour, an Indian shawl covering cold, naked shoulders, the smile of a child awakening Elena and himself at midday (7).

The flowering illogicality and sprawling absurdity would be merely laughable if they did not carry with them a sub-text of fiercely driving sexuality: in two speeches Lorenzo's verbalising has progressed from eye-contact to the love-begotten child (is he aware that this is Elena's dearest wish?) awakening them as lovers at noon!

There is nothing elsewhere in Toller's verse like this. Nowhere but in this play does he use verse in so *literary*, so consciously artificial a manner. It is important to add that the manner is literary for *dramatic* purposes. Nowhere else does he so objectify his subjective experiences. In this artificially literary style there is, too, an element of parody which further distances the situation from the everyday and ironises the dramatic viewpoint. Parody is to be found in other plays of Toller (8) but nowhere else in this key. It is tuned to the voice of the marionette, not to that of the human actor.

Despite Elena's protest the flood of sexual images pours on: the clapper in the bell, the fir-tree firmly upright in the wind, the woman as earth and soil (9).

In Elena's answer we learn that she is married, so Lorenzo's next ploy is to relate an anecdote in which Giuseppe, the husband, strutting like a turkey-cock, has revealed his basic cowardice when sword-play is in question. Finally he declares roundly in horticultural imagery that "everyone knows" that Elena, though a wife, is still a virgin:

> I'm smiling, for everyone knows that you are still a virgin bud
> And your marriage-bed a dry garden in March,
> Giuseppe blethers, but there's one thing he doesn't understand: how to look after his little flower bed (10).

Up to this point the play has operated almost exclusively through language, and above all through the artifices of language, not language as the expression of the complexities of the human character. With the unexpected return of Giuseppe action and visual impact become important: Lorenzo hidden behind the silk curtains, Giuseppe entering paunch first (*schiebt seinen Bauch ins Zimmer: shoves his pot-belly into the room*), an effect demanding the exaggerated physical distortion appropriate to marionettes.

The verbal ambiguities continue to proliferate. Elena, instead of welcoming her husband's return as an opportunity to put Lorenzo in the wrong, asks him to hide, and when Lorenzo (who, however, knows Giuseppe's cowardice) says, "I'll stay, may he stab me to death", she exclaims, "Do you want to break my heart?". Is it Lorenzo's or Giuseppe's possible death she fears? She says she wants to forget that Lorenzo made her angry: but he for his part warns her to play no tricks. All this complexity depends upon word-play accompanying very simple action, and for this combination marionettes are an appropriate medium.

This analysis of the opening sequence has already shown how suitable the marionette theatre is for this play. It has also shown the Expressionist author of *Die Wandlung* and *Masse-Mensch* successfully using a totally new means (for him) of escaping from the limitations of the naturalistic theatre. Here he is exploring aspects of human nature not touched upon in those plays of political and moral seriousness. Most remarkably the analysis has shown Toller capable of creating what was for him a completely new style of poetic expression, in which not political commitments or personal attachments and loyalties but the basic human instincts, — sexuality (the preservation of the species) and self-preservation — are examined through light-hearted (heiter) comedy in a most sophisticated manner, using theatrical and linguistic conventions which are in complete harmony with each other. These conventions are admirably suited also to exploring the play's main theme, namely, the various forms of cunning displayed by both sexes in their aims of fulfilling the two basic instincts — counterparts, if we pause to consider, of the tricks and stratagems through which the Eichstatt prisoners sought some measure of *ersatz* sexual relief and fulfilment.

It follows that this play, unlike all Toller's other plays, does not propound questions of morality but demonstrates the deviousness and ambiguity of the ways in which human beings seek the fulfilment of the fundamental animal instincts amid the restraints and conventions of a highly organised and restrictive society, whether in sixteenth century Venice or a twentieth century prison.

Thus it is arguable that this 'light' play actually studies human nature at a profounder level than those concerned with politics and morality.

Elena's deepest desire at the beginning of the play is to have a child: this her husband's impotence denies her. At the end of the play she will probably have one, not only to her own delight, but to Giuseppe's also. His closing speech is fraught with ambiguity. We are never actually told whether he noticed the mole on the left breast when his wife's body was displayed. We may, if we wish, assume that he did. Or we may believe that, as Lorenzo says, "her body was an unknown fairyland for him" (11). Giuseppe does say that he believes that "a wife" has betrayed her husband, and goes straight on:

> That's what I like about Elena (12).

What does he like about her? That she has betrayed her husband? Or does the sentence refer to what follows:

> She'll go to evening Mass
> And beg for God's rich blessing on our married bliss.
> Perhaps he will hear her and present us with a son.

As Giuseppe evidently succeeds in carrying on his line through surrogacy, has he also fulfilled his instinctive needs, despite his impotence, through "cunning", even if that cunning consists in no more than keeping his mouth shut? At his first entrance we have been made to realise that he lives through surrogates: the sword he has acquired has been (if the seller was telling the truth!) a potent and deadly weapon in another's hands. So, as with sword, so with phallus, Giuseppe can only live in the reflection of another man's prowess.

The mock duel Elena contrives between impotent husband and hidden lover is thus also charged with ambiguities. Does she intend only to frighten Lorenzo? He is actually hurt and cries out: but Elena claims the cry as her own. Is she then identifying herself with Lorenzo, and letting him know it? and in the Second Act she too hides behind a curtain — from him. The parallel is close. Indeed we may ask why she risks coming so near 'the snake', as Lorenzo calls himself in the same act. At what level is 'female cunning' operating? We never know. And the whole play is written and presented so that we never *can* know the answer to this and similar questions.

Other details could be adduced to bear out what is now clear: that the play is a light-heartedly profound study of the tortuous ways through which the human being (whether consciously or instinctively) succeeds in fulfilling basic instinctual needs. Deliberately the play frequently leaves it impossible to determine how far the individual is consciously aware of what he or she is doing. We do not even know whether what happens in the bedroom is rape or not. The gentle violin music that begins as the bedroom door shuts adds a new dimension of emotional ambiguity to the theatrical effect.

It is now clear that Toller's use of the marionette theatre for this play is part of that movement in the German theatre which Craig had initiated and that, however simple the original motives for his choice of medium may have been (e.g. possibly the practicalities of the stripping scene) the end-product exploited the artistic potential of the marionette theatre at a much more fundamental level as a means of dramatising basic instincts — those ancient strata of human nature which may be figuratively described as 'the fire of gods and demons'.

Nor are these arguments invalidated by the fact of stage productions of the play. On the contrary, that living actors should consciously play what was written with marionettes in mind only links the play more closely with Craig and his doctrine that actors should learn to acquire the positive qualities of marionettes.

Spalek lists only four productions of the play, none of them being described as by marionettes, and all in Berlin, except for the first production at Jena (13). A very favourable review of the single matinee performance at the Volksbühne on 7 September 1924 (14) does suggest that the cast should have acted more like marionettes.

Enough has also been cited of the play to indicate how it embodies the qualities Kleist saw in the marionette theatre. Morality is post-lapsarian. Toller's figures in this play are untouched by it: only *social conventions,* not questions of right and wrong, constitute the inhibiting framework within which the instincts must find their outlets. The marionette-characters do not *reflect* and therefore, as Kleist says, "grace emerges ever more radiantly and dominantly" (15), and this is seen in sharp focus in Elena's acceptance of being stripped and in her final dialogue with Lorenzo:

> ELENA: I'm angry with you. You! You have drunk up the fountain all too hastily.
> LORENZO: Was I not, a drunken man, deeply immersed in you?
> ELENA: When you raised the silken bed-cover, you did not know of a tiny blue mole on my left breast which partly adorns me like a velvet amethyst and which, I must admit, has often delighted me when bathing; you, you hasty man, overlooked this little wonder.
> LORENZO: By Dionysus! It shan't happen in future! I swear that to you with a thousand oaths!
> ELENA: Kiss me, then!
> LORENZO: And . . . may I avenge myself further?
> ELENA: You may! Oh, even if your revenge washes around me with oceans of fire, my blood will never be cooled by your revenge (16).

This is the grace, mobility and ease described by Kleist, unadulterated by moral consciousness. Toller concentrates entirely on the 'centre of gravity' of each figure's nature, and the rest, like the movements of the marionette's limbs, follows 'mechanically' — that is, inevitably and unhesitatingly: naturally. As in Herr C.'s argument in Kleist's essay, these creations of imagination have eaten again of the Tree of Knowledge in order to recover the state of innocence. The serpent's tail is in its mouth.

On a more metaphysical level than Brecht, Toller is here obliquely saying in relation to sex and the preservation of the species (or 'line') what Brecht in *Die Dreigroschenoper* said in relation to food and survival:

> Erst kommt das Fressen, dann kommt die Moral.
> (Grub first, then morality) (17)

We are also reminded of Toller's rhetorical question in *Eine Jugend in Deutschland*:

> Do moral ideas drive the masses, or do not rather poverty and hunger drive them? (18)

Morality belongs to a later phase of human experience and behaviour than the satisfaction of basic needs, without which morality becomes meaningless, because the person, or species, ceases to exist.

So far from *Die Rache* being a 'sport' unrelated to his other works with their powerful moral and political concerns, this play reveals Toller's appreciation of the primal forces whose power is at work within his morally torn protagonists — Friedrich, Sonja, the lovers in *Die blinde Göttin* — and provide the driving power which morality seeks to guide and control, as imaged in Blake's *The Marriage of Heaven and Hell.*

Lorenzo's oath, *Bei Dionysos*! in the dialogue just quoted is a perfectly placed sign that under the polished and apparently Apollonian surface, *Die Rache* is a play about the 'dark gods' and the Dionysiac, chthonian and Saturnian forces lying deep in the soil of human nature. This relates the play to another of the important influences upon Toller — the poetry of Hölderlin, and particularly to Hölderlin's great poem *Natur und Kunst oder Saturn und Jupiter*. Whatever the power of Jupiter, the law-giver, he owes it ultimately to Saturn, the guiltless God of the Golden Age:

> Denn, wie aus dem Gewölke dein Blitz, so kömmt
> Von ihm, was dein ist, siehe! so zeugt von ihm,
> Was du gebeutst, und aus Saturnus
> Frieden ist jegliche Macht erwachsen (19).

DIE MASCHINENSTÜRMER *(THE MACHINE WRECKERS)*

INTRODUCTION

The sequence of three further plays which Toller wrote during his imprisonment, *Die Maschinenstürmer (The Machine Wreckers), Hinkemann,* and *Der entfesselte Wotan (Wotan Unbound),* is remarkable both for its continuity and its discontinuity. The latter is shown in their styles, forms and genres, so unalike that one critic goes so far as to say that the three works could stem from three authors (1). The continuity becomes clearer when these three plays are placed in the context of those written before and after, and of Toller's personal political development.

Die Maschinenstürmer stands between the cautious optimism of *Masse Mensch* and the fully developed tragic vision of *Hinkemann,* as well as between the abstraction of *Masse Mensch* and the almost exact historicity of *Feuer aus den Kesseln.* After the two wholly verse plays, *Masse Mensch* and *Die Rache des verhohnten Liebhabers, Die Maschinenstürmer* moves continually between prose and verse, thus forming a significant bridge between Toller's verse and prose plays.

Hinkemann, the only play of Toller's designated a Tragedy, marks the end of a continuous process from the basic optimism of *Die Wandlung* to a deep awareness of the tragedy inherent in the human condition. *Hinkemann* indeed, occupies a central place, not only in this group of plays, but in Toller's dramatic work as a whole. With his tragedy Toller had found the resolution of the subjective problems that underlie the earlier plays, and from this point onwards his drama primarily concerned itself with objective problems and socio-political criticism, beginning with his fiercely comic anti-fascist *Der entfesselte Wotan* (2).

It is no accident that this pivotal centre is also marked by Toller's change from verse to prose (3), from the vehicle through which he expressed his inner life — culminating in *Das Schwalbenbuch,* written 1923 — to that through which he expressed his outward concerns: prose. It would be a mistake, however, to over-schematise Toller's development as a writer. To the same period that produced his greatest poetic work, *Das Schwalbenbuch,* belong also his three *Massenfestspiele (Scenes from the French Revolution, War and Peace,* and *Awakening),* 1922–1924. These, of which actual texts by Toller do not survive, belong to the realm of his public voice. They are considered in an Appendix.

PRINCIPAL SOURCES, THEMES AND CHARACTERS

Toller wrote the first version of *Die Maschinenstürmer,* at that time called *Die Ludditen,* during the winter of 1920–21. Alfred Beierle gave readings from it in May 1921 (1). Its writing was not easy. Towards the end of January he broke off writing it for, he says, the fifth time. He thought he had put into words what moved him inwardly and so 'read into' the words his own spiritual excitement; but when he looked at the words a few days later, there they stood, naked and insipid (2).

> How much in art depends upon giving form to imponderables. They are the soul of the work (3).

He did not know how the piece would develop and he noted that he was going in what were for him new ways. He was aware of a stronger "sensory" starting point, and it was doubly difficult to struggle to give this form when living a life in which every sensory stimulus was lacking (4). Here Toller gives insight into his heroic struggle to concretise the themes which concerned him, some of which he had already expressed in a more abstract form in *Masse Mensch.*

That he was aware of his artistic problem and of his ability ultimately to solve it — if not completely in this play, then in the next — is clear:

> There must be a great deal of capability and terrific will to live in me, else I could not understand how, in spite of many hours in which my will becomes weary and is near to extinction, I feel a stronger power to work (5).

The resulting play is evidence, in the strength of its parts and the complexities of its structure as a whole, both of the innate creative strength of its author and of his struggles with a deadening environment.

Lacking immediate external stimuli yet aware of the need to give ideas concrete and sensory form (6), Toller sought his particularities in books, notably in Marx's *Das Kapital*, Engels' *Lage der arbeitenden Klasse in England* and Max Beer's *Geschichte des Sozialismus in England* (Stuttgart 1913) (7). He also ordered some books (unspecified) from England, which he hoped would provide historical confirmation for what he was writing! (8)

Toller worked very closely from these sources but the contrast between his exact, often verbal, use of detail and his cavalier manner of ignoring dates and scorning historical accuracy in the realistic sense is important and significant.

First then, his close use of the sources. The final title, *Die Maschinenstürmer* (rather than *Die Ludditen*) probably came from Beer, as the word is otherwise not common and is not used by Marx or Engels (9). Lord Byron's speech is taken directly from Beer's translation of it, as is proved by certain omissions and by Toller's following Beer's rather free translation (10).

It is probable also that Toller derived his hero, Jimmy Cobbett's, name and some of his characteristics from Beer, who makes references to William Cobbett and quotes him. William Cobbett's *Political Register* (30.11.1816) describes the Luddites in Nottingham. Cobbett tries to convince the Luddites of the futility of machine-wrecking and wants to make clear to them that machinery will in the end improve the living of the workers — as does Jimmy (11).

William Cobbett, then, does belong to the period of the play and in so far as Jimmy's ideas resemble his, those scholars are wrong who describe Jimmy as an anachronism (12). Toller, however, is clearly confused as to William Cobbett's dates for in two places he refers to him as a "Chartist". Cobbett died in 1835, while the Chartist Movement only began when the London Working Men's Association was founded on 16 June 1836 (13).

But Jimmy in some other respects *is* anachronistic, as we shall see.

The name of the mill-owner Ure is also derived from Toller's reading. Dr Andrew Ure, professor of Chemistry at Glasgow, published his *Philosophy of Manufactures*, in 1835. Toller evidently did not realise that he was an academic, for he refers to him as having been historically a *Großkapitalist (capitalist on a large scale)* (14). The book and its author were direct targets for the criticism of Marx and Engels (15). Engels describes Ure as "a bourgeois *pur sang*, a man after the heart of the Anti-Corn Law League" (16). The name, an improbable one for a Nottingham mill-owner, is evidently chosen for its ideological associations. Ure's book was published two decades after the supposed events of the play, and the Anti-Corn Law League was not founded until 1838 (17).

Ure's comments to his guest, the representative of the government, in Act V Sc. 2 (18) are taken almost word for word from Dr Andrew Ure as quoted by Engels:

TOLLER	Betrachten Sie die Kinder, sehr verehrter Herr. Bemerken Sie da Müdigkeit, schlechte Laune oder gar Mißhandlung? . . . Wie heiter ihre Augen blicken! Wie sie sich am leichten Spiele ihrer Muskeln freuen! Wie sie die natürliche Beweglichkeit des jugendlichen Alters in vollem Maß genießen! Nach drüben schauen Sie! Entzückend ist die Hurtigkeit, mit der das kleine Mädchen die zerissenen Fäden wieder anknüpft! Wie alle diese lieben kleinen Kinder Freude zeigen, vor meinem Gast ihre Künste aufzuführen. Ein ästhetischer Genuß, nicht wahr?
ENGELS	Ich habe manche Fabrik besucht . . . und nie Kinder mißhandelt . . . oder nur übel gelaunt gesehen. Sie scheinen alle heiter . . . an dem leichten Spiel ihrer Muskel [sic] sich erfreuend, die ihrem Alter natürliche Beweglichkeit in vollem Maße genießend . . . Es war entzückend, die Hurtigkeit zu beobachten, mit der sie die zerissenen Fäden vereinigten . . . Ihrer Geschicklichkeit sich bewußt, freuten sie sich, sie vor jedem Fremden zu zeigen . . . (19)

Henry Cobbett, too, paraphrases Engels' own words very closely:

TOLLER	Die meisten Männer müssen wir entlassen. Aber alle eure Kinder werden eingestellt . . . Und junge flinke Weiber . . . Die Delikatesse des Gewerbes erfordert besondre Fingerzartheit . . . Gewiß, die Maschine verdrängt die Männer.
ENGELS	Die Arbeit an den Maschinen . . . erfordert keine Kraft, aber größre Gelenkigkeit der Finger. Männer sind dazu nicht nur unnötig, sondern . . . . ..sogar weniger geeignet als Weiber und Kinder und so natürlicherweise fast ganz von dieser Arbeit verdrängt (20).

Much of the material of Castlereagh's speech in the Prologue (a fictional speech, for he and Byron never clashed thus in the House of Lords (21)) is taken from Engels' account of Malthus' opinions on population (22). Although Castlereagh could have cited Malthus in this way, as the *Essay on the Principle of Population* had been published in 1798, Engels' bitter attack is related primarily to the Poor Law Amendment Act of 1834, which forbade outdoor relief (available to the poor since 1601) and established workhouses (23).

Many other details in the play are taken directly from Engels, even though they may apply to other cities three decades later (24), the adulteration of food; bedsharing; Parr's "Lebenspillen"; the clothes of working nursing mothers soaked with breast-milk; payment in goods from the "truck" shop; the atrocious fines imposed on workers; the flogging of children at work; the closing of doors and forfeiting of wages (25).

These precise, often verbally exact socio-historical details, although often used anachronistically and unhistorically, root the play firmly in factual reality and provide a solid and convincing base upon which can be constructed an expression of problems and conflicts of wide modern and contemporary validity. Writing over a decade later Toller said he had conceived the play in this way:

> Diese Konflikte und den Zusammenprall von Rebellen und Revolutionären, den Kampf des Menschen mit der Maschine und seine Gefährdung, versuche ich, in meinem Drama *Die Maschinenstürmer* zu bilden, in der Historie der Ludditen fand ich mannigfaltige Parallelen (26).
>
> (These conflicts and the clash of rebels and revolutionaries, the struggle of man with the machine, and his danger, I attempt to show in my drama *The Machine Wreckers*; in the history of the Luddites I found a variety of parallels).

In a letter of 1923, however, he had suggested a more 'historical' aim:

> Ich wollte (unter anderem) gestalten: das erste Erwachen des Volkes zu revolutionärem Bewußtsein (27).
>
> (I wanted [inter alia] to give artistic form to: the first awakening of the people to revolutionary awareness.)

These two statements of intention, divided from each other as they are by ten years of life and experience, suggest that Toller was initially aiming, at least primarily, in the direction of historical authenticity, but that as he wrote, the issues still vital in his own times became more important to him than pure history. This bears out our view of the play as transitional in style between his earlier and later work.

Toller did not only find historical data and parallels with his own times in his source-books. Surprising though it may seem, he did not have to look beyond the pages of *Das Kapital* to find the central *Dingsymbol* of his play, the machine, personified as a "monster", as he himself personifies it in the play (28):

> An organised system of working machines which are one and all set in motion by the transmitting mechanism from a central automaton, constitutes the fully developed form of machinofacture. In place of the individual machine, we now have a mechanical monster whose body fills the whole factory, and whose demon power, hidden from our sight at first because of the measured and almost ceremonious character of the movement of his giant limbs, discloses itself at length in the vast and furious whirl of his numberless working organs (29).

Here in the heart of Marx's classic of 1867 Toller could find expressed with the poetic imagination of the communist prophet, the very image which he could employ as a symbol of "our mechanistic period" (30) in his dramatic promulgation, through the character of Jimmy Cobbett, of Landauer's anti-Marxist socialist vision. Thus the ideological conflicts of the twentieth century are expressed within a dramatic framework dated 1815 and using further material from the middle decades of the nineteenth century. As Marnette says (31), Jimmy cannot be regarded as a wholly realistic figure because the author places his own anachronistic anarcho-socialist ideas in his mouth.

Similarly John Wible (32) in so far as he represents any genuine political philosophy, expresses some views associated with twentieth century Marxism. For example:

> Wir *brauchen Niederlagen*. Nur tiefstes Elend schafft Rebellen (33).
>
> (We *need defeats*. Only the profoundest misery creates rebels).

But Wible must not be identified with Marxists. Toller describes him in these terms:

> Demagoge, Phraseur, handelnder aus Ressentiment, subalterner Rebell um der Rebellion willen (34).
>
> (Demagogue, windbag, one who acts out of resentment, a subservient type, who rebels for the sake of rebelling.)

Dorothea Klein remarks that he represents no principle (35). She is therefore wrong when she says that he re-echoes The Nameless One of *Masse Mensch*: it is in fact Jimmy who says to Ure:

> Nennen Sie mich "Namenlos" (36)
>
> (Call me The Nameless One.)

But Wible's failure to represent any clear principle does justify her saying;

> Außerdem ist die Gegenüberstellung von Jimmy und Wible nicht so klar akzentuiert, als daß notwendig darin der Kernpunkt des Stücks gesehen werden müßte (37).
>
> (Anyway the confrontation of Jimmy with Wible is not so clearly stressed that the crux of the piece must necessarily be seen in it.)

Nevertheless, in terms of the plot, Jimmy is in conflict with Wible in terms of revolutionary aims and methods, while Ned Lud is torn between the two.

As the third principal rebel Ned Lud must be given some attention. Toller evidently did not know that the historical Ned Ludd, from whom the Luddite movement took its name, was an idiot boy of Leicestershire who, in 1779, unable to catch someone who had been tormenting him, destroyed some stocking-frames in a fit of temper (38). Toller believed Ludd to be one of the leaders of the movement, the original Luddite, the first of the men,

> der in der Maschine den Feind der Arbeiter sah und sie zerschlug. Ned Lud war sein Name. Er lebte bei Nottingham. Über seine Persönlichkeit ist historisch wenig bekannt (39).
>
> (who saw in the machine the enemy of the workers and smashed it. Ned Ludd was his name. He lived in Nottingham. Little is known historically about his personality.)

In December 1920 he wrote to Gustav Mayer asking if he knew of any book in German that would, in particular, give him information about the personality of Ned Ludd (40). In the following month he wrote again, evidently in answer to a reply from Mayer:

> Ihre Auskünfte [one wonders what sort of information Mayer had provided! CWD] über die Persönlichkeit Ned Luds mich sehr befriedigt. Ned Lud ist auch in meinem Drama nicht 'Führer'. Er trägt das Antlitz eines geraden, mutigen, Arbeiters, der keinerlei 'Führerqualitäten' besitzt, keine eigenen politischen und wirtschaftlichen Erkenntnisse erringt, sich treiben läßt, aber da, wo er glaubt richtig zu handeln, immer als erster handelt. (Als erster auch auf die Maschinen einschlägt) (41).
>
> (Your information about the personality of Ned Lud has satisfied me greatly. In my drama also, Ned Lud is not a 'Leader'. He bears the countenance of an honest, brave worker who possesses no 'leadership qualities' at all, who gains no political and economic knowledge of his own, allows himself to be led, but where he thinks action is correct, is always the first to act. (He is also the first to smash the machines.)

Jimmy and Wible, on the other hand, he calls "Führertypen" (natural leaders).

All the rebels are in conflict with Ure, the capitalist ideologue, and Henry Cobbett, his working-class lieutenant.

Outside the dramatic conflict, but each contributing to the pattern of diverse ideologies are two basically non-dramatic and at the same time less naturalistic figures, *Der alte Reaper* and *Der Bettler*.

Marnette remarks of these that they philosophise:

> Dadurch wird die ohnehin wenig entwickelte dramatische Handlung häufig unterbrochen, was wiederum die epischen Züge des Dramas verstärkt (42).
>
> (Because of that, the dramatic action — little developed anyway — is frequently interrupted, a fact that on the other hand reinforces the epic characteristics of the drama.)

There is truth in this, though Marnette's value-judgements here, as throughout his interesting thesis, are vitiated by his doctrinaire Marxism. These non-dramatic figures do indeed contribute to the epic character of the play, in the Brechtian sense, both by provoking thought on the themes and action, and by emphasising, through their own non-naturalism, that the apparent history is essentially a non-realistic artifact. Although structurally marginal to the story, they may therefore be regarded as keys to the understanding of the play.

Der alte Reaper is in fact given a family relationship that defines his position among the central characters: he is Mary Wible's father. He is addressed in the play only as 'grandfather' (by Teddy) and 'father' (by Mary). Only in Act III Sc. ii does he refer to himself as 'der alte Reaper' as if this were a nickname he had bestowed upon himself. To the audience he will be in effect nameless: for a dramatist can and should never rely on audiences reading the programme! We may therefore take the name rather as a hint or direction to actor and director as to how the part is to be played and presented. Despite the use of the English word (strange to a German audience and possibly suggesting a surname?) the image of the Reaper is, of course that of Death, der Schnitter (43).

Instead of the traditional scythe this death-figure has a stick which he insists is a gun, though the trigger is rusted and it will not fire (44). In Act III Sc. iv he 'plays' on it as if it were a fiddle (45). This suggests the Dance of Death, and as the imaginary dancing women cease to dance and can barely stand, the stage is darkened: a powerful theatrical image.

Der alte Reaper uses biblical phraseology throughout and relates everything he encounters to God, though in a strange manner. When we first meet him (II. ii) he is saying that he does not believe in God and will not bow the knee to him; and when his grandson, Teddy, complains of hunger, he cries out to God,

> . . . O du Kindermörder du . . . (46)
> (. . . O thou child-murderer, thou . . .)

When Teddy asks him if he has seen a Machine, — adding that it is said to have a hundred heads — he replies, "Perhaps it is God."

We meet him next in the most purely symbolic scene in the whole play, the end of Act III Sc. ii, in which he, the eighty-year old, longs to die, not to be resurrected to new life, but to become earth, the earth of an English meadow from whose lap flowers will grow, whose grass will be eaten by sheep and whose spring will bubble like a young billy-goat. It is a little lyric of the love of death set amid the harsh scenes dominated by Wible, the son-in-law. It expresses a romantic longing to be at one with Nature, 'a portion of the loveliness' (47).

In its feeling both for Death and Nature the passage is closely related to Toller's prison poems, especially to *Das Schwalbenbuch*.

But before his death the old man wants 'to know why' (48). Why is there Life, why is everything purposeless and senseless? Jimmy replies in a speech that is central to the whole play, as well as being, it would seem, its author's Credo:

> Weißt du, warum der Baum dort wächst, warum er Blätter treibt und kahl und welk im Herbst wird? Fragst du nach Zweck? . . . Fragst du nach Sinn? . . . Ich bin . . . du bist . . . wir sind . . . das, Alter, ist die letzte reiche Schau . . . Den Sinn, den gibt der Mensch dem Leben (49)
>
> (Do you know why the tree grows there, why it puts forth leaves and becomes bare and dead in autumn? Are you asking for purpose? . . . Are you asking for meaning? . . . I am . . . thou art . . . we are . . . that, old man, is the last, rich vision . . . Meaning — man gives that to life.)

"I fight, " says Jimmy, "as if I believed in God." (50)

Jimmy goes, and another 'symbolic' character enters: Louis with the barrow. Louis is a real childhood memory of Toller's, the street-sweeper of Samotschin (51), but in this tiny scene Toller transforms him into a frightening figure of petty, dehumanising ambition. Louis in Toller's autobiography is a pathetic figure, in this play an alarming one.

> "I'm not a man, ", he says, " I'm a municipal civil servant." (52)

In these few words:

> Ich bin kein Mann. Ich bin städtischer Beamter . . .

Toller epitomises something in the national character that made Hitler possible: to be *Beamter* is more important than to be a *Mann*.

Then in his bitter refusal of help he shows how individual ambition, however absurdly petty, leads to suspicion and division. A major theme of the play is the founding of Trades Unions, forbidden in England from 1800–1824 (53).

"Du willst also Gewerkschaftssekretär werden?" (So you want to become secretary of a Trades Union?), says the Beggar to Jimmy. (54)

It is insistence on trivial distinctions and differentials among workers that destroys the solidarity of the Trades Union movement and of the working-class movement as a whole.

> This organisation of the proletarians into a class, and consequently into a political party, is continually being upset again by the competition between the workers themselves. (55)

Finally, Toller brings on a blind man led by a deaf-mute (56). The former cannot *hear* God, the latter cannot *see* him: the Old Reaper, with two good eyes and two good ears, cannot *find* him (57). Here we are taken beyond socio-political considerations to a bleak summing up of the human condition and of the total impossibility of man's having knowledge of the divine (58). The scene recalls *King Lear (IV.i)* and anticipates elements in *Waiting for Godot* (59).

Two scenes later the Old Reaper appears again (60) at the end of the fearful scene of the women and Mary. His speech this time is a 'poor man's Day of Judgement' in which traditional images of the *Dies Irae* are fused with a lament for the fate of the poor (61). At the end of this he plays his *Dance of Death* already referred to.

He does not appear again until the very end of the play, when he and Teddy act a kind of Epilogue in the deserted mill. The scene is of the utmost importance for the interpretation of the play as a whole, which by this means is brought to a religious rather than a political conclusion.

The old man is now in the presence of the Machine of which he said earlier, "Perhaps it is God." (62) "Is God here?" he asks Teddy, who simply replies, 'Here is the machine."

The Old Reaper feels that the decisive moment is approaching and plainly declares that "He", God, is the Machine. Just then Teddy sees a person *(Mensch)* lying on the ground, whom he recognises as Jimmy, — Uncle Jimmy, as he calls him. The Old Reaper takes aim (it is not clear at what) and fires his 'gun', while Teddy cries that everything is broken and destroyed. Does he mean the machine or Jimmy, or both? The ambiguity is important. Seeing the body the old man cries "Hurra", as if his aim had been true: Teddy is frightened:

> Nach Haus — Ich hab' solche Angst (63).
> (Let's go home. I'm so scared.)

But the Old Reaper, he who believes himself to be the Death-bringer, sees and thinks only of Jimmy. He sees Jimmy as the Son of God, whom he has shot: but in the context 'The Son of God' can allude both to Christ and to Jimmy as the 'son' of the machine he would not destroy. Like Christ, Jimmy has died in the evening, at the going down of the heavenly sun. He, the Old Reaper, the son of a serf (64) has shot the Son of God, who must be buried, not in God's Acre but in the knacker's yard.

"Du armer, lieber Gottessohn, " he says to the dead Jimmy; and then: "Du armer, lieber Gott." Jimmy has been deified; he is seen as a Christ-figure more surely and clearly even than the Christ-figures in *Die Wandlung* and *Masse Mensch* . (65)

> Ach, du armer lieber Gott . . . Man muß für ein Begräbnis sorgen . . . man muß einander helfen und gut sein. (66)
>
> (Ah, you poor dear God . . . we must arrange a burial . . . we must help each other and be good.)

Once more Toller is led to a conclusion with a religious and ethical dimension. He remains closer to Schiller than to the Marxists, occupying the perilous middle ground between Christian and Communist (67).

The other choric figure, Der Bettler (The Beggar), can also cite scripture, but to different effect. On his first entrance he successfully uses scripture to beg Jimmy's cap. But his major function is to provide a foil to Jimmy's idealism, and his habitual imagery is earthy and sexual — as in that of the Irish who couple with their beloved pigs and produce pig-headed children, or that of Time 'riding' a young woman and making her pregnant (68). The Beggar, himself disabled, also has associations with *King Lear*, and once again with the character of Gloster, *l'homme moyen sensuel* who insensitively says in front of his illegitimate son that "there was good sport at his making" (69) and pays dearly:

> The dark and vicious place where thee he got
> Cost him his eyes (70).

The Beggar echoes Gloster in the way he refers to his own son:

> Mein Herr Sohn fand, daß ers nicht nötig habe, einen zu beherbergen, der einarmig sei und nichts verdiene. Er fand, ich hätte mich an ihm verlustiert, bevor er geboren wurde, und er wolle sich auch einmal verlustieren, nachdem er geboren sei. Dabei wäre ich ihm unbequem. Er hat so unrecht nicht (71).
>
> (My gentleman son found that it wasn't necessary for him to house someone who had only one arm and earned nothing.

> He found that I had amused myself through him before he was born, and he too wanted to amuse himself after he was born. In this respect I was inconvenient to him. He wasn't wrong.)

In his old potato-clamp (72) he warns Jimmy, the educated aristocrat among workers, that he sees the proletariat as he wants to see it; proletarians are not a new kind of God, but a mixed bunch like all other men. He points out that John Wible is hunch-backed because his working-class father threw him, when a baby, against a wall when drunk. He warns Jimmy in vain of the tricks of the fox, Wible. Thus the Beggar is a foil to the old Reaper, a bitter antidote to Jimmy's too simple faith in working-class goodness.

The Shakespearean elements in the Beggar are important in our placing of Toller in a deeper historical context. More immediately the Beggar belongs to the world of anonymous figures typical of Expressionist drama (73), and specifically to the Strindbergian heritage. Although the functions of the two characters are very different, Toller's Beggar is evidently derived from Strindberg's in *To Damascus*.

Both make their first appearance scavenging in the street or gutter (74); both deny that they are 'ordinary' beggars (75); both are interested in the relationship between property and becoming a member of parliament, though in diametrically opposed ways (76). We have already examined the close relationship between *To Damascus* and *Die Wandlung*. We see here that the influence of Strindberg on Toller is still very specific and direct, and not simply diffused through the Expressionist movement.

STRUCTURE: SHAKESPEARE AND MONTAGE. AN EPIC DRAMA

In writing this play in five acts with a prologue Toller deliberately broke away from the concept of Station Drama as associated with Strindberg and the Expressionists, and placed himself in the main-stream tradition of German, and in the broadest sense, Shakespearean drama.

Dorothea Klein in her on the whole very illuminating study of *The Change in the dramatic art form in the work of Ernst Toller (1919–1930)* says that apart from the opening and end, this formal structure is completely irrelevant to the action (1). She also refers to what she sees as a lack of unity in regard both to content and form, which, she claims, leads to a break in the manner of dramatic presentation of the principal and subsidiary actions (2).

While it is true that the five-act pattern is not developed along orthodox lines (3), this judgement is unjust. We shall proceed to demonstrate that the play does possess unity both of form and content and that the formal structure *is* relevantly used, though in a most original way.

The content is indeed complex. As we have already seen, Toller had considerable difficulty in writing this play and evidently found his chosen material intractable. He felt compelled to give artistic expression to a tangled web of social and personal forces and to write with honesty about a world whose ultimate problems were gradually revealing themselves to him as in the last resort insoluble, though he still believed in the possibility of the triumph of reason:

> Die Macht der Vernunft, glaubte ich, sei so stark, daß wer einmal das Vernünftige erkannt hat, ihm folgen muß (4).
>
> (The power of good sense, I believed, is so strong, that anyone who has once realised what is sensible, must follow it.)

In his previous plays the patterns of conflict had been comparatively simple:

In *Die Wandlung*	Man *(Mensch)* v. War
In *Masse Mensch*	Man *(Mensch)* v. The Masses
In *Die Rache*	Female Cunning v. Male Cunning

In this play the basic conflict appears simple enough:

> den Kampf des Menschen mit der Maschine (5)
> (the struggle of man with the machine)

but even as Toller made that statement he grouped around it a whole cluster of related conflicts and themes: *inter alia,* the spiritual vacillations of the masses; labour-market forces; divisions among the workers themselves; conflicts between revolutionaries. All these and more he found in the history of the Luddites, all these and more he sought to express within the limits of one play, and in aiming at a concrete, sensory expression he had to devise a correspondingly various and variously interrelated *dramatis personae*: this he had never before attempted on such a scale.

We turn to the text.

The play is visualised as being performed in a traditional theatre with proscenium arch and front curtain, though the Prologue immediately breaks down the formal separation of stage and auditorium: "it can be played with simple resources in front of the curtain" (6). There is to be a desk for the Lord Chancellor and chairs to its right and left for Byron and Castlereagh, and "in the front row of the auditorium other lords" (7). This arrangement demands that the play begin with the entrance at least of the characters on the fore-stage, and whether the other lords also make an entrance or are already seated and simply stand on the Lord Chancellor's entrance, the audience will be made aware of their presence and made to feel also that they, the audience, are participants in the debate that follows: the mould of the *Guckkasten* theatre is already broken.

> The actor playing Jimmy *could* (my italics, CWD) come on in Lord Byron's make-up, and the actor playing Ure in Lord Castlereagh's make-up (8).

Perhaps from prison Toller felt unable actually to *prescribe* this important piece of doubling. He was aware of his inability to exercise control over the productions of his plays (9), though in fact this suggestion was taken up in the first production (10). The doubling is very important. In visually identifying Byron, the poet-politician, with Jimmy, and Castlereagh with Ure, Toller effectively puts the lords' expositions of opposing views into the mouths of the characters in the play proper, thus informing the audience, through a wholly *theatrical* device, of their stances, and without holding up the actual action for wordy exposition. At the same time, of course, the Prologue shows the play's themes and conflicts as of national significance, and, through the identification of the theatre-audience with the listening House of Lords, insists on the parallels between 1815 and the 1920s (or, indeed, the 1980s or 1990s) and makes the members of the audience aware that they are being presented with problems that still face them in their own times and that are not merely past history.

Byron's warmly humanitarian speech, drawn, as we have seen, from historical records, refers to the bad example set by the rich to the poor; the loss of work owing to the use of machines; the value of working-people to the privileged classes; the vast expenditure on the Napoleonic war, a tiny fraction of which would have relieved the domestic situation; and the uselessness and utter wrongness of the death penalty for machine-breaking.

Castlereagh's fictional reply scorns Byron's humanitarianism as fitting for a poet; only economic principles are valid for the statesman; poverty is the Will of God. An exposition of Malthusianism follows, with the conclusion that the Bill is an offering on the altar of Justice.

The Bill is passed, Byron alone voting against it.

The threat of the death-penalty heightens all that follows: and what follows *immediately*, as the curtain rises, is the sight of three "gallows-like scaffolds". Their impact at this moment must be tremendous. These three scaffolds and the apathetic ragged children together present a visual image embodying the content of the Lords' debate. Jimmy enters (a lightning costume-change in the wings is demanded!) and we recognise 'Lord Byron' in the clothes of a working journeyman. He speaks, and the tone drops from the free, rhetorical verse of the debate (11) to the rhythm of everyday speech; but the density of this prose dialogue is not everyday. In a few closely packed lines the gallows are explained and facts about, and attitudes to child-labour mooted. Then as the Second Girl weeps, because "The sun shines so warmly", patches of sunlight dance on the children's faces (12). Even here in the Nottingham slums Nature, in the form of the sun, penetrates the joyless scene. Inspired by the sunshine, Jimmy begins his *Märchen* of the rich and poor children, Sorgenlos and Immerelend, and the rhythm of his speech moves into verse.

This movement from verse to prose and back again, which continues throughout the play is a symptom of the bridging position of *Der Maschinenstürmer* between the earlier verse and later prose plays. Never again would Toller write in this Shakespearean or Elizabethan manner in which scenes or parts of scenes are written in prose or verse as appropriate to the varying nature of the material.

Jimmy's fairy-tale version of social injustice is rudely interrupted by sordid reality. Under the cover of the story the Third Boy finds a bit of bread in the gutter and a fight over it ensues. Engels' "competition between the workers themselves" (13) is first shown in all its harshness through the children.

As the fighting children rush off leaving Jimmy to his thoughts, the workers' demonstration enters, led by the bearers of the effigies of strike-breakers (14). Wible's abusive speech addressed to the effigies has no political or ideological content and reaches a climax of sadistic and ugly vulgarity:

> Der Nachtmahr soll euch Äxte in die darren Brüste schlagen!
> . . .
> Mit Stricken, die in heißes Öl getränkt,
> Die Gurgel drosseln! Gekettet trag man euch vor Bottiche voll Whisky . . .
> Und wenn ihr gierig trinken wollt . . . so mögen alte Vetteln kommen und drein brunzen! (15)

> (May the nightmare strike your dry breasts with axes..
> Throttle your gullets with ropes soaked in hot oil!
> May you be carried in chains before tubs full of whisky
> And when you want to drink greedily . . . then may old hags come and piss in them!)

Amid the cheers of the crowd the effigies are hanged and there follows immediately an extraordinary, formalised Litany (16) that anticipates, as a revolutionary parody of religious ritual, *Marats Liturgie* and similar passages in the *Marat/Sade* of Peter Weiss (17). This is also linked with and set against the preceding children's scene, for its first section is a nursery-rhyme parody, "Baa, baa, black sheep!", which is followed by a three-stanza revolutionary hymn, apparently, like the parody, also to be intoned, though it invites a musical chorale-parody in the manner of Kurt Weill. The procession exits, singing and carrying the gallows with the three hanged effigies. Ned Lud, Charles and Jimmy are left on the stage and the style shifts back to prose, as the Pedlar of *Parrs Lebenspillen* crosses the stage crying his wares.

The first scene (already discussed) between Jimmy and the Beggar follows, leading through Jimmy's reference to the latter's love of schnaps to the entrance of two drunks, the first "bawling" the beginning of a strangely evocative and disturbingly poetic revolutionary song:

> Schärfet die Sichel! Die Ähren sind schwer
> Und die Kinder schreien nach Brot.
> Das Feld hat bewässert ihr Tränenmeer
> Und gedüngt ihrer Väter Tod!
> Die Hoffnung starb und das Herz, das brach,
> Sie haben den Samen gestreut . . . (18)

> (Sharpen the sickle! The ears are heavy
> And the children cry out for bread.
> Their ocean of tears has watered the field
> And their fathers' death has dunged it!
> Hope Died, and the heart — broke;
> They have scattered the seed —)

"Blessed are the poor in spirit, saith the Lord, " bawls the second drunk, more or less quoting Luther's Bible (19), and so, begging for pennies "where kings pave the latrines with pounds sterling" (20), they roll off, still bawling for rot-gut (Fusel).

Jimmy now steps up to Ned Lud and the dialogue that follows reveals the former as the returned native and therefore the probable catalyst for the development of action. Ned Lud's gut reaction against the machine and Charles' almost superstitious, "The machine is in the town" (21) are opposed by Jimmy's acceptance of it:

> Ich weiß, das die Maschine unser unentrinnbar Schicksal ist (21).
>
> (I know that the machine is our inescapable fate.)

The argument in this scene is the major argument of Robert Tressell's *The Ragged Trousered Philanthropists* (written c.1905) in which the workers argue like Ned Lud:

> Ein jeder Mensch auf Gottes Erde hat ein natürlich Recht zu Leben von der Hände mühseliger Arbeit (22).
>
> (Every person on God's earth has a natural right to live by the arduous work of his hands.)

Jimmy, though he does not yet advance his arguments (for in this act he is primarily the recipient of impressions) believes, with Tressell's George Barrington:

> . . . the reason of all the poverty and unhappiness that we see around us and endure today — It is simply because — the *machinery became the property of a comparatively few individuals and private companies, who use it not for the benefit of the community but to create profits for themselves* (23).

Now the three leading working-class views are established: Lud's instinctive feeling for the right to work; Wible's demagoguish leadership of the strike; and Jimmy's acceptance of the machine, though the rest of his view is still unstated.

To close the act, the town crier, in free, rhetorical verse, announces another new law: the rights of assembly, picketing, persuasion of strike-breakers, the right to strike, to raise money for strikes —

all are forbidden. Employers are free to fix working hours and wages according to their own estimates (24). Informers who reveal illegal funds will be rewarded with half of them.

Act 1 has contained no plot, only one short dialogue between principals, no exposition of a dramatic situation. Instead, only thematic material has been presented in a series of short contrasting scenes, each stylised to a greater or lesser extent and linked only by unity of place and the figure of Jimmy, who alone is on stage throughout the whole act. (The act may therefore legitimately also be interpreted as the accumulation of impressions received by Jimmy on his return to his native city; but this way of viewing it in no way detracts from its prologue character, but rather confirms it.)

Act 1, so closely linked to the Prologue by the gallows image and the continuity between them of Byron/Jimmy, is thus not a first act in the normal sense, but a continuation of the Prologue, a sequence of thematic statements and images analogous to the Overture of an opera into which the leitmotifs of the acts to follow are all introduced:

Humanity	Malthusianism
Byron	Castleragh

Capital Punishment
The Three Gallows
Suffering of Children
Sunshine, play, imagination (Jimmy)
Ritual Execution (Wible)
Exploitation of Gullibility (Pedlar of Pills)
Earthy Disillusionment (Beggar)
Drink
Fear of the Machine
The Power of the Law

From the beginning of Act 2 the action proper begins and continues through to the end of the play, punctuated by the "choric" scenes already examined. The manner of this action is primarily "epic" (i.e. narrative) in the sense later made current by Brecht, and thus similar to that of Shakespeare's History Plays, which were also written to provoke thought on contemporary political questions (25). Generalising scenes such as the Two Drunks, Louis with the Barrow, and the Blind and the Dumb, have similar functions to *A Son that hath killed his Father* and *A Father that hath killed his Son* (III Henry VI, II.v.) and the Gardener Scenes in *Richard II* (II.iv. lines 29ff).

Now that Act 1 has been demonstrated to be an extended Prologue of juxtaposed themes and images, a basic pattern of the remaining four acts can be discerned. It is a pattern (to use was Brecht's words) of *Montage* rather than of *Growth* (26), though not rigidly adhered to, any more than in Brecht's own plays, and dependent upon juxtapositions and contrasts. The following table shows this schematically.

MONTAGE OF ACTS II TO V

Act 2 Sc 1 The Cobbett Home Chorus: Beggar	Act 2 Sc 2 The Wible Home Chorus: Old Reaper

Leading to:
(2.2.cont'd) First Confrontation of Jimmy & Wible

Act 3, opening: Henry / Ure: Wible Later: Mary Wible & Women Chorus:Old Reaper etc.	Act 4, opening: Henry / Ure: Jimmy Later: Margret Lud & Women No Choric figure

Act 5

Introductory Chorus: Beggar	Final Chorus (Epilogue): Old Reaper

Climax of Conflicts in Action

This paradigmatic representation does not, of course, take into account the wealth of detail, the untidiness or irregularities already mentioned, which prevent the play's becoming too formalised and give it an organic, natural fluidity, nor the shifts between prose and verse according to the tone of the dialogue, shifts which often seem to have occurred spontaneously in the writing. But it does show that using at the same time Shakespearean roots and the technique of juxtaposition in order to deploy themes and provoke thought about them, Toller anticipates the later plays of Brecht. Indeed, if Brecht's schema in the *Mahagonny Notes* (1930) of the changes in emphasis between the *Dramatic Form of Theatre* and the *Epic Form of Theatre* is applied to this play, it will be found that on practically every, if not every, count *Die Maschinenstürmer* is to be classed as *Epic Drama*.

The first juxtaposition, that of the Cobbett home and the Wible home, is closely worked out in its contrasts and involves more than a simple contrast between Jimmy and Wible. One member of each family has sold out to the bosses, and each household is now dependent on that member: Henry Cobbett has betrayed his class by becoming Ure's manager, and his mother now depends on him for her standard of living; Mary Wible regularly prostitutes herself to Henry — for a mere five-pence! — and Wible depends on the continuation of this relationship in order to keep his own job. The corruption thus spreads to the dependents: Mrs Cobbett will not allow her returned son, Jimmy, to stay in her house; Wible, who accepts, indeed demands from his wife the "wages of sin", shows himself Henry's equal when he declares:

> If I were a gentleman, I'd go whoring! (27)

Henry's behaviour and Wible's words, taken together, as they are meant to be, starkly illustrate Landauer's words on this theme:

> ... der Arme und der armseliger Reiche. In der Geschlechtsnot kommen sie zusammen . . . das Lusthaus ist das Repräsentantenhaus dieser unsrer Zeit (28).
>
> (. . . the poor man and the wretched rich man. They come together in their sexual need . . . the brothel is the House of Representatives of this our time.)

Meanwhile Wible urges his wife to continue — so long as she makes sure of 'cash in advance'.

The two major choric figures are also appropriately integrated into the montage: the Beggar into the Cobbett home and the Old Reaper into that of Wible. To complete the pattern of the act comes the first confrontation of Jimmy and Wible at the weavers' meeting in the latter's house. This confrontation scene is also built upon the principle of juxtaposition and contrast, rather than of debate: Wible has his say in the first half of the scene and Jimmy in the second.

In the first section, before Jimmy's entrance, there is no ideological content; the theme is fear, almost a superstitious fear, of the machine, and the language is dominated by a vocabulary appropriate to that superstitious fear: Juggernaut, demon, devil, wages of blood, hellish mechanical monster, chains of hell, rapacious animal, pincers of hell, demon steam, tyrant, Moloch, brood of hell, tyrant steam. The machine is 'many-handed', it seizes people and crushes them, the masters have signed away their souls to the devil, the machine 'devours' the work of a thousand women, Ure has sold the workers to the devil, workers become mere hands and legs, and so on (29).

An exclamatory style of agitated, slogan-like interjections, with some speeches written as free verse, becomes more and more rhythmically rhetorical until it reaches a ritualistic climax in the manner of a *Sprechchor*:

> JOHN WIBLE:
> . . .
> Zerstörung der Maschine!
> Krieg dem Tyrannen Dampf!
> Zerstörung der Maschine!
> Krieg dem Tyrannen Dampf'
>
> DIE ARBEITER:
> Zerstörung der Maschine!
> Krieg dem Tyrannen Dampf! (30)
>
> (JOHN WIBLE:
> . . .
> Destruction to the Machine!
> War against the Tyrant Steam!
> Destruction to the Machine!
> War against the Tyrant Steam!
>
> DIE ARBEITER:
> Destruction to the Machine!
> War against the Tyrant Steam!)

Wible's emotional appeal for machine-wrecking is thus expressed through a purely rhetorical, ritualistic, non-rational medium.

On Jimmy's entrance with Ned Lud the style changes immediately to prose and remains prose to the end of the act. Thus Jimmy's speeches, passionate though they are, and though they appeal through nature-imagery to heart as well as head, eschew the cruder rhythms of demagogic rhetoric and retain the rhythms of prose, the body of rationality.

Jimmy's speech is primarily a call to the weavers to form a Trade Union. Its initial appeal is to the individual to seek the enemy within himself:

> Schaut in euch hinein, Brüder! Wie lebt ihr freudlos und dumpf und voll Unrast! Wißt ihr nicht daß Wälder sind . . . Dunkle, geheimnisvolle Wälder, die in Menschen erwecken

> verschüttete Quellen ... Wälder der schwingenden Stille ... Wälder der Andacht . . . Wälder heiteren Tanzes . . . (31)
>
> (Look into yourselves, brothers! How you live joylessly and dully and full of restlessness! Don't you know there are forests . . . dark, mysterious forests, which awaken submerged springs in men . . . forests of vibrant peacefulness . . . forests of reverence . . . forests of cheerful dance . . .)

The imagery has powerful echoes of Hölderlin. He wrote of the inner forests and secret springs:

> Wachs und werde zum Wald! eine beseeltere,
> Voll entblühende Welt! Sprache der Liebenden
> Sei sie die Sprache des Landes.
> Ihre Seele der Laut des Volks! (32)
>
> (Grow and become forest! A more soul-filled
> Fully blossoming world! Let the language of lovers
> Be the language of the land,
> Its soul the accent of the people!)
>
> und wie vom Quellengebirge rinnt
> Segen von da und dort in die keimende Seele dem Volke (33)
>
> (And as if from mountains full of springs runs
> Blessing from here and there into the stirring soul of the people.)

Both these examples of forest and spring imagery are quoted by Landauer in his celebrated Hölderlin lecture of 1916 (34). The whole speech is imbued with Landauer's attitudes. *Geist* and *Land* are key words.

> *Land und Geist* also — das ist die Losung des Sozialismus (35).
>
> (Land and *Geist* — that is the motto of socialism.)

Landauer believes that:

> nur aus dem Geiste, nur aus der Tiefe unsrer inneren Not und unsres inneren Reichtums wird die große Wendung kommen, die wir heute Sozialismus nennen (36).
>
> (only out of the *Geist*, only out of the depths of our inner need and our inner wealth will the great change come, which we today call socialism.)

And Jimmy declares, with the author's own italics:

> *Und der Tyrann Maschine, besiegt vom Geiste schaffender Menschen . . . wird euer Werkzeug, wird euer diener (37).*
>
> (And the tyrant machine, conquered by the *Geist* of working people . . . becomes your tool, becomes your servant.)

Landauer (in emphatic print) says:

> Der Kampf des Sozialismus ist ein Kampf um den Boden (38).
>
> (Socialism's struggle is a struggle for the soil)

And Jimmy cries, alliteratively:

> Den Schaffenden das Land, nicht den Schmarotzern! (39)
>
> (The land to the productive workers, not to the parasites!)

And there are many more ideological and verbal parallels (40).

For the moment Jimmy wins the workers over and is carried off shoulder-high to cries of:

> Ein jeder dient dem Volk, ein jeder dient dem Werk! (41)
> (Each one serves the people, each one serves the work!)

It is a true climax for the end of what has been effectively the first act, but John Wible's mini-epilogue, spoken when he is left alone, promises that conflict is ahead, while also revealing him as an essentially non-revolutionary rebel:

> Diese einfältigen Tölpel wollen auf Erden herrschen und wollen ein Paradies erkämpfen. Narren mögen daran glauben! Ich nicht! (42)
>
> (These simple fools want to rule on earth and win a paradise. Fools may believe in that! Not me!)

The general pattern of Act 2, namely, the presentation separately of Jimmy Cobbett and John Wible material, followed by the confrontation of the two, is repeated on a larger scale in the following three acts (see MONTAGE OF ACTS 2 to 5), with additional parallels and contrasts between Acts 3 and 4, not arranged with mechanical precision, but seeming to arise naturally in the course of the action.

Each of these two acts begins with a scene in which one of the two major antagonists gains an interview with Ure through a preliminary meeting with Henry Cobbett.

In Act 3, Sc. 1, Wible has been summoned by Henry, who wants to get Jimmy out of Nottingham before Ure discovers his identity. Wible is only too pleased to help, but asks also to see Ure. Ure mistakenly thinks he has come looking for work, but is quickly disabused of this, though deceived as to Wible's real motives, because he wants to believe that

> The living bond of community between mill-owners and workers is not a legend.
> (Das lebendige Band der Gemeinschaft zwischen Fabrikanten und Arbeitern ist keine Legende.) (43)

During the scene Ure's little daughter runs into the room, snuggles up to Ure, then runs out again. Ure complacently points out that masters and workers are alike in loving their children. Left alone, Wible reveals that in spite of appearances, he does not intend to betray the workers, even though he believes that they must be whipped out of their apathy, by defeats if necessary. As to the love of children, he sees the same contrast as was expressed in Jimmy's fairy-tale in Act 1:

> Das eine Kind wird all der Schleckereien überdrüssig, dem andern Kind ist Weißbrot ein Schlaraffenmärchen . . . (44)
> (One child is sated with sweets: to the other white bread is a fairy-tale of the Land of Cockaigne.)

This appearance on stage of Ure's child is an item of montage designed to actualise the contrast between her life and the death of Lud's child in Act 4 Sc.2.

The corresponding and contrasting scene is Act 4 Sc. 1, a scene which Klein, who failed entirely to grasp the structure of the play, describes as an "erratic boulder" within the drama (45). In structure the scene carefully parallels Act 3 Sc. 1; in content it is in total contrast. Once more Ure is reached through Henry, and once again Henry's motive in allowing the visitor to see Ure is his need to conceal Jimmy's identity. In contrast with Wible's, however, Jimmy's visit to Henry is unexpected and unwelcome.

As an anonymous representative of the workers Jimmy announces himself to Ure as *Namenlos (Nameless)* though his ideas resemble those of Sonja, and not those of that other Nameless One in *Masse Mensch*. Again Ure mistakes his visitor's motive, thinking Jimmy has come to beg. Jimmy disillusions him at once:

> Man nennt mich den landfremden Rebellen, der die Arbeiter in Nottingham lehrte . . . daß auch Arbeiter Menschen sind (46).
> (They call me the rebel stranger who taught the workers in Nottingham . . . that workers are human beings, too.)

and before Ure has recovered from his surprise at his daring, launches into an exposition of his views — in verse, thus lending additional weight to the material. Of course the scene is long when compared with the corresponding Wible scene in Act 3, but this is simply because Jimmy, unlike Wible, has got an ideology to expound and a social philosophy to express, which Ure, too has to answer in intellectual terms. The ideology and social philosophy are, in effect Toller's own and reflect his reading and his friendship with Landauer.

The argument between Jimmy and Ure is also parallel with, and can be regarded as a continuation of the Lord's debate between Byron and Castlereagh, bearing in mind that the parts are played by the same actors, without change of make-up.

Jimmy bases his own daring on personal integrity:

> Der Geist kennt keine Knechtschaft . . . .
> Wer furchtsam die Idee verläßt, verrät sein eigen Ich (47).
> (The spirit knows no serfdom . . .
> Anyone who timorously abandons the idea, betrays his own self..)

His passionate account of the poverty of the workers leads to a socialist explanation: unwoven cotton is left to rot, food decomposes in store, coal accumulates at the pit-head, because the workers have not the money to buy these commodities. It is the "murderous system" that keeps demand down. What Jimmy implies, though he does not expound it, is Marx's theory of surplus value (48). Unlike Marx, however, he sees the exploitation of labour in metaphysical terms:

> Sie töten Gott
> Wenn Sie das Leben Ihrer Brüder töten (49).
> (You kill God,
> When you kill the life of your brothers.)

Realising the unexpected intellectual ability (Fertigkeit des Geists) of his poorly clad visitor, Ure replies on the same level. First he dismisses God from the discussion:

> Gott und Geschäft verbindet nichts (50).
> (There is no connection between God and business).

He thus echoes Lord Melbourne's dictum:

> Things have come to a pretty pass when religion is allowed to invade the sphere of private life. (attributed) (51)

He then proceeds to demand why Jimmy is stirring up strife, to which the latter replies that the employers are themselves responsible for that.

> Ihr wandelt unsre Erde in ein ewig Schlachtfeld (52).
> (You change our earth into an eternal battle-field).

Ure's response, based, like Castlereagh's to Byron, on Malthus, is expressed, anachronistically, rather in Darwinian terms:

> URE:
> Im Kampfe aller gegen alle reift das Leben (53).
> (In the struggle of all against all, life comes to fruititon).
>
> DARWIN:
> A struggle for existence inevitably follows from the high rate at which all organic beings tend to increase . . . [Darwin then refers to 'the principle of geometrical increase'].. ..Hence, as more individuals are produced than can possibly survive, there must in every case be a struggle for existence . . .
> It is the doctrine of Malthus applied with manifold force to the whole animal and vegetable kingdoms (54).

Darwin read Malthus' *Essay on the Principle of Population* in 1830, "and made his revolutionary theory unique by utilizing Malthus' notion of the struggle for existence to explain why evolution occurs" (55). Though phrased positively, Darwin's theory is actually destructive in its operation.

> The 'fittest' survive because the others (by far the majority) are destroyed. Darwinian theories, applied by analogy to

> social, national and racial conflict [as in Castlereagh's and Ure's speeches. CWD] can produce rationalization of destructive plans of action (56).

It must also be emphasised that Malthus himself gave his theories a class-conscious slant. In the second, enlarged edition of his essay (1803),

> he professed to find a slackening of the pressures of population growth, due, he thought, partly to the operation of morality on the working class (a kind of voluntary birth control) (57).

Jimmy counters Ure's illustration of the stronger deer driving away its sexual rival, with one of mutual aid between such animals, taken, anachronistically, from Kropotkin (58). Then, drawing further upon Kropotkin, he points out examples of mutual aid even between classes, in slave-owning and in medieval society (59), and leads to a group of examples of mutual aid in the animal kingdom, also drawn directly from Kropotkin (60). Finally, Jimmy breaks into an attack on the power of money, its consequences, in, for example, the near extermination of the Red Indians and the Chinese Opium Wars (another anachronism: 1839!) and its being the root cause of all wars.

Ure is moved. He wishes Jimmy were on his side: a dreamer, but a man. He suddenly reverts to being a representative of his class, and drops into prose.

Acts 3 and 4 also end with big parallel scenes, based on the women: in Act 3, Henry Cobbett's speech to the women leads directly to their attack on Mary Wible, his prostitute. As so often in Toller's work (61) the most intense climax is a sexual one. Already furious with Henry and against the machine, they turn their wrath on to Mary in a series of brutally sadistic suggestions, the last of which fuses their jealousy of the whore with their hatred of the machine:

> Sie braucht was Warmes!
> Klemmt ihr heiße Kolben in die Fut! (62).
> (She needs something warm!
> Jam hot pistons [vulgarly:pricks] up her cunt.)

In Act 4 the parallels with this are found in parts of Scene 2. The fate of the faithful working-class wife and mother is exemplified in Margret Lud with her thirteen children. Then comes the scene of young Lud and his prostitute, which forms a contrasting parallel not only with the Mary Wible scene in Act 3, but also with the treatment of the Beggar by his son, described in Act 2. Later, those same women who attacked Mary come with looted bread for the children, scorning Ned Lud's moral objections, and Wible's too, when he seems for a moment to agree with Lud. Again the sexual element is used when the First Woman, Lysistrata-like, says she would not want to sleep with either of them.

These scenes are interwoven with the death of Margret and Ned's baby, in contrast with the brief appearance in Act 3 of Ure's pampered child. Toller anticipates Brecht by nearly two decades in his use of a variant of the old lullaby *Eia popeia* (63).

A further parallel between the two acts is to be found in Wible's manner of dealing with Albert (Act 3 Sc. 3) and with Ned Lud (Act 4 Sc. 2, before and after the scene with the women). He plays on the former's weak-minded fears in a scene whose non-naturalistic lighting effect stresses Albert's irrational and superstitious mind:

> *Die Szene huscht wie ein gespenstiges Flackern vorüber (64).*
> *(The scene flickers as if a ghostly light were flitting over it.)*

With Lud he deals more rationally, appealing to his sense of class loyalty and arousing suspicions about Jimmy.

The third act also contains, approximately in the middle of the play taken as a whole, the second of the three direct confrontations of Jimmy and Wible (the third is the final climax in Act 5) immediately followed by the highly stylised and symbolic choric scene already discussed (65).

Act 5 Sc. 1, already mentioned, forms a prologue to the final scene in the factory and distances the audience from the sympathetic figure of Jimmy so carefully that we realise the partiality of his vision and anticipate his tragic failure to become the effective leader of the workers. This use of the Beggar is a simple example of *Verfremdungseffekt*, designed to provoke active thought rather than mere emotional reaction. Once more in this play Toller is anticipating Brecht's methods.

In Act 5 Sc. 2 the machine is seen at last, both by workers and audience: the gigantic steam-engine and the power-looms, all in one badly-lit weaving-shed; and the working conditions of the children and women are actually put on stage in all their stark brutality. Brilliantly, Toller gives the commentary upon this to Ure, using the language of his original as quoted by Engels. In this way we see the work of the children in double-focus, both as it is and as it is made to seem to the representative of government. Thus even here a kind of montage is being used.

The rioters arrive and the rest of the scene, except for the Old Reaper's Epilogue, is a highly charged sequence of dramatic action. This does not prevent the play from belonging to the Epic category. Both *Leben des Galilei* and *Mutter Courage und ihre Kinder* have final scenes of high drama followed by quieter epilogue-like conclusions; and this despite Brecht's own contrast of *excitement as to the outcome (Dramatic Form of Theatre) with excitement as to the development (Epic Form of Theatre)* in the Mahagonny notes (66).

Shocked initially to find that the hated knobsticks are only children, the crowd halts, overpowered by the wonder of the machinery, whose various sounds, precisely described and distinguished by Toller, fill the air (67).

> Der eiserne Mann! (68)
> (The Iron Man!)

cries a voice.

> So mögen Gottes Mühlen mahlen.. (69)
> (Thus may the Mills of God grind..)

is Lud's awed response.

Then at the Engineer's command the machine is stopped: silence falls. The Engineer, in verse, praises the machine:

> Maschine ist Erlösung! (70)
> (The machine is deliverance!)

Through the machine,

> Der Mensch ward Herr der Erde! (71)
> (Man became Lord of the Earth)

It is the view of the machine as subordinate to man, as expressed, for example, in many of Max Barthel's poems:

> Brüllt auch und brüllt die rasende Maschine:
> Ich bin ihr Herr! Ein Ruck: und sie steht still.
> Aus mir springt Kraft wie stürzende Lawine.

Mein kühnster Gipfel heißt: Ich will! (72)
(And the raging machine roars and roars:
I am its master! One pull and it stops.
Power leaps out of me like a plunging avalanche.
My boldest peak is: I WILL!)

But this voice is soon drowned, and as the Engineer, Overseer, strikebreakers, women and children, flee, the Luddites storm forward. Ned Lud is the first to strike, but accidentally he strikes the starting-handle and the engine and all the looms begin to work: a *coup de théâtre,* but more, — a symbol of the futility of machine-wrecking. The rioters are frightened; but Artur crazily swings a blow with a spade at the whirling machine, is caught by the fly-wheel, and disappears screaming into the machinery. Again the crowd is silenced. Once more it is Lud who leads the attacks. This time the machinery is smashed to pieces. Just then (appropriately rather than naturalistically!) a great storm breaks out, slamming the doors and extinguishing the lights, and out of the semi-darkness we hear wild laughter. Momentarily the terrified men think the machine is laughing; but it is the weak-minded Albert, driven mad at last. Visionarily he prophesies horrors to come. Pursued by the confused mob he escapes to a distant part of the room and hangs himself: the machine has claimed another victim of Wible's exploitation of irrationality.

Jimmy bursts in, accusing them of breaking faith with him. Struck down by Lud and spat upon by Wible, he declares them all serfs and slaves who follow only those who, like Wible, whip them on. Then recovering himself, he calls upon them as workers of the world, to unite:

wenn . . . .die Schaffenden der Erde . . .
Sich nicht zur großen Menschheitstat vereinen . . .
. . Dann, Brüder, bleibt ihr Knechte bis am Ende aller Tage (73).
(if . . . the workers of the world . . .
Do not unite for the great deed of humanity..
. . Then, Brothers, you will remain serfs to the end of time).

They are Jimmy's last words before all except Wible strike him down. Now Lud sees Wible for what he is, a traitor and a coward; and as the Beggar comes to tell them what fools they are, the whimpering Wible slips away (he is not even given an exit in the stage directions) and seconds later the police knock at the door. In a last effort of defiance, Lud cries:

> Andere werden kommen . . .
> Wissender, gläubiger, mutiger als wir.
> *Es wankt schon euer Relch, lhr Herren Englands! (74)*
> (Others will come . . .
> Wiser, more faithful, braver than we are.
> *Your kingdom is already tottering, you lords of England)*

Silently they leave, giving themselves up to the police.

Only the Old Reaper's Epilogue remains, itself ambiguous, for has not the whole play proved the inadequacy, for bringing about social revolution, of his final words?

> man muß einander helfen und gut sein . . . (75)
> (We must help each other and be good).

This structural analysis of the play shows that so far from lacking "unity of content and form" (76) *Die Maschinenstürmer* is a quite brilliant, successful and original experiment in dramatic construction, based upon principles of narrative/montage that draw on the Shakespearean tradition of historical drama and anticipate Brecht's later theories and practice.

THE PLAY ON STAGE

The character of the first production of *Die Maschinenstürmer*, and particularly of its First Night (30.6.1922) was determined by three to some extent related factors: the Director (Karl-Heinz Martin), the theatre (Reinhardt's Großes Schauspielhaus) and current political events (the assassination of Walther Rathenau). It will be convenient to deal with the last of these first, as its effect gradually wore off during the run of the play. Ashley Dukes, who later translated the play into English, wrote:

> . . . the performances . . . have given rise to demonstrations from both sides, the spectators of the Left shouting, "Down with Bavaria!" while those of the right have protested against the Communist incitement implied in the speeches. On the evening when I saw the play the excitement had died down;.. (0)

But the First Night was a very different matter.

The play opened just six days after Walther Rathenau had been murdered by right-wing, anti-semitic extremists in broad daylight while being driven in his open car along the Königs-Allee on his way to the offices of the Foreign Ministry in Berlin (1). This event transformed the evening into a public meeting where the audience showed its approval or disapproval of speeches and arguments through applause or hisses (2). Fritz Engel, a critic noted for his restraint and balance — *"Criticism is not a guillotine, criticism is a pair of scales"* (3) — called the audience reaction to the play *Siedestimmung (a mood at boiling-point)* (4). Another of the older generation of critics, Hermann Kienzl (b.1865), who had actually been present at the celebrated, stormy opening performance of Hauptmann's *Vor Sonnenaufgang* in 1889 and was pre-eminently competent to judge such matters, declared that the word 'success' said in this case both too little and too much:

> It was a hurricance! An elemental mass-demonstration (5).

The like had seldom if ever been seen in a *German* theatre: similar events had occurred in Paris theatres in the early days of the French Revolution (6).

At the end, the murdered Jimmy was identified by the audience with Rathenau, as the critic Max Osborn describes:

> "Was habt ihr gemacht?" ruft ein irrer Greis, der shakespearisierend durch das Stück taumelt. "Einen Mann habt ihr getötet, der für euer Bestes kämpfen wollte. Einen, der Mutter und Bruder und eine bequeme Pfründe verließ, um für euch zu arbeiten." Da tönte es von den Bänken des Riesenhauses: "Rathenau!" (7)
> ("What have you done?" cries a crazy greybeard who staggers and Shakespeareanises through the play. "You've killed a man who wanted to fight for what is best for you. A man who left his mother and his brother and a comfortable position to work for you." Then there resounded from the seats of the enormous theatre: "Rathenau!")

After the final act Karl-Heinz Martin, as Director of the production, made a speech which rather than being concerned with art, turned the scene completely into a tribunal (8).

It is possible that any similarly motivated political murder would have produced a similar result. Political murder in Germany in this period had become an everyday event. Dr E.J. Gumbel in his booklet *Vier Jahre politischer Mord* has established, with names, the assassination of over 300 republican and leftist persons during the years 1918–1923 (9). But the links between the play and Rathenau were deeper and more significant. Max Osborn thought that most of those shouting Rathenau's name would not have realised that Jimmy's ethic for workers had much in common with Rathenau's system of thought. Osborn actually says that Jimmy's speeches are "like a paraphrase" of Rathenau; but this is an overstatement (10). Surely most of the young left-wing enthusiasts filling the theatre must have known enough about Rathenau's views to realise their significance in relation to the play, for,

> Between 1917 and 1920, according to Count Kessler, Rathenau's biographer, Walther Rathenau became the most widely read and most passionately discussed of German writers (11).

The common ground between Jimmy Cobbett and Walther Rathenau lies in their both perceiving the inevitability of mechanisation and at the same time seeking to make mechanisation the servant of the human spirit, not its master. This is encapsulated in the opening sentence of Rathenau's most celebrated book, *Von kommenden Dingen (Concerning Things to Come)*:

> Dieses Buch handelt von materiellen Dingen, jedoch um des Geistes Willen (12).
> (This book deals with material things, but for the sake of the spirit).

This book, as Kessler says, sums up

> Sein Hauptproblem, — die Überwindung der Mechanisierung durch ein "Reich der Seele" (13).
>
> (His principal problem, — how to overcome mechanisation through a "Kingdom of the Soul".)

He realised that mechanisation is the destiny of mankind and therefore the work of Nature, and consequently rational: Nature is never foolish. Mechanisation demands our reverence when we see it as part of nature's evolutionary work, but our hostility if it is seen as necessity. He believed, however, that mechanisation as necessity is disarmed as soon as its "secret meaning" is revealed. He thought that mechanisation *must* serve humanity so long as world population did not fall again to its norm in the pre-Christian millennia (14).

To serve humanity meant for Rathenau to serve humanity spiritually. For it was the inadequacy of Socialism, as he saw it, that it sought only material ends.

> . . . and because Socialism fights over institutions it remains [mere] politics. It can criticise, get rid of deplorable states of affairs, win rights: it will never remodel earthly life, for this power is due only to *Weltanschauung*, faith, the transcendental Idea (15).
>
> Every question which we think through to the end, leads to the supernatural (16).
>
> Everything we do has something prophetic about it, for every step carries us into the future . . . The condition is, that the foot never leaves the soil nor the eye the stars (17).

In the modern, industrialised world, Rathenau, the successful, powerful industrialist, saw no need for the existence of a proletariat and aimed at abolishing the conditions which helped to create it.

> Obviously he did not think of changing the ownership of the means of production: to him a distribution of wealth and equal opportunities would be sufficient to eradicate the conditions which caused the existence of a 'proletariat' (18).

Naturally enough, Rathenau seemed to some of his colleagues in industry, to the extremists of the far right and to the naive on the left, to be a socialist, and Jimmy Cobbett's Landaueresque speeches on mechanisation and *Geist* were superficially sufficiently similar to Rathenau's views to facilitate the identification.

Finally, as Foreign Minister, Rathenau had signed the Treaty of Rapallo (16.4.1922) with Soviet Russia on Germany's behalf. He had done this unwillingly and would have preferred that relationships with Russia had been worked out in conjunction with the Western Powers (19). But his signature on the treaty signed also his own death-warrant with the extreme right, while confirming his socialist image with the young left. The right wing sang their refrain:

> Knallt ab den Walther Rathenau
> die gottverdammte Judensau (20).
> (Shoot down Walther Rathenau
> the god-damned Jewish pig).

And the dwarfish Karl Helfferich spewed poison at him in the Reichstag. On 24 June, Kern's sub-machine gun and Fischer's hand-grenade ended the life of the man who in his book *Mechanik des Geistes (The Mechanism of the Mind)* had asked the question "Is mortality possible?" (21) and argued that it is not.

> Nichts Wesenhaftes in der Welt ist sterblich (22).
> (Nothing essential in the world is mortal).

That was on Saturday. On Sunday hundreds of thousands of workers marched four abreast through the streets of Berlin's West End, from early morning until late afternoon under the black-red-gold and the red flags, in silent mourning. Even in the Reichstag, which met at three, Helfferich was hounded out of the chamber with shouts of "Murderer!".

On the following Friday, Toller's play opened.

The theatre, the second determining factor in the production, made a mass-production inevitable, though critics disagreed as to whether this was wholly appropriate or to the play's advantage. For example:

> . . . Toller's stylised manner is appropriate for the arena theatre — it is one of the few cases which prove the justification and mission of the Großes Schaupielhaus (23).
>
> . . . Karl-Heinz Martin skilfully takes for granted, as something given, the theatre in which he plays. He is not successful (and nor was Reinhardt) in mastering its centrifugal spatial dimensions, but he also does not show (which Reinhardt, however, did show) the struggle with this fiendishly bursting boundlessness. But he makes sure how to accommodate an existing play, which has its own kind of spaciousness, in the simply god-willed spaciousness of the great theatre (24).

This latter critic also believed that the nature of the Großes Schauspielhaus itself, as well as the director's deliberate intentions and Rathenau's murder, contributed largely to the politicisation of the performance:

> The impressionist theatre found it easy, as we know, to create the illusion of an interior, but was troubled with scenes in the

> open air; the Großes Schauspielhaus instead has people always taking a walk in the open air, and cannot hide its embarrassment when they have a roof over their heads (25).

Even excluding the Prologue and the final scene in the weaving-shed, both, in their special ways, interiors, no fewer than six of the remaining ten scenes in the published text are interiors. The point that this theatre was in fact unsuitable for this play thus seems valid. The critic continues, moreover:

> But it [the Großes Schauspielhaus] doesn't even like forests, gardens and landscapes, for these expose with unparallelled openness the break between the arena and the rear stage, and it values to a correspondingly greater degree, streets, open, unfenced spaces, neutral areas for marches, mob-formations and demonstrations. That this house can thus be transformed from a theatre into a meeting-room is, however, not its problem, but, on the contrary, its problem is that it does not want to succeed in making a theatre out of a meeting-room (26).

That the Großes Schauspielhaus was unsuitable for a play clearly written (as we have seen) for a conventional proscenium-arch theatre, is not surprising. In an article contributed to the booklet issued on the occasion of the opening of the theatre in 1920 Carl Vollmoeller shows that it was basically an *Oresteia* theatre (27).

The very theatre, therefore, assured that the intimacy of the five interiors (Mrs Cobbett's lower middle-class living-room; Wible's damp little cottage room; the room in Ure's villa; Ned Lud's cellar dwelling; and the old potato-store occupied by the Beggar) each representing a different level in the scale of wealth and poverty, would be lost, and with it a vital dimension of the play. But, in addition, as Arthur Michel pointed out:

> Karl-Heinz Martin translated the rhetorical, demagogical character of the play, *even beyond the requirements of the Großes Schauspielhaus* [my italics. CWD] into something theatrically opera-like (28).

The material from which Karl-Heinz Martin's production can be to a considerable extent reconstructed consists of:

> The Programme
> The critiques
> Photographs
> The Second Edition of the Play (29).

Karlheinz Martin [*sic* in programme) was at that time Principal Regisseur (Oberspielleiter) for Max Reinhardt, with commitments 1920–1922, to the Großes Schauspielhaus, the Deutsches Theater and the Kammerspiele (30). The stage- and costume-designs were the work of John Heartfield, who designed many stage-settings (and, more rarely, costumes) for Reinhardt and who worked from 1920 to 1923 as artistic director for Reinhardt's décor and costume department (Ausstattungswesen) (31). Music was specially composed by Klaus Pringsheim; technician was Franz Dworsky; lighting by Paul Hoffmann (32).

The cast-lists of the two available copies of the programme show that Toller's suggestion, that Byron/Jimmy and Castlereagh/Ure might be doubled, was adopted. What is extraordinary, however, is that between Sunday 2 July (the third performance) and Tuesday 18 July, there had been no fewer than nine changes in the cast, including the leading roles of Byron/Jimmy, Ned Lud, Mary Wible, Henry Cobbett and the Beggar. It is natural to draw the conclusion that in Martin's production more importance was given to overall spectacular and rhetorical effects than to the subtlety and developed humanity of individual characters; (33) a conclusion borne out by the critiques. One or two of these describe the production quite fully, notably that by Ashley Dukes already quoted. Writing for an English readership, Dukes, while referring to the booklet we have mentioned (34), gives his impression, as a member of the audience, of the Großes Schauspielhaus:

> . . . there was a great audience in the Schauspielhaus, which may be compared roughly to the Albert Hall with the two upper balconies removed, the arena cleared of its seats, and the organ and platform occupied by a stage. Around the arena are tiers of boxes. The players enter either from the wings of the stage or from a gangway at the opposite end of the arena, which is used notably by the Reinhardt "crowds". Below the proscenium, and in place of the orchestra, is a broad flight of steps giving access from the arena to the stage, and *vice versa* . . . (35).

If the spatial qualities of the theatre unsuited it for about half the scenes — the 'domestic' interiors — of this play, its acoustic qualities certainly unsuited it for all that is subtle, intimate, poetic and unrhetorical in the text:

> The acoustics of the theatre are poor. People sitting in the lower boxes complain that the performers shout in their ears;

> in the middle boxes I heard a troublesome echo; and it must be well-nigh impossible to carry any distinction of cadence as far as the upper tiers. The place, in a word, is too large, too hard, and too resonant;. . (36)

It is not surprising that Martin, understanding the theatre's acoustic limitations, reduced Toller's text to a mere exercise in political rhetoric, for which, of course, the author was blamed by several other critics:

> . . . his lines dissolve into words, words, words (37); the rhetorical-demagogical character of the piece (38); In a word, apart from the mass-scenes and the pictures of social conditions, we have nothing but rhetoric (39); The poet shouts too loud (40); The director has also exaggerated the rhetorical element instead of playing it down. In the very first scene he let off the first rhetorical firework display . . . (41)

Dukes, clearly an admirer of Toller, thought that the play was "not imaginatively produced" (42). The visual spectacle obscured rather than heightened the intensity of Toller's text:

> The cleverness of the *mise-en-scène* made a strong momentary impression, but it shaded, like some fabric of neutral tint and indubitable good taste, the flame that burns in Toller's work (43).

Unexpectedly, when one recalls Karlheinz Martin's Expressionist production of *Die Wandlung*, Dukes complains that:

> A kind of stylistic naturalism overlaid the whole (44).

Dukes describes three scenes which he regarded as "remarkable moments in the production" (45).

<u>Act III Sc 4 (lst Ed, GW2 p.152)</u>

> . . . the surging of a crowd of factory girls against the railings of the manager's red brick house, and his sudden appearance in the doorway at the head of the steps, a sharp little figure, incredibly diminutive, with white choker and tight-waisted coat and arms akimbo, to quell the disturbance (46).

Act II Sc 1 or Act IV Sc 1 (GW2 p.144, 158) (Probably the latter)

> In another scene two such (viz: like the manager. CWD) diminutive and mannered figures sat on high stools, on either side of high desks, in the factory owner's office, while flanking the doorway in the background were painted red ledgers six feet high on colossal shelves. The ledgers were the *dramatis* personae; the men no more than bookworms (47).

Act V Sc 2 (GW2 p.176)

> The machine-wrecking scene was beautiful in comparison, with moonlight streaming through tall factory windows upon the engine, a steam-driven construction (perhaps anachronistic) of primitive flywheels, cranks and frames, with an engineer upon its bridge. The machine-wreckers are overcome by terror at the sight of this mechanical Moloch, and the first of them who takes courage to strike a blow is caught by the flywheel and mangled (48).

This final scene is the one of which we can form the clearest visual conception, for two photographs of it have been reprinted (49). Both show John Heartfield's massive and theatrically convincing steam engine, nearly twenty feet high, with its bridge and iron ladders. There is no sign in either of the power-looms at which the women and children should have been working. The images of two vast windows appear to be projected on to a cyclorama. One of the photographs shows Jimmy, fallen, but raising himself on one elbow while another worker grips his left wrist. A flywheel lies centre in front of the group and a crowd of some thirty-five or so weavers are tightly grouped in front of the engine. A figure, presumably the Engineer, is on the bridge. The impression is that of a "photo-call" grouping, though it may well approximate to an actual moment in the scene during the attack on Jimmy. The other photograph is almost certainly purely posed. In the foreground, "artistically" grouped on the steps, seven men hold the big flywheel at shoulder-height. Several figures, also self-consciously posed, are on the bridge, the iron ladder and other parts of the machine. A few others are placed around rather passively as if to complete the composition of the picture.

It is this scene which in general impressed the critics most. Max Hochdorf, highly critical of the play ("It remains a sketch and an intention") praised Heartfield for *using* the Großes Schauspielhaus *in the final scene* (50). Hermann Kienzl remarked that the machinery was even *working!* (51). Max Osborn referred to "banal sections where tendentious material in its raw state remains artistically unshaped. But," he added, "then comes the last act and brings a great improvement." His description of the scene adds much to our knowledge of it:

> The curtain rises [i.e. the curtain of the rear stage. CWD.] and before us stands a gigantic mechanical monster.

Karl-Heinz Martin here evidently understood Toller's dramatic intention in keeping the machine hidden — a monster in the imagination — until this final scene.

> With iron members, flywheels, pistons, rods, spheres [?governers. CWD], driving-belts, steam-vents, railings.

Osborn goes on to describe the looms, not seen in the photographs:

> At the sides to right and left the looms, moved by the colossus, operated by wretched children.

He points appreciatively to the extraordinary fusion of ultra-realism and symbolism in this stage setting:

> Superb reality of the everyday, and nevertheless unreal, elevated into an overwhelming symbol. The monster stares out of the mighty space of the factory cupola like fate for generations in centuries to come (52).

This is high praise, but Ashley Dukes who, remarkably for a non-German, had a better appreciation of Toller's poetic gifts than most of the dramatist's own countrymen, understood that:

> These were, however, the easy triumphs of a producer who understood the spectacular possibilities of his subject (and perhaps the limitations of his theatre where poetic drama is concerned) (53).

Apparently the English poet-critic-translator was the only journalist who understood that the Martin/Heartfield production, based on rhetoric and spectacle, concealed rather than revealed the essence of the play, and he drew the conclusion that;

> Even in the Great Schauspielhaus, Toller has not yet found his stage (54).

As to the manner of acting and performance, all the evidence points to highly drilled stylisation. Kienzl says that the "scenic, mimic and acoustic *Mystifaxen* (?a nonce word) of Karl-Heinz Martin, the Director, stood in complete contrast with the reality [of the machinery]. Nothing personal stood out from the players trained in the grotesque." (55). Artur Michel similarly comments:

> Apart from the strictly drilled vocal effort there is little particularly to praise in individual performances (56).

Osborn does indeed say it was a 'great day' (Ehrentag) for the younger players of the Großes Schauspielhaus. He mentions by name Gerhard Ritter as Ned Lud, Loni Duval (Leoni in the programme) as his "robust, rabble-rousing wife", Hans Rodenberg as the "treacherous" Wible, Esther Hagan, "his blond wife" and Paul Günther as the Engineer; and he refers to "a whole succession of characteristic figures" — which seems to imply a series of two-dimensional character parts rather than fully human, personal, *menschlich*, performances. Both Osborn and Michel, however, make an exception of Alexander Granach as Der alte Reaper, Michel saying:

> Only Alexander Granach, growing in power, created as that "Fool in God" a personally strong performance (57)

It is from Michel also that we gain the strongest impression of the way in which Martin, with the help of Klaus Pringsheim's music, gave the production an operatic quality.

> He made the procession of workers advance silently and slowly out of the depths, on to the arena, towards the stage, as if it were the question of a demonstration for the protection of the Republic. There they threw up their arms and voices in *Reinhardtish* rhythms to the declamation of the leaders and sang their Weavers' Song, now shrilly, now in a whisper. From there they separated, singing and dying away, like an operatic chorus, to the sides of the stage. From there they

> stormed towards the rear-stage in order to shatter into pieces the steam-engine which towered up into the sky. Martin used the pounding, groaning march-rhythm of the Weavers' Song at the same time as a structural refrain (58).

Großmann strongly condemns both the operatic and over-drilled aspects of the production:

> Perhaps Karl-Heinz Martin has given the play its death-blow. He has turned a play of speeches into an opera . . . For him everything becomes groups of wax-works. He creates pictures and lets the characters remain motionless in them. Then, at a military command, usually jerkily, the group is allowed to move (59).

Michel's critique reveals perhaps more clearly than any other how far this production had moved away from the performance-style implied in the original text, and this leads us to explore how that text was in fact treated.

Evidence that considerable modifications were made to the original text is to be found in the critiques, the programmes and the second edition of the play.

This second edition evidently embodies some of the changes made in production, but not all; nor is it certain that every change is derived from the production. As this edition is, surprisingly, described very inaccurately by Spalek in his bibliography, a full account of it is given in an appendix. The conclusions reached there are taken for granted in what follows.

From the programme we learn that Toller's careful construction in five acts with a prologue was ignored, and the play is described as being in *A Prologue and Eight Scenes.* The text of both editions contains a Prologue and eleven scenes (with one change in the order of scenes), so either up to three scenes must have been cut or some scenes run together. It is impossible to reconstruct these cuts or runnings-together. There was one interval, *After the fifth Scene.* Assuming no scenes were cut or linked this would have been at the end of Act III Sc. 2; but the end of Act III would seem a better place. Were Scenes 2 & 4 of Act III played without a break (bearing in mind that Act III Sc. 3 was transposed to the beginning of Act V)?

Several minor characters are omitted from the cast, so presumably these were cut: viz. the two drunks (Act I. GW2 p.128), the man with the barrow (Act III Sc. 2 GW2 p 150), Young Lud and his prostitute (Act IV Sc. 2. GW2 pp167–8). The off-stage voice of Mary Anne Walkley in the final scene is not mentioned, but these lines could have been given to any of the women (60). More importantly, in view of the content of the dialogue, Ure's guest, the representative of the Government, is omitted. But the Hawker (Act I. GW2 p.127), the blind man and the deaf-mute (Act III Sc. 2.GW2 p.150) are retained.

No children are individualised on the programme, but this does not necessarily mean that the lines given to specific children were cut. Indeed, the changes in the allocation of speeches to children which appear in the second edition suggest that some care was taken over this.

The House of Lords was probably suggested visually, for after quoting the speeches, Ashley Dukes says:

> the scene changes to Nottingham, where the weavers, already idle in consequence of the introduction of machinery or on strike against it, are hanging effigies of the strike-breakers in the streets and meditating an attack on the looms (61).

The ritual element in this scene was strongly developed. The crowd entered to the accompaniment of music and the antiphonal liturgy lengthened from two speeches to nine, with the seven-fold repetition of the response:

> Drum hängt sie auf! (62)
> (Because of that — hang them')

A number of changes were clearly designed for simplification: e.g. Wible's soliloquy in Act III Sc.1, was nearly doubled in length. The result is simpler, clearer, but less dense, less like the workings of a quick but devious mind.

The Weavers' Song was introduced whenever possible. When Jimmy was carried off shoulder-high at the end of Act II the song was sung softly. It was, of course, kept for the processional exeunt at the end of Act III (GW2 p.157.2nd Edtn. p.66) where the by now familiar – and therefore more ritualistic — first stanza was used, instead of the new one originally written. Finally, it was used for the choric entrance preceding the machine-wrecking and, defiantly, for the final exeunt of the weavers into the arms of the police cordon.

There were some major changes in the characterisation of principals. Some of Jimmy's part was rewritten so as to present him as a tactically motivated revolutionary rather than as the would-be founder of a trade union.

Margaret Lud was given a number of lines originally assigned to the First, Second and Fifth Women. These totally alter her character. In Toller's text (i.e. 1st Edtn.) she appears only in Act IV Sc.2, where her character is that of the archetypal working-class wife and mother. She sings her lullaby, grumbles at her husband and mourns her dead child. She does not speak during the scene when the women bring the stolen bread. In the production, on the evidence of the second edition, she is a leader of the group, urging the children to eat the stolen bread and publicly attacking her husband Ned in a speech taken from the Second Woman. She is also introduced into the scene in front of Ure's villa, where she takes over the First Woman's role of principal spokeswoman to Henry and leads the savage attack on Mary — who is, in both versions, rescued by Ned. So utterly different a character does this make her that it seems probable that all the private scene between her and Ned was cut along with Young Lud's entrance with his whore. Toller's beautifully arranged contrast between the Wible and Lud married couples was thus lost (63).

A third major character change involved those of Albert and the Engineer. Originally, Albert's mental instability was hinted at early in the play, and the first edition's Act III Sc. 3, with its ghostly flickerings, externalised his inner condition. But in the production his breakdown into madness was, without rhyme or reason, transferred lock, stock and barrel to the sober, clear-headed Engineer. Act II Sc. 3 was placed immediately before Act V Sc. 2, where it became fairly pointless. The concept of an engineer going mad as he experiences the destruction of his beloved machine might pass as a piece of crudely melodramatic Expressionism, but Albert's lines are inappropriate to the Engineer, and the characters of two carefully written parts are destroyed by the change.

A fourth character change, also destructive, was that the Overseer as a separate character was cut and his scene given to Henry. The coarse and brutal Overseer actually represents a cruder aspect of a worker's betrayal of his class than that embodied in the intelligent and snobbish Henry. Henry would employ others to do the harsh, dirty work of oversight on the factory floor. The fusion of the two figures meant that the essence of each was lost.

The scant respect shown to the author's text, to its intrinsic qualities and to its creator's poetic, intellectual and emotional stature, must be ascribed partly to Karl-Heinz Martin's and John Heartfield's own political enthusiasms and partly to their quite proper attempts, theatrically speaking, to accommodate the play to the Großes Schauspielhaus. But the result, however exciting, was in no way a definitive production.

There have been many subsequent productions of *Die Maschinenstürmer*, in nine countries (64). Finland heads the list with six productions; Germany has had five, plus a performance of selected scenes, the Soviet Union and Britain, four each, USA three, Hungary two, Yugoslavia and Estonia one each (65), and one scene was performed in Brussels in Esperanto in 1924.

The second German production was in the Stadttheater, Erfurt, for the Freie Volksbühne in October 1922, and the first Russian production opened on 3 November 1922.

The *Leipziger Volkszeitung* gave the Erfurt production a very favourable review, describing it as a 'social tragedy of fate'. The setting was described as a mixture of stark realism and phantasy. The reviewer thinks that the working class now knows that a poet has arisen from among them who understands the labour-pains of the birth of the proletariat (66).

The Moscow production in the Theatr Revoliutsii was directed by Vsevolod Meyerhold and P.P. Repnin, and designed by V.P. Komardenkov. New music was composed by P.V. Kartashov. The production ran for 55 performances.

The fourth production of the play was given in Ashley Dukes' translation by the Stage Society at the Kingsway Theatre, Great Queen Street, London on 6 & 7 May 1923. The original Berlin production had inspired Dukes to translate the play into English. He believed it was obviously a play for the English stage, though he thought, and continued to think, that it should be staged with more emphasis on the personal instead of the crowd scenes (67).

According to Spalek (68) the play could only be given as a closed performance by the Stage Society because of British censorship. It was directed by Nugent Monck, Director of the Maddermarket Theatre, Norwich; the scenes and children's dresses were also designed by two members of the Maddermarket, Owen P. Smyth (scenes), and Peter Taylor-Smith (dresses).

The doubling of characters in the prologue and play was abandoned, Byron being played by George Hayes and Jimmy Cobbett by

Herbert Marshall. Ned Lud (changed for some reason to Bob Lud) was played by Raymond Massey. The Third Woman was Martita Hunt. Ashley Dukes' programme note emphasised both the fact that "the play does not purport to be historical drama in the literal sense" and the authenticity of Byron's speech, which he calls "the historical motive of the play" (69).

The production was widely and on the whole favourably reviewed, and Ashley Dukes' translation received high praise, (70) though one critic blamed the translator for what he calls the "woodenness" of certain parts (71). One critic thought that though it "reads splendidly" it should have been cut in production (72). The anonymous *Daily Telegraph* critic described the production as "simple and inspired", (73) though G.D.H. Cole thought the play needed either a lavish professional production or an amateur one (74). Cole, in common with Frank Birch (75) thought the play was performed in London before the "wrong" audience. While the acting was in general favourably received, Ivor Brown, while praising the play and production (especially Monck's successful use of the small stage) found Herbert Marshall's acting not suited for an expressionist play (76). This betrays the desire to label Toller permanently as an Expressionist and at the same time suggests that Monck as producer had moved the performance in the 'personal' direction favoured by the translator. Perhaps the most striking comments came from a certain *M.A.H.* in The New Leader (77). The critique was headed *The Machine Wrecker* (sic). *M.A.H.* declares that the audience sat "in frightened attention" and describes the play as, on the one hand "shattering" because of the suffering it shows, and on the other as "uplifting" because it shows something unconquerable in the mind of man.

In June 1923, just a year after the first production, Karl-Heinz Martin took the production to the Wiener Komödienhaus. He used the same music and some of the original cast (78).

Interest in the play has revived a little in recent years, though there was no professional production of the play in Germany between 1945 and 1968 (79). However, in November 1951 a group of Berlin workers and students calling themselves the *Barrikade*, amateurs of average talent who wanted to revive the ideas and methods of the Piscator-Bühne, put the play on in the Kammermusiksaal Kreuzberg under the direction of Horst Braun (80) and though one critic thought the play had not survived the passage of time (81), another, who thought the attempt to revive the ideas of the Piscator-Bühne a mistake and found the staging primitive, wrote enthusiastically:

> And look, Ernst Toller still really is effective in spite of all the makeshifts.
> The play has power still.
> In the stalls you heard a great deal of matter-of-fact conversation about wages, contrasts between East and West in respect of work-laws (82).

One recalls Ashley Dukes' comment on the first production:

> In passion, in thought, in expression, he is the voice of his hour . . . sentence after sentence comes across to listener with an echo of something read (or, oftener, something thought) concerning the welter of Germany out-of-doors (83).

Four more productions, all post-dating Spalek's Bibliography, must be mentioned, three British, one German.

October to December 1978 saw in London a remarkable series of cultural events organised by the Goethe Institute under the title *London-Berlin, The Seventies meet the Twenties* (84). This series included, as well as a satirical revue under the Tolleresque title *Hoppla! wir leben!* at the Round House (85), a noteworthy production of *The Machine Wreckers* in a new translation by Peter Tegel, at the Half Moon Theatre (86). It is difficult to imagine two more sharply contrasting productions of the same play than Karl-Heinz Martin's original production and this at the Half Moon Theatre.

The members of the audience, the present writer included, on entering the tiny auditorium-cum-playing-space, found themselves in

> an intricate web of pipes, tunnels, ladders and tubing (87).

Instead of the machine's being monstrously built up in the imagination, to be revealed only in the very last scene of the play, this "image of the diabolic, entrailed, all-engulfing machine" designed by Mick Bearnish, formed a total three-dimensional environment for actors and audience alike. Instead of the delayed revelation of a vast piece of mechanism, impossible in an intimate theatre, the designer created a claustrophobic nightmare-octopus which seemed to wind its tentacles around every person in the theatre and, as Billington rightly prophesied:

> even when the words are forgotten I suspect that image . . . will haunt one for a long time to come (88).

Where Martin had twenty-seven named principals plus (to judge from photographs) at least twenty extras, Tim Albery cast 24 adult parts with eight actors, and used three children in addition (89). The Prologue was omitted and most of the action took place on a fairly limited floor-space. Scenes in Ure's office, however, were played on a high staging at one end, so that the audience was compelled to look far up, as if to another, more exalted, world. Effective though this and related devices were, they moved the play back into the full-blooded Expressionism of *Die Wandlung*. The exaggeratedly high desk of the Stock Exchange scene in *Masse Mensch* was not appropriate in *Die Maschinenstürmer*. The production was praised for "going all out for the right period style" (90), but for that very reason it failed to do justice to Toller's awareness of the need to give his ideas concrete and sensory form. Billington, for example, while saying that the aspect of the play dealing with the

> painful, bruising truth about the gulf between revolutionary pacificism (sic) and angry workers with teeming families, no bread and threatened jobs

is "as fresh as paint", goes on to say that

> What dates the play is its Expressionist technique (91).

But much of that "expressionist technique" is in fact Albery's, not Toller's.

Once more a Toller revival is called a "museum piece" (Billington) and is then admitted to be "fresh as paint" in essentials. Hugh Rank went as far as to call the play

> Toller's greatest achievement with the possible exception of his autobiography (92).

Julian Exner, writing up the production for German readers, drew the comparison drawn here between this production and Martin's. Having noticed the English critic's rather dismissive "museum piece", he rejoins:

> es lohnte sich in der ungewöhnlich einfallsreichen Inszenierung von Tim Albery (93).
> (it was worth while in Tim Albery's unusually imaginative production).

He recognised, too, the still contemporary importance of the theme and saw parallels with current conflicts about printing techniques on *The Times*, concluding:

> Ned Lud lebt, und für sein Land sind *Die Maschinenstürmer* des deutschen Sozialisten Toller leider doch kein Museumstück (94).
> (Ned Lud lives and for his country *The Machine Wreckers* of the German socialist Toller is still unfortunately not a museum piece).

An even more recent British production was given by the Citizens' Theatre Company, Glasgow, in the summer of 1984. This remarkable production used a cast of only five, who not only doubled all the parts but also, wearing grey masks, represented the working masses and created an illusion of numbers which made it hard to believe that the cast was so small. The set, too, was all grey and it, with appropriate lighting, conveyed the drab, poverty-stricken conditions of the workers.

> Electronic symbols looming above the nineteenth century set [were] visual pointers to the situations parallel with the technological revolution endangering employment today.

Thus the production actually incorporated the contemporary parallel noted by Julian Exner in his critique already quoted, of the Half Moon production. Giles Havergal's production was described as "a sharply sobering dose of harsh reality" [i.e. after the company's previous production, *Private Lives*] and his "dynamic treatment" is said to have made it "splendid thought-provoking theatre almost throughout" (95).

The most recent German production (probably the first since 1951) was directed by Wolfgang Lichtenstein for the Ruhrfestspiele 1985, a context which would seem very appropriate. Unfortunately the production was not satisfactory and the director was not prepared to allow the play to speak for itself. It was preceded by a monologue from the East German dramatist Heiner Müller's play *Prometheus* (after Aeschylus). A critic commented that no one could say what was being attempted through this (96). Of course it might be argued that Prometheus, as the bringer of fire to mankind , was the ancestor of all machinery, but the same critic declared that all this "Prometheus stuff"

> has not the least to do with Toller's play (97).

Bits of Brecht's verse-fragment of the Communist Manifesto were also "thundered down". There was even an industrial exhibition laid on in relation to the play and an associated leaflet, *Aus dem Museum des Fortschritts (From the Museum of Progress)*, with an article by Michael Fehr, *Idee und Realisation (Idea and Realisation)* and a colour photograph of a Claas combine-harvester on its cover (98).

Toller's play reveals its contemporary relevance better without such meretricious "aids" (99).

In no production has that relevance been demonstrated as effectively as in the English production which opened on 11 August 1995 in the Cottesloe Theatre of the Royal National Theatre, London. Directed by Katie Mitchell with Vicki Mortimer as Designer, and using (with minor changes) Ashley Dukes' translation, this production aimed, and aimed successfully, at truly fulfilling the author's intentions.

The Cottesloe Theatre, with a simple end-stage, retained the intimacy of the many domestic scenes while suggesting larger spaces when necessary. All Toller's minor characters were included and the text effectively uncut. From the moment when Colin Tierney as Lord Byron (doubling, rightly, with Jimmy Cobbett) addressed the audience in his opening speech, to the final machine-wrecking, when powerful sound-effects and strobe lighting created in their imaginations a monstrous machine filling the whole auditorium, the authenticity, intellectual clarity and emotional impact of the play gripped the entire house in tense, silent attention, punctuated only by an occasional ironic laugh when the topical parallel — never crudely emphasised on stage — was particularly striking. As *The Guardian* critic wrote: "Toller's play still shocks and grips." At the end even a mid-week matinée audience recalled the company with its warm applause.

Every character was vividly realised and sharply distinguished; it is almost invidious to single out Ron Cook (Wibley) for the special mention he merits. The irritating oddity of black faces in Nottingham families of 1815 was presumably due to the theatre's policy of 'political correctness'; but Katie Mitchell tactfully ensured that they were as unobtrusive as possible. If there is such a thing as a definitive production of a play, this, described by the *Sunday Times* as "masterful", may fairly be seen as definitive.

A plan to perform the play actually in Nottingham was frustrated as the proposed venue was not ready. I myself was privileged to be associated with this production as 'Textual Adviser'.

III

TOLLER'S USE OF LANGUAGE

TOLLER'S USE OF LANGUAGE

INTRODUCTION

A major argument of this book is that the quality of Toller's writing is a vital factor in determining the lasting worth of his dramatic work, and that this is true even of those plays whose initial reputation owed much to the directors of their first productions (1). It will therefore be valuable to relate Toller's use of language in his plays to the language of his poems, choral works and prose.

While he could always write good, clear prose for practical, journalistic or political purposes, his creative writing falls into two distinct periods, before and after 1922/1923. Until then he expressed himself creatively primarily in verse and through the medium of poetry. His earliest surviving poem was written in 1912 (2). The volume *Vormorgen* (3) shows that he was writing poetry steadily though sparingly from 1915 to 1924. The high point of his poetic output was *Das Schwalbenbuch*, conceived in 1922, written in 1923, and published in 1924. His first play, *Die Wandlung*, was partly in verse, the second and third, *Masse Mensch* and *Die Rache des verhöhnten Liebhabers*, entirely in verse, and his fourth, *Die Maschinenstürmer*, two-thirds in prose and one-third in verse. This was the last play in which he employed verse (4), and *Hinkemann*, written 1922 (5) the first to be wholly in prose. All his subsequent plays are in prose, and after *Das Schwalbenbuch* he seems to have published no new poetry apart from *Weltliche Passion* (1934) and *Die Feuer-Kantate* (1938) both of which appeared in Moscow-based German-language periodicals (6).

Thus after 1923 he wrote entirely in prose, and later, during his years of exile, produced his two prose masterpieces, the autobiographical *Eine Jugend in Deutschland* (1933) and *Briefe aus dem Gefängnis* (1935), based on his own letters from prison. At this point, therefore, when he ceases to use verse, we interrupt our examination of the plays in order to analyse the qualities of Toller the dramatist's poetry and prose.

TOLLER AS POET

Poetic Language in *Die Wandlung* and the War Poems

The selection of poems in Toller's *Gesammelte Werke* obscures the fact that he was one of the front-line war poets. His few published war-poems — actual front-line poems — are to be found in *Vormorgen* (1). They are all included in the first section of the book, *Verse vom Friedhof (Verses from the Graveyard)*. There are sixteen individually dated poems in this section, covering the period 1912 to 1918.

The first poem, *Der Ringende,* has already been discussed in relation to *Die Wandlung,* in its autobiographical aspect. There follow five poems from 1915, evidently written after Toller's being moved in March from the neighbourhood of Strasbourg to the front line before Verdun. Four poems from 1916 follow. Of these, two, *Stellungskrieg (Positional Warfare)* and *Leichen im Priesterwald (Corpses in the Bois-des-Prêtres)* are front-line lyrics of the utmost intensity: *Stellungskrieg* consists of no more than eighteen words! Of the other two, *Konzert (Concert)* was written while Toller was on leave, and *Alp (Nightmare)* is a Bosch-like dream-image of war. Strictly, these nine poems constitute the whole of Toller's output of front-war poetry. The remaining poems in *Verse vom Friedhof* are dated either 1917, when Toller was not in the army (though all three are related to the war) or 1918, when he was recalled to the army and spent three months in a military prison. Of the three poems dated 1918, two refer to this first period of imprisonment, during which the later scenes of *Die Wandlung* were developed.

There is also the MS of an unpublished poem, *Nacht im Priesterwald (Night in the Bois-des-Prêtres)* dated 21.4.1917, but based on Toller's 1916 experiences (2).

The *Verse vom Friedhof* vary greatly both in style and in quality. Wolfgang Rothe, for instance, refers to the verse of *Der Ringende* as 'clumsy' (*unbeholfen*) (3), while on the other hand he writes of *Gang zur Ruhestellung*:

> Surprising verses, which in their emphatic artlessness have nothing in common with the inflated war-poetry of those years — often written at home — and call to mind the "anti-aesthetic" tendencies of our time (4).

The 'artlessness' of the front-line poems is, however, more apparent than real, as indeed Rothe's qualifying 'emphatic' (betont) implies. Nor can all other German war-poetry be dismissed as 'inflated'.

In order to place *Die Wandlung* in the context of World War I poetry we must discriminate between Toller's front-line poems of 1915 and 1916, and those written in 1917 and 1918 when *Die Wandlung* was also written. We must also place all Toller's 1915 to 1918 poems in the wider context of German war-poetry. In practice it will be convenient first to look at that wider context.

An informed estimate suggests that there were at least 5 million German war poems of the First World War (5). Most of these have naturally found deserved oblivion and only the work of a very small number of poets needs be considered relevant to this investigation. Even the wartime poems of the two established major poets of the time, Rilke and Stefan George, evaded the issue. Rilke fell into the patriotic-romantic trap, and when he realised the enormity of the destruction he developed a mystique of *Schmerz*. War was absorbed into his private mythology. He was too far away. The best war-poetry came from front-line poets, a fact that will also contribute to how we discriminate between individual poems by Toller. George wrote objectively with little emotion, showing a brutal indifference to death, his objectivity sometimes bordering upon the inhuman. Both these poets had developed poetic modes to express private worlds — for his own, Rilke devised the untranslatable word *Weltinnenraum* — and both were committed to an outdated and irrelevant tradition. (In 1914 Rilke was 39 and George 46).

For all poets the problem of *Traditionslosigkeit* in relation to war poetry was stupendous. War poetry of the Napoleonic era was an irrelevance and that of the sixteenth and seventeenth centuries no longer part of a living tradition. In any case, where was the historical perspective to come from? The war, with its barbarous technology, was, or appeared to be, unparalleled. Its mechanical compulsory killing (*Mußmord: compulsory murder*, was a word coined) was, or seemed, without precedent. After initial idealisation of the war, parallel with Rupert Brooke's ecstatic sonnets in English, revulsion led to anti-war poetry. This change and revulsion — which Toller shares, though he seems to have written no poems expressing his early idealistic enthusiasm — can be traced even *within* the works of individual poets. Richard Dehmel (1863–1920), for example, could write in 1914 *Deutschlands Fahnenlied (Song of the Flag of Germany)* with its "lieber Tod als Schmach" (death rather than disgrace) chauvinism (6); but by 1918 he was writing *Lichter Augenblick (A Lucid Moment)* in which the soldier, home on leave, must ask his child,

war's wohlgetan
dich in die Welt zu setzen, Kind,
in diese Welt (7)?

(was it well done
to put you in the world, child,
in this world)?

Another problem faced by the potential war-poets was the German tendency to abstraction. In the context of war this all too easily led to rhetoric or even mere bombast, whether militaristic or pacifistic. Here, for example, is part of Gerhart Hauptmann's *O mein Vaterland (O, my Fatherland)*:

Doch, mein Vaterland, heiliges Heimat land,
Welche Prüfung mußt du nun bestehn!
"Kind, sie muß geschehn, muß übergehen,
Nimm du nur die Sichel in die Hand!

Denn du mußt ein Gras mähn mit fester Faust . . .

. . . .

Und es ist ein Gras, das von Blute träuft!
Kein Erbarmen kann dir sein erlaubt.
Zischend sinkt vom Halme Haupt um Haupt
Und zu Leichenbergen wirds gehäuft (8).

Clearly the poet who once wrote *Die Weber* had never in his fifty-two years seen 'mountains of corpses' or encountered the effect of sharpened steel on human flesh.

The anti-war poets could just as easily fall into similarly meaningless verbiage; witness Gerrit Engelke:

Die Welt ist für euch alle groß und schön und schön!
Seht her! staunt auf! nach Schlacht und Blutgestöhn:
Wie grüne Meere frei in Horizonte fluten
Wie Morgen, Abende in reiner Klarheit gluten,
Wie aus den Tälern sich Gebirge heben,
Wie Milliarden Wesen uns umbeben!
O, unser allerhöchstes Glück heißt: Leben! (9).

By contrast, the English Georgians were poets of particularity. Edward Thomas could move easily within the compass of one poem from the particularities of peace to the particularities of war, from

The hill road wet with rain

to

> Now all roads led to France,

or from the drunken ploughman's sleeping out of doors in Wiltshire to his sleeping,

> More sound in France (10).

So also could Wilfred Owen and the other great English war poets quickly latch on to the terrible particularities of trench warfare. For example, Isaac Rosenberg:

> The wheels lurched over the sprawled dead
> But pained them not, though their bones crunched;
> Their shut mouths made no moan.
> They lie there huddled, friend and foeman,
> Man born of man, and born of woman;
> And shells go crying over them
> From night till night and now (11).

Nevertheless some of the German front-line poets did achieve a concreteness and directness comparable with the finest English front-line poetry. Anton Schnack in his 'broken sonnets' can focus upon the details of reality:

> *Am Feuer*
>
> Septembernacht. Land zwischen Maas und ihren Bächen; Kartoffelfelder,
> quer überritten, wüst zerstampft, zertreten.
> Wer kennt sich aus? Wer war schon hier, allein, mit Damen,
> braunen Hunden? Fern: Wälder, Hügel, Allerlei, Gestirne, Tote,
> Gejohl der Reiter, dreckig, wundgeritten. Verdammt ruchloser Mund
> der dumpfen Melodie vom frühen Morgenrote! – (12).

It was August Stramm who carried to its furthest limit the concentration of particularities, reducing his words to a minimum while at the same time inventing new words and employing existing words in surprising and unfamiliar ways. For example:

> *Patrouille*
>
> Die Steine feinden

Fenster grinst Verrat
Äste würgen
Berge Sträucher blättern raschlig
Gellen
Tod (13).

This kind of intensity, but with less straining of the resources of language, Toller also achieves. Consider, as a companion piece to Stramm's *Patrouille,* Toller's *Geschützwäche (Guarding the Gun)*

. . .
Gebändigtes Untier
Glänzt mein Geschütz,
Glotzt mit schwarzem Rohr
Zum milchigen Mond (14).

In both poems intense observation of simple things — stones, window, branches, gun-barrel — and the feelings they evoke in the heightened tension of patrol or night guard duty, are expressed with the minimum number of words and the attribution of feelings to the inanimate objects. The conscious and deliberate use of the pathetic fallacy objectifies the poet's own feelings and in doing so creates poems that are both personal *and* objective. In Toller's poem natural and human sounds are expressed in natural and human terms:

Käuzchen schreit.
Wimmert im Dorf ein Kind

(An owl screeches,
A child whimpers in the village).

but the *un*natural sound — the shot — is figuratively described as a wolf, and the wolf is given human characteristics;

Geschoß
Tückischer Wolf

(A shot
Spiteful wolf)

and in this figurative form the sound of the shot

Bricht ins schlafende Haus

(Breaks into the sleeping house)

The whole poem is framed in its first and last lines by nature itself:

> Sternenhimmel
>
> (Starry sky)
>
> . . .
>
> Lindenblüten duftet die Nacht.
>
> (The night smells of lime-blossom).

This is front-line poetry at its best, comparable with Stramm in German or Rosenberg in English. In *Returning, we hear the Larks* Rosenberg similarly juxtaposes the ugliness of war with the beauty of nature:

> Dragging these anguished limbs, we only know
> This poison-blasted track opens on our camp –
> On a little safe sleep.
>
> But hark! Joy — joy — strange joy.
> Lo! Heights of night ringing with unseen larks:
> Music showering on our upturned listening faces (15).

Three more of Toller's 1915 poems are in similar style (*Morgen, Gang zum Schützgraben* and *Gang zur Ruhestellung*) though with less figurative language. In *Morgen (Morning)* the natural beauty of morning is placed in juxtaposition with the ugliness of war:

> Nebelfetzen
> Trauerfahnen
> Über Schützgraben.
> Menschenleiber
> Verstümmelte Menschenleiber . . .
> Sonne steigt empor (16).

Finite verbs are kept to a minimum (six in a poem of thirty-nine words) and the stark objectivity is achieved by what is almost a catalogue of factual observations, without comment, except that implied by the montage of natural objects and the facts of war.

Gang zum Schützgraben (Walk to the Trench) is even starker in its technique. First come two triplets, the second modelled on the first but more shocking in its content:

> Durch Granattrichter,
> Schmutzige Pfützen,

Stapfen sie.
Über Soldaten
Frierend im Erdloch,
Stolpern sie (17).

In the second half only one phrase (mit Totenfingern) is figurative, and it is this which links the second half with the first (Soldaten/Frierend im Erdloch):

Ratten huschen pfeifend übern Weg,
Sturmregen klopft mit Totenfingern
An faulende Türen.
Leuchtraketen
Pestlaternen . . .
Zum Graben zum Graben (18).

Gang zur Ruhestellung is similarly written, save that inner thought and dialogue are introduced, though with strict economy and deadly irony:

Einer träumt am Massengrab
"Solchen Haufen Weihnachtskuchen
Wünscht ich mir als Kind,
So viel" . . .
Vierzehn Kumpel zerbrach eine Mine.
Wann wars doch?
Gestern (19).

Except in parts of *Das Schwalbenbuch,* arguably his greatest work, Toller never wrote lyric poetry quite like this again, so disciplined, so unrhetorical, so self-effacing (20).

The 1916 poems, written during his traumatic "Bois-des-Prêtres" experiences — the experiences underlying the "Barbed Wire Entanglement" scene of *Die Wandlung* — show Toller having greater difficulty in retaining the poetic stance of stark objectivity in the face of ever increasing horrors. More and more he is forced into rhetorical outbursts:

O Frauen Frankreichs,
Frauen Deutschlands,
Säht Ihr Eure Männer! (21).

or more subjective straining of language in seeking to say the unsayable;

Stellungskrieg

Alltag hämmert,
Würgt Dich
Das Müdsein ins Blut dringt.
Lichter dunsten fahl.
Trotz krepiert.
Letzten Kampf ersehnst Du (22).

In *Alp (Nightmare)* he expresses himself entirely through dream-imagery, and even *Konzert (Concert),* written when on leave, transforms the concert-hall into a fluid dream-environment in which language, too, breaks its normal bounds:

In fruchtbeschwerten Augen kreist Gebären,
Geschicke brodeln hüllenlos im Raum . . . (23).

If we now turn from these wonderful and fearful front-line poems to those written in 1917 and 1918 (the years of the composition of *Die Wandlung*) we soon become aware of the changes in style and content that occur when the almost intolerable pressure of life at the Front is removed. One change is a move away from objective reality to a reliance on subjective, dreamlike imagery:

Krieg verjährte zum Gespenst,
Das knochern seine Finger
Um die gekreisten Völker krallte (24).

Another is that Toller tends to address poems to groups of persons, so that the poems become speeches or appeals, rhetorical rather than poetic. Thus one is addressed *An die Dichter (To the Poets),* another *Den Müttern (To the Mothers),* and both are rhetorical calls to action. True, the unpublished *Nacht im Priesterwald* (Munich 21.4.1917) recovers something of the objective personification used so effectively in the 1915 poems:

Der Vollmond fließt azurne Ströme
Am Bäume, die zerfetzt zerschossen,
Wie Krüppel stumm in sich verkriechen,
Von Schreckmorasten zäh umgossen. (25)

But the result is artifice, not art, especially as Toller, away from the pressures of the front line, pours the vivid imagery (reminiscent of Dante's Suicidal Wood: *Inferno XIII*) into rigid traditional verse-form.

On the other hand it must be said that two poems of 1918, written *in prison and about prison* (*not* the Front), recover much of the simplicity and immediacy of the 1915 front-line poems, as the poet-prisoner hears heavy feet above his cell or watches through the bars the children playing.

The verse scenes and passages in *Die Wandlung* are related in a variety of ways to German poetry of the First World War and to Toller's war poems in particular.

In the Ur-Wandlung (Stations 1 to 4) the use of verse was precisely related to the total pattern. It was used to heighten the opening and the close (the *Vorspiel* and the closing speeches of Sc. 7) and for the rear-stage 'dream' scenes. This created a symmetrical whole (26).

The verse of the *Vorspiel* sounds simply like staccato prose broken into line-units, and is appropriate to the two speakers. The rhythm of the speeches of *Kriegstod* is, appropriately, more marked than that of *Friedenstod*. Compare, for example the rhythm of:

> *Kriegstod:*
> In Kompagnien liegen sie begraben, /
> Am Flügel sind die untern Chargen. /
> Ganz wie im Leben schlichte Nummern, /
> Unsere tapfren Helden. /

with that of:

> *Friedenstod:*
> Ich denk' mit Wehmut und voll Schauder/
> Wenn ich die gleichen Dingen unter-
> nehmen wollte/ Mit meinen Fraun und
> Kindern-/ (27).

The verse is, so to speak, simply strongly rhythmic prose. Nor is the use of language in the scene heightened or intensified in any way that would justify the adjective 'poetic'. It is, on the other hand, fiercely satirical, and keen rhythm always sharpens the cutting edge of satire. The *Vorspiel* is therefore related to satirical war poetry, of which quite a body existed in German, though less than if Heine (the obvious model) had not been thought un-German. Not indeed that the *Vorspiel* has Heine-like qualities, and its satiric mode is remote from that of *Marschlied,* Toller's own parodistic front-line poem, which, as we have seen, (v.n. 20), has affinities with Heine, especially in the way it uses short-lined quatrains.

Very different again are the style and quality of the first verse scene in the body of the play (*Scene 2: Transportzüge*). We have already studied the rhythm of this scene and its close derivation from Toller's personal experiences. We must now relate it to the poems of 1917. It is unlike those published in *Vormorgen*: two of these are appeals (*An die Dichter, Den Müttern*), while the third (*Menschen*) is a generalised image of the third year of war, avoiding particularities. But in the unpublished *Nacht im Priesterwald* Toller writes of particularities in highly figurative language and with strict adherence to a firm verse form.

In this scene also, the poet keeps close to particularities:

> der Zug rattert (the train rattles)
> knirschende Stampfen (crunching, pounding)
> Wir irren durch endlose Räume (We wander through endless spaces) (28).

and although the predominantly four-stress lines are free, the scene itself is tightly shaped: each of the seven speakers has a speech of three to five lines, then in the same order each has a brief speech of one or two lines. The first series of speeches follows this sequence:

> The endless journey,
> desire to return to the womb,
> the wish not even ever to have been conceived,
> the speakers are already dead and the flesh is already corrupting,
> though they are only frightened children,
> no longer able to pray,
> their mothers' gentle words reduced to broken gabbling.

The passage anticipates T. S. Eliot's,

> Birth, and copulation, and death.
> That's all the facts when you come to brass tacks:
> Birth, and copulation, and death (29).

And birth and copulation and death are themselves in Toller's scene degraded and confused through war.

The second series of speeches re-iterates the same themes with even greater intensity. Here is the whole passage:

> *Erster Soldat:*
> Ewig fahren wir.
> *Zweiter Soldat:*
> Ewig stampft die Maschine.
> *Dritter Soldat:*
> Ewig gatten sich Menschen.
> Aus gieriger Lust wächst ewig Fluch.
> *Vierter Soldat:*
> Ewig gebiert Urschoß Gestirne.
> Ewig zerstört sich der göttliche Schoß.
> *Fünfter Soldat:*
> Ewig verwesen wir.
> *Sechster Soldat:*
> Ewig Kinder vom Vater geängstigt.
> *Siebenter Soldat:*
> Von Müttern geopfert.
> Frierender Not.
> *Alle:*
> Ewig fahren wir
> Ewig . . .
>
> *Die Bühne schließt sich* (30).

Regarded in this way the scene is theatrically closely related to the stylistically very different 1917 poem *Den Müttern*, in which Toller brings into juxtaposition on the one hand child-bearing and birth, and on the other death and mutual destruction.

> Mütter,
> Eure Hoffnung, Eure frohe Bürde,
> Liegt in aufgewühlter Erde, ...
>
> Mütter!
> Eure Söhne taten das einander (31).

But the scene is far better realised than the poem and embraces within its brief and simple structure, and within the Soldiers' experience in the transport train, a range of material from casual sex (or perhaps rape) in the forest to the universal process of creation and self-destruction. The cycle of life and death in individual human beings is seen as part of the universal cycle of creation and destruction. The universal vision is similar to Wordsworth's sense of eternal decay and renewal in alpine forests:

The immeasurable height
Of woods decaying, never to be decayed, (32)

but whereas Wordsworth's emphasis is on positive renewal and life, Toller's is on perpetual decay and death — the negative aspect. The poem *Den Müttern,* however, does move, in fewer than twenty lines, from the mutual destruction of the mothers' sons to the hope that out of the women's suffering — which they must accept, not evade — action and humanity may be born:

S c h m e r z   g e b ä r e   T a t !

Euer Leid, Millionen Mutter,
Dien als Saat durchpflügter Erde,
Lasse keimen
Menschlichkeit (33).

This is dangerously near Rilke's mystique of *Schmerz.* In his own newly-found pacifistic way Toller is hoping that through the pain and suffering good will come, and that this is the 'war to end war'. In his later work this guarded optimism was gradually eroded until his death by suicide on the eve of World War II.

In the scene *Zwischen den Drahtverhauen (Between the Barbed-wire Entanglements)* Toller puts into visual, theatrical form the 'dancing bones' image of his 1916 poem *Alp (Nightmare)*:

Um die Stange tanzen drei Kinderknochen

and as in that poem, sexual violence is made the focal image of war violence:

Aus dem Leib einer jungen Mutter gebrochen (34).

But now the bones are initially the bodies that Toller himself had seen rotting in No-Man's-Land. With such a powerful visual image (added to which is the sound-effect of the rhythmic clattering of bones) the language is rightly clear and straightforward, easy to grasp amid the noise and visual effects. The verse rhythm naturally corresponds with the jazzy *Niggertanz* of the skeletons:

Nun sind wir nicht mehr Freund und Feind.
Nun sind wir nicht mehr weiß und schwarz, Nun sind wir

alle gleich.
Die bunten Fetzen fraßen Würmer
Nun sind wir alle gleich.
Mein Herr . . . Wir wollen tanzen (35).

As in the *Transportzüge* scene, Toller here creates poetry, related to his own front-line and post-front-line poems, but truly theatrical in nature and demanding stage realisation for its full impact to be conveyed.

In Scene 6, *Die Krüppel,* the speeches of the Professor are written in the rather loose rhetorical verse used in the *Vorspiel,* and for similarly satirical effect. The cripples themselves, with their artificial limbs, use short lines in staccato rhythms corresponding with their jerky mechanical movements:

Blinder:
Der Tag ist grausam. Sonne sticht.
Ich fühle sie als Schwefelmeer.
Das mich mit Dämpfen ätzend beißt (36).

Their language, too, is harsh and direct, recalling the stark simplicities of the front-line lyrics:

Ich weiß nicht, bin ich Mensch noch
Oder lebende Latrine.
Gelähmt ist mein Gedärm . . .
Ich steck im eignen Kot –
Verpeste, mir und euch zum Ekel (37).

A third kind of language and rhythm is found in this scene in the speech of the Padre after he has broken the crucifix. He speaks in longer lines and more hesitant, broken rhythms expressive of his character and situation: In this speech Toller is writing purely dramatic poetry. There are no 'Military Hospital' lyrics by Toller with which the scene might be compared, but the language of the cripples arises from his direct experience of encountering such cases, and those speeches have the same objective immediacy as the 1915 front-line lyrics. (The scene ends in the satirical style in which it opened).

Thus the three scenes which made the greatest impression on critics and audience of the first production are in fact those in which Toller revealed his greatest skill and strength as a dramatic *poet* (38).

The verse passages of the latter (1918) part of the play are in general less finely crafted than those in the first part, — as indeed is the latter part as a whole. The convention that rear-stage ('dream') scenes should be in verse is retained, but much of the verse is slack and often verges on prose — and on the prosaic. The language is less condensed and less distinguished. There is, of course, no close connection between these scenes and the war-poetry: their material is not the same. However, in Scene 9, the *Prison/Factory*, where once more Toller is drawing on intense *present* personal experience (for the scenes were conceived, even if not actually written down, in the military prison) that his power as a poet, comparable with his power in the 1915 poems, again emerges.

> Die Zellenwände bergen Grauen –
> Wohin ich blickte — uferlose Sümpfe
> Nur graue Sümpfe — immer graue Sümpfe,
> In langen Dämmerstunden
> Krochen Maden aus den Eisengittern.
> Ich wehrte mich — doch dann — was konnt ich tun . . .
> An meinem Leibe zerrten graue Maden (39).

This passage has the same ring of intense authenticity as the two short prison poems written about the same time. The cell walls and iron grills have the same ineluctable reality as the *Nägelbeschlagne Schritte (footsteps of nailed boots)* of *Über meiner Zelle*; and the *Eisengitter (iron grills)* are felt to be identical with those of *Deutschland*, of which he writes:

> Durch das Gitter meiner Zelle
> Seh ich Kinder spielen (40).

Finally, the Prison / Factory identification, derived from Landauer and his 'Barracks', which forms the foundation of this scene, is hinted at in the third of the prison poems, *Ich habe euch umarmt*. As this is not patently a prison poem, Toller notes in the Table of Contents: *Militärgefangnis 1918 (Military Prison 1918)*. The first impression therefore is that the people the poet has embraced (umarmt) are prisoners; but in fact when he addresses them in the fifth line it is as

> Ihr Tausende, fabrikgemartert, Arbeitssielen (41).

The mind of the poet, writing in prison, turns directly to the workers 'imprisoned' in factories. This poem seems to be either the germ of the Prison / Factory scene or a spin-off from it.

PROSE AND VERSE IN *DIE WANDLUNG*
STATIONS I — IV

STATION & SCENE	PROSE	VERSE	FORE-STAGE	REAR-STAGE	WHOLE STAGE
VORSPIEL Totenkaserne		X			X
STATION I SCENE I Zimmer	X		X		
STATION I SCENE II Transportzüge		X		X	
STATION II SCENE III Wüste	X		X		
STATION II SCENE IV Drahtverhauen		X		X	
STATION III SCENE V Im Lazarett	X		X		
STATION III SCENE VI Die Krüppel		X		X	
STATION IV SCENE VII Atelier	X	X Last four speeches			X

PROSE AND VERSE IN *DIE WANDLUNG*
STATIONS V & VI

STATION & SCENE	PROSE	VERSE	FORE-STAGE	REAR-STAGE	WHOLE STAGE
STATION V SCENE VIII Schlafbursche		X		X	
STATION V SCENE IX Tod und Auferstehung		X		X	
STATION V SCENE X Wanderer		X		X	
STATION V SCENE XI Volksversammlung	X	X (3 short Choruses & 1 speech of Friedrich)	X		
STATION VI SCENE XII Bergsteiger		X		X	
STATION VI SCENE XIII Platz vor der Kirche	X	X A few lines of Chorus-lines within Friedrich's last speech; last 7 lines of play	X		

CHORAL WORKS AND *MASSE MENSCH*

Of Toller's front-line poems those written under the immediate stress of trench warfare expressed an intense subjectivity through the medium of stark objectivity. When the pressure of immediacy relaxed the poems began to acquire the character of rhetoric. We may thus distinguish in the poems between a private and a public voice.

Toller's first published volume of poetry, which appeared late 1920 or early 1921, is an example of the latter (1). It was no more than a stapled pamphlet and contained two choral works (*Chorwerke*), with an introductory sonnet, each dedicated to the memory of one of the socialists murdered in the early part of 1919: Karl Liebknecht (15 January), Kurt Eisner (21 February) and Gustav Landauer (2 May).

The introductory sonnet, *Unser Weg, dem Andenken Kurt Eisners (Our Way, in Memory of Kurt Eisner)*, clarifies the character and purpose of the two choral works which follow: they are secular liturgies of a new humanism which replaces the "withered" (*verdorrt*) religion of monastic asceticism. Instead of listening to the monks, whose answer to our appeals was that "redemption is the asceticism of silence, far from the world", we must struggle for the sacrament of the earth.

> "Erlösung ist Askese weltentfernter Stille.". . .
> Wir müssen um das Sakrament der Erde ringen (2).

In harmony with the concept of amateur drama to be discussed presently, these works, like ecclesiastical rituals, exist more for the sake of the participants than for the sake of passive listeners. Like such rituals and liturgies, they are written to confirm and deepen the convictions of participants and listeners rather than, like missionary sermons or speeches at the hustings, to convert the unconvinced. They are in the broadest sense of the word, religious.

> Wir haben andern Weg zu Gott gefunden (3).

But the religion is a life-affirming religion of this world:

> Das Reich des Friedens wollen wir zur Erde tragen (4).

The sonnet, then, informs the sensitive reader of what to expect, while at the same time paying tribute to Toller's debt to Eisner as one of his mentors.

The choral works were *Der Tag des Proletariats (The Day of the Proletariat)* — to the memory of Karl Liebknecht — and *Requiem den erschossenen Brüdern. Ein Chorwerk (Requiem for the shot brothers. A Choral Work)* — to the memory of Gustav Landauer. In the third edition (1925) (5) the texts of both were changed and shortened, the definite article dropped from the title of the former and the title of the latter changed to *Requiem den gemordeten Brüdern (Requiem for the murdered brothers).* This revised version of the *Requiem* had already been printed in *Vormorgen* (1924) (6).

These two choral works represent Toller's original contribution to one of the two most typical forms of amateur, workers' theatre to develop in the years immediately after the war: the *Sprechchor,* or 'speaking choir' (7).

The *Sprechchor* Before Toller

To place the *Sprechchor* in historical perspective it must be seen in relation to working-class amateur theatre in a wider sense. Not only had there always been a close association between the German social-democratic movement and drama (8), but there had also been a close association between amateur and professional theatre of the left (9).

The second decade of the twentieth century saw the development of an "anti-amateur" movement among intellectuals and middle-class youth. Instead of the existing amateur theatre *(Dilettantentheater)* which aped the professional *(Berufstheater),* this movement wanted a new kind of amateur play *(Laienspiel)* which would be clearly distinct from the professional and would find its own proper sphere and outlet. Medieval mysteries were revived and new plays written on the model of such traditional ones. In staging, simplicity was the keynote. Painted backcloths and wings were dispensed with, and forms of staging derived from the Shakespearean theatre, the Hans-Sachs theatre and the Passion Plays, were developed. Performances were often in the open air, in church porches, on flights of steps, in town squares etc. (10, 11). These amateurs used masks, avoided fussy detail and allowed scope for music, dance and mime. Rhythm and body-language were important. 'Type-casting' was avoided, as were words such as *Dilettante* and *Theaterverein* associated with the older kind of amateur theatre. Indeed they developed their own vocabulary, with newly coined words such as,

Spielchor — play-choir,
Spielgemeinschaft — play-community

Laienbühne — amateur stage (or theatre).

They avoided the word *Stück (piece)*, preferring the associations of the word *Spiel (play)*.

This young movement was taken up by churches, *völkisch* and nationalistic youth-movements, and by both the middle- and working-class youth movements. It was a protest against commercialisation and often attracted the same young people as the reaction against the *Kultur der Großstadt (Big-city culture)* which found expression in hiking, camping and in folksong and dance (12).

The working-class youth movement effectively began in 1904 (13), but in 1908 the *Reichsvereingesetz* decreed *inter alia* that youth under eighteen must not be politically active. As a result many young working-class people became involved in activities which were just like those of middle-class youth and which were, at least overtly, non-political. Within the following decade the communist left sought control of the working-class youth movement. In 1916 a left opposition developed within the *Verband der Arbeiterjugendvereine. (The Association of Working-class Youth Clubs)* which led to the formation of the *Kommunistischer Jugendverband Deutschlands (German Association of Communist Youth).*

At about the same time, the *Laienspiel* movement shifted away from its romantic position of trying to get back to a pre-capitalist, pre-bourgeois world, and the traditional artistic elements were fused with new materials.

In November 1918 the formation of the *Spartakusbund* (14) strengthened the communist left and its influence on working-class drama. Meanwhile the non-communist left, represented on the party-political side by the *Sozialdemokratische Partei Deutschlands (SPD)* and on the theatrical side by the *Freie Volksbühne (FVB)*, saw amateur theatre (*Laienspiel*) as a means of making those who participated actively in it more receptive to theatrical experience — which meant, at least primarily, receptive to experience of the professional theatre. An article published in 1924, towards the end of this initial post-war period, in *Die Volksbühne*, the organ of the FVB, under the title *Leitsätze für das neue Laienspiel (Basic Principles for the New Amateur Drama)* makes the following points:

> Amateur drama is a form of expression of the human play-instinct. It must not be combated but improved . . . The point of amateur drama lies in satisfying an inner urge . . . Amateur

> drama and professional theatre are fundamentally different in their nature: the theatre demands an audience; amateur drama can exist even without one; the aim of the theatre is to achieve the presentation of a work of art; the aim of the amateur drama group is to give expression to its own life (15).

Thus workers' theatre developed from two sides: the workers' organisations on the one hand, and the theatre-experiments of left-wing intellectuals on the other. The two most typical developments between 1918 and 1924 were the *Massenspiel* and the *Sprechchor*. Up to 1924 at least, these were considered as 'typical proletarian art-forms', as the dawn of a new 'community culture' and as an immediate expression of 'revolutionary mass feeling' (16). Unlike the *Massenspiele*, which were limited to a series in Leipzig from 1920 to 1924 (17), the *Sprechchöre* spread and enriched the repertoire of the German workers' theatre with new formal elements.

The *Sprechchöre* (the word can be applied both to the Speaking Choirs and to the works they performed) grew from the lack of suitable plays, or kindred material, for performance on "special occasions" such as May Day Festivals, revolutionary celebrations and other events such as those honouring the deaths of Karl Liebknecht and Rosa Luxemburg. The usual materials available were musical — songs, amateur orchestras and choral societies — together with speeches and recitations. Youth groups contributed folk-song and dance and the ever popular *Living Pictures*. From simple solo recitation, performers went on to reciting poems chorally, with great success. Soon they took to modifying the structure of actual poems and dividing them into passages for single voices and passages for choral speech. Finally, works were purpose-written for this type of performance, and thus the *Sprechchor* emancipated itself into a literary form in its own right.

Toller's *Chorwerke*

Der Tag des Proletariats and the *Requiem* were among the first *Chorwerke* to be specially written for *Sprechchor* use (18). Together they form a diptych of the 'optimistic' and 'pessimistic' aspects of revolution, but both share, and share with other early examples of the *genre*, a style which has been, with hostile intention, described as *pathetisch-oratorisch (histrionically-rhetorical)* (19). Their appeal is frankly and unashamedly emotional.

Der Tag des Proletariats begins with music and the muffled sound of the Full Chorus, swelling, but as if from the distance, in heavily-weighted four-stress lines, with some alliteration and some allusion to the four-stress alliterative line common to much old Germanic and Anglo-Saxon poetry:

> Wir seit Jahrhundert geknechteter Leib,
> Enterbte, Bedrückte, Mann und Weib
> Abschwören Entsagung, abschwören Verzicht,
> Wollen wirken das Werk im friedlichen Licht (20).

Single lines, given to *Voice from the Distance, Men's Choir, Women's Choir, Youth Choir, Farm-workers' Choir,* lead through to *Choruses from the Depths and from the Heights* and the *Voice from the Distance* in weighty quatrains of two-stress lines, swelling through a further eight short exclamatory lines to a climax in which the music of the *Internationale* accompanies the speaking of its opening four lines by a *Distant Voice, calling softly*. The Full Choir (powerfully) responds to the summons:

> Wir sind bereit!
> Gerechtigkeit!
> Alle für Alle!
> Alle für Alle! (21).

An organ joins in, and a little later a single violin accompanies the *Distant Voice,* speaking "visionarily":

> Ihr Mütter werdet nimmer in dumpfen Kammern
> Kinder gebären, schicksalsverflucht,
> Die Hungerhände hart umklammern,
> Von frühen Toden heimgesucht (22).

Factory workers and peasants speak in harmonious antiphony, a choric expression of Landauer's political and economic views. A joyful, triumphant climax seems to be reached, when, music breaks in and a soft and stately *Chorus from the Depths* reminds of the murdered brothers, wrapped in peace, whose legacy is fulfilled. Once more the cry of "Rejoice!" breaks out as the true climax of the work is reached:

> Masse wird Gemeinschaft (23).

It is Toller's own message, echoing Sonja's words to the Nameless in the final scene of *Masse Mensch*:

Gemeinschaft in Masse befreien (24).

After this the completion of the *Internationale* is mere rounding-off, an obvious rhetorical gesture and not, as in Scene V of *Masse Mensch,* a truly dramatic effect.

Heady stuff though it is, *Der Tag des Proletariats* is (despite the passing reference to the legacy of the martyrs) too shallowly optimistic to rank with Toller's best work, as he perhaps realised when he did not include it with the *Requiem* in *Vormorgen;* but taken *with* the *Requiem* it has its place as an introduction to that work's deeper notes and subtler use of language and rhythm. Liebknecht was for Toller a great public figure, but Landauer was a personal friend and mentor. The private, lyric voice of Toller therefore adds the richness of another dimension to the public voice of this choral work in his memory. No music is used in this and Toller relies solely on his gift of language. The work begins and ends with an identical Full Chorus:

Senkt die roten Fahnen!
Fahnen der Freiheit!
Fahnen der Liebe!
Fahnen des Anbruchs!
Senkt sie zur Erde,
Dem blutigen Schoße
Der allumfassenden Mutter! (25).

There are no groups of *Workers* or *Peasants,* only the voices of human beings *qua* human beings: men, women and children. Here is how Toller gives a child's voice appropriate form early in the work:

Traurig war von Wünschen unerfüllten,
Frühling uns und ohne Sonnenstern,
Märchenbuch und Spielzeug lag im Laden fern,
Keine Mütter, die den Hunger stillten (26).

Resignation rather than call to action is the key in which this *Chorwerk* is written, and the contrast between the two is typical of the two poles of Toller's *oeuvre* (27).

After the opening chorus a series of trochaic quatrains, rhymed *a b b a,* leads to a moment of optimism:

Morgen kommt! . . .
Tag wird! . . .

Wir grüßen die rosigen Hügel
Befreiten Tags (28).

But immediately a male voice breaks in: sentries must be placed, victory is not yet won, armoured vehicles are rolling towards them with poison gas and flame-throwers. From this point the curve is downward and the defeats of Munich are recalled: prisoners with raised hands, prisoners shot against the wall. This leads to the murder of Landauer (not by name) given by a single, distant male voice:

Hört Ihr des Bruders, des Propheten Stimme?
Von rohen Stößen wund ist sein gequälter Leib,
Sie schlagen ihn, da "Brüder!" er sie nennt,
Gemartert, angenagelt an die Erde!
Hört Ihr des Bruders, des Propheten Stimme,
Ein Stammeln ists, ein wehes Stammeln:
"Erschlagt mich doch! O, daß Ihr Menschen seid!" (29).

"Sie haben ihn getötet. " (They have killed him), cries the distant male chorus, and the Full Choir repeats the opening chorus. From here, mourning of women and youth leads to,

Requiescant in pace! (30).

from the chorus of women, and a final repeat of the opening chorus.

The juxtaposition of *Requiescant in pace* with the chorus *Lower the Red Flags* exemplifies with unusual clarity that *quasi* religious character of Toller's political beliefs which prompted Bröger to ask, "Geht sein Weg nach Damaskus über Moskau?" (31). The question might be better posed in reverse: Toller does not approach religion through socialism; he approaches socialism through a religious sensibility which is none the less deep-rooted for being heterodox and humanistic. From his Jewish roots Toller developed towards a kind of Humanist Christianity. Else Lasker-Schüler refers to Toller as,

Der Jude, der Christ ist
Und darum wieder gekreuzigt ward (32).

In prison Luther's version of the Bible was for weeks his only friend (33). He admired "the power and beauty of the Old Testament, but its ethos [was] alien to [him]", while the New Testament he considered "(with Buddha, with Lao Tse, with the Upanishads) one of the deep springs of mankind" (34) and its intensive study during his imprisonment became for him "a deeply stirring experience" (35).

Erlebnis (experience) rather than *Glaubensbekenntnis* (creed) is the heart of Toller's religiousness. This religious experience (*Erlebnis der Religiosität*) (36) found expression in Toller's Landaueresque anarcho-socialism, and throughout his writing career he was aware of the inseparability of his religious experience and his socialism. In a letter of October 1919 with reference to *Die Wandlung* (37) he says that a political poet must always be in some way a religious poet, while his very last play, *Pastor Hall,* is about a man who united in himseif a Christian and a Socialist spirit. In that play the socialist prisoner Peter Hofer says:

> Sie sind ein Rebell, Herr Pastor, Sie wissen es nur nicht.

To which Hall replies:

> Vielleicht sind Sie ein verirrter Christ und wissen es auch nicht (38).

MASSE MENSCH

The verse forms of the *Chorwerke,* often stanzaic, often rhymed, deliberately and in the best sense artificial, are not used in *Masse Mensch.* The four "realistic" scenes (I, III, V & VII) are written in irregularly stressed lines of varying length, but hovering around four stresses to a line, with some alliteration, and thus related, if only distantly, to the four-stress line of Old English and Germanic poetry and parallel with other twentieth century uses of stressed verse (e. g. by T. S. Eliot in his plays) to escape the tyranny of the pentameter.

The three "dream" scenes (II, IV & VI) which, we have argued correspond formally with the Chorus of Greek tragedy, contain practically no choral speaking. Their versification is distinguished from that of the "realistic" scenes in that the stressed lines are shorter, most having two stresses only. The effects produced by these shorter lines are remoter from everyday speech than those of the "realistic" scenes: staccato and jazzy in Scene II (Stock Exchange) with its Foxtrot finale; dreamy and musical in Scene IV, where rhyme, singing and dance are also employed; and nightmarish in Scene VI. Repetitions and near repetitions (39) recall the techniques of the *Chorwerke,* though actual choral speaking is not used in these formally 'choric' scenes.

Choral speaking as such occurs only in Scene III where, as already noticed, the *Chorus of the Masses* may well have originally been intended as Sonja's antagonist until replaced, more effectively, by The Nameless. The *Massed Chorus* is first heard "as if from the distance" (*wie aus der Ferne*) (40) at the opening of the scene, precisely as the *Full Chorus* is heard at the opening of *Der Tag des Proletariats*. The language has qualities not heard either in Scene I or Scene II. The rhythm is more heavily stressed, the alliteration more fully employed and the expression more strongly figurative:

Wir ewig eingekeilt
In Schluchten steiler Häuser.
Wir preisgegeben
Der Mechanik höhnischer Systeme.
Wir antlitzlos in Nacht der Tränen.
Wir ewig losgelöst von Müttern,
Aus Tiefen der Fabriken rufen wir:
Wann werden Liebe wir leben?
Wann werden Werk wir wirken?
Wann wird Erlösung uns? (41)

The language of this passage merits close study:

We eternally hemmed in

Not simply immer (always),
but ewig (eternally),
and literally wedged in (Der Keil=wedge)
One thinks of Caliban or Milo.

In ravines of steep houses

A Nature-image for the urban scene.

We abandoned to the mercy
Of the mechanism of mocking systems

Preisgegeben is a powerful word, a
loan-translation from French *donner en prise*,
literally, 'given up as spoils of war'.
And then the paradox: systems both
mechanical and mocking.

We faceless in a night of tears

The transfer of the tears from the
(non-existent) face to the night shows
Toller at ease with the figures of

classical rhetoric: here a kind of
hypallage.

We, eternally removed from our mothers

The four-fold repetition of 'we' (*wir*)
reinforces the subject, leading to
the inversion:

Out of the depths of the factories we call:

so that *wir* also ends the pattern.
The 'depths of the factories':
cf:'ravines of steep houses'.
After the four-fold introduction comes
the three-fold cry:

When will we live love?
When will we perform the deed?

Literally: *work the work.*

When will redemption [come] to us?

All the weight of rhythm and alliteration underlines the urgency of the words.

Close verbal parallels with the *Chorwerke* are in evidence:

Nacht der Tränen . . . . der Schweren Nacht
Aus Tiefen der Fabriken rufen wir . . . . Wir aus Fabriken
Wann werden Werk wir wirken? . . . . . Wollen wirken das Werk
losgelöst von Müttern . . . . Keine Mutter, die den Hunger (42).

The denser and more figurative style of the chorus is picked up by Sonja:

Einst Blinde noch und angefallen
Von Marterkolben saugender Maschinen,
Verzweifelt schrie ich jenen Ruf (43).

Throughout the rest of the play, in the 'realistic' scenes Sonja's language moves, in rhythm and linguistic style, between the 'poetic-choral' on the one hand and the conversational-rhetorical on the other. The speech just quoted can also accommodate, for example:

Denn seht: Wir leben zwanzigstes Jahrhundert.
Erkenntnis ist:

Fabrik ist nicht mehr zu zerstören (44).

The Nameless, when he emerges from the Chorus, adopts a dry, hard undecorated manner of speech in which short emphatic lines, devoid of figures of speech, are the norm:

Ein Ruf der Massen aller Länder:
Den Arbeitern gehören die Fabriken!
Den Arbeitern die Macht!
Alle für Alle!
Ich rufe mehr als Streik!
Ich rufe: Krieg!
Ich rufe: Revolution!
Der Feind dort oben hört
Auf schöne Reden nicht.
Macht gegen Macht!
Gewalt . . . Gewalt! (45)

It is a style shortly to be adopted by Communist *Sprechchor* writers consciously opposed to Toller and his *Sprechchöre*. Toller anticipates the style of his politico-artistic opponents!

Thus *Masse Mensch* uses five distinct styles, each with its own characteristic rhythms and language-patterns:

1. The conversational (e. g. Scene I)
2. The choral (Scene III)
3. The choral-rhetorical (e. g. Sonja's public speeches)
4. The 'Hard' rhetorical (speeches of the Nameless)
5. The Dream:
    a) Jazz-time (Scene II)
    b) Dreamy-musical (Scene IV)
    c) Nightmare (Scene VI)
       (with echoes of (a) & (b))

In this Toller is seen to be a consciously experimental artist in verse and language, devising styles, vocabularies and rhythms appropriate to the varying demands of the play.

The *Sprechchor* After Toller

The subsequent history of the *Sprechchor*, both as a branch of working-class amateur drama and as a literary form, is characterised by the conflicts between Communists and Social-Democrats which, in the broader political field tragically contributed so much to the ease with which the Nazis rose to power.

The emotional style of *Sprechchor* represented by Toller did not please the Communists and in 1922 the *Central Sprechchor of the KPD* was founded (46). Later it united with the *Proletarian Travelling Theatre* to form a sixty-strong chorus. In 1923 its leadership was taken over by Gustav von Wangenheim, who wrote and produced for it in that year his *Chor der Arbeit (Chorus of Work)*. This was written in conscious reaction against what he and his fellow Communists regarded as the *hohle Pathetik (empty histrionics)* of Toller and others of the non-Communist left.

> Gustav von Wangenheim introduced some formal innovations into the *Chor der Arbeit*. He repressed recitation in favour of dialogue and scenic insertions. In place of empty histrionics he put popular, partly even satirical verses with topical political references.
> In this way Wangenheim in *Chor der Arbeit* broke through the ideological and artistic boundaries of the *Sprechchor* as in circulation at that time. He made it into an effective instrument of agitation and propaganda (47).

That is one way of describing what von Wangenheim did. He stripped the language of his *Sprechchor* of all linguistic resonance and substituted an austere, combative style which purported to convey an ideological debate but in fact consisted of verbal confrontations which lacked substantive argument. The work opens with the Communists:

> Wir sind die Hetzer
> Wir sind die Ketzer
> Wir bringen Klarheit
> Paßt auf, Proleten!
> Wir sagen Wahrheit
> Wir Kommunisten (48).

To this the Social-Democrats reply:

> Wir sind die Christen
> Die Republikaner
> Wir sind die Mahner
> Glaubt der Belehrung:
> Der Bolschewismus
> Ist die Zerstörung . . . . usw (49).

While it is true that von Wangenheim thus set up a kind of choric dialogue, it cannot be maintained that it took the form of an intellectual, dialectic argument. Just as the clipped and austere speeches of the Nameless in *Masse Mensch* were in fact no more intellectual and no less rhetorical in their appeal than the more lyrical and overtly emotional speeches of Sonja, so the unadorned and selfconsciously plain speeches of von Wangenheim's Communists contain no more intellectual substance than the deliberately weak and unconvincing speech of his Social-Democrats.

At the conclusion of the work Stinnes, the industrialist, finds himself in conflict with Youth, now supported by the middle classes and the peasants. The language is baldly colloquial:

Alle Jugendlichen:
Halts Maul!
Die Jugend spricht
Die Jugend glaubt dir länger nicht
Die Jugend (50).

At the end the peasants declare a united front with the proletariat:

Stinnes:
Ich sterbe!
Alle:
Wir Arbeiter und Bauern
Das Volk
Ist Erbe! (51).

The language is rough and prosaic and the metre simple to the point of crudity. In his production, however, von Wangenheim paid careful attention to pitch and rhythm: the Social-Democrats were all bass voices and the Communists all tenor. He used sound effects, especially to reinforce the many passages referring to the noise of machinery: thus *Hammerschlag und Hammerschlag* was accompanied by blows on an anvil. He also employed flags and other visual properties.

Von Wangenheim's attempt to make the *Sprechchor* more dramatic and more agitational was not widely imitated — to the surprise of his admirers:

> The attempt was not much imitated at first. About 1924 the revolutionary worker-actors went over more and more to plays and mixed programmes. The *Sprechchor* was not flexible enough to take up contemporary political events quickly (52).

The Communist Left therefore developed other forms of theatre, the Revue (e. g. *Revue Roter Rummel*), Agitprop, Living Newspaper and the *Lehrstück* — none of which directly concerns us here.

A significant sequel to von Wangenheim's work was Maxim Vallentin's so-called *Kollektivreferat (Collective Report)* — a factual and didactic development of the *Sprechchor*. Vallentin's original *Kollektivreferat* was *Als die Fronten wanken . . . (As the Fronts Waver)*, written for a Liebknecht-Luxemburg Festival in 1926 and updated under the title *Third International* in January 1929 This production by *Das Rote Sprachrohr (The Red Megaphone)* had music by Hanns Eisler. The text is poor stuff. Here is a climactic moment:

Einzelsprecher:
Die dritte Internationale, sie lebe hoch!
Die UdSSR, sie lebe hoch!
Die KPD, sie lebe hoch! (53).

Other groups of the left also adopted this form. In 1931 *Die Roten Blusen*, Berlin (a group inspired by the German tour of the celebrated Moscow *Blue Blouses*) presented a *Kollektivreferat* under the title *Freidenker-Revue (Freethinkers' Revue)*. This was in three parts:

1. The role of the church in capitalism.
2. Agitation for a League of Proletarian Free-thinkers.
3. The socialist growth of the USSR.

Another production of *Das rote Sprachrohr, 'Hallo, Kollege Jungarbeiter'* (1928) was partly choral, partly in prose with oblique strokes [/] to indicate the rhythm. This was a kind of biographical sketch of the life of a worker, beginning in childhood, when he is beaten in school by a teacher who is, of course, a priest. In the second act he is a youth, and in the third act becomes a Communist (54).

Von Wangenheim himself made a further attempt in the *Sprechchor* mode. To commemorate the tenth anniversary of the outbreak of the Great War he wrote and produced an anti-war Mass-Mime (Massenpantomime) with *Sprechchöre*. A number of working-class mass-organisations were supposed to collaborate in the production, for the organisational side of which Arthur Pieck, another prominent Communist, was responsible. But during the dress-rehearsal the performance was forbidden by Karl Severing, the Social-Democratic Prussian Minister of the Interior. As a result of this ban the *Central Sprechchor of the KPD* dissolved itself in the Autumn of 1924 (55).

Von Wangenheim's attempt to change the character of the *Sprechchor* from Oratorio to Agitprop was doomed to failure from the start, for, as the *Basic Principles for the New Amateur Drama* (56) emphasised, this form was, above all, participatory.

Although the *Sprechchor* proved basically inappropriate for the purposes and methods of the Communists the debate as to the validity of the concept did not die down, and the tradition did continue to flourish among the Social-Democrats and especially in the Volksbühne movement, right up to the end of the Weimar Republic, retaining and developing the character given to it primarily by Toller.

Some important examples will illustrate this.

Bruno Schönlank was a prolific writer of poetry, plays and choral works (57). Probably the earliest of the choral works to be performed was *Erlösung (Weihespiel): (Redemption: A Play of Dedication)* (58). This uses two solo voices, one male, one female; two choruses, of the young and of the old; and an organ. As the title and the use of the organ suggest, this is "religious" in tone. It associates revolution with springtime and even with "blessing" (Segen).

In this work Schönlank shows a considerable sense of form in verse, and it contains a number of quite shapely lyrics. Here, for example, is the opening, spoken by a female solo voice:

Du Glanz,
Der aus den Augen dringt,
Du Glanz,
Der mit den Sternen singt
Urferner Welten Rätselsang.
Du Laut,
Der unsrem Mund entquillt,
Du Laut,
Der himmelstürmend schwillt
Mit aller Meere Überschwang.

Du Geist,
Der in uns wirkt und lebt,
Du Geist,
Der hoch und höher strebt
Zu der Vollendung Meisterschaft.
Du Tat,
Die unsre Hände treibt,
Du Tat,
Die jetzt und ewig bleibt,
Erfülle uns mit deiner Kraft (59).

At a climactic moment —

> Rotes Leuchten, fliege auf!
> (Red glow, fly up!) -

the organ breaks in with the *Internationale.*

The end stresses the 'religious' approach to socialism and revolution:

> Wir baun und sind
> Ein Stein der Ewigkeit . . .
> Wir wirken, baun,
> Und unser Tun
> Sei Segen! (60).

Between 1923 and 1927 Schönlank wrote eight more *Sprechchöre* (61). Even after his emigration to Switzerland in 1933 he published in 1935 *Sprechchöre* and Cantatas under the title *Fiebernde Zeit (Feverish Time),* while his latest and unpublished "Choral Play" *(Chorisches spiel) Vom König Dampf zur Atomkraft (From King Steam to Nuclear Power)* was written in 1958. He died in 1965. There is also an undated *Sprechchor*: *Weltfeiertag der Arbeit (World Holiday of Work)* (62). One of his most ambitious choral works was the *Frühlings-Mysterium,* described as a "Dramatic Choral Work in 5 Acts" (63) — (a full description in this note), while the most noteworthy production of a Schönlank *Sprechchor* was that of *Der gespaltene Mensch (The Divided Person)* at the Volksbühne Conference at Magdeburg in 1927. It was performed by the Berlin *Sprech-Bewegungschor (Speech and Movement Chorus)* supported by the Magdeburg Municipal Orchestra before an audience of 4000. The piece had been specially commissioned and was directed by Karl Vogt and Berthe Trümpy. It was an artistic picture of contemporary man, and the overwhelming spontaneous applause showed that indeed a new artistic form of expression for mass-emotion had been found. Sadly, it was also the last major production of the Berlin Volksbühne *Sprechchor* and when, two years later, in 1929, its guiding spirit, Karl Vogt, moved to Munich, it was wound up (64) (65).

Another writer of *Sprechchöre* in the same tradition as Toller was Erich Grisar, born of a working-class family in Dortmund in 1898. His poetic work reveals an ambivalent attitude to modern industry and the big city not unusual among working-class poets: on the one hand he sees the factory as a gigantic monster demanding sacrifice:

Hingeduckt wie ein Tier,
Das sein Opfer belauert,
Liegt die Fabrik
Und tatzt mit Riesenfängen in den Himmel (66).

On the other hand he is excited by engineering achievements as fulfilments of the human imagination:

Ingenieure überbrücken in kühnen Gedanken
Abgründige Täler (67).

Even within the factories, man struggles alone with the thought which brings him the greatness of being godlike:

Hier wächst der Mensch, der auf sich gestellt
In Einsamkeit mit dem Gedanken ringt,
Der ihm die Größe des Gottseins bringt (68).

Elsewhere the Big City is described as *Menschentötend (Deadly to Mankind)* (69), and Grisar longs for a return to Nature:

An deine Brüste werf' ich mich Natur.
Nimm mich zurück.
Ich, frei gewordner Sklave der Fabrik
Bin wieder dein (70).

Grisar published verse and prose from 1923 until his death in 1955, but his three *Sprechchöre* were all written between 1926 and 1930 (71).

The earliest, *Opferung (Sacrifice)*, (1927) (72) is inferior in literary quality to those of Toller and Schönlank, but is out of the same stable and is visually imaginative. In a short Preface (*Vorbemerkung*) Grisar, after referring to the original performance on 4. 9. 1926 in the large trade-fair pavilion at Köln by members of the Youth Association of the Ruhr, goes on to describe how he conceives the staging and production, for the assistance of any groups undertaking it.

The proscenium arch has a strong hold on German theatre, and *Opferung* is designed for a stage with a front curtain. Behind the curtain the stage is divided into a dark forestage and a bright rearstage. The Chorus is similarly divided, into two "dark" choruses and one "bright". The latter is kept much in the background and rarely seen. At the end, all lights are raised so that there is no longer any distinction between bright and dark or between audience and players. Inevitably the piece, which opened with gloomy organ music, ends with the Internationale or something similar.

It seems a pity that such an imaginatively conceived work should rest on a somewhat trite text, of which this is a not unfair sample:

> *Heller Chor (hinter der Bühne):*
> Es kommt ein Tag, da dröhnt ein Schlag! –
> Dann sind die Tore offen,
> und helles Licht die Nacht zerbricht.
>
> (73)

Some plays written within the social-democratic movement used the *Sprechchor* as one element among others. Examples are Grisar's own *Unser ist der Tag (The Day is Ours)*, a symbolic play based on the theme of forced labour (74), Otto Kaufmann's *Revolutionsfeier* or *Totenfeier*, in which six youths round a camp-fire celebrate the dead of the revolution (75), and Fritz Rosenfeld's *Das Herz im Asphalt (The Heart in Asphalt)*, sub-titled *A Play on the Street* (76).

There remain two major *Sprechchor* works important in relation to Toller.

The very title of the one, *Mensch und Maschine,* echoes *Masse Mensch,* and its sub-title, *Ein Schicksalsspiel für Sprech-Chöre in drei Aufzügen (A Play of Fate for Speaking-Choruses in three Acts)* suggests a thematic relationship with Toller. It was the seventh "Workers' *Sprech-Chor*" to be published by the *Arbeiter-Theaterverlag Alfred Jahn (AThVAJ) (Alfred Jahn Publishing House for Workers' Theatre)* and was written by Hans aus Sachsen.

At the beginning the people, in violet light, are crying for bread and work:

> Arbeit! Arbeit!
> Gebt uns Arbeit!
> Schafft uns Arbeit
> für die Hände (77)

The Engineer (yellow light;) says the solution is to build machines:

> Der Maschinen Riesenkräfte
> Zwingen wir in unsern Dienst!
> Herren sind wir dann

nicht Sklaven!
Neue Zeiten dämmern auf! (78).

The first act ends on an optimistic note:

Chor:
Nun ans Werk!
Zum Licht! Zur Freiheit!
Auf!
Laßt bauen uns
Maschinen
Echo:
Maschinen! Maschinen! Maschinen! (79)

Act II begins in a threatening orange light that later turns red to suggest blast furnaces at the rear of the stage. In this act the skilled manual workers (*Handwerker* as distinct from *Arbeiter*) oppose the machines that rob them of employment. *"Not" (Poverty)* is the keyword here with echo-phrases like *Not und Tod (Poverty and Death)*. Alliterative echoes reinforce the *Mensch/Maschine* dichotomy of the title. Phrases from the work's opening recur, especially:

Ewig! Ewig!
Gleicher Kreislauf!
Festgeschloss'ner Schicksalsring! (80).

But this time, instead of the Engineer with his call to build machines, an *Ausrufer (Crier)* calls for *Aufruhr (Revolt)* and machine-wrecking: then silence. The red light goes out.

In the last act the lighting reverts to the violet of the opening and once more the Chorus in its misery is calling for a Saviour (*Retter*).

This is hardly a socialist play in the accepted sense at all, as it does not profess to offer a social solution to problems of unemployment and mechanisation. Instead it recognises an eternal circle of suffering from which there is no way out, and thus impinges on the realm of tragedy. In this respect it is related to *Masse Mensch* and even to *Hinkemann*.

The last author relevant here is Felix Renker. Renker contributed several kinds of dramatic work to the social-democratic cause (81). His Sprechchor *Am Webstuhl der Zeit (On the Loom of Time)* was first performed by the Sprechchor of the Independent Trade Union Youth of the ADGB at Dresden on 14 May 1931. The characters are:

Time
The years 1890 (end of anti-socialist laws)
1914 (patriotic Unity)
1918 (revolution)
The Present
The Future
The Fighter
and World Capital,
while separate choral groups represent the Years, People, the Old, Youth, Beggars, the Unemployed, the Sceptics, the Indifferent and the Capitalists.

The performance was enthusiastically reviewed, and the *Dresdner Neue Nachricht* of 15 May admitted that:

> even someone whom the bias of the work disturbed could not escape from the power of this community play (82).

Most important in relation to Toller and his influence is the Prologue, in which the whole question of the validity of the *Sprechchor* concept is debated. It must be translated almost in its entirety, and it provides its own commentary. It was headed *Was wir wollen (What we want)* and was used at the first performance.

> The poet was found who, out of his shared experience
> in the hard and mighty past and present,
> created the work for us
> which depicts for us objectively and without bias
> the actual conditions.

A voice from the audience asks, "Why a *Sprechchor*?
Are there not plays, theatres and cinemas?"
The Chorus replies:

> But nothing is so powerful as the *Sprechchor*
> and nothing develops the community-sense as it does.
> There are two worlds, which are separated in the theatre and cinema:
> the world of the speakers and the world of the hearers!
> The stage is the barrier which insensibly separates the two.
> But we want the world of the stage, the community stage,
> to fuse firmly with the world of the hearers in inner community.

> Only the *Sprechchor* is an artistic expression of the mass will . . .

Soon a voice calls again from the audience:

> You mean that for you the choric method is not an ancient prototype?
> Is not fluctuating speech such as we get in singing
> with deep, middle and high voices,
> and is not an experiment in the manner of school drill?

The Chorus answers:

> It is none of all that!
> It is the quintessence of a man of experience,
> from whom speaks the expression of the strongest
> force of contemporary experience,
> experience of contemporary honour, strength and unity
> . . . . .

The final section of the Prologue concludes:

> The spirit of community, the will of community
> should blossom throughout the totality of our hearers.
> And out of the fire of our work, of our creation
> you should take kindling sparks for your own hearth.
> That—is—what—we—want! (83).

This prologue, which might have been written as a commentary on *Masse Mensch* a decade earlier, is remarkable as a Credo of the social-democrat writers and performers of *Sprechchöre*. It gives public utterance to a belief in objectivity, in the 'proscenium-busting' power of the *Sprechchor*, its special nature, distinct both from the classical Greek chorus and from part-singing, and in its ability to foster the spirit and will of the community in which it exists.

The continuing vitality of the Tolleresque *Sprechchor* even so late in the Weimar Republic period is indicated by the fact that no fewer than ten other *Sprechchöre* were advertised on the back of the published edition of this one.

WELTLICHE PASSION AND *DIE FEUER-KANTATE*

The only new works in verse by Toller after 1924 were published during his exile in what we have called his public voice. The earlier, *Weltliche Passion (Secular Passion)* (84) is closely related to *Tag des Proletariats* and *Requiem der gemordeten Brüder* both in subject-matter and in language and style. Apart from one speech in prose it seems on this internal evidence to have been written during the same period (1920–21) as the other two *Chorwerke* and *Masse Mensch*. It is improbable that Toller in 1933 or 1934 in exile and increasingly concerned with international questions and the Nazi threat, should have found himself passionately writing a new work almost entirely on the murders of his fellow socialists which had so moved him in 1919 (85).

The rhythms, also of *Weltliche Passion* have the variety and subtlety of Toller's best poetry before 1924. The opening chorus is elegiac:

GROSSER CHOR:

Wenn die schwingenden Hämmer
Ruhn und die kreisenden Sicheln
Wenn der Abend schweigt
Auf den reifenden Aeckern
Und die Fahnen, die roten stürmenden
Fahnen sanft sich entstraffen überm
Steingeklüft der Straßengebirge
Denken wir der gefallenen
Unbekannten Kämpfer der Revolution (86).

The *Chronist's (Narrator's)* lines are in more irregular verse, but nevertheless carefully patterned. The following passage has the character of two similarly constructed stanzas on 'seedtime' and 'harvest':

Zerstampfte die Felder Europas
Der Krieg,
Wo einst der Bauer
Die Scholle gepflügt
Und mit friedlicher Hand
Aussat gestreut und nährendes Korn
Säten die Generale
Bomben
Granaten
Haß.
Und die Ernte reifte,
Und die Ernte ward eingebracht
Und die Scheuern füllten
Zehn Millionen
Krüppel

Verwüstete Städte
Zerschossene Dörfer
Hunger
Verzweiflung
Tod. (87)

By contrast, the nature of money (the price on the heads of the revolutionaries, the bribe, the 'thirty pieces of silver') is described in an angry, rhymed, antiphonal chorus:

Geld ist Brot und ein satter Magen
Geld ist Fleisch und immer Behagen
Geld ist Schlaf in den Tag hinein
Geld ist Zeit und die Zeit ist Dein
Geld ist Macht, das Buckeln der Welt
Geld ist Glück, wer Geld hat, kriegt Geld . . . (88)

Towards the end a verse from the *Internationale,* which might well be sung, is followed by the prose speech already referred to. It has the character of secular liturgy and is given to a *Sprechstimme* (89):

> Wir gedenken der toten Revolutionäre in Europa, in Amerika und Asien, in Afrika und Australien, in allen fünf Erdteilen der Welt, über denen die Fahne der Revolution als ewige Hoffnung der Unterdrückten und Erniedrigten leuchtet, wir gedenken der toten Pioniere in Sowjetrußland, wir gedenken Lenins, wir gedenken Saccos und Vanzettis, gestorben für uns, wir gedenken Eugen Levinés, Gustav Landauers, Matteottis und Erich Mühsams
>
> wir gedenken der zahllosen Matrosen, Soldaten, Bauern, Arbeiter, Schriftsteller, Ingenieure, all der Namenlosen, gefoltert, gerädert, gehängt, erschossen, erschlagen auf den Kampffeldern der Revolution (90).

The reference to Erich Mühsam among the list of dead revolutionaries proves that this speech was written after Mühsam's murder in Oranienburg Concentration Camp in July 1934. Yet without this speech in prose the work, in verse, would flow perfectly naturally from the Internationale to the reprise of the opening chorus, *Wenn die schwingenden Hämmer,* by the Chorus of Women. *Weltliche Passion* would then contain no personal references except to Liebknecht and Luxemburg and would be purely in their memory. The conclusion seems inescapable that Toller added this prose speech to an already extant verse *Chorwerk* in order to give it clearer contemporary relevance. There is no prose in either of the earlier *Chorwerke* nor in *Masse Mensch*. Nowhere else in all his writings does Toller use a *Sprechstimme*, so this is uniquely prescribed as a means of integrating the prose interpolation with the verse.

Toller was deeply moved by his friend Mühsam's death (91) and this could have spurred him to publish *Weltliche Passion* with an additional tribute to him, linking his murder with those of earlier socialist martyrs (92).

Unlike *Weltliche Passion*, *Die Feuer-Kantate* presents no stylistic problems. Published in June 1938, (93) it must have been written in exile after 27 February 1933, the date of the Reichstag fire. This cycle of seven short poems is in fact quite unlike any other of Toller's poems. Its theme has been neatly summarised by Pittock:

> ... *Die Feuer-Kantate* ... shows skill in getting its simple point across effectively by a deliberate exploitation of the antinomies Helios (sun) and hell, latent in the concept, fire. Through their use of the swastika the Nazis identified themselves (falsely of course) with regenerative fire and by burning down the Reichstag tried to associate the Communists with destructive fire. But the poet predicts that the stratagem will rebound on themselves and the Reichstag fire will become a symbol of the fire of regeneration which will destroy them (94).

Apart from the image of the swastika and one personification of Freedom the poems are almost devoid of metaphoric expressions: their points are made as they might have been in prose. The rhythm of the poems also is indistinguishable from that of prose. The division into lines is simply a matter of giving each clause or phrase (and occasionally a single word) a line to itself. The typographical layout might assist a speaker to declaim the prose more effectively, though a good rhetorician would not need such a crutch. Here, for example, is Poem IV *(Beratung: Consultation)* written out as prose:

> Es war ein Streiten und Raufen, welches Haus am rötesten brennen würde in der mondlosen Winternacht. Und sie beschlossen, den Reichstag anzuzunden. Dort schlief die deutsche Freiheit einen schweren traumlosen Schlaf (95).

There is no evidence that this poem-cycle was intended as a *Chorwerke*, though its title suggests that Toller intended it for performance, and indeed it was set to music by Hanns Eisler (96).

Die Feuer-Kantate is the work of a former poet who has turned to prose but here feels the need to present his prose as verse in order to catch the reader's attention and create a form in which the kind of concentration of meaning appropriate for poetry is acceptable. In style it is virtually indistinguishable from some of Toller's more heightened post-exile prose, many passages of which could be similarly printed for reading aloud (97). *Die Feuer-Kantate* thus provides a bridge from the consideration of Toller as poet, to Toller as a prose-writer.

TOLLER'S DRAMATIC PROSE

Of Toller's eleven plays (1) only two, *Masse Mensch* and *Die Rache des verhöhnten Liebhabers*, are written wholly in verse; two, *Die Wandlung* and *Die Maschinenstürmer*, partly in prose and partly in verse (2); the remaining seven plays are all written in prose (3). Any estimate of Toller as dramatist must therefore take fully into account his ability to write prose and to use it in drama.

The very high quality of the best of his non-dramatic prose is unquestionable. In 1949 Herbert Jhering even suggested that his real legacy might lie in his prose writings (4). His stylistic development in prose has been divided by Jacqueline H. Roger into three stages, each with its own characteristics: Early (1917–1924); Middle (1925–1932); Late (1933-1939) (5). Roger bases her findings primarily on twenty-four selected non-dramatic texts divided almost equally between the three periods (6). The first period she describes as 'very intense, subjective, over-stated' (7). In the second phase he developed a kind of revolutionary realism. Toller was careful to distinguish this from *Die neue Sachlichkeit (The New Sobriety)* for which he had some contempt:

> I think that 'The New Sobriety' was a form of modern Biedermeier. The artist of the New Sobriety was not close to people and things, only to photography of them (8).

Even earlier he had written:

> I consider this slogan [die neue Sachlichkeit] to be false romanticism behind which hides sick sentimentality (9).

In the third period his prose was

> primarily about fascism, Nazism, the Spanish Civil War, the hardships of exile, and the impending European disaster (10).

In Roger's view the works of this period are the most accomplished:

> Toller's style is sure, balanced and graceful. His themes are formulated with great simplicity and power (11).

For our present purposes Roger's detailed findings on the development of Toller's diction in non-dramatic prose throughout the three periods are most useful.

> At the outset of his career, he took great pleasure in words for their own sake, laying emphasis on the sound as well as on the significance of his phrases. His use of language tended to be poetic and innovative (12).

He constructed new terms such as *Dinghaftigkeit* (13), devised compounds such as *persönlichkeitsbildend* (14) and *Komödianten-Heuchelei* (15), and made up phrases to which he attributed special meanings, such as *Unbedingtheit revolutionären Müssens [Synthese aus seelischem Trieb und Zwang der Vernunft]* (16). He had a penchant for superlatives and ultimate exaggerations such as *bestgehaßt* or *unendlichfaltig* (17), and for extreme and unusual phrases, especially denigrating ones; for example: *literatelendes Otterngezücht* (18).

In this early prose Roger also notes a tendency to over-use the exclamation mark [!] and the three-dot series [. . .] — punctuation typical of Expressionism (19).

The prose of *Die Wandlung* corresponds in general terms with Roger's account of the early non-dramatic prose. It is 'intense':

> Sie zünden drüben Lichter an. Kerzen der Liebe. Mysterien offenbaren sich.
> Lichtmeer der Liebe . . . (20)

It tends to over-statement:

> Ekler Zwitter . . . (21)
> Er hat mein Jugend versperrt (22).
> Lehrtest mich Haß gegen die Fremden. (23)
> Die große Zeit wird uns alle zu Großen gebären etc (24).

Exclamation marks and rows of dots are employed to excess.

As in his early non-dramatic prose Toller obviously takes pleasure in words for their own sake; and if we accept that:

> primarily poetry is an exploration of the possibilities of language (25)

then Toller's prose in *Die Wandlung* is the prose of a poet. Its style is such that when a prose scene moves into verse for a few lines, as happens occasionally, there is no sharp break or hiatus (26). In some passages the language and imagery are consciously poetic:

> Ich möchte eine gütige Fee bitten, daß sie meine groben Fäuste in Schmetterlinge wandelt, daß sie dir deine Traurigkeit nehmen könnten, die wie schwarzer Blütenstaub auf deiner weißen Stirn Schatten dunkelt (27).

Often he lays 'emphasis on the sound as well as the significance of his phrases', and frequently employs alliteration and assonance. For example:

> *E*ure H<u>ä</u>nde b<u>*au*</u>en M<u>*au*</u>ern um *eu*ch <u>*au*</u>f,
> und ihr sagt, jenseits W<u>ä</u>ren die
> Wilden.
>
> (28)
>
> *F*reudig will ich d<u>*ir*</u> *f*olgen. Nur *f*ort *v*on h<u>*ier*</u> . . .
>
> Dort *W*<u>i</u>mmern ungeborner K<u>i</u>nder, dort *W*einen <u>I</u>rrer. (29)

The concern with sound is, however, ubiquitous in the play, and indeed in all Toller's plays, for he is a dramatist writing for performance, for speech.

His interest in language for its own sake leads Toller to innovation and experiment, here as in his other prose. The play contains, even in its prose scenes, many nonce-words and unusual compounds and expressions. For example:

> *Leutedienst*, in antithesis to *Gottesdienst* (GW2 p 19)
> *Nichtalleinsein* (ibid p 20)
> *Wüstenflugsand*: a combination of *Wüstensand* and *Flugsand*. (ibid p 24)
> *in alpkeuchende Städte* (ibid p 28)
> *Lebenserfüllte*: on the model of *Haß/Liebe/Ekelerfüllte* etc. (ibid p 50)
> *Dünkelmauer* (Walls of Arrogance) (ibid p 55)
> *feinknochig und märzzart*: finely boned and tender as the month of March (describing a girl) (ibid p 58)
> *deine wünscheheißen Nächte*: your nights, hot with desire. (ibid)

All these occur in Friedrich's speeches. A few are found elsewhere, less strikingly original than these (30). Language is thus determined in part by characterisation and the most subjectively conceived character, Friedrich, shows most noticeably the characteristics of his creator's personal style. It is particularly interesting to notice that when, at the emotional climax of Station 5 Scene 11, Friedrich has one speech in verse-rhythm, this one speech contains no fewer than five innovations in vocabulary:

> Nun öffnet sich, aus *Weltenschoß* geboren / Das
> hochgewölbte Tor der *Menschheitskathedrale.* /
> . . . / Zum *nachtgeahnten* Schrein . . . . /
> . . . / Zum . . . *fruchtgeweihten* Tanz. / . . .
> . . . / So schaffe Leben *gluterfüllt* vom Geist. (31)

In this first play we thus find Toller writing a prose which is consistent both with his non-dramatic prose works of that period and with the demands of the theatre. It also harmonises with the language of his dramatic verse.

The first period of Toller's prose style, according to Roger, lasted from 1917 to 1924. This is superficially convenient in that Toller was released in July 1924; but before his release Toller had written *Die Maschinenstürmer, Hinkemann* and *Der entfesselte Wotan*. The style of none of these neatly matches Roger's analysis of the early period of prose in the way that *Die Wandlung* does.

Even in the prose of *Die Maschinenstürmer* linguistic virtuosity indulged in for its own sake, has disappeared. In general the vocabulary is concrete. The basic prose style is not rhapsodic. Jimmy enriches it with nature imagery. For example:

> Wißt ihr noch, daß Wälder sind . . . Dunkle, geheimnisvolle Wälder, die in Menschen erwecken verschüttete Quellen . . . Wälder der schwingenden Stille . . Wälder der Andacht . . . Wälder heiteren Tanzes (32).

The Old Reaper contributes a biblical element:

> Mein Leben währt nun achtzig Jahre . . . und es war nicht köstlich, trotz Mühe und Arbeit . . . (33)

This both echoes and deliberately distorts the 90th Psalm:

> Unser Leben währet siebenzig Jahre, und wenn es hoch kommt, so sind es achtzig Jahre, und wenn es köstlich gewesen ist, so ist es Mühe und Arbeit gewesen . . . (34)

Only in the Old Reaper's speeches does Toller retain the frequent use of the three dots [. . .].

According to Roger, Toller in all his prose uses more simple sentences than any other type; his complex sentences frequently have only one subordinate clause, and he uses compound-complex but little. This is borne out in his plays, though in *Die Maschinenstürmer* the short, staccato sentences and phrases lacking a finite verb give way to longer, less heavily stressed sentences. Compare for example:

> Auf Stichwort künstliches Lächeln.
> Tragikomisches Figürchen. Approbierter
> Zuschauer . . . nein . . . Stehaufclown . . .
> Länger schleppe ich nicht diese Zer-
> rissenheit mit mir umher. Was sind mir
> die! *(Die Wandlung)* (35)

and

> Wer waren die Väter? Du, deine Freunde, deine Herren, die Gold haben, sich ein Mädchen zu kaufen. Warum warfen die Mütter ihre Kinder, ihre heiligen, kleinen Kinder ins Wasser? Weil keiner der Väter ihnen hilft, ihre Kinder zu ernähren. Weil eure Kirche sie verfehmt und Schande nennt, was göttlich, unbegreiflich Wunder ist und Ehrfurcht heischt. *(Die Maschinenstürmer)* (36)

In this play Toller retains the characteristics of Expressionist prose only for certain minor characters and special effects.

In *Hinkemann* Toller was already fully competent in the 'new, or revolutionary, realism' which Roger associates with the period 1924–32 (37). This was something other than mere reporting [Reportage], which, wrote Toller, has its own significance:

> Drama, like all art, must be more [sc. than mere reporting], namely intensification, gradation and form. Only in this way does reporting also become artistic truth (38).

Rather than the thinness, as he saw it, of the new objectivity

[*Sachlichkeit*] Toller wanted "collectively valid subjectivity":

> But in spite of the law of rigorous objectification, which forms figures out of their innate necessities, the creative artist realises that he in particular achieves a collectively valid subjectivity. He does not treat all values and ideas as equal. A hierarchy is established in him which separates the higher values from the inferior (39).

He therefore wrote this play in prose, a true prose whose rhythms, while they embrace great variety, do not, like those of *Die Wandlung*, tend towards those of verse (40). The sentence-structures and rhythms are based on character and situation. The short phrases of Grete's opening speech, for example, though punctuated with the three dots [. . .], are colloquial, not 'expressionistic'; Eugen's in the same passage of dialogue arise from the intensity of his emotions in relation to the blinded bird (41). Paul Großhahn's clipped phrases are different again and express his aggressive nature:

> Essig! Wegen Betriebseinschränkung adschö! (42)

The prose of this whole short act is, however, shot through and through with Toller's poetic imagination. Without departing from the realm of dramatic prose, Toller fills the scene with dramatically relevant imagery, primarily, as in *Die Maschinenstürmer*, nature-imagery. This is introduced in terms of theatre by the use of the actual blinded songbird as a *Dingsymbol [concrete symbol]* of Eugen's own emasculation. The blinded goldfinch sets off a train of language and imagery closely related to those of *Das Schwalbenbuch* but always remaining within the dramatic context. Eugen's love for the goldfinch — *ich habe dich ja lieb* — is echoed by Grete's expression of love for him — *Ich . . . ich hab dich lieb*. Yet he must 'Play at being Fate' and kill the bird rather than let it suffer, and Grete's love for Eugen, too, ends in tragedy. The nature-imagery of the bird leads directly to that of the once-loved but now mangy old dog, who must be put down, and to Großhahns comparison of poor folk with cattle (43). The animal imagery spreads beyond these metaphoric expressions. Faces "bare their teeth" [*anblecken*] at Eugen — like animals.

> Im Nacken sitzt ein Grammophon, das
> ist wie ein unheimlich Tier . . . (44)

After Großhahn's entry the imagery quickly moves away from nature to gods and the machine. Großhahn the atheist regards the machine as an instrument through which to express his own godlike powers. Through the machine, following a Landaueresque sub-text, Großhahn moves on to Marxism:

> Er [der Prolet] verkauft seine Arbeitskraft, wie man ein Liter Petroleum verkauft und gehört dem Unternehmer, dem Prinzipal (45).

So when Großhahn refers to *die Liebe* he thinks of it purely as *Vergnügen* to be enjoyed *Bei den Frauensleuten*. This for him is Nature:

> Wie kann schlecht sein, was aus der Natur kommt? . . . sozusagen . . . aus dem Blut (46).

In this way the whole scene is held together in a train of thought and imagery that begins with the blinded goldfinch and Grete's bitter,

> Eugen, soll ich mit unserm Bett den Ofen anschüren? (47)

and ends with Großhahn's crude sexual drive. This train of thought and imagery passes through the three characters, in language both self-consistent and appropriate to each character in the changing situation. It is an excellent example of each character's being formed out of its own innate necessities yet bound together artistically by the 'collectively valid subjectivity' of Toller's imagination and sense of values expressed through his control of language.

Throughout the play each new character speaks an appropriate language, whether the Budenbesitzer, the various workmen in the working-men's bar, or the minor characters such as the Polish Jews: all are objectively conceived. Yet at the same time it is through the language that the *roter Faden* of Toller's subjective intensity runs through to the end, to a resurgence of the nature- and animal-imagery, the blinded bird:

> sinnlose, unendliche Not der blinden Kreatur (48).

Once and once only does the rhythm, reinforced by assonantal half-rhymes, trespass on to the boundaries of verse. It is at the emotional climax of the relationship of Eugen and Grete:

> GRETE:
> Sommer wird sein und Stille im Wald . . .
> Sterne und Gehen Hand in Hand . . .
> *HINKEMANN*:
> Herbst wird sein und Welken im Laub . . .
> Sterne . . . und Haß! . . . und Faust gegen Faust! . . . (49)

Grete cries that she is

> In einem Wald voll wilder Tiere allein! (50)

Nature and God are brought together, negatively, again:

> Was gegen die Natur ist, kann nicht von Gott sein. (51)

Grete and Eugen are both caught like flies in a spider's web:

> Wir sind in einem Netz, Eugen, in einem Netz. Eine Spinne sitzt da und läßt uns nicht los. Sie hat uns eingesponnen...
> Wo ist der Anfang und wo das Ende?
> Wer will das bei einem Spinngewebe sagen? (52)

In language as in other respects *Hinkemann* occupies a central place in Toller's oeuvre. In no other play is his language so consistently prose in form and poetic in its imagery and intensity.

Twice in his career as a prose dramatist Toller turned to satirical comedy: in *Der entfesselte Wotan* and in *Nie wieder Friede*. The former, his last prison play, also represented a new beginning. The Tragedy of *Hinkemann* ended the series of plays that began with the naively optimistic *Wandlung*. *Der entfesselte Wotan*, written while he was also engaged upon his highly subjective lyric masterpiece, *Das Schwalbenbuch*, is the first of the series of plays dealing primarily with objective material and ending with *Pastor Hall*.

The language of *Der entfesselte Wotan* is in itself an experiment. While his poetic imagination worked on *Das Schwalbenbuch* Toller here turned to parody and colloquialism. He parodies not only Wagner and Sternheim, but even himself (53). The style has neither the special intensity of *Hinkemann* nor the balance and grace which Roger finds in his later non-dramatic prose (54). The Sternheim parody leads to an abrupt telegraphese, an exclamatoriness totally unlike the exclamatoriness of Toller's earlier Expressionism. The vocabulary is drawn from sources hitherto alien to Toller's work: barber's gossip, right-wing politics, the vulgarity of the commercial traveller, of money-making:

> Kuppelei, seidene Höschen, man munkelt, Frisur nach Offiziersart, ungelüftete Schlafzimmer, Hurenmenscher, die lustseuchezerfressenen Beine, eine Auswanderer-Aktiengesellschaft, das Judenjoch, Golddividende, Judenzer (55).

Climaxes are rhetorical (56) or ironic (57), but beneath the comic surface the play's serious intention, its warning against the already growing power of the Nazis and their supporters, can also be felt:

> Unser großer Führer, unser hehrer
> Lichtbringer, unser Retter heil!
> Heil! Heil! Heil! . . .
> Keine Partei, kein Parlament, kein
> Programm, kein Kommunismus wird Europa retten! . . . (58)

Freed from prison and free in his own country, Toller wrote his next three plays in good dramatic prose which has stood the test of time. It has completely shed the rhapsodic rhythms and consciously experimental linguistic devices of Expressionism and moves easily among the requirements of a multitude of characters, situations and intentions. In *Hoppla, wir leben!* the language in all its variety never obtrudes, yet as will be seen in the account of post-war productions, carries the real weight of the play and has proved to have enduring quality independent of the complexities of staging.

Feuer aus den Kesseln, an historical play based on documentary sources, naturally drew its vocabulary from the records consulted, and the author's own period in the forces. Once more he showed his versatility in matching language and material in dramatic form.

The last play he wrote before his enforced exile, *Die blinde Göttin*, demanded a further extension of his dramatic prose style, for now he had to write convincing dialogue spoken by ordinary villagers and lower middle-class people in, at first, fairly normal circumstances; court procedings; a very tricky 'flashback' scene which had to be realistically convincing although staged with a life-size 'puppet'; a juryroom scene; scenes in men's and women's prisons; and a conclusion in minor key, which nevertheless had to be the climax of the whole play. In this he was wholly successful and many of Roger's comments on his exile prose are both true and relevant when applied to the style of this play:

> Toller's style is sure, balanced and graceful. His themes are formulated with great simplicity and power. They carry the weight of his own conviction but are based on rational arguments and careful analysis ... They [sc. the works] ... contain that mixture of intellectual and emotional persuasive ness which Toller considered the essential ingredients of artistic work. (59)

Toller had created in this play a strong, flexible but unobtrusive prose style that would have served as a medium for any future plays, had he been able to remain in Germany. Instead, he was forced into exile where, though his non-dramatic writings not only flourished but reached their peak of achievement in *Eine Jugend in Deutschland* and *Briefe aus dem Gefängnis*, his power as a dramatist was seriously weakened, as our study of the two plays of exile, *Nie wieder Friede* and *Pastor Hall*, in a later chapter will show. In particular, he now lacked motivation to develop the possibilities of the German language in the theatre, as he could only hope for productions in translation. *Nie wieder Friede* was Toller's second essay in satirical comedy, but it lacks the basis in fact which gave *Der entfesselte Wotan* its strength; nor is its language derived from a living vernacular. His weakest play dramatically is also his weakest linguistically.

Pastor Hall suffers less in terms of language than *Nie wieder Friede*, because it is based on the realities of Nazi Germany, but even so it does suffer. Not only was the dramatist out of touch with everyday life under the Nazis and unaware — despite accounts he had heard — of the full brutality and horror of the concentration camps, but his characters speak out of their creator's memory of how Germans spoke before 1933. It is not that the German is in any way academically incorrect, but it lacks the idiomatic and psychological edge that would have been there had Toller actually lived in Nazi Germany.

In this final phase of his writing Toller thus not only lost his gift of poetry in verse (60) but also his ability to write dramatic prose of real quality. Thus the pattern of his development as a prose dramatist is not synchronised with the pattern of his development in non-dramatic prose. Writing for the large but scattered body of German-speaking refugees and emigrés, he perfected the latter after 1933, but because he lacked a German-speaking theatre-audience in exile his use of language in drama declined from the high points reached between 1922 and 1932.

The language of drama, because of the essential intensity and concentration of dramatic form, is at its best when, even if in prose, it has the depths, concentration and numinousness of poetry. Toller's best prose plays were thus written when he still possessed his poetic inspiration as well as being in touch with the living German language.

Plate 1. The cage scene from *Masse Mensch*. Photograph by Lisi Jessen of the Volksbühne production.

Plate 2. The cage scene from *Masse Mensch.* Design by Hans Strohbach for the Volksbühne production. Photograph by Lisi Jessen.

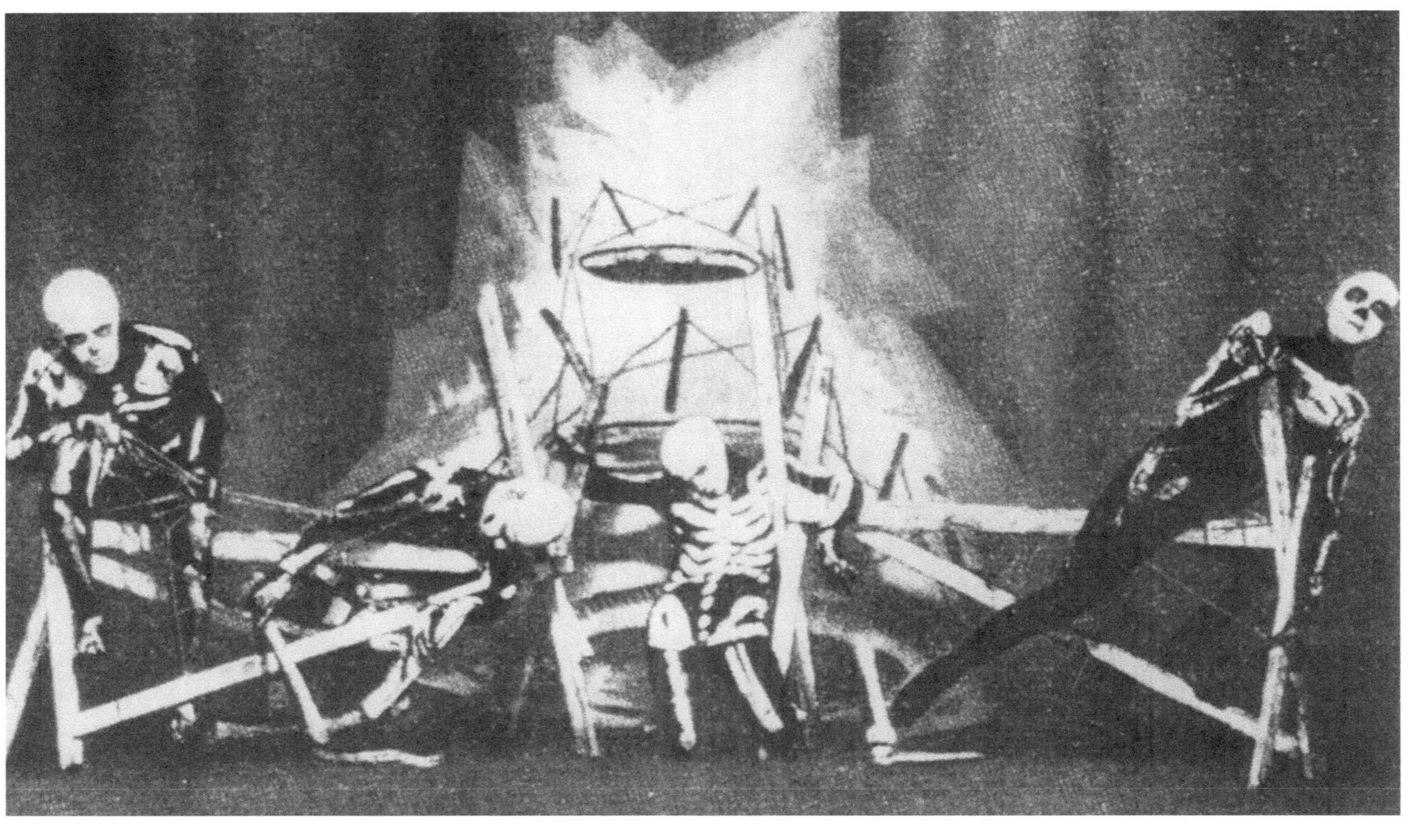

Plate 3. The skeletons scene from Karl-Heinz Martin's production of *Die Wandlung*.

Plate 4. Newspaper publicity sketch by A. Arnstam for Piscator's production of *Hoppla, wir leben!*

Plate 5. Ernst Toller (about 1918).

IV

THE PLAYS
HINKEMANN TO *PASTOR HALL*

HINKEMANN

Of the plays Toller wrote in prison *Hinkemann* is the one whose quality has been most fully appreciated and justly assessed. Even in 1922 in MS, under the title *Eugen Hinkemann,* it was described by Fritz Droop as "one of the most shattering dramas of the last decade', and as possessing "permanent worth" (1). Marxist criticism has remarked, disapprovingly, of course, upon the shift in this play from "historical optimism" to a "politically pessimistic world-view" (2). As early as 1957 Martin Reso saw the play as tragedy in the Aristotelian sense and an expression of opposition to the banal optimism that thinks that social order can solve *all* problems (3).

> The fundamental character of the work is loneliness and resignation. In the sadness of *Hinkemann* is mingled that of the poet; over the lost revolution and futile sacrifices (4).

(But he also warns against the simple identification of Toller and Hinkemann expressed by W.A. Willibrand: "Eugen Hinkemann is Ernst Toller") (5).

However, all criticism since 1968 must take account of Dorothea Klein's authoritative study of the play (6), and the comparatively brief treatment of *Hinkemann* here is to be regarded as supplementary to her work and to the later work of Wolfgang Frühwald, both of which in almost all major points are tacitly endorsed.

Klein shows that Toller was not wholly satisfied with the new dramatic form tried out in *Die Maschinenstürmer* — a dramatic form which, however, she herself did not fully grasp and which the present study has shown to be both original and consistently executed. Toller believed that his next play would "mean a critical decision" for him (7). At that time (May 1921) he thought his 'next play' would be about *Fra Dolcino* and perhaps be called *The Monk's Tragedy* (8). He must have considered this subject for a long time, for as late as 2nd February, 1922, he asks Tessa whether she can find out whether chronicles about the "Dolcino Revolt" exist (9) — yet he had already begun to write *Hinkemann* in 1921.

Klein remarks that two points emerge: 1) that Toller was drawn to historical material, 2) that he aimed to write a tragedy. But she does not pursue the matter further. It is worth while to do so in view of the fact that this material was in Toller's mind when he was occupied with the conception and writing of *Hinkemann* — a contemporary subject.

Fra Dolcino (? – 1307) was head of the *Apostolic Brethren*, one of several heretical sects which arose in Lombardy towards the end of the thirteenth century (10). In 1305 Pope Clement V ordered a crusade against the Brethren. They held out in the hills near Novara for a year and a day, but were then forced to surrender to the Novarese. Dolcino was burnt at the stake at Vercelli in 1307.

There is a reference to Fra Dolcino in Dante's *Divina Commedia (Inferno XXVIII, lines 55–59)* where Mohammed, himself regarded by Dante as a Christian heretic, tells the poet to warn Dolcino that if he does not want to be very soon in the same circle of hell himself, he must "arm himself with food" against the snow, lest the Novarese defeat him (11). The action of the *Commedia* is imagined as taking place at Easter in the year 1300, but as the *Inferno* was not finished before 1314 these lines are written with hindsight (12).

Why did this story and this character so fascinate Toller? Did he see in Dolcino and his heretical Apostolic Brethren a parallel with himself, Landauer and their group in Munich? Was he interested in the problems of a monk's celibacy, perhaps as related to the enforced celibacy of a prisoner? Had he intended to base a tragedy on celibacy (the proposed title *The Monk's Tragedy* is suggestive) even before his vision of testicles sparked off *Hinkemann*? At all events his mind was revolving around the conception of the tragedy of an 'outsider' denied normal sexual life: something undeniably close to his own situation.

The 'testicle' vision, which Toller vividly described more than once, evidently cut right across his theoretical plans for an historical play and "gave" him his subject as suddenly and vividly as he had been "given" that of *Masse Mensch*. The earlier account is in Toller's answers to a questionnaire sent to a number of authors by a literary periodical; the later is in his autobiography (13). As Klein rightly says:

> The starting point from an impression on the senses typifies the overall character of the piece (14).

That is to say, the spiritual and mental are always fully embodied in character and event, and form and content are totally harmonised. Thus, after contrasting Jimmy Cobbett's reaction to the children's hunger in *Die Maschinenstürmer* with Hinkemann's reaction to the blinding of the bird, she says:

> Hinkemann is the first figure in Toller's dramas which is drawn in its human totality as a physical-psychically and spiritually rounded person (15).

All the characters, she claims, are fully realised persons, not just representatives of ideas (16), and even more importantly:

> In *Hinkemann* Toller is for the first time successful in representing the general in the particular in that he shows a complex group of problems of central human significance in the fate of *one* figure (17).

This is, she insists, true tragedy in the full and traditional sense:

> Thus the tragedy ends in the recognition of the contradiction inherent in life. It is the cause of the "blind turmoil of the millennia" to escape which there are two possibilities only: Paradise or The Flood (18).

In this tragedy form and content are seen as a unity: the Acts really correspond with the phases of the actions, and speech is now related to character as it was not in the previous plays (19).

Klein thus clearly evaluates the play as tragedy. Of its other principal aspects, political and allegorical, she simply takes cognizance. She mentions them but neither comes to terms with them nor attempts to relate them to the concept of the play as tragedy.

Full justice has been done to these aspects by Wolfgang Frühwald (20).

What will first be attempted here is a closer examination of the relationships of these co-existing aspects of the play and how far they are artistically reconciled.

It will be shown that despite Toller's vigorous denial, *Hinkemann* is finally both tragedy *and* allegory (21).

Two months before Toller's letter to Puttkammer about the proposed Fra Dolcino play, *The Monk's Tragedy*, there had appeared in *Das Tagebuch* a single scene, apparently intended as complete in itself, called *Deutsche Revolution* (22).

The scene is a non-naturalistic representation of the reasons for the failure of the German Revolution, namely the bitter and dogmatic divisions between rival revolutionary parties, depicted as green-and yellow-robed monks whose mutual hostility is based upon the difference between *Om mani patme hum* and *Im mani patme hum*. Discussing the disputes are the Wanderer from the Evening Star and the One-eyed Man. The former wants justice for the oppressed, the class condemned to misery; but both the Greens and the Yellows cry him down as a pacifist, agent provocateur and intellectual. The latter, a disillusioned figure, points out the parallels between politics and religion: Christians have had bloody strife over mere words and letters. After the Wanderer's rejection by the Monks, the One-eyed Man says of the German proletariat.:

> Militarism lasting for centuries and five years' slavery to hunger cannot but have consequences (23).

Finally, yet another faction emerges, dressed in red and committed to *Am mani patme hum*: obviously the factional strife is to be endless.

This theme of the divided Germany, and especially of the divided German working class, is taken up in two scenes of *Hinkemann*, both of them choric in character: that is, they depict the background against which the tragedy takes place rather than advance the action. One is, of course, the "battle" of the War-wounded — in its own way as macabre a stylisation as the "battle" of the monks; the other is in Act II, Sc. 4, where the Slater and the Bricklayer dispute which trade is superior to the other, the person lost behind the functional label:

> "The Unity of the Proletariat!" cries Max Knatsch, "The Enlightened Proletariat!" (24).

We shall return to this in relation to Hölderlin.

Deutsche Revolution, as Klein remarks, anticipates the pessimism of *Hinkemann* (25). At the same time its subject-matter is not merely revolution but specifically *German* revolution. For Toller, the German Revolution is the particular representation of the general problem. Just as Hinkemann is the symbol of the *Nameless Proletarian in every society*, so too the German proletariat stands for all proletarians. Toller made this clear in the *Foreword* to the single scene published in *Volksbühne*, the earliest publication of any of the play (26). Having dedicated this *Proletarian Tragedy* to the Nameless Proletarian of all societies, he adds, indented and in parenthesis:

> (Und so Du in Deutschland lebst, wirst Du verdürsten und verhungern, lieblos verhöhnt, lieblos verlacht) (27)
> (And thus you live in Germany, you will die of hunger and thirst, unlovingly mocked and derided).

To define what Toller means by "proletarian tragedy" *Volksbühne* reprints the two final sentences of Toller's letter to Fehling (October 1921) concerning the latter's production of *Masse Mensch*:

> Proletarian art *leads into* the human, at the deepest levels it is all-embracing — like life, like death.
> Proletarian art exists only insofar as for its creator the diversities of proletarian inner life are ways to the articulation of the eternally-human (28).

Thus as we proceed with Toller from the particular to the general the sequence is: Hinkemann — German proletarian — every proletarian — all humanity. The intermediate stages in the sequence were important to Toller. Even in titling the play he strove to embody them.

The earliest recorded title is *Die Hinkemanns* (29). This emphasised the parallels between the fates of Hinkemann's mother and wife and that of Hinkemann himself: in particular, all three are laughed at ('unlovingly mocked and derided') (30) and the title aims to show that in this play Toller is dealing with an all-embracing problem, not that of an individual war casualty (31). This title might, however, mislead anyone into regarding the play as primarily a *family* tragedy. The MS read by Droop in 1922 was titled *Eugen Hinkemann*, and this is the title used for the first periodical publication of Act III Sc. 2 (32). This title focuses attention on the protagonist and, by adding his fore-name, individualises him more strongly than any of the other titles (33). Doubtless for this reason he dropped the title, as it did not lead the mind to the universal tragedy *Hinkemann* embodies and for the first edition used instead what should have been the definitive title, *Der deutsche Hinkemann*. This title is subtly balanced between the particular and the general: Hinkemann the individual is there; the definite article, however, suggests a common noun (rather than a proper name) constructed on the analogy of *Hinkebein* and *Hinkefuß* (gammy leg) and thus implies generalisation; the adjective *deutsche* on the other hand particularises again, so that in the title as a whole is epitomised the sequence from particular to general suggested above. This title was used for the first four German productions and would doubtless have been retained but for the notorious Dresden scandal on 17 January 1924 (34).

It was only after this that Toller changed the name yet again, this time simply to *Hinkemann*. It is evident that without that scandal, carefully orchestrated and related to a specific date and specific political situation, it would not have occurred to Toller to alter the title from *Der deutsche Hinkemann*. That title, subtle and revealing though it was, was also open to misinterpretation, wilful or otherwise. *Der deutsche Hinkemann* could easily be read as meaning *Der hinkende Deutsche (The Limping German)*, thus making the play into a criticism of the German nation *and nothing more*. This from a left-wing Jew was obviously too much for the nationalistic far right. The decision to change the title yet again once made, it was carried out so thoroughly that the cover and title-pages of the unsold copies of the first edition were apparently changed, and some copies even issued with only the cover altered (35), and Toller wrote in urgent terms to the Director of the Deutsches Theater, Berlin, where the play was to open in April, insisting that it be performed under the title *Hinkemann*. The letter, undated though it is, is of great importance for our understanding of how Toller saw the play at that time (36).

The title, *Der deutsche Hinkemann*, has, he says, caused such confusion that, recognising that the title is actually misleading, he must ask that the play be performed under the title *Hinkemann* and the reason for the change given in a programme note. Toller has read in a review that the play purports to be the drama of the "war-damaged German soul" . Unfortunately, says Toller, that is incorrect. Parenthetically he also remarks that because of the title's being wrongly written the play has been branded an allegory.

It is a curious letter. Certainly, if the title is genuinely confusing or misleading it should be changed: but is it? Or was Toller simply bowing here to external pressures in order to avoid trouble at future productions? If so, he would be acting contrary to his declared attitudes:

> I do not make concessions to the powers of the day (37).

The strained style of the letter, with its intrusive parenthesis and unexpected subjunctive (38) suggests that it was written under unusual stress. And is the author really certain the play is not in some sense an allegory? He had in the contribution to *Volksbühne* described *Hinkemann* as the 'symbol' of the anonymous working-man. And when he denies that the play is the drama of the "war-damaged German soul" does he mean that the German soul was not damaged by the war, or that it was damaged already? Or does he mean it is not about 'the German soul' at all?

In *Deutsche Revolution* he had already said, through the persona of the One-eyed Man, that the German proletariat was suffering the consequences of centuries of militarism as well as the hunger of the last five years, viz. the First World War and the blockade: while he told the editor of *Das Tagebuch*:

> A Preface (sc. to *Hinkemann*) already exists. Hölderlin, "About the Germans . . ." (39).

We may fairly assume, with Frühwald, that Toller refers here to Hölderlin's invective against the Germans in Part II of *Hyperion* rather than to the poem *An die Deutschen* (40).

Already in the speeches of the One-eyed Man in *Deutsche Revolution* (presumably a latter-day Wotan who has lost one eye as the price of wisdom (41)) Toller had strongly echoed Hölderlin's outburst:

The German workers have been slaves and underlings so long that they prefer to remain slaves; they do not want personal responsibility: they prefer comfortable slavery and call it freedom. They are no longer capable of religious belief. That, he says, is a spiritual (*seelisch*) fact, not a moral judgement. Unlike the Russians (i.e. the successful revolutionaries CWD) they are not naive, pure and, so to speak, addicted to belief. Instead, they welcome being mere cogs in the wheels of a European machine. The revolutionary needs to have been given *by Nature* the ability to believe in Paradise — whether here or hereafter is immaterial.

The thoughts reflect Hölderlin's. The Germans, he says, are "profoundly incapable of every god-like feeling"; they prefer the inevitable (i.e. the mechanical), their efforts are slavish, forced by necessity; they are trained like animals (cf. German militarism) and therefore their behaviour is fixed, unenthusiastic, they react as if with animal reflexes, impervious to nature and beauty.

The two visitors, the Wanderer from the Evening Star and the One-eyed Man, correspond with the visitors imagined by Hölderlin:

> And woe to the stranger who wanders because of love and comes to such folk, and threefold woe betide him who, like me, driven by great pain, a beggar of my sort, comes to such folk.

Act III Sc. 4, as already mentioned, dramatises the disunity of the German working class. The strife between the Slater and the Bricklayer which opens the scene and calls forth Max Knatsch's sarcasm, is followed by a dramatisation of the conflicts between a diversity of attitudes:

Unbeschwert's orthodox, optimistic, rationalistic party-line Communism; Knatsch's radical critique of this, which Unbeschwert denounces as Anarchism; Singegott's naive evangelical religion; and Immergleich's self-centred sloth. Woe, indeed, to *Hinkemann*, who comes to such people driven by great pain! It is *Hinkemann*'s emasculation (a direct consequence of war and militarism) that reveals the inadequacy of all these beliefs and attitudes to solve ultimate problems:

> You do not see your limits . . . there are people to whom no state and no society, no family and no community can bring good fortune. Just where your remedies end, there our affliction begins: there the person stands alone (42)

So Toller does believe in a German soul damaged by war and militarism, and he does suggest the Hölderlin passage as a possible preface to his play, while in his most recent writing before *Hinkemann* he has in an allegorical sketch, shown a strong affinity with Hölderlin.

The letter to the Director of the Deutsches Theater reveals an author torn and troubled by his own work, both in its inner essence and its outward, public effects, and the tension here exposed within the author corresponds with an unresolved tension within the play itself, a tension which, although in a sense detracting from the perfection of artistic achievement seen in it by Klein, in fact gives it the highly strung vitality which ensures its lasting greatness. For, we are arguing, Toller never did resolve the tensions between the two aspects of the play emphasised respectively by Klein and Frühwald and, on the evidence of his own letters and other statements, never himself fully appreciated the complexity of his own creation.

The unresolved tension is clearly demonstrated in the play's title (all versions) and in the Dramatis Personae. With the exception of Fränze, Grete Hinkemann's woman friend, every named character, including the titular protagonist, has a non-naturalistic type-determining surname:

Hinkemann
(Eugen, Grete, & The Old Lady) : Limping Man
Großhahn (Paul) : Big Cock

Knatsch (Max)	:	Trouble
Immergleich (Peter)	:	Always-the-Same
Singegott (Sebaldus)	:	Sing-God
Unbeschwert (Michael)	:	Carefree

Even the forename Grete, with its allusion to Goethe's *Faust,* relates this character to specifically German allegory, as Frühwald has rightly pointed out (43).

In his first two plays, *Die Wandlung* and *Masse Mensch,* only the protagonists were named, and the names were first-names only, Friedrich, and Sonja Irene L. These were the only personalised figures in the plays. All others in *Die Wandlung* were given merely descriptive, impersonal titles (e.g. Jugendfreund, Verwundeter etc.). An exception is Gabriele, who is perhaps named because of her close personal relationship with Friedrich, though she appears only in one short scene. This, as H.L. Cafferty, has pointed out, has a parallel in *Woyzeck.* In both plays all but the protagonist and his romantic partner have been "typified". Even Gabriele has no independent existence, but reflects what romantic love means to Friedrich (44). In *Masse Mensch* it is the same, except that two of the titles. *Der Namenlose* and *Der Begleiter* carry more than merely descriptive significance.

In the next two plays, *Die Rache des verhöhnten Liebhabers* and *Die Maschinenstürmer,* Toller uses ordinary personal names for all principals, and a non-naturalistic title only for *Der alte Reaper,* a semi-choric character, in the latter play. He has clearly moved towards naturalism in this respect, as he has, too, in the greater use of prose dialogue in *Die Maschinenstürmer.* It is therefore startling and new (no mere vestigial characteristic from his earlier Expressionism) when Toller fills his whole cast with type-named figures, and this suggests a definite turn in the direction of allegory.

Yet this list of 'types' is headed:

> Menschen der Tragödie (45)
> (People — human beings — in the tragedy)

This also is innovative. The earlier lists of Dramatis Personae were headed: PERSONEN (suggesting, if anything, the Persona, the mask) in *Die Wandlung* and *Die Rache des verhöhnten Liebhabers;* SPIELER (Players) and GESTALTEN DER TRAUMBILDER (Figures in the Dream Scenes) in *Masse Mensch;* PERSONEN DES VORSPIELS and PERSONEN DES DRAMAS (Persons in the Prologue; Persons in the Drama) in *Die*

Maschinenstürmer.

Now, in *Hinkemann*, Toller goes out of his way to emphasise in his Dramatis Personae, a) that his type-named figures are persons, human beings, Menschen, and b) that they are persons in a tragedy.

That a tragedy demands that its principals be truly human surely requires neither argument nor demonstration; but type-names militate *against* the fully rounded development of dramatic characters as human beings. The way, therefore, in which Toller sets out the very cast-list of this play epitomises the tension between the conflicting elements in its conception. It is difficult to believe that a twentieth century dramatist planning a tragedy would impose on himself the limitations implied in type-naming his characters.

Toller's original impetus, the testicle-vision, was towards a problem-play:

> What fate would a man live through who lacked his sex? How would it be, if this man has already been married? Must not such a fate make everything unsure which formerly seemed to him unshakeable foundations? (46)

The writing thus starts on the theme of an individual's personal problem. By the time he had finished the play, but before it had been published or produced, Toller understood that he had written something far larger in scope, — a play in which he recognised

> the tragic limits of all possibilities of happiness from social revolution . . The limits beyond which Nature is more powerful than the individual, personal will and the will of society (47).

He had discovered that tragedy has no end, that even communism has its tragedies (48). If he had not quite parted company with Marxism before this, in this sentence he did so. He saw too (and this insight resulted in the real tragic depth of his play) that:

> If there is one individual whose suffering is insoluble, then the tragedy of the one individual is at the same time the tragedy of the society in which he lives (49).

Thus Toller sees himself as having written the tragedy of a class. He realised as clearly as did and do his Marxist critics that his new insights could lead to resignation. He will have nothing of this:

> Only a weak person gives up when he sees himself incapable of giving his longed-for dream complete fulfilment. It takes nothing from the strong person's passionate will when he knows. Today we do not need people who are blind in great feeling, we need those who *will*, although they *know* (50).

He went on to say that absolute good, the Earthly Paradise, could not be created by any system of society; it was simply a matter of struggling for the *relatively best* that man can find and fulfil. More intellectually Toller had already perceived and expressed this even before *Hinkemann* was begun, in *Deutsche Revolution*. The One-eyed Man, having declared that the revolutionary must believe in paradise, here or hereafter, continues:

> Which is not to say that today's revolutionaries will still believe in paradise a hundred years after the seizure of power. Then, they no longer need that belief, it is no longer spiritually necessary for them... no, I 'm not joking... the believers become doubters, the doubters ... augurs! Christ — Paul — Pope ! The three figures are symbols. After a hundred years a new class of the oppressed, which necessarily must strive for power, has the great belief in Paradise! Eternal recurrence of forms! (51).

Another element in the internal tensions within the play is exemplified in the influence of Büchner upon it. Toller's high regard for Büchner is well documented and in a letter to Max Pallenberg in 1923 he joins Büchner in a trinity with Goethe and Hölderlin as representatives of a Germany that has nothing in common with Adolf Hitler and his like (52). Klein has pointed out many close parallels between *Hinkemann* and *Woyzeck*, not merely thematically but even verbally (53), showing that Büchner's play was never far from Toller's consciousness during the writing of *Hinkemann*. A more recent study of Büchner's influence on Toller goes so far as to declare:

> There is no question whether the basic structure of *Hinkemann* has *Woyzeck* as its model. The plots are essentially identical; the characters within each play have virtually identical relationships with each other (54).

Both protagonists, Klein points out, are *on show* as *species* — Woyzeck before the Doctor, *Hinkemann* in the fair (55). But whereas Büchner the scientist retains his objectivity throughout and Woyzeck remains incapable of reflecting on his own fate (56), Toller's Hinkemann *is* finally able to do this. This is not only because Toller has created a more articulate protagonist but, more importantly, because Toller identifies himself with *Hinkemann* in many respects: both are deprived of normal sexual life; both are front-line soldiers returning home and facing the problems of re-integration (57); Hinkemann, like his creator, is portrayed as something of a seer, a visionary:

> Toller also creates in the figure of Eugen *Hinkemann*, seer and visionary, the separation of the mental and spiritual from society, which had been a symptom of Germany since the end of the nineteenth century (58).

In Act II Sc. 4, the workers' pub, and in the scene of the war-wounded with hurdy-gurdies (1st Edtn II.2; 2nd and subsequent Edtns III.1) Toller gives objective expression to the disintegration of Germany so deplored by Hölderlin:

> I can think of no nation more disunited than the Germans (59).

At the same time Toller, German himself, shares Hölderlin's own sense of dereliction and has put this into *Hinkemann*. Toller ended both *1920* and *1921* of his *Letters from Prison* with the closing lines of Hölderlin's poem *Hälfte des Lebens:* (60)

> Woe is me! when it is winter.
> where shall I find the flowers and
> where the sunshine and shadows of the earth?
> The walls stand speechless and cold,
> the weather-cocks clatter in the wind (61).

Like Hyperion, Toller, as well as Hinkemann, is

> speaking for all who are in this country and suffer as I have suffered there (62).

Thus even the dual nature of Toller's debt to Hölderlin reflects the dual nature of the play: the objective and subjective impulses; the allegorical and the personal; the critical and the tragic.

Finally, the internal tensions are exemplified in the revisions, apart from the title, which Toller made in the second edition and its 2nd, 3rd and 4th impressions in 1924 and 1925.

Of the approximately fifty changes in the text of the second edition, only four are significant, viz:

1) The place of the action has been generalised from:

> Ort: Kleine Industriestadt in Deutschland.
> (Place: Small Industrial Town in Germany)

to

> Deutschland
> (Germany) (63)

2) The *war-wounded* sequence has been moved from Act II Sc. 2 to Act III Sc. i, immediately before the *Newspaper-boys* sequence; and the speeches of the prostitute and the pimp have been moved from their original position between the 3rd and 4th newspaper boys to a new position between the 2nd Jew's speech and the Old Waffel-Seller. Before the stage-directions for the entry of the war-wounded (64) the following Stage-direction has been added:

> Hinkemann collapses. What follows must be played as a nightmare. All the figures appear to press upon *Hinkemann* and, as if absorbed into the darkness, to detach themselves from him (65).

3) The last stage-direction concerning *Hinkemann* in the play in the 1st edition reads;

> Hinkemann goes to the drawer in the table. He takes out of it a ball of string. Quietly, matter-of-factly he twists the string into a rope (66).

This is cut in the 2nd and all subsequent editions.

4) The changes in the speech in Act III Sc 2 from "Es ist nicht um meine Krankheit" to *"Ich will nicht mehr"* (67).

All these changes indicate either changes or uncertainties of purpose. The *small industrial town* of the first edition suggests that the author visualised the play's settings and background very specifically and concretely. The change to *Germany* implies that he now recognised that a specifically small town setting was not necessary: yet he emphatically states *Germany*. The shift is from the specific to the general, but at the same time the *German* character of the play is highlighted.

The second set of alterations is far more complex in effect. In its original position in Act II Sc. 3 the war-wounded sequence is played on an otherwise empty stage. It is an expressionist intrusion inexplicably interrupting a naturalistic scene: *The stage empties*, the sequence takes place, *the stage becomes busy again* (68). It is plainly and unequivocally authorial comment embodying in theatrical language Hölderlin's "no nation more disunited than the Germans" and their being "trained like an animal (69).

In the same edition the Newspaper-boy sequence and all that follows to the end are played in the presence of the collapsed *Hinkemann*. There is no certain indication as to whether he is conscious or unconscious, and no suggestion that the sequences might be dreams of Hinkemann's: there seems no reason why they should not be treated as objective, with Hinkemann's final comment as he rises, presumably from unconsciousness, being unconsciously ironic:

> And over me the eternal heavens
> And over me the eternal stars (70).

This being so, the sequence, like that of the war-wounded, though more nearly naturalistic, is another example of authorial comment on German society about 1921. Both passages therefore, as originally introduced into the play are choric in nature, excrescences not fully integrated into its structure. Nor is the war-wounded sequence stylistically in harmony with the rest of the play, and it is very clumsily fitted into a scene which otherwise flows satisfactorily. Thus both sequences belong to the critical, satirical aspect of the play, not to the tragic.

But when the war-wounded sequence is moved and is played as *Hinkemann*'s nightmare, everything is transformed. The social criticism, indeed, is not lost. Instead its presence in the play is given artistic and psychological justification. No longer extraneous authorial comment, the passage becomes an externalisation of *Hinkemann*'s mind and, coming where it does, forms a psychological climax to the whole play, leading into the dénouement of Act III. Sc. 2.

One significant ambiguity, however, remains: in the first edition the sequence from the newspaper boys to the exeunt of all but Hinkemann takes place in the presence of the probably unconscious Hinkemann.

But unlike the war-wounded sequence it is, although relevant to Hinkemann's state of mind (71), not suddenly illuminated by the change in the second edition. There is, moreover, little in the sequence that could not pass as realistic:

1) the metonyms *Gummiknüppel* and *Flammenwerfer*.
2) the stage direction;

> Even the street lights have become small and dark on account of the incident of the soldiers (72).

But these two suffice to make it reasonable to treat the whole passage as non-naturalistic and to present it on stage as part of *Hinkemann*'s nightmare.

This scene, therefore, in its final form vividly embodies the tension inherent in the play's dual nature as social criticism and tragedy .

The third change is the omission of *Hinkemann*'s practical preparations for suicide. This is the earliest of three plays of Toller's with alternative endings involving the ultimate fate of the protagonist, the other two being *Hoppla, wir leben!* and *Pastor Hall*. In every case the alternatives are the immediate death of the protagonist or the probability of his continuing to suffer. In *Hoppla, wir leben!* the parallel is very close: Karl Thomas also, in one version, makes the 'rope' with which to hang himself. (Pastor Hall either suffers a heart attack or walks out to meet his persecutors). In each case it is the original version that includes the protagonist's death. From our perspective it is impossible not to see in these first versions foreshadowings of Toller's own suicide. That he was already considering this possibility is clear in *Das Schwalbenbuch:*

> Genosse Tod
> Genosse, Genosse . . . (73)
> (Comrade Death
> (Comrade, Comrade . . .)

He turns from death because the song of the swallows still makes it possible for him to dream:

> Daß man, nahe der dunklen Schwelle,
> Solche Melodie vernimnt, so irdischen
> Jubels, so irdischer Klage trunken . . .
> Träume, meine Seele, träume,
> Lerne träumen den Traum der Ewigkeit.
> . . .
> Fort fort, Genosse Tod, fort fort,
> Ein andermal, später, viel später (74).
>
> (That someone, near to the dark threshold,
> hears such a melody, so drunk with earthly
> jubilation, with earthly lament . . .
> Dream, my soul, dream,
> Learn to dream the dream of eternity.
> . . .
> Away, away, Comrade Death, away, away,
> Another time, later, much later.)

The subjective link with *Hinkemann* is strong:

> Wer keine Kraft zum Traum hat, hat keine
> Kraft zum Leben (75).
> (He who has no strength to dream has no strength to live).

In this play (the others will be discussed in their place) Toller apparently was able to detach *Hinkemann* eventually from his private obsession with suicide and to leave his fate more painfully open, like those of Mrs Alving and Oswald at the end of Ibsen's *Ghosts* (76).

The fourth important change, in the *Kraft zum Traum* speech, shows Toller dissatisfied with what Frühwald calls the very heart, the nucleus (*Kernstelle*) of the play, namely the speech including the sentence just quoted, which Toller also used as the play's motto or epigraph.

Frühwald believes that this key speech was suggested to Toller by something Stefan Großmann wrote about the actor Josef Kainz in *Das Tagebuch (II. 1921)*:

> Wissen wurde ihm zu Willen (77).

While this is possible, it seems to be a superfluous piece of speculation, especially as the echo, if echo it is, is one merely of rhythm and sentence structure, not of meaning:

> Alles Sehen wird mir Wissen, alles Wissen Leid (78).

A juxtaposition of *wollen* (NOT *Willen*) and *wissen* does occur in the letter to Stefan Zweig (13.6.'23) on the subject of *Hinkemann* already quoted, but the alliterative duality of Wit and Will as the two great faculties distinguishing man from the animals has its roots far back in medieval thought and, as so often, Toller in his awareness of it, shows himself part of old and central traditions rather than a mere follower of contemporary fashions.

To return to the speech itself: the first edition version, reprinted by Frühwald and Spalek in GW, reads:

> Ich habe die Kraft nicht mehr. Die Kraft nicht mehr zu kämpfen, die Kraft nicht mehr zum Traum. Wer keine Kraft zum Traum hat, hat keine Kraft zum Leben. Der Schuß, der war wie eine Frucht vom Baume der Erkenntnis . . . Alles Sehen wird mir Wissen, alles Wissen Leid. *Ich will nicht mehr* (79).

In the 2nd Edition 1st impression) as reprinted by Kiepenheuer, the latter part of the speech (after *Erkenntnis*) reads:

> Alles Sehen wird mir Wissen, alles Wissen Leid. Menschen, die alles Leid leben und dennoch wollen . . . *Ich will nicht mehr* (80).

Notice that this broken sentence is only introduced in the second edition as if to clarify the sub-textual link between the last two sentences in the first edition version. It brings out the fact that *Hinkemann* himself is not one who can live through all suffering yet keep his will intact.

But Toller was apparently still dissatisfied and in the 2nd Impression of this 2nd Edition he rewrote the 'link' as:

> . . . Einst wurde mir alles Leid: Wille . . . (81)

This is more strongly personalised than the generalised reference to *Menschen*, but it is less clear: the vital *und dennoch wollen* has disappeared. Toller allowed this to stand in the 10,000 copies that constituted the 3rd Impression, but in the 4th Impression (24th–28th thousand) he finally fixed upon a shortened version of the 2nd. Edition, 1st Impression:

> . . . Alles Leid leben und dennoch wollen . . . (82)

Here at last Toller has forged an intelligible link between:

> Alles Sehen wird mir Wissen, alles Wissen Leid.
>
> and
>
> *Ich will nicht mehr.*

which through its very fragmentariness and grammatical incompleteness invites both the objective (*Menschen*) and subjective (*mir*) interpretations. In saying:

> To live through all suffering and still have will

Hinkemann can be thinking both about the possibility that perhaps there *are* people who can do this, and about the fact that *he* cannot.

The long struggle with this key sentence (the 4th Impression of the 2nd Edition was not published until 1925) reveals perhaps more vividly than any other evidence how keenly Toller experienced the tension between the play as critical allegory and as tragedy. He was clearly aware of its artistic ambiguity, both in aim and in achievement.

We conclude that although the judgement that this is Toller's most fully realised dramatic achievement up to this point, and perhaps the actual peak of his work as a playwright, is correct, the play is nevertheless a transitional one. As tragedy it marks the end of the early optimism, based upon moral and political idealism and shown so strongly in *Die Wandlung* and with decreasing certainty in the plays that followed. In it Toller at last faces the uncompromising reality of the human predicament in all its harshness and insolubility. As dramatic criticism of his own nation this play (his first wholly prose play) anticipates all his later plays except the unsuccessful *No More Peace,* the collaborative *Wunder in Amerika* and perhaps *Die blinde Göttin,* in which the critique of the operations of the law are more generalised.

The play thus occupies a central place in its author's oeuvre, not only as one of his finest plays but as the key-stone in the bridge between his earlier expressionist/poetic dramatic work and his later objective/prose plays. As such it inevitably carries within itself the stresses of its key position.

HINKEMANN ON STAGE

The 'theatre scandal' at Dresden on 17.1.1924 coloured all subsequent attitudes to *Hinkemann* and influenced all later critical assessments either directly or indirectly. The productions that preceded this have, therefore, particular importance and the critiques of them, when available, are of special interest. Of these six productions, two were in Russia, one (2 performances only) in Karlsruhe, and the other three geographically close together in Leipzig, Altenburg and Glauchau (1).

Fortunately several periodical criticisms survive of the first production, which opened on 19 September 1923 in the Altes Theater, Leipzig, under the title *Der deutsche Hinkemann* and ran for about fifty performances. The production was directed by Alwin Kronacher. The extant critiques include a celebrated and contrasting pair by Herbert Ihering and Alfred Kerr. Both these, however, review *Hinkemann* together with Brecht's *Baal* which, interestingly enough, had its world premiere at the same theatre when Toller's play had already been played about twenty times (2). Thus even in these first and highly influential critiques Toller's play was not assessed purely as itself but also as a foil to the first play (written 1918) of his younger contemporary.

Kerr's and Ihering's critiques of *Baal* and *Hinkemann* constitute classic examples of their work and an illuminating illustration of their critical duelling throughout the period of the Weimar Republic.

Kerr notes that *Baal* 'had little luck', but was greeted by whistling, laughter, stamping of feet and cries of derision lasting half-an-hour (3). He summarises the play dismissively (So *Baal*) (4), concluding:

> The talented Brecht is a frothy epigone. (5)

He concedes — perceptively, in the light of Brecht's late poems — that Brecht is 'talented in the lyrical'(6) and that despite other faults he is 'a poet'. The play itself Kerr considers to be undergraduate stuff, its prominent characteristics being ballad-like; it is an 'illustrated broadsheet', street-singer's material —

> "All in all: an elephantine idyll." (7).

While Rühle is broadly correct in saying that Kerr, though in general open to everything that promised creative originality, remained closed against the early Brecht, this brief judgement has penetrating insight.

Ihering also regards *Baal* as a 'scenic ballad' with 'fine lyrical passages'. He declares that, in spite of an inadequate production, the impression was unusual and, at the end, overpowering so that finally resounding, long-drawn-out applause overcame the earlier hostility.

He rather artificially relates *Baal* to *Hinkemann* through their contrasting protagonists, the eunuch and the 'super-virile' Baal, and rather than assess each play or production he uses the juxtaposition as a peg upon which to hang an essay on what he calls 'productive' and 'unproductive' dramatists, concluding that Brecht is typical of the former and Toller of the latter. This is the logical outcome of his concept of the nature of dramatic criticism. He criticised a production from the point of view of the requirements of the theatre of the future, which for him was to be artistic, fundamental and corresponding with the spirit of the age. Theatre for him was a factor in politics which moulded consciousness. He did not write primarily for the newspaper reader but in order to influence the theatre, and even though he overestimated the degree to which the theatre could be perfected through 'systems', his criticisms exercised great influence upon directors and actors (8).

His critique thus tells us little about either the play or the production. After making a careful distinction between sympathy (*Mitgefühl*) and pity (*Mitleid*), he goes on to argue that the dramatist's emotion is more 'elemental' than either. Toller, he argues, is 'merely the sympathetic spectator', unable to experience ' a tragic complex'. Because the play possesses 'merely human authenticity' and 'merely sympathetic love', 'it remains rationally banal' and 'becomes false and tasteless'. He claims that Toller possesses neither 'the great anger which could have made the play biassed, but magnificently biassed and unjust, nor the unifying power which serves a higher justice'. Ihering gives no evidence for these assertions. They are his own subjective reactions to the play, brilliantly disguised as rational critique. From this he can with deceptive facility falsely conclude:

> All the leading articles of recent years can be found again in *Hinkemann*. An impotent, provocative piece of empty talk (9).

Kerr, two decades Ihering's senior, approaches Toller with greater natural sympathy:

> A socialistically determined ethic caused him to stand up for Hauptmann and later for Toller and Piscator without surrendering himself to a 'tendency' (10).

But like Ihering, he asserted rather than described. He already admired Toller's work but found that in this play the things that concerned the times were adulterated with *Kitsch*. Toller seemed to him to be for the first time uncertain; the transition to semi-naturalism was not easy. He finds two essentials in the play: 1) a symbol of Germany: not, as seems obvious, the emasculated warrior as symbol of post-war Germany, but the 'outwardly abundant' (*äußerlich Strotzenden*) as symbol of pre-war Germany. 2) Anger directed against Priapus. Critical of the play's alleged long-windedness and repetitiousness, Kerr continues:

"And nevertheless. . .". With Toller, says Kerr, there is always 'nevertheless'. Toller is more truly a 'contemporary' writer than Brecht: "He writes as people live today" — though limited at present by the restriction of his view from prison. Kerr sees the play as educational, as a folk-play, a poetic Apocalypse, a vivid, bold play that goes on resonating long after the actual performance is over.

In a passing, but welcome, reference to the production Kerr says that Leipzig has presented *Hinkemann* with provincial ham-acting (*mit Provinzpathos*), but that in any case it is a fine thing that such material should be performed for a serious audience: 'serious' gives a clear impression of how the play was received.

Summing up his judgement on both plays, Kerr concludes:

> All in all: the critic is not enthusiastic but he raises his hat. . . and finally, both are poets: the descendant as well as the explorer (11).

And for Kerr, Brecht is the epigone, Toller the trail-breaker.

After our examination and comparison of these two critiques — each in its own way tendentious — notices by reviewers less committed to publicly known ideological approaches to theatre help to piece together a clearer notion of first impressions of the play uninfluenced by its later notoriety.

A notice in the *Leipziger Volkszeitung* (12) apparently written on behalf of the *Arbeiter Bildungsinstitut*, for which the play was put on, regards Toller as "the greatest dramatist of the working class and the most successful author of the post-war generation." The review notes Toller's criticism of the working-class movement and sees *Hinkemann* as the symbol of Germany (13). This is the kind of assessment and reasonable comment one might have expected from such a source. Two days later, in the same newspaper, E. Delpy noted Toller's 'spiritual sensitivity' (*seelische Zartheit*) and 'intellectual independence' (*geistige Unabhängigkeit*), qualities he would not expect from a 'former revolutionary', though he has also found them in Toller's earlier work

(14). On the same day in the same paper Erwin Jahn briefly and favourably reviewed the play, describing it as the equal of Büchner's *Woyzeck* and Hauptmann's *Fuhrmann Henschel* " in the portrayal of the simple and helpless man" (15). Finally the anonymous author of an *Afterword on 'Hinkemann'*, five days later in the same paper, comments favourably on the realism of the play and production. While realising that the pessimism is atypical of most proletarian attitudes, he refuses to reduce any author to a formula, points out that no single work can express all the ideas of an author, and that "pity for the suffering and the socialist aim to better their lot go together." (16)

Thus this local newspaper printed no fewer than four separate notices of this production within a week of its opening, and none of them even hinted that the play's subject-matter or treatment might be either scandalous and objectionable or unpatriotic and insulting. One of these reviewers (Erwin Jahn), later called this production the most important in the season promoted by the *Arbeiter-Bildungsintitut* (17).

Similar comments were made by Erich Michael in *Die schöne Literatur*. He picked out the (naturalistic) fairground and tavern scenes as the best, noted Toller's ideological independence and considered Hinkemann to be a symbol of defeated Germany.

To conclude the critiques of the Leipzig production, here in full is an undated notice, newspaper unknown, signed *L.St.* It is not listed by Spalek.

> The three-act tragedy *Hinkemann* by Ernst Toller, whose world premiere took place in the Altes Theater, is a dramatic Book of Job. Only that Hinkemann, having been struck down by Fate, does not find the way back into life like his Old Testament forebear, but succumbs to a higher power through no fault of his own. It is a work of gloomy pessimism, a yearning cry for justice, a cry of the tormented creature. This work full of tears, sympathy, love and renunciation directs at the same time bitter criticism against the time in which it has come into being. Literary threads run from Hinkemann's fate to *Wozzeck [sic CWD]* and *Fuhrman Henschel.* Tolstoy's influence, too, makes itself felt (18)

Here is a spontaneous reaction to the play itself. For this critic the play has deep religious and literary roots reaching back through Hauptmann and Tolstoy, not only to Büchner's *Woyzeck,* but even to the Book of Job — a book which modern criticism sees as a *dramatic* poem, perhaps influenced by Aeschylus. This appraisal of the play suggests what its future assessment could have been but for the short perspective in which it was viewed after the Dresden troubles, and even before these by the prominent critics anxious to express and promote their personal and ideological notions of the pattern of development of contemporary German theatre.

For this critic Toller's 'bitter criticism against the time in which [the play] has come into being' is secondary to "tears, sympathy, love and renunciation", a play epitomised in one great phrase:

> ein Aufschrei der gepeinigten Kreatur. (19)
> (a cry of the tormented creature)

Here, at the very outset of the play's stage-history, is a critic who sees *Hinkemann* as not less than a tragedy in the Aristotelian sense, arousing in the audience the ancient feelings of pity and terror. That *L.St.* immediately relates the play to *Woyzeck* is a guarantee of his perceptiveness. The parallels with Hauptmann's *Fuhrmann Henschel* are of particular interest in relation to Toller's clear shift here towards naturalism (20). Henschel and Hinkemann are physically similar in their outward strength. Henschel is described as 'an athletically built man' (21). Hinkemann's physique has been such that even now his spongy muscles can fake a bear-like strength (22). Like Hinkemann, Henschel realises his betrayal in an inn scene. Hauptmann's is a dialect play, a true *Volksstück*, and, as we have seen, Toller's was early perceived to have some *Volksstück* elements.

The pre-Dresden critiques provide a picture of the immediate and spontaneous reaction of critics and audiences before the deliberately orchestrated Dresden riot had thrown over the play a false aura of sexual scandalousness and political extremism, and what emerges is, through all the differences of approach, self-consistent.

The play is imbued with a sense of pity. It may be seen as tragedy. Its author is a sensitive, independent, non-party socialist, critical, perhaps bitterly critical of his own times. The play is thoroughly contemporary and artistically exploratory while at the same time based on living traditions of German drama, especially as exemplified in Büchner and Hauptmann. The author is indeed a poet who has written a play symbolic of the problems of post-war Germany and having within it distinct elements of the folk-play tradition. His pessimism is not resignation, and his pity is consistent with his socialist ideals.

It was good that such material should be presented to a serious audience — namely the Workers' Educational Institute — and even though the standard of acting was provincial, the *Pathos* (over-emotional declamation) was honest in the case of the actor Engst and restrained in Hans Zeise-Gött (23). The production emphasised the realism of the play rather than its expressionistic elements.

Recorded Russian critiques earlier than the Dresden scandal serve to confirm the German ones.

Even Spalek lists no notices of the first Russian production, Moscow, Autumn 1923 (24), but he summarises three of Sergei E. Radlov's Leningrad production of December 1923 and three of Adrian Piotrovski's translation, published in Petrograd in 1923 (25).

Predictably all three reviews of the book publication have reservations on Toller's ideology. More interestingly, two interpret the play as the tragedy of an individual set against a social background. The reviewer, *B.I.* (26), who thinks this Toller's best work, says it has 'the force of ancient tragedy' and remarks also upon the relationship of the play to the naturalistic drama and to Hauptmann in particular, from whom, he says, the main character comes (presumably meaning from Fuhrmann Henschel). Both *B. I.* and *Ch. T.* see theatrical potential in the play , the latter referring to 'new and original elements' (27). The third reviewer, M. Kuzmin (28), discusses *Hinkemann* as a typical example of Expressionist Drama in an article on that wider theme, and his view of the play is inevitably distorted by the assumption from which he starts.

Of the three recorded reviews of the first Leningrad production, all praise the production itself, two having reservations about the acting: e.g. Hinkemann too cerebral and the Budenbesitzer disappointingly acted (29). The 'nightmare', singled out by Eduard Stark as the best-staged scene of all (30), evidently made a great impression on I. Rabinovich also, for in his thoughtful and favourable review, in which he compares Toller with Hamsun, to the former's advantage, he suggests that the whole play should have been staged as a monodrama with a (realistic) Hinkemann clearly separated from his (expressionistic) background (31). The third review, by Gr. Avlov (32), gives us little help in reconstructing the production.

It should by now be clear that before Dresden *Hinkemann* was well understood, justly and rationally praised and faulted, and treated as a natural development from Toller's earlier work. There is in the reviews no trace of the hysteria that was later to dog the play and lead both audiences and theatre-managements (even that of the Berlin Freie Volksbühne) to prejudge and misjudge it.

It is not necessary here to retell the story of the Dresden disturbance. This and its political aftermath in the Parliament of Saxony have been very fully documented and are easily accessible (33). In particular, Frühwald has convincingly demonstrated that the play was made a pawn in the political conflicts that were threatening to tear the Weimar Republic apart. The autumn of 1923, the crisis-year of the Weimar Republic, had seen Bavaria, under the extreme right-wing emergency government of Gustav Ritter von Kahr, on the verge of civil war both with the central government of Stresemann and Ebert and with the left-wing governments of Thuringia and Saxony. In November the political atmosphere had so deteriorated that Hitler believed the time to be ripe for 'National Revolution'. After the failure of the 'Beerhall Putsch' (8–9 Nov. 1923) the conflict between Bavaria and the central government was settled peacefully (34).

On the very day (27.Oct.1923) that the central government had issued its ultimatum to Bavaria, it also issued one to Saxony, demanding that its communist-dominated Popular Front government should be dissolved, as Stresemann no longer regarded it as a 'Land' government in the sense of the Weimar constitution. As in Bavaria, so too in Saxony the ultimatum was rejected. Stresemann and Ebert took direct and successful military action. On 29.10.1923 the Dresden Ministries were occupied by troops of the Reichswehr and an acceptable social democratic government was formed (35).

Against this background the production of *Hinkemann* was seen as a protest against the action of the central government, and indeed the theatre of Saxony saw itself as a rear-guard defendant of the socialist revolution. Hostility from the extreme right was intensified by the fact that the production opened on 17th January (1924) on the eve of the anniversary of the founding of the Second German Reich when Wilhelm I was proclaimed German Kaiser in the Hall of Mirrors, Versailles, on the 18th January, 1871, a date revered by all German Nationalists. Fearing the total defeat of the Right in Saxony following the failure of the Hitler-Putsch in Bavaria, Nationalists and National-Socialists united in a deliberately orchestrated demonstration in the auditorium, so that, as Frühwald remarks (referring also to subsequent productions):

> At the productions in Dresden, Vienna, Berlin and Jena auditorium and street provided each time not only a commentary on what happened on the stage, but its actual documentation . . . Allegory became reality (36).

In these circumstances reviews inevitably concentrated primarily upon the disturbance and only secondarily upon the play — already published and widely read — virtually ignoring the production and individual performances, which, in any case, were, as several critics pointed out, rendered largely inaudible (37). We know that Decarli, the actor who played *Hinkemann*, pleaded in vain with the audience for attention to be paid to the work of the players (38).

Friedrich Kummer (39) compares the impression with the paintings of Otto Dix, presumably thinking of such pictures as *Kartenspielende Kriegskrüppel* (1920) (40), but it is not clear whether he is referring to the actual visual impact of the production or merely in general literary terms to the play.

From the parliamentary proceedings of 24.1.1924 we know that some passages (the word actually used is *Szenen*) that had been performed in Leipzig without trouble were cut by Wiecke in Dresden (41).

An extant photograph evidently shows the Newspaper-sellers scene. *Hinkemann* lies awkwardly by the lamp-post and six men are grouped pyramidally about him, brandishing papers. It looks suspiciously as if specially posed for the photographer and may not accurately represent a moment in the production. But costumes and make-up are naturalistic even in this 'nightmare'. Only the faces and papers are highlighted (42).

Otherwise from all the contemporary reviews examined and the comments of scholars these are the only shreds of information to be gathered about the production. But from this time onwards all pre-1933 criticism, and even some post-war-criticism, is, at the least, modified by consciousness of the 'Dresden Scandal'. Here we shall try to extract from criticism what some later productions were actually like.

There were eleven further productions of *Hinkemann* in the year 1924 (43). Some of these are well documented; of others little firm information can be gleaned from the reviews.

In Vienna (44) attempts by Swastika-bearing members of right-wing student and gymnastic associations to enter the theatre and disrupt the performance were foiled by the police, but despite a sympathetic review by Felix Salten and a serious 'puff' by Ludwig Marcuse, the quality and character of the production remain hidden (45).

After further troubles in Jena (30 3.'24) and Delitzsch (9.4.'24) the play opened on 11.4.'24 in the Berlin Residenz Theater. (The first performances were closed; the first public performance 14.4.'24). The production was directed by Emil Lund and Erwin Berger, design César Klein.

Heinrich George had been released by the Staatstheater to play *Hinkemann,* and the part soon became inseparable from his name. To him much of the credit for the success of the production was given: too much, inasmuch as the quality of Toller's writing was under-rated.

> He [George] enlivened even those passages which suffer from oratorical monotony. He pulsated through the rhetoric and filled, so to speak, the empty vessel of speech with blood.

Renée Stobrawa

> formed a Frau *Hinkemann* into a shattering proletarian figure with sparely condensed gestures and economical use of vocal power.

Klein

> provided very quiet settings which were very effective in their tragic gentleness.

The production

> united in itself Emil Lund's clever diplomacy and Erwin Berger's creative initiative (46).

The same critic also singles out Hugo Döblin's performance as the Booth Proprietor for special mention.

George was the only actor mentioned in F.E's review in the Berliner Tageblatt, where he is called Toller's "shattering interpreter" (47).

So once more it is impossible to form any visual, practical image of the production; nor can one, from Spalek's excellent summaries of important reviews gain any clear idea of the styles chosen by the many foreign directors from USSR to USA. Some seem to have emphasised the 'expressionist' elements more than others . In an account of the first English production (48) the play was said to have 'sincerity and beauty but also unbearable realism', a comment which must also reflect the style of the production (49).

It is therefore most profitable to concentrate upon the Volksbühne production of 1927, directed jointly by Toller and Ernst Lönner (a pupil of Piscator's), with Edward Suhr as designer. With Toller's personal involvement in the direction this can be regarded as an authoritative production of the play (50).

Although Toller had been refused leave from prison to attend the opening of *Hinkemann* in Berlin in 1924 he had seen the production only three days after his release on 15th July and had been given a hero's ovation by the audience.

Lönner had already directed the play with great success in Vienna in January 1927: four performances in three different venues (51). It was seen to be 'a mighty accusation against war . . free from party-political colouring . . . too differentiated psychologically, its thoughts too much broken through finely-cut prisms . . . for one to be able to speak of it as a directly propagandist piece' (52). Toller was at the first performance "deadly pale and with tears in his eyes". The play was greeted with cries of "No more war!". Toller gave the company all the credit for the success of the performance (53). Clearly this experience promised well for his co-directing with Lönner in Berlin.

The Volksbühne production, which Toller had long desired, opened on 25th November 1927, nearly three months *after* the celebrated but controversial Piscator production of *Hoppla, wir leben!,* Toller's first post-prison play. Toller had learnt much, both positively and negatively, from Piscator during the preparation of this play for the stage, despite, and indeed also through the serious conflicts with Piscator — to be examined in their place.

Inevitably, and especially because Lönner was joint director, "the ghost of Piscator hovered in the wings" (54). This influence was seen most clearly in the nonrealistic, visionary scenes (55). There were no interpolated film-sequences in Piscator style, but there was an effective adaptation of this technique when gigantic shadows of marching soldiers were projected on the wall of a house (56).

The revolving stage, beloved of Piscator, was used with great effect in the Rummelplatz (fairground) scene, thought by several critics to be the high-point of the production (57). A photograph gives a good impression of this scene (58). The fairground is set in the working-class area of a big city: the lighted windows of multi-storey blocks of flats (the typical Berlin *Mietskasernen*) are simply projected on a dark background. This exemplifies the impact made by Edward Suhr's settings as a whole. They

> painted the whole wretchedness of the concrete jungle [lit: stony wilderness] of the big city in which today's proletarian is buried (59).

Stage right [actor's viewpoint] Heinrich George as *Hinkemann*, wearing only a sort of 'tiger-skin' leotard and brandishing the cages holding the rats, stands on a podium in front of a booth labelled *KULTUR THEATER*, with a drummer, a trumpeter and a short-skirted woman. He is watched by a mixed crowd, many with balloons, back and three-quarter back to the audience. Left centre, further upstage is a white-faced, white-clad clown-figure in front of another booth, and behind this a hint of a Big Wheel. Down stage extreme left are Grete Hinkemann and Paul Großhahn, the former tense and unhappy, avoiding looking towards Hinkemann, her hands clasped in front of her; the latter, darkhaired and moustached, in contrast with Hinkemann, is leering ironically and obviously try to get Grete to look at Hinkemann.

But although one critic (60) would have liked more 'Piscator' stage-effects, the weight of praise lies in the other scale, that of speech and acting:

> In the main the production managed without Piscator's principal makeshifts. It was based upon the word, it guarded the overall tone, it disciplined the individual performance outstandingly (61).

The unity and clarity of the production were more impressive than mere stage effects:

> The clarity of all events in their sequence, the dialogue forcefully carried forward, the interrelation between spiritual and scenic reflexes . . . All those taking part, served, almost without exception, the idea of the ensemble (62).

Within this united ensemble individual performances were clearly appreciated and assessed, above all those of Helene Weigel and Heinrich George.

Weigel portrayed a hard, working-class wife. Her performance was, even by the standards that must be applied to her, unified, unforced and convincing (63).

But above all it is the performance of Heinrich George, returning to the part after a lapse of three and a half years, that critics praise unstintingly and which many thought of as carrying the whole production. From photographs and descriptions we can form an unusually clear idea of his performance both visually and aurally.

There is a certain naivety in Hinkemann's character, and George emphasised this in that he "spoke in the manner of a great helpless child" (64). In his speeches he was undoubtedly helped by the fact that the play had been "ruthlessly cut . . . much to the advantage of the whole" (65). It was advantageous that Toller, who was aware that in the solitariness of prison he had written too many words, was now as co-director in a position to cut his own text.

There is an almost unbearably moving photograph of Heinrich George as Hinkemann (66). He sits with his arms resting on a table, holding a bunch of chrysanthemums in his large, soft hands. His top-coat, waist-coat and collarless shirt are loosely unfastened, his hat tilted at a slightly rakish angle, with pathetic effect. He gazes before him with widely opened, uncomprehending eyes. His face is full but pale, and his drooping, fair moustache lends sadness to his full, sensual lips. The photograph accurately bears out the most vivid description we have:

> His figure is bloated, his face bloated and white, whiter, so to speak, under his straight, fair hair, made puffy by the weary-looking fair moustache — that is Heinrich George's Hinkemann. One who draws his breath audibly from deep in his chest. One who carries a leaden yoke on his shoulders (67).

Even a very hostile critic, who left at the interval rather than endure the play again, granted that George,

> once more lent the misery of the emasculated Hinkemann his very great strength and art as an actor (68).

Under Toller's own direction the play revealed itself not as political theatre but as "unpolitical, very human tragedy" (69), "a drama of love" (70), "the tragedy of an individual fate" (71). Toller's "mysterious post-war drama rose more strongly than ever before to spiritual significance. It gained new light, it secured warmer participation" (72).

> Yesterday evening brought to the fore the tragedy of the individual person, as it could take place at all times, with or without war, under any regime whatsoever (73).

The effect was not revolutionary, but purely and profoundly human. Advanced stage techniques, epitomised by the revolving stage, were united with vision to create an organically completely interrelated action. In spite of all the social accusations in the play the audience realises that "God lays this leaden yoke on Hinkemann's shoulders with his own hands" (74). The 'Yoke' recalls Aeschylus' Agamemnon and the 'yoke-strap of necessity', but Heilborn, while retaining the classical image of burnt sacrifice to symbolise Hinkemann's injury (75) sees another *Leitmotif (roter Faden)* revealed in the play through Toller's direction:

> And in spite of all reproaches against society, both when it makes war and endures peace — sympathy with animals becomes decisively also sympathy with the poor animal, Hinkemann. It runs like a red thread through this production, sympathy with the animal, a red thread, reddened by the blood of animals, from the drop of blood which flowed from the eyes of the blinded siskin to the blood of the mice and rats whose heads Hinkemann must bite off, to the blood of the shattered Grete Hinkemann. Blood of creatures ..the sacrifice blazes.
> It is as if Ernst Toller, directing his play in such a way, reworks his *Hinkemann* spiritually (76).

This was the definitive production in Toller's lifetime and other pre-war productions are therefore of less interest.

Revivals since the war, however, have a new kind of interest: whereas the Toller/Lönner production was welcomed for its realism and its social and ethical seriousness, as being more appropriate for the *Volksbühne* than Holl's confected and opera-like *Peer Gynt* which had preceded it, the director of the first post-war revival — and the first German production since 1932 — Hansgünther Heyme [Heidelberg 1959] — went all out for Expressionism. Heyme, for over a quarter of a century one of West Germany's most original and controversial regisseurs, was only twenty-three at the time. He was a student of Piscator's — of the post-war Piscator! — and he himself had suggested to the intendant, Paul Hagar, that they should put on the play, under his direction: it was in fact only the second production he had undertaken! (77).

Using surrealistic montages he directed the play in a manner more suited to *Die Wandlung*, distancing the play through 1920s-style Expressionism. It was not what the author intended (as critics realised), but Hansgünther Heyme carried it through consistently to the end. He laid the symbolism on too heavily and some of his scenic devices were clumsy, but he showed unusual talent, which was well supported by the actors. Toller himself was described by a critic as 'the angry young man of 1922' and compared with John Osborne (78).

In the following year, 1960, a student group from the Freie Universität Berlin performed *Hinkemann* as the opening production of a special series *Youth plays for Youth* at the Ruhrfestspiele, Recklinghausen. The director, Dietrich von Oertzen, brought the motif of Hinkemann's tragedy into the foreground' with burning intensity'. Both he and the designer, Peter Umbach, emphasised the expressionist style (79). More than one critic regarded the play as being now a period piece or even an anachronism (80), an opinion for which the expressionist production may well be to blame. One, however, also points out the play's frighteningly prophetic quality as Hiroshima, twenty years later, showed by causing genetic damage to thousands (81).

A third production, a French one by Francois Joxe, who also played Hinkemann, was performed in Paris in 1975 and at the Avignon Festival in 1976. Once more the director of the revival seized the opportunity for 'expressionistic turbulence'. The Fairground scene was boisterous with acrobats, fireworks, dance and song. The *Fate* motto from Beethoven's Fifth was hammered out far too heavily! Flore Hofmann, who played Grete, made her bewilderment, but above all her love, credible (82).

Thus, ironically, the very play in which Toller moved, though not all the way, from expressionism towards realism, has been used in post-war revivals as an occasion to attempt to revivify the expressionist techniques of the 1920s: and even in 1959 a critic of Heyme's production wondered whether the play would still cause a scandal (ghosts of Dresden!) if produced realistically (83).

DER ENTFESSELTE WOTAN (WOTAN UNBOUND)

In the Introduction to *Die Maschinenstürmer* it was noted that *Hinkemann* marked the end of the earlier of the two major phases into which Toller's dramatic oeuvre naturally divides itself. In the tragic vision of *Hinkemann,* the vision of a world in which, irrespective of political reforms, the leaden yoke is, in the words of Ernst Heilborn, laid on a man's shoulders by God's own hands (1), Toller had reached a conclusion beyond which advance in the same direction was impossible: the sequence, Friedrich, Sonja, Jimmy Cobbett, Hinkemann, was complete. From now on, even though his plays continue to contain 'victims' — Karl Thomas, Reichpietsch and Köbis, Dr Frank Färber and Anna Gerst, and Pastor Hall — they are primarily studies in the misuse of power and the closely related theme of the miscarriage of justice. The second phase also resembles the first in that it begins quite hopefully, almost optimistically, with the comic treatment of a defeated demagogue and ends with the death of Pastor Hall in the shadow of a Nazi concentration camp, though the progress from tenuous hope to despair is less direct.

Wotan Unbound was, says Toller,

> Written in the cheerful power of growing early springtime in the year 1923 in the fortress-prison of Niederschönenfeld (2).

It was therefore being written at the same time as Toller's lyric-cycle *Das Schwalbenbuch,* his finest poetic achievement and effectively his last (3). The first nine months of 1923 were thus a period of extraordinary creative activity and change, before that strange onset of apathy that almost overcame his spirit during the last 300 days or so of his imprisonment (4).

As the swallows developed in his imagination as a symbol of freedom, life and love, he dedicated the new play *To the Ploughmen (5),* alluding to the words of the Young Workman in the *Allegro* scene, who, when Wotan calls Europe *a field of corpses, a graveyard,* replies:

> What does *your* Europe matter? Every field of corpses becomes a fallow field. To the fallow field comes the ploughman . . . (6)

Having accepted the burden of the leaden yoke of the human condition, Toller turns again to the task of ameliorating it; from the tragic vision he turns to the comic:

> What was once tragedy becomes farce,
> What was once writhing pain becomes laughter (7)

Once freed from prison Toller himself set out to be a 'ploughman', labouring prosaically in the external world until, with Franco's victory, the tragic vision finally overcame him and he too *disappeared into timelessness* (8).

Like the tragedy which preceded it, the farce had its origin in something actually experienced by Toller in prison, though he did not reveal this in public until January 1926, when the play had already been produced in Moscow (Nov. 1924) and — in German — in Prague (Jan. 1925), and was about to open in Berlin (Feb. 1926).

The play's close relationship to the work of Sternheim has tended to lead critics, even since 1926, to regard it as purely derivative, a mere imitation of Sternheim, and to underestimate its originality (9). But truth is stranger than criticism and as Toller has told us, his basic source was not literary but experiential.

Toller's best work indeed always grew from particulars — his friend Sonja Lerch, the image of testicles, the naval revolt, the pair of swallows — and this play, even though it cannot be numbered among his greatest, owes its strength to its foundation in a specific experience: a fellow-prisoner in Niederschönenfeld (10), a one-time barber, later an aircraft builder and later still a leader of revolutionary troops, had, while in prison, a fantastic plan of founding an Emigrants' Co-operative (11). Many of the details in the play are taken directly from the ex-barber's fantasies. Wotan's motto, *In Arbeit, Freud und Leid sind wir vereint* (12) is derived directly from that of Toller's fellow-prisoner *In Freud und Leid sind wir vereint*. Wotan's interest in a machinery catalogue (13) and his 'invention' of a wooden gate for use in Brazil (14) have the same source. Helped by a fellow-prisoner and his paper-work paid for from pocket-money he received from a sister in America, the prisoner became victim of his own imagination and felt himself actually to be the Director of the Co-operative. He even seems to have made contacts in Switzerland (15). The Emigration Office in the Reich Ministry somehow got to know about this and he was warned that if after his release he tried to recruit emigrants he would be prosecuted. So he dropped his plans and seems to have forgotten about them.

Of course, this is not to imply that Toller simply set out to dramatise his fellow-prisoner's fantasies: these were only the starting-point, the catalyst activating Toller's imagination. Just how truly and acutely Toller's imagination developed the initial material is strikingly illustrated in his account of what happened when the prisoner got hold of a copy of the play. (It was published, as well as written, in 1923). After reading only a few pages he hurled the book into a corner and, threatening Toller with his fist, shouted,

> Kerl, Du willst mich lächerlich machen vor der deutschen öffentlichen Meinung (16).

But as Toller points out, remarkably enough that sentence stands, almost word for word, in the play (17). Now whether Toller knew his man so well that he had exactly foreseen or 'fore-heard' the way he would express himself, or whether the sentence printed had caught, the prisoner's eye so that he unconsciously echoed it, in either case the truth of Toller's imagination is, in a small way, exemplified. The prisoner, without finishing his reading of the play, went away and altered his plans so as to win over the Bavarian government to support them. But Toller had anticipated this also in the final scene! (18).

Toller also realised, however, that his Wotan was a type of wide, perhaps universal validity, though flourishing in the atmosphere of Germany (19), but critics interpreted the play more narrowly. The most authoritative critic of the first German-language production described it as,

> Propaganda against the swindlers of postwar Germany who use nationalistic clichés in order to do business at the expense of the German people (20).

From the post-Hitler perspective it is astonishing that even when the play was directed by Fehling at the Tribüne in Berlin in 1926 (21) *after* the publication of Vol. I of *Mein Kampf* and over two years after Hitler's 'Beerhall' putsch, some critics still regarded the play as an already dated satire on the immediate post-war period.

> Why has Toller written this so-called comedy?
> Mass-suggestion as a theme for comedy — in what period did Toller live, when he teased this out of his brain? This theme had already been completely worn out the day before yesterday (22).

Obviously Toller's warning in his Prologue, *Don't laugh too soon,* was given in vain (23). Several critics still saw the play as only derivative from Sternheim and Kaiser (24), and even Kerr in his extensive and sensitive critique, sees Wotan primarily as a "swindler . . . with certain hazy theories about the depression" (25).

However, apart from a 'rogue' critic who saw Ibsen's Hjalmar Ekdal as Wotan's prototype and thought Toller warmly sympathetic to his hero's dreams (26), others did perceive the 'Hitler' element. One said it was typical of the aims of the Volksbühne as it convincingly showed the masses the fundamental nature of the Hitler movement (27), while another was disappointed because of what he saw as the inadequacy of the play as political satire against the Nazis:

> At first we hope that populist Teutonism à la Hitler together with his followers will be pilloried and executed in respect of its perilous and hollow bombast and *dementia praecox.*
> We are expecting great political satire of the pathological barber who is drunk on his own words (28).

Instead, he says, we get 'bloodless dialogue' (blutleeren Dialog) and newspaper leading articles.

This brings us to the crux of 'Wotan' criticism: the relation of the play and its protagonist to Hitler.

When the play was revived in a series of productions from 1959 through into the 1960s, and later again in the 1970s and 1980s, critics were impressed by its prophetic qualities:

> One is compelled, by this accuracy, to believe that it was written after the event (29).

> It is one of the most astonishing visions in the history of the political theatre. The warning that was expressed in this comedy of 1923 by the clairvoyant Toller was not understood, any more than it was in his other numerous works for the theatre (30).

> This comedy, so seldom revived, is not exactly a showpiece out of the dramatic workshop, but it has politico-prophetic drive (31).

But like the critic in 1926 whose expectations of a 'great political satire' of 'populist Teutonism à la Hitler' was disappointed (32), the critics of post-Nazi productions felt that in the light of history Toller had trivialised the Nazi menace:

> Nowadays the play easily arouses false merriment. Toller could afford to under-rate Hitler in 1923 and aim at superficial absurdity (33).
>
> Did he [viz. the Director Koch] make Wotan remind us too much of the person of Hitler? That is a question that remains hard to answer. The eternal remnant in us of the petty-bourgeois gone wild, which becomes a dangerous dream in the hands of an astute demagogue is thereby perhaps too much trivialised (34).

Certainly had Toller in 1923 primarily intended Wotan as a Hitler figure he would have had more excuse for under-rating him than had Chaplin in *The Great Dictator* (1940), but even so, as Rothe well expresses it,

> If Hitler had really been directly intended by Wilhelm Dietrich Wotan, the barber without customers, then Toller would have hopelessly under-rated this excretion of the bourgeoisie tormented by existential fear, and rendered him innocuous as a non-political demagogue and profiteer (35).

But Toller did not actually and directly intend Wotan to represent Hitler. Wotan is based on the fantasies of Toller's anonymous fellow-prisoner. That the theatre both sides of the footlights so soon made the *Wotan=Hitler* equation is tribute to Toller's extrapolating imagination which moved accurately beyond the limited terms of the given data; for the play includes a series of startling minor anticipations of the Hitler story. For example, Wotan more than once hints that he will get support from Stinnes (36). Hugo Stinnes was the most notorious speculator of the period of inflation, amassing a huge fortune, and described by W.R. Castle, American Secretary of State for Western Europe, as "the strongest man in Germany . . . and one of the most dangerous men in the world". Obsessed by the threat of Bolshevism, he conspired to create a Dictator, and after the NSDAP (Nazi) Congress of 1923, he headed the group of right-wing industrialists with whom Hitler had consultations (37).

When Wotan is arrested the police officer assures him that "he is recognised by the authorities as a citizen whose basic convictions are conducive to the well-being of the state" (38). He has nothing to fear from the law and will soon be freed; and meanwhile his Wife may bring in dainties from her kitchen (39). Wotan declares that while in prison he will write a book, his memoirs, with the title *The Stab in the Back, shortly before the Goal, Memoirs of Wilhelm Dietrich Wotan* (40).

Hitler, as a result of the Beerhall Putsch, was condemned (1.4.1924) to five years' fortress imprisonment at Landsberg: he was released *less than nine months later (20.12.1924).* In prison "high above the River Lech . . . treated as an honoured guest, with a room of his own and a splendid view" (41), he began to dictate a book to Rudolf Hess. Hitler's own title for the book (abbreviated to *Mein Kampf* by his Nazi publisher) is reminiscent of Wotan's: *Four and a half Years of Struggle against Lies, Stupidity and Cowardice* (42).

Although Hitler's obsession with *Lebensraum* was a European one (43), his attitude to those (primarily the Russians) whose land he intended to overrun and annexe was as ruthless as that of Wotan to the Brazilian natives.

According to Frühwald (44) Wotan was first played with "Hitler characteristics" (Die Züge Adolf Hitlers) in Fehling's production of 1926. He cannot mean make-up (Maske) for a photograph of Rolf Arthur Roberts in this production shows no particular likeness to Hitler (unless later in the play he combed down the typical Hitler forelock) and his moustache extends beyond his mouth, drooping a little at the ends (45). This corresponds with Toller's own description of Wotan's drooping moustache which he twice during the play gives the *Es-ist-erreicht* style: presumably the upturned style of Kaiser Wilhelm II (46). It is thus evident that Toller did *not* intend Wotan actually to be modelled upon Hitler.

Therefore, rather than interpret the play as a Hitler-satire trivialised by lack of imaginative depth, we must see it as a swindler-comedy extended into politico-prophetic satire through the working of the author's imagination upon the contemporary Germany of 1923.

From this firm basis of understanding of the original theme and the direction of its imaginative growth, we are in a position to see the play in true perspective and assess it rightly as a text and upon the stage.

The fundamental mode of *Wotan Unbound* is parodistic: not a simple parody of one particular style or genre but an attempt to weave into a single comic pattern a number of distinct critical threads. The assessment of the artistic success of the play must therefore depend to a great extent upon how far this is achieved.

The title parodies that of the lost second play of Aeschylus' *Prometheus* trilogy, *Prometheus Unbound* (47). The play, however, bears no relation at all to the supposed content of the Greek p]ay (48). Instead, the title introduces the second thread of parody, the Wagnerian. The substitution of Wotan for Prometheus is in itself parody. Instead of the Greek demigod,"the champion of mankind . . . the type of the highest perfection of moral and intellectual nature, impelled by the purest and truest motives to the best and noblest ends" (49), we have the principal Germanic god "symbolic [sc.in Wagner's *Ring*] of greed for wealth and power" (50); instead of "the creator of mankind" (51), we have "the chief of the gods, a race marked out by fate for annihilation" (52) (53).

The play opens with full-blooded Wagner-parody: the god Wotan in Valhalla riding a fire-breathing black horse *BUT* "swinging a lasso" cowboy fashion and crying *in English: "Come on!"*, thus emphasising from the outset that, as Toller later wrote,

> The figure of Wotan, although flourishing in the teutonic atmosphere, is a universal one — at least European and *American* (my italics) (54).

Dragged on-stage by the lasso, Wilhelm Dietrich Wotan is dressed in exaggeratedly Wagnerian style — though as photographs of earlier Bayreuth productions show, the exaggeration is not excessive! (55).

The God Wotan's speech which follows, while not a close parody of Wagner's verse and vocabulary, is recognisably a travesty of Wagnerian rhythm and language (56). The parodistic intention is plainly stated:

> Let what once was tragedy become farce (57)

Wilhelm Dietrich Wotan is invited to play as "an epigone of himself" (58), and finally the closing, climactic word *HELDENFAHRT (Hero's Journey)* is printed in large capitals and in the form of an arch, suggesting the Rainbow Bridge in the closing scene of *Das Rheingold* (59). Toller, however, offers no suggestion as to how the typographical device could be translated into theatrical terms, though obviously this could be done.

With this Wagner parody Toller was entering upon a tradition that went back as far as 1854, when a Dr H. Wollheim from Breslau based a parody of *Tannhäuser* on student songs, a parody upon which Johann Nestroy based another, more substantial one in 1857, which Wagner himself is said to have enjoyed (60). Only a year before Toller wrote *Der entfesselte Wotan,* Carl Sternheim had brought together his comedies and plays written since 1908 under the ironical general title: *Aus dem Bürgerlichen Heldenleben. (From the heroic life of the middle classes)* (61), and Toller's use of the nonce-word *Heldenfahrt* may be seen as an allusion to Sternheim, whose best known plays, *Die Hose (Knickers)* and *Bürger Schippel (Paul Schippel Esq.),* are shot through with Wagnerian Parody (62). In the former, Mandelstam "can only come to terms with the world through seeing it *sub specie Wagneri*" (63), while the latter is closely related to *Die Meistersinger von Nürnberg,* complete with a male-voice quartette as Mastersingers (64). Toller thus in effect invites his audience to associate Wilhelm Dietrich Wotan with Sternheim's 'family' of petit-bourgeois pseudo-Wagnerian anti-heroes. Moreover, as Kerr noted:

> Toller, who indeed found his own language, here uses Sternheim's language almost like a parody (65).

Sternheim's style is remarkable in its terseness, almost amounting to telegraphese:

> His extreme, elliptical language also was antiromantic, deliberately heartless and matter-of-fact (66).

His language, however, like his satire, is ambiguous, being "part parody, part pre-Expressionist earnest" (67). With Toller there is no doubt but that parody is intended, and in this play Toller goes so far as to parody his own works. Even the kernel of *Hinkemann,* "He who has not strength to dream has not strength to live" (68) is parodied in Bankier Karauschen's speech:

> But man does not live by figures alone. Man needs a dream. Mine is: Brazil . . . I have kept my dream to myself. It lies safely in a drawer (69).

Colonial war, so bitterly regarded in *Die Wandlung,* is treated satirically:

> They steal from the officer his right to war. In Brazil he can make war against the natives to his heart's content (70).

In the *Andante* scene Toller parodies the dream scenes in *Masse Mensch* in which Sonja realises in visionary form the implications of her husband's political position. This is just what happens, in the manner of a "street-ballad, a dreamlike grotesque charade "(ein Moritát-Traumspuk) -with barrel-organ accompaniment — in Mariechen's absurd, yet basically true foreboding of Wotan's future triumph and defeat. (This is, of course, also a more general parody of Toller's earlier Expressionism and of Expressionism in general).

In this scene, too, the 'Colonial War' material is parodistically presented.

The "Sternheim" style does in general terms parody the more heavily rhetorical passages of Toller's earlier plays, as well as parodying: in a wider sense the *O-Mensch* style, but in some places the verbal parodistic parallels are so close that they cannot be accidental (71).

In our examination of *The Scorned Lover's Revenge* we saw how frequently Toller uses sexual and marital relationships climactically. This element is also woven into the 'Dream Scene' of this play, when Mariechen, the wife, watches as

> Natives . . . lead in dark-skinned virgins.
> Wotan, pawing them, makes them form a
> picturesque group. He gives a signal!. .
> a majestic, imperious gesture! . . .
> A photographer enters the scene.
> Dance of the Virgins before Wotan.
> A plaintive cry from Mariechen rings out.
> MARIECHEN: Wilhelm! (72)

The sexual / marital motif runs in fact through the play. Wotan assumes that the customer, the Strange Gentleman, is looking for a brothel or other sex-adventure. In fact the customer is disgusted with the doomed country,

> which offers its gaping vagina for sale in exchange for gold marks, and lecherously couples in orgies like those before Noah's Flood (73).

Wotan, quickly converted to the idea of emigration, also uses sexual imagery to express the alleged corruption of society:

> Women dress their pox-ridden legs in silk knickers (74).

The dramatic climax of the play is in fact Wotan's rejection of his wife (at Schleim's insistence) so that he may be free to marry the wealthy religious bigot, Gräfin Gallig. Wotan's wooing of the Gräfin is the most farcical scene of the play, highlighted by the real pathos of Mariechen. Of this character in the first Berlin production, Alfred Kerr wrote:

> Fatally moving when he [viz. Roberts as Wotan] puts his wife away. When the consciousness of mean behaviour breaks its way over the hushing-up and self-deception — and he chokes it down. The ego does not want to know — and yet does. Stobrawa plays his subordinated wife excellently. This woman, who is the best verse speaker in the realm of Penthesilea [Queen of the Amazons. CWD], mouths and worrits here as a delightfully care-worn poor middle-class wife. Even to the turned-in toes, to the stupid, ill-educated look; to the niceness and neatness that, for all that, still show through (75).

Like all the best comedy, *Der entfesselte Wotan* includes not only some broad farce but also touches of real feeling:

Oh yes, it was very funny, very sad (76). In this area, and in general, the self-critical faculty seen in Toller's self-parodies is one of the play's greatest strengths and reveals a by no means obvious trait in our author's character.

Woven into the main pattern of parody are several minor strands which enrich the total effect. Of these perhaps the most important is the musical. Probably taking his cue from the Wagnerian parody Toller has cast the play in a four-movement symphonic mould:

> Allegro
> Andante
> Scherzo Furioso — Rondo Finale

preceded by the

> Wotanisches Impromptu

as Prelude (77).

This mock-symphonic pattern reflects the movement and tempo of the plot:

> *Allegro*: Exposition. Wotan *quickly* develops his plan
>
> *Andante*: The action slows, and various new 'themes' are developed.

> *Scherzo Furioso — Rondo Finale*: The Scherzo covers the comic and farcical climaxes (as it should) up to the flourish of trumpets (Tusch) and Chorale (78) which lead straight into the headlong catastrophe of the Rondo Finale: a mere three pages of text and in the view of some critics, too rapid.

Music, as comic and parodistic motif, is also introduced throughout the play and makes an important, contribution to the overall effect:

1) Sound of hunting-horns at the end of the *Impromptu*.
2) Barrel-organ music accompanies the 'dream' scene.
3) Naval song and wind band at the end of that scene.
4) At the end of the Andante Wotan, hearing a jazz band, declares:

> I really do hear the Music of the Spheres.

5) During the Interval Toller prescribes, with some irony:

> So that the deeply moved audience may blow their noses and get over their emotion, a barrel-organ can churn out familiar tunes and military pot-pourris (Battle Marches, King Frederick etc).

6) Towards the end of the Scherzo an approaching band is heard in the distance accompanied by the heavy beat of masses of people marching. This comes to a climax with the Flourish and the Chorale, *Ein' feste Burg* that lead into the *Finale*.
7) The Director seems to be encouraged to use a military march to accompany the final exeunt:

> While all three march off into timelessness in traditional quick goose-step, the stage closes (79).

Thus the whole play is shot through with musical effects, all parodistically or satirically intended (80).

To a lesser extent literary references other than the major Wagnerian and Sternheim ones already mentioned, are also used in the comic texture.

Wotan, who appears to read nothing but "exotic novels" (81) which affect his view of the real world rather as Gothic novels affected Catherine Morland's (82), likes to imply his familiarity with serious literature. His declaration:

> Des starken Mannes Anfang: Tat!

echoes Faust's

> Mir hilft der Geist! auf einmal seh' ich Rat
> Und schreibe getrost: Im Anfang war die Tat. (83)

and later he absurdly expresses sympathy with Karauschen's speech on figures and dreams by using the word *Wahlverwandtschaft (Elective Affinity),* the title (in the plural) of Goethe's psychological novel. For the benefit of the American journalist he can quote a hackneyed line from Walt Whitman and claims acquaintance with the most recent world-literature (84).

In his use of symbolism in this play also Toller turns to comic and satirical effect the love of symbolism evinced in his earlier plays. Manfred Durzak considers that the jungle (*Urwald*) conjured up in conjunction with dictatorship (85) by General von Stahlfaust becomes "a socio-political allegory, a great metaphor of regression" (86). But this way of putting it ignores the comic and satirical aspect (87).

Even though Wotan is not, and is not intended as a portrait of Hitler, the figures with which he surrounds himself do closely parallel the individuals and groups with whom the German Dictator surrounded himself.

> More dangerous than this undaemonic barber appear all sorts of sinister figures who gather round him (88).

Schleim, even if his name owes something to Schleich in Unruh's *Platz* (89), grimly foreshadows Goebbels; von Wolfblitz and von Stahlfaust caricature the military men, especially Ludendorff, who supported Hitler; and although Ernst von Bussard-Baldrian in no way resembles Gustav Gründgens his inclusion anticipates the support given to the Nazis by "Mephisto" (90) and other artists. Of course there is the Banker Karauschen, eager to help, though to Schleim he is just a "gold mine", a "filthy Jew" (91).

The Gräfin Gallig anticipates all those religious people who were prepared to give the Nazis their support and Schleim lists several more, whom history can see as prototypes of Hitler's supporters:

Herr Assessor Biersumpel: the typical anti-semitic graduate civil servant.

Herr Zuchthausaufseher Neuland: the prison officer who offers good references . . . a later KZ boss?
Frau Konsistorialrat von Schimmelmark: the administrator's wife who wants to see things started.
Chemiker Gelbkreuz: the scientist who offers his patents for use against the natives.
The brothel-keeper Gretchen Nudel, eager to supply supervised prostitutes (92).
— Toller has prophesied all too clearly how many and how various will be the classes and professions who will support the Nazis.

Finally and most importantly, *Der entfesselte Wotan* is a satirical critique of

> certain psychic susceptibilities of the Germans, their need for substitute religions and every kind of irrationality, pseudomyths, and their susceptibility to doctrines of redemption (93).

This search for a 'redeemer' to whom they can subordinate themselves is another aspect of Hölderlin's invective against the German people which Toller considered a suitable Preface to his tragedy *Hinkemann* (94). Here, of course, he is giving the theme comic, satiric treatment, and so once more this play reveals self-parody and Toller's new objectivity.

As Rothe says:

> Toller dramatised the religious wave which surged up powerfully in the early 1920s and which betrayed the emotional undernourishment of a people whose previous idols, ideals and ideas of value had been taken from them, and whose need to worship and to pay honour was wandering without a goal (95).

Rothe suggests that Toller's isolation in prison actually heightened his ability to recognise the contemporary danger, and asks whether the German theatre's virtual rejection of the play was due to Toller's having touched a sensitive nerve, as 1933 would show (96).

The gullibility of the public, whether German or American, under the influence of phoney religious leaders was a theme Toller took up again in his and Kesten's attack on Mary Baker Eddy in *Wunder in Amerika* and in a little known prose account of another similar false prophetess, *Aimée, die Prophetin*, published in a popular periodical in June 1930 (i.e. a year before *Wunder in Amerika*) (97).

No wonder then that in 1933 Rainer Schlösser, a Nazi, included *Der entfesselte Wotan* in a violent attack upon what he called "System-Theatre", along with plays such as Paul Zech's *Verbrüderung* and Alfons Paquet's *Sturmflut*, as

> An art which has nothing to do with German blood and which did not come out of our soul (98).

This vicious attack on *Der entfesseite Wotan* as a play in which

> a man of foreign blood gives full rein to the profound hate of his race for the Germans (99)

is the best testimonial it could receive from such a source, and proves that those critics, both in the 1920s and in the post-Nazi world, who thought the play treated its terrible theme too trivially or inadequately, were wrong.

Der entfesselte Wotan marks the watershed in Toller's career both as dramatist and political writer. Up until now he has written subjectively, chiefly in verse and primarily as a revolutionary — after Munich, a failed revolutionary. From now on he writes objectively, almost exclusively in prose, and primarily as an anti-fascist (100).

HOPPLA, WIR LEBEN! *(WHOOPS! WE'RE ALIVE)*

BACKGROUND AND DEVELOPMENT

In the four years between October 1919, when he began *Masse-Mensch* and the publication of *Der entfesselte Wotan* in 1923, Toller wrote five plays, not to mention the Leipzig *Massenspiele*, two *Sprechchöre*, and a considerable body of poetry, including *Das Schwalbenbuch*; but then over three years elapsed between his release from prison on 15 July 1924 and the first nights of *Hoppla, wir leben!* on 1 Sept. (Hamburg) and 3 Sept. (Berlin) 1927, — three years of intense activity, during which he had to discover and come to terms with the world he had for five years known only at second-hand from behind prison bars.

During this period he travelled widely, visiting Palestine (March 1925), England (December 1925), the Soviet Union (Early March to mid-May 1926), France (from June to October, 1926), Austria (January 1927), Brussels (10 to 14 February 1927), Denmark and Norway (February to March 1927). These tours involved lectures and readings. He worked against injustices, for example on behalf of the imprisoned Max Hölz, (1) and published his book *Justiz: Erlebnisse* in May 1927. He became deeply involved in theatre controversies, helped to direct *Der entfesselte Wotan* (January 1925), joined the *Group of Revolutionary Pacifists*, and supported the *League against Colonial Oppression*. The imprisoned dramatist and poet of Niederschönenfeld had become a world-figure and he responded eagerly to the demands and rewards of this new role. From now until his death his outward life was primarily that of a politically and morally motivated publicist.

It is against this background of adjustment and expansion that the merits and shortcomings of his next completed play, *Hoppla, wir leben!*, are to be interpreted.

It was early 1926 before he even attempted any new dramatic writing. A short notice published in February 1926 stated that Toller was working on a new drama called *Sturm über der Erde* (2). This may or may not have been an early title for *Hoppla, wir leben!*. In the spring of the same year he planned a new *Massenstück* which he is said to have intended to discuss with Piscator during its actual writing (3). At first this was to be called *Komödie über das Scheunenviertel* but later became *Berlin 1919*. It was about Karl Liebknecht and Rosa Luxemburg, but was never finished. The subject suggests that Toller was moving towards the use of contemporary documentary material, as in *Feuer aus den Kesseln*. Five short scenes from it were published in *Die Volksbühne* in March 1927 (4).

In August 1926, *Die Volksbühne* published an open letter from Toller about another new play on which he was working. This would seem to refer to *Hoppla, wir leben!*, whose earlier title was *Barrikaden am Wedding* (5). Part of the open letter runs:

> I am reluctant to make statements about the content of the piece so long as it is not finished. Let me just say that I have tried to find a new form for a *Collective-Drama*, as I believe that the inner character and outward atmosphere, the ups and downs of a great modern mass-movement, cannot be given form with the usual means of dramatic construction. For example, the new mass-drama must also be able to show happenings which are very intimately connected, almost simultaneously — a possibility in which film has the advantage over drama. To make the dynamics and movement of the twentieth century perceptible it is not a question of imitating the noise of machinery with stage-props. The inner tempo and diversity of plot are elements which the audience must absorb as an integrated whole (6).

Clearly Toller intended, even at this date, 1) that the play should be concerned with a mass-movement, 2) that some sort of simultaneous or multiple setting was envisaged, 3) that, whether or not the play *used* film, techniques should be borrowed from that medium.

The earliest surviving version of the play consists of an unbound set of proof-sheets, corrected in Toller's own handwriting, in the possession of John M. Spalek. Its title-page reads: *Hoppla, wir leben! Ein Vorspiel und vier Akte von Ernst Toller. Gustav Kiepenheuer Verlag. Potsdam 1927* (7).

This consists of 122 pages, as against 141 pages in the version finally published, and had evidently reached this proof-stage before Toller, in response to Piscator, began his major revisions. It may well be the version that Piscator first read in the spring of 1927, though he calls what he saw merely "a draft. " (8). It has not been possible for this copy to be examined by the present writer, but its vitally important final scene (Act 4, Sc. 4) is reprinted by Frühwald (9).

Toller's own description of his original ending agrees approximately with this:

> In my first version Thomas, who did not understand the world of 1927, ran into the asylum to the psychiatrist, recognised in discussion with the doctor that there are two kinds of dangerous fools: one, those who are held in solitary confinement in padded cells; the other, those who as politicians and army officers rage against humanity. When he understands his old comrades, who carry on the idea through dogged everyday work, he wants to leave the asylum, but because he has understood, because he has achieved the relationship of a mature person to reality, the psychiatric civil-servant will no longer release him: now for the first time he has become "dangerous to the state", not earlier, when he was an awkward dreamer (10).

The proof-sheet ending and this description are in harmony with Toller's summing-up of his original theme:

> Once more it was the collision of the man who wishes to translate the absolute into reality unconditionally and now, with the powers of the time and with contemporaries who give up that fulfilment out of weakness, betrayal and cowardice, or prepare for later days through strength, fidelity and courage (11).

Piscator on the other hand, was not looking for a play with this theme, nor indeed for any "available, ready-made scripts" (12). Instead, he wanted a revue, a collaborative script written by his own intellectual group (13). Having been disappointed by the opening scenes of a commissioned piece by Wilhelm Herzog submitted in July, he turned again to Toller's play, which, he says, approximated to the original aim of the revue he had planned and which offered an opportunity "of giving a social and political outline of a whole epoch" (14). Thus from the start Piscator regarded *Hoppla, wir leben!* not as a play to be interpreted through a stage production but as a foundation upon which to construct a revue-like creation of his own.

As C. N. Innes suggests, Piscator was not content to create an individual style on the basis of his interpretation of plays but tried to create what Ehm Welk protested was "a style of production . . . politically and artistically an end in itself" (15).

By August 10 many of the changes and developments wanted by Piscator were clear and were fully described by him in his letter to

Toller of that date (16) and the next day August 11 Toller wrote in a letter to Kerr:

> Will you be in Berlin on September 1st? The rehearsals in the Piscator-Bühne have begun. Granach plays Karl Thomas; Sima — Kilman; Sybille Binder — Eva Berg; René Stobrawa — Frau Meller; Graetz — Pickel; Steckel — Professor Lüdin. Meanwhile I have worked through the piece yet again; a short fifth act has been written: Thomas does not finish up in the madhouse (17).

Evidently Toller had by this date accepted the new ending — not that finally used by Piscator but that printed in the first edition and used in the Hamburg production.

But, as the *Regiebuch* shows, Piscator was not yet satisfied and continued to alter the text throughout the rehearsal period. Nearly half-a-century later Gerda Redlich, an eighteen year old member of the cast playing a small part, "just a very tiny citizen or a girl walking along the streets" recalled the conflicts between Toller and Piscator:

> I remember a terrible row between Toller and Piscator. Piscator being extremely quiet and cold — and Toller . . . a terribly excitable man — these two men absolutely standing there glaring at each other. We thought they would be fighting any moment, but it didn't come to that! But I cannot tell you what it was about. Toller didn't want all that technical to-do; he wanted everything very much simpler; that's what it was all about fundamentally. Piscator wouldn't give an inch to anyone (18).

Soon after August 11, however, Toller as author must have decided that the text was now definitive and have gone ahead with publication, for the printed book was available in time for Piscator to use it as the basis of his greatly modified production.

Although it is through Piscator's production that *Hoppla, wir leben*! has usually been described in later books (19), contemporary reviews of the Hamburg and Leipzig productions show that even then critics not carried away by Piscator's political enthusiasms and experimental stage-machinery recognised his production to be an aberration and fundamentally a falsification of Toller's play. For example, Fritz Mack, reviewing the Leipzig production, begins by saying how Piscator (in Berlin) had "altered and falsified" the play; and Hermann Kienzl, who thought the play's success in Hamburg was due to the 'excellent production', said that "in Berlin, Piscator's mechanical madhouse made the audience half-crazy". He also remarked that Granach was frequently inaudible, though he suspected that the inaudibility might have been intentional (20). Another critic, evidently without having seen Piscator's production, described the first night in Hamburg in glowing terms:

> . . . The full house celebrated the poetic drama most vividly in the scenes whose profoundly human content compelled rapt, breathless silence, particularly in Karl Thomas's movingly simple story of the dreadful suffering of the war. A brilliant production and masterly representation as regards acting helped to get over the all too everyday treatment and weakening impression of the sequence [of scenes] particularly in the second part, so that the artists and author, who was present, were greeted at the end with stormy and honest applause (21).

That Toller quickly regretted having re-written the end of the play (with the added Act 5) even as in the published text, is evidenced by the fact that for the Leipzig production of October 7 he again re-wrote the ending, evidently restoring his original version (22), and three years later he declared:

> I regret now that, prejudiced by a contemporary fashion, I destroyed the structure of the original work in favour of the structure of the production. Its form, as aimed at, was stronger than that which was shown on the stage. I alone am responsible for that, but I have learned, and today I prefer that a director extracts too little from a work than that he puts too much into it (23).

Obviously Toller's conflict with Piscator was far deeper than disagreement over technical elaboration, as Gerda Redlich suggested.

There is profound irony in the nature of Toller's conflicts with Piscator over this play, for during the same year Toller was publicly defending Piscator for similarly distorting Ehm Welk's *Gewitter über Gottland* at the Volksbühne in March. That production had brought to a head the conflict between Piscator and his contractual employers, the Volksbühne, resulting from Piscator's aim of turning that theatre into a vehicle of leftwing, not to say Communist, propaganda, rather than a theatre with left-wing sympathies (24). Piscator developed *Gewitter über Gottland*, an admittedly 'political' play set in the later middle-ages, into "a communist election and propaganda meeting" (25). Welk did not himself disapprove of Piscator's attempt to strengthen the political impact of the play, but of the manner in which this was done (26).

Toller quickly became involved in the resulting *Storm over the Volksbühne (Gewitter uber der Volksbühne)*. Piscator's phrase (27).

Ehm Welk's play opened at the Volksbühne on 23 March 1927. Alfred Kerr gave the production very high praise, claiming that in the face of this new experience,

> One's own political attitude scarcely matters. The emotional fact speaks, speaks, cries out (28).

On March 29 Toller wrote to Kerr:

> I was very pleased with what you wrote on behalf of Piscator. The Volksbühne threatens, through the influence of various 'Baberlababs', to become an instrument of the law-and-order petty bourgeoisie (29).

By *Baberlababs* Toller means the supporters of Julius Bab (1881–1955), critic, essayist, publicist, dramaturge, whose influence within the Volksbühne was very strong. Throughout his life he belonged to the liberal left and was a passionate supporter of the ideals of the Volksbühne. In an essay published at the end of June, 1927, he makes the reasons for his enthusiasm plain:

> If it were only a consumers' co-operative, a cleverly devised set-up for making it cheaper to go to the theatre, I certainly would not have devoted two hours of my life to the Volksbühne . . .
> That the economic advantages of this organisation should be above all for the benefit of the proletariat, that the whole institution was first created in order to make a high level of culture accessible to the disinherited from middle-class society, — that was really of great significance . . .
> But even that could not be decisive, as, becoming politically aware, I came to know the greater and more appropriate way to satisfy my feeling of social responsibility.
> The Volksbühne idea must more enduringly fascinate a dramaturge who had recognised that every theatre, as a basic act of society, can be built up organically only from its audience, and who saw here, for the first time in centuries, an attempt to renew the theatre not through artistic genius and gifts from wealthy patrons, but in the only natural way — through the creation of an audience (30).

Piscator and his supporters did, of course, accuse the Volksbühne of being a mere consumers' co-operative. That it was not, despite these accusations, is plain from a study of its history (31). The curious, and rather sad fact that Toller aligned himself with the Communist Party (which had so bitterly opposed him in Munich) rather than with Bab (with whose sympathetic humanism Toller obviously had a great deal in common) is probably due to the fact that at that juncture Bab and the Volksbühne *appeared* to represent 'the establishment' and Piscator the underdog: Toller's heart was always with the underdog.

The article by Bab just quoted was, of course, written at the height of the *Storm over the Volksbühne* and with Piscator's accusations in mind.

Toller's first public act in the battle was to sign, along with over 40 other public figures — writers, actors, critics etc. - a statement of solidarity with Piscator addressed to the management of the Volksbühne (32). In fairness it must be said that the list of signatories indicates support for Piscator from quite a wide spectrum of progressive opinion (33).

His second public act was to speak at a meeting of the left wing of the Volksbühne on Wednesday 30 March (the day after his letter to Kerr) held in the ballroom of the Herrenhaus (the former upper chamber of the imperial government), also addressed by Arthur Holitscher, Erwin Kalser, Victor Blum, Karlheinz Martin, Piscator and Kurt Tucholsky.

> Ernst Toller, who was greeted with loud applause, spoke on *Drama — Idea- Message*: 'Drama means conflict, means we must be radical if we are to be anything at all. The proletarian who walks the stage today carries a flag — and that disturbs the petty bourgeois. The proletarian of today is no longer a man of feeling, he is the bearer of an idea. The Volksbühne has no face, no character, has not the courage to make itself disliked.' Toller then spoke on his own account, which was unnecessary. (It is well known that Toller is involved in a lawsuit against the Volksbühne, which accepted one of his plays but failed to stage it.) (34)

Toller spoke again on behalf of Piscator at the Eighth Volksbühne Conference held in Magdeburg, 23 to 26 June, 1927.

Bab gave a major lecture on *Theatre and Politics*.

> In a spirited manner and yet with the greatest objectivity he showed the boundaries between dramatic art and political

> propaganda, without overlooking in the process the threads which connect them. With convincing eloquence he expounded the tasks presented to art and theatre to collaborate in the "Education of the Human Race" (35).

Toller, not himself a delegate at the conference, though highly regarded in the movement, made himself the "Spokesman of the Opposition".

> Toller and one or two of his friends did not speak undiplomatically. But no doubt could ever arise that the vast majority of the delegates stood behind the official speakers at the conference (36).

Piscator's dispute with the Volksbühne was not about the choice of Ehm Welk's play (which had been agreed) but about Piscator's cavalier treatment of it. Toller reacted very differently when his own play was subjected to similarly ruthless re-working.

Whatever may have been the artistic merits of Piscator's production when judged in its own terms, it is now clear that the author regarded the re-working as artistically damaging to his play. Had a second edition appeared in his lifetime he would certainly have used the original ending: but it was not reprinted until 1962, in East Germany (37).

The contemporary critiques already quoted also make it clear that the success and quality of Toller's play were never dependent upon Piscator's scenic elaborations and filmic additions. Of the Leipzig production Fritz Mack goes on to refer to the "good technique" for the many scene changes in W. Dobra's setting. Unfortunately he does not describe this, though it was clearly simpler than Piscator's machinery. Nor did the Regisseur, Alwin Kronacher, think it necessary to use film. He did, however, project 'titles'. Again Mack does not clarify this. So while it remains generally true that *Hoppla, wir leben*! is, as John Willett has said, "an underestimated play" doubt can be thrown on the same scholar's assertion (admittedly more cautious than C. N. Innes' adulation of Piscator) that Piscator made his production of the play "into something of a technological masterpiece" (38).

FURTHER STAGE HISTORY

After its initial run in the Theater am Nollendorfplatz the Piscator production went on tour, apparently with the organisational and promotional support of local branches of the Communist Party (KPD) which, according to the hostile right-wing press, turned "the performances into propaganda through calls from the audience, the sale of propaganda materials, etc. " (1). In Frankfurt am Main, where the play opened 16 January 1928, the performances were in the Schumann Theatre, a large theatre whose bad acoustics were made even worse by the deadening effects of huge drapes (2): a "cave for the masses" in which the players' voices were completely lost and where many of the audience thought they must smoke and chat whatever was happening on stage; according to Bernhard Diebold, it must have been Piscator's worst enemy who advised him to bring *Hoppla, wir leben!* here: the place was fit only for "Mammoth-shows", not for human ones (3).

The critic "-ng" (? Ihering), quoted above, said the play and production constituted a demonstration rather than a creation, but

> a demonstration with the enormous force of agonising and completely naked truth.
> Piscator elevated the demonstration into something enormous. He almost destroyed the play itself with his accumulated force, and overwhelmed the audience — a veritable "knock-out" (4).

Ludwig Marcuse, referring to Toller as "a thwarted lyric poet", described the production as "an encouraging fanfare" (5).

Three sketches of the production in Frankfurt show the use of scaffolding to create 'levels' and suggest a high degree of naturalism in costume and acting style. It is not possible to judge whether the whole vast machinery of the Berlin setting was toured (6).

After the tour, which also included Mannheim (7), the production returned, in March 1928, to Berlin, this time to the Lessing Theatre (8), where critics continued to notice it, unfavourably:

> The stage-technical trick has been trivialised by over-use (9).
> The shortcomings of the piece are known to everyone (10).
> The set makes an hotel look like a prison (11).

(Toller, of course *intended* it to look like a madhouse!)

While the "Piscator-Swindle" (12) toured Germany, Toller's play, in his own, revised, 'Leipzig' version, was produced by Rudolf Beer at the Raimund Theatre, Vienna, opening 11 November 1927 (13).

In studying the reviews of this production of Toller's 'own' latest version of the play — though based upon the earliest (14) — in Vienna, with its own literary and theatrical traditions and away from the politically over-heated atmosphere of the Berlin of the Weimar Republic, we can begin to ascertain the direct impact of Toller's work upon a theatre public.

A full and detailed critique by Felix Salten makes some imaginative reconstruction of the production possible (15). Toller, he thinks, is no dramatist. His play will not last like *Kabale und Liebe* or even Sardou's *Tosca*, but Toller, "God help him" can write in no other way: it is the consequence of his imprisonment — a view also expressed by Leopold Jacobsohn in *his* review, published on the same day as Salten's: the martyr's halo, his inability to free himself from his experience of imprisonment, that is his trade-mark (16). Unlike Piscator, whose explosive production disintegrated the play and left little of it intact., Beer tries to draw it together.

> The plot itself is very simple, completely plain in its humanity, completely genuine in its fundamental attitudes (17).

Jacobsohn says that Beer has used few technical tricks and that though he has lost a few "moments" (i. e. in comparison with Piscator) he has done more justly by the author — he and his designer, Kunz, have given the fundamental melody a firmer rhythm. Referring to such stage devices as Beer does use, Salten interestingly suggests that the transparencies, inscriptions and "allegorical figures" really all go back to the techniques of Raimund's fairy-plays. It is illuminating to realise that, viewed from an Austrian perspective, techniques appropriate for this modern, highly political play, can be seen as having their origins in the *Wiener Zauberspiel*: it also helps one to see Piscator in truer perspective and less as an utterly new and original phenomenon in the theatre.

Jacobsohn, evidently familiar with Piscator's production, regards the play as a pamphlet, a sort of contemporary film, adding that it was as such that Piscator had produced it from the very start. Piscator's production, in fact, seems to have conditioned this critic's approach to the play. For others the emotional impact is of greatest importance. Rudolf Holzer says:

> There are scenes which remain almost unforgettably in the memory (18).

Salten picks out two scenes, an 'inward' and an 'outward'. The former, which is also one of Holzer's 'unforgettables', is the scene with the children, their failure to understand what the war was like, and their dismissal of Thomas's attempts to change things as "*dumm*". The latter is when, as he tells us, five different types of persons, from five different "stages", cry in turn, "*Hoppla, wir leben!*". There is no such scene in any version of Toller's text. In Act 4 Sc. 4 of the version used in Vienna, however, Lüdin does present and number five types of '*Normality*' — but the five-fold repetition is of "*Normal . . . Normal . . .*" not of "*Hoppla, wir leben!*" (19). Either Salten is describing this scene or, less probably, Beer used Mehring's *Chanson* and presented it in this way. (Holzer picks out *Irrenhaus* as an 'unforgettable' scene.)

In this production, not overweighted with technical tricks, the figure of Karl Thomas was more clearly seen. Karl Thomas, says Salten, is true, because Toller understands him through his own five-year imprisonment: but, he goes on, whether Toller really sees the other characters as he draws them, is another matter. Most valuable of all other evidence, therefore, is that of the actor Loibner, who played Karl Thomas. Interviewed for the *Neue Freie Presse,* he said:

> Thus I was clear from the very start that I would give my role a somewhat softer conception than my Berlin colleague.

Of course, as we now know from his subsequent admission, Piscator deliberately miscast Alexander Granach as Thomas in order effectively to turn him into a proletarian type (20). Loibner presumably did not know this. He continues:

> I had to create the revolutionary more out of feeling than with sharp, naked intellect. But I believe that I was able to get on to close terms with the part by this route also.
>
> And as Karl Thomas there is one thing I am as little as possible, viz: an actor. One can create this man with the heart, one can also create him entirely with the brain, but one can absolutely not create him by purely histrionic methods and professional finesse. And I am an emotional actor, always have been; I have truly little or nothing to do with the theatre as a private person, I can't "play" anything, and I don't want to, and that damages one a little now and then in present day show-business. So, too, I've not become what we call a 'Star', although I've actually already played a whole series of good parts under Dr Beer.

Asked about his favourite part he said it was Selbitz in Goethe's *Götz von Berlichingen*, in which he came on with his own son and which he played practically as himself. From this he brought the interview back to the subject of Karl Thomas:

> And as I can always characterise my favourite parts as those which can be played quite simply straight from the heart without further contortions and mental acrobatics, I haven't first fetched an intellectually constructed conception from afar for Toller's character either. And what you want to feel as new and especially contemporary in this figure is hardly clear to me. I play a man who, whether he has come out of an asylum or not, stands instinctively in the strongest opposition to the world which surrounds him, a world shaped by compromise and regulated by the economic situation.

This actor's understanding of the leading role in *Hoppla, wir leben*! is complete. He goes on to describe how he acts such a part:

> I do not understand how you could play something of this sort "well" or less well. You must feel, that is all. And I have never conceived of acting in any other way. I could never work with mere "methods", and if don't feel something, I'd rather keep my hands off it! . . . . (21)

Loibner's approach could scarcely be more diametrically opposed to Piscator's, of which Gerda Redlich says:

> He had no time for any human touch or any human weakness, or anything like that. It was a bit like a parade ground, like drill for the small-part actors . . . A very hard man on the surface . . . oh . . . he was obsessed. There was no human feeling at all. I don't ever remember him saying a human word or cracking a joke . . . (22)

Loibner's emotional approach to acting was capable of penetrating straight to the core of Toller's characterisation, where Piscator's intellectual and functional view missed the essential in the part while exploiting Karl Thomas's figure in the play's ideological pattern (23).

Between this production and 1930 Spalek lists 9 productions in various parts of the USSR. 4 in Nordic countries, 2 in Germany. 2 in England and one in Ireland (Abbey Theatre). Of the German productions that at Zwickau, 11.2.'28, had only about three performances (24).

The production at the Essen Schauspielhaus opened early in December, 1929, directed by Friedrich Sebrecht, decor by Caspar Neher, with Walther Reymer playing Karl Thomas. The published version was used, ending in Karl Thomas's suicide. A contemporary critic, O. G. , thought the play did not reveal the poetic Toller, but the documentary:

> A phosphorescent mirror shimmered, out of which the times stared back at you as a crazy grimace. A whole civilisation was unmasked as being uncivilised. The accusation waved on high like a flag. Threateningly (25).

Technically the production left something to be desired and the still projections between scenes looked like the work of a beginner.

Reymer, like Loibner, evidently gave an emotional performance:

> Often melodious, not always hard enough when driven into a corner, then again enormously human, crazily, openly vulnerable. A rebel of the heart, not of the head. He moved us more than he convinced us. Sympathy flowed to him a hundred-fold (26).

The critic concludes:

> A production worth seeing, more, — an important one. And one for the public. The applause was in keeping with the sold-out house (27).

In this production both the character of the protagonist and the social-critical elements in the play, were evidently well developed and balanced.

Hoppla, wir leben! was translated into English by Hermann Ould and published by Ernest Benn in September, 1928 (28) and produced twice in the following year, 1929 (29) in London and Cambridge.

The London production was at the Gate Theatre Studio, directed by Peter Godfrey under the title *Hoppla!* It ran from 19 February to 16 March. The cast included Graveley Edwards (Karl Thomas), Beatrix Lehmann (Eva Berg), Keith Pyott (Albert Kroll), Ronald Simpson (Kilman), Joan Pereira (Mrs Meller), Robert Newton (Pickel).

A programme note by David Joseph indicates the direction in which interest in the play was weighted:

> *Hoppla!* is interesting from a technical standpoint for the manner in which it utilises the film, not only to act as a commentary on the stage action but so that it performs an individual function towards the obtaining of a full common dramatic effect.
>
> The moving pictures shown in this play were made with a Cine-Kodak, and are projected by a Kodascope "B". Only non-inflammable film is used (30).

The setting has been preserved in a newspaper cutting where a photograph shows that four simultaneous scenes were staged (two up, two down) on what the caption says is "the smallest theatre stage in London" (31).

Ould's translation is uninspired and occasionally incorrect (32). Toller's more poetic passages suffer particularly badly (33). The inadequacy of the translation, together with the emphasis on technical novelty, may in part account for the hostility of the reviews; but the actors must also have been at fault, even though *The Times* praised Graveley Edwards and Beatrix Lehmann as Karl Thomas and Eva Berg (34). For that anonymous reviewer the play was:

> intolerably tedious . . . . weighed down with stage mechanisms masquerading as an experimental technique.
>
> It is hard to believe,

the reviewer says,

> that it was written in passion; yet, if passion is not the explanation it is altogether unpardonable.
>
> The dialogue, when it does not smack of a communist Sunday School, is jerky and lifeless.
>
> It is all very like the performance of a nasty-tempered child whom no one prevents from inflicting his nonsense on the world, and who continues his elephantine pranks for hours and hours and hours (35).

Another anonymous critique was nastily hostile to Toller and ended:

> A pretentious evening, during which the audience was completely bored (36).

Ivor Brown reviewed the production in *The Saturday Review* of 23. 2. '29 (37) and again on 24. 2. '29, presumably in *The Observer* (38).

Brown thought there was too much movement and activity:

> The patron saint of the Gate Theatre is evidently St. Vitus (39).

He pointed out that the 4-scene simultaneous stage was unoriginal. It had been started in Drury Lane and familiarised by Eugene O'Neill (40). He referred to the celebrated seventeenth century controversy between Inigo Jones and Ben Jonson on the relative importance of staging and language: in this play "Inigo Jones" had won. The play had missed tragedy and become tiresome and trivial, and this was no one's fault but the author, who had "genuine passion and dramatic aptitudes" but "smothers his own talent".

Clearly, on a tiny stage in a small studio an opportunity had been missed to free *Hoppla, wir leben*! from its mechanical trappings and to emphasise the qualities of the author's language — which were also destroyed by Ould's unsatisfactory translation.

The other English production was Terence Gray's at the Cambridge Festival Theatre. It is noteworthy for the fact that Gray used the production as a medium for ridiculing the theatre censorship exercised in England by the Lord Chamberlain's Office. Toller wrote an unsigned article about this (41). A Programme Note informed the audience that the printed full text of the play was on sale in the theatre, but that the Lord Chamberlain had forbidden certain scenes. Members of the audience were encouraged to read the whole play and, if they could not find immoral passages, to write to the Lord Chamberlain. He would explain their full obscenity. Do not blame Toller or us, begged the note!

At the start of the performance this statement was projected:

> Scenes which show how people are shot at
> Scenes which show persons are shot
> Scenes which show how people lie killed:
> Forbidden by order of the Lord Chamberlain (42).

During the second scene the actors suddenly froze and an amplified voice said that a scene followed which the audience was not allowed to hear. The response was shouts and laughter. A love-scene was 'acted' behind closed front curtains!

It is difficult to imagine what can have survived of the feeling and passion of the play!

No productions of the play are recorded between 1929 and

1951, when it was directed by Giorgio Strehler at the Piccolo Teatro, Milan, in an adaptation by Strehler and Emilio Castellani (43). The German critic Horst Rüdiger wrote several review articles on this, which he described as 'an outstanding production' (44), though he considered the play, about a generation after its being written, to be

> the tragic mistake of a dramatist of great ability (45).

The next production, in the Théâtre Municipal Gérard-Philipe, St. Denis, in 1966, was more interestingly reviewed by Georges Schlocker as 'Toller's Victory in Paris' (46). He regarded the play as still topical, especially in France. The audience was interested in whether the political events of Germany after the First World War could be repeated, and he believed that Toller himself was more interested in asking perennial questions than in mere propaganda. In this the reviewer is clearly right, and it is interesting that he says that the French production staged the play as a modern work, asking such questions. He does not tell us *how* this was done.

Eight years later the play was performed in the Staatstheater Kassel under the direction of Charles Lewinsky (47). The revival showed that the play had lost nothing of its power to arouse controversy. On the one hand Helmut Schmitz in the *Frankfurter Rundschau* declared that

> the Kassel 'Toller' seems like the exhumation of a theatrical corpse,

and asked rhetorically,

> What in the Devil's name is intended today by this opus, stumbling between Documentary and Expressionism, in which under the direction of Erwin Piscator, the regisseur of the original production (1927) in film-montage style, glaring highlights were thrown on the contemporary scene (48).

On the other hand Klaus Colberg (49), while saying that the result was mixed, especially in the uneasy movement of the language between "naive, idealistic emotional rhetoric" and "expressionistic and trivially realistic idioms" (50), nevertheless discusses the play — in "Toller's original version" (Urfassung): presumably the Leipzig version — seriously and rationally. At the present time,

> an instinct to defend the much-maligned Weimar Republic is aroused in the audience (51).

He thinks that Toller fails to appreciate the positive aspects of the Weimar Republic;

> Does not this disappointed revolutionary see it exactly as the Nazis later saw it — merely as a system of weakness and horse-trading — only from the left instead of from the right? (52)

Colberg here falls into the trap of identifying Toller and Karl Thomas: Toller's comment on the inadequacy of Karl Thomas's reactions and attitude to Kilman is the fact that these lead him to exactly the same course of action as that of the right-wing student: the attempt to assassinate the Minister. Toller understood, as Karl Thomas does not, that the imperfections of the Weimar Republic would lead not back to Wilhelmine imperialism and old-fashioned capitalism, but 'forward' into fascism:

> We are moving towards a period of fascism which will last for *years* and at whose end war is threatened not against France but against Soviet Russia (53).

Toller of course understood, as Colberg says, that Weimar was

> a first attempt at democracy, even if a feeble one (54).

He did not have "crooked optics" (schiefe Optik) because of his long imprisonment, but understood the complex political perils of the late twenties very clearly.

The production and decor reflected the varying styles within the text. Herwig Lucas played Thomas with youthful — perhaps too youthful — naivety, while Michael Rademacher's Kilman was discreetly caricatured.

A production in Wuppertal in 1980, directed by Horst Siede, was said by Lothar Schmidt-Mühlisch to be a cliché-ridden and unsuccessful attempt to ape Otto Dix and George Grosz, — and the heading of his review, *Aus der Konservendose (Out of a Tin)* suggests that the play was directed as a museum-piece of the 1920s (55).

Of much greater interest is the first production of *Hoppla, wir leben*! in the German Democratic Republic in June 1984. In order to distance the theatre, — the Kammerspiele of the Deutsches Theater in East Berlin — from Toller's political 'heresies', the programme included a carefully worded note:

> This production is to call to mind Ernst Toller, who would not compromise when one must not compromise (56).

It also quoted the *DDR-Theaterlexicon*.

> He had never been able wholly to overcome the contradiction between his idealistic ethical postulates and the real demands of class-war (57).

Apparently further to sanitise Ernst Toller the programme reprinted Piscator's 1965 essay *Mein Freund Toller* (58) in which he recalls his being with Toller the day before his death. Toller had packed his luggage:

> He had wanted to leave New York — in fleeing from himself (59).

Thus recalling Toller's suicide, Piscator goes back to *Hoppla, wir leben*! and criticises Toller for the fact that Karl Thomas commits suicide, — quite forgetting that he himself had been responsible for this ending (though he claims to understand better now the arguments about the ending). In line with the Marxist view of Toller, Piscator says:

> It is the paradox of Toller's life that the will to revolution and resignation, escapism and combativeness, were combined with each other and against each other (60).

There was also a contribution from the dramatist Ferdinand Bruckner in which he spoke of his twenty-year friendship with Toller. The only thing he could never understand was the suicide of such a fighter as Toller (61).

In the text there were cuts, including some lines obviously unacceptable in East Berlin, e. g. Gewalt ist immer reaktionär (62). Yet in spite of the cuts the production was long-winded, according to W. Mommert (63). He said he thought Toller still worth playing in the West, and wondered whether this production might make East German audiences thoughtful about their 'Here and Now' and what its future would be (64).

Thus in the mid-1980s it was still the 'perennial questions' raised by Toller that were the lasting element in the play and which remained valid under differing political systems. This indeed has been borne out in all these post-war productions and the critiques quoted.

One year before this last production, in 1983, an interesting experiment was carried out at the Akademie der Künste, Berlin, whose success strongly bears out the argument here advanced that the strength of *Hoppla, wir leben!* lies not in spectacle, stage machinery or film sequences, nor even in the panoramic view it offers of a whole society (important though that is), but in the quality of Toller's writing.

This experiment was a straight reading of the play: even the major stage-directions and the details of films were read (65). The readers were a strong team, including Joanna Maria Gorvin, Martin Benrath, Martin Held and Boy Gobert (66). Friedrich Luft, whose reviews of Toller had often been hostile (67), and who still had reservations about aspects of Toller's style which he regarded as dated, gave a 'rave' review:

> Toller's language today often seems shrill to us, and often fragmented in an over-emotional kind of rhetoric . . . The evening was sensational . . . unrepeatable! . . . A great, rare evening, so beautiful (68).

That the play emerged strong and intact from the reading is clear from the concluding sentence of Hedwig Rohde's enthusiastic review:

> Why doesn't any present-day theatre actually dare to put on this unjustly forgotten play? (69).

The reading took place in June and was also later broadcast (in November 1983). It made good radio — sure proof, if more were needed, that its strength lies in the spoken word, the author's words (70); indeed, Willi Schmidt, writing in the popular radio-periodical *Hör zu*, emphasises the present-day validity of the play:

> We found that Toller's 'Station-drama' which requires an enormous number of players, has lost nothing of topicality and that we can still identify with his "negative hero", a deceived idealist (71).

That reading and its broadcast, nearly a half a century after the original production, is the final proof that the lasting qualities of the play are those contributed by its author through the medium of language.

A RE-ASSESSMENT

This examination of the background, development and stage history of *Hoppla, wir leben!* has shown that a re-assessment of the play through its text is long overdue. Many students of drama will still be introduced to it through Raymond Williams' superficial, inaccurate and critically untenable account in *Drama from Ibsen to Brecht* (1). What is now needed and will be attempted here, is an examination and evaluation of the text with the primary emphasis upon Toller's basic work: the structure, dramatic techniques, characters and dialogue. Lacking a sight of the ur-text in Spalek's possession (2) we base this study on the published text (3), but regard the published ending of the ur-text (4) as the authentic version preferred by the author (5).

Dorothea Klein's analysis of the structure of the play (6) is very perceptive, especially in view of the fact that she was not permitted to look at Piscator's *Regiebuch* and was not aware of the ur-text now in Spalek's possession (7). Her principal insight is that the play is built upon the principle of balance, and she illustrates this in many ways.

She understands, as many critics have failed to do, that Karl Thomas is not Toller (8) and is not a mouth-piece for his ideas. In his prison plays, as in the earlier *Die Wandlung*, the protagonist had also been the "bearer of the central idea of the play" (9). Now the protagonist is a 'negative hero' (negativer Held) — what more recent critical jargon terms an 'anti-hero' — who is set over against a group of characters — Kroll, Meller, Eva Berg — which embodies the positive element (10) and express Toller's views. (This is an over-simplification of the truth.)

She also perceives balance in Toller's attempt "to be fair to all sides" (11). This reflects his developing interest in justice, both in the sense of the administration of justice (Justiz) and that of the principle of justice (Gerechtigkeit). It was, as Klein realises, no coincidence that in this same year, 1927, Toller published his closely documented polemic against injustice, *Justiz: Erlebnisse (Justice: Experiences)* (12), — two series of cases of injustice: one, *The Experiences of Others: Objective Facts of the Case*, the other, *My Own Experiences; Experiences of my Cell-Neighbours*. In the Preface Toller says that the book contains documents about the administration of justice in Bavaria, but that neither Prussians, Württemburgers, Romanians, Hungarians nor Americans dare cry pharisaically,

> That could happen in Bavaria — not with us! (13)

He continues:

> In every country in which privileged classes defend their prerogatives of property — injustice of property — the same thing happened, and will happen again (14).

It is thus also no coincidence that in the preliminaries to *Hoppla, wir leben*! we read:

> The play takes place in many countries (15).

In the Preface to *Justiz* Toller cites the 'white-hot' words of Kleist's Michael Kohlhaas:

> Whoever denies me the protection of the laws drives me out to the wild beasts of the wilderness and puts in my hand the cudgel with which to defend myself (16).

He goes on to prophesy that the way in which democracy has begun to undermine and destroy its own foundations, in the realms, *inter alia*, of law, will lead to fascist rule:

> The democrats can't complain if tomorrow fascism counts them as wild beasts who may be hunted and hounded, tortured and murdered (17).

Kilman as representative of this self-undermined democracy, specifically the democracy of the Weimar Republic, is in fact murdered by the fascists; but Thomas, too, feeling that the just society for which he suffered, has been betrayed, also, though ineffectually, seeks to become a Michael Kohlhaas and take the frustrated law into his own hands.

Klein then turns to the symmetry of the play's structure. She begins by claiming that Toller is again using "Station" technique, though more closely wrought than in the earlier plays (18). Her subsequent analysis, however, does not bear out this claim. There are, indeed, one or two vestiges of Station Drama, but the concept is not a useful basis on which to build.

Klein knew at first hand only the one (the published) version of the play, in five acts. She therefore quite rightly drew attention to the symmetry of this version, which she saw in this form (my diagram, not hers):

Vorspiel	Imprisoned Revolutionaries	Prison (Rand) A
Act 1 Sc. 1	Release	Asylum (Lüdin) B
Sc. 2	Thomas & Kilman	Exposition 1 C
Act 2 Sc. 1	Thomas and Eva	Exposition 2 C
Sc. 2	Thomas, Kroll & Meller	Exposition 3 C

INTERVAL

Act 3. Scs. 1 & 2	Main Action	(Student's Room) & Hotel D
Act 4 Sc. 1	Arrest	Consequences 1 E
Sc. 2	Police Interrogation	Consequences 2 E
Sc. 3	Judicial Interrogation	Consequences 3 E
Sc. 4	Psychological Investigation	Asylum (Lüdin) B
Act 5 Scs 1, 2, & 3	Imprisoned Revolutionaries	Prison (Rand) A

This pattern of scenes, leading towards and then away from a central (multiple) scene, Act 3, sc. 2, and returning to its twin starting-points of Prison and Asylum, does indeed recall the pattern of Strindberg's *To Damascus*, which we have already related to the structure of *Die Wandlung*.

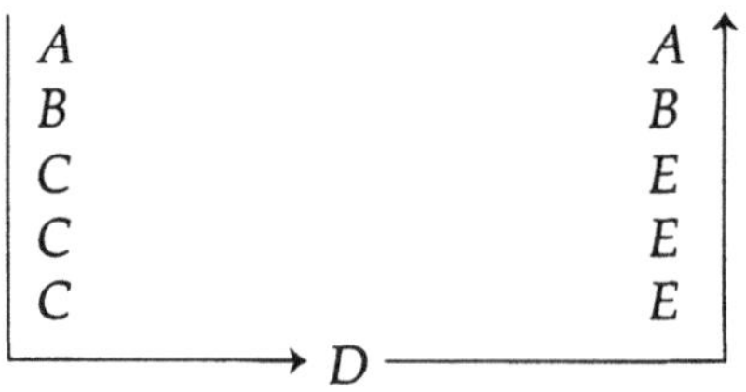

```
| A              A ↑
| B              B |
| C              E |
| C              E |
| C              E |
|______→ D ________|
```

But Act 5 is in effect an epilogue added under Piscator's influence and quite radically changes the play's meaning. Toller, both in the published text and in the 4-act ur-text deliberately detached the Vorspiel (Prologue) from the main body of the play on his title-pages, and the 4-act version (19) offers an equally symmetrical pattern:

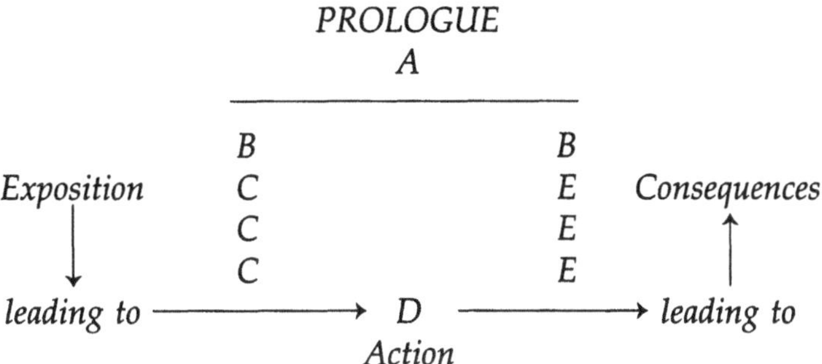

But the resemblance to the pattern of *To Damascus* is superficial and, as we shall see, the real structure of *Hoppla, wir leben!* is dramatic, with important elements, especially montage, of epic theatre — in Brecht's sense (20).

Finally, Klein demonstrates the balance of the "constellation" or grouping of characters (21):

Karl Thomas "radical from a socialist direction" Isolated	BALANCES	Graf Lande & Student "radical, reactionary from a conservative direction." Also somewhat isolated in their own circle.
Kroll, Berg, Meller: Left wing of a group who want to change the state legally, without violence. (Represent the political message of the play.)	BALANCE	Baron Friedrich & Wandsring Also oppose existing state but from the Right.

Seen as traitor ⟶ KILMAN ⟵ Seen as parvenu.

This is useful as far as it goes, but it includes only nine characters out of a cast of about fifty. There are many other symmetries yet to be noted. Klein valuably singles out one, that of Pickel and Karl Thomas, already noted by Piscator, who refers to:

> . . . the tragic hero and the comic hero of the piece, the petit bourgeois Pickel, who is looking for the ideal embodiment of the republic, and the worker Thomas [presented as such by Piscator in his production. CWD], who wants to complete the revolution (22).

Klein, who of course does not fall into Piscator's 'deliberate error' of seeing Karl Thomas as a "worker", and who draws attention to the way in which Pickel is linked with the comic elements in the play, says,

> Pickel is a projection of Karl Thomas distorted into comic form; he is Thomas's caricatured mirror-image (23).

She examines the parallels in some detail. Both men come to the capital from isolation — one from the asylum, the other from *Holzhausen, Bezirk Waldswinkel* (roughly suggesting *Log-Cabin Village, Corner-of-the-Forest*). She sees the whole railway problem as an anachronism which parallels Karl Thomas's lost years. Like Karl Thomas, Pickel brings an *idée fixe* into the political situation and like him he constantly poses fundamental questions, but in such a way that they sound comic. The intentional comedy of the correspondence between the two figures comes to a climax in a dramatically explicit false identification at the police head-quarters. There, as she points out, Pickel is at first suspected of the assassination and, like Karl Thomas, gives the Police Chief the impression of being mad (24).

As a final link between these two she refers to their language. She appreciates that in this play Toller is distancing himself from the linguistic expression of his earlier phase of writing (25) and adds:

> Pickel's and Thomas's manner of speech stands out clearly from the background of the predominantly bare and realistic style (26).

The principle of balance upon which Klein bases her valid, though limited analysis of the structure of *Hoppla, wir leben*! is only part of the broader principle at work in the play, namely that of creative juxtaposition, montage, more fully and more clearly developed here than in *Die Maschinenstürmer*.

This is seen most obviously in the "Grand Hotel" sequence of Act 3, originally, but in the modern theatre not necessarily, portrayed by means of Piscator's "scaffolding" (27). But the montage principle is applied much more generally in the play both spatially and — as in *Die Maschinenstürmer* — temporally.

Piscator may have had some inkling of the significance of the juxtaposed settings. He had already worked with John Heartfield as early as 1920 (28), though he had not yet directed one of Brecht's plays (29). Toller was in fact using a technique that had not yet been given a name in theatrical terms. In his unclear justification for having used the patented Kreisler-Bühne (30), Piscator writes:

> This multilevel stage is not identical with the Kreisler stage. Despite a certain superficial similarity it was in principle the direct opposite. If the Kreisler stage, at least as it has been used up till now, signifies nothing more than creating a multiple stage-set by dividing the set up, the multilevel stage is a self-contained, independent framework for the acting, to which the proscenium opening is only an external impediment. The multilevel stage actually already belongs to a different system of stage architecture (31).

Setting aside the somewhat inflated claim of the final sentence, what Piscator appears to be saying is that whereas the Kreisler-Bühne was simply a device for instantaneous scene change — a development of the multiple settings familiar, for instance, from medieval mystery plays — his *Etagenbühne* was intended to show a single, unified setting composed of several parts or sub-sets. This implies, though it does not state explicitly, that the total effect on the audience depends upon the simultaneous impact of the different sections of the setting: in other words, montage.

Spatial montage — which in drama also inevitably has a temporal element — is not seen only in the Grand Hotel sequence, but in varying degrees throughout the play. Thus Act 1 Sc. 2 is based upon the contrast and interaction between what happens in the Minister's private office (Arbeitszimmer) and the ante-room or outer office (Vorzimmer), both of which are seen as the curtain rises, though subsequently only the room where characters are speaking is fully lit (32).

A verbal signal is immediately given that we must be alert to the interrelation of the two locations:

> *In the Private Office*
> WILHELM KILMAN: I sent for you.
> EVA BERG: Yes, of course.

> *In the Ante-room*
> BANKER'S SON: Will he receive you? He hasn't sent for you. (33)

In the opening sub-scenes (34) Kilman's attitude and veiled threats towards Eva Berg, the Trade Union activist, his one-time revolutionary colleague, are contrasted with and related to the attitudes and expectations of the banker and his son, the representatives of capital and heavy industry who anticipate obtaining credit from the government and plan their offensive against the unions, hoping by a lock-out to kill two birds with one stone, gaining at one stroke overtime and lower wages.

This is simple, but the complexity of the pattern quickly evolves as Kilman in his office exercises his shadowy and precarious political power while von Wandsring, Minister of War, Graf Lande, and later Baron Friedrich in the ante-room blatantly plan the overthrow of democracy and the establishment, by legal means of course, of an "honest dictatorship" (35). Their contempt for Kilman is boundless.

The whole scene, with its dual setting, is shot through with similar juxtapositions. The servant's announcement to Kilman in the private office that his wife and daughter are waiting to see him, is immediately countered in the ante-room by Friedrich's and Lande's scornful comments upon them:

> BARON FRIEDRICH: Please, said the little daughter and uncovered her knee.
> GRAF LANDE: And her mother?
> BARON FRIEDRICH: Thought that was refined behaviour, blushed and said nothing.
> GRAF LANDE: The capital is worth straining one's virginity for (36).

Karl Thomas's fruitless interview with Kilman is immediately followed by Pickel's equally fruitless one.

Baron Friedrich and Graf Lande also are constantly used to highlight the differing facets of the Right, which they represent, and their rivalry for Lotte parallels and symbolises their political rivalry (37).

All this, it must be reiterated, is more than mere balance: it is montage, in which the various elements reacting together convey a meaning that is more than the sum of the parts.

Act 3 Sc. 2, the Grand Hotel, is naturally the major example of spatial montage.

Apart from a couple of linking sub-scenes on corridors (38) and the Vestibule, with jazz music and dancing couples, also used momentarily between individual scenes (39), the sub-scenes take place in a montage of six locations:

SERVANTS' ROOM (OFFICE)	used 3 times Karl Thomas, Meller & other servants)
PRIVATE ROOM	used 3 times (Kilman's private party)
RADIO STATION	used once (links Karl Thomas with a wider world)
CLUB ROOM	used once (the intellectual debate, with related entries of Pickel & Karl Thomas)
WRITING ROOM	used once (Friedrich's press conference)
HOTEL ROOM NO. 96	used 3 times (Graf Lande & Lotte)

The private room, where Kilman entertains the Banker, is used near the beginning of the scene, almost exactly in the middle, and at the end, and thus provides the firm framework for the whole act:

1. The attempted bribery and Kilman's compromise. Thomas helping to serve.
2. Kilman still resisting the Banker's attempts to corrupt him. Thomas present, serving. Pickel's intrusion.
3. The assassination.

Among these three sub-scenes are grouped the others, thus:

<u>Introductory:</u>
<u>The Grand Hotel above-& below-stairs:</u>

1. Vestibule

______________________________Montage

2. Servants' Room

1st Private Room sub-scene.

<u>The Wider Background:</u>

1. Outer contemporary world of technical advance. (Radio Station)

______Montage

2. Ideological Background: the inner world of ideas. (Club Room)

2nd Private Room sub-scene.

<u>Converging Assassination Plots:</u>
<u>a) Thomas, b) Lande & Student</u>
<u>Interwoven</u>

____________Montage

1. Press Conference. Friedrich as Kilman's PR man.
2. Bedroom 96. Lande with Lotte (lesbian drug user)
3. Servants: bad food, inflation, homosexual molestation.
4. Momentary meeting of tragic & comic anti-heroes, Thomas & Pickel.
5. Bedroom 96: ordering wine
6. Servants' Room: Thomas finally determines to "wake them up". (6 is in parallel with 7 & 8)
7. Bedroom 96: a knock, leading to
8. Lande & Student in corridor

3rd Private Room sub-scene.
Thomas & Student BOTH come to assassinate Kilman.

There is, as already remarked, a sequential side to this montage, but the spatial aspect predominates, as each element always recurs in the same facet of the setting, and this spatial montage is given a theatrically powerful additional dimension in Act 4. Sc. 4, both in the ur-text and the published version, though more fully and effectively in the former (40):

The facade (of the scaffolding) is transformed into that of the asylum. The ground-floor right opening becomes Professor Lüdin's consulting room and as the scene proceeds, what *were* in Act 3, various rooms in the Hotel "become" the corresponding rooms of the asylum. The trick is not, of course intended to be naturalistic, but to allow the audience to see the 'madness' of the contemporary world through the eyes of Karl Thomas. In the ur-text, apparently trying to preserve an illusion of naturalism, Toller has Lüdin actually getting an attendant to set up a ciné projector, but this clumsy device is dropped in the published text. Then, each room being lit in turn, we see the Banker in the Private Room ruined and driven mad as he tries in vain to sell falling shares; the hotel servant, in the Servants' Room, driven mad when he puts his inflated savings on a losing horse (in the published version he also stabs himself); in the Radio-station the radio-telegraphist is driven mad through not being able to communicate his invention; the Examining Judge — in the 'opening' where his room was (Act 4 Sc. 3) — is victim of the illusion that he is on the track of all unsolved crimes; Kilman, in the Private Room, is mad with the illusion of power:

> He's got the idea into his head that it isn't the engine that drives his car, but he himself — with the horn (41).

But for Lüdin every one of these is "Normal".

Finally, and with wonderful irony, Lüdin's own mad face appears on the facade! When Karl Thomas addresses this, Lüdin himself accuses Karl Thomas of playing tricks, but the latter retorts:

> Now I see the world clearly again. You have turned it into a madhouse. There's no dividing wall between 'in here' and 'out there'. The world has become a pen in which the healthy are trampled under foot by a small herd of galloping madmen. *You* normal! Ha-ha! (42)

At this moment of Karl Thomas's illumination all the rooms are lit up and the squatting inmates all bend down towards the consulting-room chorusing:

> Ha, ha! . . . Normal! (43)

This wonderfully skilful sequence is truncated in the published text to the Banker, Servant and Telegraphist, followed immediately by the chorus, an unexplained and meaningless explosion in the 'hotel', and blackout: thus much of the significance is lost.

The multiple stage and the way Toller exploits it contribute the most striking, as well as the most consistently used application of the montage principle, but even apart from the groupings of characters noted by Klein, the whole play is pervaded by it e. g. :

Release from Prison (Prologue)	Release from Asylum (Act 1 Sc. 1)

Release from Asylum (Act 1 Sc. 1)	Return to Asylum (Act 4 Sc. 4)
Thomas & Eva in Eva's Bedroom (Act 2 Sc. 1	Lande & Lotte in Bedroom No. 96 (Act 3 Sc. 2)
Apparent political power (Voting Scene: Act 2. Sc. 2)	Real political power Lande & Student plot assassination (Act 3 Sc. 1)
(Last scene before Interval)	(First scene after Interval)

These and other structural pairings are reinforced by words. For example:

> *End of Act 1 Sc. 1: Release from Asylum.*
> KARL THOMAS: ... draußen vorm Fenster wachsen wirklich Buchen . . . keine Gummiwände. (*Karl Thomas hinaus.*)
> PROFESSOR LÜDIN: Schlechte Rasse. (*Dunkel*)
>
> *End of Play, Act 4 Sc. 4 (ur-text): Return to Asylum.*
>
> PROFESSOR LÜDIN: ... Führen Sie ihn in die Isolierzelle, In seinen ... Buchenwald. (*Karl Thomas wird vom Wärter abgeführt*)
> PROFESSOR LÜDIN: Lebensunfähig. (44)

The basic structural principle of the play having been established, any re-assessment must look anew at the characters, not only in their groupings, but individually.

Piscator regarded all the characters, with the exceptions of Thomas and Pickel, as 'sharply outlined expressions of social classes'. Their private dispositions and individual complexes were not what mattered; what mattered was the type, the representative of a certain social and economic viewpoint (45). While this is a just judgement of the right-wing characters (46), the functionaries of law and psychiatry, and other minor figures, it is not adequate for Kroll, Eva Berg, Frau Meller and Kilman, all of whom are introduced in the Prologue (47).

We have already seen that Pickel and Thomas are distinguished from all other figures by their language. They are 'outsiders'. Piscator suggests that they are both *déclassé*. It is not clear in what way the peasant Pickel is 'severed from his class roots'. Karl Thomas is, but not in a way in which Piscator is willing to admit: he turned Karl Thomas into a worker and described and cast him as such. But Toller's Karl Thomas is middle-class; he has been a university student, was 'slung out of the university' (presumably because he was a political activist) and afterwards learnt to be a compositor, a skilled tradesman (48). His education gives Toller justification for Karl Thomas's expressing his fundamental romanticism verbally: for this is what distinguishes his speech from the plainer speech of the others, not 'expressionism'. Piscator excused his cavalier treatment of the text on the grounds that Toller had been unable to shake off the expressionism that dominated his formative years (49). But this was untrue. *Hoppla, wir leben!* belongs to *die neue Sachlichkeit*. Its style and language, apart from Karl Thomas's poetic romanticism, are sober. (John Willett, in his book on that period and movement refer to the play's being written in "relatively sober terms for this author" and categorises the exceptions as "romanticism" (50).)

To return to the Prologue. Here at the very outset of the play the five revolutionaries (Thomas, Kroll, Berg, Kilman and Meller) are introduced as individuals: indeed, in his few lines the anonymous Sixth Prisoner also becomes a person, able to arouse our sympathy as a mere type could not. In this densely compact scene each figure is distinctly characterised. Of course, the extremely tense situation of the prisoners, who have waited ten days for their death-sentence to be carried out, reveals their characters, their strengths and weaknesses, vividly and nakedly.

Karl Thomas is emotionally sensitive to atmosphere and tension. "Verfluchte Stille"' (Damned silence!), his opening words, show him immediately articulating the strain affecting them all. But when next he speaks it is to reveal his powers of alert observation, intelligence, initiative and leadership, when he notices the broken plaster at the window and instantly plans and organises the attempt to escape, taking the initial risk himself. It is he who later defends both Eva and Kilman from Kroll's sharp tongue, though he also has the perception to suspect that Kilman has begged for mercy, and forces upon the latter the grim logic of their situation. In passages cut by Piscator in his production he expresses deep and sympathetic understanding of Eva's youthful dread of death, scepticism about the very existence of 'ultimate causes', and realistic, uncynical awareness of the many reasons why people becomes revolutionaries. His intense love for Eva is revealed in few words:

> KARL THOMAS: Deine Hände.
> EVA BERG: Du.
> KARL THOMAS: Ich liebe dich sehr, Eva.
> EVA BERG: Ob sie uns zusammen begraben, wenn wir sie drum bitten?
> KARL THOMAS: Vielleicht. (51)

And when Kroll, under strain, coarsely abuses him through her (52) his self-control breaks and he attacks Kroll — preluding his breakdown into uncontrollable, hysterical, braying laughter when the commutation of the death sentences is announced.

Albert Kroll, unlike Karl Thomas, is of the working-class. At the age of six he used to be pulled out of bed at five in the morning to deliver fresh rolls to better-off people. He has acquired a certain hardness, is often coarse in speech (53), ironic (54), anti-romantic (55), anti-religious (56), yet pitiful of the Sixth Prisoner. He is courageous and will be last to escape, yet cautious (57), impatient with the emotions of Karl and Eva, but as warm and spontaneous in reconciliation as in anger. He, who attacks Kilman most fiercely for his not joining in when they stormed the Town Hall, is manly and generous in his farewell, when he believes that Kilman alone has not been reprieved.

Frau Meller, 'Mother Meller', as they call her, is in fact the true 'mother' in the play, in contrast with Frau Kilman. In his anxiety Kilman turns to Mother Meller for comfort and reassurance, and she talks to him as to a son -"Ruhig, mein Junge" — "Quiet, my boy" — and offers a warmly feminine stoicism:

> Life and death flow together. You come out of one womb, you journey into another womb (58).

But it is a womb where there is no future life:

> The teachers beat that belief out of me (59).

She lost her husband and both sons in the war, but hoped for different times. They did come, but were lost. Now others must carry on the struggle. As Kilman's cowardice becomes evident she scorns him, calling him 'Cowardy-custard' (Bangbüchs) and offering him her place in the order of attempted escape. She seeks to check the quarrels among the men, comforts Eva while telling her to prepare for death, boldly turns on Rand, when he asks if anyone wants to see a parson:

> The worms don't recognise any brand of religion: I know that. Tell your parson, Jesus drove money-changers and profiteers out of the temple with whip-lashes. He can write that in his Bible — on page one! (60).

Yet she rebukes Kilman for his cheap jibes at the Sixth Prisoner.

Mother Meller is not as intelligent as Kroll: she thinks their reprieve a sign of government weakness; Kroll realises that it is one of government strength.

Eva Berg is only seventeen and at this age deeply romantic. She, the young revolutionary, would like to emulate the French aristocrats who danced the minuet on the way to the guillotine. She is passionately in love with Karl ("I'll kiss you to death!") and cannot forbear from weeping. But she cries shame at Kroll's attack on Kilman. Thomas echoes her, thus provoking Kroll's coarse attack on them both:

> Lie down in the corner with your whore and make a child for her. Then it can creep out in the grave and play with the worms (61).

When Karl is led off to see a doctor, Eva, apparently unhindered, goes with him.

Finally there is Kilman. His weakness, his tendency to lean on others, his fear of taking risks, his subservience to the powerful, his readiness to compromise, to keep his head down and then join the winning side, all these are demonstrated in this one scene. His baser hypocrisy emerges in his bitter onslaught upon the Sixth Prisoner (whom, however, Karl Thomas also condemns as "Judas"). He ventures to criticise Kroll over the shared cigarette and brings down a storm of invective on his own head (62). As the curtain falls he virtually crawls to Lieutenant Baron Friedrich:

> Danke gehorsamst, Herr Leutnant (63).

In the play proper all the characters in the Prologue (except the anonymous Sixth Prisoner) re-appear after a lapse of eight years as fully developed characters, not mere types. The Prologue is thus much more than a preliminary stage in the narrative, for each person now reappearing in the play is seen in relation to his or her character as first introduced in the Prologue: Montage technique again.

Karl Thomas has evidently been kept in total ignorance of the world outside the asylum and has even lost track of time. However improbable these two facts are, they are necessary premisses if the play is to function as the author intends (64). Although Karl Thomas learns the date, Lüdin quite deliberately, almost as if playing a practical joke on his patient, does not tell him the full truth about Kilman. So Karl Thomas goes out into the world of 1927 in the mental as well as the physical clothing he brought into the asylum in 1919.

The rest of Act 1, already examined, deploys Kilman, Eva, Baron Friedrich and Karl Thomas in new inter-relationships and in relationships with other, newly introduced, more 'typically' conceived characters.

Kilman is now Minister of the Interior and apparently powerful. Eva is a civil servant (Beamtin), a secretary in the Department of Finance; but she is also on the committee of the Association of Women Employees (65). No longer the tearful teenager, she is a confident young woman, sure of her constitutional rights, prepared to confront Kilman with his own revolutionary past, and yielding nothing to him.

Baron Friedrich, no longer mere Lieutenant, holds a position close to Kilman in the Ministry of the Interior, evidently as a bribe to conceal the Minister's past. Contemptuous of Kilman, his working-class origins and his ignorant, *nouvelle riche*, wife, he has evidently set out to seduce the daughter, who for her part has read his personal file and decided that Graf Lande will be the better conquest, while both Friedrich and Lande wait only for the day when "other times come again" (66).

Only Karl Thomas remains unchanged and interprets everything he encounters in the uncompromising light of revolution. The eight years incarceration and isolation provide the naturalistic justification for presenting —

> a man who, whether he has come out of an asylum or not, stands instinctively in the strongest opposition to the world which surrounds him, a world shaped by compromise and regulated by the economic situation (67).

To this grouping of characters is added one other, that of the second 'innocent', Karl Thomas's comic counterpart, Pickel, who comes not from the 'beech wood' of the padded cell, but from the other isolation of an actual 'corner of the forest' (Waldwinkel). The presence of the second innocent adds verisimilitude to the first, and throughout there is an interplay of comedy and pathos between the two: in the light of

Karl Thomas, Pickel cannot be taken as purely comic, while in *his* light Karl Thomas becomes not simply tragic, but tragically comic.

Act 2 Sc. 1, which follows, is one of the most important in the play — indeed it is in the literal sense, essential — yet it has been conspicuously ignored by critics. Piscator does not mention it, and only two of the critiques seen make any reference to it at all (68).

The scene falls into two clear parts: the scene between Karl Thomas and Eva, and the scene between him and the children, which Holzer and Salten both found memorable in the Vienna production.

Neither part of the scene appreciably advances the action. Structurally the scene corresponds in the play as a whole with the Radio Station and Club Room sub-scenes in Act 3 Sc. 2. In both cases, the act and the whole play, Toller sets the action in motion and then, having aroused our interest, holds up its development in order to present the deeper issues, both personal and ideological, which underlie it. In the act, he uses contemporary technology and political discussion as his media. In this scene he uses, and links, what are for him two key aspects of life: sexual relations and children.

Once more in this play, as in every previous play, the sexual relationship is made the focal point: in this case primarily that of Eva and Karl (69). In the Prologue it is their passionately romantic mutual attraction which triggers the climax when Karl sets upon Kroll and which now forms the basis of audience expectation when curtain-up on this scene discovers them in bed together. The romantic illusion is quickly shattered when Eva jumps out of bed and hastily begins to dress in order to take the 'copy' for a new leaflet to the Trade Union before going to work. She concentrates on the final revisions while Karl admires her (to him unfamiliar) short hair-style, whose nakedness, he muses, suits her, but is more than most commonplace faces can bear. She is curious to know about the sense of sexual deprivation in an institution, but appreciates that sex may be no more than a game — though a game worth taking seriously. She will not accept that her having slept with Karl means that she 'belongs' to him or even that they are lovers. If she found herself pregnant, she would have an abortion: pregnancy would simply be an accident, not a necessity. Revolutionaries, she says, don't have to renounce life's thousand little pleasures. Eight years of work, of experience of men and situations and of making all her own decisions, have made her what she has become. But it has not been easy and often in the loneliness of furnished rooms she has wept and felt at the end of her tether.

In his characterisation of Eva as a left-wing activist of the 1920s

Toller reveals great insight. It was not easy for the newly liberated women to come to terms with the price of freedom. Rosa Luxemburg also, alone in Berlin in the late 1890s "cringed" at the thought of furnished rooms unfamiliar and constantly changing (70), and she too admitted that she felt "like having a good cry" (71). Like Rosa Luxemburg, Eva could have quoted Schiller:

> In *großes* Unglück lehrt ein edles Herz
> Sich endlich finden, aber wehe tut's,
> Des Lebens kleine Zierden zu entbehren (72).

But unlike Luxemburg, Eva has destroyed or suppressed her romanticism nor can her utter honesty permit her even at the end of the play in Act 4 Sc. 3, to respond with warmth to Karl's last declaration of love.

He for his part carries into 1927 the passionate intensity of 1919, both in sex and in politics. His inability to accommodate himself to the non-romantic "sex-for-fun" ethos of the 1920s is matched by his inability and unwillingness to accommodate himself to the politics of elections, trade unions, patience and compromise. He cannot accept that the failed revolution was an episode which has passed into history.

> I found you in days when we heard the heart-beat of life because the heart-beat of death knocked loudly and inexorably. I cannot find my way in this time. Help me, help me! The flame which burned has gone out (73).

Eva understands his problem and its dangers:

> Either you gain strength for a new beginning or you are done for. It would be a crime to keep you in false dreams out of pity (74).

Karl, unable to face and come to terms with the world of the Weimar Republic, would like to escape — as Toller's swallows escaped — to an earthly paradise in Greece, India or Africa. Surely, he says,

> There must be somewhere where people still live, childlike people who *are*, just *are*; in whose eyes the heavens and sun and stars circle, shining; who know nothing of politics, who live, who don't always have to be fighting (75).

But Eva truly tells him that this paradise of which he dreams does not exist. She herself was a mere child in 1919: now we can't just be children any longer. And as she leaves the room, the children — the *real* children, idealised by Karl, — appear.

This was the second time Toller had used the device of confronting his protagonist with children. In *Die Maschinenstürmer*, immediately after the Prologue, Jimmy Cobbett encounters the children and seeks to capture their imaginations with the *Märchen* of Sorgenlos and Immerelend, but a crust of bread in the gutter is enough to turn the starving innocents into ravenous savages. The child victims must eat before they can even begin to seek a more moral society.

Here Fritz and Grete regard themselves as relatively poor (their mother, the landlady, has to let out rooms), but they have cinema tickets, are going to a boxing match and think the Charleston and Black Bottom important. Of the Great War they have learnt only the dates of battles and of the revolution virtually nothing. Karl Thomas tries to stimulate their imagination with the realities of war: the poison-gas factory at the end of the street, and then with Toller's own experience of a man's slow death in the barbed-wire entanglements, which had already inspired the Skeleton scene in *Die Wandlung*, (76) and which he later described, using many of the same words and phrases, in *Eine Jugend in Deutschland* (77). It had been a turning point in Toller's life, and as Karl Thomas says, it is no *Märchen*. Here Toller fuses it with another incident described immediately afterwards in *Eine Jugend in Deutschland*, when he first realised that a dead man is simply a dead man — whether friend or foe is immaterial.

Karl Thomas has aroused the children's sense of pity, but when he tells them of the struggle for a world in which all children 'have it good' — they reject him as stupid because he hoped a minority might win. They lose interest and go. The image of the childlike is shattered. Even the innocents are corrupted by the values of power. There is no escape to a childlike paradise.

When Eva unexpectedly returns, having been sacked because of her Union activity, and ironically says she *could* go away with him now, he still clings to the idea. But Eva retorts:

> Do you seriously believe I'd leave the comrades in the lurch? (78)

Wouldn't Karl like to work with her and the others? — Let him think it over.

Thus analysed, Act 2 Sc. 1 presents a series of vital steps towards Karl Thomas's determination to take the law into his own hands. From the moment in Act 1 Sc. 2 (79) when he realises that Kilman is not a covert revolutionary but takes his ministerial office seriously, Karl Thomas is potentially his assassin:

> If only they had put you up against a wall and shot you! (80)

In the discussion that follows, Kilman is not unsympathetically presented. He is not complacent in his position, admits to difficulties and doubts. He even realises that

> Power is always reactionary (81),

though it is the power of the Left he fears, while Karl Thomas prophetically sees that Kilman is helping reaction into the saddle and that, important though he believes his office of Minister to be, he is in fact

> A powerless puppet, a football (82).

The end of the interview, through the use of the telephone, introduces the name of Eva, whom Karl Thomas has not yet rediscovered, and in revealing Kilman's attitude to the object of Karl Thomas's still lively passion, takes the play an emotional stage further and preludes Act 2 Sc. 1.

In Act 2 Sc. 2, Karl Thomas, evidently following Eva's proposal that he should work with his old revolutionary colleagues, seeks out Kroll at the polling station and sees an election in progress with all its razzmatazz, bureaucratic muddle, trickery, intimidation and frustration. Kroll is trying to work within the democratic system, protesting at abuses of authority and fighting corruption. He is disillusioned by the apathy of the 100,000 (!) workless:

> When hunger comes in by one door, good sense goes out by the other (83).

Karl Thomas sees Kroll, with his cautious, patient use of the imperfect machinery of democracy for the time being, as the mirror-image of Kilman. Both are playing charades while the right-wing forces are moving towards power.

With hindsight this aspect of Karl Thomas's understanding (the aspect which is Toller's own) is seen to be true. In 1919 the Government's identification of the German socialists with the Russian Bolsheviks

> was no doubt a clever and, in the short run, successful move. In the long run it helped to pave the way for Adolf Hitler (84).

Noske's *Freikorps* can now be seen as the forerunner of the *SS Einsatzgruppen* (85). Not Toller alone, but Rosa Luxemburg had foreseen all this, as early as January 1919:

> Ironically entitled *Order Reigns in Berlin*, Luxemburg's last article appeared on 14 January 1919 in *The Red Flag*. An order, she wrote, whose survival depends on ever more bloodshed "inexorably proceeds toward its historical fate — annihilation. " She was right. The fighting lasted another year, was followed by the tormented Weimar Republic, and ended in Hitler's ascent (86).

Disillusioned by the democratic process and the attempts of the former revolutionaries to work within it, Karl Thomas decides on a course of martyrdom. If one person sacrifices himself "the lame will run". He knows now what he has to do. He whispers to Kroll, who replies aloud:

> You're no use to us! (87)

But Karl Thomas answers:

> That's the only way I can help myself. I'm suffocating with disgust (88).

Karl Thomas has now met three of his four old revolutionary comrades: his meeting with the fourth, Mother Meller, is decisive when she is brought in unconscious, having been clubbed with a rubber truncheon when she was sticking up an election leaflet. As she recovers she tells them that Eva has been arrested. The wielder of the rubber truncheon is none other than Rand, the former prison warder. Karl leaps at him in fury but is restrained by the others.

Rand, of course, was 'only obeying orders'. They have taken away his revolver. Karl Thomas grabs it and aims it at Rand: this will be his great sacrificial act — but Kroll prevents him from shooting, while at the same time he finds Rand's waistcoat stuffed with anti-semitic leaflets.

In the closing exchanges, as Kroll tells Karl Thomas to find work and get once more into everyday life, Frau Meller tells him of the jobs available as extra waiters in the hotel where she works, thus unwittingly giving him the opportunity he seeks. In the confusion as the election of Wandsring is announced on the radio, Karl Thomas is left with Rand's revolver.

Karl Thomas's encounters with his four old comrades have now fully prepared him, inwardly and outwardly, to become an assassin: completely failing to see that in adopting their own terrorism he is opening the door to the Nazis. 'The bow is bent and drawn' and we reach the Interval suggested by Toller (89).

In contrast with the length of a Prologue and two full acts, it requires only one short scene (Act 3 Sc. 1) to establish the background and motivation of the right-wing student. His memory of the shame and suicide of his uncle, the General, when ordered by a member of the Soldiers' Soviet, Kilman, to remove his epaulettes (a common incident during the Munich *Räterepublik*) is pregnantly conveyed in a single, moving paragraph. Graf Lande exploits the student's understandably revengeful feelings. More is not needed.

Act 3 Sc. 2 has already been examined in some detail. It leads straight into Act 4 Sc. 1 and thence to the final sequence of three scenes.

Act 4 Sc. 1 begins with the final twist to Karl Thomas's failure to grasp the world of 1927: that the student's motive has been politically the polar opposite of his own is so incomprehensible to him that his reaction is:

> Has the world become a madhouse? (90)

– a line which provides the key to the last act of the play and is given its full theatrical expression in Act 4 Sc. 4, already discussed, in which the 'normal' world is actually presented as a madhouse.

Left alone, Karl Thomas is forced to question the reality of the objective world and the validity of his relationship with it. If the world is really a madhouse, is this beech tree actually the wall of a padded cell? Do his own actions contradict his aims? Is everyone but him asleep? Does he alone see the murderers and their secret plots? He runs awake through the streets, but his thoughts collide with the beams of the arc-lights and injure themselves: the subjective and objective are no longer clearly distinguished. He even asks himself if he had not been better off in the asylum "in spite of the North Pole and the wingbeat of grey birds" (91). He no longer belongs to the world in which he lives. He sums up his situation in a memorable epigram:

> Ich bin der Welt abhanden gekommen
> Die Welt ist mir abhanden gekommen
> (The world has lost me
> I have lost the world) (92).

His alienation is complete. Arrested — or, as the police claim, taken into protective custody — he answers the officer's questions out of his subjective condition. What to the officer is impertinence carries its inner meaning for the audience:

> Even the revolver turns against the perpetrator and out of its barrel spurts laughter (93).

Already he specifically identifies the hotel and the asylum, thus preparing the way for Scene 4. The path straight across the park leads not into the hotel but the asylum.

The three final scenes constitute an ever-deepening investigation into Karl Thomas's outward actions and inner condition: his objective and subjective relationship with the world which has lost him and which he has lost.

First there is the shallow police investigation, in which Pickel's inability to communicate with and to understand this world of the big city, and the confusion of his identity with that of Thomas convey the craziness of the world in a manner that anticipates the Theatre of the Absurd. Preconceptions and false assumptions make total nonsense of the Police Chief's interrogation of both his suspects.

Second comes the investigation carried out by the Examining Judge. This is, in its way, rational. Nor does Karl Thomas display any symptoms of alienation. He answers every question factually and rationally. The first witness is Rand, who testifies that he himself had not fired the revolver. Karl Thomas admits that he discharged two shots — aimed at the assassin: but the Judge does not even believe in the student's existence. The head waiter can only bear witness that Karl Thomas had merely grumbled about Kilman as Minister. Frau Meller, the next witness, denies that Karl Thomas, whom she describes as a friend and comrade, had said to her:

> You're all asleep! Someone must die. Then you'll wake up (94).

The Pikkolo, however, says that he did hear this, though comically forced to admit that he was hiding under the table at the time, to avoid work (95).

The last witness is Eva, independent, fearless. She refuses to be bullied as to her sexual relationship with Karl Thomas, asking the judge whether he is living in the fifteenth century. She witnesses strongly on Karl Thomas's behalf, while at the same time, as already noted, she retains her crystal-clear honesty.

The judge, still convinced of Karl Thomas's guilt, and having read his case-history, sends him to the psychiatric department to determine whether he is of sound mind. In a prejudiced world Karl Thomas is assumed to be guilty.

Before proceeding to the final scene, a device used in the scene just discussed merits note. Eva says:

> I've been in custody for weeks (96).

It would seem that Toller is using here the Shakespearean device of a double time-scale by which as the play proceeds, each scene appears to follow immediately upon the previous one, thus maintaining dramatic intensity, while backward references often imply considerable lapse of time, thus assisting probability and conveying epic breadth. It is during the election scene that her arrest is reported. Only during the Interval following this could a lapse of weeks occur. But in the forward movement of the play, Karl Thomas's engagement at the hotel is felt to come immediately after the election (97).

After the police enquiry, with its false conclusions, and the judicial enquiry, also with its false conclusions, comes at last the psychological enquiry.

(We examine this in the early version (98), ignoring, however, the device of setting up a projector, abandoned in the published text and surely never restored.)

Like the Police Chief and the Judge, the Psychiatrist assumes Karl Thomas to be guilty of the murder, and his enquiry is dominated and distorted by this false assumption. Karl Thomas gives a clear and completely rational account of his own re-encounter with the world after eight years of being cut off from it. He speaks of Kilman, now 'a pot-bellied wheeler-dealer', of Kroll, playing a waiting game, of the

Hotel:

> It stank of corruption, of lecherousness, of arrogance, of filth. My colleagues found it all in order and were proud of it (99).

He describes his plan to stir people out of their sluggishness by shooting the Minister, and how another had shot him instead, as being a revolutionary bolshevik: how at that point — in Act 4 Sc. 1 — he began to doubt his own sanity.

Lüdin assures him that the masses are a greedy herd of swine, wallowing in their own filth; that inequalities are the law of nature. There follows the montage scene already carefully examined. At the end Lüdin tells Karl Thomas he will be sent to prison: obviously he does *not* think Karl Thomas is mad. Indeed, Karl Thomas himself now sees clearly, if only for a moment:

> I see everything clearly. In times like those we marched under the Banner of Paradise. Today one has to wear out one's boots on the earthly highway. *You* believe you are alive. It drives you into the abyss if you simply pretend that the world will always remain as it is today (100).

At this moment distant singing is heard, which gradually is broken off. We hear the sound of marching people, a demonstration on behalf of the prisoners, shouting:

> Long Live Karl Thomas! (101).

By the use of film a vast procession of silent demonstrators is now seen. It is Karl Thomas's fault, with his crazy assassination, says Lüdin.

> But I haven't done anything! (102).

cries Karl Thomas as the total absurdity of the situation becomes manifest, and he bursts into his hysterical, braying laugh. This ultimate contradiction between fact and reality is too much for his tormented psyche. He is led off to the padded cell.

> Not capable of living! (103).

says Lüdin, and as the people walk silently past, the curtains close.

Karl Thomas, according to Lüdin, is in the strictly scientific sense of the word 'Not viable' (Lebensunfähig).

Mad though the 'normal' world is (and in this scene we are convinced of the madness of its false values) Karl Thomas is also mad. He lacks the qualities needed to survive in the world as it exists.

Kroll, with his dogged political patience, Frau Meller, with her warm courage and loyalty, and Eva, with her brave independence and utter honesty: these three can at least live in the world, opposed to its madness and representing human sanity, but there is no guarantee that they will succeed politically. Indeed, the tone of the play as a whole and the disappearance of the three into the silence of prison in this authentic version, suggest that the author already knew in his heart that Nazism was on its way.

Thus re-assessed, *Hoppla, wir leben*! is seen as far more complex, profound, subtle and pessimistic than it appears in traditional criticism, influenced as that is by Piscator's falsifications, mechanical complications and thematic simplifications. Karl Thomas is the counterpart of Eugen Hinkemann: the former's lack of viability corresponds with the latter's loss of potency. Each reveals that the society in which he finds himself is suffering from the same vital lack as he is; it is a society without potency or viability, unable to beget its own continuation or even to exist. It was finally destroyed in 1933.

Despite the many positive qualities to which we have drawn attention however, there are uncertainties in this play, places lacking sureness of touch, some raggedness, — all evidently due to the external pressures brought to bear on the author, principally but not only by Piscator. Despite its fame this play is less surely unified, less finely crafted than Toller's best work. The many revisions and re-revisions it underwent have left their mark, and no edition representing the author's final and authoritative version was ever published. In working on it, however, he came to terms as an artist with the realities and responsibilities of being a dramatist writing at liberty in the contemporary world and theatre. His next plays show the confidence he had now gained.

FEUER AUS DEN KESSELN (DRAW THE FIRES)

INTRODUCTION

It is characteristic of Toller's restless temperament that he used his new freedom to explore various modes and media of dramatic expression. After his experience of attempting to collaborate with a distinguished and strong minded director, he tried to enter the field of socially critical musical theatre in the wake of Brecht's *Dreigroschenoper* (August 1928) (1). In collaboration with Walter Hasenclever he based his text on Molière's *Le Bourgeois Gentilhomme* under the title *Bourgeois bleibt Bourgeois*. Hermann Kesten wrote the song-lyrics and Friedrich Holländer the music. Alexander Granowsky directed and Max Pallenberg and Trude Hesterberg played the leads. With such a team, "A triumph was generally expected", as Kesten recalled nearly thirty years later (2). The Propyläen Press wanted the publishing rights, foreign agents were interested, and even Hollywood was said to have made enquiries. "All Berlin" attended the first night on 2 February, 1929. But the reviewers were highly critical and after about eight performances the work was sunk without trace: not even one copy of the script remains!

It is impossible in these circumstances to apportion blame for the failure. Critics were divided between those who primarily blamed Granowsky and those who blamed the authors. The setting and costumes by Victor Trivas were lavish, too lavish in some opinions, and stylised in a manner unsuited to the play (3). Several critics expressed the view that the authors had had to give way to the director (4). Kerr, normally always Toller's supporter and advocate, was unable to praise either play or production. He commented on the degree that authors are at the mercy of directors, and thought that "Toller avenged his mistreatment at the hand of Piscator on Molière" (5).

But the text was severely criticised, especially the second part, which one critic called "shallow repetition" (6). Holländer thought the text departed too far from Molière (7). Kesten, writing nearly thirty years after the event, was unkindly dismissive of his former colleagues (8).

The authors' declared intention,

> To give shape to contemporary events and at the same time to preserve the parallels with Molière's comedy of character in the dramatic structure,

was completely unfulfilled, wrote Franz Köppen (9).

According to another critic the authors were inconsistent in their criticism of the contemporary bourgeoisie and pandered to public taste (10).

At this time Toller was also becoming interested in film, not merely as an adjunct of theatre productions, but as a medium in its own right. In his answer to a question which *Die Welt am Montag* addressed to various prominent figures, "Who will make the film of the German revolution?", Toller suggested the case of the sailors Köbes (sic) and Reichpietsch as the central event of such a film (11). Indeed, he evidently began to write a screenplay on this theme (12). In doing so Toller began his contribution to that remarkable series of plays on naval themes (and especially on the theme of naval mutiny) which spanned a period from the middle of the Great War to the end of the Weimar Republic, a series which included Reinhard Goering's *Die Seeschlacht* (1917), Rudolf Leonhards *Segel am Horizont* (March 1925), Günther Weisenborn's *U-Boot "S4"* (1928), Plievier's *Des Kaisers Kulis* (1930), Friedrich Wolf's *Die Matrosen von Cattaro* (1930), and Karl Lerb's *Die Fahrt des U.B.116* (1931).

The use of the theme was also given impetus by the impact of Eisenstein's film *The Battleship Potemkin*, which made an enormous impression on Berlin in 1926 (13) and perhaps motivated the question posed in *Die Welt am Montag*.

Hope that the proposed film would be financed by the Trade Unions and the Volksbühne having been dashed, Toller reworked his material for the stage, greatly reducing the historical breadth, and concentrating upon the Köbis-Reichpietsch case; and whereas the film was to have been purely documentary, the play, though it drew heavily upon the documentary evidence, was not. In describing it as an *Historisches Schauspiel* Toller explained:

> I have altered some scenes of action (Köbis was a stoker on the *Prinzregent Luitpold*, Reichpietsch a naval rating on *Friedrich der Große*), shifted events in time, invented characters, because I believed that the dramatist ought to give the image

> of an epoche and not, like the reporter, photograph each historical detail (14).

In this Toller once more shows himself an heir of Schiller, who was always ready to invent events and people and to shift them in time and place in order to give a theatrically true 'image of an epoch' (15).

Toller's 'inventions' are in no way as drastic as Schiller's, however, and he emphasises that "there is documentary corroboration for all substantial events" (16). The documentary appendix to the published edition confirms this (17).

SCHOLARLY CRITICISM

Although, as will appear, the first production won much critical acclaim, scholarly recognition of the play's quality has been slower to develop. The pioneering Toller scholar, W.A. Willibrand, who thought that the main purpose of the play was "to expose unfair methods of criminal procedure" (18), failed altogether to appreciate the structure of the play, which he dismisses as "extremely episodic". He continues:

> . . . there is little evidence of successful dramatic concentration . . . In the hurried shift of scenes very little happens that makes a lasting impression on the reader. [Note: 'the reader'. Willibrand had no opportunity of seeing the play on stage. CWD]. It is also disturbing to have a play begin and end with scenes that are but remotely connected with the main plot. Too much ground is covered to permit a full realisation of all the implications of miscarried justice, and too little attention in given to the sound psychological development of the main characters (19).

Seventeen years later, Martin Reso, whose dissertation is markedly Marxist throughout, disagreed with Willibrand and thought the play to be not a critique of justice, but a presentation of revolutionary events in the fleet (20). Reso draws attention to the epigraph:

> He who prepares the paths
> Dies on the threshold,
> Yet Death bows before him
> In reverence (21).

In doing so he shows his understanding of the connection between the 'frame' (Scenes II & XII) and the story enclosed by it.

Dorothea Klein, in 1968, recognised both the 'revolutionary' and 'justice' aspects of the play. She did not attempt to relate these, though she did strongly contest the Marxist view of the play as 'historically optimistic' (22).

In the following decade, Rosemarie A.J. Altenhofer, who thought this play to be Toller's best stage work (23), came back to the view that it is primarily about legalised murder ('Justizmord') (24). She saw it as an early example of Documentary Theatre, but written thirty years too soon, when epic structure was not fully accepted and there was no theory of documentary drama (25).

More recently (1981), Thomas Bütow has drawn many of these critical threads together in a perceptive but in some ways controversial paper (26). Bütow's major conclusions are as follows:

The play becomes not only a drama of Revolution, but a drama about Justice, including justice in the Weimar Republic, and thus also a contemporary tribunal which challenges living persons, especially Dobring (27).

In this play Toller deals for the first time with class-conflict rather than conflict *within* the revolutionary movement.

The members of the marine proletariat are clearly differentiated as individuals.

The contrast between Reichpietsch and Köbis is of special importance:

Reichpietsch is fundamentally a pacifist whose pacifist ethic has a basis in religious conviction. Köbis on the other hand comes to believe that only stupidity and cowardice have prevented the sailors from using violence to obtain their ends. Bütow regards this as more positive than Reichpietsch's Christian pacifism:

> Köbis is the first of Toller's protagonists who justifies the evil method of force in order to fight against another evil — war. Köbis is therefore Toller's first rationally ethical hero . . .
> However, Köbis is the first of Toller's positive figures who at the same time has a positive relationship to power. Köbis recognises that the power of the system can in turn be opposed only by power.
> Finally, in the trial scene, when it is too late, Köbis is also prepared to use such counter-force (28).

Bütow notes with surprise [!] the persistence of the concept of self-sacrifice in Toller's plays. (He evidently does not appreciate the implications of the epigraph and dedication, which imply that Reichpietsch and Köbis are pioneers and trail-breakers).

Finally, he notes what he sees as an inner contradiction between the revolutionary play and the 'justice' play:

> If Toller wishes to make the 'Idea' apparent, he must open up from the sailors' revolt the perspective towards the great revolution. If on the other hand he wishes to make an attack on Lösch and Dobring as to the court's verdict, Toller must show that Köbis and Reichpietsch were not revolutionaries (29).

Even if one rejects some of his value-judgements, Bütow's analysis must form the basis of any subsequent study and evaluation of the play, so precisely has he isolated its essentials and apparent paradoxes.

Three of his major judgements must certainly be questioned:

1. That Köbis is the "apex of the pyramid" of characters (30).
2. That there is an unresolved contradiction between the themes of revolution and justice in the play.
3. That Toller intended the play to have an "optimistic tendency" (31).

1. Bütow argues that Reichpietsch's character, apart from being true to the documentary sources, has the aesthetic function of forming a contrast with Köbis: he does not also say that Köbis has the function of forming a contrast with Reichpietsch. In fact, both characters are presented sympathetically and positively, and though Köbis in his exasperation during the trial, exclaims,

> We were too stupid and too cowardly to do what that charge accuses us of. Today I regret that (32),

it is he, not Reichpietsch, who opposes a suicide pact of the prisoners, because he appreciates the positive value of sacrifice:

> No, lads, hands off! It is bitter to be put up against a wall again by these people . . . Our blood will not flow in vain (33).

Apart from this internal textual evidence it is not reasonable to suppose that in 1930 Toller would have deliberately made an advocate of violence the single hero of his play. Toller at this time was still a committed pacifist and remained so until about 1935/6.

The evidence for this is to be found in a speech delivered at Friends House, Euston Road, London, at a lunch-hour meeting (1.20–2.00 p.m.) on Tuesday, 13 February 1934, entitled *Masses and Man: the Problem of Non-violence and Peace,* and published in that year for the London and Middlesex Quarterly Meeting Peace Committee of the Society of Friends (Quakers) (34). This precisely dated printed version of the speech is not in Spalek's Bibliography and is categorically "not known" by Frühwald, who prints, under the modified title, *Man and the Masses: The Problem of Peace,* a later version from a Yale University typescript, which he merely dates as "evidently before 1937" and which he says was "presumably utilised as a speech" (35).

We learn from Spalek (36) that there are five versions of the speech in the Yale typescript and that the revisions include the change of title already noted. Frühwald does not say which version he prints, but it must be the third or the fifth, as only these correspond with his statement that it consists of nine sheets. It is reasonable to suppose that he used what appeared to be the final version.

Neither Spalek nor Frühwald gives any grounds for the statement that the typescript is earlier than 1937. Internal evidence suggests that the version printed in GW1 may be as late as 1939 (37).

For our present purpose the essential difference between the two versions is that Toller adapted a pacifist speech of 1934 to make a non-pacifist speech several years later.

In 1934 Toller declared:

> When the welfare of the soul, the absoluteness of the moral law, the divine command, the sanctification of life are at stake, then earthly, material aims must stand back (38).

In the later version this declaration has become a question. Both versions emphasise the dangers of Nazism (though not by name in 1934). Both say:

> Today after thousands of years of human history, certain states [later version: "dictators"] are still in the condition of the undeveloped child.
> To teach them, activity is needed, a curative compulsion. Otherwise they will hurl themselves and [italicised 1934] us into the hell of another war (39).

In 1934 Toller continued:

> This curative compulsion is the vigorous proscription, the real outlawing of the spirit of violence and war (40).

and went on to declare that "the word is stronger than weapons".

In the later speech he omitted all this and called for a

> united world ... which is willing to punish the attacker ... a bloc of strong countries which would defend freedom collectively (41).

These changes reflect Toller's change of conviction after February 1934. Indeed, he says in the later version:

> I was a convinced pacifist, but reality set me right (42).

Bütow is thus wrong in saying that in 1930 Toller made an advocate of violence the hero to his play. He could not have done this at that time. Indeed Bütow recognises that Köbis' 'positive' attitude to power — as Bütow sees it — does not lead *in this play* to the acute problems of revolutionary violence propounded in *Masse Mensch* and *Die Maschinenstürmer*. He also recognises that Toller expressed views similar to those of Köbis when, in exile, he took up the struggle against Nazism.

However, Köbis is a new phenomenon in Toller's plays, though already foreshadowed in the special case of Karl Thomas, viz: a *sympathetic* presentation of a man prepared to use violence in the last resort.

It is therefore surely not fanciful to see in Reichpietsch and Köbis embodiments of Toller's past and future attitudes to force. Toller never wore his pacifism complacently — witness his military leadership of the Red Army to Dachau in April 1919. The 1934 speech, too, is filled with passionate, ethical self-doubts and questionings. The author's own inner condition is expressed both in the tension between Reichpietsch and Köbis and in the common cause that unites them.

2. Bütow concludes that the *antithesis* between Toller as politician who soberly and sceptically stresses that in the sphere of justice the Wilhelmine system continues to operate in the post-revolutionary Republic, and Toller as poet who wants to make manifest the

"Idea" of opposition to such a system, constitutes an actual inner *contradiction* between the two aspects of the play. He evidently does not think it to be consistent to support the idea of revolution and at the same time demand genuinely just treatment for failed or defeated revolutionaries. Toller on the other hand had in his own person and life carried on that dual struggle: for revolution and for justice.

His major work on this dual theme, *Justiz: Erlebnisse (Justice: Experiences)* had been published at the end of May 1927 (43). The book is primarily a documentation of injustices perpetrated by the Bavarian Government against the left-wing revolutionaries, himself and his cell-neighbours included. Contrasted with these experiences is the treatment meted out to, for example, Graf Arco-Valley, Eisner's assassin, and to Hitler in 1921 and 1923 (44).

That he himself, Landauer, Leviné and the rest were revolutionaries, Toller never seeks to deny, but

> The bourgeoisie, its power threatened by the pioneers of future social structuring has, whether consciously or not, given up its concept of justice (45).

He quotes a memorandum of the Bavarian Government on accusations raised in parliament about the treatment of the revolutionaries in prison:

> The Administration of Justice finds itself in respect of these violent prisoners in a situation of emergency. Because of that, and from this viewpoint also, all measures necessary for the maintenance of order in the institution and for the protection of state security are justified (46).

Toller's clarity of mind and utter sincerity are nowhere more clearly demonstrated than in his account of *The Judicial Murder of Eugen Leviné (47).*

Leviné was Toller's own bitter opponent within the revolutionary movement, and what he overthrew was not the constitutional government but the Soviet Republic (the Phoney Soviet Republic — *Scheinräterepublik* — according to Leviné and other hard-line communists) with Toller at its head. Leviné was nevertheless found guilty of high-treason and was executed. This, said Toller, was only made possible by the prosecution's alleging that the original Soviet Republic set up in 4 & 5 April ("Toller's" Soviet Republic) was merely 'a revolt against the continuing constitutional government' (48) and that therefore Leviné's revolutionary actions in the night of 13–14 April, directed against the 'Phoney Soviet Republic', were in fact high-treason against the constitutional government. Had the facts been correctly presented, argues Toller, Leviné could only have been found guilty of being an accessory to high-treason, for which the maximum sentence was 15 years imprisonment.

Toller's attitude to the judicial murder, as he construed it, of a fellow revolutionary who was also his own personal and political opponent, illustrates his perfectly logical position as a supporter both of revolution and of justice — including justice for revolutionaries. *Feuer aus den Kesseln* thus reflects two actual and in no way contradictory attitudes of its author.

3. Marxist critics have argued that in this play Toller's intention was based upon "historical optimism": this special pleading cannot be sustained either in the light of Toller's earlier and later work or through the examination of the text itself. Let one example of the latter suffice, from Scene IX, the prison scene.

> *Distant singing is heard outside.*
> BECKERS: Quiet!
> REICHPIETSCH: The International!
> KÖBIS: It really is!
> REICHPIETSCH: The comrades are coming!
> SACHSE: They'll set us free!
> ALL (*sing softly*):
> Peoples, hear the signal,
> Up, to the final fight!
> The Internationale
> Conquers for human right!
> *They break off; listen. The singing outside falls silent.*
> KÖBIS: Drunken shipyard workers. They only remember the Internationale when they're tight.
> *Silence* (49).

That "historical optimism" was evidently not his intention has already been well argued by Klein. Though the play is based on documentary evidence, Toller's selection of facts is calculated to reflect his particular personal perspective (50). Even his use of documents in the Appendix is such that:

> In the overall effect this factual testimony itself has an even harder and more polemic effect than the play (51).

And the author's *intention* in his selection and presentation of facts is, she says, the same as in all his plays; only the *method* is different. This intention she defines as *Aufrüttelung (arousing, stirring up),* — the title of the prefatory poem to his very first play, *Die Wandlung*.

While it is true that *Die Wandlung*, written before his actual experience of revolution, ends on an optimistic note, no subsequent play had done so, and Toller never fell into a facile optimism or a Marxist belief in historical determinism.

FEUER AUS DEN KESSELN AND *DES KAISERS KULIS* (THEODOR PLIEVIER)

The origins and first productions of these two works based in part upon the Reichpietsch/Köbis case are so closely linked that some comparison must be made before Toller's play can be independently assessed.

Theodor Plievier, less than two years Toller's senior, was born on 12 February 1892 in Berlin-Wedding and was brought up unhappily in brutalised and degrading poverty. He left home at 17 to follow the life of a tramp and vagabond, eventually going to sea.

> I followed the sea until the first World War, and then the only difference was that I had to leave a merchant ship and join the Imperial Navy for four years (52).

In the course of his compulsory service he endured a voyage of 444 days on the auxiliary cruiser *Wolf*, which sank a record 300,000 tons of shipping and laid mines outside Capetown, Colombo, Bombay, Singapore and off the coast of Australia. In November 1918 he took an active part in the sailors' revolt at Wilhelmshaven.

Plievier saw Spartacism and Bolshevism as destructive and self-destructive, and became an idealistic anarchist. He went into exile in 1933; lived in the Soviet Union during World War II, returned to Germany with the Red Army in 1945, and fled from the Soviet Occupation Zone to the American in 1947.

Des Kaisers Kulis (The Kaiser's Coolies) was published at the end of 1929 (dated 1930); a second impression followed in 1930 with the addition of the chapter *S.M. (Seine Majestät)*. It is a novel based upon both documentary and autobiographical material — a method which he developed in modified form in his great trilogy of the Second World War, *MOSKAU STALINGRAD BERLIN: Der große Krieg im Osten (Moscow Stalingrad Berlin: The Great War in the East)*. The earlier novel, regarded as a masterpiece of the *Neue Sachlichkeit*, is much more than that. The starkly documentary and autobiographical material is heightened by the author's brilliantly inventive imagination, as, for example, in the passage at the end of the *Skagerrak* (Battle of Jutland) chapter (53) in which a drowning sailor holds a dialogue with a mine, which finally explodes and kills him: a scene which anticipates, for example, Golding's *Pincher Martin*.

The first edition of *Feuer aus den Kesseln* was published about May 1930 (54).

Then on 31 August 1930 occurred the noteworthy double premiere:

At the Lessing (later 'Waldorf') Theatre, Piscator's production of a stage version of *Des Kaisers Kulis;*

At the Theater am Schiffbauerdamm, *Feuer aus den Kessseln.*

This sequence of events makes it impossible to consider Toller's play without some reference to the rival production: even the critics had to choose which first night they attended.

Piscator clearly found Plievier's long and epic novel impracticable as stage material. "Plievier is no dramatist", commented one critic (55).

Piscator found himself forced to use film not merely as a colourful and atmospheric accessory but as central to the action. (Interesting, in view of the filmic origin of Toller's play).

> The Battle of Jutland, which is really a crucial point in the piece, is shown cinematographically. Photographs which presumably stem from military archives and are very gripping. Sometimes Piscator de-natures and de-emotionalises the film also: he presents the climax of the battle through a matter-of-fact cartographical sketch in which the naval battlefronts are only moving lines. Plievier, from a box at the left-hand side of the stage, speaks at the same time a colourless account of the phases of the battle. All this, no longer dramatic, and no longer epic either, had a tremendous effect (56).

Kurt Pinthus also wrote a full account of Piscator's production (57) which is much more critical of it. Plievier's novel, he says is one of the great post-war books and perfect material for sound-film. Piscator realised this but unfortunately tried to make a stage-play instead. The stage material was poor alongside the film, which eclipsed the live actors. It was bad, too, in his opinion, to have bits of the book read out:

> What Piscator shows is no longer theatre (58).

Nor did Piscator achieve anything new. Out of all these mixed elements he made only

> a laboriously strung-out montage that fluttered in every wind.
>
> Piscator was powerless in the face of Plievier's mass of material.
>
> I've seen working-class amateur companies to whom fanaticism gave more power than these hard struggling professional players could show. Among them the author himself spoke rather than acted the part of Köbis.
>
> It is bitter that we must reject the great cause of humanity — that of winning human rights — especially when we passionately endorse it, when it is presented in such a false and feeble performance. It is bitter to say that Piscator, who is now striving forward towards simplicity, fell back this time into confusion.
>
> For here it is not only a question of a bold but unsuccessful attempt, but the danger exists that the weapons which the historical facts place in the hands of the champions of an idea, will, through all too childish implementation, be torn out of well-intentioned hands by enemies and turned to reactionary use.
>
> Nevertheless the splendid material called forth much applause. But the material would have had a thousand-fold stronger effect if it had either been totally remodelled as a sound-film or used with theatrical means only — as on the same evening, in another theatre, Toller successfully attempted, often with the same scenes, — yes, often with the same speeches (59).

Toller's working of the material, so far from being 'laboriously strung out', was closely and symmetrically organised in a form that the simple division into 12 scenes does not bring out clearly.

Scene I (1926, The Reichstag Committee of Investigation) is a Prologue to the whole, as even Willibrand saw (60).

Scenes II & XII (the identical boiler-room, 1916 and 1918) form the Frame.

Scenes III to X are the play within the frame, with Scene XI an Epilogue to that inner play. (See Diagrammatic representation below).

Thus, as always, Toller paid close attention to form. The Reichstag Prologue recalls the use of the House of Lords in *Die Maschinenstürmer* in that it places the whole play in the context of national politics. The two 'boiler-room' scenes provide a 'frame' in the manner of the *Rahmenerzählungen* so frequent in German Novellen and thus familiar at least to the reading public who read the printed version.

So far from having virtually 'no connection with the play' (61), these two scenes reveal the *effect* of the events of the inner play and above all of the sacrifice of Reichpietsch and Köbis, upon the sailors and stokers. The Battle of Jutland, which was the climax and centre-piece of Plievier's novel, in which the casualties and sufferings of the 'coolies' were starkly contrasted with the official view of the naval commanders, becomes in Toller primarily an image of the bravery and endurance of the common sailors and stokers, unacknowledged by the officer class, while the second boiler-room scene shows their ultimate revolt, inspired by the self-sacrifice of the protagonists.

DIAGRAMMATIC REPRESENTATION

SCENE I PROLOGUE
(1926: The Reichstag Investigation)

FRAME

SCENE II
Boiler-Room
31.5.1916
The Battle of Jutland

INNER PLAY
Sc. III. June 1917 Corridor
SC. IV. July 1917 Casemate
SC. V. July 1917 Bar
SC. VI August 1917 Interrogation
SC. VII August 1917 Admiral Scheer
SC. VIII August 25th 1917 Court Martial
SC. IX August/Sept 1917 Prison
SC. X Sept 5th 1917 Execution

SCENE XI
EPILOGUE
to the Inner play
End Sept. 1917
News brought to Reichpietsch's parents

SCENE XII
Boiler-Room
2nd Nov.1918
Naval Mutiny.

Scene XI, the bringing of the news to Reichpietsch's parents is not only an Epilogue to the inner play but also, as an additional structural refinement, a deliberate contrast, using montage technique, of the private consequences of the executions with their public effect: the revolt.

FEUER AUS DEN KESSELN ON STAGE

The 'acting version' used in the first production (62) survives as mimeographed copies, not for sale. This version is reprinted in GW3. Spalek in his Bibliography says it "must be considered the authoritative edition of the play" (63), apparently simply because it is the later version and because he personally regards the changes as "improvements" (64).

More thoughtfully, a note in GW (Frühwald and Spalek) suggests that the two versions have two different aims:

> Toller follows, — particularly through the different versions — the tendency of the "political theatre" to have an effect upon the audience through the dramatically intensified stage version and at the same time upon the reader through an epically elaborated book version (65).

This seems more reasonable, and indeed, George Bernard Shaw, one of the founding fathers of political theatre, deliberately wooed the reading public with his Prefaces, novelistic stage directions and appendices; but most plays are cut and modified in production, and a close study of the cuts and alterations made to *Feuer aus den Kesseln* shows them to be no more than might be expected for a stage production, and it is perfectly natural that some passages cut should be 'explanatory' (66). The changes and cuts in songs seem to have no special significance; the shortening of the cast was probably for economy, the changes in names may well have been on legal advice: the agent provocateur Dames becomes Birgiwski and the Reichstag Member Scheidemann becomes Kleidermann. It goes without saying that the Documentary Appendix in the published version was a conscious appeal to the reading public.

More drastic than any of the cuts in the mimeographed version was the cutting in the production itself of Scenes XI and XII. Toller evidently fought long and hard against this butchery but, according to Ernst Josef Aufricht, the Producer, recalling the events after a lapse of 36 years, he finally gave way late at night during a rehearsal. He handed Aufricht a copy of the play inscribed:

> Such and such a date
> Twelve o'clock at night.
> In memory of the hour, in which
> a man made a sacrifice.
>
> Signed *Ernst Toller* (67).

Once more Toller as author had been defeated by a theatre director.

The cut, as several critics pointed out (68), made the title meaningless. It pleased those, Aufricht, of course, among them, who wanted Toller's political message to be muted. Aufricht wrongly recalls the last scene (Sc. XII) as

> The final apotheosis: red flags and tirades of communist propaganda (69).

The cut also, of course, destroyed the balance of the parallel themes of revolution and justice and turned the play primarily into a 'justice' play. The emotional mood induced by ending the play with the execution was remote from that intended by the author's true ending. Critics already knew the published play and were able to comment on the cut.

Moritz Loeb in a sympathetic review, thought the cut wise. The political message went without saying. It was not

> spread on our bread and butter in film or through inflammatory tirades (70).

Praising the cut, he wrote:

> Toller is too serious a dramatist not to know that what is self-evident falls flat in stage lighting (71).

Bernhard Diebold, who does not compare the production with the printed version, does contrast the conclusion, as played, with *Des Kaisers Kulis*:

> Piscator and Plievier end with a political programme and a proclamation of 'humanity'. Toller and Aufricht end with shattering sorrow over the death of beloved persons (72).

Clearly the altered ending was theatrically effective, but as so often in earlier productions of Toller's plays, the meaning of the play was distorted.

As an array of talent this production outstripped even that of *Bourgeois bleibt Bourgeois*. Ernst Josef Aufricht was Producer and Hans Hinrich, Director. Caspar Neher constructed highly naturalistic settings: even a direct hit on the engine-room was actually shown.

The tradition of ultra-realistic naval settings went back to Richard Goering's *Die Seeschlacht* (1917). Goering does not prescribe the style of setting for his expressionist drama taking place in the gun-turret of a warship. Indeed, "in some productions of the play, the gun is not even there: the puppet-like slaves go through the balletic motions of aiming and firing a non-existent gun while the action towards the end is punctuated by flashes, bangs and screams" (73). But in Reinhardt's 1918 production in the Deutsches Theater, Berlin,

> Little coloured lights twinkled on the control panel, there was the hum of the engines, the dim glitter of machinery . . . Alarm bells rang, signals flashed, the engines raced, and the sound of gunfire shook the theatre. Guns 10 miles off, guns on stage, the flash of explosions, smoke pouring through the shattered metal, dead men falling back soaked in blood (74).

And a photograph of the production in the Königliches Schauspielhaus, Dresden, in the same year, shows a highly realistic gun, iron ladders and so on (75).

More realistic naval settings followed, several under Piscator's direction: Paquet's *Sturmflut*, 1926 at the Volksbühne, when film and live action were combined (76): Leonhard's *Segel am Horizont*, 1926, Volksbühne (77); Ehm Welk *Sturm über Gotland*, 1927, Volksbühne (78). Another was Günther Weisenborn's *U-Boot 'S4'*, 1928, Volksbühne, for which Edward Suhr designed a wonderfully realistic submarine interior backed by film projection of the sea (79).

After Toller's play came Karl Lerbs' *UB 116*. Photographs of three different sets for this all show realistic constructions of the claustrophobic interior of a submarine (80).

To return to *Feuer aus den Kesseln*:

Felix Holländer wrote the music; there was a superb cast;

Albert Hörrmann	Köbis
Hermann Speelmann	Reichpietsch
Erich Ponto	Schuler
Heinrich Gretler	The Mate
Theo Lingen	Lieutenant

> For the great number of sailors we chose actors who were not stagey under Hanns Hinrich's realistic direction (81).

Photographs of the production confirm the impression of realism (82). In the interrogation scene Schuler sits rigidly in his uniform gripping his white gloves in his left hand, his eyes fixed on the two sailors. He wears a neat moustache and small beard. He breathes cruelty. The two sailors stand there, neither looking at him. Köbis stares into space, while Reichpietsch looks up at him enquiringly.

In a picture of Sc. V, Lucie sits on the bar displaying her wide-stretched legs, her left arm round Reichpietsch's neck. Two prostitutes sit at a small table in the background, and the Wachtmeister stands firmly, hand on hip. The few details of the high stools, the hanging oil-lamp, serve to set the scene.

Another photograph shows the cleanliness inspection in Sc. IV. Lieutenant Hoffmann, knife-edge creases in his trousers, inspects eleven naval ratings, while the Mate stands at the side with his notebook. Open girders above convey the feeling of a ship's deck-room (83).

Aufricht claims that the production had sensational success both on the first night and in the press, but admits that the tickets did not sell. Thousands of complimentary tickets were distributed to Trade Unions and workers' organisations, but even these were not taken up. Rather rhetorically he concludes:

> The theatre of contemporary realism of the twenties had died (84).

In reality the response from the press was mixed.

One critic concludes a heavily ironical article by declaring that

> Without massive documentary help every one of Toller's scenic inventions turns into a dreary revolutionary idyll (85).

The right-wing critic Ludwig Sternaux said the play was a boring failure, so crudely done that one had to laugh.

> . . .
> [in his anti-war views] Toller was of course not great. And how should he understand, foreign as he is to the country and the people [Ger:Volk] whose language he misuses into the bargain? (86).

The critic "P.W." said that, lacking the end, it was merely an "episode", a "German Potemkin" (87). Only those parts which corresponded with the author's own experiences were of value. Scheidemann, Scheer etc.,

> are only intermezzi in a dark satire (88).

Another anonymous critique, undated, declared that

> For lack of better intellectuality the theatre becomes a political wax-works.

and concludes,

> No more about this Toller, he is only the product of a party (89).

The critic in the *Berliner Tageblatt* of 1.9.'30, regrets that Toller, the poet, is content this time to allow actions to speak for themselves. The theatre should not be content with that.

> Then we cannot share his contentment. We wanted and want to hear a poetic person speak. To do without the poet means killing art, and art is just as necessary to us as humanity and justice (90).

A certain "A.Ltg" concluded a very hostile review:

> There are much more cheerful communist election meetings nowadays at which to amuse oneself better (91).

A majority of critics reacted favourably. Even when the play was not liked ideologically (92) the author's skill was recognised:

> Toller is in control of all stage devices . . . and when Jannings is looking for a part again he may turn to Toller (93).

Manfred Georg, who contrasted the play with *Des Kaisers Kulis*, thought that Toller was once more wholly himself (94):

> Toller's political effect is indirect. The documentary reality is only a component in a poetic truth . . . He succeeded in writing a poetic work which absorbed the political idea and then made it shine out with doubled force from within . . .

> Person speaks here to person. The person is first — then the age (95).

The play was thought 'clever' and in some parts more than merely clever — particularly the prison scene, which had a plain fine tone which carried the audience along with it (96).

Felix Holländer, who, having written the music may have started with a favourable bias, wrote the fullest and most penetrating critique of this production. He too praised the gripping and shattering effect of Toller's unadorned presentation of the crudeness and naivety of the 'tormented creatures', his avoidance of all spiritual nonsense and all Piscator-fuss.

> The effect lies in the toughness of the unvarnished facts (97).

Reichpietsch, in Toller's hands, became the representative of a whole stratum of society:

> A man pure to the very marrow shows the collapse of a whole régime, and just because he avoids any extra ingredients, he succeeds (98).

Holländer wrongly prophesied that the play would remain a long time in the repertoire and that thousands would want to see it (99).

The same critic placed Toller's work rightly in the traditions and perspectives of German drama, saying that this play could not have existed without Büchner's *Dantons Tod* and Hauptmann's *Die Weber*, though he thought Toller lacked Büchner's rapturous verve and Hauptmann's poetic impact. The prison scene was heir to Büchner, the bar-room scene to Hauptmann.

He concluded by declaring the play to be honest both in its outer techniques and inner motivation.

Perhaps the strongest evidence of the dramatic authenticity of the play comes from Head Stoker Sachse, one of those condemned to death (27.8.1917) and then reprieved (1.9.1917), who travelled from Leipzig to Berlin to attend the first night. He had suffered greatly in prison from undernourishment. (Weber, one of his colleagues, had died from this cause). He had served eight years, a forgotten man, as another Sachse, a coiner, had been released by mistake instead of him. After the play he talked with the actors:

> Yes, you see, Erich Ponto made the greatest impression on me as the official of the Court Martial. Outwardly he did not resemble our Judge, Herr Gerichtsrat Dobring who now holds a position in the District Court in Moabit; but this sudden transition from courtesy to cruelty, — *that* you recognised. Yes, Dobring. I shall never forget how he came to me in the prison cell with a photo of the place of execution of our two poor shot comrades, Köbis and Reichpietsch. (The corpses had been strewn with lime). 'Just you see,' he said, 'I've saved you from this fate'.
> Of course, during the trial where we were examined as witnesses, he'd achieved nothing by this method. When I once asked him, during another interrogation, whether he did not regret his methods of interrogation, he replied 'No, if I could bring the two mutineers to life again today, I'd act in the same way again' (100).
>
> (101)

After the box-office failure in Berlin there was only one more production of *Feuer aus den Kesseln* in Germany before the Nazis came to power. This was by the Volksbühne in Plauen, Saxony, in 1932. No details or reviews are available. Saxony at this time was "a 'Volksbühne Province' of the first rank" with 41 Volksbühne Societies and over 63,000 members. Plauen Volksbühne, founded in 1924 through the fusion of two existing organisations, had over 1,000 members. It is therefore not surprising that Toller's play should be performed in that area (102).

A production at the Workers' Theatre, Riga (Latvia) which opened on 1 May 1931 (103) was highly praised even by those critics who had reservations about the actual play. It was evidently well acted and produced, and the choice of 'best' scenes is predictable. The work is compared with that of Remarque and of the Latvian Upits. One reviewer perceptively noted the filmic style. Only one Latvian critic, Arweds Stirajs, thought it 'literary Marxist propaganda' (104), but a Russian-language review criticised it for not showing the ideological motivation behind the 1917 revolt (105).

The play had a second Latvian production in the People's Theatre, Liepaja, in 1932, which was well and warmly received (106). There was also a Tokyo production in 1931 of which details are not available (107).

But by far the most important production of this play was in Manchester in 1935, jointly directed by Dominic Roche, Director of the Manchester Repertory Theatre, and Toller himself.

From Stephen Wardale, who acted in this production and worked on the stage-management side also, we have not only many details of the production but also a unique impression of Toller as a Director (108).

The production opened at the Rusholme Repertory Theatre, Wilmslow Road, Manchester on 10 February, 1935 and ran for three weeks, of which the first two were packed out (109). It was taken also to the Grand Theatre, Oldham, where it was played twice nightly[!] and 'did fairly well' (110). On 12 May it was taken to London for a single Sunday performance for the Arts Theatre Club at the Cambridge Theatre (111).

The Manchester production was given two weeks' rehearsal, — considered fortunate for an English repertory company at that time.

Toller gave Wardale the impression of being 'on the down grade' and of not having 'got great knowledge of production'. He 'tried to copy other producers: Reinhardt, Piscator'. Although his command of English was 'fairly good' he was naturally unacquainted with English technical terminology.

> When he wanted lighting he didn't know whether front battens or back battens; he didn't know. When someone said. "Front batten, " then he would echo it: "Front batten" (112).

Toller would lose his temper and was notably undiplomatic to colleagues, including Hanns Eisler, who wrote and conducted the music for this production, which included an Overture *Going to Sea* (113). Toller was apparently cavalier in his attitude to Eisler. The Manchester Playgoers' Club had invited Toller to speak to them. It seems that Toller could not be bothered to do so and said to Eisler, "You go down and play the piano for them" (114).

Wardale was much aware of Toller's intensity — a quality which obviously had positive effects as well as negative on his work as Director.

> He took everything so much to heart, though, didn't he? You can tell with those eyes, can't you? (115).

But above all Wardale latched on to W.H. Auden's adjective 'egotistical' (116) and his reaction to an account of Toller's suicide had in it an element of black comedy:

> Yes, he *would* do that: no consideration for anybody else but himself. No, that's just it. I think you've got him there. No consideration. That's it. All his ideas — they're very subjective characters. Thinking of his own, — thinking of what-d'y'call-it. He would never think of the woman's coming up. There was no mercy there, was there? There was no kindness there. All this what-d'y'call-it about loving-kindness, never thinking about his secretary having to find him (117).

But he was innately an actor:

> Toller had to be dramatic, though, didn't he? . . . There was the actor *in* him (118).

Such was the impression Toller made on an actor working under him. In Wardale's recollections of details one sees Toller's imagination having to be disciplined by the practical theatre people.

The production opened with Scene II, the Boiler-room: the 'Reichstag' scenes were cut: that is, Scenes I & III. As the curtain went up the furnace doors were opened and the fires glowed red. Then:

> We had a sort of ballet, — impressionistic: open the door; one man shovelled coal into the fire, straight off; another shovelled coal to the other man: there was no coal there.
> CWD: You mean imaginary coal?
> WARDALE: Yes. But it brought the place down when it came up. Every night it brought the place down . . . (119).

Much was evidently made of the explosions in this scene and Toller had considerable staging problems. Wardale again:

> I was in this, I played — I was in the boiler-room. One boiler's blown up and a man shouts out, "Minna, Minna!" — he's a bit of a sick man, well, he's blown up and they carry him out dead; we, of course, stayed in the boiler-room, but Toller wanted us to clean up the boiler. We used to say to him, "Now, Toller, if this boiler's been blown up and a man's been killed, these men would not be *able* to get up, it would kill everybody". Eventually what he had done was — when the blow-up, he had a sort of slide come across, the lights went out and a slide came across as though — and a painted scene, as though it was ruined, you know; they only brought one man out screaming about "Minna, Minna", and then . . . (120).

After this inside view of the production, with the tensions and struggles typical of rehearsal work, it is interesting to turn to the successful result, already recognised in Wardale's account of the 'stoking ballet'.

Even before the opening night the forthcoming production was hailed as an intellectual event (121). Toller's 'infectious enthusiasm and dynamic energy' were commented upon. Toller is reported as saying that this is the first production of his life with all his ideas in it (122). His initial doubts about the potential of the theatre were evidently overcome after a few days (123). The reviews were consistently favourable towards both play and production (124), and the author / director, too, was virtually fêted.

> His terrific, violent intensity of pacifistic purpose takes possession of the Manchester Repertory Theatre (125).

When, only four years later, the *Manchester Guardian* had to write an obituary of Toller, the drama critic, Arthur S. Wallace, who had written a very long and favourable review of *Draw the Fires* in Manchester in 1935, added a retrospective account of this production, which evidently echoes his original review (126). He said that:

> The production brought out to the full Toller's attitude towards drama, that its purpose should be not to afford an escape from life but to seize upon and interpret the great movements that for good or evil shake the civilised world to its foundations.

Wallace also adds the information that the Left Theatre Group joined with the regular players to fill the large cast needed.

On Sunday 12 May in the same year the production was given one performance for the Arts Theatre Club at the Cambridge Theatre, Cambridge Circus, London. This time the Manchester Repertory Company was augmented by members of the Theatre of Action (Manchester), the Left Theatre and the Toynbee Players (127). 'Heralded as an event of intellectual importance' it drew a large audience including notabilities (128). An advance leaflet gave enthusiastic extracts from ten major reviews of the production in Manchester (129). But the London performance was comparatively unsuccessful. Perhaps it had not been adequately re-rehearsed since Manchester and Oldham (130). There were other difficulties, too. Toller interfered with the casting

(131), and there was trouble with the Stage Manager, Arthur Johnson, who resented being given orders by Toller, a German, and had 'a blazing row' with Toller at the dress-rehearsal in London, for which he was afterwards sacked. He also took the curtain up too soon on the final scene. Several actors, including Stephen Wardale, had played in Scene X (the Execution Scene) and then had to change in time for the final boiler-room scene (XII) during Scene XI. Before they could all get back on stage, Johnson sent up the curtain with about two men in the boiler-room (132).

Of the cast, only Keith Pyott and Noel Morris were praised (133). The performance in general was described as 'poor, halting and spiritless' (134), and its style as 'crude as an old-fashioned touring revue' with 'some attempt at grim realism' (135). The *Observer* critic back-handedly excused what he called 'the emergency nature of the production' (136).

These journals were doubtless hostile to the political messages of the play. Much more balanced judgements came from the *Times* and *Sunday Times*. Toller himself was seen by the latter as 'a fine and lofty spirit' whose 'passionate love of life and hatred of war' had 'gone to the making of this play' (137). The former felt there was a certain inconsistency between Toller's personal advocacy of non-violence and his support for armed revolt in the play. The alleged 'inconsistency' is, of course a reflection of the permanent struggle in Toller's heart between the pacifist and the revolutionary anti-fascist.

> It is odd that a dramatist who, at the end of his play, had the grace and courtesy to thank this country for having given him the opportunity to work, and whose spirit appears to be one of liberal tolerance, should in his writing have given so little attention to the virtues of compromise (138).

Feuer aus den Kesseln does not seem to have had another production until 1958 (139), when it was produced almost simultaneously in Quedlinburg and Radebeul, a suburb of Dresden, both in the German Democratic Republic. The latter was given by the Landesbühnen Sachsen and was directed by Wolfgang Böttcher. It opened on 9 November 1958 and had 42 performances. According to the radio-critic Walther Pollatschele, it was inferior to the Quedlinburg production (140) which opened on 4 November 1958 at the Städtische Bühnen and had 28 performances as well as giving a guest performance at the Leuna Werke, Halle (141).

This production was jointly directed by Heiner Blume and Curt Trepte, Intendant of the Städtische Bühnen, who as a young actor had played in the 1930 Berlin production. As an emigré in Sweden during the Nazi period he had interpreted Toller's plays at the Independent Theatre there and had exchanged letters with Toller precisely about this play. The play was a big undertaking for his small stage. Trepte, in preparing his production, talked with and engaged four sailors who were actual survivors of that period (142). Original films of the Battle of Jutland were used, along with contemporary photographs. As in London in 1935, the cast was augmented with amateur 'extras' and a good rapport was obtained between them and the professional ensemble. The climaxes of the production were apparently the trial scene and the bringing of the news of her son's death to Mother Reichpietsch, played by Erna Buck. Helmut Frensel as Köbis was the strongest of the five revolutionary sailors. The setting by Harald Reichelt was technically good, but the scene changes sometimes inevitably broke the tension and were disturbing (143). As might be expected, most East German critics found fault with the play ideologically, blaming Toller for not motivating the revolt politically (144). One particularly favourable critic, writing on the guest performance at Halle, said:

> The particular effectiveness of the piece lies in the intensity of its message, in its dramatic structuring, which embraces truth and reality, structuring which unites theatre and life (145).

Quoting the heading of Manfred Georg's review of the 1930 production, *Genuine Contemporary Theatre,* (146), Döll continues:

> The piece is 'Genuine Contemporary Theatre' for us, too (147).

Another favourable review, if slightly more cautious from the ideological point of view, came from Schenk, who wrote that 'Toller's concern for historical truth is remarkable' (148). He said that Toller stood as an opponent of war, an anti-fascist, and

> as a champion of socialist ideas. But it would be wrong to say "as a socialist" (149).

Schenk thinks that Toller was at fault not to include in the play Reichpietsch's cry,

> Up, break the fetters in Russian style! (150).

It is interesting to note that this play, in which Toller does, through Köbis, seem to question his own pacifist convictions, should be twice chosen for production and be especially praised in Communist Germany.

The play had to wait another twenty years for a production in West Germany, when it was put on, very appropriately and doubtless deliberately, at Kiel. It was a non-realistic production, unspectacular, and so tightly produced that it could be played without an interval, powerfully and emphatically. It was a careful production, exact in every detail, while at the same time gripping and atmospheric.

> You can smell the sweat: the sweat of work and fear (151).

Various projections were used, all seen through the portal of the Reichstag Chamber, apparently a sort of false proscenium.

At the end of the play a Tucholsky/Eisler song was sung: *Ja, damals — Yes, THEN!*, with the implication:

> *Ja, damals — ! Und heute? — Yes, THEN — ! And today?* (152).

No better testimonial to the lasting and broadly based relevance of this play exists than the fact that this relevance was recognised in the 1950s and again in the 1970s and in both Germanies, on both sides of the Iron Curtain.

Of all his plays this is the one in which virtually all Toller's deepest concerns find artistic integration: his hatred of war and experiential sympathy with the sufferings of combatants; his commitment to the German Revolution at the end of World War I and his subsequent disillusion with the Weimar Republic; his lifelong stress, torn between pacifism and doubt as to the effectiveness of pacifism to oppose tyranny; his passionate concern for justice, with his realisation that the injustices of Wilhelmine Germany lived on in the Weimar Republic, embodied, for example in Dobring; his fervent belief in the inspirational effectiveness of personal sacrifice combined with his recognition that the actions inspired by it do not bring Utopia; his critical appraisal of the machinery of democracy, and his understanding of the distorting sexual consequences of forced single-sex communities such as battle-ships and prisons.

In style, too, this play is his own, earlier influences now woven into a seamless texture. Toller himself, as we have noticed, confirmed this evaluation of the play when he told the *Daily Dispatch* that the Manchester production of it was "the first production of his life with all his ideas in it" (153).

DIE BLINDE GÖTTIN (THE BLIND GODDESS)

INTRODUCTION: A PERIOD OF RE-ADJUSTMENT

After *Feuer aus den Kesseln* Toller wrote only one more stage play, without collaboration, before his exile. The intervening period was one of experimentation, development and the coming together of a new grouping or constellation of themes and interests already alive in his work. Although he was never again to achieve the dramatic and poetic intensity of his prison plays he could now broaden both his own experience and the forms and content of his writing and public speaking.

His concern about the effects of imprisonment on sexuality — implicit, as we have seen, in his prison plays — was now directly expressed in his speech on *Imprisonment and Sexuality* to the Fourth Congress of the World League for Sexual Reform in Vienna, 16–23 September, 1930.

His reactions to Soviet Russia and the United States found expression in *Quer Durch* (1).

His continued interest in film led to his collaboration with Walter Hasenclever in making the German version, *Menschen hinter Gittern*, of the MGM sound-film of prison life, *Big House*.

His interest in Spain, crucial to an understanding of the closing months of his life, evidently began at this time with his long visit there (end of October 1931 to beginning of March 1932 (2)) in the company of Lotte Israel, on which he contributed a series of five articles, *The New Spain*, to *Die Weltbühne* (3). He was disappointed in the Spanish Republic, observing that it was following in the footsteps of the German one (4). He saw Spanish Republicans being beaten with rubber truncheons by the Civil Guard.

> And where have I seen that before? (5).

Characteristically Toller writes a scathingly critical account of the sexual *mores* of contemporary Spain, for which he considered the Moorish occupation partly to blame (6). In old families even engaged couples might never meet alone, and it would be unthinkable that they should kiss. A woman on her own in a café must be a demi-mondaine.

> The reverse side of strict sexual morality is prostitution and venereal disease (7).

In Madrid alone 3,000 girls are registered as prostitutes, the smallest towns have brothels, and very poor parents, especially in Andalusia, sell their daughters into prostitution. The bookstalls are full of pornography. Men do not bother about the spiritual life of women, so women turn to the church: no wonder, remarks Toller, that women do not understand the Republic very well, when their only friend is the church! Yet the women are not particularly religious: they go to church mechanically (8).

Toller, again pursuing one of his primary interests, visited prisons in Spain (9). Though he had himself suffered imprisonment in Bavaria and had visited prisons in Prussia, Scandinavia, Switzerland, the USA and Soviet Russia, all his experiences paled before the prison in Seville, a sewer where 350 men and women, in a prison built for 200, had no beds, one tap, and a hole in the courtyard in lieu of a toilet.

With the support of the German League for Human Rights (*Die Deutsche Liga für Menschenrechte*) he broadcast readings both from his Spanish and his African reports. He was a good broadcaster, fluently rhetorical in his rather high-pitched voice (10), and was obviously keenly interested in this medium, as his use of it in *Hoppla, wir leben!* had already shown. His unscripted, live debate with the National Socialist Alfred Mühr, editor of the *Deutsche Zeitung*, on the Cultural Bankruptcy of the Bourgeoisie (11) shows the sharpness and quickness of his mind in debate. The discussion ranged widely once the two men, who had never met before, had taken each other's measure, and it covered such widely diverse topics as the relationship of politics and capitalism, abortion, education, the family backgrounds of Hitler and Goebbels, the relationship of the concepts *Class (Klasse)* and *People (Volk)*, Piscator's theatre, *Romeo and Juliet*, Schiller's *Die Räuber*, censorship, Marxism and National Socialism.

Toller argued that the viewpoints represented by right-wing leaders could "only be effective in the capitalist system" (12). Inflation was only one consequence of bourgeois bankruptcy,

> whose clearest political expression was the World War with its millions of dead and mass of misery, greater than inflation (13).

He exposes the fallacy of personifying Marxism.

> Revolutions are not "made". Breakdowns precede them (14).

The revealing and characteristic conclusion of the discussion merits full quotation:

> T. You will permit me, Herr Mühr, to find your expressions of opinion — which indeed are not your personal ones, but those of the Nationalsocialist party - pretty unclear.
> Nationalsocialism has taken some demands from the doctrine against which it fights most vigorously, namely the Marxist doctrine, and mixed these into a muddled, falsely romantic farrago, with ideas which stand in total antithesis with these demands.
> But it is not the intention of either of us to convince the other. We have both, from different intellectual stances, tried to demonstrate in which areas of bourgeois culture symptoms of decline manifest themselves. You will agree with me on the sentence: The philosophers have interpreted the world variously; what matters is, to change it.
> M. Yes, certainly.
> T. This sentence is by Karl Marx. Good evening, Herr Mühr.
> M. That is a rhetorical squib, and the curtain-line of a radio-play. You are not a dramatist in vain. Good evening, Herr Toller (15).

And indeed in this same year Toller entered the field of broadcast drama with his radio-play, *Berlin – letzte Ausgabe! (Berlin — latest edition!)*, written, as Richard Dove has conclusively shown, between late July and late September 1930 (16), and broadcast in the Funkstunde Berlin, 4 December 1930 (17). A second radio-play *Indizien (Circumstantial Evidence)*, broadcast on Radio Austria Verkehrs-AG (RAVAG) on 7 May 1932, was apparently a radio version of *Die blinde Göttin* (18). The script does not seem to have survived.

Berlin – letzte Ausgabe! was published in 1982 (19) and has been very fully examined by Richard Dove (20). Dove sees this montage or juxtaposition of "a series of unrelated events arbitrarily connected through the headlines" as containing "an implicit critique of the medium which retails these events" and "implicit criticism of a social system which condemns people to despair", but goes on to argue that "its criticism is largely vitiated by the moralising conclusion of the Gast's final monologue . . . an appeal for imaginative empathy, not social revolution" (21). Dove evidently prefers Brecht's presentation of suicide in the film *Kuhle Wampe* (1931) as "the delusion of one who fails to find 'den Anschluß an die kämpfende Arbeiterschaft'" ("contact with the fighting work-force") (22). But since the epiphany of testicles which inspired the creation of *Hinkemann* Toller could never return to the naivety of a socialist optimism that believed all human problems can be solved by changing society, or despair resolved by political allegiance.

Dove argues with some cogency that the 'montage of disparate facts and events is used to suggest the contradictions of capitalist society' (23). But by no means all the headline material in the play points the finger at capitalism in particular. The "public appetite for disaster (Eisenbahnunglück, 70 Tote), the thirst for entertainment, epitomised by the cinema and the prize-fight" (24) are not peculiar to capitalist societies; nor is bureaucratic heartlessness (25), nor fraudulent bigamy (26). Rather is Toller characterising twentieth century mass-society in which everything is retailed at second-hand through what are now called 'the media'. The contrast Toller makes is not between capitalist and socialist societies but between mass-society, where all news is mediated and denatured into consumer entertainment, and earlier, smaller communities in which events were more immediately perceived:

> A hundred years ago a whole town was thrown into a state of excitement if a barn burnt down (27).

In this play, as in his prose writings of the same year, Toller broadens his canvas to include his post-prison awareness of an international dimension. His original opening scene (after the introduction with the newspaper-boys) showed the incident in the British House of Commons when on 17 July 1930 Fenner Brockway had, by remaining standing, challenged the authority of the Speaker when trying to force a discussion on the imprisonment in India of those taking part in Gandhi's campaign of civil disobedience by defying the salt-tax, after which John Beckett seized the Mace and attempted to remove it from the House. This original opening scene is a key to the whole play. Fenner Brockway, a friend of Toller's and a member of the Independent Labour Party, the British political party closest to Toller's own convictions, was challenging the imperialist policies in India of Ramsay MacDonald's *Labour* Government.

> I was shocked that a Labour Government should besmirch the record of the British working-class in this way and took all Parliamentary opportunities to protest . . . (28).

Fenner Brockway's stance *vis-à-vis* a Labour Government was thus parallel with Toller's *vis-à-vis* the German Social Democratic Government, and the occasion of his stance was related to Toller's own belief in non-violence, his admiration of Gandhi and his opposition to imperialism. The scene provides the play with a positive political starting-point, balancing the positive call for personal "imagination" in the Guest's closing speech.

With the 'Brockway' opening the play would thus have had resonances which were lost when, because the incident had recently been fully covered by the same radio station, Toller substituted a condensation of disarmament discussions at the League of Nations in 1928 (29). This retained the international, anti-imperialist element but was more negative in impact. There is no ideological equivalent of Fenner Brockway, no allusions to Gandhian non-violence, and the necessity to present Litvinoff as the most positive figure gave the play an apparently 'Communist' start (instead of an 'Independent Labour' one), which was naturally in disharmony with the ending.

Dove rightly says that in this play Toller had taken documentary realism to the limit of its possibilities (30). His plays in exile, even if based on real persons and events, do not reproduce documentary sources (31).

Once more also, in the summer of 1931, Toller collaborated in the writing of a play: he and Hermann Kesten together wrote *Wunder in Amerika,* in which Mary Baker Eddy, founder of the Christian Science Churches, is shown both as a charismatic but ruthless leader and as a fraudulent charlatan.

As the proportion and nature of Toller's contribution to this play cannot be determined, a detailed analysis is not appropriate here, though some account of it and an examination of certain aspects are relevant.

The play is a narrative of major events in the life of Mary Baker Eddy (b. 1821) from 1865, when Quimby, a mesmerist, cures her paralysis, to her death in 1910.

There is little pattern in its overall structure and the dramatised narrative rambles on from decade to decade and setting to setting (there are as many settings as scenes — nine — all conceived in naturalistic terms) without either Aristotelean or Brechtian unity (32). Only

Mary Baker Eddy herself runs through the play from start to finish, forming a rôle in which no actress could fail, *eine Bombenrolle,* as Fritz Droop described it in praising Ellen Widmann's performance in the first production (33). Droop's praise must be assessed in the light of his long commitment to Toller, whom he clearly admired. His book, *"Ernst Toller und seine Bühnenwerke"* (34) was the first book to be published on Toller.

> Toller's Dichtung aber ist die Beichte eines Menschen, der mit sich selbst in heißen Kampfe rang und der uns aus einem sterbenden Jahrhundert in ein neues Zeitalter fuhrt (35).

Yet even this rôle does not and cannot develop as it should, because it begins on too high a note. Ellen Widmann was blamed for this in the first production, but the fault is surely inherent in the text:

> The sensual frenzy, as visible expression of spiritual possession was too unrestrained from the beginning. The ecstasy not developed, but sustained with an effort (36).

Nor does the play contain an antagonist anywhere nearly equal in stature to Mary Baker Eddy and consequently there is no continuous line of dramatic conflict (37).

No doubt because jointly written the play lacks a fitting and consistent style. If, argues *f. t. g.,* its intention is indeed to demonstrate, through arousing laughter, that human welfare cannot be brought about through a sect which does not bring its economic order into congruence with its spiritual teaching, then the spiritual aspect must be granted another status from the outset.

> In the shadow of Voltaire this joke has too little light to shine into the darkness of the heart where blood and *anima* dwell. The piece is cold. The exemplary element is destroyed by cheap comedy (38).

Similar comment was provoked by the London production in 1934 (39). The play does not fulfil the promise of its opening:

> . . . as the play proceeds, much of the effect is lost by what seems to be ill-placed satire even malice — on the original authors' part (40).

English critics on the whole saw the play as a mere attack on Mary Baker Eddy. The authors were:

> a trifle too anxious to underline the unpleasant side of what was undoubtedly a tremendous personality (41).

Indeed its promoters seemed anxious to disclaim the implied criticism in the play of Christian Science itself, for a Programme Note stated:

> The play would not have been chosen had it been an attack on the religion which Mrs Baker Eddy founded, or

the note astonishingly continues,

> if it had questioned her own essential integrity (42).

More perceptively, the German critic, *f. t. g.*, already quoted, understood (perhaps simply because he was a German and appreciated better the character of German drama) that the play was a *Lehrstück* — a piece of didacticism:

> . . . it is a piece that wants to enlighten and redeem, redeem from these strange, dark, irrational movements which today are seizing hold of people violently and mysteriously; redeem from doctrines of salvation which are none and which drive people away from real blessing and salvation, namely an intelligent ordering of material life, in order to confuse them with illusions (43).

That one sentence places the play correctly in Toller's life and *oeuvre.* It is the successor to *Der entfesselte Wotan* and the forerunner of *Pastor Hall,* both anti-fascist plays. The period was plagued by religious movements such as Moral Re-armament (44), which appealed to the emotional religious idealism of the young, but which revealed themselves during the 1930s as instruments of capitalism and the policies of the extreme right. Toller realised the close kinship between the religious and political movements of the time and saw that the relationship of charismatic but false religious leaders, like Mary Baker Eddy, and the Nazi and Fascist dictators was closer than mere parallelism. In *Der entfesselte Wotan* he had already emphasised the element of *ersatz* religion in fascism.

Nor is *Wunder in Amerika* an isolated example of Toller's directly attacking this type of religious leader. In June 1930, — that is, a year before his collaboration with Kesten — Toller published a narrative-article, *Aimée, die Prophetin (Aimée, the Prophetess)* (45).

This is an account — apparently true, for he cites information from Upton Sinclair — of Aimée Semple McPherson, who founded *The Church of Smiling Light* in Los Angeles. (What else can you expect, asks Toller rhetorically, of a country that puts make-up on its dead?)

The daughter of a farmer, she married a missionary and went to China. The missionary died. She returned and met McPherson. Unhappy with him, she left him and founded this church.

Aimée went bathing. (A line illustration shows her saucily on the beach displaying her apparently naked buttocks.) She staged a disappearance, re-appearing later with a corny tale of having been abducted: actually she had been having a sexual affair. Toller describes her "musicals", on religious themes but with plagiarised music, such as *The Merry Widow*. She baptised her followers, and used the usual revivalist's ploy: "Everyone who loves Jesus, raise your hands". Like Mary Baker Eddy she performed 'cures'. According to Upton Sinclair she actually paid people to say they had been cured. She had a private bank account also, in which she kept money she had embezzled from church funds. She was very beautiful, and always well dressed.

There are two other illustrative drawings. One shows her as *Sailor Girl* — with Jesus as Sailor; the other is of the scene when Adam and Eve eat the apple: but they are not nude! (46). These, of course, are scenes from her 'religious musicals'.

Toller's account ends at the point when Aimée is about to make a pilgrimage to the Holy Land — arranged by Thomas Cook's travel agency!

Wunder in Amerika can thus be seen to be no aberration but an integral part of Toller's literary and ideological development, and its links with *Der entfesselte Wotan* and with his later passionate anti-fascism when in exile, show that his friend Emil Ludwig was wrong when he declared in a radio talk soon after Toller's suicide that Toller had lost his way politically after 1930 and that Hitler "gave him a new enemy, a field of action" (47).

Hitler was no new enemy of Toller's; nor had Toller been at any time "following will-o'-the-wisps". On the contrary, his political development, through all its profound changes, was both consistent and rational.

THE DEFEAT AND TRIUMPH OF JUSTICE

In September 1931 Toller made a journey to Switzerland to visit the alleged poisoners Max Riedel and Antonia Guala in the Remand Prison (Untersuchungsgefängnis) at Burgdorf, where they were awaiting the re-hearing of their case promised by the Court of Appeal. Riedel, a successful doctor, and his housekeeper, Antonia Guala, had been convicted in 1926 of the murder of Riedel's wife by administering arsenic and had each been sentenced to twenty years' imprisonment. The evidence was entirely circumstantial and now scientific research had thrown serious doubts upon the toxological evidence, while the discovery of a lost diary of Frau Riedel confirmed the view that she had suicidal tendencies. Toller was much exercised by this apparent case of gross injustice and immediately published an article about it (48).

He must quite soon have decided to dramatise the subject, for the radio-play *Indizien (Circumstantial Evidence)* broadcast from Vienna on 7 May 1932 was apparently a radio version of it, though whether an adaptation of an already written stage play or an independent work written before *Die blinde Göttin* cannot be determined. No script survives, nor does any typed or duplicated acting version of the stage play earlier than the First Edition, though the First Edition post-dates the first production. With the growing power of the Nazis, Toller was already having to look outside Germany both for printers and productions. This play, though the last of his with copyright by Kiepenheuer, Berlin-Charlottenburg (1933), was printed in Salzburg, his first book in German to be printed outside Germany (49).

In style and structure *Die blinde Göttin* marks a new stage in Toller's development as a playwright, one which might well have led on to a major phase of dramatic writing had not the Nazi *Machtergreifung* and Toller's enforced exile deprived him for the rest of his life of a German-speaking theatre-audience.

In style the last traces of expressionist rhetoric and of deliberate poeticism or overt stylisation of dialogue have disappeared (50). Language and style in this play derive purely from character, situation and function (51). In structure it is firmly based on the tradition of five acts, but uses this form with a certain originality. As Felix Salten wrote:

> A dramatically perfect first act, bubbling with life, shows how the two, the doctor and the woman he loves, fall into the pitfall of suspicion (52).

Integrated in this act with this central story-line are the tributary sub-plots involving Marie, Pflasterer, Max Franke and Blasenkleffer. The second act, inevitably and traditionally, is the trial; the third, predictably, the prisons; the fourth the turning-point of new evidence; and the fifth the resolution, in which all the sub-plots of Act I are re-introduced and resolved, while the main story is given a final, carefully prepared but nevertheless unexpected and theatrically unconventional twist in conclusion (53).

Within this broad pattern, in which the inner three acts are framed by the two outer, the acts themselves are most carefully and meaningfully structured. In Act I Marie, the maid-servant, is the figure through whom the interdependence of the main and sub-plots is designed and made manifest. Except for one passage of dialogue between Anna and Färber immediately after Betty's death (54), Marie is on stage or eavesdropping throughout the entire act, and she is the thread which binds the Pflasterer, Max and Blasenkleffer themes to each other and to the main plot. She is also the only character, apart from Anna and Färber, to appear in every act of the play.

Each of the three inner acts is divided into two scenes — in each case to provide a contrast:

> ACT II: Contrast between the formal and dignified outward process of justice and the prejudices and ignorance that determine the secret discussions of the jury.
> ACT III: Contrast between the fates of the two prisoners and their differing reactions to imprisonment.
> ACT IV: Contrast between the belated but nevertheless genuine correction of the original injustice done to the lovers, and the persisting corruption of petty officialdom in their home town.

Thus each of these acts is based on the principle of montage, as each scene gains its significance through its juxtaposition with the other.

In Act IV the montage is intensified and given a spatial dimension through the use of a divided stage (simplified *Hoppla* effect). In Act III the juxtaposition of the separate character-developments of Färber and Anna highlights their basic incompatibility and prepares the way for Act V.

That last act, in which the several plots are again brought together, is shaped almost as a play within the play:
Scene I (55) is a kind of Prologue in which Anna and Färber meet for the first time on the eve of their release, and their final estrangement is adumbrated.

Scene II falls into three mini-acts and an Epilogue:

> i. The preparationss for the homecoming and the resolution of the sub-plots involving Pflasterer, Max and Marie. The departure of Marie, her function in the main plot being now concluded.
> ii. The Procession. The bitterness and disillusion of the welcome — interrupted by a rainstorm.
> iii. Blasenkleffer and Pflasterer attempt unsuccessfully to re-relate themselves to the doctor. The Bailiff's demands make a mockery of the compensation Färber and Anna have received.
> EPILOGUE: Anna, disillusioned with Färber, leaves him. In a memorable curtain-line she declares that she *has* loved him so deeply that she really could have killed his wife!

Within this firm, naturalistic design, Toller employs techniques, adapted from his earlier plays, which extend the convention without destroying it. The boldest of these are in the Court scene, Act II Sc. I, where the action gradually penetrates space, time and significance.

First he uses the non-dimensional radio-technique. In darkness, the radio voice states the bare facts, placing them on a par with the weather forecast and sporting results — an effect similar to the use of news-paper headlines in the radio play *Berlin, letzte Ausgabe.*

Then the house-lights come up on a forestage scene where members of the 'public' clamour vulgarly for entry to the court for this sensational trial (an implied comment on the nature of public opinion).

The curtain then rises on the Court room. The auditorium lights remain on, so that the audience, including the 'public' in the forestage scene, are all, so to speak, actually *in* the Court Room. Initially, evidence is given by Färber and Anna. Then Marie, in prison clothing, as she is serving a sentence for abortion, gives hers, followed by Pflasterer and Max. At this point the judge announces his intention of reconstructing the scene on the day that Frau Färber fell ill, thus bringing the past to life on stage through genuinely theatrical means: not a narrator but 'gesticulating actors' (56). Court servants bring on a table and chairs; a life-size puppet (a live actress) representing Betty, is brought on in a wheel-chair, also the child, Lore (57). Anna and Lore sit with the 'puppet' at the table. All lights, including the house-lights, go off, except for a pool of light on the table and chairs. Färber enters the pool of light and sits. They all, including the 'puppet', mime eating the meal. The judge asks what Färber then said, and the scene begins, re-enacting the past, occasionally interrupted by calls from the auditorium and the judge's voice demanding order. Toller handles the convention with tact. When dialogue occurs between Färber, and the judge and the prosecuting counsel, whose voices speak out of the surrounding darkness, the 'puppet' freezes; when the flashback scene continues, the puppet comes to life again. At the end of the flash-back, the stage lights (apparently not the auditorium lights) come up, the 'puppet' freezes, Anna takes her place in the dock, and the judge orders the 'puppet', table and chairs to be removed. The trial then proceeds with the expert evidence of the professor, and the closing speeches.

This play thus shows Toller's craftsmanship as a playwright, if not at its most exciting and original, then certainly at its most flawless.

Thematically *Die blinde Göttin* expresses the new constellation of interests and priorities which had taken shape since the writing of *Feuer aus den Kesseln*. Toller as a dramatist has at last turned his back on the failed German revolution and its immediate consequences. Justice, which had still been thematically linked to the revolution in *Feuer aus den Kesseln*, now becomes a subject in its own right:

> Ernst Toller's play this time remains completely free from political leanings of any kind. *The Blind Goddess*, that is to say, Justice, whose eyes are blindfolded, is fateful simply because of her blindness (58).

Once again, as in *Hinkemann*, the sexual relationship, never absent from his plays, becomes central. The case to embody a critique of the imperfection of human justice — the continual failure of *Justiz* to achieve and express *Gerechtigkeit* — is one concerning an unhappy, unsuccessful marriage and an extra-marital love-affair whose great power is eventually broken by the weakness of the man's character and the strength of the woman's.

This central plot, with the death by poisoning of the wife, is placed in a context shot through with the sexual. Pflasterer values his cow more than his nagging wife — and tries to paw Marie; Max, the Parish Clerk, who rises to be Bürgermeister, is an unprincipled womaniser. Marie for him is 'sheer flesh' with ' a nice pair of boobs' (59). When he learns she is pregnant by him he sardonically plays a funeral march on his mouth-organ — but it is she who goes to prison for aborting her child with the help of Blasenkleffer's wife (also evidently one of Max's women).

He pinches Barbara's calf as she stands on a ladder hanging a lantern, and plans to meet her at the barn near the churchyard, while at the same time he has been having an affair with the postman's wife. When Marie returns from prison, anticipating marrying him, he rejects her out of hand.

In the prison scenes Toller uses his personal knowledge of the effects of sexual frustration on prisoners. In the women's prison lesbianism leads to jealousy, bitterness and potential violence. The First Prisoner, Lotte, unbuttons her prison blouse and tries to admire her reflection in the shiny blade of a pair of scissors; but she does not want to sleep with the Third Prisoner, who is jealous of 'the newcomer'. In one breath she threatens to kill Lotte, in the next she offers her the extra jam she has been allowed on medical grounds. She wants Lotte to give her a tuft of her hair, presumably pubic hair (60), so that she will have something of her to feel and smell. Anna is deeply frustrated when her loveletter to Färber is intercepted, while Färber himself is nearly driven mad by the informer who lies to him that there are male warders in the women's prison and that they sleep with the prisoners. Anna, the true lover, woman of strength and integrity, and Färber, true lover also within the limits of his weak character, are thus set against a background of sexual corruption and betrayal in a society rotten with sexual prejudice and hypocrisy (61). The social criticism that runs through the whole play is independent of specific political systems and is of universal validity. Indeed, the specificity of the case and its details is the firm foundation for the expression of general themes.

While the prison scenes do illustrate the harshness and futility of prison life, it is the miscarriage of justice that is the basic theme, with special weight laid on the deceptiveness of circumstantial evidence (62), the unreliability of 'scientific' evidence, and the terrible flaws in the jury system, in which ignorance, prejudice and the sheer mental laziness of the 'ordinary' people who constitute the average jury, lead to ill-founded verdicts. Closely linked with the narrower criticism of the operation of the law is the wider criticism of the venality and corruption of 'ordinary' society, and the montage of the Färber / Anna case set against the small-town world of Max Franke and the rest is a major structural feature of the play: here again Marie the maid is the key figure — the only character who is both agent and victim of prejudice and corruption.

Deeper even than the social critique is the moral critique. This is not merely expressed through the exposure of the moral corruption of Max and other minor characters, but more profoundly in the relationship and characters of the lovers themselves. These are clearly revealed in their only private dialogue in Act 1, immediately after Betty's death. In this both Färber's weakness of character and Anna's open-eyed understanding of him are unequivocally presented (63). These factors are re-emphasised by their testimonies in the trial (Act II) and their reactions in prison (Act III). Nevertheless the material of Act IV and the manner of the early part of Act V are such that an audience is still conditioned to expect a 'happy end'. But instead, Anna declares that she does not and cannot love Färber any more.

> But now, after prison, after the mockery of the village reception, now she can no longer love the man on whose account she has suffered, cannot begin again there, where she formerly supported him, can no longer live as if nothing had happened, can 'no longer simply think of herself' (64).

She leaves him, and the audience is deprived of a conventional ending. Felix Salten remarks that Toller dares to write this ending because he is driven by conscience more strongly than by practical considerations of theatre (65). This is true, but it must be added that not only has Toller, as we have seen, prepared for this ending throughout the whole play, but also that the theatrical effect he actually does achieve is far more striking and durable than a superficial 'happy-ever-after' could have been. To the additional dimension of tension between the lovers arising from Farber's moral weaknesses (66) Toller adds that of Anna's having developed in prison a social conscience:

> I know that I have no longer any right to live as I did earlier, for myself, for you, for the saving's bank (67).

Her moral revulsion from Färber has become also a physical revulsion:

> Then when you really lay down beside me, I froze with repulsion and loneliness (68).

What she will do, how she will implement her new sense of social purpose, she does not yet know:

> I know now what I cannot do any more.
> What I *must* do — I shall know (69).

But the ending has yet a final twist as Anna continues her curtain-speech:

> Good-bye, Franz. [She says "Leb wohl" not "Auf Wiedersehen"] I loved you very much . . . I loved you so much, that I really *could* have killed your wife (70).

The closing line of Act IV, spoken by the corrupt Bürgermeister, Max, was:

> Justice has always triumphed, and it will triumph now (71).

Justice: the word he uses is *Gerechtigkeit,* the great principle of Justice, not *Justiz,* the mere workings of the law. When spoken, the line brings down the curtain with a sense of bitter irony; but Act V bears out that Max has spoken more truly than he knows: Färber has never merited such a love as Anna could offer him, and he obtains his deserts when he loses her. Anna has been punished for a crime she did not commit and has learnt through her experience a need to work for justice, not just for herself and Färber, but in a wider sense. At the same time, however, her unjust punishment has had some moral justification, for unlike the weak and indecisive Färber, who would never have made up his mind even to commit a crime, she knows that in a moral, in a biblical sense, she is guilty of the murder of Betty because she has committed it in her heart (72).

The curtain-line, as well as being theatrically effective, expresses not only the intensity of her now dead love for Färber, but also gives a new meaning to her imprisonment, to the play, and to the idea of Justice expressed by the play.

> Die Gerechtigkeit hat immer gesiegt,
> sie wird auch jetzt siegen.

THE PLAY ON STAGE

The first production of *Die blinde Göttin* opened in the Raimund-Theater, Vienna, on 31 October 1932, under the direction of Jürgen Fehling (73). It was the last German-language production of any of Toller's plays until *Pastor Hall* at the Deutsches Theater, Berlin, 27 Jan. 1947 (74). There is no record of any subsequent German-language production of *Die blinde Göttin.*

Even at this date and in the Austrian capital, letters to Jarno, the theatre director, threatened demonstrations on the first night (75), but though Fehling was on strange ground and with an ensemble he did not know,

> his enormous intensity, his feverishly nervous rush of work, overwhelmed all these obstacles and drove the actors to such a height, that a production of altogether rare brilliance was achieved (76).

In the event, the first performance, given in the presence of the Bürgermeister, other city worthies, and numerous detectives, went off peacefully — though not quietly: an enthusiastic audience called for all the actors and the author at the end of Act II.

Fehling's earlier Toller productions, *Masse Mensch* (1921) and *Der entfesselte Wotan* (1926), had not prepared him for the tactfully modified naturalism used in this new play, which he so directed, especially in Act II, as to give the flash-backs an affinity with Strindberg, the Strindberg of *The Ghost Sonata*:

> Here . . . Toller . . . shows for the first time [!!!CWD] that he has read Strindberg: it has become his "Justice-Sonata" (77).

This assessment was chiefly based on the use of the Puppet, which evidently was so presented as to recall *The Mummy* in *The Ghost Sonata* (though there is really little or no parallel), but also on Fehling's conception of the flash-back not simply as a more truly dramatic method of presenting evidence in court than mere narration, but as a fearful re-enaction of the past by the living with the dead:

> In a mystic light the puppet in the court-room suddenly becomes the actual doctor's wife; during a minute of terror the ruined life of this house is enacted before us (78).
>
> Toller's idea of presenting the confrontation of the accused with a wooden puppet representing the allegedly murdered woman is heightened by Fehling to mass-suggestion, from whose horror no one remains exempt (79).

It would appear that Fehling deliberately sought out opportunities to depart from the fundamental naturalism of the piece, for we also read that,

> the final scene, too, under the triumphal arch, borders on unreality (80).

Even Toller's highly naturalistic prison scenes are described by one reviewer (rather unsympathetic to Toller in general) as

> naturalistically-fantastic scenes whose undeniable power does not in the least stem from the author's experience before more than one court and in more than one prison (81).

The first act which should in fact set the key for the whole production, did not lend itself in any way to revivals of Toller's earlier Expressionism, and Fehling evidently allowed it to speak clearly in its own realistic voice:

> Especially in the first act, which is written with virtuosity, poet and director together show that Gerhart Hauptmann has lived and is living (82).

The production did not conceal the fact that in this play, more than in any previous one, Toller simply 'states' (konstatiert) and neither accuses nor psychologises; but in summing up, the full and thoughtful critique that points out this 'step forward' of the author's, concludes that Fehling's production was good on atmosphere but weak on bringing out the meaning (83).

ENGLISH PRODUCTIONS: PREWAR

Apart from two productions in eastern Europe, Sarajevo and Skopje, in 1933 (84) all other productions traced of *Die blinde Göttin* have been in English. Even these have been fewer than might be expected, because of the intrusion of a play by the Irish dramatist, Denis Johnston, *Blind Man's Buff*, which was advertised and published as being *By Ernst Toller and Denis Johnston* although, as Spalek correctly says, it

> is not an adaptation of *Die blinde Göttin*; it is a play by Denis Johnston in which the opening and closing situations are based on *Die blinde Göttin* (85).

Spalek records four productions of it up to 1953 and no fewer than fifty-three articles, reviews and announcements about it as compared with seven, in English, on *The Blind Goddess* (86). It has no place in any assessment of Toller, and Spalek says he only includes it "because it was published and produced jointly under both names" (87).

Edward Crankshaw's translation of *Die blinde Göttin* was first published on 13.4.1934 by John Lane and reprinted in *Seven Plays* in the following year (88). It was first produced by an amateur group, The Welwyn Folk Players, at the Barn Theatre, Welwyn Garden City, on 3 December 1934, directed by Frank Herbert and designed by Stanley Herbert (89). Toller attended the first night. The reactions of critics were curiously mixed: the *New Statesman and Nation* called the play 'sincere and moving' but criticised the production (90), while two reviews in *The Welwyn Times* published together on 13 December 1934, one by a certain F. J. O. , and the other by the well-known critic C. B. Purdom, both praise the director and actors while dismissing the play as 'imperfectly digested' and 'not a great work' (91).

The first professional English production was given in June 1935 by the Manchester Repertory Theatre. Neither this production nor any review of it is recorded by Spalek. It opened on Monday 3 June 1935 and ran for one week as part of a normal season of "weekly rep" (92). Toller should have directed it, presumably as a follow-up to his successful production of *Draw the Fires* with the same company, but in fact did not (93), and it was directed by the company's own director, Dominic Roche, who, according to Toller, had been very eager to have his company perform the play (94).

The *Manchester Guardian* gave the first night a full and thoughtfully critical review. Its theatre-critic, M. C. , took the play seriously. What made it impressive, in his view, was a

> sense of blind fate, by which the story of ordinary people is lifted all the time to tragedy (95).

Indeed, this critic, in a philosophical preamble to his review, saw the play as expressing simultaneously,

> Two conceptions of the world, of the creatures in it . . .
> . . . we have separate characters, in a way their own masters, each with his own strength or weakness, and his own personality (96).

Yet at the same time,

> The people in *The Blind Goddess* are like flies to wanton boys in their lying at the mercy of chance (97).

Like Fehling in Vienna, Roche evidently took all possible opportunities of using non-naturalistic techniques in his production, especially in the trial scene. Of the flash-back in this scene, M. C. says:

> The judge, the counsel, the witnesses, the prisoners, the scenes re-enacted from the lives of the prisoners are all or should be, like disembodied voices (98).

The tell-tale phrase in this assessment is "or should be". Neither in the English translation nor in Toller's original text is there anything to suggest these "disembodied voices". The Judge says in perfectly matter-of-fact language that he wants to "reconstruct" the scene. The table and chairs, together with the Puppet are brought on and taken off by court servants. There is nothing ghostly or "expressionistic" in this. Only through the Puppet's coming to life does Toller, drawing on his own interest in film techniques, subtly transform the scene from what could be a somewhat crude court reconstruction to a filmic flash-back (99). But Roche, like Fehling, evidently wanted to stress the vestiges of expressionism and of Strindbergian influence in the text, although, as already argued above,

> Toller employs techniques, adapted from his earlier plays, which extend the [naturalistic] convention without destroying it (100).

The play's own style was resisting Roche's effort to present it in part expressionistically. M. C. realised that,

> . . . this play . . . may easily fall between the realistic and the expressionist, and not always fall on the right style at the right time (101).

Significantly, he praises most highly the scenes (especially the prison scenes) which were played naturalistically. The court-room scene, on the other hand, he says,

> . . . did not hit off the right mood; it was sometimes slow and laboured, and had not sufficient unity of movement (102).

The last act he criticised for having "too much of pantomime" instead of seeming "like a tragic masque" (103). The acting, he said,

> . . . had the understandable fault of stressing the individual too much (104).

The critic was not prepared to let Toller transcend his expressionist beginnings. In this play the actors' stress on individuality was not a fault: its universality is achieved, not through expressionistic generalisations but through "labouring well the Minute Particulars" (105).

The key role of Marie, the maidservant, was played by Joan Littlewood, whose acting was described as "excellent". Yvonne le Dam as the Puppet "gave the right suggestion of impersonality" (106), and Montague Beaudyn as President of the Court was "good". The two leads, Keith Pyott as the Doctor, and Enid Hewitt as Anna,

> . . . had that intensity and yet restraint which could achieve best the atmosphere of the play (107).

Critical though it was of aspects of the production, the review concluded that the play

> . . . is one which Manchester playgoers need hardly be urged to see (108).

On the third night (Wednesday 5 June) Toller went up to Manchester to see the production. He said in public, presumably in a curtain speech, that he did not like the way the first three scenes were produced, though he liked the rest (109). As these scenes were Act I, Act II Sc. 1 (the court-room scene), and Act II Sc. 2 (the Jury-room scene), Toller himself apparently disliked Roche's treatment of the most experimental scene in the play. But it was, at the least, tactless, to say so in public (110).

His comments gave the cue to the (anonymous) critic of *The Manchester City News*, a weekly paper, who was present that night (111). That critic deeply admired Toller, describing him as

> A relentless force bending a masterful command of technique to the needs of a mind crammed with the problems of real life and urgent to express its views on them (112).

As for the play:

> Toller drives home all along the line, with violence at times

> approaching crudity, what a cross-tangle of personalities and motives enwraps justice and how little likely are our legal methods to unravel the truth (113).

But he slams the production unmercifully, faintly praising only Enid Hewitt's performance as one that "got nearest to the right key" and enabled one to 'feel something more than personal tragedy" (114). Dominic Roche,

> ... hardly glimpses even the technical values of the play... produces altogether too timidly . . . (115)

Apart from "odd scenes", the thing is unimaginatively humdrum (116). The critic wants to see "one of the big experimental amateur societies on the job" (117).

Toller's undiplomatic criticisms and the *City News* review caused a deep rift between author and director, and Roche wrote angrily in defence of his production, which, he claimed,

> has lifted this play somewhat above the ordinary and actually led you to suppose there is more in it than exists (118).

Not content with this, he attacked the play roundly, but without any detailed justification for his opinion. The play, he declared "is very, very bad". So far from Toller's having "a remarkable command of technique",

> To anyone who understands the theatre, and more particularly play production, it must be instantly obvious that technique is distinctly lacking throughout the construction of the whole work . . . .
> Actually it is the play itself that is humdrum (119).

He added for good measure that,

> *The Blind Goddess* was actually first produced in this country by one of the best experimental amateur societies and was hopelessly ineffective (120).

The unhappy critical and personal squabble was continued a fortnight later by Toller, who wrote a bitter letter to the *City News*.

> Sir, – With great interest I have followed the controversy between your dramatic critic and Mr. Roche. You have asked your readers to take part in the discussion. May the author, too, say a few words?
>
> I do not like to quarrel with Mr. Roche. I only want to state some facts. Mr. Roche has accepted this "very, very bad play" months ago. For reasons which I do not want to tell here, I refused later on that the play is produced by him.
>
> Mr. Roche has then rung me up, has pressed me and my agent by letters and telephone calls to let him produce this "very, very bad play".
>
> When the *Blind Goddess* was first published in England as a book, it had mostly very good reviews. When it was first actually produced in this country by the Welwyn Garden Players it was extremely effective and successful and had a long run before crowded houses.
>
> After I saw the letter of Mr. Roche, I really regretted very much that he accepted the play and produced it against his better judgment. More I don't want to say.
>
> Yours faithfully,
> ERNST TOLLER
> c/o John Lane,
> Vigo Street, W. 1
>
> (121)

It was sad that the relationship with Roche should end on this note; but Toller's connection with the Manchester Repertory Company was destined to continue even after the author's death.

Another aspect of Toller's 'Manchester links' is mentioned in the previous week's issue of the same periodical, where it is announced that Toller, provisionally in late August, is to preach a sermon in Cross Street Chapel, "to appeal for support of the new Cross Street Chapel Fellowship". Toller wrote to the Minister of this famous Unitarian Chapel, the Rev. C. W. Townsend, that he was looking forward to speaking in his church. The columnist adds:

> Toller does not speak English very well, but he knows how to get his message over even so (122).

Whether the sermon was actually delivered is uncertain. The Rev. Raymond Cook, for many years Minister of Cross Street Chapel, says that in his very full researches of the chapel archives he has never come across a reference to it.

ENGLISH PRODUCTIONS: POST-WAR

The Blind Goddess was revived twice in England during the early 1980's.

In 1981 the play, in an adaptation by Michelene Wandor, was taken on tour by *Red Ladder*, a "small scale" company with a strong sense of social purpose, subsidised by the Arts Council. The adaptation appeared to keep close to the original both in text and spirit (123). The following description of the production is based upon the performance at Ilkley College of Education on 4 November 1981, a 'one night stand' which played to an audience of about 100, practically all students (124).

The company had devised a very simple but effective mode of presentation in the round. A table, centrally placed, served for all settings, whether domestic, court or prison, with simple changes of a lamp or table-cloth, or both, to indicate the change of scene. The pattern of movement and grouping was entirely based upon an X, or St. Andrew's Cross, four corner entrances and four basic corner positions defining the space and providing a firm framework. It was simply lit; there were some unobtrusive but emotive sound effects. The adaptation, and the skill of the company, enabled it to be played with a cast of six, four of whom played Dr Färber, Anna, Marie and Max Franke, while the other two doubled for everything else! The Jury consisted of the whole company of six, in simple masks.

The young audience was totally held by the production, and Toller's approach to a complex moral and legal problem evidently made a direct appeal to these students — who probably regarded themselves as fairly sophisticated (125).

In the following year the play was presented by the Octagon Theatre, Bolton, from 1–26 June 1982, as part of its 2nd International Season. It was directed by the Theatre Director, Wilfred Harrison, who brought out very strongly the issues and principles involved in it. Compared with his production, that of *Red Ladder*, effective though it was, seemed naive. For example, *Red Ladder* made the innocence of Färber and Anna absolutely clear from the beginning; the Octagon production deliberately played these characters "externally" until the interval, so that the audience shared the uncertainties and doubts of the jury as to their guilt or otherwise. This called for considerable professional skill in alienation technique from the cast and brought out Toller's intellectual strength. The second half, when Färber and Anna gradually revealed their legal innocence and their moral strengths and weaknesses, became all the more deeply moving because of the emotional control exercised by the director in the more intellectually presented first half. Anna's curtain line, "I loved you so much I *could* have murdered your wife", 'cut like a keenly honed knife' (126).

The cast of ten (as against *Red Ladder's* six) played all the required characters, the principal ones being stated in the programme (127).

The performance was on an open stage where a massive but simple architectural structure which set the keynote even before the performance began and both projected and symbolised the play, was dominated by a vast pair of scales high above the action. Every element in the unified design of this semi-abstract setting by Edward Furby served at some point a practical or symbolic end, while William Roberts' lighting transformed it from house, to court, to prison and to open street as required.

The visual impact was strengthened by the interpolation into the production, otherwise faithful to Edward Crankshaw's translation, of one wordless scene in which the women prisoners, threatened by menacing shadows, took their exercise in a monotonous round reminiscent of Wilde's *Ballad of Reading Gaol* or Gustave Doré's engraving of prisoners at exercise, and which at the same time recalled the Dream Scenes of *Masse Mensch* (128).

Harrison also seized on Toller's direction that Max Franke plays a mouth-organ, to create a musical background in which passages from six different works for the mouth-organ were used, with extraordinary atmospheric effect. "The mouth-organ is a lonely instrument," Harrison commented.

It is noteworthy that Toller had also used the mouth-organ in Scene IV (a Dream Scene) of *Masse Mensch,* where the Nameless One accompanies on the mouth-organ the Dance of the Condemned (129).

It is evidence of the poetic potential that lived on into this play, in which, as we have seen, Toller had shed the last remnants of expressionist rhetoric, that a director faithful to the text, but sensitive to its under- and over-tones, should use visual and aural effects stemming from the early phase of the dramatist's development and that these effects should blend harmoniously with the humanity and faithfulness to authorial intention that are the hall-marks of Harrison's style of direction.

Both these English productions of the 1980's have proved the enduring worth of this particular play. Both were presented in association with the Goethe Institute (the Octagon Production with the

Goethe Institute Manchester), but it is particularly appropriate in view of Toller's growing internationalism in the early 1930's that half a century later the Octagon Production should also be supported by the European Cultural Foundation (130).

NIE WIEDER FRIEDE *(NO MORE PEACE)*

INTRODUCTION: THE EFFECTS OF EXILE

Through being in Switzerland on 27 February 1933, the night of the Reichstag Fire, to give a broadcast, Toller escaped arrest and never returned to Germany. His works were burnt on 10 May, and on 23 August he was deprived of his German citizenship and his property was confiscated.

The exiled writer and political activist, though he failed in his aim of uniting all German exiles in a disciplined anti-fascist body (1), became even more important and influential internationally than he had been before. The Nazis regarded him as one of their principal opponents abroad and followed and recorded his every movement until his death (2). He delivered at least two hundred lectures and addresses, attended and addressed PEN-Club congresses and, apart from his literary writing, published very many important political articles and pamphlets.

But, for several reasons, exile almost destroyed Toller as a dramatist. First, it deprived him of a German-speaking theatre-audience and thus of the incentive to give full rein in his plays (which would now be performed only in translation) to his command of the resources of language, which for him had to be his native German. Instead, he put his creative energy and linguistic power into his prose autobiographies, *Eine Jugend in Deutschland* and *Briefe aus dem Gefängnis* (3). Second, it removed him from direct contact with specific German political subject-matter (4). Third, the nature of the cause of his exile — Fascism — at first shook and later undermined his pacifist convictions, born on the Western Front in World War I. Last, the socialism that had provided the ideological and intellectual backing for his basically emotional pacifism, seems to have receded from the foreground of his consciousness as he became more attracted by the freedom of the American way of life and disillusioned with Stalinist USSR, leaving him only with the uncongenial mission of promoting the need for war against Fascism.

The two plays he wrote in the last six and a half years of his life reveal all too clearly the adverse effects of exile upon him as a dramatist.

THE ENGLISH VERSION *NO MORE PEACE* AND ITS PRODUCTION

The sole authority for the original German text of the play is an unbound typescript in the Toller Collection at Yale University (5). The typescript is undated, but as the first scene was published in *Das Neue Tagebuch* in December 1934, at least that much must have been written at that time, and it must have been finished by the spring of 1936 (6). No production of it in German is known and it was not printed before its inclusion in GW (7).

It was almost immediately translated into English by Edward Crankshaw with lyrics "adapted" by W.H. Auden and music by Herbert Murrill (8). The music for the original German text was by Hanns Eisler (9). The English text varies greatly from the German, with many added phrases and sentences, and it is in general less taut and economical than the original. The version is loose and sloppy, which is not surprising in view of the way in which it was arrived at. As Edward Crankshaw himself informed Malcolm Pittock,

> The way Toller produced his manuscript for us to work on was so patchy that I doubt if I ever saw the whole thing in one piece . . . We would all meet at the Gate Theatre, where rehearsals were in progress, and changes would be made by Toller himself in his original German, by me in the translation, by Auden in the verses, while rehearsals were actually in process (10).

The play opened at the Gate Theatre Studio, London, on 11 June 1936, produced by Norman Marshall and designed by Scobie Mackenzie. Hanns Eisler's Overture was used, but the settings to Auden's versions of the songs, whose rhythms and verse-forms were largely unlike Toller's, were by Herbert Murrill. Christiane Grautoff played Rachel, pacifist daughter of Laban the Banker (11).

Critical reaction was unenthusiastic and sometimes patronising. Apart from the settings being "economical and effective" (12), Christiane Grautoff's performance ("a pleasing first appearance on the English stage", she "impresses us with her clean-cut charm") (13), and

Auden's "neatly turned", "well-written, good-tempered" lyrics (14), the critics found little to commend. "Mildly entertaining", "easy-going satire" are the highest praise offered (15). "Satire . . . on hob-nailed boots", "little to feed the sense of comedy or to minister to moral indignation", "Cheap skit on war", "a clumsy little skit", "recalled one of those unevenly inspired charades of our youth", are typical phrases (16).

Audience reaction was thus ironically described:

> It was received on Thursday night with indulgent warmth by such an audience as might be relaxing, one felt, from the more rigorous demands of, say, Surrealism or the Ballet (17).

Understandably the *Evening Standard* critic, "M.N.", cried:

> Surely the author of *The Machine-Wreckers* could have stated a more effective case by taking his theme more seriously (18).

The Rev. "Dick" Sheppard, founder of the Peace Pledge Union (1934), and a certain Ellis Roberts, wrote to the *Sunday Times* complaining about its review, which had called the play "a clumsy little skit which pokes awkward fun at all things sacred and profane", and the reviewer "GWB" defended himself (19).

Crankshaw's translation was published in England and the USA in 1937, the American edition showing a number of changes in the text and Stage Directions. During that year it had five American productions, but few actual performances (20). It has since had two further American productions, in 1939 and in 1963 (5 performances) (21). Reviews on the whole were unfavourable and the heaviness of touch particularly criticised. Several reviewers thought it could never get a full professional production but would stay in colleges and Little Theatres.

Only one scholar, Malcolm Pittock, appears to have written seriously on the play (22) and he had only read the English version. Thus, although he makes some cogent observations, his most acute criticisms are based on speeches and words which do not appear in the original German but were introduced in the haphazard way that Crankshaw himself has described. Pittock sees the "basic propagandist intention of the play" as "a covert appeal for Communists and Christians to unite against Hitler . . . ". His evidences for this are, 1) St. Francis' favourable reaction to the *Internationale,* which the Angel in charge of the switchboard accidentally switches on (23); 2) St. Francis' agreement with the Marxist dictum, cited by Napoleon, "Hitherto philosophers have sought to explain the world. Our task is to change it" (24); 3) St. Francis' statement that "Peace on earth", will come "When the clever stop talking and the wise begin to act" (25).

Not one of these is in the original German. Therefore they could not represent the "basic propagandist intention of the play". They represent additions and alterations made or agreed to by Toller during rehearsal conferences with his translator and thus are no more than afterthoughts, perhaps even ill-considered ones.

To know what Toller actually said in the play and to judge its quality as dramatic writing, we must turn to the original German, now made available in the Collected Works.

THE GERMAN TEXT

Despite fundamental weaknesses the play Toller actually wrote is in many ways superior to the hitherto more widely known English version. It is more terse and concise. Not only does the "translation" continually add words, phrases and whole sentences (26); even scenes are added. An entirely new scene is introduced between Socrates, Napoleon and Francis, which contains over thirty speeches: just over four pages of the English text (27). In it Socrates argues that his 'bravery' in history was pretence and that he played that part out of vanity. The scene contributes nothing to the central issues of the play, and only confuses the whole "Socrates" theme.

To do justice to the author we must therefore examine the play as he first wrote it, paying particular attention to where it differs from the translation. Even if it still emerges as Toller's poorest play the reappraisal will be justified.

The play's title parodies the slogan *Nie Wieder Krieg (No More War)*, which was widely used by pacifist and anti-war movements in many countries and languages during the period between the two World Wars. The parody is more effective in German than in English as the two words *Krieg* and *Friede*, with their common central phonetic element, *-rie*, constitute a half-rhyme. It anticipates the major theme of the play, namely the ease with which popular enthusiasm for peace can be manipulated politically into popular enthusiasm for war. In the play itself Toller reiterates this in the self-parody of *Das Friedenslied (Peace Song)* as *Das Kriegslied (War Song)*, and in the simple reversal of the placard *Nie wieder Krieg/Es lebe der Krieg* in Scenes II & VI (28).

Toller does not, however, develop this theme organically within the play. Instead he uses a trivial mechanical device to end the war-fever engendered by Napoleon's initial telegram, namely that the female angel in charge of the Olympian switchboard informs Laban of the falsity of the declaration of war in exchange for

> Pariser Flügel. Klein. Elegant. Plissiert
> Mit Goldstickerei in der Mitte (29).

This triviality undercuts the serious satire. Nevertheless, Toller does shape his comedy with a certain symmetrical elegance, lost in the English version. In effect the seven scenes fall into three "Acts" (30).

THE DRAMATIC STRUCTURE

[Act I]

Scene I (Prologue)

OLYMPUS. Franziskus & Napoleon.
The Switchboard Angel.
Napoleon's Bet: the War Telegram.

Scene II

A HALL IN DUNKELSTEIN.
Peace becomes War.

[Act II]

Scene III

OLYMPUS.
The Angel wants modish wings.
Franziskus sends Socrates to Dunkelstein.

Scene IV

PRISON CELL
Rahel & Jakobo awaiting execution.
Noah.
Socrates is brought in.
The wisest of men learns worldly wisdom from Noah the beggar.

Scene V

OLYMPUS
The Angel arranges the bribe to send the Peace Telegram.

[Act III]
Scene VI
THE HALL IN DUNKELSTEIN, as in Sc. II.
War becomes Peace.
Scene VII (Epilogue)
OLYMPUS
Franziskus & Napoleon, as in Sc. I.
Napoleon discovers the Angel's betrayal.
Franziskus concludes that only the fools can bring peace on earth.

The structure thus revealed is fully symmetrical and its keystone is the scene in the Prison Cell. In it Toller, himself the former political prisoner, writes at a level of genuine humanism belied by the rest of the play. The potentially farcical situation when the lovers Rahel and Jakobo in the darkened cell each mistakes the other for the executioner, suddenly ceases to be funny. Rahel's impending execution takes on the character of Eva's in *Hoppla, wir leben!*:

> Ich bin so jung, es ist so schrecklich so jung zu sterben (31)

she cries, recalling Frau Meller's words,

> . . . das sieht sich nur so schlimm an, wenn man noch jung ist (32).

But Jakobo, she feels, has betrayed her in Scene II:

> Ich bin militärpflichtig . . . Ich muß mich bei der Gesandtschaft melden (33).

"Rühr mich nicht an!" she cries, repeating exactly the words of the risen Jesus to Mary Magdalene in Luther's translation (34) — "Noli me tangere" — an allusion that immediately and inevitably lifts the dialogue on to a new plane. Like her creator in Niederschönenfeld, the poet of *Das Schwalbenbuch,* she turns in spirit from man to nature, her language breaking through the shell of the play's overall style:

> Warum habe ich nicht an Steine geglaubt, an Tiere, an Blumen? Es ist schön Blumen zu lieben. Sie sind was sie scheinen, sie scheinen was sie sind. Morgens wenn sie erwachen und der

> stille Tau fällt auf die samtnen Kelche, abends wenn sie schlafen im verdämmernden Licht. Nur die Menschen stören ihren Frieden (35).

Then she learns that Jakobo is her fellow-prisoner because he believed her anti-war words: she really is, in a moral sense, his executioner. When the doctor comes to offer her the escape of pleading insanity, and Jakobo too tries to save her, she realises what his character really is.

> Ist es nicht schöner zu sterben als zu töten? (36).

she exclaims. She is expressing Toller's deepest conviction, the conviction he embodied in Friedrich and in Sonja (37) and which surely motivated his suicide in the face of the coming anti-Nazi war, which he, the pacifist, was to advocate. In Munich in 1919 Toller had seen his friends and colleagues murdered and executed, and he himself had stood in danger of the death-sentence. This scene draws upon his own deepest traumas and his close encounters with death.

Touching for a moment spiritual depths lacking in the rest of the play, Rahel says:

> Es war finster und weil es finster war hattest Du Furcht, und Du glaubtest ich sei der Henker. Du hattest Furcht, Jakobo. Ich bin glücklich, daß Du Furcht hattest, fürchte Dich nicht vor Deiner Furcht, ist es nicht Menschlich Furcht zu haben? (38).

It is indeed human to feel fear, and so, when Noah reveals himself as seeking prison to avoid the war, we are inclined to accept his 'self-arrest' as human, too.

Just as the first half of this scene embodies the emotional heart of the play, so the second, in a totally different style, more closely related to that of the play as a whole, is its intellectual, cerebral, centre. The wisest of the ancients, Socrates, whom the authorities are uncertain whether to regard as criminally subversive or mad (39), disputes with Noah, the cynic. Socrates' abstract logic is no answer to his own or the world's practical problems. Noah offers instead "the wisdom of this world": that the same group of people stands to gain both in peace and in war.

> Für die einen regnet es Mannah im Frieden, für die einen im Krieg. Die einen und die einen sind meistens die einen (40).

Socrates finds he still has something to learn and wants to become Noah's student. Their closing duet reaches the negative conclusion that one must learn worldly wisdom and that this does not dwell among the stars:

> Die Weisheit dieser Welt
> Sie wohnt nicht auf den Sternen,
> Die Weisheit dieser Welt
> Mußt Du erlernen (41).

Thus the central scene of the play is essentially negative, for there is no suggestion, as in *Die Wandlung* or *Masse Mensch*, that the acceptance of death is itself creative; and neither the wisdom of Socrates nor the worldly wisdom of Noah offers any solution to the socio-political problems of war and peace (42).

Sadly, the rest of the play fails to match in dramatic quality the bleak nihilism of this key scene. It opens on Olympus, where Napoleon, bored with the eternal peace of the life of the blessed, bets Franziskus (St. Francis of Assisi) that with a single telegram he can immediately arouse war-fever in the most peaceful city on earth (43). The chosen 'city' is Dunkelstein, presumably parodying 'Liechtenstein', and is a tiny country (in the geographical position of Andorra) which lives on its banking and has everything to fear from war (44).

Thus from the outset Toller distances his play from the realities of the threat of war as it actually existed in the 1930s, that is to say, the deliberately aggressive and expansionist policies of the "Rome-Berlin Axis" (45) and presents us instead with an imaginary aggressor who is unmotivated and anonymous — though the Dunkelsteiners suspect Brazil (46). At the same time, far from covertly encouraging a Christian-Communist Anti-Fascist Front, as Pittock, on the strength of the English version, suggested, Toller seems quite deliberately to try to keep any specific or contemporary politico-ideological content out of the play (47). In this first scene Franziskus rejects Napoleon's suggestion that Karl Marx should be invited up from Hell for an hour, adding that he has read *Das Kapital* and did not enjoy it (48).

In using this 'Olympian' framework, Toller was following a fashion of the time. In Jean Giradoux' *Amphitryon 38* (1929) Zeus involves himself in human affairs, and more specifically, as Pittock has pointed out, Toller's own friend, Walther Hasenclever, had written a play, *Ehen werden im Himmel geschlossen (Marriages are made in Heaven)* (49) in which,

> . . . the heavenly powers manipulate human beings into situations that will illustrate their weaknesses and the intractable problems arising from them (50).

The second scene begins with the burial of war (a table with black cloth and funereal candle), and the slogan parodied in the play's title, *Nie wieder Krieg*, prominently displayed. A tight, sharp exchange between Noah, the beggar, and James, the model servant, which emphasises the contrast between the 'insider' and the 'outsider', leads to Noah's Song, omitted here in the English version and introduced instead into Act II Scene ii (Scene IV of the German text), to the detriment of that scene, of course. It is a neat, Brechtian quip in the tradition of Wedekind and the cabaret *chansons*.

> . . . Jedem hat das Schicksal seine Gaben
> In das Bett der Frau Mama gelegt,
> Wer nichts hat, der soll nichts haben,
> Wer viel hat, der hats mit Recht verdient (51).

Noah's characterisation, too, owes something to Brecht's *Dreigroschenoper*. His clothes, so *abgerissen* and *zerlumpt* are necessary to his profession, the customers demand it.

The festival procession enters, with banners, and Laban the financier introduces Herr Robert, delegate from the League of Nations. Noah's bitter song began and ended:

> Weil der Mensch vom Affen abstammt
> Will der Mensch nicht gleich sein.
> Weil der Mensch eine Seele hat,
> Will der Mensch auch reich sein (52).

Robert's Song (reduced to mere declamation in the English version) uses the same Darwinian basis (which Darwin, in Scene I, is said to have recanted) to draw instead naively optimistic conclusions:

> Als die Menschen einst in Waldern
> Auf die Bäumen lebten, nackt und bloß

. . .
Schlugen sie mit diesen Keulen
Auch den Nachbarn tot.
. . .
Erst zweitausend Jahr nach Christ
Ward der Mensch ein Pazifist
. . .
Und die Menschheit lebt in guter Laune,
Denn der Krieg ist abgeschafft (53).

The deliberate juxtaposition of these two lyrics shows Toller still employing the montage technique.

These songs, and the others in the play, contribute to its character a bite that is wholly lacking in what a critic called Auden's "good-tempered" lyrics (54). There appears to be no record of Eisler's music to the lyrics, but its character can easily be imagined by anyone familiar with his work. Herbert Murrill's settings of Auden's lyrics are relatively bland and in the softer tradition of English musical comedy (55).

The Festival of Peace is linked with the engagement of Laban's daughter Rahel to a young Brazilian, Herr Jakobo (56). Toller thus alludes through the names and relationships of these central characters in his plot, to the biblical story related in the Book of Genesis, Chapters XXVIII to XXXI, but not, it seems to any purpose (57).

A ceremonial 'sacrifice' by those present of their 'war symbols' — medals, uniforms, sabres, children's toy soldiers — disturbed by Noah, the only person there who has actually been sacrificed in war, through the loss of a lung, is followed by a dance-scene in which the *Friedenlied* is played in waltz time. While Laban's cronies discuss the price of peace in cynical terms, Rahel and Jakobo dance, and Emil the hair-dresser (a reincarnation of Wotan) emerges as Rahel's disappointed lover and a xenophobic Dunkelsteiner (58).

The war-telegram arrives and Laban's three associates, Der Dicke, Der Hagere and Der Kleine (59), plan, patriotically of course, to flee the country to feather their own nests. Their Trio, *Man muß das Rechte zur rechten Zeit tun* (60) is particularly crisp in its rhythmic irony (61).

There is even a side-swipe, though a politically inept one, at the League of Nations, as Robert leaves with the words,

> Der Völkerbund wird dafür sorgen, daß dieser Krieg der letzte Krieg sein wird.
> Es lebe der letzte Krieg (62).

The elected government resigns and the Peace Song is re-written as the War Song:

> Was liegt am Inhalt? Nur die Form ist entscheidend. Die Form ist das Ewige (63).

Emil immediately takes over the Leadership (die Führung) and the Doctor passes everyone "k.v."(kriegsverwendungsfähig: A.1.) in a brief song (64).

Emil forbids Rahel's marriage with an alien; Jakobo goes off to the Brazilian Legation to enlist if required; Noah prefers imprisonment to the army, purely for reasons of his own safety; Tomas, author of the Peace/War Song, is made Minister for Propaganda and Popular Enlightenment, and Leader of Counter-Espionage.

There follows a short, very funny, but irrelevant scene in which Male, the Nanny, describes how she had to tie her dog Napoleon to her bed; she is mistaken by Emil first for a violent lover and then for a lesbian (65).

Rahel is arrested for distributing the New Testament and shouting *Nie wieder Krieg*; Emil woos her, absurdly:

> EMIL: . . . Rahel, heiraten mich!
> RAHEL: Ein knieender Diktator. Lächerlich (66).

She is taken off to prison; Jakobo has been arrested; all corn-fields are to be burnt (67) in case spies hide in them (68).

This scene, written at the level at best of political cabaret, ends the first "Act" and is followed by the second Olympian scene (Sc. III), in which the Female Angel expresses her desire for fashionable wings and Franziskus sends Socrates to earth.

Scene IV, already fully discussed, follows.

In the third Olympian scene (Sc. V) the angel hints at her negotiations with Laban for new wings: but it must be said that this crude device to manipulate the earthly plot is actually handled with tactful obliquity and anything but crudely (69).

Scene VI, which in the structure of the play begins the third "Act" and which balances Scene II, of which it is the approximate mirror-image, reverts to the style of that scene. The opening sequence is based upon spy-phobia, corresponding with the closing lines of Scene II (70).

A neat Spy Song (71) is followed by a long, untidy scene involving: the mysterious disappearance of Socrates (now regarded as a spy); Male's passionate appeal to Emil on behalf of Rahel; Laban's telegram from the Angel and a brief introduction of popular racism: "Down with the foreigners!" (72). Emil is prepared to bomb his own country:

> Lieber durch eigene Bomben verbrennen als durch feindliche (73).

Noah is brought in and condemned to death. But at this point the heavenly telegram arrives:

> Alle Kriegsoperationen einstellen.
> Krieg Mißverständnis. Friede auf Erde (74).

This leads to a sequence of farcical knockabout which ends when Emil declares that war is nevertheless to continue:

> Nie wieder Friede! Ich lasse Ihnen drei Minuten Bedenkzeit. Verweigern Sie dem Staat Ihre Hilfe, sperr ich Sie ins Gefängnis (75).

He goes; and the three financiers, after a reprise of their Trio (very appropriate at this moment, and neatly pointing the reversal of Scene II) decide that at this juncture peace will be more profitable than war. They produce the copy of a birth certificate proving that Emil is not a true Dunkelsteiner as his mother was a pure-blooded Brazilian.

He is sent off into banishment, on an expedition to discover the South Pole! (As the South Pole was reached by Roald Amundsen on 15 December 1911 this distances the play even further from the actualities of the 1930s).

Once more Male comes on with her poodle, Napoleon (76). The reprieved lovers return, but their sparse expressions of affection are eclipsed by Rahel's Song, whose twin themes are that sorrows end with death and that mankind's stupidity is boundless.

> Wenn der Tag vergeht
> Endet alles Leid.
> Und das arme Herz
> Ruht in Heiterkeit

Grenzen hat das Meer,
Und die Welt ist klein,
Ohne Grenzen dumm
Ist der Mensch allein (77).

It is indeed a negative song, for in it not only is death (the end of the day) the only escape from sorrow, but there is no hope for mankind, whose stupidity is boundless.

Noah, too, is reprieved; the placard *Es lebe der Krieg* is once more reversed to *Nie wieder Krieg*, and the Peace Song is sung — with bitterly ironical impact, surely!

As the play began with a kind of Prologue on Olympus, so it ends with a kind of Epilogue on Olympus (78). The action of the play has achieved nothing. Napoleon and Franziskus begin their dialogue with the identical four speeches with which they opened the first scene. We are, the play is telling us, back where we started. But the dialogue between Napoleon and Franziskus, interrupted by Napoleon's interrogating the corrupt little Angel, is a serious attempt to provide the play with a conclusion.

In the first part of the discussion Franziskus asks why, if people have the courage to die, so few have the courage to live. Even for peace, he says, they are more ready to die than to live: and this the central scene and Rahel's Song have already shown. Napoleon's answer is that peace is not an ideal worth living for. Franziskus then wonders whether what the statesman call peace is true peace.

In the second part of the discussion Franziskus wonders when peace on earth will come. Napoleon replies that for millennia clever people (die Klugen) have known that peace is a fool's dream (ein Traum der Toren). The play ends:

> FRANZISKUS: Eines Tages wird der Traum sich erfüllen. Die Liebe wird stärker sein als der Haß, die Wahrheit stärker als die Lüge, und die Menschen werden sehen und sich erkennen, und es wird Friede sein auf Erden.
> NAPOLEON: Wann wird dieser Tag sein?
> FRANZISKUS: Wenn die Klugen schweigen. Wenn die Toren Handeln (79).

"When the clever are silent and the fools act". The conclusion is biblical. In the English version Toller altered this to a Marxist conclusion. The 'fools' become the 'wise' (as distinct from the merely 'clever') and Napoleon gets Franziskus to agree with the Marxist slogan used by

Toller in 1930 to disconcert his debating opponent, the Nazi Alfred Mühr:

> Hitherto philosophers have sought to explain the world. Our task is to change it (80).

But the original, unrevised ending is biblical. The New Testament (especially in Paul's First Epistle to the Corinthians) repeatedly asserts the positive value of so-called foolishness.

The verbal parallels with the biblical text in Luther's translation are strikingly close:

> Wo sind die Klugen? Wo sind die Schriftgelehrten? Wo sind die Weltweisen? Hat nicht Gott die Weisheit dieser Welt zur Thorheit gemacht?
>
> . . . die Griechen nach Weisheit fragen. Wir aber predigen den gekreuzigten Christum . . . den Griechen eine Thorheit.
> (1. Cor. 1. v. 20, 22, 23)
>
> Denn die göttliche Thorheit ist weiser, denn die Menschen sind.
> (1. Cor. 1, v. 25)
>
> Niemand betrüge sich selbst. Welcher sich unter euch dünkt weise zu sein, der werde ein Narr in dieser Welt, daß er möge weise sein.
> Denn dieser Welt Weisheit ist Thorheit bei Gott.
> (1. Cor. 3. vv. 18,19)
>
> And similarly:
>
> Zu derselbigen Zeit antwortete Jesus,
> und sprach: Ich preise dich, Vater und
> Herr Himmels und der Erde, daß du solches
> den Weisen und Klugen verborgen hast,
> und hast es den Unmündigen geoffenbaret.
> (Matt. 11. v. 25)

Thus Toller did not give his play a Marxist conclusion, but a Christian one, though he did not, and evidently could not, give this Christian conclusion a contemporary political application: this had to wait until his next and last play, *Pastor Hall*. Moreover, the rejection of rationality, of both Noah and Socrates, *Klugheit* and *Weisheit*, is for Toller, despite its positive implications in the biblical context, a gesture of pessimism, and Franziskus' closing line is therefore double-edged, capable of both positive and negative interpretation, and thus an expression of the spiritual conflict from which Toller was suffering.

Hence the play's negative impact: the human protagonists have only learnt that it is better to die than to kill, not that it is better to live than to die; that human stupidity is boundless, and that all

> Life death does end and each day dies with sleep (81).

For Toller, as for the agonised Jesuit, Gerard Manley Hopkins, hope, as expressed by Franziskus, lies in a yet unrealisable future.

As a play *Nie wieder Friede* is deeply flawed, but through the cracks in its brittle comic mask stare the ever more despairing and tragic eyes of its author, Ernst Toller (82).

PASTOR HALL

No More Peace opened in London on 11 June 1936; five weeks later (17/18 July 1936) the revolt of the Spanish Army in Morocco under the leadership of Emilio Mola and Francisco Franco set in motion the Spanish Civil War, prelude to World War II, which more and more dominated the last three years of Toller's life and whose outcome in the victory of the fascists finally led to his suicide on 22 May 1939, three days after Franco's great victory parade in Madrid on 19 May 1939.

It would not be appropriate here to trace in detail the course of Toller's restless activity during these years, from the great anti-fascist lecture tour through the USA and Canada (October 1936 until February 1937) (1), to the huge international relief action for the civilian population of Spain which he initiated through a personal appeal to President Roosevelt broadcast on Madrid Radio, 26 August 1938 (2), and to which he devoted himself almost exclusively until it was wrecked by Franco's victory and the recognition of his regime by the western powers only weeks before Toller ended his own life (3).

During these three tormented years Toller wrote little other than his political speeches and articles. *Die Feuerkantate,* a cycle of seven poems on the Reichstag Fire, though published in 1938, may well have been written earlier (4). Under contract for a time to MGM he worked on two film scenarios, but neither was used (5).

His one play from this period, his last, was begun early in 1938 (6). His own statement is that it was written during 1938 in "New York, Barcelona and Cassis" (7). This declaration that the play was written in America, Spain and France was no doubt symbolic as well as factual. He returned from his Mexican trip and was in New York from 10 February 1938 (8). It would seem that the play was begun then. On 25 July he addressed the PEN Club Congress in Paris. Afterwards he travelled to Spain, where he was flown from Barcelona to the besieged city of Madrid. He must have worked on the play in Barcelona at this time. On 26 August he made his broadcast appeal to President Roosevelt over the Madrid Radio (9). He was in France again by 4 September (10) and about this time must have occurred the incident described by Harold Hurwitz when Toller heard in Paris of the plight of a group of

Spanish Republican Airmen who were to be sent back to Franco Spain. Within hours Toller flew to the south of France to help them (11). It could have been now that he completed the play (12).

In this first version Hall dies through a heart-attack before he can be re-arrested and returned to the concentration camp (13). Some time before the end of 1938 a group of exiled German writers met in a New York flat to hear Toller read the play. These literary friends expressed sensitive criticism of its conclusion. They told Toller:

> That is not true as regards the best in Germany, the best of us and of people like you (14).

Toller accepted the criticism and re-wrote the ending (15).

The play was translated into English by Stephen Spender, and with the original ending, before the end of 1938, for it was rejected on 6 December 1938 by Barrett H. Clark, Executive Director of Dramatists Play Service Inc., primarily on the ground that the translator's language was too 'English' (i.e. not American):

> . . . no doubt it is English, but English is no longer our language here (16).

By the time the translation was published the ending had been re-written and the second version was used.

There was no German edition, of course, until much later. In 1946 Henschel issued a mimeographed edition, not for sale, in two versions, one with each ending. The first German publication for sale is GW3 pp. 245–316, which derives from a previously unpublished typescript, with Toller's hand-written corrections (and therefore considered to be authoritative) in Yale University. It has the second ending, the first ending being given in the bibliographical notes (17).

While the second version must clearly be regarded as authoritative, the first throws light upon authorial intentions and was used for the first German production: for these reasons it must be given consideration in a critical evaluation of the play.

We have said that exile almost destroyed Toller as a dramatist, and our examination of *Nie wieder Friede*, together with the fact that in the last six and a half years of his life he wrote only two plays is evidence enough of this. That *Pastor Hall*, written in the midst of travels and civil war, and of psychological turmoil not helped by the breakdown of his marriage (18), could still be regarded by Willibrand in his pioneering thesis of 1940 as in some respects "Toller's best play" (19), is in the circumstances all the more remarkable. Nevertheless the play has incontrovertible shortcomings, summarised succinctly by Rothe:

> *Pastor Hall* shares the weaknesses of nearly all literature of exile: as direct observation of the changed realities of life and personal experience of the dictatorship are lacking, atmosphere and accuracy of detail tend to suffer. There are disturbing inconsistencies, and sheer improbabilities betray both the author's geographical distance as well as his inner estrangement from the scene of the events portrayed (20).

It is in one sense 'outwardly observed' (21). Seen after the war, the gas-chambers and the atom bomb, it now reveals that Toller could not know and failed to prophesy the final horrors of war and mechanised mass-murder, though he did, in October 1938, foresee the slaughter of the Jews (22). The language is "strangely colourless" (23), the effect, obviously, of exile. Even when written,

> . . . the play was also in some respects out of date. The Germany of 1938 was not that of 1935, the time at which the action takes place. It was worse (24).

Despite these weaknesses, however, the play has artistic worth and power. In his material, however second-hand it might be, Toller found an objective correlative for his own, ultimately insoluble, inner conflict. As a result the play derives from its subjective element the strength and immediacy lacking in the un-experienced objective material. As Rothe rightly says:

> For a writer who works primarily out of feeling the lack of a basis in concrete experience was bound to have a negative effect (25).

But though Toller lacked the concrete experience of living and suffering in post-1933 Germany, he shared with Pastor Hall the experience of inner conflict as to whether evil can be opposed with non-violent means or whether violence is in the last resort unavoidable. Was he right when he told the American people that Hitler

> only understands one language, the language of will and power (26)

or when he wrote

> No one may kill people for the sake of a cause (27)?

The moral dilemma in which he and his created protagonist, Sonja, found themselves in relation to revolutionary struggle Toller now faced in the new and even more challenging context of Fascism. At the outbreak of the Spanish Civil War he had wanted — or part of him had wanted — to join the International Brigade: his 'non-violent' contribution to the Spanish people's struggle, his Relief Action, he felt as the repayment of a debt (28) because he had not done so. That it was not for lack of courage that he had not volunteered is witnessed by his flying into besieged Madrid. But had Toller now got himself into the position of effectively advocating a war against Fascism in which he personally would find it impossible to take part?

Pastor Hall is a Toller-persona. As Pittock has pointed out, Toller gives the three women in the play names of women very close to him in his own life: Ida (his mother), Christine (his wife, Christiane) and Jule (the family servant of his childhood); he gives Hall something of his own background as a volunteer in the First World War converted to pacifism by his experience in the trenches (29). Then Hall's escape from the concentration camp results in the death of a guard (actually the one who helps him). Toller himself had rejected a plan of escape from prison which would have involved the death of a guard, and Sonja acts similarly in *Masse Mensch*. Moreover, he gives Hall the significant Christian name of the author-persona in his first play, *Die Wandlung*, — Friedrich.

Another autobiographical element, unremarked in previous studies of the play, is to be found in the character Erwin Kohn, whom Toller links with Hall by making the two men new arrivals in the concentration camp in Act II Sc. i (30). Kohn is linked to Toller through his name. Toller's mother's maiden-name was Cohn, which is how Egon Freundlich spells out the prisoner's name. Cohn has Germanised his Jewish name by changing the C to a K. The child Ernst had felt himself to be as German as he was Jewish:

> Against the Poles, Jews and Germans showed a united front. The Jews looked upon themselves as the pioneers of German culture ... When the others cry 'Polak' I cry 'Polak' with them (31).

But he was made to feel conscious of his Jewishness, and though never baptised (as Kohn claims to have been) he had tried to associate with an evangelical Christian group:

> I am blissfully happy. I am not a Jew any more, and I have a Christmas verse to learn; nobody will ever be able to call "Dirty Jew!" after me again (32).

Kohn is an artist (33) who has returned to Germany from France because he was homesick. Toller, though he knew he could not return to Germany, was desperately homesick for Europe. When Christopher Isherwood visited him in New York in the Spring of 1939, Toller told him:

> I long greatly to return to Europe (34).

However much America had at one time appealed to him, his feelings had by now totally changed. When Isherwood asked,

> You don't like it here?

he replied,

> 'I hate it'. He said this quietly, quite without passion, stating a simple fact (35).

Kohn similarly says quite simply,

> Mir war nicht wohl in Frankreich (36).

Harold Hurwitz also tells of Toller's longing for Europe, even though he realised it was less safe for him than America, foreseeing as he did the fall of France and a Nazi victory.

> In the dead Toller's pocket were found tickets which he had bought with his last money, to travel to Europe the next day. He had written to Hermann Kesten that he wanted to meet him in Normandy and that they would go together to England if France fell. That was his premonition. This did not prevent him from writing his last work, expressing his belief in another Germany even while he anticipated a Nazi victory (37).

A further expression of Toller's awareness of being both Jew and German is to be found in one of Hall's closing speeches (in the second version):

> Du (i.e. Gen. Grotjahn) hast nicht geschwiegen, das haben wir nämlich den Juden voraus, die haben keine Wahl. Wir dürfen uns entscheiden (38).

Thus though Hall is the principal Toller-persona he is not the only one. Peter Hofer, the communist, is also that facet of Toller's character that made him declare in his American speeches that he was no longer a pacifist (39) and which tormented him because he had felt unable to join the International Brigade in the Spanish Civil War (40).

Central to the dramatisation of Toller's internal conflict is the dialogue in Act II Sc. iii (GW3 p. 289) between Hall and Hofer. This is parallel with the debate between Sonja and The Nameless One in *Masse Mensch* and the arguments between Jimmy Cobbett and Wible in *Die Maschinenstürmer*, but not exactly like either, for Wible is a treacherous rogue, not an ideological revolutionary, and The Nameless One, as his designation shows, lacks Hofer's humanity. Hofer is sympathetic to human weakness, even quoting scripture in support of his views, and is aware of the shallowness and inadequacy of his pre-camp communism:

> The spirit was willing, but the flesh was weak . . . We called Freedom a petty-bourgeois cliché — so little did we know what slavery is (41).

He sees the weaknesses and shortcomings of individual workers though he rejects Hall's idea that we must reform individuals rather than the system as "too Christian" for him. Hall changes the subject and asks:

> Would you, if you had power, revenge yourselves and torture and torment your enemies?
> HOFER: Kill, if it must be . . Maltreat, no (42).

Hall then describes his Toller-like conversion during the Great War, concluding:

> Today I believe only in the way of understanding and love. There is no question on earth that cannot be solved without violence, be it never so entangled and involved (43).

To Hofer's reply that it takes two to reach a non-violent solution and that he would rather die than tamely allow himself to be robbed of his rights, Hall replies:

> The courage to die has become cheap, so cheap that I often ask myself if it is not a flight from life (44).

He is questioning the position reached by Rahel in the cell and in her song; and through him Toller is asking himself whether he has the greater courage, the courage to live. Hofer, in reply, says,

> It is a question of what you live for and how you die (45).

And he tells the true story of Toller's friend Erich Mühsam.

> The spirit lived in Mühsam (46)

declares Hall, and the dialogue ends with Hofer's recognising the rebel in Hall, and Hall recognising the Christian in Hofer.

Mühsam's heroic martyrdom, felt by Hall as inspiration, is the positive centre of the play, as the scene in the marsh (II. ii) is the negative. It is Mühsam who inspires Hall (in both versions of the ending) with courage to emerge from his hiding-place to face what he expected to be a brutally cruel death. In the first version Toller then allowed his protagonist to evade the consequences of the final existential Either/Or. It is true that Hall has decided to face his flogging and death, but he is saved by Nature's swift and merciful death: he has, as Gerte angrily exclaims "escaped", as Toller himself was voluntarily to "escape" from his own intolerable dilemma. In the revised version he does not escape but has to make a further, absolutely committing decision: to go and speak in the church. This is not "suicide", as Christine claims; it is fulfilment of duty: the parallel with the author's actual suicide is in the first version (47), Hall's death through a heart attack being one which lacks the moral and inspirational dimensions of Mühsam's (48).

Toller's personal tragedy was the tragedy of the twentieth century. As Herbert H. Hofner, quoting Walter Mehring, wrote in 21 May 1954, the fifteenth anniversary of Toller's death:

> The rift in the age went through his heart (49).

Hall, in the revised version, achieves heroism of Mühsam-like, of Christ-like proportions (50), which his own daughter calls "madness" (Wahnsinn). Hall's "mad" action fulfils Franziskus' final words in *Nie wieder Friede*:

> When the clever are silent. When the fools act (51).

He fulfils them not by rejecting wisdom, but by rejecting "Vernunft", so-called "common-sense".

> GROTJAHN: Ist das nicht wirklich unvernunftig, Friedrich?
> HALL (*lächelt*): Mit Vernunft hast du den Gerte nicht gerade vor die Tür gesetzt (52).

"Vernunft", escape down the back stairs (53), is not the way to life. Hall has his "Pflicht" (that profoundly German concept of indisputable duty) to live, and therefore may not be a deserter. The demands of Hall's non-violence are as ineluctable as military commands: his language shows that he feels himself to be a soldier of Christ. He is to be an example to others. In the earlier version this is merely stated in the closing lines of the play:

> CHRISTINE (*softly*): What remains for us?
> IDA (*softly*): A grave.
> CHRISTINE (*strongly*): An example (54).

In the later version that 'example' is dramatised, demonstrated upon the stage. We see Hall walk out, we hear the marching tread of the approaching column: but not only that. We also actually see Hall's example being followed — by Grotjahn in his General's uniform, with his orders and decorations. Pittock says that although "astonishingly" (!) this is prophetic, it was at that date "quite inconceivable" that the old General should oppose Hitler "on principle" (55). True, it was not until 20 July 1944 that Claus Schenk Graf von Stauffenberg placed the brief-case bomb almost at Hitler's feet; but he had seen through the system by the end of 1943, and said to Jakob Kaiser:

> We have to put ourselves to the test before God and before our conscience, it must be done, for this man is evil incarnate.

Grotjahn foreshadows von Stauffenberg, though he chooses almost certain martyrdom rather than high-principled assassination, and it might be said of him as Thom Gunn wrote of Claus von Stauffenberg:

> And though he fails, honour personified
> In a cold time where honour cannot grow,
> He stiffens, like a statue, in mid-stride
> – Falling toward history, and under snow (56).

Pastor Hall and Grotjahn are patriots, as their creator also was. The play is no mere anti-Nazi tract but also (apart from its vital subjective content) an affirmation of the traditional values of German patriotism and Lutheranism.

The principal symbol of these is the old musical-box which, when it manages to produce anything but crackling noises, plays Ernst Moritz Arndt's famous patriotic song of the Napoleonic War, ("Der Befreiungskrieg" as it is known to Germans) *Der Gott, der Eisen wachsen ließ/Der wollte keine Knechte* (57). This song is peculiarly appropriate in the context of the play. Apart from his war-like songs of 1812/13, Arndt fought tirelessly for the social rights of the people, especially for the peasants still oppressed by feudalism. He sought to link the national ethos with Christian convictions, and this song, in common with his others, is written in a style that recalls Luther's hymns in energy and sturdiness (58). It thus symbolises the friendship and unity of the General and the Pastor, and while the half-broken musical-box itself symbolises the breakdown of the traditional German values in the Nazi state, the General, too, speaks the words of the song "unrhetorically" while the musical-box is playing the tune.

Traditional German values are further symbolised by two pictures in the General's living-room: a portrait of Frederick the Great, and Anton Werner's painting, *The Founding of the German Reich at Versailles* (59). Another reference to the period of Frederick the Great may well be intended in the use of the name Johann Herder for the bible-student flogged to death in the concentration camp and whose real-life name was Albert Stein (60).

Willibrand claimed to see a further depth in this play which he called a 'mystical tendency' (61). He quotes an article contributed by Toller to the *New York Times* (24.1.1937) in which he refers to the 'timeless elements in art' and refers particularly to

> consciousness of that last-of-all which Angelus Silesius called the "Unio Mystica", the union with the whole (62).

He finds an interpretation of this 'union with the whole' in Hall's speech on marriage, in which he refers to living in the "Brotherhood of God"

> In which all men are equal and need love and salvation; in which they show faithfulness, honesty and an open heart, instilling trust and being worthy of trust, and rejoicing in meadows and clouds, animals and flowers and light (63).

This expresses a certain sense of unity with nature and one's fellowmen, but Willibrand is stretching a point to call it "mystical" and to compare it with the sense of identity with God, characteristic of the Catholic, Angelus Silesius (64).

Carel ter Haar also sees a kind of unity in the play, but in another sense, in that it

> unites all the insights that Toller had gained in exile (65).

Above all this critic refers to the wide human sympathies he now shows, whether for the weak, like Jule and Erwin Kohn, or the strong and understanding, like Peter Hofer and Paul v. Grotjahn. It is a humanistic rather than a politically based play.

> Socialism and conservatism — Toller knew himself to be bound up with both — fuse in this play to a unity, whose expression is the human attitude (66).

ter Haar quotes perceptively the conclusion of a letter to Tessa from prison:

> I discover conservative elements in me. One could perhaps say that the revolutionary only becomes revolutionary out of a love for a utopian conservatism (67).

Hall is a synthesis of weakness and strength, fear and confidence, past and future — *and* he knows his responsibility:

> He mounts the pulpit in order to preach and show his congregation the way to humanity (68).

ter Haar concludes:

> His life and death become a demonstration in support of mankind (69).

This universalising element ter Haar goes as far as to call "strongly allegorising" (*allegorisierend* not *allegorisch*).

This also contains some truth, for despite its largely naturalistic mode *Pastor Hall* shares with Toller's other plays — and especially with *Masse Mensch* — the power of conveying human truths and problems of wider and more universal significance than the specific subject of the play. But in the terminology of English literary and dramatic criticism 'allegorising' suggests *a=b* relationships which are not to be found in this play. Nevertheless the universalising element is present and is further emphasised in its structure.

Like every other play of Toller's *Pastor Hall* reveals itself upon examination to be both skilfully and appropriately constructed. In fact its structure closely resembles that of the preceding play, *Nie wieder Friede*, with one central scene before and after which all others are symmetrically arranged.

THE STRUCTURE OF *PASTOR HALL*

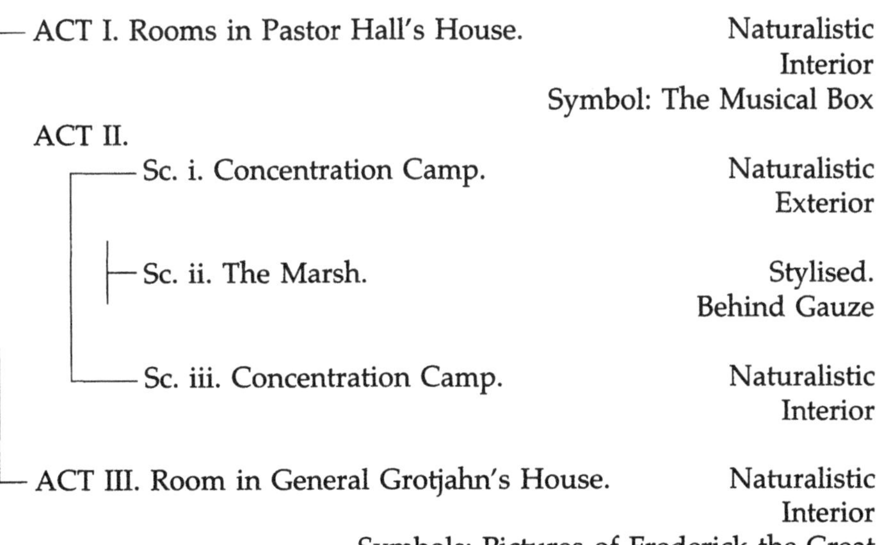

The Concentration Camp (Act II) is the centre of the play, and the mechanical, dehumanising labour of the prisoners (Act II. Sc. ii) the centre of the Camp, the Act and the play. To isolate and universalise this scene Toller finds a valid use for the expressionistic techniques of two decades earlier:

> In order to give the realism of this short scene the monotony of *without-beginning-and-without-end*, it should be played muffled, behind gauze.
> After the end of the scene the impression must remain that it continues — for months, for years (70).

In a brilliant theatrical touch Toller uses the command *One . . . Two . . . One . . . Two* that accompanies the punishment march at the double at the end of the (naturalistic) first scene of the act to link this scene through a blackout with the ("expressionistic") Marsh scene in which the prisoners dig mechanically to the same command.

The Marsh scene is framed between the other two concentration camp scenes, the first an exterior setting, and also 'external' in its presentation, the second an interior setting with interiorised subject-matter: the intimate conversation of the prisoners, Hall's four important dialogues (with Hofer, Ida and Christine, the S.S. Man and Fritz Gerte) and the communal expression of suppressed rebellion in *Das Moorsoldatenlied* (71).

This whole act is in turn framed by the two wholly naturalistic acts, I & III, in both of which the 'true Germany' is presented through concrete symbols (*Dingsymbole*).

The play begins as domestic drama, though the immediate presence of Fritz Gerte in S.S. Uniform sets this at once fully in the context of Nazi Germany. The initial plot material is domestic and private, which at least one critic of the 1947 production found irritating (72), but which really shows how impossible truly 'private' life is under a totalitarian regime.

When the play returns to a realistic domestic setting in Act III (Grotjahn's home balancing Hall's in the first act, — the religious and secular aspects of German values) it is permeated by the audience's experience of Act II.

The whole shape of the play thus embodies and dramatises its theme. There is no waste, no distraction, every character and incident is relevant and is precisely placed within the total pattern.

> From the viewpoint of plot continuity and stage economy this is Toller's best play . . . There is no padding, no crowding in of unnecessary material (73).

For Altenhofer Toller's plays have come full circle. Noting the parallels between the conversion to pacifism of Friedrich in *Die Wandlung* and of Friedrich Hall, she also points out that whereas Friedrich had at the end of *Die Wandlung,* preached revolution *outside* the Church (74), Friedrich Hall will call the people to resistance *inside* the church (75).

The final tableau of the play (and of Toller's whole dramatic oeuvre) is not actually presented on the stage, — where Jule, whose weakness set the plot in motion, kneels down and prays, — but is evoked in our imagination. From without we hear evermore loudly the march-step of the approaching column; but in our mind's eye we see the two representatives of Germany, the Pastor and the General, standing side by side before the assembled congregation. It is a fitting conclusion to Toller's creative life (76).

THE PLAY ON STAGE AND FILM

The World Première of *Pastor Hall* was not, as previous studies have stated, in Berlin in 1947, but in Manchester in 1939 (77). It was thus the third Toller play to be presented by the enterprising Manchester Repertory Theatre.

The theatre should have re-opened early in September after its usual summer break, for a new season: but on 3 September 1939 war between Great Britain and Germany was declared, and this theatre, in common with virtually all others in the country, was closed. The blackout was imposed, and heavy air-raids, with the probable use of poison gas, were expected to come almost at once. After a few weeks, however, the theatre was permitted to re-open, which it did, starting with a weekly repertory programme of light, entertaining plays (78).

Then on Monday 20 November, 1939, the World Première of *Pastor Hall* opened for a two-week run of sixteen performances (i.e. with matinées on Thursdays and Saturdays at 2.15 as well as evening performances at 7.15). It was advertised in the *Manchester Evening News* as the World Première of

> Ernst Toller's last play.
> A sensational drama about Nazi Germany and the concentration camps, by a famous German refugee.
>
> Every Britisher must see this play (79).

It was a difficult time for theatres. J. Lea Axon, the Chairman of the Repertory Theatre, feared that the blackout would reduce attendances, and the Lea Axon Guarantee Scheme was introduced under which guarantors undertook to indemnify the theatre against loss to the extent of £10, spread over the next five years, not more than £2 to be called upon in any one year. The response had clearly been good: the list of guarantors covers three pages of the programme in two columns (80).

The fear of air-raids was very real, though in fact the 'blitz' was still many months away (81). The programme explained the A.R.P. [Air Raid Precautions] Regulations in relation to the theatre. In the event of an Air-Raid Warning patrons could remain or go to the nearest shelter, "which is very close to this building". The performance would be continued "after the least possible delay". The comparative safety of the building "owing to its unusual construction" was emphasised, and members of the audience were asked to remember to take their gas-masks with them when they left the theatre (82).

These were the circumstances of the first production of Toller's last play, exactly six months after his death and less than three months after the outbreak of the war, and when the content of the play was still of intense contemporary importance.

The play was produced and the production designed by James Bould, Director of the Theatre. Rafe Thomson played Hall and Patricia Jessel his wife; Bould himself played Dr Werner von Grotjahn, who appears only in the first act (83).

The review by A.S.W. (A.S. Wallace) in the *Manchester Guardian* congratulated the theatre on staging this play for the first time and recalled Ernst Toller's own direction of a "vigorous" production of *Draw the Fires*. Wallace sees and describes the play in very simple terms as

> the tragedy of a German clergyman who puts the worship of God before obedience to a tyrant (84).

He retells the story straightforwardly. The only hint he gives of the style of the production is that

> In the second act, in which Mr Bould's production uses well the expressionist technique, we are given a glimpse of the brutality of the guards and the courage of the prisoners in a concentration camp (85).

He describes the final curtain as "memorable". He advances only two adverse criticisms. One is the character of Pipermann:

> A tiresome, crafty and enigmatic old gossip of a church-warden on whom the author has spent some pains (86).

Pipermann,

> . . . does not quite emerge in the round, though Mr Leslie Jackson fills him with fawning malice (87).

Another is

> The difficulty of making natural the prisoners' songs (88).

For this he blames Stephen Spender's translation and the production.

Otherwise, he praises Rafe Thomson's "manly, urgent and unaffected Pastor", Patricia Jessel's "distraught but loyal wife" and the proud conservatism of Noel Morris's General von Grotjahn, saying that in these three,

> Toller has the vehicles he would have wanted to convey a drama of contemporary history through which the passion for freedom and justice shine as they did through his own radiant personality (89).

This production was the only one of the play during the Nazi period, but in 1940 an English film was based upon it using a screen play written by Leslie Arliss, Anna Reiner and Haworth Bromley. It was produced and directed by the Boulting Brothers. It was a "small budget production" (90), but made a very powerful impact whether it was received favourably or unfavourably. In England the *New Statesman and Nation* called it the "first really successful anti-Nazi film" (91). The cast was outstanding, with Wilfred Lawson, whose restrained "underacting" was commended (92), as Pastor Hall, Sir Seymour Hicks as General von Grotjahn, Nora Pilbeam as Christine Hall, and Marius Goring as Fritz Gerte (93).

As well as being shown in England, the film was distributed in the United States (by United Artists for James Roosevelt) and in Mexico, where it was called *El Martir*. Both in USA and Mexico it ran into considerable difficulties, even though for US distribution Mrs Eleanor Roosevelt had spoken a foreword to it written by Robert E. Sherwood and filmed at 20th Century Fox Studios in New York. It must be borne in mind that US did not declare war on Germany until 11 December 1941, three days after the Japanese attack on Pearl Harbour, while Mexico did not declare war on the Axis until 2 June 1942, and that there were many groups of Germans in both these countries.

In Mexico the film was shown at the Cine Chino Palacio in Mexico City. Press advertisements compared the Pastor's sacrifice with that of Christ, and showed a prisoner hanging in chains resembling Christ on the Cross (94). The film itself, which was shown in the week preceding 1 December 1940, provoked riots and was withdrawn on the sixth day because of bomb threats from "a group of Germans". The campaign included advertisements attacking United Artists, Toller and Mrs Roosevelt (95).

In US the biggest scandal was caused by the film's being banned in Chicago, though a pro-Nazi film, *Blitzkrieg in Poland*, was shown uncensored (96). It appears that there were two very active groups of Germans of opposing political views in Chicago at the time (97). Some days after the banning, a private showing was sponsored by the Civil Liberties Committee (98). At the same time Dr Eric von Schroetter, head of the German-American League for Culture, accused Chicago politicians of playing up to Germans with pro-Nazi leanings (99). The ban was eventually lifted and responsibility for censorship in Chicago changed (100). These events occurred between early June and mid-September 1940.

Nevertheless, the reviews in USA were generally favourable. Cecilia Ager in *P.M.* (N.Y.) was moved to tears (101). Edwin Schallert in *Los Angeles Times* called it the "strongest offering in its particular field" (102). T.S. in the *New York Times* praised the film, "for uncovering the naked spiritual issues involved" (103). All this American praise is in the face of the interesting fact that the *Variety* critic in Hollywood found it "too British in speech and mannerisms to be successful on the American market" (104).

Toller dedicated *Pastor Hall* to the day "on which this drama can be played in Germany" (105). That day was 24 January 1947 when it was performed at the Deutsches Theater, Berlin, directed by Thomas Engel and designed by Heinrich Goertz, with music by Wolfgang Langhoff (106). This was believed at the time to be the World Premiere (Uraufführung) and this misinformation has frequently been repeated authoritatively ever since (107). The first performance was preceded by a commemorative speech by Günther Weisenborn, subsequently published, in which he remembered Toller as a lifelong fighter against war and as a successful public speaker (108).

The production was given with the earlier ending, apparently because only that version of the Henschel duplicated edition (109) was available and "by an unfortunate chance Toller's latest version of the piece was not known to the producers" (110). In the opinion of Harold Hurwitz the consequence was to place Toller's life and his significance for Germany in a false light.

> Toller's last word is therefore [viz. in the 2nd version] not a vague moral appeal. He shows an example which others can follow (111).

Nevertheless, the production, in spite of its comparatively short run of 33 performances, aroused considerable critical interest. Spalek lists and comments upon nine reviews, and the present writer has read press-cuttings of sixteen more, not listed by Spalek.

In this production Act II was, rightly, presented as "the heart of the drama" (112). Its "sinister setting" (113) dominated the whole play:

> The concentration camp was projected into the pastor's living-room like a giant shadow, as if disaster was already darkening the idyll (114).
>
> The middle act is entirely activist theatre as Toller himself called it into life. The fantastic back-cloth . . . which towers up above the walls of the rooms in the first and last acts stretches out as the back wall of a concentration camp which rotates on the revolving stage (115).

The projection of the barbed wire fence presides over all three acts:

> It is a striking symbol (116).

The two principal adverse criticisms brought against the play were the colourlessness of the language (117), — the result of Toller's having lived in exile — and an alleged weakness of form:

> What Toller puts round the concentration camp act, is of course theatrical artifice (118).

Although there were critics who found it "superficially observed, not a 'Toller' piece" (119), who referred to the "milieu often not distinctly constructed because seen from the distance" (120), and who pointed out that Toller, prophetic though he was, did not experience the final horrors of war and mass-murder (121), the majority reacted positively, even to the extent of crediting Toller with the ability to dramatise what he had not experienced:

> Toller has seen it, although he was not present (122).
> Truth, not routine-theatre, because everything is experienced and suffered (123).

It was "the most shattering event in the Berlin Theatre since the end of the war" (124). Walter Lemming (125) also makes the point that the concentration camp is so horribly realistic that you might believe Toller had been a victim in one. Friedrich Luft also said that the material was "shattering", and,

> where it is a matter of homesickness, where the guards' whips batter the many victims into a spiritual unity, there was authenticity and the drama of itself seized the conscience directly (126).

It was a play that *had* to be performed (127); it was not just a memory, but had contemporary importance: it taught that in the divided post-war Germany,

> all well-intentioned inhabitants of this miserable "camp" called "Germany" should reach out the hand to each other, as the Parson Hall and the worker Hofer do in Toller's play (128).

It taught that:

> It is always necessary to comprehend the inconceivable. *That* was possible in Germany. It must never again be possible

> . . . The play's purpose is only attained when every member of the audience understands why it is being performed today (129).

Mario Thomas, critical of the play in many respects, concludes on this note:

> Truly he never ran away from his time and remained the constant activist of his period — yet Ernst Toller was also artist enough always to hit upon the universal in the contemporary, to comment upon the deprivation of heart and freedom throughout the centuries and to portray man's longing for salvation. *Pastor Hall* from another hand — perhaps it would be unbearable (130).

Pastor Hall was produced again in East Germany on 1 May (May Day) of the same year by the Landestheater Rudolstadt-Arnstadt, in Rudolstadt. The Director was Martin Homburg and the Designer Max Pohle (131). It was not well reviewed. The performance was inferior, the setting inappropriate, and the director and actors were blamed as being not equal to the task in ideological and artistic respects. As a result the play was said to be turned into "a tragicomedy, a pathetic farce". The revised version of the ending was used and some reviewers disapproved of this for ideological reasons (132) (133).

For a production in West Germany *Pastor Hall* had to wait until 1983, when it was produced in Osnabrück under the direction of Goswin Moniac. The production apparently vacillated between a realistic period piece and expressionistic "confession" drama (134). Perhaps for this reason one critic thought the play too schematised (135), while another thought it only had a *succès d'estime* (136). A critic remarked on accuracy of detail despite Toller's exile and saw the play as a forerunner of those of Rolf Hochhuth (137). This, if the comparison is made, particularly with *Der Stellvertreter*, is an insight with considerable truth in it. Too few critics and scholars have drawn attention to Toller as innovator (138) and this critic indicates a real anticipation by him of some post-war drama.

The most enthusiastic critic, Sonja Luyken (139) said that this "Trouvaille in Osnabrück" *must* be played in Germany,

> because it makes the present-day audience familiar with everyday life in the Nazi period, with the conditions of life — and does this without false rhetoric, without sentimentality and without feelings of resentment — but excitingly (140).

A few passages, such as the visit of Ida and Christine to the concentration camp were cut as being untrue to reality: Toller's exile accounted for them. It was not "heroic drama" (*Heldendrama*) but a play about people such as there were many of at that time and always will be.

> Nothing is tear-jerking, nothing is exaggerated, there are neither angels nor devils in it (141).

The play was well received even by those who came with reservations:

> And in the auditorium: great and justifiable approval, even from members of the audience who at first regarded the play with scepticism (142).

Luyken evidently did not know the earlier ending and imagined that in it *Pastor Hall* survived! The ending used, however, is, she says "positive":

> The man has in the end become what he already was within: upright. To paraphrase Hebbel's Notebook:
> "What a man can become, he already is" (143).

V

CONCLUSION

CONCLUSION

Der Riß der Zeit ging mitten durch sein Herz

wrote Walter Mehring of Toller in 1952 (1): and not only through his heart, but through his entire oeuvre, and above all through his plays, — for drama is the genre *par excellence* of inner and outer division and conflict. His plays, like his life, present a chronological paradigm of the fissures that for two decades tore apart not only their author but German society, and ultimately, in World War II, the comity of nations. In them, as in Toller's life, the tragic course of German history from World War I until the debacle of 1939, can be traced.

First of all the Jew in *Die Wandlung*, divided by religion and culture from his compatriots, seeks identity with the German, but when the price of this is to identify with German militarism, he identifies himself instead with the underdogs of German society and the anti-militaristic proponents of socialist revolution. But the socialist synthesis thus achieved out of the antitheses of the first play is found in the second to contain, as in Toller's own Munich experiences, its own inherent conflicts and contradictions: the ethical values relevant to the individual and leading to non-violence and self-sacrifice on the one hand, and the political aspirations of the masses, which are to be achieved by violent revolution, on the other. Sonja's attempted synthesis:

Masse soll Gemeinschaft sein
(The masses should be community)

(2)

is not fulfilled in this play or subsequently, any more than the conflict was ever resolved in Toller's own life.

The irreconcilability of the sexual urge as pure instinct and the restraints upon it demanded by organised society is not a problem peculiar to any time or place, but certain circumstances, such as imprisonment, can bring it into sharp focus. Already in his first two plays Toller had used marital and sexual relationships to highlight political and moral issues; now he left the central ethical problem of *Masse Mensch* unresolved and turned in deceptively lighter vein to this universal and perpetual conflict.

The principal ethical problems of *Masse Mensch* are examined again with greater complexity in *Die Maschinenstürmer*, whose setting in early nineteenth-century England evidently did not dilute its contemporary message for German audiences, and whose further theme of the social implications of advancing technology had obvious significance at that time. By now Toller was avoiding any facile synthesis of irreconcilable political and moral antitheses, and in the tragedy of *Hinkemann* (originally, we remember, *Der deutsche Hinkemann*) he squarely faces the existence of tragically insoluble problems and, by implication, of political theses and antitheses whose synthesis can be achieved, if at all, only through human suffering and tragedy. The play therefore does not only refer back to the consequences of World War I but is obliquely prophetic of World War II in that Toller, in recognising that problems and conflicts incapable of solution are essential elements in the human condition, was admitting, whether consciously or not, that the already intensifying strife between the parties of left and right in the Weimar Republic might not be soluble through rational political means, and it is therefore no surprise that his next play, *Der entfesselte Wotan*, is a bitterly satirical warning of the increasing strength of the irrational forces which were leading the country towards fascist dictatorship, nor that his first play after his release from prison, *Hoppla, wir leben!*, shows a Minister of the Weimar Republic assassinated simultaneously, as it were, by representatives of the extreme right and left. No other playwright of the period dramatised the internal contradictions of the politics of the Weimar Republic with Toller's acuteness, accuracy and tragic understanding.

Through the deaths of his Munich colleagues, the injustices he saw inflicted on his fellow-prisoners, and through his own five-year incarceration, Toller was made painfully aware both of the political bias of 'justice' in the Germany of his time, and of the fortuitousness of 'justice' in general, and the last two plays written before his exile reflect his awareness of the conflict between justice and political expediency (*Feuer aus den Kesseln*), and of the arbitrariness both of the causes and of the effects of imprisonment (*Die blinde Göttin*) (3).

During his exile Toller shared the moral and political concerns and conflicts of other exiles and of his British and American friends, and tried imaginatively to share the struggles, sufferings and sacrifices of his anti-Nazi friends still in Germany. His deep-rooted pacifism and his conviction that Nazism must be destroyed, by war if necessary, were impossible to reconcile and repeated in new terms the stances of Sonja and The Nameless. The very faults of his 'pacifist' play, *Nie wieder Friede*, reveal this fissure in Toller's mind and heart, and though *Pastor Hall* is unequivocally an anti-Nazi play, the Pastor can in the end meet Nazism only as Toller himself did — with his own death.

Thus Toller expresses, certainly more comprehensively than any of his contemporaries in drama, the rifts and conflicts of the period. Except for the two plays of his exile the texture of every play is rich in detail, and the major dialectical themes already outlined gather round themselves a host of related topics, such as: the generation gap; the position of the artist in society; the experience of war in the front-line and in the military hospital; poverty; prostitution; abortion; factory conditions; both the humdrum and the rhetoric of politics; marriage; sexual cunning; the exploitation of child-labour; trade-unionism; sexual prejudices; the everyday lives of working men and women; the life of the 'Grand Hotel'; drugs; the impact of radio and the future impact of television; courts of law; tensions between lovers; small-town pettiness; naval life on ship and on shore; the machinations of financiers and politicians . . . the list could be extended. Toller's plays not only dramatise those major problems of the period which his own life embodied, but, through all their varieties of style, are rooted in the real lives of real people, and present a spectrum or cross-section of Weimar Germany.

Just as the themes of the plays epitomise the dominant problems and conflicts of the period, so too the varieties of style, both theatrical and linguistic, are effectively a panorama of the drama of the period, with Toller appearing sometimes in the rôle of innovator, sometimes in that of consummator of a style or technique. Sometimes these rôles are combined, as in *Die Wandlung*, where Toller draws creatively on the existing style of literary Expressionism and at the same time uses his theatrical imagination with an originality that enabled Karl-Heinz Martin to present the play as a new kind of genuinely theatrical Expressionism. Martin's celebrated production could not have come into existence save on the twin bases of Toller's conceptions of such scenes as *Transportzüge, Zwischen den Drahtverhauen* and *Die Krüppel*, and on the language of these scenes — especially their rhythms. Thus *Die Wandlung* can fairly be regarded as a model Expressionist play and Toller as much as Karl-Heinz Martin as responsible for its *theatrical* expression.

Toller, as one of the first to write works specially for use by the amateur Speaking Choirs, was similarly innovatory in the choral passages of *Masse Mensch*, and this play, so suitable for the *Jeßner Steps* used by Fehling, becomes, like its predecessor, a model of its kind. Once more Toller draws on existing traditions — the subtle re-creation of a classical form, and the Strindbergian 'dream' scenes — while at the same time developing from Expressionism his own style of language and rhythm.

He was emphatically no mere epigone of his expressionist forerunners, and when both the material and the intended medium of *Die Rache des verhöhnten Liebhabers* demanded decorative language expressed in elegant rhyming couplets, so as to be evocative of earlier times, the time of the original novella and that of the Blütezeit of puppet theatres, he met this stylistic challenge with a relaxed nonchalance — a considerable achievement amid the tensions and squalor of prison life.

As part of the major shift in the arts, including the art of the theatre, from Expressionism to the New Sobriety, verse as a dramatic medium was being succeeded in mainstream live theatre by prose, and Toller contributed to this trend in *Die Maschinenstürmer* in which he moved with apparently casual ease, Shakespearean fashion, from verse to prose and from prose to verse, his vocabulary, sentence structure and rhythmic patterns all showing a developing flexibility. In this play Toller also employs montage as a major structural principle which he uses naturally, without needing the support of theory, even before Brecht had consciously adopted and described the technique.

Prose now rapidly became established as the principal medium for drama, and Toller evolved for *Hinkemann* a strong, flexible prose style capable of moving between the colloquial conversation of a workmen's bar and the requirements of an expressionist 'dream'. No verse was needed even for the most intense scenes.

Unlike many dramatists of the 1920s and 1930s upon whom naturalistic prose exerted a stranglehold, Toller, after achieving the austere theatrical style appropriate to *Hinkemann*, was never confined within the limitations of naturalistic, or even apparently naturalistic prose and its associated style of staging. Instead he next introduced his satire of the burgeoning force of National Socialism with a swingeing Wagnerian parody in verse, complete with fire-breathing black steed, cowboy lasso and hunting-horns:

> Was einst Tragodie, werd zur Posse
> (Let what was once tragedy become farce) (4)

In the same play Toller wishes if possible to introduce a film sequence which he wants to be accompanied by a barrel-organ and to glide past like the grotesque dream-charade of a streetballad (ein Moritat-Traumspuk), thus anticipating both Piscator and Brecht (5), and though *Der entfesselte Wotan* is not a 'musical', Toller uses music both here and elsewhere in the play as an integral element in the satire (6).

In collaboration with Piscator, Toller was a pioneer of multiple setting. Their somewhat stormy partnership represents Toller's one experiment in "Director's Theatre"; but time has proved that the basic strength of *Hoppla, wir leben!* lies in the author's own text: in Toller's writing, his use of language.

In no play was Toller so far in advance of his time as in *Feuer aus den Kesseln*. In spite of the changes made from the source material, this is a documentary drama that anticipates those of the post-World War II period, and in this he demonstrates his ability not only to give documentary sources dramatic form but to convert their language to that of dramatic dialogue.

His technical inventiveness, for example in his use of the living puppet, and his control of language, were still developing when he wrote *Die blinde Göttin*, and but for his exile would doubtless have continued to develop, but though the two plays of exile still reveal his experimental abilities, their language has lost contact with a German-speaking audience, and it is for this reason primarily that, in spite of their biographical and ideological interest, they are to be regarded as inferior to the others.

Apart from these two, Toller's plays are as stageworthy today as they ever were. *Die Wandlung*, admittedly, in view of the naivety of its conclusion, might stand only as a period piece, but in all the rest the particulars have been given universal significance, and because their strength is inherent in the playwright's language — in the actual words spoken — rather than in any particular theatrical styles or tricks of production, they are as relevant today as when they were written and, as the all-too-few revivals prove, as effective. They should be as integral a part of the repertoire of the modern theatre as those of Brecht, and although, as with Brecht, much must be lost in translation, they should have an established place not only in the repertoire of the German theatre, but of the European. It is regrettable that even today there is no complete translation of the plays available in English, though one is in preparation.

Toller's principal themes — militarism and pacifism, the problems of ethnic minorities, conflicts of ends and means whether in achieving socialism or in destroying totalitarianism, the sexual drive and social restraints upon it, trade unionism, technological development and consequent unemployment, the tragedy of the insoluble in the human condition, demagogy and dictatorship, justice and injustice — these are living issues and likely to remain so. Toller treats them with intellectual passion, in well and always appropriately constructed plays conceived and executed in terms of the theatre, but written in language which not only provides a 'blueprint for the stage' but also has intrinsic literary worth able to be reinterpreted in the theatrical modes of successive generations.

No simple label can be attached to Toller or to his plays without devaluing both him and them. As a practising playwright he is unusually versatile, but his oeuvre is given unity by the passionate humanity which runs through it as a continuous thread.

However, the tendency to belittle Toller's achievement as a dramatist dies hard. Even the close relationship between his life and his work is used as an argument to underrate the latter:

> If he possessed greatness, it is possibly not to be sought first of all primarily in his printed oeuvre (7).

Because it is difficult to encapsulate his work in a few unambiguous phrases, because he was a lower middle-class provincial Jew, he is alleged in an authoritative study of 1983 to have been,

> in almost every respect an amateur, if not a dilletante (8).

The present study has had the aim of showing through cumulative evidence, that Toller's plays, far from being the work of an amateur, establish him as arguably *the* representative German dramatist of the two decades 1919–1939, and that through his themes, the versatility of his methods, his traditional and innovatory skills, and finally through the quality of his writing for the theatre, he showed

> the very age and body of the time
> his form and pressure.
>
> *(Hamlet III ii)*

NOTES

I INTRODUCTION

1. Ernst Toller was born 1.12.1893 in Samotschin, Posen. He hanged himself in the Mayflower Hotel, Central Park, New York, on 22.5.1939.
2. Richard Dove, *The place of Toller in English Socialist Theatre 1924–1939*. German Life and Letters 38: 2. January 1985 p. 125.
3. Großmann, Stefan: *Der Hochverräter Ernst Toller. Die Geschichte eines Prozesses*. Berlin, Rowohlt, 1919. (Spalek 1071). Reprinted in: *Ernst Toller: Prosa, Briefe, Dramen, Gedichte*. Rowohlt 1961.
4. GW2 p. 50.
5. PBDG p. 488.
   Nie hat er die Menge zu den Taten gedrängt, für welche er sie innerlich nicht reif gefunden. In der Stunde des scheinbaren Siegs in München, als Leviné und Lewien von dem gefährlichsten Applaus betrunken wurden, ist in seinem Kopf der bitterste Zweifel eingezogen.
6. *Ernst Toller und seine Bühnenwerke. Eine Einführung von Fritz Droop*. Schneider Bühnenführer. Berlin & Leipzig 1922.
7. ibid pp. 12/13.
   Tollers Dichtung aber ist die Beichte eines Menschen, der mit sich selbst in heißem Kampfe rang und der uns aus einem sterbenden Jahrhundert in ein neues Zeitalter führt.
8. ibid p. 14.
   . . . sein Traum ist die ideale Anarchie, die uns Dehmels prophetischer Geist verhieß.
9. ibid p. 25.
   Die Phantasie Tollers ist im Schmerz verankert.
10. ibid p. 30.
    Masse Mensch gehört nicht zu den Werken, die sich auf eine theatralische Handlung stützen. Das Drama wurzelt ganz im Gedanklichen, und es ist schwer, das tiefe Ethos, das den Anschlag gibt, in einer Inhaltsskizze anzudeuten.
11. ibid p. 43: kein Tendenzstück.

12. ibid p. 14.
    . . . das Mechanische auf Erden muß dem Seelischen untergeordnet werden.
13. ibid p. 15.
14. ibid p. 17.
15. Two other studies appeared in 1924: Paul Signer (Spalek 1079) & Herman Lieberman (Spalek 1072).
16. v. Spalek 1080.
17. William Anthony Willibrand, *Ernst Toller and his Ideology*. Iowa City 1945. University of Iowa Humanistic Studies Vol. VII. (Spalek 1082).
18. Martin Reso, *Der gesellschaftlich-ethische Protest im dichterischen Werk Ernst Tollers*. Unpub. Ph. D Thesis. Univ. of Jena 1957. (Spalek 1077).
    Hans Marnette. *Untersuchungen zum Inhalt-Form-Problem in Ernst Tollers Dramen*. Unpub Ph. D Thesis, Pädagogische Hochschule Potsdam, 1963.
19. Marnette p. 4.
    Unsere marxistische Literaturwissenschaft geht in ihrer Forschung von den Bedürfnissen des sozialistischen Aufbaus in unserer Republik aus und orientiert daher ihre Arbeit entsprechend den Empfehlungen der führenden Kraft in diesem Aufbau, der Sozialistischen Einheitspartei Deutschlands.
20. In *The German Quarterly* XXXIX, No. 4 Nov. 1966, pp. 581–598.
21. John M. Spalek, *Ernst Toller and his Critics. A Bibliography*. Univ. of Virginia 1968. Reprinted by Haskell House Publishers Ltd, New York, 1973.
22. Spalek: *Ernst Toller, The Need for a New Estimate* pp. 589–591.
23. Tankred Dorst, *Toller*. Suhrkamp Verlag, Frankfurt/M, 1968.
24. Already in 1966 Dorst had published an anthology of material on the Munich Soviet Republic: *Die Münchner Räterepublik. Zeugnisse und Kommentar. Herausgegeben von Tankred Dorst*. Suhrkamp Verlag, Frankfurt/M 1966.
25. Ernst Toller, *Gesammelte Werke*, in 5 Volumes. Edited by John M Spalek and Wolfgang Frühwald, Hanser Verlag, München, Wien, 1978 (cited as GW 1–5).

    The title *Gesammelte Werke (Collected Works)* is misleading as the collection is by no means complete. Major omissions are: *Die blinde Göttin, Justiz: Erlebnisse* (except for 16 pages of extracts from this book of 145 pages), *Quer Durch* (except for the section *Arbeiten*

and about 14 pages of extracts on Toller's visits to USSR and USA), *Vormorgen* (containing some of Toller's best poems), the *Chorwerke.* His short stories are not represented, and we have to be satisfied with selections from his critical and political articles and speeches.
Die Rache des verhöhnten Liebhabers is also omitted.

26. Malcolm Pittock, *Ernst Toller,* Twayne Publishers, Boston, 1979.
27. Richard Dove, *Revolutionary Socialism in the Work of Ernst Toller.* Utah Studies in Literature and Linguistics, Vol 26. Peter Lang, New York, Berne, Frankfurt am Main 1986.
28. ibid p. 8.
29. *Arbeiten* in *Quer Durch,* 1930. GW1 p. 138.
Jeder Autor will in sein erstes Werk alles, was er weiß, alles was er erlebt hat, hineindrängen. Das tat ich auch.
30. GW1 p. 139. das Private, das Lyrische.
31. GW1 p. 137.
damals war er eine notwendige künstlerische Form.
32. ibid.
. . . wollte er diese Umwelt vom Wesen her neu gestalten . . . diese Umwelt . . . wollte er ändern, ihr ein gerechteres, helleres Gesicht geben.
33. The major exception is *Nie wieder Friede.*

II THE PLAYS: *DIE WANDLUNG* TO *DIE MASCHINENSTÜRMER*

Die Wandlung

1. Michael Ossar, *Anarchism in the Dramas of Ernst Toller,* Albany, State University of New York Press, 1980. p. 16.
2. Cf. Michel Bataillon: "Par sa fable, *Die Wandlung* apparaissait comme un *Erlebnis-Drama,* comme un *Ich-Drama.* Son économie interne, sa structure en faisait un *Stationen-Drama.* Par son éthique, son idéologie, elle était un *O Mensch-Drama".*
Michel Bataillon, *Die Wandlung de Toller. Un exemple de Stationen-Drama,* in *L'Expressionisme dans le Théatre Européen.* Paris 1971. Editions du Centre National de la Recherche Scientifique. pp. 153–175. p. 159.

3. G.W. 2 p. 360. 1917 war das Drama (viz. *Die Wandlung*) für mich Flugblatt.
4. ibid. Wenn politisches Flugblatt Wegweiser, geboren aus Not der äußeren Wirklichkeit, Gewissensnot, Fülle der inneren Kraft bedeutet, so mag *Die Wandlung* getrost als *Flugblatt* gelten.
5. It is not possible to determine exactly when the later scenes were actually written down: Toller tells us (GW2 p. 96) that verses 'formed themselves in his mind' in the prison yard, and that these were the *Lieder der Gefangenen* and the last scenes of *Die Wandlung*.
6. Seit Schiller's *Räubern*, seit *Kabale und Liebe* war das Theater nie mehr so Tribüne zeitlichen Geschehens gewesen, so umwogt vom Streit und Widerstreit der öffentlichen Meinung. GW1 p. 128.
7. Spalek 65, & GW2 p. 351
8. Das Drama ist der geistige Ausdruck unserer Zeit. Der heutige Mensch liest das Drama, wie man gestern noch die Erzählung las, als fesselndes, einfaches Buch. GW2 p. 351.
9. Diese Arbeit entstand in ihrer ersten Niederschrift 1917, im dritten Jahr des Erdgemetzels. GW2 p. 360.
10. ibid.
11. GW4 p. 84.
12. Rosemarie A.J. Altenhofer, *Ernst Tollers Politische Dramatik*. Ph. D. Thesis, Washington University Dept. of Germanic Languages and Literature. 1976 pp. 26ff.
13. *Außerhalb der Universität* muß Dozenten *und* Studierenden unbeschränkte politische Bewegungsfreiheit zustehen.
    Frühwald & Spalek *Der Fall Toller: Kommentar und Materialien*. Munich. Carl Hanser Verlag, 1979, p. 30. (cited as 'Fall').
14. Wir wissen, daß er kein Programm darstellt. Das ist auch nicht unsre Absicht. Fall p. 32.
15. Jeder wirke, ausströmend Seele und Geist, als Mensch zum Menschen. GW1 p. 32.
16. Nur aus innerlicher Mensch-Wandlung kann die Gemeinschaft, die wir erstreben, erwachsen. ibid.
17. Wir fordern Revolutionierung der Gesinnung! GW1 p. 34.
18. . . . Äußerung unklarer Köpfe ohne geschichtliche und politische Bildung . . . *Deutsche Tageszeitung* 11.12.'17. v. Fall p. 33.
19. Was ich tue, tue ich nicht aus Not *allein*, nicht aus Leid am *häßlichen* Alltagsgeschehen *allein*, nicht aus Empörung über politische und wirtschaftliche Ordnung *allein*. Das alles sind Gründe, aber nicht die einzigen. Aus meiner . . . lebendigen Fülle

heraus kämpfe ich. Ich bin kein religiöser Ekstatiker, der nur sich und Gott und nicht die Menschen sieht, ich bin kein Opportunist, der nur äußerliche Einrichtungen sieht . . . GW1 p. 34–35.

20. Zu einer Erkenntnis, wie ich sie verstehe, muß man durch Not, Leiden an seiner Fülle, gekommen sein, muß geglaubt haben *entwurzelt* zu sein, muß mit dem Leben gespielt und mit dem Tode getanzt, muß am Intellekt gelitten und ihn durch den Geist überwunden — muß *mit dem Menschen gerungen haben.* GW1 p. 35.
21. In *letzten* seelischen Dingen müssen wir unsere Einsamkeit, d. h. unser Alleinsein mit Gott nicht "tragisch", sondern *freudig* empfinden. GW1 p. 36.
22. Zum Schluß nur das noch, daß ich in meinem innersten Kern eine Ruhe spüre, die *ist* und mir Freiheit gibt, daß ich in größter Unruhe leben, daß ich gegen Schmutz oder beschränkten Unverstand hitzig und erregt ankämpfe kann und mir diese innerste Ruhe noch bleibt. GW1 pp. 36–7.
23. Ossar *op cit* p. 46.
24. Gustav Landauer, *Aufruf zum Sozialismus*. Berlin 1911, pp. vii–viii. (cited as *Aufruf*).
25. Der Sozialismus ist ein Bestreben, mit Hülfe eines Ideals eine neue Wirklichkeit zu schaffen. ibid. p. 1.
26. . . . keinerlei Fortschritt, keinerlei Technik, keinerlei Virtuosität wird uns Heil und Segen bringen; nur aus dem Geiste, nur aus der Tiefe unsrer inneren Not und unsres inneren Reichtums wird die große Wendung kommen die wir heute Sozialismus nennen. ibid p. 12.
27. ibid. p. 6.
28. Der Vater des Marxismus ist nicht das Geschichtsstudium ist auch nicht Hegel, ist weder Smith noch Ricardo noch einer der Sozialisten vor Marx, ist auch kein revolutionär-demokratischer Zeitzustand, ist noch weniger der Wille und das Verlangen nach Kultur und Schönheit unter den Menschen. *Der Vater des Marxismus ist der Dampf.*

    Alte Weiber prophezeien aus dem Kaffeesatz. Karl Marx prophezeite aus dem Dampf. ibid. p. 51.
29. Hunger, Hände und Erde sind da, alle drei sind von Natur aus da. Und außer ihnen brauchen die Menschen nur was *zwischen* ihnen hergeht anständig zu ordnen. ibid. p. 141.
30. Die Erde müssen wir wieder haben. Die Gemeinden des Sozialismus müssen den Boden neu aufteilen. Die Erde ist

niemandes Eigentum. Die Erde sei herrenlos; dann nur sind die Menschen frei . . .
Auch die Aufhebung des Eigentums wird im Wesentlichen eine Umwandlung unsres Geistes sein . . .
Der Geist wird sich Formen schaffen; Formen der Bewegung, nicht der Starrheit . . .
Land und *Geist* also – das ist die Lösung des Sozialismus . . .
Der Kampf des Sozialismus ist ein Kampf um den Boden; die soziale Frage ist eine agrarische Frage. ibid pp. 143–151.

31. FRIEDRICH (*im Fieber*): Wo seid ihr andern . . . o der Wüstenflugsand . . . gekörnter Nebel . . . nicht ruhen . . . weiter . . . kenne dich nicht . . . wer bist du . . . Ahasver . . . Armseliger . . . schleich dich zurück . . . in alpkeuchende Städte, hier findest du nicht Höhlen . . . ich wandre nicht mit dir . . . nein (*schreit*) nein. GW2 p. 28.
32. Roy Pascal, *From Naturalism to Expressionism. German Literature and Society 1880–1918*, London, Weidenfeld and Nicholson, 1973. Especially Chap. 4: *The Jew as Alien and Bourgeois.*
33. ibid p. 67.
34. ibid p. 67.
35. ibid.
36. ibid p. 73.
37. ibid p. 74.
38. . . . Das Vaterland weiß Ihre Dienste zu schätzen. Es sendet Ihnen durch mich das Kreuz. Fremder waren Sie unsrem Volk, nun haben Sie sich Bürgerrechte erworben. GW2 p. 29.
39. . . . Durch zehntausend Tote gehöre ich zu ihnen. Warum quirlt nicht Lachen? Ist das Befreiung? Ist das die große Zeit? Sind das die großen Menschen? (*Augen starr gerade aus*)
    Nun gehöre ich zu ihnen.
    (*Dunkel*). ibid.
40. / Wir könnten uns die positive Branche nennen, / Die negative ist die Rüstungsindustrie. / Mit andern Worten: Wir Vertreter der Synthese, / Die Rüstungsindustrie geht analytisch vor. GW2 pp. 30 & 34.
41. Brecht *Gesammelte Gedichte,* Frankfurt / M, Edition Suhrkamp, 1967. Vol 1. pp. 256–7.
42. Marianne Kesting, *Brecht,* Hamburg, Rowolt, 1959, p. 14.
43. Ohnmächtig, junger Mann, beim Werk der Liebe, / Wie wärs denn draußen, auf dem Feld der Schlacht. GW2 p. 31.
44. Man fand Sie an einen Baum gebunden. Der einzig Überlebende.

FRIEDRICH: Nicht an ein Kreuz . . . Der einzig Überlebende. GW2 p. 29.

45. Wedekind, *Frühlings Erwachen,* Stuttgart, Reclam 1971. *Nachwort* von George Hensel p. 75 (and the frequently reproduced photograph of the scene).
46. Deuteronomy 30.19.
47. Sie kleiner Tod! / Sie Heuchelprotz mit militärisch aufgestutzten Phrasen. / Empfehlen Sie mich Ihrem Herrn, dem Kriegssytem. / GW2 p. 18.
48. Zu Gott, der Geist und Liebe und Kraft ist, Zu Gott, der in der Menschheit lebt. GW2 p. 40.
49. Marnette: 'Die folgenden drei Szenen bilden eine Einheit, sie enthalten in Traumbildern die "Menschenwerden" Friedrichs'.
50. e.g. Adolf Löhr, treasurer of the Neue Freie Volksbühne, 1897–99, was such a man. v. Cecil W. Davies, *Theatre for the People. The Story of the Volksbühne,* Manchester 1977, p. 65.
51. Als ob ich eine schwere Grabesplatte fortgewälzt / Und auferstehe. GW2 p. 46.
52. Marnette *op cit* p. 186.
53. Ich weiß den Weg zur Arbeitsstätte / Nun weiß ich ihn. GW2 p. 46
54. . . . solange wir in uns Individuen nicht das Menschtum gefunden und neu geschaffen haben. Vom Individuum beginnt alles; und am Individuum liegt alles.
Landauer, *Aufruf,* Berlin 1911, p. 154; also Berlin 1919, p. 145. Also quoted by Marnette p. 186.
55. Seit einst die Nachricht kam, / Der große Hammer habe ihn zermalmt, / Stöhnt sie in jeder Nacht, / Das elfte Kind, die sie noch mit sich trug, / Erbrach sie – war natürlich tot, / Ein großes Glück. GW2 p. 41.
56. DER NÄCHTLICHE BESUCHER: . . . Beim ersten Anblick wähnst mit Freude du / Oho – hier blüht ja ein Gefängnis – / Streng deine Augen an! / Schon sind wir angekommen! / Siehst du das Schild? / Du zitterst – laß sich lesen – / Ich betrug dich nicht: / *Die große Fabrik,* GW2 p. 43.
57. Fabrikkasernen, Mietskasernen, die Kasernen der Bureaukraten, die Kasernen der Soldaten . . . and "die weiteren Kasernen": die Arbeitshäuser, die Gefängnisse und Zuchthäuser, und die Geschlechtshäuser, in denen die Prostituierten kaserniert sind. Landauer, *Aufruf,* passim.
58. . . . die Dampfmaschine, die die Arbeitsmaschinen und die

arbeitenden Menschen bei sich, dem Kraftzentrum, in der Nähe haben muß und darum die großen Fabrikbetriebe und die raffinierte Arbeitsteilung geschaffen hat . . . Die technischen Notwendigkeiten der Dampfmaschine also waren es, die die großen Fabrikkasernen und Mietskasernen erzeugt haben.
Op cit p. 51 (1911).

59. Minutenlang Dröhnen hämmernden Kolben, Sausen wirbelnder Räder, Zischen glühenflüßiger Metallströme . . . GW2 p. 43.
60. Der Geist zieht sich in den Einzelnen zurück . . . jetzt lebt er in Einzelnen, Genialen . . . , die ohne Volk sind: vereinsamte Denker, Dichter und Künstler, die haltlos, wie entwurzelt, fast in die Luft stehen. Landauer, *Aufruf* (1919) p. 8. Quoted Marnette p. 186.
61. 2. BERGSTEIGER: Zu weit schon gingst du / Denk an dich - / Ich habe Furcht um dich.
1. BERSTEIGER: Weil ich mich nicht verlassen will / Verlaß ich dich . . . / Leb wohl! . . . GW2 p. 54.
62. But unprotected, here on the mountains of the heart. L. Forster (ed). *Penguin Book of German Verse.* Harmondsworth 1957 p. 407.
63. *Aufruf* (1911) p. 49.
64. . . . reden aus dem Geist heraus zum Volke und vom kommenden Volke. ibid (1919) p. 8
65. Und diesen isolierten Wenigen, in die sich der Geist geflüchtet hat, . . . entsprechen die voneinander Isolierten, die atomisierten Vielen, denen nur die Geistlosigkeit geblieben ist und die Öde und das Elend:
Die Massen, die das Volk heißen, die aber nur ein Haufen Losgerissener, Preisgegebener sind . . . die Massen, in die der Geist wieder strömen muß. ibid.
66. Was soll uns Bildung, da der Geist gemartet wird? GW2 p. 51
67. Volk ist aber für ihn Masse. Denn er weiß nichts vom Volk. GW2 p. 50.
68. Das Volk ist Gott! . . . Gott ist eine Maschine. Darum ist das Volk eine Maschine. Er wird sich trotzdem freuen an den schwingenden Hebeln, wirbelnden Rädern, hämmernden Kolben. ibid.
69. Geist ist etwas, was in den Herzen und Seelenleibern der Einzelnen in gleicher Weise wohnt; was mit natürlicher Nötigung, als verbindende Eigenschaft, aus allen herausbricht und alle zum Bunde führt. Landauer, *Aufruf* (1919) p. 30.
70. ich . . . wünschte euch seelische Not. GW2 p. 50.
71. ich will, daß ihr reich seid, Lebenserfüllte. ibid.
72. . . . nur aus dem Geiste, aus der Tiefe unserer inneren Not und

unseres inneren Reichtums wird die große Wendung kommen, die wir heute Sozialismus nennen. *Aufruf* (1911) p. 12.

73. Ich weiß . . . Um dich, du Reicher, der du Geld anhäufst, und alle verachtest, die andern und dich selbst. GW2 p. 59.
74. Geht hin zu den Reichen und zeigt ihnen ihr Herz, das ein Schutthaufen ward. Doch seid gütig zu ihnen, dann auch sie sind Arme, Verirrte. GW2 p. 61.
75. Viel zu wenig weiß auch der Arbeiter, was für furchtbare, was für unwürdige und erdrückende Sorgen der Kapitalist hat; was für ein völlig unnötiges, ganz und gar unproduktives Quälen und Abracken ihm aufgeladen ist und viel zu wenig beachten die Arbeiter diese ähnlichkeit zwischen sich selbst und den Kapitalisten. *Aufruf* (1919) p. 94.
76. GW2 p. 60.
77. ibid.
78. see Marnette *op cit* p. 188.
79. *Aufruf* (1919), *Vorwort* p. X.
80. Spalek p. 79.
81. Marnette p. 161.
82. Hölderlin, *Gedichte*, ed. J. Schmidt, Frankfurt/Main, Insel Verlag 1984 p. 17ff.
83. Schmidt ibid. p. 299.
84. There! loathsome beasts creep murdering, spitting flame, on the earth. GW2 p. 9.
85. Heavy with dreams, blinking, we looked up
And heard the man crying out beside us. ibid.
86. ibid.
87. St John's Gospel 2. 19–20. Luther's version. Psalm 24.7. Luther's version.
88. *Christ*: Away with you! I wish this desecrated place to be given back to the worship of the Father!
Zadok: With what authority do you do that?
Voices: Through what miracles can you prove that you have the power to do that?
Christ: You demand miracles? Yes, I can give you one: Destroy this Temple here, and in three days I will build it again.
Ezekiel: They took forty-six years to build this temple, and you will build it up again it three days?
Passionsspiele Oberammergau 1634–1984. Textbuch. Oberammergau, 1984. p. 23 (Text written 1810–11. 1984 version).
89. Marnette *op cit* p. 161.

90. GW2 p. 8 (In the 1st Edition the 'motto' had a whole page – 4 – to itself, the poem *Aufrüttelung* occupying 5 & 6).
91. Tollers *Wandlung* ist kein Revolutionsdrama.
    Marnette *op cit* p. 189.
92. Die Arbeiterklasse . . . wird von Toller überhaupt nicht gestaltet. ibid.
93. Die Kritik am Krieg bleibt abstrakt und gleitet zum Teil ins Irrationale ab. ibid.
94. ibid.
95. Toller *Eine Jugend in Deutschland,* Chap X passim.
96. As is Landauer's *Aufruf.*
97. Wolfgang Rothe, *Ernst Toller,* Reinbek bei Hamburg 1983, p. 7ff.
98. Im Jahre 1834 siehet es aus, als würde die Bibel Lügen gestraft. Es sieht aus, als hätte Gott die Bauern und Handwerker am fünften Tage und die Fürsten und Vornehmen am sechsten gemacht, und als hätte der Herr zu diesen gesagt: "Herrschet über alles Getier, das auf Erden kriecht", und hätte die Bauern und Bürger zum Gewürm gezählt . . . .
    In Deutschland stehet es jetzt, wie der Prophet Micha schreibt, Kap. 7, V. 3 and 4: "Die Gewaltigen raten nach ihrem Mutwillen, Schaden zu tun, und drehen es, wie sie es wollen. Der Beste unter ihnen ist wie ein Dorn, und der Redlichste wie eine Hecke". . . Ihr Bautet die Zwingburgen, dann stürzt ihr sie und bauet der Freiheit Haus. Dann könnt ihr eure Kinder frei taufen mit dem Wasser des Lebens. Und . . . wachet und rüstet euch im Geiste und betet ihr selbst und lehrt eure Kinder beten: "Herr, zerbrich den Stecken unserer Treiber und laß dein Reich zu uns kommen – das Reich der Gerechtigkeit. Amen".
    Gesammelte Werke pp. 169, 173, 181. v. Bibliog. (lst & 3rd begin & end the pamphlet; all probably written by Pastor Weidig, Büchner's collaborator, with his approval).
99. Schiller *Sämtliche Werke,* Munich, Hanser Verlag, 1967, Vol V p. 818. The lecture was given in Mannheim, 26.6.1784 and published in *Heft 1* of *Rheinische Thalia,* 1785. When he republished it in *Kleinere prosaische Schriften, 4. Teil* (Leipzig, 1802) he omitted the original introduction and altered the title, significantly to, *Die Schaubühne als moralische Anstalt betrachtet (The Theatre considered as a moral insititution).*
100. Menschlichkeit und Duldung fangen an, der herrschende Geist unsrer Zeit zu werden; ihre Strahlen sind bis in die Gerichtssäle und noch weiter – in das Herz unsrer Fürsten gedrungen. Wie

Anteil an diesem göttlichen Werk gehört unsern Bühnen? Sind sie es nicht, die den Menschen mit dem Menschen bekannt machten und das geheime Räderwerk aufdeckten, nach welchem es handelt?
ibid. p. 828.

101. Eine merkwürdige Klasse von Menschen hat Ursache, dankbarer als alle übrigen gegen die Bühne zu sein. Hier hören die Großen der Welt, was sie nie oder selten hören – Wahrheit; was sie nie oder selten sehen, sehen sie hier – den Menschen. ibid p. 828.
102. Die Schaubühne ist der gemeinschaftliche Kanal, in welchen von dem denkenden bessern Teile des Volks das Licht der Weisheit herunterströmt und von da aus in milderen Strahlen durch den ganzen Staat sich verbreitet. ibid p. 828.
103. Ich gehe in die Streikversammlungen, ich möchte helfen, irgend etwas tun, ich verteile, weil ich glaube, daß diese Verse, aus dem Schrecken des Krieges geboren, ihn treffen und anklagen, Kriegsgedichte unter die Frauen, die Lazarett- und Krüppelszenen aus meinem Drama *Die Wandlung*. GW4 p. 88.
104. Schiller *op cit* p. 824. *Cinna* by Corneille. The reference is to Act V Sc. 3. *Franz von Sickingen* (1481–1523). Schiller is referring to a play of that name concerning which the Intendant of the Mannheim Theatre, von Dalberg, asked his opinion in September 1783. (Also the title of a play by Ferdinand Lassalle).
105. Ich ging in die Versammlungen Eisners, in denen Arbeiter, Frauen, junge Menschen nach dem Weg suchten, der den Frieden bringt, das Volk rettet. In diesen Versammlungen sah ich Arbeitergestalten, denen ich bisher nicht begegnet war, Männer von nüchternem Verstand, sozialer Einsicht, großem Lebenswissen, gehärtetem Willen, Sozialisten, die ohne Rücksicht auf Vorteile des Tages der Sache dienten, an die sie glaubten. GW4 p87–88.
106. Fritz Martini, *Deutsche Literaturgeschichte*. Stuttgart, A Kröner Verlag, 1965. p. 390.
107. Die Kunst hat es mit dem Leben, dem innern und äußern, zu thun, und man kann wohl sagen, daß sie beides zugleich darstellt, seine reinste Form und seinen höchsten Gehalt.
Friedrich Hebbel, *Mein Wort über das Drama*, 1848. In *Sämtliche Werke* in 12 Bd. , Leipzig, Hesse und Becker verlag, n. d. , but *Vorwort* by Emil Kuh dated October 1867, Vol. 10, p. 13. (All references here to *Mein Wort* and the *Vorwort* to *Maria Magdalena* are to this volume of this edition).
108. *Mein Wort* p. 13.

109. *Vorwort* p. 43.
110. . . . Daß es uns das bedenkliche Verhältnis vergegenwärtigt, worin das aus dem ursprunglichen Nexus entlassene Individuum dem Ganzen, dessen Theil es trotz seiner unbegreiflichen Freiheit noch immer geblieben ist, gegenübersteht. *Mein Wort* p. 13.
111. Arthur Miller, *On Social Plays* in *A View from the Bridge*, London, 1957 p. 9.
112. *Mein Wort* p. 14.
113. . . man hat erkannt, daß das Drama, nicht bloß in seiner Totalität, wo es sich von selbst versteht, sondern daß es schon in jedem seiner Elemente symbolisch ist und als symbolisch betrachtet werden muß, eben so wie der Maler die Farben, durch die er seinen Figuren rothe Wangen und blaue Augen gibt, nicht aus wirklichen Menschenblut destilliert, sondern sich ruhig und ungefochten des Zinnobers und des Indigos bedient.
ibid p. 15.
114. Aber der Inhalt des Lebens ist unerschöpflich, und das Medium der Kunst ist begrenzt. ibid p. 16.
115. . . . und dies ist der Punkt, den Goethe allein im Auge haben konnte, als er aussprache, daß alle ihre Formen etwas Unwahres mit sich führten. ibid.
116. Nun ist noch ein Viertes möglich, ein Drama, das die hier charakterisirten verschiedenen Richtungen in sich vereinigt und eben deshalb keine einzelne entschieden hervortreten läßt. Dieses Drama ist der Ziel meiner eigenen Bestrebungen, und wenn ich, was ich meine, durch meine Versuches selbst, durch die *Judith* und die nächstens erscheinende *Genoveva*, nicht deutlich gemacht habe, so wäre es thöricht, mit abstrakten Entwickelungen nachzuhelfen. ibid p. 18.
117. . . . die dramatische Kunst soll den welthistorischen Prozeß, der in unseren Tagen vor sich geht, und der die vorhandenen Institutionen des menschlichen Geschlechts, die politischen, religiösen und sittlichen, nicht umstürzen, sondern tiefer begründen, sie also vor dem Umsturz sichern will, beendigen helfen. Hebbel, *Vorwort* p. 49.
118. GW5 p. 67
119. . . . die Kunst. . ist die realisierte Philosophie, wie die Welt die realisierte Idee . . . Hebbel, *Vorwort* p. 56.
120. Sir P. Sidney *Apologie for Poetrie*, ed. J. Churton Collins, Oxford, Clarendon Press 1907 (imp. 1947) pp. 16–17.
121. Hebbel *Vorwort* p. 61.

122. Es ist an und für sich gleichgültig, ob der Zeiger der Uhr von Gold oder von Messing ist . . . ibid pp. 62–63.
123. *25 Jahre Theater in Berlin*. Theaterpremieren 1945–1970. Herausgegeben im Auftrag des Senats von Berlin. Berlin, Heinz Spitzing Verlag 1972, passim.
124. L. A. Willoughby, *German Literature from 1805 to 1880* in *A Companion to German Studies* ed. Jethro Bithell, London, Methuen & Co. 5th Edtn, 1955 p. 276.
125. Die Arbeiterklasse verband ihr Theater mit der neuen Kunst der Naturalismus. Eine Kunst, die vorgab, das Leben zu schildern wie es wirklich ist, durfte wohl geeignet erscheinen, sich mit revolutionärer Politik, die Wirklichkeit verändern will, zu verbinden. Heinrich Braulich, *Die Volksbühne. Theater und Politik in der deutschen Volksbühnen-Bewegung*. Berlin. Henschelverlag, 1976, p. 37.
126. Die revolutionären Arbeiter nahmen die kritischen Elemente der naturalistischen Stücke zum Anlaß, sich in ihren Klassenkampf mit der Bourgeoisie zu bestätigen. Sie politisierten das naturalistische Theater. ibid p. 39.
127. ibid pp. 252–275.
128. A. Strindberg *Author's Foreword* to *Miss Julie* in *Six Plays of Strindberg*, Trans. E. Sprigge, New York, Doubleday and Co. Inc, 1955, p. 64.
129. ibid pp. 63–64.
130. ibid p. 66
131. Eric Bentley, *The Modern Theatre*, London, Robert Hale, 1948 (2nd imp. 1950) p. 34. (N. B. First published in US as *The Playwright as Thinker*).
132. ibid p. 35.
133. ibid p. 62.
134. Bataillon *op cit.* p. 160.
135. See *Das Oberammergau Passionsspiele 1984*. Gemeinde Oberammergau 1984. Title Page and Vorwort p. 15f. (All references to the play are to this edition).
136. ibid p. 48.
    The same inclination hardened Jacob's sons so that they mercilessly sold their own brother into the hands of foreign profiteers, for a pitiful price. Where the heart pays homage to the idol of money, there every nobler inclination has disappeared; honour is saleable, and one's word, and love and friendship.
137. Clemens Haertle-Dedler, *Rochus Dedler, der Komponist der*

Passionsmusik zu Oberammergau. Festschrift zum 200. Geburtstag des Komponisten. Herausgeber: Gemeinde Oberammergau. 1979. p. 7.

138. *Oberammergau Passionsspiele* pp. 19–20.
139. Bentley *op cit* p. 35.
140. Ich liebe die Bücher, die die Schule verbietet: Hauptmann und Ibsen, Strindberg und Wedekind. GW4 p. 34.
141. August Strindberg *The Road to Damascus, A Trilogy*. English version by Graham Rawson. London 1939. p. 23.
142. See *Brewer's Dictionary of Phrase and Fable* 2nd Revised edition, London 1981, p. 1016, under catchword *Seven*.
143. See Bataillon *op cit* p. 161.
144. e.g. Mark 2. 15–16. Matt. 11. 19. Mark 14. 3 etc.
145. Der Kirche christliche Gebot
Hat zweimal er in Sünde übertreten. GW2 p. 43.
146. Nicht Römer schlugen ihn ans Kreuz/Er kreuzigte sich selbst. GW2 p. 44.
147. Wir selber gingen schmerzende Stationen/Und schicken Kinder aus/Zur eignen Kreuzigung. GW2 p. 45.
148. Hilflose schaun wir dem Passionsweg zu. GW2 p45.
149. Vielleicht, gekreuzigt kann es sich erlösen,/Zu hoher Freiheit auferstehn. GW2 p. 45.
150. Mir ist, als ob ich heut/Zum erstenmal erwache,/Als ob ich eine schwere Grabesplatte fortgewälzt/Und auferstehe. GW2 p. 46.
151. Ich weiß den Weg zur Arbeitsstätte , /Nun weiß ich ihn. GW2 p. 46.
152. cf note 62.
153. GW2 p. 57.
154. Geht hin zu den Soldaten, sie sollen ihre Schwerter zu Pflugscharen schmieden. GW2 p. 61. cf. Isaiah 2.4.
(Luther: Da werden sie ihre Schwerdter zu Pflugscharen . . machen).
155. In connection with the religious aspects of the play (which are seen most clearly when it is considered as a Station Drama) it is to be noted that the word *Wandlung*, apart from its general meaning of *transformation*, is also the word used for the transubstantiation of the elements in the Mass. This fact links the play not only with the drama of the Passion itself, but also with the rite of the Mass, the root of European religious drama.
156. Goethe, *Faust*. Herausgegeben und kommentiert von Erich Trunz. Munich. C. H. Beck. 1972. p. 464.

157. Hartnoll. *Oxford Companion to the Theatre.* Oxford 1951, p. 234.
158. Trunz. *loc cit.*
159. Goethes Tagebuch, 11 Juni 1818: *Dr Faust* von Marlowe. See Trunz *op cit* p. 433.
160. J. Q. Adams, *Chief Pre-Shakespearean Dramas.* London. Harrap n. d. p. 266.
161. Trunz *op cit* p. 464.
162. . . Der erste Teil ist fast ganz subjektiv. Es ist alles aus einem befangenern, leidenschaftlichern Individuum hervorgegangen . . . Goethe, *Gespräch mit Eckermann.* 17 Februar 1831 . . . Trunz, *op cit* p. 455.
163. Im zweiten Teil aber ist fast gar nichts Subjektives, es erscheint hier eine höhere, breitere, hellere, leidenschaftslosere Welt. ibid.
164. (Vordere Bühne. Städtisch verunstaltetes Zimmer. Dämmerung weht Formen und Töne verwischend. In den Häusern jenseits der Straße werden die Lichter an Weihnachtsbäumen angezündet. Am Fenster lehnt Friedrich). GW2 p. 17.
165. ibid
166. Ihr naht euch wieder, schwankende Gestalten,
Die früh sich einst dem trüben Blick gezeigt . . . .
Ihr drängt euch zu! nun gut, so mögt ihr walten,
Wie ihr aus Dunst und Nebel um mich steigt; . . .
Goethe, *Faust* (ed. Trunz) p. 9.
167. Es wölkt sich über mir –
Der Mond verbirgt sein Licht –
Die Lampe schwindet!
Es dampft – Es zucken rote Strahlen
Mir um das Haupt – Es weht
Ein Schauer vom Gewölb herab
Und faßt mich an!
ibid p. 23 (11. 468–474)
Note the verbal echo in the word *weht.* cf note 164.
168. Es mag bei Euch wohl Augentäuschung sein. ibid p. 42. (1. 1157).
169. Ungeheures Getöse verkündet das Herannahen der Sonne. ibid p. 147. S. D. after line 4665.
170. Hinaufgeschaut! – Der Berge Gipfelriesen
Verkünden schon die feierlichste Stunde. ibid p. 148. (11. 4695f).
171. So bleibe denn die Sonne mir im Rücken!
Der Wassersturz, das Felsenriff durchbrausend,
Ihn schau' ich an mit wachsendem Entzücken . . . .
Allein wie herrlich, diesem Sturm ersprießend,

Wölbt sich des bunten Bogens Wechseldauer, . . .
Am farbigen Abglanz haben wir das Leben.
ibid p. 149. (11. 4715–17; 4721f; 4727).

172. Zu Gott, der in der Menschheit lebt. GW2 p. 40.
173. FRIEDRICH:
Sonne umwogt mich,
Freiheit durchströmt mich,
Meine Augen schauen den Weg.
Ich will ihn wandern, Schwester,
Allein, und doch mit dir,
Allein, und doch mit allen,
Wissend um den Menschen.
(Schreitet ekstatisch zur Tür hinaus)
ibid.
174. Bataillon *op cit* p. 160.
175. GW2 p. 17. War nicht Hauch des Mitleids . . . . etc.
176. GW4 p. 21.
177. ibid p. 38.
178. Der gute Vater . . . er hat meine Jugend versperrt! . . . ja, mein wirtschaftliches Fortkommen ist gesichert. Was aber tatest du für meine *Seele*?
GW2 p. 18f.
179. Mutter nannte ich dich, weil du mich gebarst. Kann ich dich heute noch Mutter heißen, da du meine Seele aussetztest, wie törichte Mütter ihr nacktes Kind? GW2 p. 19.
180. Mother, Mother, / Why are you not my mother? / If I cannot with an honest heart call that woman 'mother' / Who lent me my heartbeat with her blood / In the dark nights, / I will journey in distant ways.
Toller, *Vormorgen*. Potsdam, Gustav Kiepenheuer Verlag, 1924, p. 9.
181. GW2 p. 17.
182. Franz Norbert Mennemeier, *Modernes Deutsches Drama. Kritiken und Charakteristiken*. Bd. I. 1910–1933. Munich, Wilhelm Fink Verlag, 1973, p. 47.
183. ibid p. 54.
184. This and other biographical statements about Hasenclever are taken from Kurt Pinthus' introduction to his edition of Hasenclever's *Gedichte, Dramen, Prosa*, Hamburg, Rowohlt Verlag, 1963, quoted by Günther Rühle, *Zeit und Theater. Vom Kaiserreich zur Republik, 1913–1925*. Bd. I, Berlin, Propyläen Verlag, 1973, pp.

852–853.

185. You are guilty *(intimate, family plural)* he groaned, you are guilty *(intimate singular, addressed to Ernst)*. GW4 p. 35.
186. GW4 p. 15.
187. Meine Mutter konnte nicht fassen, daß ihr Sohn wegen Landesverrats angeklagt war, furchtbar schien ihr die Anklage, furchtbar die drohende Strafe, sie begriff nicht, wie ein Mensch aus Bürgerlicher Familie sich den Kampf der Arbeiter zuwenden konnte, er muß krank sein, dachte sie, ich will ihm helfen, sie alarmiert die Hausärzte, sie schickt Atteste ans Gericht, ich sei schon als Kind nervös gewesen, die Folge war diese psychiatrische Untersuchung. GW4 p. 104.
188. Karl Strecker, *Tägliche Runschau* 1.10.1919.
189. see Mennemeier, *op cit* pp. 55–56.
190. Although Hasenclever's history in relation to the war was very like Toller's, he did not use this directly in his writing.
191. GW4 p. 50.
192. GW4 p. 53.
193. GW4 p. 57.
194. GW2 pp21–22.
 Hildebrandslied Line 3. *Penguin Book of German Verse* ed. L. Forster, Harmondsworth, Penguin Books Ltd. 1957, p. 3.
195. GW4 p. 53.
196. KORPORAL: . . . Wer meldet sich hier bei euch?
 FRIEDRICH: Ich. *Ich will trotz euch.*
 GW2 p. 25.
197. Nun sind wir nicht mehr weiß und schwarz. (Now we are no longer white and black).
 Die Wüste trieb die Scham zum Teufel. (The desert drove shame to the Devil).
 GW2 p. 26.
198. Compare Scene 3: Wir sind ja schließlich alle ohne Vaterland. Wie die Dirnen. (In the end we are all without a fatherland. Like prostitutes).
199. Carel ter Haar, *Ernst Toller. Appell oder Resignation*? tuduv-Studien. Reihe Sprach- und Literaturwissenschaft Band 7. Munich. tutuv-Verlagsgesellschaft, 1977. pp. 1–2.
200. Walter von Molo, *So wunderbar ist das Leben. Erinnerungen und Begegnungen*. Stuttgart 1957 p. 217.
201. Fremder waren Sie Unserm Volk, nun haben Sie Bürgerrechte erworben. GW2 p. 29.

202. GW4 pp. 99–102.
203. Ich komme ins Lazarett nach Straßburg. In ein stilles Franziskanerkloster. Schweigsame, freundliche Mönche pflegen mich. GW4 p. 73.
204. Hauptmann studied sculpture in Breslau in 1880, and made a final attempt at sculpture in the autumn of 1883 in Rome, where this incident occurred.
205. v. Spalek p. 889. This whole section owes much to: Walter-Jürgen Schorlies, *Der Schauspieler, Regisseur, szenische Bühnenbauer und Theaterleiter, Karl-Heinz Martin. Versuch einer Biographie*. PhD Dissertation, Köln, 1971. Seen in Theatermuseum, Köln.
206. *Neue Hamburger Zeitung*, 1918, Nr. 230. From a typescript in Theatermuseum, Köln.
207. ibid.
Der Expressionismus ergreift leidenschaftlich und ohne Rücksicht auf das natürliche Weltbild Besitz von dem inneren Wesen, der Seele der Natur, der Weltseele, und erst wenn er diese leidenschaftlich *auszudrücken* vermag, da er sie erlebt hat, wird ihm sein Erlebnis zur Erschaffung. Er fühlt den kosmischen Mittelpunkt der Welt in jedem Ich und fixiert ihn in jedem ichberechtigten Werk.
208. ibid.
Denn das Theater ist weder eine literarische Anstalt, noch ein Ort des Amüsements, noch eine Bude für technische Sehenswürdigkeiten, sondern einzig und allein die Stätte eines *künsterlischen Erlebnisses.*
209. ibid.
Denn das Wort, das rhythmisch beschwingte, gedanklich gegliederte Wort, das mimisch erlebte Wort ist die Brücke zum Geistigen, zum Seelischen, zum Metaphysischen.
210. ibid. Im Menschen ist das Drama der Welt.
211. ibid. Dem Expressionismus wieder kann die neue Bühne wesentliches Ausdrucksmittel werden: Kanzel seiner neuen Verzückung, Katheder seiner neuen Logik, Tribüne seinem neuen Pathos.
212. These two paragraphs ('In 1919. . . . *literary* Expressionism') are taken verbatim from: Cecil W. Davies, *Working-Class Theatre in the Weimar Republic. 1919–1933. Part II. Theatre Quarterly, Vol X No. 39. 1981*, pp. 81–82.
213. Herbert Jhering, *"Die Wandlung". Fünf Stationen von Ernst Toller. Uraufführung der Tribüne. Der Tag,* 1.10.1919. Press cutting,

Theatermuseum. Köln.
214. Photographs can be seen in the Theatermuseum, Köln.
215. Er griff über die Grenzen der Bühne und sprengte den Raum. Jhering *loc cit* (n. 213).
216. Kortner spielte nicht *Die Wandlung*, sondern die Empörung. ibid.
217. Die Aufführung war ein theatergeschichtliches Ereignis. Dr A. Kober. Press cutting, Theatermuseum, Köln. Periodical not named. n. d.
218. Das war ein Abend, der im Gedächtnis bleiben wird . . . Willi Handl, *Der Tag* 1.10.1919. Press cutting, Theatermuseum, Köln.
219. Die unfaßbare Tragödie des Weltkrieges brannte sich in heißer Symbolik im Bewußtsein.
Emil Faktor, *Nachlese* (i.e. *Further Thoughts*). Press cutting, Theatermuseum, Köln. Periodical not named. n. d.
220. Die Tribüne hat mit der Aufführung von Tollers *Wandlung* ihre theater-geschichtliche Mission erwiesen.
Kober. *loc cit*.
221. Mann kann ein verrannter politischer Phantast und doch ein großer Künstler sein. Und es muß zugestanden werden, daß Toller im letzten Punkt, der für uns der erste ist, Hasenclever auf Nimmerwiedersehen überragt.
Karl Strecker. *"Die Tribüne". Zur Erstaufführung der "Wandlung" von Ernst Toller. Tägliche Rundschau,* 1.10.1919. Press cutting, Theatermuseum, Köln.
222. *Neue Zürchner Zeitung*, 6.10.1919
The image off the teeth of the dead dog is probably derived from C. F. Meyer's *Angela Borgia* (Chap. 6):

> Eines Tages trat der Heiland mit seinen Jüngen aus dem Tore einer Stadt. An der Landstraße lag in der Sonne ein toter Hund, dem die Jünger mit Ekel und Schmähungen auswichen. Der Heiland aber blieb bei dem Aase stehen, und das einige, was daran rein geblieben war, hervorhebend, sprach er; 'O sehet, wie blendend weiß seine Zähne sind'.
>
> (One day the Saviour walked with his disciples out of the gate of a town. On the country road there lay in the sun a dead dog, which the disciples avoided with disgust and abuse. The Saviour, however, remained standing by the rotting carcass and, stressing the only thing about it that had remained pure, said, 'O look how brilliantly white its teeth are').

223. Nackt steht der Mensch dem Menschen gegenüber . . . .
Ernst Tollers Menschentum hat etwas von dem Menschentum am ersten Schöpfungstage. Es ist sehr stark und rein.

E.H. Critique under the dateline *Berlin den 1. Okt*, so presumably not in a Berlin periodical. Press cutting Theatermuseum, Köln. Periodical not known. n.d.

224. Toller ist ein Dichter. Kober *loc cit.*
225. Nicht als Drama kann diese formschöne, von Traumkraft und Gefühlswärme durchströmte Dichtung gewertet werden.
Emil Faktor. Periodical not named. 1.10.1919. Press cutting, Theatermuseum, Köln. (cf n. 219).
226. E.H. *loc cit.*
227. "R", Berlin Correspondent, *Neues Wiener Journal*, 7.10.'19.
228. In Wahrheit endet dieses Stück mit der Geburt des Künstlers Toller. ibid.
229. In Wahrheit ist er überhaupt kein Sozialist, und sogar in diesem Stück burleskiert er die Agitatoren vom Schlage Liebknechts und Levinés. ibid.
230. Alfred Kerr, *Ernst Toller: Die Wandlung. Tribüne. Berliner Tageblatt.* 1.10.1919. Press cutting, Theatermuseum, Köln. Spalek 3724.
231. Der Held von Tollers 'fünf Stationen' ist so dumm. So erschütternd. So umleuchtet. So unreif. So anmaßend. So kenntnislos. So ganz mit dem Blick des Beginners. So wundervoll. So heilig. Und er soll gesegnet sein, für und für, heut und immerdar. ibid.
232. Hier ist zum ersten Male wieder ein Dichter, der nichts anderes als ein Mensch ist. Dessen Künstlertum nichts anderes als Intensität des Persönlichen bedeutet, Jhering. *loc cit.*
233. Ihn rütteln die Dämonen auf, die hinter den Erscheinungen stehen. ibid.
234. Sein Drama ist nicht das philiströse, kleinbürgerliche Spiel von Schuld und Sühne. Es ist das Schauspiel tragischer Notwendigkeit: der Totentanz der Zeit. Und die Musik, die zu dem Gespensterreigen aufspielt, ist der Glaube an die Auferstehung. ibid.
235. Das Gewagteste ist einfach, Grauenhafteste schlicht. Toller verschmäht die Originalität. Seine Sprache hat keine Gebärde, seine Gedanken kein Funkenregen. ibid.
236. Er hat die Dämonisierung des Sachlichen erreicht. ibid.
237. Press cutting in Theatermuseum, Köln. Periodical not named. n. d.
238. Sie haben Menschen durch eine Idee getötet; Toller, können Sie das verantworten? ibid.
239. Lassen wir uns überzeugen von den Gedanken, der Mensch sei zur Liebe geboren . . .
Tollers Wandlung von der Gewalt zur Liebe, zum Wort, das sei

sein nächstes Werk. ibid.

240. Hamburg: Kammerspiele. Sept. 1, 1920. Director, Erich Engel. 35 performances. (Spalek p. 889). Leipzig: Altes Theater. Aug 3 1924. Director, Alwin Kronacher; Design, Thiersch. Ca. 14 performances. (ibid).
241. *Vossische Zeitung*. No. 369. 5.8.'24. Spalek 3693.
242. Evidently he spoke the introductory poem, *Aufrüttelung*. v. Spalek 3742, 3719.
243. Spalek 3742.
244. Stuttgart, Deutsches Theater. Design, Wilhelm Baumeister. Spalek p. 889.
245. Details from Spalek 3722.
246. Detalls from Spalek 3670 and 3739.
247. Und über die Bühne geistert eine schwanke Gestalt:
Der Dichter vor dem Demos.
'F. H.' *Eine Toller-Feier der Volksbühne. Berliner Lokal-Anzeiger* 8.9.24. Press cutting in Akademie der Kunste, Berlin.
248. Danish (1925); Finnish (1928); English (before 1935); Gujarati [India] (1961); Japanese (1922); Russian (n. d). and Yiddish (1923). Spalek: 77, 120, 131, 138, 158, 170, 191.
249. A notice in *Vorwärts*, 18.2.1920, (Spalek 3689) refers to a production by "a British workers' theatre". No other record of this found. The same notice refers to translations into French, Spanish, Swedish and Dutch. Spalek records none of these.
250. See Spalek 3678, 3679 and 3698.
251. Tollers *Wandlung* unsittlich.
Verbot für die Schulbüchereien.
Das Revolutionsstück Tollers, *Die Wandlung* soll nach einem Antrag der Deutschen Volkspartei, der heute vom Unterrichtsausschuß des Landtags angenommen wurde, aus allen Schulbüchereien entfernt werden. Der Antrag wurde damit begründet, daß das Buch in vielen Schilderungen das *sittliche* Gefühl, besonders der Jugendlichen gröblichst verletze.
Periodical unknown. Dated: November 1931 (actual date not legible, but evidently 25th). Press cutting in Theatermuseum, Köln.

Masse Mensch

1. Das Drama *Masse-Mensch* ist eine visionäre Schau, die in zweieinhalb Tagen förmlich aus mir "brach". GW2 p. 353.

2. Ein Jahr währte die muh-*selige* Arbeit des Neuformens und Feilens. ibid.
3. In Tollers nächstem, künstlerisch weit schwäche Schauspiel *Masse-Mensch . . .*
   F. N. Mennemeier, *Modernes Deutsches Drama I*, Munich, Wilhelm Fink Verlag, 1973, p. 197
4. For details of the omission of the hyphen in the First Edition and the subsequent distortion to *Die Masse Mensch*, see GW2 p. 352 and Spalek pp. 45ff. GW prints the title unhyphenated.
5. *Masses and Man*, translated by Vera Mendel, London, The Nonesuch Press, 1923.
6. H. D. F. Kitto, *Greek Tragedy*, London, Methuen, 3rd Edition, reprint 1968, p. 22.
7. GW2 p. 82.(Mendel p. 18).
8. Landauer, *Aufruf*, pp. 143 & 151.
   Die Erde müssen wir wieder haben . . . Die Erde ist niemandes Eigentum. Die Erde sei herrenlos; dann nur sind die Menschen frei . . . Der Kampf des Sozialismus ist ein Kampf um den Boden; die soziale Frage ist eine agrarische Frage.
9. Aus der Masse im Saal eilt der Namenlose auf die Tribüne . . . GW2 p. 84.
10. R. A. J. Altenhofer, *Ernst Tollers Politische Dramatik*, Ph. D. Thesis, Washington University, 1976, p. 57.
11. Wolfgang Rothe, *Toller*, Reinbek bei Hamburg, Rowohlt, 1983, p. 64.
12. Rothe *op cit* p. 128.
13. GW4 p. 89.
14. The preliminary material as printed both in PBDG and in GW2 p. 66, is faulty and incomplete. In particular, it is Scenes II, IV and VI that are 'dream' scenes, *not* Scenes III, V & VII.
15. Throughout his subsequent career Toller headed his cast lists in ways he clearly regarded as appropriate to the particular play, e.g.
    Die Maschinenstürmer: Persons in the Prologue, Persons in the drama.
    Hinkemann: People (i.e. *Menschen*, with emphasis on their humanity) in the Tragedy.
    Der entfesselte Wotan: Figures.
    In other cases he normally put: Persons.
16. cf. the diagram *Formal Scheme of "Masse-Mensch"*.
17. v. note 10.

18. Ernst Toller, *Masse Mensch*. Stuttgart, Reclam 1979 pp. 57–77.
19. ibid p. 76–77.
20. *Masse Mensch* war nach Erlebnissen, deren Wucht der Mensch vielleicht nur einmal ertragen kann, ohne zu zerbrechen, Befreiung von seelischer Not, Befreiung, die den Zwiespalt nicht selbsttrügerisch durch irgend eine Formel aus der Welt verbannte, sondern die zum Zwiespalt "ja" und "Schicksal" sagte.
GW5 p. 36. Letter to Theodor Lessing.
21. Der einzelne Mensch kann den Tod wollen. Die Masse muß das Leben wollen. Und da wir Menschen und Masse in einem sind, wählen wir Tod und Leben. ibid.
22. Ich habe einen der schwersten Konflikte unserer revolutionären Zeit, der immer wieder an den Menschen herantritt, der die Notwendigkeit des Umpflügens erkannt hat, zu gestalten versucht. ibid. Letter to Frau T. D.
23. Ich stehe dem Drama *Masse Mensch* heute kritisch gegenüber, ich habe die Bedingtheit der Form erkannt, die herrührt von einer trotz allem! inneren Gehemmtheit jener Tage, einer menschlichen Scham, die künstlerischer Formung persönlichen Erlebens, nackter Konfession, scheu auswich, und die doch nicht den Willen zu reiner künstlerischer Objektivation aufbringen konnte.
GW2 p. 353. In *Briefe aus dem Gefängnis*, apart from other minor alterations, the whole of the sentence after the word Scham is omitted. In the intervening years Toller had come to appreciate that he had in fact given purely artistic form to his personal experience. v. GW5 p. 38.
24. *Arbeiten (Works)* in *Quer Durch*, Berlin, Kiepenheuer, 1930 pp. 277ff. v. GW1 p. 135ff. *Arbeiten* does not seem to have appeared before its publication in *Quer Durch*, 1930, and as it refers to *Feuer aus den Kesseln* (lst performance 1.8.'30) it could not have been written before that year.
25. Jeder Autor will in sein erstes Werk alles, was er weiß, alles was er erlebt hat, hineindrängen. Das tat auch ich. Und so ist es nicht verwunderlich, daß das Private, das Lyrische, sich stärker hervordrängt, als dramatische Architektonik es zulassen darf. GW1 pp. 138–9.
26. Schon in *Masse Mensch* ist die Form reiner. Es war sehr merkwürdig: nach der Aufführung des Stückes sagten die einen, es sei konterrevolutionär, weil es jede Gewalt verwerfe, die andern es sei bolschewistisch, weil die Trägerin der Gewaltlosigkeit untergehe, und die Masse zwar im Moment unterliege, aber auf

die Dauer Sieger bleibe. Nur wenige erkannten, daß der Kampf zwischen Individuum und Masse sich nicht nur draußen abspielt, daß jeder in seinem Innern Individuum und Masse zugleich ist. Als Individuum handelt er nach der als recht erkannten moralischen Idee. *Ihr* will er leben, und wenn die Welt dabei untergeht. Als Masse wird er getrieben von sozialen Impulsen und Situationen, das *Ziel* will er erreichen, auch wenn er die moralische Idee aufgeben muß. Dieser Widerspruch ist heute noch für den politisch Handelnden unlöslich, und gerade seine Unlöslichkeit wollte ich zeigen. ibid.

27. Ich war gescheitert, ich hatte geglaubt, daß der Sozialist, der Gewalt verachtet, niemals Gewalt anwenden darf, ich selbst habe Gewalt gebraucht und zur Gewalt aufgerufen. Ich haßte Blutvergießen und habe Blut vergossen. GW4 p. 222.
28. GW4 p. 77. *Fall* p. 13.
29. Muß der Handelnde schuldig werden, immer und immer! Oder wenn er nicht schuldig werden will, untergehen? GW4 p. 222.
30. Treiben die Masse sittliche Ideen, treiben sie nicht vielmehr Not und Hunger? GW4 p. 222–3.
31. Erst kommt das Fressen, dann kommt die Moral. From *Denn wovon lebt der Mensch (In Die Dreigroschenoper)*. Bertolt Brecht, *Gedichte und Lieder aus Stücken* Frankfurt/M, 1963 p. 35.
32. Die sinnliche Fülle der Erlebnisse war so stark, daß ich ihrer nur Herr werden konnte durch Abstraktion, durch die dramatische Auflichtung jener Linien, die den Grund der Dinge bestimmen. GW4 p. 223.
33. *epei d'anankas edu lepadnon.*
Aeschyli, *Septem Quae Supersunt Tragoedias*, Ed. Denys Page, Oxford 1972 p. 146. (*Agamemnon* line 218)
34. Aeschylus, *The Oresteian Trilogy*, Trans. P. Vellacott, Harmondsworth, Penguin Books, 1956, p. 49.
35. A Note on *ananke/Schicksal*.
ananke: Latin, *necessitas*: force, constraint, necessity. (Liddell & Scott, *Abridged Greek-English Lexicon*, 22nd Edtn. Oxford, 1887).
necessitas: that which is inevitable, fate. *mors est necessitas naturae*, Cicero. (*Cassell's Latin Dictionary*, Revd. Marchant & Charles, London 270th thousand, n. d).
fate: *Schicksal*: Langenscheidt's *Encyclopaedic Dictionary, English-German, German-English (The New Muret-Sanders, Ed. O. Springer)*, Berlin-Schöneberg, 1962).
Schicksal: alles, was dem Menschen widerfährt . . . das menschl.

Leben lenkende Macht. (Wahrig, *Deutsches Wörterbuch,* Berlin 1968, 1972) (everything which happens to a person . . . the power directing human life).

36. B. Russell, *History of Western Philosophy,* London, 1954, p. 737.
37. "Kant, the founder of German idealism". ibid p. 730.
38. A. Schweitzer, *Civilization and Ethics,* Tr. C. T. Campion, Rev'd Mrs C. E. B. Russell, London Unwin Books & A. C. Black, 1961, passim and esp. Chap IX.
39. ibid p. 103.
40. Karl Marx, Foreword to *Capital Vol. I,* quoted in *A Textbook of Marxist Philosophy,* London, Gollancz, n. d. (c. 1935) p. 184.
41. ibid p. 22.
42. GW2 p. 85.
43. GW2 p. 84.
44. GW2 p. 86.
45. ibid.
46. *pathein ton erxanta*
    Aeschylus, *Agamemnon,* 1. 1964 (Ed. cit. p. 194)
47. See note 29.
48. Kitto *op cit* p. 70.
49. GW4 p. 223.
50. v. P. W. Harsh, *A Handbook of Classical Drama,* Stanford, 1944–67 p. 13ff.
51. See note 49.
52. That Toller did learn this is understood by, I think, all commentators on *Hinkemann.* That he expressed it also and earlier in *Masse Mensch* does not seem to have been fully appreciated.
53. See, *Toller's Use of Language.*

Masse Mensch on Stage

1. *Fall* p. 111
2. Karl Bröger, newspaper review (? *Zeitung*) 19.11.1920. Seen in Theatermuseum, Köln. Also reprinted in part in G. Rühle, *Theater für die Republik.* Frankfurt/Main, 1967, p. 321.
3. *Fall* p. 111ff.
4. Both are in the press-cutting collection in the Theatermuseum, Köln. The names of the newspapers are either not given or are

illegible. Rühle thinks one may be from the *Zeitung*. v. Note 2. Spalek lists 15 periodical references to this production, including these two, but most are short announcements or comments on the political or public order aspects. Only 4 others are in any real sense 'critiques'. One of these is short and unfavourable (Spalek 3132), but the other 3 are both favourable and interesting. One (in the *Neue Augsburger Zeitung*, Spalek 3136) "acknowledges the aesthetic and ethical value of the play and recognises that Toller's ideal is *Gemeinschaft* (community), and not *Masse*". One in the organ of the Independent Social-Democrats (Spalek 3157) is thoughtfully and predictably favourable. Toller is seen as a "revolutionary poet", not as a mere "politicising man of letters". The other appreciates Toller's talent and symbolism. He suggests, interestingly, though I think incorrectly, that The Nameless One and Sonja represent the old and new Toller respectively. Perceptively, this reviewer "fears that the language of the play, though effective, will not be understood by the general public because it is too condensed".

5. Schatten aus der Münchener Räterepublik laufen durch die Bilder. Rühle *op cit* p. 322.
6. Sein Herz ist mit dem Menschen, sein bewußter Wille, scheint es, mit der Masse. Geht sein Weg nach Damascus über Moskau? ibid.
7. Die im szenischem Ausdruck hervorragende Leistung des Regisseurs Friedrich Neubauer zusammen mit der Darstellung Marg. Hannens und Fischer-Streitmanns ließ keinen Wunsch unerfüllt. ibid p. 323.
8. Lionel Richard (ed)., *The Concise Encyclopaedia of Expressionism*, trans. Stephen Tint, Ware (Omega Books) 1984. (Copyright Editions Aimery Somogy, Paris, 1978) p. 183.
   Caption: TOLLER, ERNST, *Masses and Man* (*Masse Mensch*) Staadtheater (sic. CWD) Nuremberg, 1921. No further details given. Source not acknowledged.
9. W. Rothe, *Toller*, Reinbek bei Hamburg, 1983 p. 69. Picture supplied by Spalek.
10. Spalek p. 884 and no. 3164a.
11. Spalek p. 884
12. Das Bühnenbild von Hans Strohbach zeigte vorne die übliche Stufenanlage, in der Mitte eine leichte Plattform; oben im Hintergrund eine braune Mauer, mit Torbogen in der Mitte als Eingang zum Palast; links daneben ein stilisierter einsamer

Blütenbaum vor einem ebenen, dunkelblauvioletten Himmel. Sehr schön wirkte das Verhältnis der Menschengröße zu dem ganz hoch geöffneten Bühnenbild. Das unsichtbare Schicksal war hier lediglich durch eine stumme Raumwirkung fühlbar gemacht. *Deutsche Allgemeine Zeitung* 11.4.1921, in Rühle *op cit* p. 300.

13. Rühle *op cit* p. 324.
14. ibid p. 300
15. Paul Wiegler, *Berliner Zeitung (BZ) am Mittag,* in Rühle *op cit* p. 301.
16. Man braucht ja den komplizierten Bau der Antike nicht sklavisch nachzuformen (obwohl auch das geht, wie man in Hölderlins Übersetzung nachlesen kann). Rühle *op cit* p. 300.
17. *Berliner Lokal-Anzeiger* 10.4.1921. Reprinted in Rühle *op cit* p. 301.
18. Sophocles. *Antigone,* lines 781–799 of the Greek text. (Sophocles, ed. Jebb. Cambridge 1906 p. 145).
    English: Sophocles, *The Theban Plays* tr Watling, Harmondsworth (Penguin Books) 1947 p. 161.
19. Jürgen Fehling, *Note on the Production of "Masses and Man"* in Toller *Masses and Man* (tr. Mendel), London 1923 p. 57.
20. Es gibt Kritiker, die bemängeln, daß Sie, obschon die Traumbilder Traumantlitz trugen, den "realen Bildern" visionäres Antlitz gaben und so die Grenzen zwischen Realität und Traum milderten. Sie haben, ich möchte es Ihnen eigen sagen, in meinem Sinn gehandelt. Diese "realen Bilder" sind keine naturalistischen "Milieuszenen", die Gestalten (bis auf die Gestalt Sonjas) nicht individual betont. *Was kann in einem Drama wie "Masse-Mensch" real sein? Nur der seelische, der geistige Atem.*
    GW2 p. 352.
21. M. Patterson, *The Revolution in German Theatre 1900–1933,* London and Boston 1981 pp. 106–7.
22. ibid (using material from K. MacGowan and R. E. Jones, *Continental Stagecraft,* New York 1922).
23. die Geburtsstunde des Bühnenexpressionismus und der Lichtregie. *Fall* p. 118.
24. Patterson *op cit* p. 107.
25. v. Note 19.
26. ibid.
27. ibid.
28. ibid.
29. ibid pp57–58.
30. Der Höhepunkt, wie die Masse dem Gewehrgeknatter ihr

Schlachtlied entgegensingt – ehern, rasend, fanatisch, aufgepeitscht, über sich hinausgetrieben, in Weißglut erhitzt. Man bebt. Der Autor fragt: Ohne mein Verdienst? – Ja – denn man versteht keine Silbe, braucht keine zu verstehen . . . Siegfried Jacobsohn in *Die Weltbühne. Fall* pp. 118–119.

31. Fehling *op cit* p. 58.
32. v. Spalek 3408, 3365.
33. L. Richard (ed). *op cit* p. 28.
34. ibid.
35. Fritz Martini, *Deutsche Literaturgeschichte*, Stuttgart, 1965 p. 328.
36. Paul Vogt, *Expressionism. German Painting between 1905 and 1920.* Cologne 1979. Plate 37.
37. Georg Trakl, *Das dichterische Werk*, Munich, DTV, 3. Auflage, 1974, pp. 73, 74 and 65.
38. H. G. Scheffauer, *The New Vision in the German Arts*, Benn, London, 1924 p. 236. Quoted by Patterson *op cit* p. 107.
39. Patterson *op cit* p. 107.
40. ibid. Plates 24, 25, 26.
41. This is a photograph of a design: but Lisi Jessen was also the photographer who took the production photograph of the Volksbühne production (the 'cage' scene) captioned THE GUIDE AND THE WOMAN, used as the frontispiece of the same edition.
42. Patterson *op cit* p. 107.
43. *Masses and Man* (tr. Mendel) London 1925 p. 25.
44. L. Richard (ed). *op cit* pp. 158, 164, 209, 216.
45. Mendel (tr). *op cit* p. 41.
46. Patterson *op cit* p. 106.
47. ibid p. 107.
48. ibid.
49. G. Rühle, *Theater in unserer Zeit*, Frankfurt/Main 1976, p. 280.
50. ibid p. 75.
51. ibid p. 76.
52. v. L. Richard (ed) *op cit* p. 195 (Picture).
53. ibid.
54. Rühle *op cit* (in note 49) p. 56.
55. Symbolisch wirkt sie falsch. Die Menschen der Tiefe müßten ja rechtens aus der Tiefe steigen: während sie hier weit eher von oben nach unten gravitieren. A. Kerr, *Berliner Tageblatt* 30.9.1921. In Theatermuseum Köln. Reprinted in part in Rühle, *Theater für die Republik*. pp. 323–324.
56. Spalek: 3156, 3157, 3162, 3163, 3165, 3167, 3168, 3169, 3173, 3174,

3192, 3193.
57. Gehen Sie nach der Volksbühne – wenn Sie zu den ausverkauften Vorstellungen noch einen Platz erwischen – und sehen Sie sich die Inszenierung von Tollers *Masse-Mensch.*
Press cutting in Theatermuseum, Köln. Source not given . . . Apparently not in Spalek.
58. Die Aufführung von *Masse-Mensch* war die beste Aufführung dieser kürzen Spielzeit.
Press cutting in Theatermuseum, Köln. Spalek 3169, *Berliner Börsen-Courier* 1 Oct. 1921.
59. Press cutting in Theatermuseum, Köln. Source not given. Apparently not in Spalek.
60. Press cutting in Theatermuseum, Köln. Apparently the same as Spalek 3174. *Vossische Zeitung No. 460 Morgen-Ausg.* 30. Sept 1921.
61. Press cutting in Theatermuseum, Köln. Apparently the same as Spalek 3167, *Das literarische Echo,* 1.11.1921.
62. Press cutting in Theatermuseum, Köln. Not in Spalek.
63. Could that possibly mean *Linksgerichteter*?
64. Press cutting in Theatermuseum, Köln. Source not given. Not in Spalek.
65. In *Crime and Punishment.*
66. Rühle, *Theater für die Republik,* p. 326.
67. ibid.
68. Press cutting in Theatermuseum, Köln.
69. See for example, Piscator, *Das politische Theater, Chap 5.*
70. In Fehling liegt die Zukunft der Volksbühne.
71. Siegfried Nestriepke. *Neues Beginnen, Die Geschichte der Freien Volksbühne Berlin 1946 bis 1955.* Berlin 1956, p. 71.
72. ibid. p. 87. For details of this production v. 25 *Jahre Theater in Berlin. Theaterpremieren 1945–1970,* Berlin, 1972, p. 266.
73. Nestriepke *op cit* p. 88.
74. ibid p. 182.
75. In einem nicht alltäglichen Gefühl innerer Bewegtheit folgten alle diesen sieben Bilder. Der Ernst eines Dichters, nicht sein Schicksal, packte das Gewissen der Hörer.
Auch solcher, denen, wie mir, diese Friedenslehre zu friedsam vorkommt.
In jedem Fall war es der stärkste von allen Eindrücken des jetzigen Kunstwinters – und ein Sieg der Volksbühne.
Den immer aufs neue dankenden Scharen versprach der glückliche Spielwart, Jürgen Fehling, einen Gruß an Ernst Toller zu senden.

Über Werk und Darstellung noch ein Wort.

K . . r

Press cutting in Theatermuseum Köln. Source not given.

76. Press cutting in Theatermuseum Köln. Reprinted in part in Rühle *op cit* p. 323.
77. Und wenn man dennoch tiefbewegt ist; wenn eine fast religiöse Stimmung über die Menschen kommt; wenn politisches Erörtern, Abwägen, Meinungsaustausch fast zum Oratorium wird: so läßt sich kein anderer Grund hierfür feststellen, als daß ein Mensch mit einem . . . unfeststellbaren Fluidium nämlich ein Dichter, dies schuf. ibid. § VII.
78. Das ist kein Theater mehr. Dichtung ist es. (Mag auch ein Politikus dahinter stehen, der mit vierundzwanzig Jahren schon ein Iphigenie ward). ibid.
79. Seltsames Gefühl, wenn man den Wert dieses Dichters mit dem Wert seiner Schergen vergleicht . . . Und er predigt Sanftmut. ibid.
80. Die Ferne bekommt gewissermaßen einen Klang bei ihm. ibid. § VIII.
81. Tallinn, Hommikteater, 23.2.1922. 4 performances only. Spalek p. 884.
82. Spalek p. 884.
83. v. Spalek 3429 especially.
84. Spalek 3428.
85. Spalek 3442.
86. cf. Patterson's criticism of Constructivism, already quoted.
87. Spalek p. 885.
88. Lee Simonson *The Art of Scenic Design* N. Y. 1950, p. 130.
89. Spalek 3390, 3271 & 3288.
90. v. note 88.
91. v. Spalek 3180.
92. Programme seen in Victoria and Albert Museum (Theatre Museum).
    The title used was *Man and the Masses.*
93. Spalek 3160.
94. Spalek 3327.
95. Spalek 3248.
96. J. T. G. in *The Sketch,* 28 May 1924. Press cutting seen in Victoria and Albert Museum.
97. J. C. Trewin, *Sybil Thorndike,* London (Rockliff) 1955, pp. 111 ff. (*Hecuba,* Oct. & Dec. 1919 and Feb/Mar 1920. *Medea,* Feb/Mar

1920. She played *Hecuba* again in Oct. 1924).
98. Press cutting seen in Victoria & Albert Museum. n. d.
99. *The Sketch,* 28.5.1924. Press cutting seen in Victoria & Albert Museum.
100. See Note 98.
101. *Sunday Times,* n. d. Press cutting seen in V & A.
102. Press cutting seen in V & A.
103. Spalek 3374.

Die Rache des verhöhnten Liebhabers

1. M. Pittock, *Ernst Toller,* Boston 1979.
2. ibid p. 145.
3. Fall p. 17.
4. Spalek p. 62.
5. *Die Weißen Blätter,* VII No. 11 (1920) 489–504. Spalek 51.
6. However, he lists only 2: Freie Volksbühne Jena, 8.5.'23, and Freie Volksbühne Berlin, 7.9.'24, (one performance only) Spalek p. 888.
7. Pittock *op cit* p. 146.
8. ibid p. 147.
   In prisons and concentration camps from the Nazi period onwards it has been normal in non-democratic countries for prisoners to be compelled to sleep with their hands and arms outside the bed-covers. e.g. "We had to sleep with our hands above our heads, you see – in case we tried to knock ourselves off". C. Bielenberg, *The Past is Myself* pb ed Dublin 1982 p. 260.
9. Pittock *op cit* p. 146.
10. ibid p. 147.
11. see supra: *Masse Mensch* note 32.
12. *loc cit* note 23.
13. v. D. G. Rees in *Penguin Companion to Literature Vol 2,* Harmondsworth 1969 p. 80.
    A complete translation of the Novella by W. I. Hyslop is given as an Appendix.
14. Zuerst spielerische und harmlose, dann fiebrige, leidenschaftliche, wirre. Was sich in der Abgeschlossenheit, in Träumen, in Wünschen, in Phantasien gesammelt hatte, drängte hin zu dieser Frau. GW5 p. 17.
15. ibid p. 18.

16. Sie, liebe Freundin, begreifen das. Sie sagten einmal, daß die feinsten privaten Erlebnisse einen Hauch haben, der sie nur durch winzige Nüancen vom Banalen unterscheidet. ibid
17. GW4 pp. 209–10.
18. "Impotence is not funny". Pittock *op cit* p. 147.
19. Ernst Toller *Die Rache des verhöhnten Liebhabers,* Berlin 1925 p. 5
20. Fall pp. 124–5.

The Play in Relation to its Source

1. *Die Rache* T. P. "Frei nach".
2. ibid p. 60.
3. V. Appendix.
4. Schiebt seinen Bauch ins Zimmer. *Die Rache* p. 22.
5. I am indebted to W. I. Hyslop for pointing this out.
6. Ben Jonson *Volpone,* Act III, Sc. V.
7. *Die Rache* p. 52:

   Ihr starken Lenden, Ihr Gefäß der fruchtbeschwingten Welle,
   Du blonder Märchenhain, gelobtes Land der heilgen Schwelle,
   Ersehnter Altar Du, in dem der heiße Kämpfer selig ruht,
   In dir zerbrechend löst sich Gott in keuscher Liebesglut . . .

   (Ye strong loins, receptacle of the wave, the shaft, vibrant with fruit,
   Thou fair-haired, fairy-tale grove, Promised Land of the holy threshold,
   Thou longed-for altar, in which the impassioned warrior blissfully rests,
   Breaking into thee, God dissolves in chaste ardour of love . .).
8. W. I. Hyslop's translation tries to preserve something of this quality in modern English.

A Puppet Play

1. I am using the term *puppet* as a general term including *all* types, and *marionette* only for articulated puppets controlled by strings.
2. Max von Boehn, *Puppen und Puppenspiele, Vol II, Puppenspiele,* Munich 1929 p. 117.
3. ibid p. 113.
   . . . da "nichtswürdige Landstreicher durch unanständige Zweideutigkeiten Beifall zu erhalten suchen".
4. ibid p. 113–4.
5. ibid p. 115–6.
6. ibid p. 126.
7. E. T. A. Hoffmann, *Werke Vol I,* Frankfurt/M, Insel Verlag, 1967

p. 520.

8. Boehn *op cit* p. 134 (*Die Totenglocke um Mitternacht, Die Leichenräuber von London, Der Mord im Weinkeller*).
9. ibid p. 115 (*Die öffentliche Enthauptung des Fräulein Dorothea*)
10. ibid p. 144 (Trotzdem es doch unanständig genug für den Pariser Geschmack war).
11. Spalek p. 889.
12. Spalek 3628.
13. Boehn p. 221 Die Renaissance der Marionette.
14. ibid p. 206.
15. ibid.
16. ibid.
17. ibid p. 212. Illustration: ibid No 176, p. 205.
18. Janet Leeper, *Edward Gordon Craig*, Harmondsworth, 1948 p. 13
19. ibid p. 35.
20. ibid p. 19.
21. ibid.
22. ibid p. 18.
23. v. Cecil W. Davies, *Theatre for the People*, Manchester 1977 p. 68
24. Leeper *op cit* p. 15.
25. Edward Gordon Craig, *On the Art of the Theatre*, 5th imp. London 1957 pp. 55–6.
    Craig's argument concerning the incalculability of the human being also has applications to language. It is significant that for Craig space and light appear to be more important than a text.
26. Craig *op cit* p. 89.
27. ibid.
28. ibid pp. ix–x.
29. Heinrich von Kleist, *Über das Marionettentheater* in *Sämtliche Werke und Briefe 2. Bd*, Munich, 4th Rev. Edn. 1965 p. 340. . . . daß sich der Maschinist in den Schwerpunkt der Marionette versetzt, d. h. mit andern Worten, *tanzt*.
30. ibid p. 343 . . . wo die beiden Enden der Ringförmigen Welt in einander griffen.
31. ibid p. 345.
    Wir sehen, daß in dem Masse, als, in der organischen Welt, die Reflexion dunkler und schwächer wird, die Grazie darin immer strahlender und herrschender hervortritt. – Doch so, wie sich der Durchschnitt zweier Linien, auf der einen Seite eines Punkts, nach dem Durchgang durch das Unendliche, plötzlich wieder auf der andern Seite einfindet, oder das Bild des Hohlspiegels,

nachdem es sich in das Unendliche entfernt hat, plötzlich wieder dicht vor uns tritt: so findet sich auch, wenn die Erkenntnis gleichsam durch ein Unendliches gegangen ist, die Grazie wieder ein; so, daß sie, zu gleicher Zeit, in demjenigen menschlichen Körperbau am reinsten erscheint, der entweder gar keins, oder ein unendliches Bewußtsein hat, d. h. in dem Gliedermann, oder in dem Gott.

Mithin, sagte ich ein wenig zerstreut, müßten wir wieder von dem Baum der Erkenntnis essen, um in den Stand der Unschuld zurückzufallen?

Allerdings, antwortete er; das ist das letzte Kapitel von der Geschichte der Welt.

32. Boehn, our source for many historical facts, writes in total disparagement of Kleist's essay, saying that it has nothing to do with the puppet theatre and would have been forgotten long ago but for the fame of its author. (*op cit* p. 128). It does not concern us here whether Kleist's theory as to how marionettes are controlled is true and practical or not. What matters for us are his philosophical approach to puppetry and his relating it to wider theatrical issues.

An Examination of the Text

1. John Mortimer, *Clinging to the Wreckage*, Weidenfeld and Nicholson, and Penguin 1982. Quoted in National Theatre Programme of *A Little Hotel on the Side* (Feydeau, Trans. John Mortimer) 1984.
2. Joe Orton, quoted by John Lahr. Programme cit.
3. Craig *op cit* p. 89
4. *Die Rache* pp. 13–14

ROSA
Wie Ihr befahlt, wies ich die angekommenen Besucher fort.
Doch draußen drängt ein Herr, drängt immerfort,
Er will Euch sprechen.
Und sollt man tausend Riegel vor die Tore bringen,
Er würde sie zerbrechen
Und sich den Weg zu Euch erzwingen –
Und, ich gesteh, der Herr ist schön.
ELENA
Sag Deinen Herrn, ich wolle niemand sehn.
ROSA
Wenn ihn die Antwort nicht zufriedenstellt?

ELENA
Mir scheint, es ist ein Herr, der dir gefällt.
ROSA
Ich sagte schon, der Herr ist schön.
ELENA
Du langweilst mich. So heiß ihn weitergehn.
(Rosa verläßt das Zimmer)
ELENA (singt)
Nella tua cuna
Sparsa di rose
Dormi fanciulla
Mio dolce amore.
(Herein stürzt Lorenzo, ihm folgt Rosa)

5. ibid p. 15.
Ohnmächtig war ich, Mona, dienstbeflissen.

6. ibid p. 16

Schlürfe ich den Duft der Augen, die ich dürstend trinke,
In die ich wie in hyazinthne Juninacht versinke,
Strom von roten Flammenfackeln stürmt mein Blut,
Ihr seid der Kelch, in dem der Unrastpilger ruht,
. . . .
Mein Wille, eben schneidend Schwert . . . .
Demütig bin ich wie Blumen zu Füßen Unsrer Lieben Frau,
Ein zitternd flüchtig Wölkchen im mittaglichen Blau.

7. . . . O wär ich Flügelwehen von San Marcos Tauben,
O wär ich süßer Atem der jasmin'nen Lauben,
Ein Tuch aus Indien, das frierend nackte Schultern deckt,
Lächeln eines Kindes, das uns mittags weckt.

ibid

8. e.g. *Wotanisches Impromptu.* GW 2 p. 253

9. *Die Rache* p. 17

Kann sich die Glocke, deren Klöppel schwingen,
Wehren und sagen: Ich will nicht klingen?
Kann sich die Tanne, die der Wind zersaust,
Aufsteilen trotzig: Ich will nicht, daß Du mich umbraust?
Wenn ich selbst wollte, ach, gekettet sind die Füße,
Ich wachse hier und blühe, Du meine Erde, wundersüße.

10. ibid p. 19.

Ich lächle, denn ein jeder weiß, daß Ihr noch Knospe unberührt,
Und Euer Ehebett ein märzlich herber Garten,
Giuseppe schwätzt, doch eins versteht er nicht:
sein Blumenbeetlein warten.

11. ibid p. 58

Für ihn gewiß war Euer Leib ein unbekanntes Märchenland.

12. ibid pp61–2

Ich irr mich nicht, heut hat ein Weibchen ihren Mann betrogen.
Da lobe ich mir Elena. Sie wird zur Abendmesse gehn
Und Gottes reichen Segen auf unser Eheglück erflehn.
Vielleicht erhört Er sie und schenkt uns einen Sohn.

13. Spalek pp888–9
14. Spalek 3623
15. v. A Puppet Play, note 31 . . .
16. Die Rache pp59–60

ELENA
Ich zürn Dir, Du! Du hast den Bronnen
Allzu flüchtig ausgetrunken.
LORENZO
War ich nicht, ein Berauschter, tief in Dich versunken?
ELENA
Als Du das seidne Bettuch hobst, hast nicht gewußt
Von einem winzigen blauen Muttermal an meiner linken Brust,
Das mich, ein samtner Amethyst, vorwitzig schmückt,
Und das mich, ich gestehs, beim Baden oft entzückt
Du hast dies kleine Wunder, Flüchtiger, übersehn.
LORENZO
Bei Dionysos! Es soll in Zukunft nicht geschehn!
Mit tausend Schwüren will ich es versprechen!
ELENA
So küsse mich!
LORENZO
Und . . . darf ich mich ferner rächen?
ELENA
Du darfst!
O, Deine Rache mag mit Feuermeeren mich unspülen,
Doch . . . nie wird sich mein Blut an Deiner Rache kühlen.

17. Brecht, *Gedichte und Lieder aus Stücken*, Frankfurt/M 1963 p. 35
18. GW4 pp. 222–3.
Treiben die Masse sittliche Ideen, treiben sie nicht vielmehr Not und Hunger?
19. Hölderlin, *Gedichte* (ed. J. Schmidt), Insel Taschenbuch, 1984 p. 78

For as your [sc. Jupiter's] lightning comes out of the clouds, so does what is yours come from him. See! thus what you command is begotten from him, and from Saturn's peace is every power developed.

Die Maschinenstürmer

Introduction

1. Wolfgang Rothe *Toller* Reinbek bei Hamburg 1983 p. 87
   Rothe classifies Toller's first 6 plays thus:
   Die Wandlung: expressionist station-drama
   Masse Mensch: idea-drama without "flesh"
   Rache . . . : kindly-innocuous(!) burlesque
   Die Maschinenstürmer: pseudo-realistic mass play
   Hinkemann: existential problem piece
   Der entfesselte Wotan: satirical contemporary comedy
2. Thus:

   Hoppla, wir leben!: socio-political criticism
   (Bourgeois bleibt Bourgeois): social criticism
   Feuer aus den Kesseln: objective, historical criticism
   (Wunder in Amerika): criticism of phoney religious authority
   No More Peace!: anti-war satire
   Pastor Hall: anti-fascist celebration of the inner-resistance
3. v. *Toller's Use of Language* (passim)

Principal Sources, Themes and Characters

1. Fall p. 16 & 113.
2. Letter to Tessa 23 & 27.1.'21. GW5 p. 59.
3. ibid. 'Wie sehr kommt es in der Kunst auf die Gestaltung der Imponderabilien an! Sie sind die Seele des Werks.'
4. cf an unpublished letter (Yale University Archives) addressed to Kurt Wolff and written only two days before the letter to Tessa, and quoted by Dorothea Klein *Der Wandel der dramatischen Darstellungsform im Werk Ernst Tollers (1919–1930) Ph.D Thesis Bochum 1968, p. 80:*

   Nicht das Abstrakte, das Programm, sondern *das Sinnliche* wird wieder Ausgang und Ton werden.
   (Not what is abstract, not the 'programme', but *the sensory* will again become the starting-point and tone).
5. GW5 p. 60
6. His actually having achieved this in *Rache* may well have alerted him to its importance in drama.
7. GW5 p. 60 & Klein *op cit* p. 76

8. GW5 p. 60
9. Klein *op cit* p. 76
10. *loc cit*
11. Klein *loc cit,* quoting Beer *op cit* p. 155, suggests that Jimmy Cobbett is based on William Cobbett and his son James. That he is based on William is certain. The name may come directly from the son.
12. e.g. Reso pp. 158–159
13. GW2 p361: *Jimmy Cobbett* (sein wirklicher Name war William Cobbett) ein Führer aus den späteren Chartistenkämpfen.
    Carel ter Haar *Ernst Toller: Appell oder Resignation?* Munich 1977 p. 216:
    'ein Chartist, der unverstanden von den Arbeitern erschlagen wird.'
14. GW2 p. 361
15. Rothe *op cit* p. 88
16. F. Engels *The Condition of the Working-Classes in England in 1844* translated by F. K. Wischnewetzky, London 1892 pp121ff.
17. 1838 in Manchester; 1839 nationally. Coincidentally a revised Corn Law was actually passed in 1815 prohibiting imports of foreign corn to Britain when the price fell below 80 shillings per quarter, but allowing duty-free imports when that price was exceeded. v. N. Williams *Chronology of the Modern World 1763 to the present time.* London 1966 p124.
18. GW2 pp. 177ff
19. Marnette p. 226
    Translation of quotations:

    > Look at the children, most honoured sir. Do you see weariness there, or bad temper or indeed ill treatment? . . . How happy their eyes look! How they rejoice in the easy play of their muscles! How they enjoy in full measure the natural mobility of youth! How delightful is the nimbleness with which the little girl re-ties the broken threads! How all these dear little children enjoy showing off their arts before my guest. An aesthetic pleasure, is it not?
    >
    > I have visited many factories . . . and never seen children ill-treated . . . or merely ill-tempered. They all seem happy . . . rejoicing in the easy play of their muscles, and enjoying in full measure the mobility natural to their age . . . It was delightful to observe the nimbleness with which they joined the broken threads . . . Conscious of their skill, they enjoyed showing it in front of every stranger . . .

20. GW2 p. 153f & Marnette p. 226.

Translation of quotations:

We must dismiss most men. But all your children will be taken on... and nimble young women . . . the delicacy of the work demands particular delicacy of the fingers... Indeed, the machine displaces men.

The work on the machines . . . does not demand strength but greater agility of the fingers. Men are not only unnecessary for it but... actually less suitable than women and children and so naturally they are almost entirely displaced from this work.

21. Rothe 88.
22. Engels *op cit* pp. 284ff.
23. Marx's account of Malthus' famous essay is delightfully dismissive: "a schoolboyish, superficial and parsonic declamatory plagiarism . . . did not contain a single sentence thought out by Malthus himself". Capital Vol 2 p. 679. v. Note 29.
24. Letter to Gustav Mayer 7.2.1921.
    GW5 p. 60.
25. GW2 p. 153: Engels p. 65/GW2 p. 127: Engels p. 104/GW2 p. 166: Engels p. 143/GW2 p. 169: Engels p. 182/GW2 p. 169: Engels p. 179/GW2 p. 176: Engels p. 151/GW2 p. 177: Engels p. 179.
26. GW4 225.
27. GW5 p. 160.
28. GW2 p. 140.
29. Marx. *Capital* Trans E & C Paul. London 1930 Vol I p403
30. GW5 p. 60.
31. Marnette pp. 230f.
32. Is this perhaps an aural corruption of the Nottingham name *Wibberley*? In the production at the Half-Moon Theatre, London, the form *Wibley* was used.
33. GW2 p. 148.
34. ter Haar p. 216.
35. Klein p. 78.
36. GW2 p. 159.
37. Klein *loc cit*
38. See under *Luddite Rioters* in *Everyman's Encyclopaedia*, London, 1953.
39. GW2 p. 361.
40. ter Haar p. 216
41. *loc cit.*
42. Marnette p. 242
43. cf C. F. Meyer *Die Versuchung des Pescara*, 1 Kap. 3rd Para. In

describing a fresco of the Feeding of the 5000:

> . . . während sich im Vordergrunde eine lustige Gesellschaft ausbreitete, die an Tracht und Miene nicht übel einer Mittag haltenden lombardischen Schnitterbande glich . . .

W. D. Williams in his edition (Blackwell, Oxford, 1958) adds the note:

> The choice of the word *Schnitterbande* is also not without significance, since Death as a reaper is one of the oldest and most widespread symbols in literature.

44. GW2 p. 137.
45. GW2 p. 157.
46. GW2 p. 136.
47. Shelley, *Adonais* line 379.
48. I have in mind the first line of Faust's great opening speech in *Faust in Hell* by R. H. Ward (2nd edition, London 1945).:

> *Cognoscere rerum causas*: to know why;
> Could one know why the sun and why the stars
> Hang in their spheres and move within their bounds,
> Why spring must answer winter, migrant birds
> Make from far Egypt their mysterious flight,
> Why from the acorn hidden in the earth
> The forest oak uprises ring by ring;
> Could one know why the living cell increases
> And in its life already carries death;
> Could one know why men suffer, why they love,
> Why they grow old and fail, and why they die;
> Then were there reason in our blind unreason,
> Contempt of fate and whole belief in God.

49. GW2 p. 149.

For a philosphical statement of this view, almost exactly contemporary with the play, see Albert Schweitzer *Civilization and Ethics*, first pub. in German 1923. English translation London 1961 *passim*.

e.g. p. 9f:

> If we take the world as it is, it is impossible to attribute to it a meaning in which the aims and objects of mankind and of individual men have a meaning also. Neither world- nor life-affirmation nor ethics can be founded on what our knowledge of the world can tell us about the world . . . . Every world-view which fails to start from resignation in regard to knowledge is artificial and a mere fabrication, for it rests upon an inadmissible interpretation of the universe.
>
> When once thought has become clear about the relation in which world-view and life-view stand to each other, it is in a position to reconcile resignation as to knowledge with adherence to world- and

life-affirmation and ethics. Our view of life . . . can safely depend upon itself alone, for it is rooted in our will-to-live.

50. cf Bonhoeffer's view that mankind has come of age and must learn to live as if God did not exist.
51. GW4 p. 32.
52. GW2 p. 150.
53. Marnette p. 225. Marnette is wrong about English Trade Unions, which he says were first founded in 1830.
54. GW2 p. 135.
55. Marx/Engels *Communist Manifesto* (1848). English edition, London 1988 p. 29.
56. GW2 p. 150.
57. Der Blinde hört ihn nicht . . . Der Taube sieht ihn nicht . . . Ich hab' zwei gute Augen und zwei gute Ohren . . . ich find' ihn nicht . . . ibid.
58. cf John I. 18. and T. W. Ogletree, *The 'Death of God' Controversy*, London SCM 1966 passim.
59. In *King Lear* (IV. i) the blinded Gloster is led on his way to Dover by Edgar, who, in the guise of Poor Tom, is in effect dumb, being unable to express his real thoughts and feelings. The third character, the Old Man, gives his age as 80, the same as that of the Old Reaper. 'Tis the times' plague, when madmen lead the blind', says Gloster, underlining the symbolism of the scene, so close to that of Toller's. The themes of the two scenes are also closely related: the remoteness of the divine and the struggle for social & economic justice.
"As flies to wanton boys are we to th' Gods;
They kill us for their sport".
"So distribution should undo excess
And each man have enough".
How far the parallels were deliberate and conscious, and whether Toller hoped the allusion would deepen and enrich the scene for the perceptive in the audience cannot now be determined, but whether intentional or not, the Shakespearean reverberations place Toller firmly in the greatest of dramatic traditions.
In *Waiting for Godot* (Act II) Pozzo 'now blind' enters led by Lucky, now dumb: "He can't even groan" says Pozzo. Again a major theme, as of the whole play, is the inaccessibility of the divine; others are social injustice (Pozzo/Lucky) and lack of solidarity among the dispossessed (Estragon kicking Lucky).
60. GW2 p. 157.

61. ibid. Wenn Posaunen Siegestriumph blasen . . . Aber die Armen haben keine . . . Posaunen . . . etc
62. GW2 p. 137.
63. GW2 p. 190.
64. ibid. Ich, der Sohn einer Leibeigenen.
Is there perhaps here an echo of Strindberg's four-volume autobiography *Tjänstekvinnans (The Son of a Servant)?*
65. GW2 pp. 43ff. Sonja in *Masse Mensch* passim.
66. GW2 p. 190.
67. Klein interprets the Old Reaper rather differently: . . . er ist als Repräsentant der alten Zeit in ihrem Wahn, ihrer Müdigkeit and ihrer verirrten Suche nach der Wahrheit anzusehen. (Klein p. 79) . . . he is to be looked upon as the representative of the old time in its delusion, weariness and lost search for the truth.
68. GW2 p. 134.
69. *King Lear* I. i. 64.
70. ibid V. iii. 172–3.
71. GW2 p. 135.
72. GW2 p. 173.
73. Wolfgang Rothe *Expressionism in Literature* in *German Art in the Twentieth Century*, RAA London & Prestel-Verlag 1985 p. 101.
74. GW2 p. 127.
Strindberg, *The Road to Damascus* Trans. G. Rawson, London 1939 p. 31.
75. GW2 p. 127: Ich bin auch kein gewöhnlicher Bettler.
Strindberg *loc cit*: Why do you call me that? I'm no beggar.
76. GW2 p. 127f:

    Ich suche den Wohltäter, der mir Land schenkt, das 300 Pfund Sterling wert ist. Ich habe in meiner Jugend Westminster von außen gesehen. Ich möchte das Haus von innen betrachten.
    Strindberg *op cit* p. 38: I refused to pay taxes because I didn't want to become a member of parliament.

Structure: Shakespeare and Montage. An Epic Drama

1. Klein, p. 83.
2. ibid, p. 84, "[ein] Mangel . . . an inhaltlicher wie formaler Einheitlichkeit, die zu einem Bruch in der dramatischen Darstellungsweise von Haupt- und Neben-handlung führt . . ".

3. viz: 1. Exposition; 2. Development; 3. Turning-point 4. New Development; 5. Denouement.
4. GW1 p. 225.
5. *loc cit.*
6. GW2 p. 119. Das Vorspiel kann mit einfachen Mitteln vor dem Vorhang dargestellt werden.
7. *loc cit.* In der ersten Reihe des Zuschauerraums andere Lords.
8. *loc cit.* Der Darsteller Jimmys könnte in Lord Byrons Maske auftreten, der Darsteller Ures in der Maske des Lord Castlereagh.
9. see GW5 p. 159. The passage will be discussed in relation to the first production.
10. v. Programme, reproduced in *Weimarer Republik* p. 773. See later.
11. The Lord Chancellor's three brief speeches are in a clipped, formal prose, suggesting the ritual of parliamentary proceedings and punctuating the eloquence of the two main speakers.
12. GW2 p. 124. Die Sonne scheint so warm. *Sonnenkringel tanzen auf den Gesichten der Kinder.*
13. See note 55 (PRINCIPAL SOURCES, THEMES & CHARACTERS)
14. Wible uses the English word *Knobsticks,* common in the 19th Century. v. , e.g. E. Gaskell *North and South* passim. *Scab* is of US origin, first recorded in England in 1811.
15. GW2 pp. 125–6.
16. Toller uses the word *Litany* in respect of the form, not the content, of the Litany, viz. antiphony and intonation.
17. Peter Weiss, *Die Verfolgung und Ermordung Jean Paul Marats dargestellt durch die Schauspielgruppe des Hospizes zu Charenton unter Anleitung des Herrn de Sade.* Suhrkamp Verlag, Frankfurt/ Main, 1973.
   (author's revised version of 1965) p. 39 and passim.
18. GW2 p. 128.
19. Toller: Selig sind die geistig Armen.
   Luther: Selig sind, die da geistlich arm sind. (Matt. 5.3)
20. GW2 p. 128. Wo Könige mit den Pfunden der Easterlinge die Latrinen pflastern.
21. a) GW2 p. 129 b) GW2 p. 130.
22. GW2 p. 129.
23. Robert Tressell, *The Ragged Trousered Philanthropists,* Panther Books, London 1965, reprint 1985 p. 471 . . . Similar conflicts and arguments could be seen in the newspaper industry in the 1980s.
24. This is apparently a reference to the repeal in 1813 & 1814 (under the influence of the new doctrine of *laissez-faire*) of the Eiizabethan

Statute of Artificers, which gave magistrates powers to regulate wages & apprenticeships.

25. cf Marnette p. 242. In Shakespeare the political issues are primarily the Tudor Myth and the dangers of civil war. v. E. M. W. Tillyard, *Shakespeare's History Plays,* Harmondsworth 1962 (lst edn. Chatto & Windus 1944) pp. 54–70 & passim.
26. German: *Montage; Wachstum.* v. B. Brecht, *Anmerkungen zur Oper Aufstieg und Fall der Stadt Mahagonny* (1930) in *Aufstieg und Fall der Stadt Mahagonny,* Suhrkamp, Berlin, 1963 (text of 1955) p. 89.
27. GW2 p. 137. Wär ich ein Herr, ich würde huren.
28. *Aufruf* pp. 19–20.
29. GW2 pp. 138–141: Juggernaut, Dämon, Gott-sei-bei-uns, Teufel, Blutlohn, das höllische Maschinenungeheuer, Höllenketten, das reißende Tier, Höllenzange, der Dämon Dampf, Tyrann, Moloch, Höllenbrut, Tyrann Dampf; ein Dämon, der uns packt und rasch zermalmt; Dem Gott-sei-bei-uns haben sich die Herren verschrieben!; das höllische Maschinenungeheuer / Frißt tausend Weibern die gerechte Arbeit; Dem Teufel hat euch der Ure verkauft! Ich werde Bein! / ich werde Hand! etc.
30. GW2 p. 141.
31. GW2 p. 142.
32. *Die Liebe.* Hölderlin, *Gedichte,* Frankfurt / Main 1984 p. 74.
33. *Der Archipelagus.* ibid p. 131.
34. Gustav Landauer, *Friedrich Hölderlin in seinen Gedichten* Potsdam 1922. pp. 53 & 41 . . . Thus the 1916 lecture was not published until after this play had been written.
35. *Aufruf* p. 149.
36. ibid p. 12.
37. GW2 p. 143.
38. *Aufruf* p. 151.
39. GW2 p. 143.
40. GW2 pp. 141–143: Ein Gott dünkt euch die Maschine, ein Dämon. Ein Feind . . . wandelte euren Geist in Starre und Dumpfheit . . . Schau in euch hinein . . . Eure Schuld ist, daß ihr euch nicht eintet zum Arbeitsbund . . . Wollt der Gemeinschaft allen Werkvolks . . . Einet euch im Bund der Schaffenden . . .

    Aufruf: Darum ist der Geist in den Völkern immer in Verbindung mit dem Ungeist, das tiefe Denken des Symbols immer zusammen mit dem Meinen des Aberglaubens (p6); von Individuen beginnt alles; und am Individuum liegt alles (p. 154); Sozialismus ist die

Willenstendenz geeinter Menschen (p. 4); wo Geist ist, da ist Gesellschaft (p. 20).

41. GW2 p. 144.
42. *loc cit*. Wible here refers to Jimmy as an Irishman (Ire), as did the Beggar in Act 1 (GW2 p. 128). This is not to be taken literally but as a term of abuse. Engels (p. 67 etc) describes how Irish immigrants accepted even worse conditions than the indigenous workers. They were often brought in as strike-breakers. See, for example, E. Gaskell, *North and South* Chap XXII *et al.*
43. GW2 p. 146.
44. GW2 p. 147.
45. Klein p. 78.
46. GW2 p. 160.
47. ibid.
48. K. Marx *Das Kapital* Pt. III passim.
49. GW2 p. 161.
50. ibid.
51. Attributed to Lord Melbourne (1779–1848).v. D. C. Browning *Everyman's Dictionary of Quotations and Proverbs* London 1955 p. 199.
52. GW2 p. 161.
53. GW2 p. 162.
54. Charles Darwin *The Origin of Species* 6th Edtn, London, 1901 p. 79.
55. Angus Ross in *Penguin Companion to Literature* 1971 Vol II Harmondsworth 1971 pp. 133–4.
56. Ross *loc cit.*
57. Ross *op cit* p. 345: article on Malthus.
58. GW2 p. 162. cf Kropotkin *Mutual Aid,* Harmondsworth 1939 p. 54.
59. cf Kropotkin pp. 74–128 passim & p. 158.
60. GW2 pp. 162–3. Eagles: Kropotkin pp. 34–5; Ants: Kropotkin p29; Beetles: Kropotkin pp. 27–8.
61. v. Chap. on *Die Rache . . .* passim.
62. GW2 p. 155.
63. GW2 p. 165, cf *Mutter Courage und ihre Kinder* Berlin 1974, p. 106
64. GW2 p. 151.
65. GW2 pp. 149–50.
66. v loc cit in N. 26. Spannung auf den Ausgang. Spannung auf den Gang.
67. GW2 p. 176. das Surren der Transmissionen. Verschiedenartigste

Summlaute schwingen. Hellklingendes Singen schnellaufender Wellen. Tiefen Brummen der Steuerhebel. Taktmäßiges klirrendes Klappern der Schiffchen.
(the whirr of the transmission. Humming noises of the most various kinds are vibrating. The clear singing of the fast-running shafting. The deep drone of the control levers; the rhythmic rattling clatter of the shuttles).

68. GW2 p. 180.
69. ibid.
70. ibid.
71. GW2 p. 181.
72. Max Barthel *Beginn.* In *Die Faust,* Potsdam 1920. Reprinted in Günter Heinz (ed) *Deutsche Arbeiterdichtung 1910–1933* Stuttgart 1974 p. 148.
73. GW2 p. 187.
74. GW2 p. 189.
75. GW2 p. 190.
76. Klein p. 84.

The Play on Stage

0. *The New Statesman* 4.11.1922, p. 138.
1. See, Harry Graf Kessler, *Walther Rathenau, Sein Leben und sein Werk,* Wiesbaden 1962 pp. 354–369 for a full account of the plot and murder. Count Kessler's book was originally published in Berlin, 1928.
2. Artur Michel, *Vossische Zeitung,* Berlin, 13.7.1922. (Also in Rühle p. 387)
3. Quoted in Rühle p. 1163.
4. Press cutting in Theatermuseum, Köln, 13.7.22, almost certainly from *Berliner Tageblatt.*
5. *Steglitzer Anzeiger* 1.7.22. Press cutting in Theatermuseum, Köln; reprinted in Rühle, pp. 383ff.
Es war ein Orkan! Eine elementare Massendemonstration
6. Ihresgleichen hat sich in einem *deutschen* Schauspielhaus kaum jemals zugetragen. In den ersten Jahren der großen Französischen Revolution ging es in den Theatern von Paris ähnlich her. (Kienzl. *loc cit).*
7. Max Osborn, *Berliner Morgenpost* 13.7.22.
Osborn quotes inaccurately from memory and attributes the speech to Der alte Reaper instead of to the Beggar. It is, of course,

also possible that Karl-Heinz Martin had made changes in the text, perhaps in the last days of rehearsal.

8. Kienzl, *loc cit.*
9. Kessler *op cit* p. 356
10. Osborn, *loc cit*
11. *Walther Rathenau, Industrialist, Banker, Intellectual, and Politician, Notes and Diaries 1907–1922*. Ed. von Strandmann. Trans. Pinder-Cracraft. Oxford, 1985, p. 10.
12. Walther Rathenau, *Gesammelte Schriften*. Berlin, 1918, Vol 3, p. 13
13. Kessler *op cit* p. 195
14. W. Rathenau *op cit* Vol 3 p. 33–34: Wer ist der Mensch, der von einer Torheit der Natur berichten wüßte? Die Mechanisierung aber ist Schicksal der Menschheit, somit Werk der Natur; sie ist nicht Eigensinn und Irrtum eines einzelnen noch einer Gruppe; niemand kann sich ihr entziehen, denn sie ist aus Urgesetzen verhängt. Deshalb ist es kleinliche Zagheit, das Vergangene zu suchen, die Epoche zu schmähen und zu verleugnen. Als Evolution und Naturwerk gebührt/ihr Ehrfurcht, als Not Feindschaft . . . . . . Mechanisierung als Not aber ist entwaffnet, sobald ihr heimlicher Sinn offenbart ist.

    Mechanisierung als Form des materiellen Lebens hingegen wird der Menschheit dienen müssen, solange nicht die Volkszahl auf die Norm der vorchristlichen Jahrtausende zurück gesunken ist.
15. *loc cit* p. 17–18:

    . . . und weil der Sozialismus um Einrichtungen kämpft, bleibt er Politik; er mag Kritik üben, Mißstände beseitigen, Rechte gewinnen: niemals wird er das Erdenleben umgestalten, denn diese/Kraft gebührt allein der Weltanschauung, dem Glauben, der transzendenten Idee.
16. *op cit* Vol 2 p. 9.

    Jede Frage, die wir zu Ende denken, führt ins *Überirdische*.
17. *Op cit* Vol 3, p. 27.

    All unser Tun hat etwas Seherisches, denn jeder Schritt trägt in die Zukunft . . . Bedingung ist, daß der Fuß den Boden, das Auge die Gestirne nie verliere.
18. *Notes and Diaries* (v. Note 11) p. 19.
19. Kessler *op cit* p. 344. (For text of Treaty of Rapallo v. *Weimarer Republik p. 264*)
20. ibid p. 356
21. Rathenau *op cit* Vol 2 p. 177: Ist Sterblichkeit möglich?

22. *ibid* p. 180.
23. . . . die stilisierende Art Tollers dem Arena-theater entgegenkommt – es ist einer der weniger Fälle, welche die Berechtigung und Mission des Großen Schauspielhaus erweisen. Max Osborn. *Berliner Morgenpost* 13.7.22.
Press cutting in Akademie der Künste, Berlin. Also reprinted in *Rühle*).
24. . . . nimmt Karlheinz Martin das Haus, in dem er spielt, handfertig als etwas Gegebenes hin. Ihm gelingt nicht (was auch Reinhardt nicht gelang), die auseinanderflüchtenden Dimensionen des Raumes zu bezwingen, doch er zeigt auch nicht (was aber Reinhardt zeigte) den Kampf mit dieser teuflich zerberstenden Grenzenlosigkeit. Sondern er sieht zu, wie man es möglich macht, ein vorhandenes Stück, das seine Art von Räumlichkeit hat, in der nun einmal gottgewollten des großen Hauses unterzubringen. (Critic: *Lg*. Press cutting in Theatermuseum, Köln. Periodical and date not given).
25. Das impressionistische Theater hatte es, wie man weiß, leicht die Illusion eines Innenraumes zu erzeugen, plagte sich aber mit den freien Gegenden; das Große Schauspielhaus läßt dafür die Leute immer im Freien ergehen und kann seine Betretenheit nicht verbergen, wenn sie ein Dach überm Kopfe haben. (ibid).
26. Aber selbst Wälder, Gärten und Landschaften liebt es nicht, denn diese demaskieren mit unvergleichlicher Offenheit den Bruch zwischen Arena und Hinterbühne, um so mehr aber schätzt es Straßenzüge, freie, ungezäunte Plätze, neutrale Gegenden für Aufmärsche, Zusammenrottungen und Demonstrationen. Daß diese Haus sich so aus einem Theater in einem Meetingraum verwandeln kann, ist aber gewiß nicht sein Problem, sondern im Gegenteil, daß es nicht gelingen will, aus diesem Meetingraum ein Theater zu machen. (ibid).
27. Carl Vollmoeller: *Zur Entwicklungsgeschichte des großen Hauses*, in *Das große Schauspielhaus. Zur Eröffnung des Hauses* herausgegeben vom Deutschen Theater zu Berlin. Im Verlage der Bücher des Deutschen Theaters. Berlin 1920. Redaktion: Heinz Herald. (Copy in Theatermuseum, Köln).
28. *Vossische Zeitung* 13.7.22. Press cuttings in Theatermuseum, Köln and Akademie der Künste, Berlin. Also reprinted in *Rühle*. pp. 387–9.
29. a. Programmzettel der Uraufführung am Großen Schauspielhaus, 1922. aus: Blätter des Deutschen Theaters, Ausgabe für

das Große Schauspielhaus. (Jg. 8, H. 17). Reproduced in *Weimarer Republik* pp. 773–4.
This programme is dated Sunday, 2 July 1922.

b. Programme. Copy in Theatermuseum, Köln, dated Tuesday 18 July (amended in hand-writing to Wednesday 19 July).
c. Critiques as quoted.
d. Photographs: see later note.
e. 2nd Edition

30. See: Walter-Jürgen Schorlies, *Der Schauspieler, Regisseur, szenische Bühnenbauer und Theaterleiter, Karl-Heinz Martin. Versuch einer Biographie. Diss. Ph. D. Köln 1971.*
31. Michel Töteberg, *Heartfield,* Reinbek, 1978, p. 41.
32. v. Programme (N. 29 a & b).
33. Cast List 2.7.22. (Changes in programme for 18.7.22 given in brackets).

Lordkanzler	Aribert Wäscher (Hermann Greid)
Lord Castlereagh	Carl Wallauer
Lord Byron	Wilhelm Dieterle (Ferdinand Hart)
Ure, Fabrikant	Carl Wallauer
Offizier	Kurt Lukas (Kurt Müller)
Ingenieur	Paul Günther
Ned Lud	Gerhard Ritter (Max Nemetz)
Margret, seine Frau	Leoni Duval
John Wible	Hans Rodenberg
Mary, seine Frau	Esther Hagan (Friedel Harms)
Teddy, beider Kind	Gertrud von Hoscheck
Der alte Reaper, Marys Vater	Alexander Granach
Jimmy Cobbet	Wilhelm Dieterle (Ferdinand Hart)
Henry Cobbet	Aribert Wäscher (Hermann Greid)
Jimmys und Henrys Mutter	Elise Zachow-Vallentin
Bettler	Sigmund Nunberg (Fritz Rasp)
Georges	Erich Fiedler
William	Willi Fritsch

	(Gerd Elinen)
Bob	Max Kowa
Albert	Gerhard Bienert
Artur	Karl Hannemann
Charles	Walter Redlich
Eduard	Wilhelm Hiller
Tom	Fritz Hahn
Erstes Weib	Lotte Fließ
Zweites Weib	Else Lorenz
Drittes Weib	Käte Nevill
Hausierer	Richard Martienssen
	(Bruno Klein)
Blinder	George Hilbert
Taubstummer	Gustav Deimling

34. see note 27
35. Dukes. *loc. cit.*
36. ibid
37. seine Linien zerfließen in Worte, Worte, Worte. (Hermann Kienzl). *Steglitzer Anzeiger* 1.7.22, in *Rühle p. 385*
38. . . . den rhetorisch-demagogischen Charakter des Stücks . . . (Michel *loc. cit*).
39. Kurz, außer den Massenszenen und den Zustandsbildern haben wir nichts als Rhetorik. (Michael Charol. Press cutting in Theatermuseum, Köln. Date and periodical not given).
40. Max Hochdorf *Vorwärts* Berlin 3.7.22
41. Der Regisseur hat auch das Rhetorische übertrieben, statt abzuschwächen. Schon in der ersten Szene ließ er das erste Redner-Feuerwerk abbrennen. (Stefan Großmann in *Das Tagebuch III*, Berlin 15.7.1922. Reprinted in Fall pp. 135 ff).
42. Dukes, *loc. cit.*
43. ibid
44. ibid
45. ibid.
46. ibid.
47. ibid.
48. ibid.
49. 1. in *Weimarer Republik* p. 774.
    2. in Rothe p. 86.
50. Auch dieses Drama bleibt Entwurf und Absicht.
    (*Vorwärts*. Berlin, 3.7.22).
51. die Räder im Betrieb! (*Steglitzer Anzeiger* 1.7.22).

52. . . . es gibt auch banale Stellen, wo Tendenziöses im Rohzustand künstlerisch ungestaltet bleibt. Aber dann kommt der letzte Akt und bringt eine großartige Steigerung.
Der Vorhang hebt sich, und vor uns steht ein riesenhaftes Maschinenungetüm. Mit Eisengliedern, Schwingrädern, Kolben, Stangen, Kugeln, Treibriemen, Dampfmäulern, Gittern. Zur Seite rechts und links die von dem Koloß bewegten Webstühle, von jämmerlichen Kindern bedient . . . Grandiose Wahrheit des Alltags, und dennoch unreal, in ein überwältigendes Symbol emporgehoben. Wie ein drohendes Schicksal für Generationen in Jahrhunderten glotzt das Ungeheuer aus dem mächtigen Fabrikkuppelraum. (*Berliner Morgenpost*. 13.7.22. Reprinted in *Rühle*. p. 386).
53. Dukes. *loc. cit.*
54. ibid.
55. In vollem Gegensatz zu dieser Wirklichkeit standen im übrigen die Szenischen, mimischen und akustischen Mystifaxen Karl-Heinz Martins, des Regisseurs. Aus den auf Groteske abgerichteten Schauspielern ragte nichts Persönliches hervor. (Kienzl. *loc. cit*).
56. Michel. *loc. cit.*
57. ibid.
58. Er ließ aus der Tiefe, die Arena hinauf, den Arbeiterzug schweigend-langsam nach der Bühne sich vorschieben, als gelte es eine Demonstration zum Schutze der Republik. Dort warfen sie zur Deklamation der Führer die Arme und Stimmen im Reinhardtschen Takt empor und sangen bald gellend, bald flüsternd ihr Weberlied. Von dort verteilten sie sich singend, verklingend, wie ein Opernchor, nach den Seiten. Von dort stürmten sie nach der Hinterbühne, um die himmelragende Dampfmaschine zu zertrümmern. Den stoßend-stöhnenden Marschrhythmus des Weberlieds benutzte Martin zugleich als Refrain zur Gliederung. (ibid).
59. Vielleicht hat Karlheinz Martin dem Drama den Todestoß gegeben. Er hat das Redespiel in eine Oper verwandelt . . . Alles wird ihm zur Wachsfigurengruppe. Er stellt Bilder und läßt die Figuren bewegungslos verharren. Dann, auf militärisches Kommando. möglichst ruckweise, darf die Gruppe sich bewegen.
(Großmann, *loc. cit.* in *Fall* pp136–7).
60. The name Mary Anne Walkley is taken from a real person. She was not a mill-worker, but a seamstress who died in 1863 from over-work in an ill-ventilated room. *Punch* published a bitter

cartoon on the theme: *The Haunted Lady, or The Ghost in the Looking-glass*. (Eric de Maré *The London Doré Saw*. London 1963. p. 110).

61. Dukes. *loc. cit.*
62. *Die Maschinenstürmer* 2nd Edtn. pp. 15–16.
63. The 2nd Edition, which prints the domestic scene while also reallocating the lines, thus presents a split and inconsistent character.
64. v. Spalek pp. 882–884, up to 1951.
65. Estonia, 1924. Estonia did not become part of USSR until 1940.
66. soziale Schicksalstragödie. . . . daß ihrem Geschlecht ein Dichter erstanden ist, der die schmerzlichen Wehen der Geburt des Proletariats nachfühlt. (Reviewer: rr. *Leipziger Volkszeitung* No. 246. Oct. 1922. *Feuilleton*. Spalek 3073).
67. Details from Spalek 3100.
68. Spalek p. viii & pp. 687ff.
69. All facts from copy of programme in Victoria & Albert Museum. (A pencilled note alongside Martita Hunt's name may imply that this was her first professional appearance).
70. In The Daily Review (NY). Spalek 3082; *TLS*, Spalek 3087; *The Times*, Spalek 3090.
71. Frank Birch, *The Nation & the Athenaeum* XXXIII, No. 6 (May 12, 1923) 204 (Spalek 3093).
72. *The Daily Review* (NY) 2.6.1923.
73. *Daily Telegraph*, late ed., 8.5.'23. Spalek 3083.
74. *The New Statesman* XXI 12.5.'23, p141. Spalek 3097.
75. Birch, *loc. cit.*
76. *Manchester Guardian* 8.5.1923.
77. 11.5.1923. Spalek 3101.
78. See Spalek 3075.
79. See Spalek; also *25 Jahre Theater in Berlin. Premieren* 1945–1970. Berlin 1972.
80. 22 Nov, 1951. Spalek p. 884.
81. W. K. in *Kurier* 23.11.'51. Press cutting in Theatermuseum, Köln.
82. Und siehe da, Ernst Toller hat wirklich noch seine Wirkung, trotz allen Behelfs . . . Das Drama . . . hat noch Kraft . . . Im Parkett hörte man viele sachliche Unterhaltungen über Löhne, arbeitsrechtliche Gegensätze zwischen Ost und West.
    (S-F in *Die Neue Zeit*. Berlin 23.11.'51).
83. Dukes. *loc. cit.*
84. A comprehensive brochure (n. d). was produced, published pre-

sumably by the Goethe Institute. Referred to here as *Brochure*.

85. 23 Nov. to 9 Dec. Songs and texts by Brecht, Mühsam, Tucholsky, Eisler, Weill, Kollo, Heyman and others, including, of course, Walter Mehring's song, *Hopla, wir leben,* which was used in Toller's play and provided its final and definitive title. *Brochure* p. 54.
86. At 27 Alie Street, London E. 1. The production ran from 27 Nov. to 23 Dec. *Brochure* p. 49. The Brochure reproduced a photograph of the final scene of the original production at the Großes Schauspielhaus, 1922, wrongly captioned: *Krakov production 1924. Cf Weimarer Republik* p. 774 where the same picture is correctly captioned. No *Krakov 1924* production is listed by Spalek. The Brochure's error is apparently derived from *Theatre Quarterly* Vol II No. 5, Jan-Mar 1972, p. 80.
87. Michael Billington, *The Guardian,* Wed. 29 Nov. 1978.
88. ibid.
89. The Cast, as given in the programme:

Lizza Aiken	Mary Wibley, Ure's daughter, Louis with the barrow
Janet Amsden	Mrs Cobbett, Margaret Lud, a man, a blind man, a woman
Simon Callow	Ure, The Old Reaper, a drunk
David Fielder	John Wibley, a drunk, a woman
John Hartley	Ned Lud, a deaf and dumb man
Jim Hooper	Jim Cobbett, a woman
Robin Hooper	Henry Cobbett, Albert, a woman
Maggie Steed	The Beggar, a woman, a man

(Also two groups each of three children performed on alternate days).

The Programme made or perpetuated a number of errors: Toller's own error in *Eine Jugend in Deutschland* that Rathenau was murdered ON the day of the first performance; Max Reinhardt was credited with Karl-Heinz Martin's production (an error repeated by Billington in his review); the relationship between Toller and Piscator is inaccurately expressed; the Goethe Institute is called the German Institute.

90. Billington. *loc. cit.*
91. ibid.
92. *The Guardian* 28.11.'78.
93. *Der Tagesspiegel.* 6.1.'79.
94. ibid.
95. Quotations and facts from Winnie Lees in *The Stage* 7.6.'84.

Other information:

Stage Design	Kenny Miller
Lighting	Gerry Jenkinson

Cast:

Patrick Hannaway, John McGlynn, Yolanda Vasquez, Derwent Watson, and Laurance Rudic as Jimmy: "showing in a beautifully conceived portrayal of an idealist, that he is maturing into a very fine actor indeed".

96. von dem niemand sagen kann, was hier zu suchen ist. (Kathrin Bergmann in *Die Welt*, 7.5.'85).
97. ibid.
98. Copy in *Fritz Hüser Institut*, Dortmund.
99. The play was given an imaginatively conceived amateur production as part of the Edinburgh Festival Fringe 1987 by the Bulmershe Revival Theatre Company, students of the Bulmershe College of Higher Education, Reading, produced by Tom Wild, a member of the college staff. The immaturity of the cast, except for Kevin Naghten (Ure/Castlereagh) was a major weakness, but the design and choreography were most effective. The whole production was in red and grey, punctuated occasionally by black. When the audience entered, they were faced with a tableau of masked, red-robed figures grouped pyramidally: The House of Lords. Instead of a 'property' Machine, members of the cast performed a kind of symbolic ballet, rhythmically handling a great strip of red cloth that dominated the stage as surely as any mechanism. Instead of Toller's ending the cast formed a defiant tableau, dominated by the Red Flag: theatrically striking, but Agitprop rather than Toller. In Ashley Dukes' translation the play, in the words of the programme note, spoke "as powerfully to us in 1987 in the aftermath of the miners' strike . . . as it did to its German audiences".

III TOLLER'S USE OF LANGUAGE

Introduction

1. e.g. *Die Wandlung*: Karl Heinz Martin. *Hoppla, wir leben!*: Piscator.
2. *Der Ringende*. In *Vormorgen* p. 9.
3. E. Toller, *Vormorgen*, Potsdam, Kiepenheuer Verlag 1924.
4. Except in songs. e.g. in *Nie wieder Friede*.

5. A scene from 'the unpublished drama *Eugen Hinkemann*' (the scene between Hinkemann and the Budenbesitzer in which he takes on the rat-killing job) was published in *Blätter des Deutschen Theaters,* Jg. 8.1921/22, Heft 7, pp. 182/3, with an editorial note that implies that the whole play was already written.
   (Seen in Deutsches Literaturarchiv, Marbach).
6. *Weltliche Passion* in *Internationale Literatur*, Nr. 4 1934. *Internationale Vereinigung Revolutionärer Schriftsteller*, Zürich, Paris, Amsterdam and Copenhagen.
   (Seen in Deutsches Literaturarchiv, Marbach)
   Die Feuer-Kantate in *Das Wort* Jg. 3 Nr6, Moscow, June 1928. (Seen in Akademie der Künste, Berlin).

Toller as Poet

Poetic Language in *Die Wandlung* and the War Poems

1. *Vormorgen* is a nonce-word of Toller's formed on the analogy of *Vorgestern* (the day before yesterday), *Vormittag* (fore-noon); *Vortag* (the day before, the eve of) etc. It therefore refers to the period before morning, 'the darkness before dawn', a title reflecting Toller's political hopes for the future.
2. Deutsches Literaturarchiv, Marbach.
   Facsimile in W. Rothe, *Toller,* Reinbek 1983, p. 36.
3. Rothe op cit p. 27.
4. Überraschende Verse, die in ihrer betonten Kunstlosigkeit nichts mit der (oft in der Heimat geschriebenen) inflationären Kriegspoesie jener Jahre gemein haben und an "antiästhetische" Tendenzen unserer Zeit erinnern. ibid p. 32.
5. For this and many of the facts and suggestions in what follows I am indebted to a lecture, *German Poetry of the First World War,* delivered by Prof. P. Bridgwater in the Conference Centre, John Rylands University Library, Manchester, 8.10.'84.
6. Walther Killy (ed) *Epochen der Deutschen Lyrik,* Bd 9, 1.Teil. Munich 1974, p. 123.
7. ibid p. 167.
   Translation, Cecil Davies, *Stand,* Vol 24 No 3 p. 44.
8. Killy op cit p. 121.
   Yet my Fatherland, holy Homeland, what test must you now come through? "My child, it must happen, it must pass over. Only take the sickle in your hand! For now you must mow grass

with a firm hand . . . And it is a grass that drips with blood! You can be permitted to have no pity. Head after head sinks hissing from the stalk and is heaped into the mountains of corpses . . ".

9. Gerrit Engelke, *An die Soldaten des großen Krieges* in Günter Heintz (ed), *Deutsche Arbeiterdichtung 1910–1933*, Stuttgart, Reclam 1974 p. 77.
This world is for you all, great and beautiful, and beautiful! / Look here! Look up in astonishment! After the battle and groaning in blood: / How green oceans flood to the horizon / How mornings and evenings glow in pure clarity / How mountains rise from the valleys / How milliards of beings tremble around us! / O, our highest joy of all is: to live! /
10. Edward Thomas, *Collected Poems*, London, Faber 1936. *Roads*, pp. 181 / 183; *A Private*, p. 202.
11. Isaac Rosenberg, *Dead Man's Dump* (lines 7–13). B. Gardner (ed) *Up the Line to Death*, London, Methuen. Rev. edtn 1976. 3rd Printing 1980, p. 133.
12. Dietrich Bode (ed). *Gedichte des Expressionismus*, Stuttgart, Reclam, 1976 p. 207.
By the Fire
September night. Land between the Meuse and its tributaries. / Potato fields, ridden across, desolate, trampled upon, crushed under foot. / Who knows his way around? Who was here already, alone, with ladies, with brown dogs? In the distance: forests, hills, all sorts of things, stars, dead men, / The howling of the riders, filthy, riding wounded. Damned dastardly mouth of the muffled melody of the redness of early morning. /
13. ibid p. 195
Patrol. The stones are hostile / A window grins treacherously / Branches choke / Mountains of bushes rustle their leaves rapidly / Scream shrilly / Death / .
14. *Vormorgen* p. 12.
. . . Tamed monster / My gun gleams, / Stares with its black barrel / At the milky moon. /
15. Gardner (ed). op cit p. 104.
16. *Vormorgen* p. 11.
Wisps of mist / Mourning banners / Over trenches. / Human bodies / Mutilated human bodies . . . / The sun rises. /
17. ibid p. 13.
Through shell-holes, / Dirty puddles, / They plod. / Over soldiers / Freezing in the fox-hole / They stumble. /

18. ibid.
Rats dart squeaking across the path,/Rainstorm knocks with dead fingers/On rotting doors./Signal rockets/Plague lanterns . . ./To the trench to the trench. /
19. ibid p. 14.
One man is dreaming at the mass-grave/"Such a heap of Christmas cookies*/I wanted for myself as a child,/So much" . . ./A mine blew fourteen lads to bits./When was it, anyway?/Yesterday./
(*Presumably *Lebkuchen* are meant: the gingerbreads cut into shapes of little men).
20. The remaining 1915 poem, *Marschlied,* is a bitter parody of a soldiers' Marching Song. This was first published in *Die Aktion, Wochenschrift für Politik, Literatur, Kunst,* edited by Franz Pfemfert, 6.4.1918 p. 172. This version has four stanzas, the extra stanza placed between stanzas 1 & 2 of the *Vormorgen* version; otherwise it is identical. The whole poem reads:

Wir Wand'rer zum Tode
Der Erdnot geweiht,
Wir kranzlose Opfer,
Zu Letztem bereit

Wie fern aller Freude
Und fremd aller Qual.
Wir Blütenverwehte
Im nächtlichen Tal.

Wir Preis einer Mutter
Die nie sich erfüllt,
Wir wunschlose Kinder,
Von Schmerzen gestillt,

Wir Tränen der Frauen,
Wir lichtlose Nacht,
Wir Waisen der Erde
Ziehn stumm in die Schlacht.

We travellers to death/Dedicated to the affliction of the earth/We ungarlanded sacrifical victims,/Prepared for the end//We, far from all joy/And alien to all agony,/We scattered with flowers/In the valley by night.//We the reward of a mother/Who was never fulfilled/We, contented children/Relieved from pain./We tears of women,/We lightless night,/We the orphans of the earth/March dumbly into the battle./

The editor, Franz Pfemfert, wrote an introductory paragraph to the poem:

Wenn ich doch endlich allen Ahnungslosen einhämmern könnte, daß es mir nicht um Literatur, jüngste oder älteste Dichtung geht! . . . . . .
. . . . . . Hier spricht kein "Dichter", kein Hoffnungsvoller der Reinhardklique oder der Wolfensteinethiker:
ein Mensch spricht, hinter dessen Worten sein Schicksal steht.
(If only I could drum into all clueless people that I'm not concerned with Literature or with Poetry, whether the most contemporary or the most ancient! . . . ..Here it is not a 'Poet' who is speaking, not some starry-eyed member of the Reinhard-clique or of the moral philosphers of the Wolfenstein group: a human being is speaking, behind whose words stands his destiny).

Two months later, on 15.6.1918, the same periodical carried a poem by Toller not subsequently reprinted. It is somewhat turgid, but does express Toller's belief in the spiritual importance of language and his awareness of how it is debased in wartime:

An die Sprache

Sprache,
Gefäß göttlichen Geistes.
Weltorgel!
Brausende in allen Registern!
Hauch der Erfüllten,
Stammeln wunder Mütter,
Seziermesser furchtloser Denker,
Dichtergeliebte!

Sie haben Dich geschändet,
In allen Pfützen Europas
Taten sie Dir Gewalt.
Sie schändeten Dich!
Zeig Dein Gorgonenantlitz den Tempelräubern!
Weh, daß Du Mordschweiß perlst!
Tauch in geheiligten Quell geäderte Glieder
Voll göttlichen Bluts!
Steige verjüngt,
Geheiligt empor!

Language/Vessel of the divine spirit./Organ of the world! Thundering out in all registers!/Breath of those who are fulfilled,/Stammering of wounded mothers/Dissecting-knife of fearless thinkers,/Beloved of poets!//They have defiled you,/In all the puddles of Europe/They have violated you./They have defiled you!/Show your Gorgon-countenance to the despoilers of the temple! Alas, that you sweat the sweat of murder!/Immerse veined limbs filled with divine blood in the sanctified spring!/Rise up rejuvenated, sanctified!/
(*Marschlied* may owe something to Heine. The only other important war poet to show Heine's influence was Alfred Lichtenstein, killed in September 1914).

21. *Vormorgen* p. 17.
O women of France, / Women of Germany, / If you saw your men! /
22. ibid p. 15.
Positional Warfare. Everyday life hammers, / Chokes you, / Weariness penetrates into the blood. / Candles smell wanly. / Defiance dies. / You long for the final battle. /
23. ibid p. 16.
Child-bearing revolves in eyes heavy with fruit, / Fates swirl unclothed in the room. /
24. ibid p. 19.
War lapsed into a ghost / That bonily clutched its fingers / Around the circled peoples. /
25. v. note 2.
The full moon sheds azure streams / On trees which, lacerated, shot to pieces, / Creep away dumbly into themselves like cripples, / Glutinously surrounded by morasses of terror. /
26. See the schematic representation on pp. 227/8.
27. GW2 pp. 13/14.
28. GW2 pp. 21/22.
29. T. S. Eliot, *Sweeney Agonistes* (1932) *in Collected Poems 1909–1935*, London, Faber, 1936 (2nd Imp. 1937) p. 127.
30. GW2 p. 22.
1st Soldier: We travel eternally./*2nd* S. The engine pounds eternally./*3rd* S. People marry eternally. / Out of greedy pleasure grows the eternal curse./*4th* S. The primeval womb bore stars eternally. / The divine womb destroys itself eternally./*5th* S. We rot eternally./*6th* S. Children frightened by the father eternally./ *7th* S. Sacrificed by mothers. / Freezing affliction. / *All*. We travel eternally / Eternally . . . / *The Scene closes.*
31. *Vormorgen* p. 21.
Mothers! / your hope, your happy burden / lies in churned-up earth / . . . Mothers / Your sons did that to each other. /
32. W. Wordsworth, *The Prelude*, Bk VI lines 556 / 557 (1805), 624 / 625 (1850).
33. Let pain give birth to action! / Let your suffering, millions of mothers, / Serve as seed for the ploughed-up earth, / Let humanity / Germinate. *Vormorgen* p. 21.
34. ibid p. 18.
Around the pole dance three children's bones / Broken out of the body of a young mother.
35. GW2 p. 26

Now we are no longer friend and enemy. / Now we are no longer white and black. / Now we are all equal / Worms ate the multi-coloured tatters. / Now we are all equal. / Sir . . . we want to dance.

36. ibid p. 31.
Blind Man: The day is cruel. The sun stings. / I feel it as a sea of sulphur. *That* bites and cauterizes me with vapours. /

37. ibid p. 32.
I don't know whether I am still a human being / Or a living latrine. / My bowels are crippled . . . / I'm stuck in my own shit - / I pollute myself and you disgustingly. /

38. The verse passage with which Toller closed the Ur-Wandlung has already been examined, and we have seen that its poetic ancestry is to be found in Goethe.

39. GW2 p. 44.
The walls of the cell hide horror — / Wherever I looked — boundless swamps, / Only grey swamps — always grey swamps, / In long hours of twilight / Maggots crawled out of the iron grills. / I defended myself — yet then — what could I do . . . / Grey maggots tore at my body. /

40. *Vormorgen* pp. 23/24.
Through the grill of my cell / I see children playing. /

41. ibid p. 22.
You thousands, tortured in factories, harnessed to your work.

Choral Works and *Masse Mensch*

1. *Tag des Proletariats*, Potsdam, Kiepenheuer, 1920 Spalek 60.
2. ibid p. 7.
3. ibid. We have found another way to God.
4. ibid. We want to bring the Empire of Peace to the earth. (The last three lines of the sonnet are alexandrines).
5. Spalek 62.
6. Spalek 64. Spalek states incorrectly under 62 (p 75) that "The revised version of *Tag des Proletariats* was also published in *Vormorgen*". He also refers under 64 (p 78) to "the two Chorwerke". But his own bibliographical description, p. 77, and an examination of the book itself (copy stamped: *Stiftung — Staatsbibliothek — Preuß. Kulturbesitz*). prove that only the *Requiem* was printed in this volume. References and quotations are from the 3rd Edition.
7. The other was the Massenspiel, to which Toller also made impor-

tant contributions.

8. v. Knilli F. & Münchow U., *Frühes Deutsches Arbeitertheater 1847–1918 Eine Dokumentation,* Munich 1970 passim.
9. L. Hoffmann & D. H. Hoffmann-Oswald, *Deutsches Arbeitertheater 1918–1933. Eine Dokumentation.* Berlin, Henschelverlag, 1961 pp. 13–14.
10. ibid pp. 25–26.
11. A parallel movement occurred in the professional theatre, e.g. Hofmannsthal's *Jedermann* (1911) and Reinhardt's Salzburg Festival (from 1920).
12. Hoffmann op cit pp. 26–27.
13. ibid.
14. The *Spartakusbund* became the *Kommunistische Partei Deutschlands (KPD)* in January 1920.
15. *Die Volksbühne.* 1924.
    Das Laienspiel ist eine Ausdrucksform des menschlichen Spieltreibes. Es darf nicht bekämpft, sondern muß veredelt werden . . . Der Sinn des Laienspiels liegt in der Befriedigung eines inneren Dranges . . . Laienspiel und Berufsbühne sind ihrem Wesen nach grundlich verschieden: Das Theater verlangt Zuschauer, das Laienspiel kann auch ohne Zuschauer leben; Das Theater will ein Kunstwerk zur Darstellung bringen, die Spielschar will ihr eigenes Leben aussprechen.
16. Hoffmann op cit p. 32.
17. v. Appendix.
18. Other pioneering *Chorwerke* were by Max Barthel (b 1893), Karl Bröger (b 1886), Bruno Schönlank (b 1891) and other worker-poets. They were taken up enthusiastically both by Communist and by Social-Democratic groups. At first they were performed by *ad hoc* groups, but soon actual *Sprechchorgruppen* were established and in 1922 and 1923 many were formed. The *Freie Volksbühne,* for example, worked in conjunction with A. Florath's *Sprechchor* until 1924, then, through the enthusiasm of Fritz Holl (Friedrich Kayssler's successor as Director of the Theater am Bülowplatz) established its own, which was very active for the next five years under the direction of Karl Vogt.
    cf. C. W. Davies, *Theatre for the People,* Manchester 1977, p. 111
19. Hoffmann op cit p. 35
20. *Tag des Proletariats* 1925 edtn, p. 11.
    For centuries a subjugated body,/Disinherited, oppressed, we, man and woman/renounce renunciation, renounce sacrifice,/

We wish to effect the work in the light of peace.

21. ibid p. 13.
We are ready, / Justice! / All for all! / All for all! And cf *Masse Mensch*: GW2 p. 85.
22. ibid p. 14.
You mothers will never bear children / In gloomy little rooms, cursed by fate, / Or strongly clasp hungry hands / Overtaken by early death.
23. ibid p. 16.
The masses become community.
24. GW2 p. 108.
To release community into the masses.
25. *Tag des Proletariats* ed. cit. p. 19.
Lower the red flags! / Flags of Freedom! / Flags of Love! / Flags of Daybreak! / Lower them to the earth, / To the blood-stained lap / Of the all-embracing mother!
26. ibid.
Sad, with unfulfilled desires, / Was Spring for us, and lacking the sun's star, / Fairy-tales and playthings lay in the shop afar, / No mothers, who satisfied our hunger.
27. cf the title of Carel ter Haar's book: *Ernst Toller: Appell oder Resignation?*
Munich 1977
28. *Tag des Proletariats* ed cit pp. 19–20.
Morning is coming! / . . . Day is breaking! . . . / We welcome the rosy hills / Of liberated day!
29. ibid p. 22.
Do you hear the voice of your brother, the prophet? / His tormented body is sore from brutal blows, / They strike him when he calls them "Brothers!", / He is tortured, nailed to the earth! / Do you hear the voice of your brother, the prophet, / It is a stammer, a woeful stammer: "Do strike me then! O, that you are men!" / The last line exactly quotes Landauer's reported last words. v. *Justiz* p. 29.
30. ibid p. 23.
31. v. note 6 of *Masse Mensch on Stage.*
32. Quoted by ter Haar op cit pp. 239–240.
The Jew who is a Christian / And because of that was crucified again. /
33. ter Haar op cit p. 92.
34. ibid.

Written in English by Toller. Ter Haar misspells 'one' as 'ohne'.

35. 'ein aufwühlendes Erlebnis'. Toller's own expression, quoted by ter Haar op cit p. 91. Source, p. 240 n. 40.
36. The word *Religiosität* is not pejorative in German.
37. ter Haar op cit p. 240 n 45. ,
38. GW3 p. 291.
    You are a rebel, Herr Pastor, only you don't know it . . . Perhaps you are a Christian gone astray and don't know it either.
    Also quoted from another version by ter Haar op cit p. 240 n 43. In that version *Rebell* reads *Revolutionär*, and *verirrte* is omitted.
39. GW2 pp. 87 & 100.
40. GW2 p. 80. *Tag des Proletariats* p. 11.
41. GW2 p. 80.
42. *Tag des Proletariats*: p. 11, ibid, ibid. *Requiem*: p. 19
43. GW2 p. 81.
    Once, a blind woman and assaulted/By the torture-pistons of (blood-)sucking machines,/I cried that cry* in despair./
    *Down with the factories!
44. ibid.
    See then: We live in the twentieth century./It is recognised that/ The factory can no longer be destroyed.
45. ibid p. 85.
    A call to the masses of all countries:/The factories belong to the workers!/All for All!/call for more than a strike!/I call: War!/ call: Revolution!/The enemy up there does not listen/To fine speeches./Power against power!/Force . . . Force!/
46. Hoffmann op cit.
47. ibid p. 102.
48. ibid.
    We are the rabble-rousers/We are the heretics/We bring clarity/ Watch out, Proles!, We tell the truth/We Communists.
49. ibid p. 103.
    We are the Christians/The Republicans/We are the admonishers -/Believe the teaching:/Bolshevism, Is destruction . . . etc.
50. ibid p. 124.
    All Youth:/Shut your gob! Youth is speaking/Youth believes in you no longer/Youth.
51. ibid p. 125.
    Stinnes:/I am dying. /*All:*/We workers and peasants/The People/Is heir!
52. ibid p. 102.

53. ibid p. 361.
A single voice: / Three cheers for the Third International! / Three cheers for the USSR! / Three cheers for the KPD!
54. ibid p. 275.
55. ibid p. 102.
56. v. n. 15.
57. Bruno Schönlank was born in 1891 as son of Bruno Schönlank, a writer and social-democratic politician. He was arrested and forced into military service for having organised a workers' peace demonstration in Berlin in 1915. He supported the Spartacist movement, but dissociated himself from it in 1920 and worked for social-democratic newspapers. v. G. Heintz (ed) *Deutsche Arbeiterdichter 1910–1937* Stuttgart 1972 pp. 403 ff.
58. Dated 1920 by Heintz op cit., but copy seen in Theatermuseum, Köln, published by E Laub'sche Verlagsbuchhandlung is dated 1924.
59. *Erlösung*. Berlin 1924 p. 7.
Thou gleam / That comest through, out of the eyes, / Thou gleam / That singest with the stars / The mysterious song of most distant worlds. / Thou sound / That streamest from our mouth, / Thou sound / That swellest boundlessly / With the exuberance of all oceans. / / Thou spirit / That workest and livest in us, / Thou spirit that strivest high and higher / To the mastery of fulfilment. / Thou deed / That drivest our hands, / Thou deed / That abideth now and eternally, / Fill us with thy power.
60. ibid. Final Page.
We build and are, / A stone of eternity . . . We act, build, / And our action - / Let it be blessing!
61. *Der Moloch (1925), An die Erde (To the Earth) (1923). Großstadt (Big City) (1923), Ein Frühlings-mysterium (A Spring Mystery-play) (1925). Jugendtag (Day of youth) (1925), Neujahr (New Year) (1926), Seid geweiht (Be initiated) (1927), Der gespaltene Mensch (The Divided Person) (1927).*
62. This appeared in the *Merkblätter der Jugendarbeit im DGB.*
63. Schönlank B., *Ein Frühlings-Mysterium*. Verlag für Sozialwissenschaft, Berlin, SW68, 1925. Copy seen in Theatermuseum, Köln.
This secular Mystery Play adopts the multiple setting so often employed in the Middle Ages. In front of a *Grey Factory Town* stand four gates, before and behind which the action takes place, thus:

Morning	Midday	Midnight	Evening
Gate	Gate	Gate	Gate
Acts I & V	Act II	Act IV	Act III

The action is primarily a conflict between *The Watchman,* who summons to the factories, and *Spring,* who appears as a character. In Act I the Chorus of children, girls, are enjoying the spring. The figure of Spring calls to the town:
Du große Stadt / Ich will dich fassen / In allen Herzen will ich sein / Will Sonne geben euren Gassen / Und euren Seelen goldnen Wein. /
(You, great city, / l want to seize upon you, / I want to be in all hearts, / To give sunlight to your alleys / and to your souls golden wine).
The Watchman's voice replies:
Was singst du vor dem Morgentor, / Die Stadt ist Stahl, die Stadt ist Stein / Und kämst du tausendmal herein, / Du singst vergeblich ihr ins Ohr. /
(Why are you singing before the Morning Gate? / The city is steel, the city is stone; / And if you came here a thousand times / You sing in vain into her ear. /)
The girls want a day's holiday, but at the end of the act, when the sirens howl, they turn back into the town, saying they will see Spring at the Midday Gate.
After brief Acts (II & III at the Midday and Evening Gates, comes Act IV, at the Midnight Gate. Dreary music opens the act, soon to be drowned by a jazz band. Over the town lies mist and a reddish light. Midnight bells sound.
Death enters accompanied by the *Organ-Grinder (Leierkastenmann),* a frequent figure in street-scene drawings of the period (crippled ex-service-men often played the hurdy-gurdy) and a symbolic figure of long lineage: e.g., the Leiermann who ends Wilhelm Müller's *Die Winterreise* (1823):
Baarfuß auf dem Eise / Schwankt er hin und her; /
Und sein kleiner Teller / Bleibet immer leer. /
(Barefoot on the ice / He staggers to and fro; /
And his Little dish / Always remains empty. /)
(v. W. Killy (ed). *Epochen der deutschen Lyrik.*
Bd. 7.1800–1830, Munich, 1970, p. 281)
It is *Death* who dominates this act. He is given very short lines, often of single words, that recall the short lines used by von

Wangenheim, and those of *The Nameless*:
Frühling (zum Tod): / Höre auf mit deinem Schlagzeug. / *Tod:* / Pauke / Trommel / Alles Schlagzeug / Kreischt / Und wirbelt / Schillt / Und dröhnt. /
(*Spring [to Death]:* / Stop your drumming. / *Death:* / Kettledrum / Side-drum / All percussion / Screeches / And rolls / Rings / And rumbles. /)
Death is trying to claim a girl's life (perhaps evoking memories of Matthias Claudius' *Der Tod und das Mädchen*. v. for example. L. Forster (ed) *Penguin Book of German Verse*, Harmondsworth, 1957, p. 178). but *Spring* says that instead she will turn the girl into a tree.
In Act V (Morning Gate, as Act I) the *Watchman* tries to fell the flowering tree, but is stopped: *Spring* is stronger than *Death*.

64. A. Brodbeck, *Handbuch der deutschen Volksbühnen-Bewegung*, Berlin, 1930 p. 142.
By an extraordinary irony this performance of a *Sprechchor* in the mode which Toller had helped to establish and which had become typical of Social-Democrat amateur drama, took place at the very Conference of the Volksbühne at which Toller, though not a member of the Volksbühne movement, became "spokesman for the Opposition" (Sprecher der Opposition) in support of Erwin Piscator and the Communist faction within the movement against the Social-Democratic management committee led by Siegfried Nestriepke. (v. Brodbeck op cit p. 379).
65. Precisely how Toller, the Independent Social-Democrat, came to align himself with the Communist element within the Volksbühne does not concern us here: it was typical of his character that emotionally motivated impulses in the face of what seemed to be conservative oppression of an 'underdog' should drive him at that time into alliance with the Marxists.
66. *Die Fabrik* in Heintz op cit p. 204.
Crouching like an animal / That eyes its victim / Lies the factory / And paws the sky with gigantic talons. /
67. *Der Gesang der Fabrik*. op cit p. 208.
In bold thoughts engineers span with bridges / Precipitous valleys. /
68. ibid p. 210.
Here grows the man, who, fending for himself, / In solitariness struggles with the thought / That brings him the greatness of being a god. /

69. *Großstadt.* ibid p. 289.
70. Heintz op cit p. 332.
I throw myself on thy breasts, Nature./Take me back./I, the liberated slave of the factory,/Am thine again./
71. ibid p. 338. *Opferung,* Dortmund, 1927; *Das Tor,* Waldenburg-Altwasser, 1929; *Der Tag des Lichts,* Waldenburg-Altwasser, 1930.
72. Copy examined in Theatermuseum, Köln.
73. ibid p. 6.
Bright Chorus (Behind the Stage):/A day comes, as a blow resounds!/Then the gates are open,/and bright light shatters the night./
74. Leipzig, 1924.
75. Alfred Jahn, Leipzig, n. d. Copy seen in Theatermuseum, Köln.
76. As n. 75.
77. As notes 75, 76.
Work! Work!/Give us work!/Create work for our hands./
78. ibid.
We force the gigantic powers of the machines/Into our service!/Then are we lords,/not slaves!/New times are dawning!/
79. ibid.
Chorus:/Now to the work!/To the light! To freedom!/Up!/Let us build/Machines./*Echo:*/Machines! Machines! Machines!/
80. ibid
For ever! For ever!/The same cycle!/The firmly closed ring of Fate!/
81. His *Um Recht und Freiheit (For Justice and Freedom)* is a good well-constructed one-acter of family conflict, with convincing characters. It has the Kapp-Putsch of 1920 as its background.
Im Reiche des Sozialismus (In the Realm of Socialism) is an ambitious three-act play set in the Past, Present and Future:
Act I: 1890. The last day of Bismarck's anti-socialist laws. A naturalistic prose act about a printer and his family.
Act II: 1920 (The Present).The same characters thirty years later struggling for the young Republic, against the forces of reaction.
Act III: 100 years later. In verse. An idyllic setting of autumn woods and meadows, which nevertheless feels like a day in May.
"War! it is a word from a foreign language", says Fischer, aged 60. Ferra, his 20–year-old daughter explains that a century ago the world-dominating power of capital caused wars. Würfel, her lover, is now a Grade I worker and is being received today into the Council of Masters: they can marry. With the ambivalence so

frequent in writers of this movement, heavy industry flourishes without destroying the pastoral idyll:

Die Fabriken rauchen.

(The factories are smoking).

But that is safely off-stage! And though working hours have been reduced,

Es stieg die Produktion zu ungeahnter Höhe, / Weil in der Brust des Schaffenden Gesundheit wohnt. / (Production rose to undreamt-of heights / Because health dwells in the breast of the labourer. /)

82. Renker *Am Webstuhl der Zeit*, Leipzig (Alfred Jahn) n. d. Quoted on p. 2.
auch der, den die Tendenz des Werkes störte, konnte sich der kraft dieses Gemeinschaftsspieles nicht entziehen,

83. Renker op cit.
Der Dichter war gefunden, der aus seinem Miterleben / in schwerer und gewaltiger Vergangenheit und Gegenwart / das Werk uns schuf, / das objektiv uns die tatsächlichen Verhältnisse / tendenzlos schildert. /
Doch nichts ist so gewaltig als der Sprechchor, / und nichts ist so gemeinschaftswachsend als wie er. / Zwei Welten sind's, die im Theater sich in Kino trennen: / Die Welt der Spielschar und die Welt der Hörer! / Die Rampe ist die Schranke, die beide fühllos trennt. / *Wir* aber wollen, daß die Welt der Bühne, der Gemeinschaftsbühne, / sich mit der Welt der Hörer in inniger Gemeinschaft fest verschmilzt. / Des Massenwills künstlerischer Ausdruck ist allein der Sprechchor. /
/ / Du meinst, es sei das Chorische euch kein antikes Vorbild? / Kein Sprachgewoge, wie es der Gesang uns gibt / mit tiefern, mittleren und hohen Stimmen, / und kein Experiment in schulgedrillter Art? /
Das alles ist es nicht . . . / Es ist Zusammenfassung von Erlebnismenschen, / aus dem der Ausdruck stärkster Zeiterlebniskraft, / zeitehrliches, zeitstarkes und zeitgebundenes Empfinden spricht. /
. . . .
Gemeinschaftsgeist, Gemeinschaftswillen / soll'n durchbluten die Gesamtheit unser Hörer. / Und aus dem Feuer unsres Werkens, unsres Schaffens / sollt ihr euch zündende Funken holen für den eignen Herd. / Das——wollen——wir! /

84. *Internationale Literatur. Zentralorgan der Internationalen Vereinigung Revolutionärer Schriftsteller*. Nr. 4, 1934. Moscow. pp. 3–8. Spalek

328. Copy seen in Deutsches Literaturarchiv, Marbach.

85. *Tag des Proletariats* is dedicated to the memory of Karl Liebknecht; *Requiem* to that of Landauer; the introductory Sonnet to that of Kurt Eisner. *Weltliche Passion* has no dedication, but, unlike the earlier publication, it refers to Karl Liebknecht and Rosa Luxemburg by name.
It introduces a variant of the chorus, *Senkt die roten Fahnen* which opens and closes the *Requiem*: Senkt die Fahnen/Fahnen des Kampfes/Fahnen der Freiheit/Senkt sie zur Erde/Zum Schoß der Mutter./(*Weltliche Passion* p. 7).
Like *Tag des Proletariats* it introduces lines from the Internationale. As in *Requiem* the opening chorus is repeated at the end (though in this case a few lines from the very end).
There are many close parallels in words and images with the two other *Chorwerke*, *Masse Mensch* and the war poems. e.g. Nicht unser die Scholle (*Tag*): Wo einst der Bauer/Die Scholle gepflügt/(*Weltliche Passion*).
Hammer und Sichel . . . (*Tag*): Wenn die schwingenden Hämmer/Ruhn und die kreisenden Sicheln/(*Weltliche Passion*).
The seed and harvest of corn, contrasted with those of war:
Euer Leid, Millionen Müttern/Dien als Saat durchpflügter Erde/(*Den Müttern. Vormorgen* p21): Säten die Generale/Bomben/etc (*Weltliche Passion*). Schluchten steiler Häuser (*Masse Mensch. GW2 p80*): Steingeklüft der Straßengebirge (*Weitliche Passion*).

86. *Wettliche Passion* p. 3.
When the swinging hammers/Rest, and the circling sickles/When the evening is silent/On the ripening fields/And the banners, the red stormy/Banners gently droop [*sich entstraffen* seems to be a coinage of Toller's] over the/Stony ravines of the mountain ranges of streets/Let us think of the fallen/Unknown fighters of the revolution./
Malcolm Pittock curiously regards this opening chorus as "a celebration of achieved revolution". (M. Pittock, *Ernst Toller*, Boston, 1979. p. 149).

87. *Weltliche Passion* p. 3.
War/Trampled upon the fields of Europe/Where the farmer once/Had ploughed the soil/And with peaceable hand/Scattered the seed and nourishing grains/The generals sowed/Bombs/Shells/Hate. And the harvest ripened,/And the harvest was gathered in,/And ten million/Cripples/Devastated Towns/Villages shot to pieces/Hunger/Despair/Hate/Filled the barns.

88. *Weltliche Passion* p. 5.
Money is bread and a full belly / Money is meat and contentment always / Money is sleep right into the day / Money is time and the time is yours / Money is power and being kow-towed to by the world / Money is happiness, he who has money gets money. /
89. *Sprechstimme*: 'Sprechgesang', the older form, is properly singing tinged with a speaking quality whereas 'Sprechstimme' is rather speech tinged with a singing quality. (P. A. Scholes *The Oxford Companion to Music* 10th edn, Ed. J. O. Ward, London, reprint 1974 p. 968 f. n).
The juxtaposition of the *Internationale* and the *Sprechstimme* shows that music was an integral element in *Sprechchor* works. (e.g. the close of *Tag des Proletariats*, where the *Internationale* is both played and sung).
Toller's *Requiem*, for example, was performed on 21.11.1928 by the Volkschor Dortmund, conducted by Hans Salger, with the Städtisches Orchester and four soloists, to music composed by Artur Wolff, as part of a concert of works by living *composers.* The other two items were E.G. Elsaesser's *Die Hekatoncheiron* (Text by Karl Weiser) and Isr. J. Olmann's *Arbeitsauferstehung* (Dutch by Margot Vos, translated into German by Franz Landé). Obviously all three texts were sung. (Programme in Fritz Hüser Institut, Dortmund).
90. *Weltliche Passion* p. 7.
We commemorate the dead revolutionaries in Europe, in America and Asia, in Africa and Australia, in all five continents of the world, over whom shines the flag of revolution as eternal hope to the oppressed and humiliated; we commemorate the dead pioneers in Soviet Russia, we commemorate Lenin, we commemorate Sacco and Vanzetti, who died for us, we commemorate Eugen Leviné, Gustav Landauer, Matteotti and Erich Mühsam / we commemorate / the countless sailors, soldiers, farmers, workers / writers, engineers, all the Nameless Ones / tortured, broken, hanged, shot, struck down / on the battle-fields of the revolution.
(Note: towards the end the prose breaks into lines of very loose pentameters).
91. In an interview with a Swedish newspaper, *Svenska Pressen*, on 9 October 1934, Toller said how deeply Mühsam's death had affected him: '. . . daß ich ihnen niemals verzeihen kann, daß sie meinen Freund Erich Mühsam ermordet haben. Dies hat mich

tiefer geschmerzt als Verbannung und Verfolgung. '(. . . that I can never forgive them for having murdered my friend Erich Mühsam. This has hurt me more deeply than being banished and persecuted). (v. Fall p. 217).

92. Significantly Mühsam's is the final name in the roll-call of dead revolutionaries. As these are *not* in strictly chronological order Mühsam's name seems deliberately chosen as the climax.
(Landauer: murdered 2.5.1919; Leviné: shot 5.6.'19; Lenin: d. 21.1.1924; Matteotti: murdered 1924; Sacco & Vanzetti, executed 1927).
Note: no great problem need be attached to Toller's having in 1934 a MS from this earlier period. It might, for example, have been in the small box of MSS rescued from his rooms in Berlin by his secretary, Dora Fabian, whose bravery and loyalty cost her imprisonment. (Rothe, p. 109). Richard Dove has recorded regular performances in England, 1935–39, under the title *Requiem*.
93. In *Das Wort*, Jg 3 Nr 6 S Moscow, June 1938, pp. 35–36.
Copy seen in Akademie der Künste, Berlin. Spalek 218.
94. Pittock pp. 148–149.
95. Es war ein Streiten und Raufen,
welches Haus am
rötesten brennen würde
in der mondlosen Winternacht
Und sie beschlossen,
den Reichstag anzuzünden.
Dort schlief die deutsche Freiheit
einen schweren traumlosen Schlaf.
(There was argument and quarrelling,
which house
would burn the reddest
in the moonless winter night.
And they decided
to set fire to the Reichstag.
There German Freedom slept
a heavy dreamless sleep).
96. Pittock p. 148.
97. Here, for example, are two paragraphs from *Eine Jugend in Deutschland* (GW4 p64) set out in this way:

Zerschossener Wald,
zwei armseliger Worte.
Ein Baum ist wie ein Mensch.

Die Sonne bescheint ihn,
er hat Wurzeln,
die Wurzeln stecken in Erde,
der Regen wässert sie,
die Winde streichen
über sein Geäst,
er wächst,
er stirbt,
wir wissen wenig von seinem Wachsen
und noch weniger von seinem Sterben.
Dem Herbststurm neigt er sich
wie seiner Erfüllung,
aber es ist nicht der Tod
der kommt,
sondern der sammelnde Schlaf des Winters.

Ein Wald
ist ein Volk.
Ein zerschossener Wald
ist ein gemeucheltes Volk.
Die gliedlose Stümpfe
stehen schwarz im Tag,
und auch die erbarmende Nacht
verhüllt sie nicht,
selbst die Winde
streichen fremd über sie hinweg.

(Shell-blasted forest, two pitiful words. A tree is like a person. The sun shines on him, he has roots, the roots are set in the ground, the rain waters them, the winds waft over his branches, he grows, he dies, we know little of his growth and even less of his death. He bends to the autumn storm as if to his fulfilment, but it is not death that comes, but the gathering sleep of winter.
A forest is a people. A shell-blasted forest is an assassinated people. The limbless stumps stand black by day and even the merciful night does not hide them, even the winds waft away over them as strangers).

Toller's Dramatic Prose

1. Not including the collaborative *Wunder in Amerika*
2. *Die Wandlung* well over 50% prose; *Die Maschinenstürmer* over 70% prose.
3. *Der entfesselte Wotan* has a 32–line prologue in mock-heroic verse; *Nie wieder Friede* contains a number of songs.
4. J. H. Roger *Ernst Toller's Prose Writings*, PhD thesis. Yale 1972. p. 24.
5. Roger p. 93.

6. ibid.
7. Roger p. 97.
8. *Arbeiten* in *Quer Durch* (1930). GW1 p. 138.
   Ich glaube, daß die Neue Sachlichkeit eine Form modernen Biedermeiertums war, nicht den Menschen und Dingen war der Künstler der Neuen Sachlichkeit nahe, nur ihrer Photographie.
9. *Berliner Tageblatt* No 606, Dec 23, 1928. Quoted by Roger p. 98 f. n.
   Ich halte dieses Schlagwort [neue Sachlichkeit] für verlogene Romantik, hinter der sich sieche Sentimentalität verbirgt.
10. Roger p. 99.
11. ibid. Roger ignores or fails to perceive, the inner tension in much of the later prose between Toller's deep-rooted pacifism and his awareness of the profound evil of Nazism and the virtual inevitability of World War II.
12. Roger p. 109.
13. GW1 p. 31.
14. ibid.
15. GW1 p. 37.
16. GW2 pp. 360/1.
17. Roger p. 110.
18. ibid.
19. cf not only almost any typical play of German Expressionism, but also the plays of Eugene O'Neill, *passim*.
20. GW2 p. 17.
    They are lighting lights over there. Candles of love. Mysteries are revealed. An ocean of light and love.
21. ibid. Disgusting hermaphrodite.
22. GW2 p. 18. He obstructed my youth.
23. GW2 p. 19. You taught me to hate foreigners.
24. GW2 p. 21. The Great Age will make us all great.
25. Michael Roberts *The Faber Book of Modern Verse*, London 1936, 15th Imp. 1948, p. 3.
26. e.g. GW2 p. 51.
27. GW2 p. 36.
    I'd like to ask a kind fairy to turn my coarse fists into butterflies, so that they could take away your sadness, which forms dark shadows like black pollen on your white forehead.
28. GW2 p. 59.
    Your hands erect walls around you, and you allege there were savages on the other side.

29. GW2 p. 39.
I will follow you joyfully. Only, away from here! . . . There the whimpering of unborn children, there the weeping of madmen.
30. e.g.
unsere sieggekrönten Brüder (Alter Herr. GW2 p47).
die eiserne Wahrheit (Pfarrer. GW2 p. 48).
Glutenströme (Studentin. GW2 p. 51).
schweißzittert; Rothund (Die Dame. GW2 p. 57).
31. GW2 p. 51.
Now, born from the womb of the world, the high-vaulted gate of the cathedral of humanity opens . . . to the shrine known by night . . .
. . . to the fertility rite . . (lit. The dance dedicated to fruitfulness) . . .
. . Thus create life filled with spiritual heat . . .
32. GW2 p. 142.
Do you remember that there are forests . . . Dark, mysterious forests which awake buried springs in men . . . Forests of vibrant peacefulness . . . Forests of worship . . . Forests of cheerful dance.
33. GW2 p. 149.
My life has lasted eighty years . . . and it was not exquisite, in spite of effort and work . . .
34. Psalm 90 v. 10. Luther's Translation. cf AV:
The days of our years are three-score years and ten; and if by reason of strength they be four-score years, yet is their strength labour and sorrow; for it is soon cut off, and we fly away.
35. GW2 p. 17.
An artificial smile on cue. Tragicomic little figure. Approved onlooker . . . no . . . a Kelly-man . . . I won't drag this inner conflict around with me any longer. What are they to me?
36. GW2 p. 133.
Who were the fathers? You, your friends, your bosses, who have gold to buy a girl for themselves. Why did the mothers throw their children, their sacred little children into the water? Because none of the fathers helps them to feed their children. Because your church outlaws them and calls disgraceful what is a divine, incomprehensible miracle demanding reverence.
37. Roger p. 97.
38. *Berliner Tageblatt* No 606, Dec 23, 1928. Quoted by Roger p. 98.
Das Drama wie alle Kunst muß mehr sein, nämlich Verdichtung, Stufung und Gestalt. Erst dadurch wird Reportage auch

künstlerische Wahrheit.

39. GW1 p. 142 (Quoted by Roger p. 98).
Aber trotz des Gesetzes strenger Objekivation, das Gestalten aus den ihnen eingeborenen Notwendingkeiten formt, ist der Schaffende sich bewußt, daß gerade er zum kollektiv giltigen Subjektivismus gelangt. Er stellt Werte und Ideen nicht gleich. In ihm ist angelegt eine Hierarchie, die höhere Werte von minderwertigen sondert.
40. With one exception, GW2 p. 245.
41. GW2 p. 195.
42. GW2 p. 199.
It's all off! On account of less business: so long!
43. GW2 pp. 196, 197, 199.
44. GW2 p. 198.
There's a gramophone breathing down my neck, like a sinister animal . . .
45. GW2 p. 200.
He [the proletarian] sells his labour as one sells a litre of paraffin, and belongs to the employer, the proprietor.
46. GW2 p. 203.
How can anything be bad which comes from Nature? . . . as it were . . . from the blood.
47. GW2 p. 195.
Eugen, am I to stoke up the stove with our bed?
48. GW2 p. 244.
meaningless, endless affliction of the blind creature.
49. GW2 p. 245.
GRETE:
It will be summer and peace in the forest . . .
Stars and walking hand in hand . . .
HINKEMANN:
It will be autumn and the leaves will wither.
Stars . . . and hate! and fist against fist.
50. ibid
Alone in a forest full of wild animals!
51. ibid
What is contrary to Nature cannot be from God.
52. GW2 p. 246.
We are caught in a spider's web, Eugen, in a spider's web. A spider is sitting there and doesn't let us go. It has spun a web around us . . . Where is the beginning and where is the end? Who

will say, where a spider's web is concerned?

53. v. Chapter on *Der entfesselte Wotan*, passim.
54. Roger p. 99.
55. All these from the first scene: GW2 pp. 255–268. procuring, silk knickers, it's rumoured, Officer's hair-style, unaired bedrooms, sluts, legs eaten away with pox, an Emigrants' Joint-Stock Company, the yoke of the Jews, gold dividends, Jewboy.
56. e.g. GW2 p. 297.
57. e.g. GW2 p. 301.
    Ich werde Leiden. Ein Märtyrer wird für seine Idee leiden. Auch Jesus von Nazareth litt. Auch Bismarck litt . . .
    (I will suffer. A martyr will suffer for his idea. Jesus of Nazareth suffered, too. Bismarck suffered, too . .).
58. GW2 p. 280.
    Our great Leader, our noble* light-bringer, our Saviour: Hail! Hail! Hail! Hail!
    No party, no parliament, no programme, no communism will save Europe . .
    (*Notice Toller's use of the literary adjective *hehr*, much used by Wagner. e.g. *das hehre Pfand* (Das Rheingold, Vorspiel, Sc. 2).; *Den hehrsten Helden dürft' ich dich heißen* (Die Walküre, Act I, Sc. 3).
59. Roger pp. 99–100.
60. Except for the keen satirical lyrics of *Nie wieder Friede*.

IV THE PLAYS: *HINKEMANN* TO *PASTOR HALL*

Hinkemann

1. 'eines der erschütternsten Dramen des letzten Jahrzehntes.' 'Ewigkeitswert.' Fritz Droop *Ernst Toller und seine Bühnenwerke*. Berlin & Leipzig 1922. p. 18.
2. 'historische [r] Optimismus'.'politische [r] und weltanschauliche [r] Pessimisimus.' Marnette. p. 279.
3. Reso. p. 95, 96.
4. 'Grundcharakter des Werkes ist Einsamkeit und Resignation. In die Traurigkeit des Hinkemann mischt sich die des Dichters über die verlorene Revolution und die sinnlosen Opfer'. Reso p. 103.
5. Willibrand, *Ernst Toller and his Ideology*, Iowa 1945 p. 66.
6. Dorothea Klein *Der Wandel der dramatischen Darstellungsform im*

Werk Ernst Tollers 1919–1930. Bochum 1968 p. 85–116.

7. 'kritische Entscheidung für mich bedenken'. Unpublished letter to A. Puttkammer, 22.5.1921 in Toller Archive, Yale University, quoted by Klein p. 85.
8. ibid. 'Tragödie des Mönches'.
9. GW5 p. 93.
10. C. W. Previté-Orton *Shorter Cambridge Medieval History* London 1955. Vol II p. 680.
11. Or di' a Fra Dolcin dunque che s'armi,
 tu che forse vedrai lo sole in breve,
 s'egli non vuol qui tosto seguitarmi,
 Sì di vivanda che stretta di neve
 non rechi la vittoria al Noarese,
 ch'altrimenti acquistar non saria lieve.

 Dante *Inferno 28. lines 55 ff.*
12. v. note in *Dante, The Divine Comedy* translated by Dorothy L. Sayers. I. Hell. Harmondsworth 1949 p. 296 & 317.
13. a) *Die Literarische Welt* No. 30. Jan. 1928, p. 3f.

 Prof. Magnus Hirschfeld posed 9 questions which were sent to about a score of contemporary writers. The first question was:

 I. *Erste Inspiration:* Können Sie uns merkwürdige Beispiele nennen, wie Ihnen der erste Einfall zu einem Werke kam?

 (I. *First Inspiration:* Can you mention curious examples of how the first idea for a work came to you?)

 Toller's reply to this:

 1. Der merkwürdigste: der erste Einfall zu "Hinkemann" Ich sitze in Niederschönenfeld an meinem Zellentisch. Vor mir auf der Wand flirren zwei Sonnenflecke. Ich sehe sie zum erstenmal, schauend, ohne Assoziation. Senke den Blick, sehe wieder hin und denke: "Kurios. Wie zwei Eier". Einen Moment später: Welches Schicksal würde ein Mensch leben, dem das Geschlecht fehlt? Wie, wenn dieser Mensch verheiratet gewesen ist? Müßte nicht solches Geschick Alles wanken machen, was ihm vorher unverrückbares Fundament schien? Eine Stunde später war in großen Umrissen das Stück aufgebaut.

 (The most curious: the first idea for "Hinkemann". I am sitting in Niederschönenfeld at the table in my cell. Before me on the wall shimmer two spots of sunlight. I see them for the first time, looking, without association. My glance sinks, then I

look again and think: "Curious. Like two eggs". [*N. B. The German slang for 'Testicles' is not 'balls' but 'eggs'*]. A moment later: What fate would a man live through who lacked his sex? How would it be, if this man has already been married? Must not such a fate make everything unsure which formerly seemed to him unshakeable foundations? An hour later the piece was constructed in broad outline).
(From a photocopy of the original made by me at the Deutsches Literaturarchiv, Marbach).

b) *Eine Jugend in Deutschland.* GW4 p. 226.:
An der Wand meiner Zelle flirren Sonnenlichter. Zwei eirunde Flecke bilden sich, wie sähe der Mensch das Leben, den der Krieg entmannt hat, ist der gesunde Mensch nicht mit Blindheit geschlagen? Minuten später schreibe ich die Fabel zu meinem Drama "Hinkemann". Auch der Sozialismus wird nur jenes Leid lösen, das herrührt aus der Unzulänglichkeit sozialer Systeme, immer bleibt ein Rest. Aber soziales Leid ist sinnlos, nicht notwendig, ist tilgbar.
(Sunlight shimmers on the wall of my cell. Two egg shaped spots are formed; how would a person whom war has emasculated, see life; is the healthy person not struck by blindness? Minutes later I am writing the plot of my drama 'Hinkemann'. Even socialism will only solve the suffering that stems from the inadequacy of the social system; a residue always remains. But social suffering is senseless, not necessary, can be wiped out).

14. . . . (daß) der Ausgang von einem Sinneneindruck für den Gesamtcharakter des Stückes kennzeichnend ist. Klein p. 88.
15. Hinkemann ist die erste Gestalt in Tollers Dramen, die in ihrer menschlichen Totalität, als physisch-psychisch und geistig abgerundete Person gezeichnet ist. Klein p. 97.
16. Klein p. 110f.
17. Im *Hinkemann* gelingt es Toller also zum ersten Mal, das Allgemeine im Besonderen darzustellen, indem er einen komplexen Problemkreis von zentraler menschlicher Bedeutung am schicksal e i n e r Gestalt aufzeigt. Klein p. 103
18. So endet die Tragödie in der Erkenntnis der dem Leben innewohnenden Widersprüchlichkeit. Sie ist die Ursache für den "blinden Wirbel der Jahrtausende", dem zu entrinnen es nur zwei Möglichkeiten gibt: Paradies – oder Sintflut. Klein p. 101

19. Klein pp. 101 & 114ff.
20. W. Frühwald, *Hinkemann* in *Zu Ernst Toller, Drama und Engagement*, Ed. Jost Hermand, Stuttgart 1981 pp. 148–160.
21. GW5 p. 152.
22. In *Das Tagebuch* II, No. 12, March 26, 1921. Printed by Marnette as Appendix I of his thesis.
23. Marnette, Anhang I.
24. GW2 p. 215.
25. Klein p. 89. Klein, however, regards *Deutsche Revolution* as a 'fragment' rather than as a complete work.
26. Act II Sc. 1. *Volksbühne II. 3 Jan/Feb 1922.*
27. ibid.
28. GW2, 354 & 362.
29. GW2 p. 362.
30. cf one of the Yiddish titles, *Der blutike gelekhter*, i.e. *Bloody Laughter*.
31. Klein p. 109, 110.
32. Szene von Ernst Toller. Aus dem unveröffentlichten Drama "Eugen Hinkemann". *Blätter des Deutschen Theaters. Ausgabe für das Große Schauspielhaus*. Jg. 8, 1921–22, Heft 7 pp182–183. The scene is preceded by a note (Anmerkung), part of which reads: "Eugen Hinkemann ist ein Invalide, den eines Bruders Schuß zum höheren Ruhm (gloire – glory – gloria) der Vaterländer entmannte. Seines Schicksals Tragödie zu zeichnen versuchte der Autor".
(Eugen Hinkemann is a disabled man whom a shot fired by a brother has emasculated for the greater glory (gloire – glory – gloria) of the Fatherlands. The author attempted to portray the tragedy of his fate).
Copy seen in the Deutsches Literaturarchiv, Marbach.
This is NOT listed by Spalek in his Bibliography.
NOTE: When the same scene (Act III Sc. 2) was printed in the following year (1923) in *Die Neue Dichtung* the title given was *Der deutsche Hinkemann*. See Spalek p. 137 no. 294.
33. Did Toller also intend a terrible irony in the juxtaposition of Eugen *[Gk. eugenes, well-born, of noble race]* and *Hinkemann?*
34. v. Fall pp. 142–155, and Frühwald / Hermand pp. 158f.
35. v. Spalek 23 and 22.
36. GW5 p. 152.
37. "Ich mache keine Konzession an die Tagesmächte". GW5 p. 191

38. (noch dazu durch falsches Schreiben zur Allegorie gestempelt). Sei es aber leider nicht. GW5 p. 152.
39. "Es gäbe schon ein Vorwort. Hölderlin, "Über die Deutschen..". It is interesting that Toller in making this statement uses 'The Subjunctive of Modest Assertion' (v. A. E. Hammer, *German Grammar and Usage* London 1971 §475, and cf *Der Große Duden* 2nd Edtn. Mannheim 1966 Bd. 4 Grammatik. p. 188: §§965, 970).
40. a) Hölderlin, *Hyperion*, Reclam, Stuttgart 1983 pp. 171–175.
b) Frühwald/Hermand p. 156.
c) Hölderlin, *Gedichte*, Insel, Frankfurt/M, 1984, p. 64.
41. "Weil ich das zweite Auge verlor, das den Wünschen Sklave ist? weil ich skeptiker bin?" (v. Marnette, Anhang I).
(Because I lost my second eye, which is a slave to desires? because I am a sceptic?).
42. GW2 p. 226.
43. Grete Hinkemann ist schon durch die Namengebung der Deutschland-Allegorie zugeordnet . . . Frühwald/Hermand p. 152.
44. H. L. Cafferty, *George Büchner's Influence on Ernst Toller*. PhD Dissertation, Michigan, 1976.
45. GW2 p. 193.
46. see Note 13.
47. GW5 p. 152.
48. . . . Darum wird Tragödie niemals aufhören. Auch der Kommunismus hat seine Tragödie. (ibid).
49. Und gibt es ein Individuum, dessen Leid nie enden kann, ist die Tragik des einen Individuums gleichzeitig die Tragik der Gesellschaft, in der es lebt. (ibid).
50. Nur der Schwache resigniert, wenn er sich außerstande sieht, dem ersehnten Traum die vollkommene Verwirklichung zu geben. Dem Starken nimmt es nichts von seinem leidenschaftlichen Wollen, wenn er wissend wird. Not tun uns heute nicht die Menschen, die blind sind im großen Gefühl, not tun uns, die wollen – obwohl sie wissen. (ibid).
51. Womit nicht gesagt ist, daß die Revolutionäre von heute hundert Jahre nach der Machtergreitung noch paradiesgläubig sind. Sie haben es dann nicht mehr nötig, es ist nicht mehr ihr seelisches Bedürfnis . . . nein, ich scherze nicht . . . Die Gläubiger werden Zweifler . . . Auguren! Christus – Paulus – Papst! Die drei Gestalten sind Symbole. Nach hundert Jahren hat eine neue Schicht

von Unterdrückten, die notwendig nach Macht streben muß, den großen Paradiesglauben! Ewige Wiederkehr der Formen! (*Deutsche Revolution.* v. Marnette, Anhang I).

52. GW5 p. 154.
53. Klein pp. 91–95.
54. Cafferty p. 219.
55. Klein *loc cit.*
56. This is true despite Cafferty's assertion that both Woyzeck and Hinkemann become more articulate as the plays proceed. (v. Cafferty p. 225).
57. See also Frühwald/Hermand for a comparison between Hinkemann and Brecht's Kragler (*Trommeln in der Nacht*) as the problem of the *Heimkehr der Fronttruppen.*
58. ibid p. 153.
59. . . . ich kann kein Volk mir denken, das zerrißner wäre, wie die Deutschen.' *Hyperion.* Reclam p. 171.
60. GW5 56 & 88.
61. Weh mir, wo nehm ich, wenn
Es Winter ist, die Blumen, und wo
Den Sonnenschein,
Und Schatten der Erde?
Die Mauern stehn
Sprachlos und kalt, im Winde
Klirren die Fahnen.
(Hölderlin *Gedichte* (ed. J. Schmidt Frankfurt/M 1984).
62. '. . . ich sprach für alle, die in diesem Lande sind und leiden, wie ich dort gelitten.' Hölderlin, *Hyperion.* Reclam, Stuttgart, 1983.
63. GW2 p. 193. *Hinkemann,* Kiepenheuer, Leipzig & Weimar 1979, p. 6. *Hinkemann,* Kiepenheuer, Potsdam 1924 (14th to 23rd Thousand) opp. verso of t. p.
64. *'Von allen seiten kommen . . . usw'*. Kiepenheuer 1979, p. 53; Kiepenheuer 1924 (14th to 23rd Thousand) p. 40.
65. *Hinkemann bricht zusammen. Das Folgende muß sich wie ein Traumalp Hinkemanns abspielen. Alle Gestalten scheinen Hinkemann zu bedrängen und vom Dunkel aufgesaugt, sich von ihm zu lösen . . .* (Kiepenheuer 1979 p. 53. Kiepenheuer 1924 p. 40).
66. GW2 p. 247.
67. GW2 p. 244–5. Kiepenheuer 1979. pp. 72–3. Kiepenheuer 1924, pp58–59.
68. *Die Bühne leert sich . . . Die Bühne belebt sich wieder.* GW2 p. 211 & 212.

69. 'kein Volk . . . das zerrißner wäre, wie die Deutschen' . . . 'abgerichtet'. (*Hyperion*. edtn. cit. p. 172).
70. GW2 p. 233. (cf. Kiepenheuer 1979 p. 59 and Kiepenheuer 1924, p. 45).
71. That is to say, the themes mentioned in the newspaper headlines, the commercial sex of the prostitute, pimp and quack merchant, and the other street dialogues, while relevant to the theme of the play and the background to Hinkemann's state of mind, are not necessarily *in his mind*, and some, notably the dialogue of the Polish Jews, are unlikely to occupy Hinkemann's thoughts, though they clearly occupy the author's.
72. *Selbst die Laternen sind ob des Soldatenereignisses klein und dunkel geworden.* (GW2 p. 233. Kiepenheuer 1979, p. 58. Kiepenheuer 1924, p. 45).
73. GW2 p. 327.
74. ibid.
75. Epigraph to all editions. Cf. GW2 pp. 244–5.
76. I refer to Mrs Alving's indecision as to whether to give Oswald the overdose of morphia he requests. Ibsen ends her last speech 'No, no, no! Yes! – No, no!" She *may* change her mind later, and the matter is left open. v. Ibsen: *The Pillars of Society and other plays*, Edited with an introduction by Havelock Ellis, London (Walter Scott) 1888. p. 198.
77. Fall p. 142.
78. GW2 p. 245.
79. GW2 p. 244.
80. Kiepenheuer 1979, pp. 72–3.
81. Spalek no. 25, p. 28.
82. Spalek No. 27.

Hinkemann on Stage

1. Spalek p. 875.
2. *Baal* opened 8.12.1923.
   (Rühle, p. 486, wrongly credits Paul Wiecke with the production of *Hinkemann*. Both plays were directed by Alwin Kronacher)
3. Brechts hat wenig Glück: Skandal, Gelächter, Trampeln, halbstündige Ulkrufe . . . (*Berliner Tageblatt* 11.12.'23, v. Rühle p. 490).
4. ibid.
5. Der begabte Brecht ist ein schäumender Epigone. (ibid).

6. Begabt im Lyrischen (ibid).
7. Alles in allem: ein Elefantenidyll (ibid. p. 491).
8. v. Rühle pp. 1167–8.
9. Alle Leitartikel der letzten Jahre finden sich im "Hinkemann" wieder. Ein ohnmächtiges, aufreizendes Geschwätz. (*Berliner Borsen-Courier* 9, 10, & 11.12.'23. Rühle p. 488).
10. v. Rühle p. 1170.
11. Und dennoch . . . Mit alledem ist Ernst Toller dennoch . . . Doch Toller schreibt, wie man heute lebt . . . Alles in allem: der Kritiker schwärmt nicht — hebt aber den Hut . . . Beide Poeten schließlich auch: der Nachfahr wie der Landsucher. (v. Rühle pp. 492–3).
12. 18.9.'23. Spalek 2603.
13. Spalek ibid.
14. Spalek 2614.
15. Spalek 2635.
16. Spalek 2636.
17. "Einführung zu den Schauspielen des ABI im Februar", *Kulturwille*, I, No. 1 (Feb. 1, 1924) 10. Spalek 2637.
    (It is worth noting that the *Arbeiter-Theaterverlag Alfred Jahn*, which published scores of working-class, non-communist plays during the 1920s, was based in Leipzig).
    The *Arbeiter-Bildungsinstitut*, with a large membership, was for many years the principal theatre-audience organisation in Leipzig, arranging scheduled performances for its members in the municipal theatres, as indeed did some other Leipzig organisations. It was so strong that when in 1926 a *Freie Volksbühne* was founded in Leipzig, it did not grow as might have been expected, though relationship between the organisations was friendly.
    See Albert Brodbeck *Handbuch der Deutschen Volksbühnenbewegung*, Berlin 1930, p. 296.
    See aso Cecil W. Davies *Working-Class Theatre in the Weimar Republic, 1919–1933: Part I*, in *Theatre Quarterly Vol X No. 38, 1980*, especially pp. 88ff on *Alfred Jahn Publications* and p. 91ff on *Audience Organisations* in the provinces.
18. Die dreiaktige Tragödie *Hinkemann* von Ernst Toller, deren Uraufführung im Alten Theater stattfand, ist ein dramatisches Buch Hiob. Nur daß der von Schicksal geschlagene Hinkemann nicht den Weg ins Leben zurückfindet, wie sein alttestamentarischer Ahne, sondern unverschuldet höherer Gewalt erliegt. Es ist ein Werk düsteren Pessimismus, ein Sehnsüchtiger Ruf nach Gerechtigkeit, ein Aufschrei der gepeinigten Kreatur. Dieses

Werk voll Tränen, Mitleid, Liebe und Entsagung übt zugleich bittere Kritik an der Zeit, in der es entstanden ist. Von Hinkemanns Schicksal gehen literarische Fäden zu Wozzeck [sic] und Fuhrmann Henschel: auch Tolstois Einflüsse machen sich geltend. (Signed: L. St., n.d., periodical not known. Press cutting seen in Theatermuseum Köln).

19. v. note 18.
20. cf Kerr: Der Übergang zum Halbaturalismus ist nicht leicht. (Rühle p. 491).
21. Athletisch gebauter Mann. *Fuhrmann Henschel* Act I. Gerhart Hauptmann *Das dramatische Werk* Erster Band, Propyläen Verlag Frankfurt/M 1974, p. 930.
22. GW2 p. 205.
23. Kerr, in Rühle p. 492.
24. Spalek p. 875.
25. Spalek 164.
26. Spalek 2712.
27. Spalek 2715.
28. Spalek 2725.
29. Spalek 2711, 2733, 2736.
30. Spalek 2736.
31. Spalek 2733.
32. Spalek 2711.
33. v. Fall 143–149 and Frühwald/Hermand 157–160.
34. With hindsight it can be seen as ominous that even at this date Hitler was an important political figure. A factor in the tension was General von Lossow's refusal to carry out the ban on Hitler's newspaper, *Der Völkische Beobachter*, and even earlier (7.10.23) Kahr had appointed one of Hitler's most faithful henchmen, the former Munich Police Chief Pölner, as civil commissar for Saxony and Thuringia in the event of the Bavarian army's being called upon to "re-establish order" in those states. (v. Frühwald/Hermand 158).
35. For Stresemann's attitude at this time see: *Rede in Halle/Saale* (11.11.'23). *Mitteldeutsche Kurier (Halle) Sonderblatt*, 12.11.'23. In *Gustav Stresemann, Schriften*. Ed. A Hartung, Berlin 1976, pp. 297ff.
36. Bei den Aufführungen in Dresden, Wien, Berlin und Jena lieferten Zuschauerraum und Straße jeweils nicht nur den Kommentar, sondern die reale Dokumentation zu dem Geschehen auf der Bühnen . . . die Allegorie wurde Realität. (Frühwald/Hermand

160).

37. e.g. Friedrich Kummer. *Ein stürmischer Theaterabend. Schauspielhaus: Hinkemann. Von Ernst Toller. II, in Dresdner Anzeiger* Jan. 19, 1924. (Spalek 2646). In an artistically not unsympathetic, though politically hostile review, Kummer says he could not hear and judges the play after reading it as well. (Press cutting seen in Theatermuseum, Köln).
38. Decarli, der Darsteller des Hinkemann, bat um Achtung vor der Arbeit des Schauspielers. (Erich Weise in *Weltbühne* 2.2.24, in: Rainer Hajan *Das politische Theater in Deutschland zwischen 1918 und 1933*. Doct. Diss. Ludwig-Maximilian Universität, Munich. (Hamburg 1958)).
39. ibid.
40. *Crippled war veterans playing cards*. Private Collection. v. *Neue Sachlichkeit and German Realism of the Twenties*. Arts Council of Great Britain 1978, Plate 33.
41. Fall 145.
42. Photograph in possession of Spalek. Reproduced in Rothe p. 91.
43. Vienna, Delitzsch, New York, Berlin, Paris, Magdeburg, Hamburg, Frankfurt/M, Moscow (2), Cracow. v. Spalek pp. 875–6.
44. Raimund Theater. 10.2.'24. One performance for the Sozialdemokratische Kunststelle.
45. Felix Salten: *Neue Freie Presse* 11.2.'24. Ludwig Marcuse: *Dem Dichter des* Hinkemann! Apparently a programme note. Photocopy made at Theatermuseum, Köln.
46. J. Roths. *Vorwärts* 15.4.'24. Reprinted in *Fall* 149–155.
47. In Heinrich George hatte er einen erschütternden Dolmetsch. *Berliner Tageblatt*. 15.2.'24. Morning Edition. Seen in Akademie der Künste, Berlin.
48. London. Gate Theatre. 24 May 1926. Production and Direction Peter Godfrey. 12 Performances. Spalek p. 877.
49. Spalek 2687.
50. Details of production, as performed on Friday, 23 December, 1927 at 8 p. m. (Photocopy made from Programme seen at Theatermuseum, Köln).

    HINKEMANN / Tragödie in 4 Akten (6 Bildern) von Ernst Toller / Regie: Ernst Toller und Ernst Lönner / Bühnenbilder: Edward Suhr. / Hinkemann .... *Heinrich George* / Grete Hinkemann, seine Frau ... *Helene Weigel* / Die alte Frau Hinkemann .... *Johanna Koch-Bauer* / Paul Großhahn ... *Peter Ihle* / Max Knatsch ... *Sigmund Nunberg* / Peter Immergleich .... *Friedrich Gnaas* / Sebaldus

Singegott . . . *Jacob Sinn*/Michel Unbeschwert . . . *Fritz Staudte*/ Schieferdecker . . . *Georg Czimeg*/Ziegeldecker . . . *Gustav Roos*/ Fränze, Gretes Freundin . . . . *Margarethe Mahr*/Budenbesitzer . . . *Viktor Schwanneke*/Eine tätowierte Frau . . . *Edda Lindborg*/ 1. Ausrufer . . . *Georg Kaufmann*/2. Ausrufer . . . *Ernst Notbaar*/ Invaliden . . . *Fritz Klaudius, Fritz v. Wödte, Willy Koblank*/ Zeitungsjungen . . . *Günther Ruschin, Heilo Boelen, Erich Wander*/ *Hilde Weber, Frieda Bohm*/Zeitungsverkäufer . . . *Marie Burke, George Kaufmann*/Zwei Juden . . . *Sigmund Nunberg, David Turner*/ Händler . . . *Rolf Gunold*/Dirnen . . . *Steffi Spira, Elisabeth Geyer, Nina Tokumbet*/Stehumlegekragen . . . *Paul Kaufmann*/ Technische Leitung: Hans Sachs. Beleuchtung: Hugo Diesner/ Pause nach dem 2. Akt (4. Bild) . Ende nach 10 Uhr/.

51. 1.1.'27, Hotel Hietzinger; 24, 25.1.'27. Lustspieltheater; 26.1.'27, Kasino Zögernitz.
52. K. Sid. in *Neue Freie Presse* 3.1.'27.
53. ibid.
54. Piscator geistert durch die Kulissen. Friedrich Hussong, *Berliner Lokal-Anzeiger* 25.11.'27. Seen in Theatermuseum, Köln. Spalek 2632.
55. v. H. L-g in *VZ* 26.11.'27, and Ernst Degner in *Vorwärts* 26.11.'27.
56. Act III Sc. 1, GW2, p. 233. v. Bruno E. Werner, *DAZ* 25.11.'27.
57. v. "F", 4.12.'27, newspaper not known. Not in Spalek. Seen in Theatermuseum, Köln; Julius Knopf, n. d., newspaper not known. Not in Spalek. Seen in Theatermuseum, Köln.
58. Photograph in Theatermuseum, Köln. Copy in present writer's possession.
59. Ernst Degner, in *Vorwärts* 26.11.'27.
60. H. L-g. *loc cit.*
61. In der Hauptsache kam die Regie ohne Piscators prinzipielle Behelfe aus. Sie war auf das Wort gestellt, sie umhütete den Gesamtton, sie disziplinierte hervorragend das Einzelspiel . . . Emil Faktor in *Berliner Börsen-Courier* No 554, 26.11.1927. seen in Theatermuseum, Köln. Spalek 2617.
62. ibid.
63. v. Degner, *loc cit* & Faktor *loc cit.*
64. Er spricht die Sprache des großen hilflosen Kindes. Degner, *loc cit.* Toller applies the phrase 'helpless child' (hilfloses Kind) to Grete, Act III Sc. ii, GW2 p. 245 (wie ein hilfloses Kind weinend).
65. Rücksichtslos haben sie am Buch gestrichen, sehr zum Vorteil des Ganzen. Degner, *loc cit.*

66. In Theatermuseum, Köln. Copy in present writer's possession. A reversed, stylised version of this picture, which loses the emotional impact of the original, is on the front cover of *Theatre Quarterly* Vol X, 1980 No. 38.
67. Gedunsen die Gestalt, gedunsen und bleich das Gesicht, bleicher gleichsam unter dem glatten Blondhaar, aufgedunsen durch den müden, blonden Schnurrbart – das ist der Hinkemann Heinrich G e o r g e s. Einer, der den Atem hörbar aus tiefer Brust zieht. Einer, dem ein Joch aus Blei auf den Schultern lastet.
    Ernst Heilborn in FZ 2.11.27 (?) N. B. On press-cutting seen in the Theatermuseum, Köln, date and periodical were not given. 2.11.'27 is the date given by Spalek, but as the play did not open until 25.11.27, this is probably an error for 2.12.'27.
68. Heinrich George leiht der Erbärmlichkeit des entmannten Hinkemann auch diesmal wieder . . . seine ganz große darstellerische Kraft und Kunst. Hussong. *loc cit.*
69. Critic "F", 4.12.27. Periodical illegible. Seen at Theatermuseum, Köln. Not in Spalek.
70. Degner. *loc cit.*
71. ibid.
72. Emil Faktor. *loc cit.*
73. Anonymous press-cutting dated 26.11.27. Theatermusseum, Köln.
74. Heilborn. *loc cit.*
75. Unter freiem Himmel die lodernde Flamme, und der Beraubten, einer stellt sich selbst als Opfer dar. Heilborn. *loc cit.*
76. Und trotz aller Vorwürfe auf die kriegführende und friedenleidende Gesellschaft — bestimmend wird das mitleid mit den Tieren, das Mitleid auch mit dem armen Tier Hinkemann. Wie ein "roter Faden" zieht es sich durch die Aufführung, das Mitleid mit dem Tier, ein roter Faden, von Tierblut gerötet, von dem Tropfen Blutes, der den Augen des geblendeten Zeisigs entfloß, zu dem Blut der Mäuse und Ratten. denen Hinkemann den Kopf abbeißen mußte, zum Blut der zerschmetterten Grete Hinkemann. Blut der Kreatur . . . das Opfer flammt.
    Es ist, als hätte Ernst Toller, derart Regie führend, seine *Hinkemann* seelisch umgedichtet.
    Heilborn. *loc. cit.*
    In this production Hinkemann did NOT prepare to hang himself. Rudolf Kayser's programme note says specifically: "Die Frau geht in den Tod, Hinkemann muß auf der von ihm gehaßten Erde bleiben.'(The wife goes to her death, Hinkemann must remain on

the earth which he hates). Programme seen and photocopied in Theatermuseum, Köln.

77. v. H. L-g. *loc cit.* & Emil Faktor *loc cit.*
78. v. Ulrich Seelmann-Eggebert in *Stuttgarter Nachrichten* 18.2.'59.
79. Anonymous. *Herner Zeitung.* 7.7.'60.
80. Bernhard Bole, *Recklinghäuser Zeitung* 6.7.'60.
81. Josef Reding, *Essener Tageblatt* 7.7.'60.
82. Gerhard Weber *Pariser Kurier* 15.10.'75
83. Seelmann-Eggebert, *loc cit.*

Der Entfesselte Wotan

1. v. *Hinkemann on Stage,* Note 74.
2. Geschrieben in der heiteren Kraft wachsenden Vorfrühlings im Jahre 1923 im Festungsgefängnis Niederschönenfeld. GW2 p. 250.
3. v. Chap. V passim, especially references to *Die Feuerkantate;* also *Briefe aus dem Gefängnis,* GW5 p. 161:
   Es wächst ein eigenttumliches Buch, das "Schwalbenbuch" wächst ohne daß ich viel dazu tue, wächst nach seinem eigenen Rhythmus, nach seinen eigenen Gesetzen. (29.7.'23).
   Ich schicke Dir heute "Das Schwalbenbuch". (15.9.23).
4. v. GW5 pp. 162, 168, 170 etc. Also GW4 pp. 232–233:
   . . . ich fühle, wie meine Lebenskraft sich mindert, tagelang liege ich apathisch in meiner Zelle, ich freue mich nicht auf die Freiheit, ich ängstige mich vor ihr. usw.
5. Den Pflügern. GW2 p. 251.
6. Was liegt an *Eurem* Europa! Jedes Leichenfeld wird Brachfeld. Zum Brachfeld kommt der Pflüger. GW2 p. 262. *Leichenfeld* suggests both *Leichenacker* (graveyard) and *Schlachtfeld* (battlefield). Wotan belongs to the war generation, the Young Workman to the post-war.
7. Was einst Tragödie, werd zur Posse,
   Was einst gekrümmtes Leid, werd zum Gelachter . . .
   GW2 p. 253.
8. . . . bevor ins Zeitenlose du verschwindest, . . . GW2 p. 253.
9. Max Brod in a long and favourable review of the Prague production said it reminded one of Sternheim. (Fall p. 166).
   Of later critics, see for example Manfred Durzak, *Zur Posse gewordene Politik* in Hermand *op. cit.* p. 142:

Der Wagner verehrende Barbier Mandelstam aus Sternheims 'Hose' erlebt in Tollers Friseur . . . seine Wiederauferstehung.

10. Toller does not, for obvious reasons, name him.
11. v. GW2 p. 363, where all the details mentioned here may be found.
12. GW2 p. 284.
13. GW2 p. 282.
14. GW2 p. 285.
15. Wotan's wild use of international telegrams may also owe something to Toller's sobering experience of Dr Lipp, the Commissary for Foreign Affairs at the beginning of the Munich Revolution. GW4 pp. 126–128.
16. You swine, you want to make a laughing-stock of me before the German public.
17. WOTAN: Sie wollen mich verlassen? Mich lächerlich machen vor der öffentlichen Meinung. GW2 p. 274.
18. VON WOLFBLITZ: In München gestern abend Gründung Ortsgruppe der wotanischen Auswanderergenossenschaft. Bayern unsere Basis! GW2 p. 295.
19. Aber die Gestalt des Wotan, obwohl in der teutschen Atmosphäre sich blähend, ist eine universale, zum mindesten eine europäisch-amerikanische. GW2 p. 364. It is significant that Toller introduced an *American* journalist into the play.
20. Max Brod, *Berliner Tageblatt* 5.2.'25:
    Tendenz gegen die Schieber Nachkriegsdeutschlands, die die nationale Phrase benützen, um auf Kosten des deutschen Volkes Geschäfte zu machen.
    Fall p. 166.
    Only two other reviews of this production have been seen, of which only one is listed by Spalek:
    Jo Lhermann, n. d. newspaper unknown. Spalek 2430.
    E. F. n. d. newspaper unknown. Not in Spalek. Newspaper cutting seen in Theatermuseum, Köln.
21. 23.2.'26. Spalek p. 872.
22. Warum hat Ernst Toller diese sogenannte Komödie geschrieben? Die Massensuggestion als Komödienmotif – in welcher Zeit lebte Toller als er dies seinem Hirn entquälte? Vorgestern schon war dies Motif gänzlich verbraucht. Ludwig Sterneaux in *Lokal-Anzeiger* No. 93, 24.2.'26.
    Spalek 2432.
    Mysing in *Kölnische Zeitung* 4.3.'26 (not in Spalek; newspaper

cutting seen in Theatermuseum, Köln) takes the same view, referring to this production.

23. Lach nicht zu früh. GW2. p. 254.
24. e.g. Manfred Georg in *BVZ* 24.2.'26; Felix Hollaender, *Berliner Abendblatt* 24.2.'26.
25. ein . . . Schwindler . . . Mit den gewissen dunstigen Theoremen der Niederung. Kerr. *Berliner Tageblatt* No. 93. Abend Ausgabe. Newspaper cutting photocopied in Theatermuseum, Köln.
26. Franz Köppen *Berliner Börsen-Zeitung* No. 92. Mittwoch 24.2.'26, Spalek 2429.
27. Es ist ein typisches Stück für die Zwecke der Volksbühne, für Massen, denen hier Wulle-Hitlersches Grundwesen überzeugend gezeigt wird.
    Manfred Georg *loc. cit.* note 24.
28. Zuerst hofft man, daß völkischer Teutonismus à la Hitler samt Gefolgschaft an den Pranger gestellt und in seinem gefährlichen Phrasenschwulst und seiner *dementia praecox* hingerichtet werden soll.
    Man erwartet die große, politische Satire vom pathologischen Schaumschlager, der am eigenen Worte sich berauscht. Hollaender, *loc. cit.* v. Note 24.
29. Man muß, bei dieser Treffsicherheit, meinen, er sei post festum geschrieben.
    Hans Schwab-Felisch, in *FAZ* 11.1.1960.
30. Das ist eine der erstaunlichsten Visionen in der Geschichte des politischen Theaters.
    Die Warnung, die in dieser Komödie von 1923 von dem Hellseher Toller ausgesprochen wird, ist nicht verstanden worden, wie auch nicht in seinen anderen, zahlreichen Bühnenwerken.
    Alfred Baresel in *Vorwärts* 22.1.'60.
    (Both this and the previous review, N. 29. refer to the Frankfurt/M producticn of 9.1.1960. Spalek p. 873).
31. Diese so selten hervorgeholte Komödie ist nicht gerade ein Prunkstück aus dramatischem Werkstatt, aber sie hat politisch-prophetische Drive.
    Rose-Marie Borngässer in *Die Welt* 11.11.'83, reviewing a production in Munich (later than Spalek's bibliography).
32. v. note 28.
33. . . . animiert in der Gegenwart leicht zu falscher Lustigkeit.
    Jürgen Althoff in *Abendpost* 15.3.'62 reviewing a production by *theater 53* in a Hamburg Keller.

(Neither the production nor the review are in Spalek. Newspaper cutting seen in Akademie der Künste, Berlin).

34. Ließ er den Wotan zu sehr an die Person Hitlers gemahnen? Das ist eine Frage, die schwer zu beantworten bleibt. Der ewige Rest des wildgewordenen Kleinbürgers in uns, der zum gefährlichen Phantasten in der Hand von geschickten Demagogen wird, ist damit vielleicht zu sehr bagatellisiert. Schwab-Felisch *loc. cit.*
35. Wäre mit Wilhelm Dietrich Wotan, dem Barbier ohne Kundschaft, tatsächlich Hitler direkt gemeint, hätte Toller diese Ausschwitzung des von Existenzängsten gequälten Bürgertums hoffnungslos unterschätzt und als unpolitischen Demagogen, Geschäftemacher verharmlost.
    Wolfgang Rothe *Toller,* Reinbek bei Hamburg 1983.
36. GW2 pp. 265 & 285.
37. Simon Taylor *Germany 1918–1933,* London 1983, pp. 54 & 68.
38. Herr Wotan ist der Behörde als ein Bürger von staatserhaltender Gesinnung bekannt. GW2 p. 300.
39. GW2 pp. 300 & 301.
40. Der Dolchstoß kurz vorm Ziel. Memoiren von Wilhelm Dietrich Wotan. GW2 p. 302. The *Dolchstoß* is historically the right-wing myth that Germany at the end of World War I was betrayed by her own politicians.
41. W. L. Shirer *The Rise and Fall of the Third Reich* Book Club Associates Edition 1973. p. 79.
42. Shirer *op. cit.* p. 80.
    There even seeems to be an extreme example of self-parody in the scene of Wotan's arrest, with the latter's hiding under the table behind his wife's skirts, his moustache dishevelled, being possibly seen as a farcical parody of Toller's own experience when he hid in a secret room in Lech's house, his hair reddened with peroxide, and finally emerged to give himself up, that being the safest course to take. v. GW4 pp. 168–171.
43. 'Territorial policy cannot be fulfilled in the Cameroons but today almost exclusively in Europe". Hitler, *Mein Kampf, Vol. II,* quoted in Shirer, *op. cit.* p. 8.
44. Fall p. 166.
45. Photograph in Theatermuseum, Köln.
46. GW2, pp. 263 & 301.
47. H. J. Rose, *A Handbook of Greek Literature,* London 1964. p. 153.
48. v. ibid. & P. B. Shelley *Poetical Works,* ed. T. Hutchinson, OUP, London 1908, p. 201.

49. Shelley, *loc. cit.*
50. Gustav Kobbé *Wagner's Music Dramas Analysed,* NY 1923, p. viii.
51. Robert Graves *The Greek Myths,* Harmondsworth 1955, Vol I p. 143.
52. Kobbé *op. cit* p. xv.
53. This Wotan contains no hint of *der Einäugige* in *Deutsche Revolution,* who seems to allude to Wotan's wisdom.
54. cf. Note 19.
55. see, for example, illustrations in Kobbé *op. cit.*
56. e.g.
    Brüllt Heil! und Hoch! . . .
    In teutschen Trinkhorn füllen teutschen Met . . .
57. Was einst Tragodie, werd zur Posse.
    GW2 p. 253
58. ibid.
59. v. Kobbé *op. cit* pp. 27–28 and *Das Rheingold* Sc. 4:
    FROH
    Zur Burg führt die Brücke,
    leicht, doch fest eurem Fuß:
    beschreitet kühn ihren schrecklosen Pfad!
    WOTAN
    Abendlich strahlt der Sonne Auge;
    in prächt'ger Glut prangt glänzend die Burg.
    In des Morgens Scheine mutig erschimmernd,
    Lag sie herrenlos hehr verlockend vor mir.
    and cf:
    Und morgen früh, wenn Frigga rosig lächelt,
    Weckt dich der lichte Baldur zur befohlnen
    HELDENFAHRT. (GW2. p. 254).
60. Raymond Furness, Wagner and Literature, Manchester 1982, pp. 111–112.
61. cf. the — non-ironic — title of Richard Strauss' tone-poem *Ein Heldenleben,* 1899.
62. *Heldenfahrt* also echoes *Siegfrieds Rheinfahrt* in *Götterdämmerung.*
63. Furness *op. cit.* pp. 116–117.
64. v. Furness ibid.
65. Fast wie eine Travestie verwendet hier Toller, der doch die eigne Sprache fand, Sternheims Sprache.
    Kerr. *loc. cit.*
66. Antiromantisch, betont herzlos und sachlich war auch seine äußerst verkürzte Sprache.

Fritz Martini *Deutsche Literaturgeschichte,* Stuttgart, 1965, p. 546.

67. P. Bridgwater & A. K. Thorlby in *Penguin Companion to Literature Vol. 2,* Harmondsworth 1969, p. 742.
68. Wer keine Kraft zum Traum hat, hat keine Kraft zum Leben. GW2 pp. 194 & 244–245.
69. Aber der Mensch lebt nicht allein von Ziffern. Der Mensch braucht einen Traum. Meiner heißt: Brasilien . . . Meinen Traum hab ich für mich behalten. In einer Schublade liegt er verwahrt.
GW2 p. 278.
Note also the Biblical parody here:
Der Mensch lebet nicht vom Brode allein. (Matt. 4.4).
Man shall not live by bread alone (Matt. 4.4).
70. Dem Offizier stiehlt man sein Recht auf Krieg. In Brasilien kann er Krieg führen gegen Eingeborene nach Herzenslust! GW2 p. 261.
71. For example:
   a) HINKEMANN . . . . jede Nacht die Sintflut (GW2 p. 247).
   WOTAN: Nach uns die Sintflut (GW2 p. 259).
   b) DER NAMENLOSE: Die Bruckenpfosten eingerammt, Genossen!
   Wer in den Weg sich stellt, wird überrannt.
   Masse ist Tat!
   WOTAN: Des Starken Mannes Anfang: Tat!
   . . . . .
   Wir brücken die Brücke!
   (For the Faust allusion, see below).
72. *Eingeborene . . . führen dunkelhäutige Jungfrauen herbei.*
Wotan läßt sie, tätschelnd, sich malerisch gruppieren.
Winkt! . . . Majestätische Herrschergeste! . . .
Ein Photograph tritt in Aktion.
Tanz der Jungfrauen vor Wotan.
Es ertont ein Klageruf Mariechens).
MARIECHEN: Wilhelm!
(GW2 pp. 271–272).
73. . . . das / seinen klaffenden Schoß gegen Goldmark feilbietet und an Sintflutorgien geil sich kuppelt. (GW2 pp. 256–257).
74. Frauen bekleiden die lustseuchezerfressenen Beine mit seidenen Unterhosen. (GW2 p. 259).
It is habitual for right-wing politicians and demagogues to attack the sexual mores of contemporary society. This was well illustrated in the case of Anderton, Chief Constable of Manchester in

1986 and the comments of other right-wing leaders on victims of AIDS.

75. Fatal ergreifend, wenn er die Gattin abschiebt. Wenn über die Vertuschung, die Selbsttäuschung sich das Bewußtsein schoflen Handelns dennoch Bahn bricht . . . und er es unterwürgt.
Das Ich will es nicht wahr haben — und weiß es doch. Die Stobrawa macht ganz herrlich seine untergeordnete Gattin. Diese Frau, mitten in Penthesileas Reich die beste Sprecherin für Verse, mault und ängstelt hier ein arm Spießerweib, sorgenvoll ergötzlich. Bis auf die einwärts gekehrten Füße; bis auf den dümmlich verzogenen Blick; bis auf die, bei allem, noch durchscheinende Nettheit, Adrettheit.
Kerr. *loc. cit.*
NOTE: Renée Stobrawa also played Grete opposite Heinrich George in *Hinkemann* at the Residenz Theater Berlin, April 1924.
76. Ach ja, es war sehr lustig, sehr traurig.
Gerhard Schön in *Der Tag 14.1.1964*, in a review giving high praise to a midnight matinée in Frankfurt/M. Neither production nor review in Spalek. Newspaper cutting in Akademie der Künste, Berlin.
77. GW2 pp. 255, 269, 282 & 253.
78. GW2 p. 298.
79. GW2 pp. 254, 271, 272, 281 (Ich höre wahrhaftig Sphärenmusik)., 281 *(In dieser Pause kann, damit das ergriffene Publikum seiner Rührung sich entschneuzt ein Leierkasten traute Weisen und militärische Potpourris (Schlachtmärsche, Fridericus Rex usw) dudeln), 297, 298, & 302 (Während alle drei im traditionellen leichten Parademarsch ins Zeitlose abmarschieren schließt sich die Bühne).*
80. Perhaps we may also treat Wotan's inability to distinguish the song-thrush from the hens as a pendant to the musical motif as well as being a parody of Toller's own swallow-experience.
81. exotische Romane. GW2 p. 257.
82. In Jane Austen's *Northanger Abbey*.
83. The strong man's beginning: Deeds!
GW2 p. 261.
The spirit helps me! suddenly I understand
And write confidently: In the beginning was the deed!
(Goethe, *Faust I, Studierzimmer*).
84. GW2 p. 291. Schleim, the 'Goebbels' brain of the enterprise, can allude to Tagore and quote the Bible [The Devil can cite scripture], as well as being able to drop names like Caesar and Nero.

85. GW2 p. 277.
86. Durzak *loc. cit.* p. 145.
87. Compare Toller's use of the jungle image with Thomas Mann's in *Der Tod in Venedig*. v. *Der Tod in Venedig*. ed. T.J. Reed, OUP 1971, p. 64. Mann's use of the *Urweltwildnis* is indeed a 'great metaphor': Toller's is a satirical one.
88. Gefährlicher als dieser undämonische Bartkratzer scheinen allerlei sinistre Gestalten, die sich ,um ihn scharen.
Rothe. *op. cit.* p. 92.
89. Durzak. *loc. cit.* p. 144.
90. v. Klaus Mann's Novel *Mephisto.*
91. Eine Goldgrube für uns, der Dreckjude. (GW2 p. 279).
92. GW2 p. 280.
93. . . . von gewissen psychischen Dispositionen der Deutschen, ihrem Bedarf an Ersatzreligionen und jeder Art Irrationalismen, Paramythen, ihrer Anfälligkeit für Erlösungslehren. Rothe, *op. cit.* p. 92.
94. See chapter on Hinkemann N. 40.
95. Toller dramatisiert die mächtig aufschweppende religiöse Welle der frühen zwanziger Jahre, die eine emotionale Unternährung des Volkes verriet, dem gerade seine bisherigen Idole, Ideale, Wertideen genommen worden waren, dessen Bedürfnis nach Anbetung und Verehrung ziellos vagierte. Rothe *loc. cit.*
96. ibid.
97. *Volksblatt-Illustrierte* 13.6.1930. See below in section on *Wunder in Amerika* in chapter on *Die blinde Göttin.*
98. Eine Kunst, die nichts mit deutschem Blut zu tun hat, und die nicht aus unserer Seele kam. Rainer Schlösser in *Völkische Beobachter* 14.2.1933. Not in Spalek. Newspaper cutting in Akademie der Künste, Berlin.
99. . . . in dem ein Fremdblütiger den abgründigen Haß seiner Rasse gegen das Deutschtum die Zügel schießen läßt. (ibid).
100. List of productions and reviews not listed by Spalek (1968). *This list does not claim to be exhaustive. The list of productions is based upon the list of reviews seen during research, which follows.*

PRODUCTIONS

1. Theater '53, Hamburg, 1961. Directed by Hans-Günter Martens.
2. A Midnight Matinée. Frankfurt/M, 1964.
3. Deutsches Theater, Berlin, 1979.
4. Munich (no further particulars), 1983.

REVIEWS

1. E.F. n.d. Newspaper not known. Prague production, 1925. Newspaper cutting, Theatermuseum, Köln. Says he happened to be in Prague, but it would not have been worth the special journey from Berlin.
   "Eine angesagte Hakenkreuzdemonstration blieb aus".
2. Mysing. *Kölnische Zeitung*, 4.3.'26.
   On Tribune, Berlin, 1926. Thinks play already dated and belonging to inflation period. Concludes:
   "Einige erotische Geschamlosigkeiten durften in den Stuck nicht fehlen; sie brachten aber durchaus nicht die beim Publikum erhoffte Wirkung hervor".
3. E. H. [? Possibly Ernst Heilborn or Otto Ernst Hesse] *Frankfurter Zeitung*, 6.3.'26. On Tribüne, Berlin.
   "Und doch möchte man sich mit Toller zum Glase niedersetzen, denn er weiß um den Menschen und hat es hinter Gitterfenstern gelernt, selbst über dies völkische Fratzengesindel, das ihm schlug, zu lächeln".
4. H.H.B. *Germania* 25.2.1926 on Tribüne, Berlin.
   Sees play as derivative from Sternheim and Kaiser.
5. Rainer Schlösser, *Völkischer Beobachter* 14.2.1933. Nazi attack on Toller, Zech, Paquet etc.
6. Dr. Fehrenbach. *Badische Neueste Nachrichten*, Karlsruhe, 17.1.1961. On Tübinger Keller-Theater [almost certainly identical with 'Zimmertheater', Spalek p. 273]. A production of students and intellectuals.
   "Ernst Toller . . . war anfangs einer der "Hitzigsten" unter den hitzigen Expressionisten. Durch jahrelang Gefangenschaft wegen illegaler Pazifisten-Untergrundwühlerei allmählich zermürbt, wurde er zunächst ein weltverbessernder *homo politicus*, um dann aber zum Dichter zu reifen. Während seiner zweiten Gefangenschaft, nach der von ihm betriebenen und dann gescheiterten Installierung einer Art kommunistischen Musterstaates in Bayern, mischt sich in die grausam zerstörten Ideale viel Zynismus. Aus dieser Zeit stammt seine Komödie, *Der entfesselte Wotan*.
7. Richard Evers, *Holsteinischer Courier*, 16.12.1961. On Theater '53, Hamburg, 1961. The production is described as the first of a series under the general heading: *Auf Gegenkurs*.
   "Und, o Wunder, mit welch genialischer Hellsichtigkeit zeichnete

Toller seinen späteren Henker, dessen Leben er ja nicht kennen konnte, das er höchstens in schöpferischer Phantasie erahnte!" Evers quotes part of Toller's essay in *Die Szene*, January 1926 [GW2 pp. 363–364] from "Man wird in der Öffentlichkeit . . . . to . . . Eine Figur, die uns heiter macht". And adds:
"Hier irrte Toller. Sie machte uns übel, und tut's heute noch".

8. Jürgen Althof, *Abendpost* 15.3.1962.
On Theater '53, Hamburg-Keller.
See Note 33.
"Toller konnte es sich 1923 noch erlauben, Hitler zu unterschätzen und in eine oberflächliche Lächerlichkeit zu zielen". He adds that a present-day director must take steps to avoid this, but that Hans-Günter Martens does not succeed.
9. Friedrich Luft, *Die Welt* 18.9.1962. On Forum Theater. Press cutting in Akademie der Künste, Berlin. Very hostile to Toller.
"Das Stück ist mehr ein Gegenstand für das germanistische Seminar als eine Möglichkeit fürs lebendige Theater".
"Er schrieb expressionistisch und zugleich den Expressionismus selbst satirisch übersteigend . . ".
". . . die Komik des eralteten Kabaretts . . . Theater wird es nicht".
"Tollers hektische Stil ist so kaum nicht mehr goutabel".
10. Anon. *Morgen Zeitung, Kiel,* 17.9.1962.
On Forum Theater. Press cutting in Theatermuseum, Köln.
Says it did not fill an evening and would have been better had it remained a cabaret sketch. Klaus Hoser, Director, worked with imagination and wit. Piscator, "Volksbühne Intendant und sonstiger Toller-Regisseur" was in the audience. The applause was friendly.
11. Anon. *General Anzeiger*, 29, 9.1962.
As No. 10, but shorter.
12. Gerhard Schön, *Der Tag,* 14.1.1964.
On Midnight Matinée, Frankfurt/M. Praises it highly.
13. Michael Stone, *Der Tagesspiegel,* 3.10.1979.
On Deutsches Theater, Berlin. Unenthusiastic.
14. Rose-Marie Borngässer, *Die Welt,* 11.11.1983. On Munich production.
Points out that the performance was on the anniversary of *Kristallnacht*.
Would have been better if Wotan had not been made so much like Hitler, amusing though that was.

Hoppla, Wir Leben!

Background and Development

1. GW1 pp. 86–90.
2. *Neue Dramen. Berliner Tageblatt.* Morgen-Ausg. 6.2.'26. 3:1. Spalek 1340.
3. Klein p. 117.
4. ibid. Spalek 289. *Die Volksbühne* 2. 1.3.1927. Note this is not to be confused with the radio play *Berlin, letzte Ausgabe,* written later.
5. Spalek p. vii. Wedding is a district of Berlin.
6. Es widerstrebt mir, Mitteilungen von dem Inhalt des Stückes zu machen, solange es nicht fertig ist. Nur soviel läßt sich sagen, daß ich versucht habe, eine neue Form für ein *Kollektivdrama* zu finden, da ich glaube, daß mit den üblichen Mitteln dramatischer Formung inneres Gesicht und äußere Atmosphäre, Auf und Ab einer großen modernen Massenbewegung nicht gestaltet werden kann. Was beispielsweise der Film dem Drama voraus hat, die Möglichkeit, Geschehnisse, die innigsten Kontakt geben, fast gleichzeitig zu zeigen, muß auch das neue Massendrama können. Um die Dynamik und Bewegung des 20. Jahrhunderts spürbar werden zu lassen, kommt es nicht darauf an, mit Bühnenrequisiten Maschinengestampf nachzuahmen. Das innere Tempo und die Vielfältigkeit der Handlung sind Elemente, die der Zuschauer als gebundene Ganzheit aufnehmen muß.
   Die Volksbühne No. 16 15.8.'26, p. 2. Spalek 499. Quoted by Klein p. 130. Klein adds a note, p. 277, Note 53: The expression Mass- or Collective-Drama is not to be confused with the term 'Mass-play'. The Leipzig 'Mass-plays' were 'Festival Plays'. (Die Bezeichnung Massen-oder Kollektivdrama ist nicht zu verwechseln mit dem Terminus Massenspiel).
   (The Leipzig *Massenspiele* were *Festspiele*).
7. The title here is already *Hoppla, wir leben!*, that of Walter Mehring's Chanson interpolated into Piscator's production but never printed in the text of the play. It was first printed in the *Leipziger Volkszeitung* 14.9.'27 as, *Hoppla, wir leben! Intermezzo zu einer Hotelszene des Tollerschen Stückes.* (Fall p. 332) If, as is often assumed, Toller's new title is derived from that of the Chanson it is strange that no mention of it is made. May not Toller have himself invented the title *Hoppla, wir leben!* and Walter Mehring taken it up for that of the Chanson?

8. Rorrison p. 207. PT p. 147. The word used is *Entwurf.* A completed, printed version in proof cannot properly be called a draft.
9. GW3 pp. 318ff.
10. In meiner ersten Fassung rannte Thomas, der die Welt von 1927 nicht verstand, ins Irrenhaus zum Psychiater, erkennt in der Unterredung mit dem Arzt, daß es zwei Arten von gefährlichen Narren gibt, die einen, die in Isolierzellen festgehalten werden, die andern die als Politiker und Militärs gegen die Menschheit lostoben. Da begreift er die alten Kameraden, die in zäher Alltagsarbeit die Idee weiterführen, er will das Irrenhaus verlassen, aber, weil er begriffen, weil er zur Wirklichkeit die Beziehung des reifen Menschen gewonnen hat, läßt ihn der psychiatrische Beamte nicht mehr hinaus, jetzt erst sei er "staatsgefährlich" geworden, nicht vorher, da er ein unbequemer Träumer war. GW1 p. 147
11. Wieder war es der Zusammenprall des Menschen, der das Absolute unbedingt, noch heute verwirklichen will, mit den Kräften der Zeit und Zeitgenossen, die die Verwirklichung aus Schwäche, Verrat, Feigheit aufgeben oder aus Kraft, Treue, Tapferkeit für spätere Tage vorbereiten. GW1 p. 145.
12. 'die fertig vorliegenden Werke'. Rorrison p. 206. PT p. 146.
13. ibid.
14. Rorrison and PT *loc. cit.*
    Frühwald (Fall p. 19) says that Toller worked with Piscator on *Hoppla, wir leben!* from the end of May until the beginning of July. This does not agree with Piscator's own statement (which itself may of course well be inaccurate, like so much in *Das politische Theater*) that it was after his disappointment with Herzog's drafts submitted in July that he turned again to Toller's, which had been "submitted in the spring" (Rorrison 207, PT 146. ". . . den Toller mir im Frühjahr gegeben hatte".)
    Toller took a holiday on the island of Sylt during July. It is unlikely he would have done this had he been already involved in reworking his new play, due to open on September 1!
15. Innes pp. 68–69. Rorrison p. 152. PT p. 108.
16. Photocopy from Akademie der Künste, Berlin. Also reprinted in Fall pp. 182ff.
17. Werden Sie am 1. September in Berlin sein? Die Proben in der Piscator-Bühne haben begonnen, Karl Thomas spielt Granach, Kilman — Sima, Eva Berg — Sybille Binder, Frau Meller — Réne Stobrawa, Pickel — Graetz, Professor Lüdin — Steckel. Ich habe

das Stück inzwischen noch einmal durchgearbeitet, ein kurzer fünfter Akt ist entstanden, Thomas endet nicht im Irrenhaus. (Photocopy made from Toller Archive, Akademie der Künste, Berlin). September 1 was the planned 1st night. Note that Graetz is stated as playing Pickel. This is confirmed by Gerda Redlich (taped interview).
Cf. Cast as given in Programme, where Pickel is played by Erwin Kalser.

18. Tape-recorded interview with present writer, 10.5.'74. Also printed in Cecil W. Davies *Theatre for the People*, Manchester 1977, p. 111.
19. e.g. by Willett, Innes, & in *Weimarer Republik*.
20. Mack: "verändert und verfälscht". Leipziger Neueste Nachrichten, 9.10.'27. Spalek 2825. Press cutting in Theatermuseum, Köln.
Kienzl: In Berlin machte das mechanische Tollhaus Piscators die Zuschauer halb verrückt. (Press cutting seen in Theatermuseum, Köln. Almost certainly identical with Spalek 2814: *Leipziger Neueste Nachrichten* 7.9.'27).
21. . . . Das volle Haus feierte die Dichtung am eindringlichsten in den Szenen, deren tief menschlicher Inhalt andächtigstes, atemlos Schweigen erzwang so namentlich in der ergreifend einfachen Erzählung des Karl Thomas von den ungeheuren Leiden des Krieges. Eine glänzende Inszenierung und meisterhafte schauspielerische Wiedergabe halfen über den namentlich im 2. Teil allzu tagesgeschichtlich behandleten abschwächenden Eindruck der Widerfolge hinweg, so daß die Künstler und der anwesende Dichter zum Schluß mit sturmisch und ehrlichen Beifall begrüßt wurden.
Critic: "F" in *Berliner Tageblatt* 2.9.'27.
Press cutting in Theatermuseum, Köln.
22. V. Spalek p. 33 & Fall p. 181.
23. Ich bedaure heute, daß ich, von einer Zeitmode befangen, die Architektonik des ursprünglichen Werkes zugunsten der Architektonik der Regie zerbrach. Seine erstrebte Form war stärker als jene, die auf der Bühne gezeigt wurde. Verantwortlich dafür bin nur ich, aber ich habe gelernt, und es ist mir heute lieber, daß ein Regisseur zu wenig aus einem Werk herausholt, als daß er zuviel hineinlegt. GW1 p. 146.
24. v. *Theatre for the People* pp. 95–112 for the present author's account of this and Braulich pp. 108–129 for a Marxist view
25. *Der Tag.* v. *Theatre for the People* p. 107 and PT pp. 101–2.
26. v. PT p. 108:

Ich habe protestiert gegen das Überwuchern des Films und des szenischen Beiwerks; gegen die Durchsetzung des Textes mit Banalitäten, Parteischlagworten und Funktionärsphrasen: gegen das Übermaß revolutionärer Prophezeihung. Genau gesagt, also nicht gegen eine politische Inszenierung – ich wollte die denkbar größte Schärfe –, sondern gegen die zum politischen und künstlerischen Selbstzweck gewordene Art der Inszenierung, durch die Regie und Stück getrennt wurden, durch die die Regieleistung zu einer rein optischen, vom Stück unabhängigen, ja, das Stück vernichtenden Wirkung gebracht werden mußte.
(I protested against the excessive development of film and scenic additions; against the insertion into the text of banalities, party slogans and bureaucratic jargon; against the excessive number of revolutionary prophecies. So, to put it precisely: not against a political production (I wanted the greatest pungency conceivable) but against the style of the production, which became a political and artistic end in itself and which unavoidably turned the achievement of the production itself into a purely visual one, independent of the play and indeed destroying the play altogether).
(Trans. CWD. See also Rorrison p. 152).

27. PT 106. Rorrison 150.
28. Wie einer politisch dazu steht, fällt kaum noch ins Gewicht. Die Gefühlstatsache redet, redet, schreit.
PT p. 102. Rorrison p. 146.
29. Ich habe mich sehr über Ihre Worte für Piscator gefreut.
Die Volksbühne droht durch den Einfluss der verschiedenen Baberlababe ein Instrument der Ruhe- und Ordnung- Spiesser zu werden.
(Photocopied from letter in Akademie der Künste Berlin)
30. Wäre es nur eine Konsumgenossenschaft, ein geschickt aufgezogener Apparat zur Verbilligung des Theaterbesuches, ich hätte bestimmt der Volksbühne nicht zwei Stunden meines Lebens gewidmet . . .
Daß der wirtschaftliche Vorteil dieser Organisation vor allen Dingen dem Proletariat zugute kommen soll, daß die ganze Institution zunächst geschaffen wurde, um den Enterbten der bürgerlichen Gesellschaft ein hohes Kulturgebiet zugänglich zu machen, das war schon von größerer Bedeutung . . .
Aber auch das konnte nicht entscheidend sein, da ich im allmählichen Erwachen zur Politik den größeren und gemäßeren

Weg kennenlernte, um sozialen Verantwortungsgefühl zu genügen. Dauerhafter schon mußte die Idee der Volksbühne einen Dramaturgen faszinieren, der erkannt hatte, daß jedes Theater als ein elementarer Gesellschaftsakt organisch nur vom Publikum aus aufgebaut werden kann, und der hier nach Jahrhunderten zum erstenmal einen Versuch sah, die Bühne nicht durch künstlerische Genialitäten und mäcenatische Opfer, sondern in einzig naturgemäßer Weise durch Schaffung eines Publikums zu erneuern.

Julius Bab: *Uber den Tag hinaus*. Darmstadt 1960. p. 306.

31. v. *Theatre for the People*, passim.
32. PT 105–6; Rorrison 149–50.
33. Joh. R Becher; Bernard v. Brentano; Paul Bildt; Ernst Deutsch; Tilla Durieux; Erich Engel; Fritz Engel; Gertrud Eysoldt; Erwin Faber; Emil Faktor; Jürgen Fehling; Lion Feuchtwanger; S.Fischer; Manfred Georg; Alexander Granach; George Grosz; Wilhelm Herzog; Herbert Ihering; Erwin Kalser; Alfred Kerr; Kurt Kersten; Egon Erwin Kisch; Fritz Kortner; Leo Lania; Heinrich Mann; Thomas Mann; Karlheinz Martin; Edmund Meisel; Gerda Müller; Traugott Müller; Max Osborn; Alfons Paquet; Max Pechstein; Kurt Pinthus; Alfred Polgar; Ernst Rowohlt; Leopold Schwarzschild; Hans Siemsen; Ernst Toller; Kurt Tucholsky; Paul Wiegler; Alfred Wolfenstein. (PT. p.106).
34. Ernst Toller, der mit starkem Applaus begrüßt wurde, sprach über Drama — Idee — Tendenz: "Drama, das heißt Kampf, radikal oder gar nicht sein. Der Proletarier, der heute auf der Bühne steht, trägt eine Fahne — das stört die Kleinbürger. Heute ist der Proletarier nicht nur Gefühlsmensch, er ist Träger einer Idee. Die Volksbühne besitzt kein Gesicht, keinen Charakter, hat nicht den Mut, sich unbeliebt zu machen". Toller sprach dann in eigener Sache, was unnotwendig war. (Bekanntlich führt Toller einen Prozeß gegen Die Volksbühne, da sie eines seiner Dramen angenommen hat, aber nicht herausbringt).

Berliner Volkszeitung, quoted in PT p. 111–112. Rorrison 158.

The play concerned was *Die Wandlung*. Some idea of Toller's anger and bitterness over this matter (which may in part account for his championing Piscator so heartily) may be gained from this exchange of letters with Heinrich Neft (for the Volksbühne).

On 23.12 '25 Neft wrote to Toller offering 1000M for performances of *Die Wandlung* and referred to a possible extension of the contract. (Carbon copy of letter, in Akademie der Künste, Berlin).

Toller replied the next day (24.12.'25). First he confirmed the new conditions: the contract to be extended to 20.3.'26. If the play were produced later than that but before 15.11'26, Toller must give permission in writing.He went on to attack bitterly Neft's policy:

The idea of the Volksbühne appears to me more important than the failure of the most distinguished theatre of the *Volksbühnenbund**. When Herr Neft explains that the administration cannot perform *Die Wandlung* at present because "the piece has too strong a propaganda message", "the piece is too radical", because "he is bound to be afraid that he would frighten away the Volksbühne membership with the production" — these are for me symptoms of a decline in the original Volksbühne concept. Until now I was used to such replies only from commercial theatres, which the Volksbühne could not combat bitterly enough on account of their anxious considerations for the trends of the day . . .

I had to tell Herr Director Neft that I don't write bright and cheerful plays about soldiers . . .

I know too well why you are afraid. In *Die Wandlung* it is not a question of trying to show abstract things; nor is it about abstract problems or the abstract course of destiny; it is about concrete things, immediate things, things which force each individual to decide "for" or "against". That is why you are afraid. The negotiations with the Volksbühne were for me the most unpleasant theatrical experience in my not small practical experience of unpleasant theatrical matters.

(Die Idee der Volksbühne erscheint mir wichtiger als das Versagen des bedeutendsten Theater des Volksbühnenbunds. Wenn Herr Direktor Neft erklärte, die Direktion könne die "Wandlung" gegenwärtig nicht spielen, weil "das Stück eine zu starke Tendenz habe","das Stück zu radikal sei", weil "er Angst haben müsse, dass er mit der Aufführung die Mitglieder Volksbühne [sic] weggraule", so sind das für mich Symptome eines Verfalls des

---

*By *Volksbühnenbund* Toller must mean, the *Bühnenvolksbund*, an organisation founded in 1919 by Wilhelm Karl Gerst, closely modelled upon the Volksbühne but starting from the Christian-National rather than from the Socialist-International position. (v. *Theatre for the People* Appendix D, ppl65ff. Also Anton Strambowski *Bund der Theatergemeinden*, Düsseldorf, 1978.)

ursprunglichen Volksbühnen-Gedanken. Solche Entgegungen war ich bisher nur von Geschäftstheatern gewohnt, die die Volksbühne wegen ihrer ängstlichen Rücksichtnahme auf Tagesströmungen nicht scharf genug zu bekämpfen wusste . . .
Ich musste Herrn Direktor Neft sagen, dass ich frisch-fröhliche Soldatenspiele nicht schreibe . . .
Ich weiss nur zu gut, wovor man sich fürchtet. In der "Wandlung" geht es nicht um abstrakte Dinge, dort werden nicht abstrakte Probleme oder abstrakte Schicksalsabläufe, zu zeichnen versucht, dort geht es um Konkretes, um Unmittelbares, das jeden Einzelnen zum Für oder Wider zwingt.
Darum fürchtet man sich.
Die Verhandlung mit der Berliner Volksbühne war für mich die unerfreulichste Theatererfahrung meiner an unerfreulichen Theatererfahrungen nicht armen Praxis.
(Carbon of Tollers letter of 24.12.'25 "An die Direktion der Volksbühne", in Akademie der Künste, Berlin).

Toller was obviously still preoccupied with this dispute in the spring of 1927. In the letter to Kerr of 29.3.'27 already quoted he refers to the matter and asks Kerr if he may name him as an expert witness if the matter comes to court.

35. Temperamentvoll und doch mit größter Sachlichkeit wies er die Grenzen zwischen dramatischer Kunst und politischer Propaganda auf, ohne dabei die verbindenden Fäden zu übersehen. Mit überzeugender Beredsamkeit entwickelte er die der Kunst und dem Theater gestellten Aufgaben, mitzuwirken an der "Erziehung des Menschengeschlechts". (Brodbeck p. 378)
36. Toller und ein, zwei seiner Freunde sprachen nicht ungeschickt. Aber nie konnte ein Zweifel darüber bestehen, daß die übergroße Zahl der Delegierten hinter den offiziellen Rednern der Tagung stand. (ibid p. 379).
37. With *Feuer aus den Kesseln*. Leipzig. 1962. Spalek 30.
38. John Willett. *The New Sobriety*, Thames & Hudson 1978 p. 151. cf. C.D. Innes *op cit*. e.g. pp. 94, 99–100 et passim.

Further Stage History

1. v. Spalek 2769.
2. The critic "-ng". (Perhaps Herbert Ihering, who sometimes signed articles in this style). In *Frankfurter Volksstimme* 17.1.1928. Press

cutting in Theatermuseum, Köln. Not in Spalek.

3. 16.1.1928. Periodical not known. Press cutting in Theatermuseum, Köln. Not in Spalek; but cf Spalek 2778.
4. -ng. *loc cit.*
5. Press cutting in Theatermuseum, Köln. Periodical and date not known. Not in Spalek.
6. *Frankfurter Volksstimme* 17.1.1928. "Der *Wahlakt* aus Tollers Drama". "Im Hause des Ministers". "Rosa Valetti" (apparently as Frau Meller).
7. Apollo Theater. Spalek p. 880.
8. Spalek p. 879.
9. Der bühnentechnische Trick hat sich zudem in der vielfältigen Abnutzung oft zum Klischee verflacht.
   Tägliche Rundschau 21.iii.'28. Press cutting in Theatermuseum, Köln. Spalek 2765.
10. Die Mängel des Stückes sind allbekannt. 'Ad' in Germania, 20.iii.'28. Press Cutting in Theatermuseum, Köln. Spalek 2768, where date is given as 10.iii'28.
11. ibid
12. v. Spalek 2769.
13. Spalek p. 879 and No. 2763.
14. Spalek 2760.
15. Felix Salken, [erroneously for "Salten"] *Feuilleton," . . . Er kann nicht anders"* in *Neue Freie Presse* 12.xi '27. Press cutting in Theatermuseum, Köln. Spalek 2841, where the critic's surname is given as 'Salten', correctly.
16. Leopold Jacobsohn. *Neues Wiener Tageblatt* 12.11.'27. Press cutting in Theatermuseum, Köln. Spalek 2809.
17. Diese Handlung ist ganz einfach; sie ist ganz rein in ihrer Menschlichkeit, ganz echt nach ihrer Gesinnung. Salten. *loc cit.*
18. Press cutting in Theatermuseum, Köln. Periodical not known. Not in Spalek.
19. GW3 pp. 321–323.
20. Rorrison p. 209. PT p. 148.
21. Ich war also im Vorhinein klar, daß ich meiner Rolle eine etwas weichere Auffassung als der Berliner Kollege geben werde. Ich mußte das Revolutionäre mehr aus dem Gefühl als mit dem scharfen, nackten Verstand gestalten. Aber ich glaube, daß man auch auf diesem Wege der Figur nahezukommen vermag.
    Und eines bin ich als Karl Thomas so wenig als möglich:

Schauspieler. Man kann diesen Mann mit dem Herzen, man kann ihn auch ganz aus dem Gehirn, aber man kann ihn absolut nicht mit rein schauspielerischen Mitteln und Finessen des Metiers gestalten. Und ich bin Gefühlsschauspieler, bin es immer gewesen, habe als Privatmensch mit dem Theater wahrhaftig wenig oder gar nichts zu schaffen. Ich kann und mag nichts"machen", was einem im heutigen Theaterbetrieb mitunter ein bißchen schadet. So bin ich auch nicht das geworden, was wir heute einen "Prominenten" nennen, obwohl ich bei Dr Beer eigentlich schon eine ganze Reihe guter Rollen gespielt habe . . . . . .
Und als meine Lieblingsrollen kann ich immer nur die bezeichnen, die man ohne weitere Verrenkungen und Gehirnakrobatik ganz schlicht aus dem Herzen spielen darf, so habe ich mir auch für die Figur Tollers nicht erst von weither eine gedanklich konstruierte Auffassung geholt. Und was man an dieser Gestalt als neu und besonders modern empfinden will, leuchtet mir kaum ein. Ich spiele einen Mann, der, ob dem Irrenhaus entsprungen oder nicht, in gefühlsmäßig stärksten Gegensatz zu der ihn umgebenden, aus Kompromissen gefügten und nach Konjunkturen regulierten Welt steht.
Wie man so etwas "gut" oder weniger gut spielen könnte, verstehe ich nicht. Man muß empfinden, das ist alles. Und anders habe ich meine Schauspielerei nie aufgefaßt. Mit bloßen "Mitteln" könnte ich nicht wirken, und wenn ich etwas nicht fühle, lasse ich lieber die Hand davon ! . . .
Neue Freie Presse. 27.11.1927.

22. Gerda Redlich. *loc. cit.*
23. Rudolf Holzer, *loc cit,* did not approve of the revised ending, saying of Karl Thomas, "er *muß* sterben": he *must* die.
24. Spalek p. 879. Stadttheater. Directed by Barth; Design by Cajo Kühnly.
25. Ein phosphorner Spiegel flimmert, aus dem einem die Zeit als wahnwitzige Grimasse entgegenglotzt. Eine ganze Kultur wird als kulturlos demaskiert. Wie eine Fahne flattert die Anklage hoch. Drohend.
General Anzeiger. 5.12.1929. p. 3.
(Aus den Beständen des Institut für Zeitungsforschung der Stadt Dortmund).
26. Manchmal melodisch, nicht immer hart genug in die Ecken getrieben, dann wieder ungeheuer menschlich, irrsinnig offen

verwundbar. Ein Rebell des Herzens, nicht des Kopfes. Mehr als er überzeugt, bewegt er. Sympathie fliegt ihm hundertfach zu. ibid

27. Eine sehenswerte Aufführung, mehr, eine wichtige. Und eine fürs Publikum. Den Beifall entsprach dem ausverkauften Haus. ibid.
Rest of cast given in this source: Hans Raabe, Fritz Günzel, Hanns Olsen, Bruno Nepach, Lotte Kleinschmidt, Nora Reinhardt, Reinhold Jungermann (Pickel).
28. English title: *Hoppla!*. Spalek 92. Reprinted as *Hoppla! Such Is Life!* in *Seven Plays*, London, The Bodley Head, 1935. Spalek 120.
29. Spalek p. 880.
30. All quotations and information above, from copy of Programme seen in Victoria and Albert Museum.
31. Press cutting, source not given, seen in Victoria and Albert Museum.
32. e.g. GW3 p. 89:
LOTTE KILMAN: Bitte. Die kleine Blonde wär mir lieber oder Koks.
Seven Plays p. 252:
LOTTE KILMAN: I should prefer the blonde girl — or a fire.
(Correctly: Thanks! I'd rather have the little blond girl, or cocaine).
33. e.g. GW3 p. 96:
Wo die andern Nacht umfängt mit braunen Schatten, seh ich den Mörder sich ducken, nackt und mit entbloßtem Hirn . . .
Seven Plays. p.257:
When others creep into the shadowy bosom of the night
I see murderers lurking everywhere, the evil workings of their brains exposed to my gaze.
(A more acceptable translation might be: Where night envelops the others with brown shadows, I see the murderer cowering, naked, his brains exposed. [In 1927 the adjective *braun* was already closely associated with the Nazis, through *die Braunen*, the Brown-shirts]).
34. *The Times* 20.2.1929. Anonymous. Not in Spalek. Press cutting seen in Victoria and Albert Museum.
35. All these quotations: ibid.
36. Press cutting seen in Victoria and Albert Museum. Monday, February 18, altered to 19 in pencil. No source named. Not in Spalek.

37. Spalek 2885.
38. Press cutting seen in Victoria and Albert Museum. Name of paper not given. Not in Spalek.
39. ibid.
40. In *Desire Under The Elms*. 1924.
41. *Zensur in England*. Seen in Akademie der Künste, Berlin.
42. ibid.
43. Spalek p. 881. Italian title: *Oplà, noi viviamo!*.
Design: Gianni Ratto. Music, Fiorenzo Carpi, Negri, Weill, Hollaender.
44. 'eine hervorragende Aufführung': Horst Rüdiger, *Italien gräbt Ernst Toller aus*. In *Mannheimer Morgen* 5.12.'51. Press cutting in Theatermuseum, Köln. Spalek 2872.
45. . . . den tragischen Irrtum einer hohen dramatischen Potenz. ibid.
46. Production, v. Spalek p. 881. *Hop la, Nous vivons!*
Dir: José Valverde; Design, Camille Osorowitz; Costumes, Marianne Pade; Music, César Gattegno; Photography, Jacques Citles.
47. Decor, Franz Koppenhofer. Karl Thomas: Herwig Lucas; Eva Berg: Sabine Schmalhausen; Kilman: Michael Rademacher. Information from Klaus Colberg, *Revolutionäre gestern und heute. Der Tagesspiegel* 27 Feb. 1974.
48. 13.2.'74. p. 37. Press cuttings in Theatermuseum, Köln, and Fritz Hüser Institut, Dortmund.
49. *Der Tagesspiegel* 27.2.'74. Press cutting in Theatermuseum, Köln.
50. vom naiven idealistischen Pathos zu expressionistischen und dann wieder zu trivial realistischen Redewendungen. ibid.
51. Da wehrst sich im Zuschauer zunächst eine Art von Verteidigungsinstinkt für die Weimarer Republik, die vielgeschmähte. ibid.
52. Sieht dieser enttäuschte Revolutionär sie nicht, genauso wie später die Nazis, bloß als System der Schwäche und des Kuhhandels — nur von links statt von rechts? ibid.
53. . . . wir gehen einer Periode des Faschismus entgegen, die *Jahre* dauern wird und an deren Ende der Krieg nicht gegen Frankreich, sondern gegen Sovietrußland droht.
Zur deutschen Situation (1932) GW1 p. 75.
54. ein erster Demokratieversuch, wenn auch ein schwacher. Colberg. *loc cit.*
55. *Die Welt*. 4.10.'80. Press cutting in Akademie der Künste, Berlin.
56. Mit der Aufführung soll an Ernst Toller erinnert sein, der sich

nicht abfinden wollte, wo man sich nicht abfinden darf. Quoted by W. Mommert. See N.63, below.

57. Der Widerspruch zwischen seinen idealistischen ethischen Menschheitspostulaten und den realen Erfordernissen des Klassenkampfs hat er nie ganz überwinden können. ibid.
58. In Erwin Piscator, *Schriften 2*, Henschall Verlag, Berlin 1968 pp. 34 ff.
59. Er hatte — auf der Flucht vor sich selbst — New York verlassen wollen. ibid.
60. Es ist das Paradox des Tollerschen Lebens, daß in ihm revolutionäre Wille und Resignation, Weltflucht und Kämpfertum miteinander und gegeneinander gepaart waren. ibid.
61. Programme. Deutsches Theater, Kammerspiele. 5.6.'84. In Akademie der Künste, Berlin.
62. Power is always reactionary. GW3 p. 41.
63. W. Mommert of the Deutsche-Presse- Agentur (dpa) in *Volksblatt* Berlin 7.6.'84. Press cutting in Akademie der Künste, Berlin.
64. Hier und Heute. Und wie es weitergehen könnte. ibid.
65. Christine Gregor. *Die Tageszeitung*, Berlin, 15.11.'83. Press cutting in Akademie der Künste, Berlin.
66. F. Luft. *Berliner Morgenpost* 28.6.'83. Press cutting in Akademie der Künste, Berlin.
67. e.g. his review of *Der entfesselte Wotan* in *Die Welt* 18.9.'62. Press cutting in Akademie der Künste, Berlin.
68. Tollers Sprache, heute erscheint sie uns oft schrill, manchmal auf pathetische Weise mürbe . . . Der Abend wird sensationell . . . unwiederholbar! . . . . Ein großer, rarer, — ein so schöner Abend. Luft. *loc. cit.*
69. Warum wagt sich eigentlich kein Theater von heute an dieses zu Unrecht vergessene Stück?
Tagesspiegel, Berlin. 28.6.'83. Press cutting in Akademie der Künste, Berlin.
70. Gregor. *loc. cit.*
71. *Hör zu*, Hamburg, 12.11.'83 . . .

A Re-Assessment

1. 1st published as *Drama from Ibsen to Eliot*, Chatto & Windus 1952; revised edtn, Peregrine Books 1964; 2nd Revised edition published as *Drama from Ibsen to Brecht* (a signal of changing critical

fashion!), Chatto & Windus 1968. Published in Pelican Books 1973 and reprinted 1976, 1978, 1981 & 1983.

Williams evidently knows the play only in Ould's translation, from which he quotes. He treats the whole text, with films and stage-directions, as being the simple and sole work of the author: Piscator is not mentioned. This play is presented as the book's principal specimen of Expressionism — but as Williams classifies Brecht as expressionist we need not be too surprised. e.g.' It is a fact that there is a general historical development from Ibsen to Brecht, from dramatic naturalism to dramatic expressionism". (1983 ed. p. 13). Or again: "Brecht's expressionism is unusually open". (1983 ed. p. 331).

Williams describes Thomas as having suffered 'imprisonment' and his being 'released from detention'. The madness is lost, though Williams does refer to 'a lunatic asylum' without explaining its place in the story.

2. GW3 p. 318.
3. GW3 pp. 7–117.
4. GW3 pp. 318–325.
5. He reverted to this for the Leipzig production.
6. Dorothea Klein. *Der Wandel der dramatischen Darstellungsform im Werk Ernst Tollers 1919–1930*. Doctoral Thesis, Bochum 1968.
7. She thought that the Hamburg production used the *original* ending, (i.e. the ending used at Leipzig) and could not know precisely how Piscator had altered the last scene of Act 5.
8. Klein pp. 122ff.
9. Träger der zentralen Idee des Dramas. ibid p. 129.
10. das positive Element verkörpert. ibid.
11. allen Seiten gerecht zu werden. ibid p. 131.
12. E. Laubsche Verlagsbuchhandlung G.m.b.H. Berlin 1927.
13. Justiz p. 8.
14. ibid
15. GW3 p. 10.
16. Wer mir den Schutz der Gesetze versagt, der stößt mich zu den Wilden der Einöde hinaus, der gibt mir die Keule, die mich selbst schützt, in die Hand.

    Justiz p. 8.

    Toller is quoting from memory. The passage actually reads: Verstoßen, antwortete Kohlhaas, indem er die Hand zusammendrückte, nenne ich den, dem der Schutz der Gesetze versagt ist! Denn dieses Schutzes, zum Gedeihen meines friedlichen

Gewerbes, bedarf ich; ja, er ist es, deshalb ich mich, mit dem Kreis dessen, was ich erworben, in diese Gemeinschaft flüchte; und wer mir ihn versagt, der stößt mich zu den Wilden der Einöde hinaus; er gibt mir, wie wollt Ihr das leugnen, die Keule, die mich selbst schützt, in die Hand.
(Heinrich von Kleist, *Erzählungen*. DTV, Munich 1964–74 p. 38.

17. Die Demokraten mögen nicht jammern, wenn morgen der Faschismus auch sie zum Wilde zählt, das man jagen und hetzen, quälen und morden darf. (*loc cit*).
18. Klein p. 134.
19. *Ein Vorspiel und Vier Akte.* GW3 p. 318.
20. The earlier sections of this chapter have already shown that the elements of epic theatre in Piscator's sense are superficial, primarily mechanical and largely dispensable.
21. Klein p. 136ff.
22. . . . der tragische und der komische Held des Stückes, der Kleinbürger Pickel, der die ideale Verkörperung der Republik sucht, und der Arbeiter Thomas [presented as such in Piscator's production. CWD], der die Vollendung der Revolution will. PT p152. v. Rorrison p. 214.
23. Pickel ist eine ins Komische verzerrte Projektion von Karl Thomas, ist dessen karikiertes Gegenbild.
Klein p. 141.
24. Act 4 Sc. 2. GW2 p. 97ff.
25. Distanzierung vom Sprachgestus der Frühphase. Klein p. 143.
26. Vom Hintergrund der vorherrschenden nüchtern-realistischen Sprechweise hebt sich die von Pickel und Thomas deutlich ab. *loc cit.*
27. The 'scaffolding' was an appropriate, if cumbersome, technique for the proscenium-arch stage. In the late 20th Century appropriate staging techniques for open, thrust and in-the-round stages could easily be developed and even for the proscenium stage less clumsy methods could well be used.
28. Piscator's Proletarian Theatre opened on 14.10.1920 with a Triple Bill. Designer: John Heartfield.
29. The first was *Schweik,* 23.1. to 12.4.1928, immediately after *Hoppla, wir leben!*. The full *Aufstieg und Fall der Stadt Mahagonny* (as distinct from the *Kleiner Mahagonny,* produced in Baden-Baden in 1927) to whose published edition Brecht appended the notes that included the word *Montage* as one of the characteristics of epic theatre, was written 1928/9 and first produced 9.3.1930.
30. *Kreisler-Bühne* is the name given to the simultaneous setting with

multiple subdivisions and three storeys used in 1922 in the Berlin Theatre on the Stresemannstraße for the performance of the piece after E. Th. A. Hoffmann, *The marvellous story of Bandmaster Kreisler.* A supplementary device for the incorporation of lantern-slides was added. The sequence of scenes unwound, alternately lit up, in part successively, in part simultaneously.
The *Kreisler-Bühne* found a continuation on the similarly constructed *Piscator-Bühne* (named after the regisseur E. Piscator) after 1923 in the Nollendorf-Theatre in Berlin.
Incidentally a stage divided vertically or horizontally for plays that needed simultaneous action in performance, had already been used earlier.
(Translated from Wilhelm Koch *Deutsches Theater-Lexikon 2. Bd).* The name *Piscator-Bühne* is used here for the *Hoppla* setting, properly called the *Zugbühne* or the *Etagenbühne*. The *Piscator-Bühne* was the name given to the Theater am Nollendorf-platz itself.)

31. Diese Etagenbühne ist nicht identisch mit der Kreislerbühne. Trotz einer gewissen äußerlichen Ähnlichkeit war sie ihrem Prinzip nach direkt das Gegenteil. Bedeutet die Kreislerbühne, wenigstens in ihrer bisherigen Verwendung, nichts weiter als eine Vervielfachung des Bühnenbildes durch eine Aufteilung, so ist die Etagenbühne ein in sich geschlossenes selbständiges Spielgerüst, für das der Bühnenausschnitt nur noch ein äußerliches Hemmnis bedeutet. Die Etagenbühne gehört in Wirklichkeit bereits einer anderen Bühnenarchitektonik an.
(PT. p. 150) v. Rorrison p. 211).
32. In Piscator's production the characters in the 'non-speaking' room 'froze' and were thus in silhouette throughout the scene acted in the adjoining room. This helped to emphasise the montage technique.
33. Im Arbeitszimmer
WILHELM KILMAN: Ich ließ Sie rufen.
EVA BERG: Bitte.
Im Vorzimmer
SOHN DES BANKIERS: Wird er dich empfangen? Er hat dich nicht rufen lassen.
(GW3 p. 27).
34. We use the term 'sub-scene' to indicate each section of dialogue in a specific sub-section of the set, here *Private Office* and *Anteroom*.
35. No entrance is given for Baron Friedrich in the text, an omission

repeated in *Seven Plays*.
36. GW3 p. 34.
37. GW3 pp. 37 & 38.
38. *Flur* GW3 p. 90; *Halbdunkel Korridor* GW3 p. 92.
39. GW3 p. 78.
40. GW3 pp. 321–324 and GW3 pp. 106–110. Piscator, though he gives stage-directions for this scene, probably cut it completely during rehearsal as irrelevant to a version ending with Karl Thomas's suicide in prison.
41. GW3 p. 323.
42. GW3 p. 324.
43. ibid.
44. KARL THOMAS: . . . . outside the window beech trees are really growing . . . . not padded walls. *(Karl Thomas off)*
PROFESSOR LÜDIN: Bad stock.

PROFESSOR LÜDIN: . . . Take him to the padded cell. To his . . . . beech-wood. *(Karl Thomas is led off by the warder)*
PROFESSOR LÜDIN: Not capable of living!
(GW3 p. 26 and p. 325).
It is an historical coincidence that Buchenwald was a notorious Nazi concentration camp, but the association is bound to affect a modern reader or audience as if it were prophetic.
45. Hier war jede Rolle tatsächlich der scharf umrissene Ausdruck einer gesellschaftlichen Schicht. Nicht die private Veranlagung, der individuelle Komplex war ausschlaggebend, sondern der Typus, der Vertreter einer bestimmten gesellschaftlichen und ökonomischen Anschauung.
PT p. 152. v. Rorrison p. 214.
46. Though even the anonymous student is given powerful and convincing *personal* motives for his political stance and action.
47. It is also worth remembering that in this play Toller does not give his characters 'type' names, as he does in *Hinkemann*.
48. GW3 p. 63.
49. PT p. 149. Rorrison p. 210.
50. John Willett, *The New Sobriety*, Thames & Hudson 1978 p. 151
51. KARL THOMAS: Your hands. *(The use of the intimate form implies: 'My darling').*
EVA BERG: You. *(The intimate form 'Du' implies, 'My darling')*
KARL THOMAS: I love you very much, Eva . . . *(intimate form)*
EVA BERG: Would they let us be buried together, if we ask them?

KARL THOMAS: Perhaps.
(GW3 p. 17)

52. Was pfui! Leg dich mit deiner Hur in die Ecke und mach ihr ein Kind. Das kann dann im Grabe auskriechen und mit den Würmen spielen.
GW3 p. 20.
53. Man hätte ihr Unterzeug untersuchen sollen. Der Duft wird nicht nach Lavendel gerochen haben (GW3 p. 13).
54. Blaue Bohnen gefällig?
(GW3 p. 14).
55. Romantischer Schwindel. GW3 p. 13.
56. Choräle singen gefällig? (ibid).
57. Er wird uns nicht verraten? GW3 p. 16.
58. GW3 p. 13.
59. ibid.
60. GW3 p. 16.
61. GW3 p. 20. And v. Note 52.
62. His speaking to the masses from the Town Hall balcony recalls the well-known photograph of Philipp Scheidemann proclaiming the Republic on 9 November 1918 after the SPD had decided to throw in its lot with the revolutionaries. (Picture. *Weimarer Republik* Elefanten Press Berlin 1977, p. 117. See also Simon Taylor *Germany 1918–1933* London 1983 p. 8).
63. Almost untranslatable! 'I thank you obediently'.
GW3 p. 21.
64. Improbabilities asserted as data at the beginning of a play have always been acceptable within theatrical conventions.
65. Verband weiblicher Angestellter. German distinguishes sharply between *Beamter* and *Angestellter*. The latter is any salaried employee *not* in government service. The former is any salaried employee *in* government service. The term covers a much wider range of occupations than the approximate English translation 'civil servant'.
66. wenn wieder andere Zeiten kommen. GW3 p. 32.
67. Loibner, quoted above. *Neue Freie Presse* 27.11.'27.
68. Piscator in *Das Politische Theater* merely lists Eva as one of the three "who represent the positive side of the revolution" (Rorrison p. 209): even this sentence was omitted in Felix Gasbarra's revised 1963 edition (Rowohlt Verlag, Reinbek bei Hamburg). The critics Felix Salten and Rudolf Holzer (see *Further Stage History* at Note 15). both refer only to the scene with the children. The

first half of the scene was almost certainly the scene `played' behind closed tabs at Cambridge.

69. Though Lotte, Lande, and the complaints of the Pikkolo focus the sexual perversity of the period.
70. Elżbieta Ettinger *Rosa Luxemburg, A Life,* London 1987, p. 83–84.
71. *Comrade and Lover: Rosa Luxemburg's Letters to Leo Jogiches*. Edited & translated by Elżbieta Ettinger, Cambridge, Mass. , and London, England, 1979.
72. In *great* misfortune a noble heart learns to find itself at last, but it is painful to do without life's little ornaments.
    Schiller *Maria Stuart* Act 1 Sc. 1 lines 52–54. Quoted by Rosa Luxemburg in a letter from prison, February, 1915 v. Ettinger *A Life* p. 202.
73. GW3 p. 52.
74. ibid.
75. GW3 p. 50.
76. Sc. 4 GW2 p. 25ff.
77. GW4 p. 69.
78. GW3 p. 58. Another parallel with Rosa Luxemburg, who might have left Berlin even the very day before her murder:
    "Was she right in refusing to leave Berlin? Perhaps not; but she could not leave the victims behind and seek safety for herself. Once she had quoted from a legend: 'O Adonai, Adonai . . . Let us never speak these words: "Let us save ourselves and leave the weak to their destiny".'".
    Ettinger *A Life* p. 244.
79. GW3 p. 40.
80. ibid.
81. GW3 p. 81.
82. Ein ohnmächtiger Popanz, ein Spielball! GW3 p. 42.
83. GW3 p. 64.
84. Ettinger *A Life* p. 236.
85. ibid
86. op cit p. 244.
87. GW3 p. 66.
88. ibid.
89. In Piscator's production the second half was preceded by Walter Mehring's Chanson *Hopla, wir leben,* sung to Edmund Meisel's music. This brilliantly satirical song, worthy a place in any political cabaret, bears little relation to Toller's play. v. GW3 pp. 332–335. It did fit, of course, into Piscator's production, in which

Toller's complex questions and largely negative and pessimistic conclusions were obscured and often eliminated in exchange for a simplistic revolutionary message summed up in the closing slogan Piscator evidently wrote (or had written by his dramaturge) for Frau Meller:

Damned World! We must alter it.

Verdammte Welt! — Man muß sie ändern.

The Chanson must be ignored in any serious re-assessment of the play.

90. GW3 p. 95.
91. . . . trotz Nordpol und Flugelschlag der grauen Vögel. GW3 p. 96. Toller here uses his own prison experience and draws on the imagery of *Das Schwalbenbuch*: Die raschelnden Blätter Schneefelder am Nordpol endloser Ohnmacht.
    GW2 p. 326.
92. GW3 p. 96.
93. Sogar der Revolver kehrt sich gegen den Täter, und aus dem Lauf spritzt Gelächter. ibid.
94. Ihr schlaft alle! Es muß einer hinwerden. Dann werdet ihr aufwachen. GW3 p. 103.
95. Karl Thomas did not use these exact words and never said "Someone must die" (Es muß einer hinwerden). The relevant passage is:
    Ihr schlaft! Ihr schlaft! Aufwecken muß man Euch . . .
    Euch alle muß man wecken! (GW3 p. 91–92).
96. Seit Wochen stecke ich in Haft. GW3 p. 105.
97. Less successful is Toller's attempt to add a dimension by reference to an earlier encounter of Eva and the Judge. This works badly, as it has not been prepared for, and the listener is distracted by wondering when this has occurred — in 1919, or early in her present custody?
98. GW3 p. 318ff.
99. GW3 p. 319.
100. GW3 p. 324.
101. Hoch Karl Thomas! Hoch Karl Thomas! ibid.
102. ibid.
103. GW3 p. 325.

Feuer aus den Kesseln

1. v. *Fall* pp. 188–189.

2. Man erwartete allgemein einen Triumph. H. Kesten in the Berlin *Tagesspiegel* 15.9.1957. v. *Fall* p. 188.
3. Emil Faktor (Spalek 2336): Willi Haas (Spalek 2337); F. Holländer (Spalek 2338); Alfred Kerr (Spalek 2341); Kurt Pinthus (Spalek 2348).
4. e.g. W. Haas (Spalek 2337).
5. A. Kerr. *Spanische Rede vom deutschen Drama oder Das Theater der Hoffnung* (Aus dem Französischen rückübersetzt) Berlin: S. Fischer, 1930, 19. (Spalek 2342).
6. Faktor *loc. cit.*
7. Holländer *loc. cit.*
8. "Molière läßt sich nicht korrigieren. Erinnerungen an Walter Hasenclever", *Der Tagesspiegel* (Berlin), No. 3655. Sept. 15. 1957, 4. (Spalek 2343)
9. Zeitgeschehen zu formen und dabei in der dramatischen Struktur die Parallele zur Molièreschen Charakter-komödie zu wahren". *Berliner Börsen-Zeitung* Feb. 21, 1929.
10. Paul Wiegler. *Berliner Zeitung am Mittag* Feb. 21, 1929. Spalek 2350.
11. "Wer schafft den deutschen Revolutionsfilm?" *Die Welt am Montag.* 5.11.'28. v. GW1 pp. 117ff & 274–5.
12. "Jetzt schreibe ich meinen ersten Film". Beilage der *Vossischen Zeitung*, Berlin, No. 153, 31.3.'29, p. 1.
13. v. Jay Leyda (ed).: *Eisenstein, Three Films*, London, 1974, p. 45.
14. Ich habe Schauplätze verändert (Köbis war Heizer auf "Prinzregent Luitpold", Reichpietsch Matrose auf "Friedrich der Große"), Ereignisse zeitlich verlegt, Personen erfunden, weil ich glaube, daß der Dramatiker das Bild einer Epoche geben, nicht wie der Reporter, jede historische Einzelheit photographieren soll". Ernst Toller, *Feuer aus den Kesseln* Berlin, 1930. p. 7.
15. The supreme example, especially in the eyes of English-speaking readers and playgoers, is, of course, the meeting of Mary Stuart and Elizabeth I at Fotheringhay in *Maria Stuart* Act III Sc. 4. The essence of the play is the conflict between the two queens. The theatre's strength in representing conflict lies in personal confrontation. Therefore Schiller uses the strongest theatrical technique to represent his theme, even though, historically, the two queens never met.
    (Incidentally, he also brings Fotheringhay near enough to Westminster for an afternoon's hunting-party).
16. Alle wesentlichen Vorgänge sind . . . dokumentarisch erhärtet.

Ref. as N. 14.
17. *Feuer aus den Kesseln*, Berlin, 1930, pp. 105–168.
18. Willibrand *op. cit.* p. 90.
19. ibid p. 93.
20. Reso p. 119.
21. Der die Pfade bereitet, / stirbt an der Schwelle, / Doch es neigt sich vor ihm / in Ehrfurcht der Tod. *Feuer aus den Kesseln*, Berlin 1930, p. 5. v. Reso p. 110ff.
22. Klein *op. cit.* pp. 147–160.
23. Altenhofer *op. cit.* p. 210.
24. ibid. p. 199.
25. ibid. p. 209.
26. in Hermand (ed). *op. cit.*, pp. 179–190.
27. On 1.10.1930 there appeared in *Die Weltbühne* an open letter from Toller to Landrichtsrat Dobring (Schuler in the play) challenging him to meet the author face to face on the stage on 5 October in order to defend himself. Apparently Dobring did not reply.
28. Köbis ist der erste Protagonist Tollers, der das böse Mittel der Gewalt legitimiert, um ein anderes Böses — den Krieg — zu bekämpfen. Bütow, *loc. cit.* p. 188.
29. ibid. p. 190.
30. ibid. p. 185.
31. eine optimistische Tendenz. ibid. p. 190.
32. *Feuer aus den Kesseln*, Berlin 1930 p. 82.
33. ibid. p. 88.
34. Photocopy in present writer's possession, kindly supplied by Friends House, London.
35. GW1, pp. 78–85. Note on p. 273.
36. Spalek 761.
37. The final 4 paragraphs begin with a reference to 'July 1914' and proceed to draw parallels between the Kaiser's aggression and Hitler's threat, leading to the conclusion:
"The last 25 years of European policy have the motto: 'Too late'. Let us hope that future historians will not say of our epoch , that the [*sic*] which ultimately must be done, was done 'too late'". GW1 p. 85.
Unless Toller is using "25 years" very loosely, this suggests 1939 for the final version of the speech.
38. Photocopy (N. 34) p. 6.
39. ibid p. 7. GW1 p. 84.
40. ibid.

41. GW1 p. 84.
42. GW1 p. 82.
43. E. Laubsche Verlagsbuchhandlung G.m.b.H. Berlin W 30. Fall p. 19.
44. *Justiz* pp. 39 & 53ff.
45. Das Bürgertum, in seiner Macht von den Pionieren künftiger Gesellschaftsgestaltung bedroht, hat, sehend oder blind, seine Idee der Gerechtigkeit preisgegeben. ibid. p. 7.
46. ibid. p. 77.
47. ibid. pp. 35–38.
48. ibid. p. 37.
49. *Von draußen ferner Gesang*
BECKERS: Still!
REICHPIETSCH: Die Internationale!
KÖBIS: Wahrhaftig!
REICHPIETSCH: Die Kameraden kommen!
SACHSE: Sie befreien uns!
ALLE (*singen leise*):
"Völker, hört die Signale!
Auf zum letzten Gefecht!
Die Internationale
Erkämpft das Menschenrecht!" . . .
Sie brechen ab, lauschen. Der Gesang draußen verstummt
KÖBIS: Betrunkene Werftarbeiter. Nur im Suff erinnern sie sich an die Internationale.
Schweigen.
Feuer aus den Kesseln Berlin 1930 p. 89.
50. Klein p. 155.
51. Im Gesamteffekt wirkt diese Aussage der Fakten selbst sogar noch härter und polemischer als das Stück. ibid p. 158.
52. Plievier, quoted by HH Müller in Plievier, *Des Kaisers Kulis* DTV Munich 1984 p. 337.
53. ibid. p. 236ff.
54. Toller's Introduction is dated April 1930. Spalek says " The first edition was published shortly before the opening of the play on Aug 30 [sic] 1930. Spalek p. 20.
55. Plievier . . . ist kein Dramatiker. Walter Steinthal, *Zeittheater an der Spitze der Saison. Pliviers und Tollers Matrosenstücke. Gesprach über zwei Aufführungen von Walter Steinthal und Rolf Nürnberg.* Press cutting in Theatermuseum, Köln. Date and periodical not known.

56. ibid.
57. Press cutting in Theatermuseum, Köln. Date and source not known.
58. Was Piscator zeigt, ist kein Theater mehr. ibid.
59. ibid.
60. "Presumably the eleven scenes that follow are a dramatic portrayal of the results of this investigation". Willibrand p. 90.
61. ibid.
62. Oddly described by Spalek (17) as the "Second Edition".
63. Spalek p. 21.
64. ibid.
65. Toller folgt — gerade durch die Fassungsdifferenz — der Tendenz des 'politischen Theaters', durch dramatisch zugespitzte Buhnenfassung auf den Zuschauer und gleichzeitig durch eine episch ausgearbeitete Buchfassung auf den Leser zu Wirken . . . GW3 p. 327.
66. Spalek p. 21.
67. Den soundsovielten zwölf Uhr nachts. Zur Erinnerung an die Stunde, in der ein Mann verzichtete. Gezeichnet Ernst Toller. Fall p. 189. Spalek 2481.
68. e.g. K. Kn. *Die Welt am Abend,* Berlin 1.9.30. Press cutting in Akademie der Künste, Berlin.
69. — die Schlußapotheose: rote Fahnen mit kommunistischen Propaganda. Aufricht, *loc. cit.*
70. *Berliner Morgenpost* 2.9.'30. Press cutting in Akademie der Künste, Berlin.
71. ibid.
72. Press cutting. Theatermuseum, Köln. 5.9.'30. Periodical not known.
73. J. M. Ritchie in *Vision and Aftermath: Four Expressionist War Plays,* London 1969 p. 12f.
74. John Wells, *Berlin's Drama of the Absurd: Playing Both Sides of the Wall for the forseeable [sic] Future. The Independent.* Saturday 3 October 1987 p. 13.
75. *Weimarer Republ*ik p. 771.
76. Picture in *Piscator: The Political Theatre* Translated. Rorrison. London 1980, between pp. 110 & 111.
77. ibid.
78. ibid between pp. 150 & 151.
79. Picture: *Weimarer Republ*ic p. 798.
80. Bremen, Schauspielhaus, Designer, Max Gschwind, 1931; Hamburg, Deutsches Schauspielhaus, designer Heinz Daniel, 1931;

Berlin, Schillertheater 1933. All in WR pp. 795, 796.
81. Aufricht. Fall p. 189.
82. Copies in the writer's possession from Theatermuseum, Köln.
83. Wrongly captioned in Theatermuseum, Köln, as taking place in a submarine.
84. Das realistische Zeittheater der zwanziger Jahren war gestorben. Fall p. 190.
85. Ohne die mächtige Hilfe des Dokuments gerät ihm jede szenische Erfindung zum lahmen revolutionären Idyll. Press cutting of 8.9.1930 in Theatermuseum, Koln. Author and periodical not known.
86. *Berliner Lokal-Anzeiger*. Sept (probably 1st Sept) 1930.
87. *The Battleship Potemkin* was originally planned only as one episode of 44 shots in a 900–shot film of *The Year 1905*. Leyda op. cit p. 13.
88. Press cutting in Theatermuseum, Köln. n. d. Periodical not known.
89. Press cutting, Theratermuseum Köln.
90. Press cutting in Akademie der Kunste, Berlin.
91. 1.9.'30. Periodical not known. Press cutting in Akademie der Künste, Berlin.
92. He makes a pacifist movement out of the revolt. 'Ermacht aus der Erhebung eine pazifistische Bewegung.' K. Kn. in *Die Welt am Abend, 1.9.'30.*
93. ibid. Jannings had played one of the sailors in Goering's *Seeschlacht*.
94. Toller ist wieder ganz er selbst. *Echtes Zeittheater* in *Tempo,* Berlin, 1.9.'30.
95. ibid.
96. Emil Faktor *Börsen Kurier* Berlin 1.9.'30.
97. *8–Uhr Abendblatt* 1.9.'30. In der Härte der ungeschinkten Tatsachen liegt der Effekt.
98. ibid.
99. ibid.
100. Hans Tasiemka, *Der zum Tode Verurteilte erzählt*. Press cutting in Theatermuseum, Köln. Date and periodical not known.
101. For further reviews confirming those quoted here, v. Spalek 2476ff.
102. v. Brodbek p. 288ff.
103. Director, Juris Jurovskis; Translator, Janis Sudrabkalns; Music, Melli; Dances, Sam-Khior. Spalek p. 874.
104. Spalek 2549.
105. Spalek 2550. Latvia was an independent state at this time. v. Spalek 2544, and 2546–50.

106. Spalek 2545.
107. Tsukiji Theater. Spalek p. 874.
108. Taped interview with the present author made at 68 Banks Court, Ridgeway Park, Timperley, on Friday 11 May, 1984.
Inevitably much of Wardale's material is presented in anecdotal form. It has seemed best to retain this for its vividness.
109. Wardale. Spalek, p. 874, says 'at the Opera House. Ca. 20 performances'. Wardale is correct. The Rusholme Theatre closed in 1940.
110. Wardale. No reference to Oldham in Spalek.
111. Spalek, p. 874 does not indicate that this was the Manchester production.
112. Wardale.
113. This music, 75pp of score, and Toller's actual production copy of Edward Crankshaw's translation are in the Toller Collection at Yale University. Spalek 88. It has not been practicable to consult these for the present study.
114. Wardale.
115. ibid.
116. "one who was egotistical and brave" *In Memory of Ernst Toller (d. May 1939)* in W. H. Auden. *Collected Shorter Poems 1930–1944*, London 1950 (2nd impression 1953) p. 136.
117. Wardale.
118. Wardale.
119. Wardale. This is confirmed by a lady in Altrincham who was taken to see the production when she was a girl. The lasting impression is of the stoke-hole scenes.
120. Wardale.
121. *Daily Dispatch* (Manchester) Feb 8, 1935. Spalek 2518.
122. Same periodical Feb 11, 1935. Spalek 2519.
123. *Manchester Evening Chronicle* Feb 9, 1935, Spalek 2535.
124. v. Spalek pp. 553ff.
125. G. M. in *Manchester Evening News* Feb 12, 1935. Spalek 2539.
126. *Manchester Guardian* Feb 12, 1935. Spalek 2542.
Spalek (1795) attributes the obituary *Ernst Toller's Career* to A.S.W. and does not mention the separate, signed article that followed under the heading: Toller's "Draw the Fires", A *Manchester Performance.*
127. M Wilson Disher, *Daily Mail* 13.5.'35. Press Cutting in British Theatre Museum. Seen at Victoria and Albert Museum. Not in Spalek.

128. ibid.
129. Copy seen in Victoria and Albert Museum. Extracts from: *Times, Observer, Sunday Referee, Daily Dispatch, Manchester Evening News, Daily Mail, Daily Express, Sunday Times, Times Literary Supplement and The New Statesman*. The review in the last was by Sean O'Casey, who wrote: "Toller is a dramatist and that's the thing that counts. England will be striding nearer to a finer drama when Toller has his London Season".
130. W. A. Darlington, *Daily Telegraph*, 13.5.'35. said the company as a whole lacked confidence and authority, and that as it had already had its Manchester run it was "odd" that it seemed under-rehearsed.
131. There was a young actor in the Manchester company, Tony Allingham, who had trained under Reinhardt at Salzburg and was consequently made a fuss of by Toller. At some point before the London performance he was sacked, but he wrote to Toller asking for a part in it. Toller got him to play the anonymous Sailor who brings the news of Reichpietsch's death to the parents in Scene XI. Toller simply told the actor who had been cast in the part, "I don't want you to play that". Wardale.
132. Wardale. His comment: 'It was disgraceful; it was a disgraceful thing.'
133. Other members of the cast included: Dominic Roche, Edward Midgeley, Brian Melland, Eileen Draycott, John Byrne, Helen Dunlop and Margot Webster. Also in the cast was A. F. Johnson, presumably Wardale's Arthur Johnson.
134. Darlington *loc cit.*
135. Disher *loc cit.*
136. *Observer* 19.5.'35.
137. *Sunday Times* 19.5.'35.
138. *The Times* 13.5.'35.
139. But see below on Trepte's work in Sweden.
140. *Theater 47*. Critique on Radio DDR II, Nov. 1958. 4pp of typescript. Spalek 2515.
141. Spalek p. 874.
142. Spalek 2517.
143. Information from M. Döll, Liberal-Demokratische Zeitung Halle, 11.11.'58 Press cutting in Akademie der Künste, Berlin. Not in Spalek.
144. v. Spalek 2512–2515.
145. Döll *loc cit.*

146. see note 94.
147. Döll *loc cit.*
148. Schenk (no initials) *DDR-Erstaufführung in Quedlinburg* in *Freiheit*, Halle, 13.11.'58. Press cutting seen in Akademie der Künste, Berlin. Spalek 2516. Tollers Bemühung um historische Treue ist bemerkungswert.
149. ibid.
150. Auf, sprengt die Fesseln nach russischem Muster. ibid.
151. man kann Schweiß riechen: Arbeits- und Angstschweiß. Susanne Materleitner, *Kieler Nachrichten* 1.7.78.
152. All information from Materleitner, *loc. cit* and Doris Maletzke, *Holsteinischer Courier* 4.7.78.
153. Spalek 2519.

Die blinde Göttin

1. *Quer Durch. Reisebilder und Reden*. Berlin 1930.
2. Fall p. 20.
3. *Das neue Spanien. Die Weltbühne*. 1932. Nr. 15 p. 550: *I L'España es Republica*. Nr. 17. p. 622: *II Männer und Frauen*. Nr. 18. p. 667: *III Spanische Gefängnisse*. Nr 20 p. 749: *Spanische Arbeiter*. Nr 25 p. 929: *Spanische Miniature*. Press cuttings seen in Deutsches Literaturarchiv.
4. Die spanische Republik tritt in die Fußstapfen der deutschen. *L'España es Republica*. v. GW1 p. 241. (Only this first essay is reprinted in GW).
5. Wo habe ich das doch gesehen? GW1 p. 245. See N. 4.
6. *Männer und Frauen*. See N. 3.
7. Die Kehrseite der strengen Gesellschaftsmoral heißt Prostitution und Geschlechtskrankheit. *Die Weltbühne* Nr 17 p. 624.
8. ibid.
9. *Die Weltbühne* Nr 18 pp. 668–9.
10. *Sprechstunden Deutscher Geschichte II, 1918–1930*.
    A record produced by the German pharmaceutical industry for trade promotion. This includes an excerpt from the Toller/Mühr radio-discussion of 1930. Taped copy kindly provided by Prof. Frühwald.
11. *NATIONALSOZIALISMUS. Eine Diskussion über den KULTURBANKROTT DES BÜRGERTUMS zwischen ERNST TOLLER und ALFRED MÜHR, REDAKTEUR DER DEUTSCHEN ZEITUNG*

. . . Kiepenheuer Verlag Berlin 1930.

12. . . . sich nur im System des Kapitalismus auswirken können. ibid p. 9.
13. dessen klarsten politischer Ausdruck der Weltkrieg mit seinen Millionen Toten und seiner Fülle von Elend war, größer als die Inflation. ibid.
14. Revolutionen werden nicht "gemacht". Ihr gehen Zusammenbrüche voraus. ibid. p. 11.
15. Sie werden mir erlauben, Herr Mühr, Ihre Ausführungen, die ja nicht Ihre persönliche, sondern die der nationalsozialistischen Partei sind, reichlich unklar zu finden. Der Nationalsozialismus hat der Lehre, die er am heftigsten bekämpft, nämlich der marxistischen, einige Forderungen entnommen und sie mit Ideen, die im völligen Gegensatz zu diesen Forderungen stehen, zu einem verworrenen, unecht-romantischen Allerlei vermischt. Aber es liegt ja nicht in unserer Absicht, daß einer den anderen überzeuge. Wir haben beide von verschiedenen geistigen Haltungen her versucht aufzuzeigen, auf welchen bürgerlichen Kulturgebieten sich Verfallserscheinungen zeigen . . . Sie werden mit mir dem Satz zustimmen: "Die Philosophen haben die Welt verschieden interpretiert, es kommt darauf an, sie zu ändern".
    M. Jawohl.
    T. Dieser Satz ist von Karl Marx. Guten Abend, Herr Mühr.
    M. Das ist ein Knalleffekt und Hörspiel-Aktschluß. Sie sind nicht umsonst Dramatiker. Guten Abend, Herr Toller. (ibid. p. 35).
16. R. Dove. Fenner Brockway and Ernst Toller: *Document and Drama in "Berlin — letzte Ausgabe!"* in *German Life and Letters* 38: 1. October 1984 p. 45.
17. ibid
18. ibid pp. 54–55.
19. in *Frühe Sozialistische Hörspiele,* ed. S. B. Würfel. Fischer Verlag, Frankfurt/M 1982 pp. 95ff.
20. Dove *op. cit.*
21. ibid 46–47.
22. ibid p. 47.
23. ibid p. 46.
24. ibid pp. 46–47.
25. Würfel *op. cit.* p. 107.
26. ibid 109–111.
27. Vor hundert Jahren geriet eine Stadt in Aufregung, wenn eine Scheune brannte . . (ibid p. 113).

28. Fenner Brockway *Inside the Left: Thirty Years of Platform, Press, Prison and Parliament.* London 2nd impr. 1947. Post-war edtn. pp204–205. (1st pub. 1942).
29. Dove *op. cit.*
30. ibid p. 53.
31. Dove, *op. cit.* p. 51, referring to Toller's use of Hansard, writes: "There is one obvious discrepancy. The motion to suspend Brockway was carried by 260 votes to 26 (*Hansard* col. 1463), though the figures could not actually be announced in the prevailing confusion. Toller's text gives the figures as 200–26 (*BLA* p. 115), which is probably the result of a simple error of transcription".
But a photocopy in the Deutsches Literaturarchiv of a copy of the script in the possession of Pinthus gives the correct figures of 260 to 26. The error in the published version of 1982 is thus not Toller's but the editor's.
32. The critic 'f. t. g. ' (see note 36 below) finds some pattern, viz. Act I in the nature of a Prologue, followed by four acts, each separated by a long period of time and each containing two scenes. But in fact Act IV has 3 scenes, so any pattern is less regular than f. t. g. suggests.
33. At the National Theatre, Mannheim, 17 October 1931; Dir. Richard Dornseiff. Design, Eduard Löffler. v. Spalek p. 889.
Fritz Droop: *Toller und Kesten: 'Wunder in Amerika'.*
Uraufführung im Mannheimer Nationaltheater.
Berliner Tageblatt No. 495,
Abend -Ausgabe 20.10.1931, 2–3. Press cutting in Theatermuseum, Köln. Spalek 3756.
34. Fritz Droop *Ernst Toller und seine Bühnenwerke.* Franz Schneider Verlag. Berlin & Leipzig. In the series: *Schneiders Bühnenführer.* 1922.
35. But Toller's poetry is the confession of a man who struggled in passionate strife with himself and who leads us out of a dying century into a new age. Ibid pp. 13–14.
36. Die sinnliche Raserei als sichtbarer Vorgang für die geistliche Besessenheit war von Anfang an zu hemmungslos. Die Ekstatik nicht entwickelt, sondern mit Anstrengung durchgehalten. f. t. g *Wunder in Amerika. Schauspiel in 5 Akten von Hermann Kesten und Ernst Toller. Uraufgeführt im Mannheimer Nationaltheater.* Press cutting in Theatermuseum, Köln. Frankfurter Zeitung No 786/ 787 22.10.'31. Spalek 3758.

37. Droop. *Toller, Ernst und Kesten, Hermann: Wunder in Amerika (Mannheim 17 Okt)* in *Die Neue Literatur* XXXII, No. 12. Dec. 1931 pp631–632. Spalek 3757.
38. f. t. g. *loc cit.* Im Schatten von Voltaire hat dieser Scherz zu wenig Licht, um in die Dunkelheit des Herzens, wo Blut und *Anima* wohnen, hineinzuleuchten. Das Stück ist kalt. Das Exemplarische zerbricht an einer billigen Komik.
39. London Stage Society, members only, at the Gate Theatre Studio, 1.10.1934, 18 performances. Translation by Edward Crankshaw under the title *Miracle in America.* Producer Norman Marshall. Design: Hedley Briggs. The part of Mary Baker Eddy was played by Dorothy Holmes-Gore at short notice. (v. Spalek p. 889. Further details from copy of Programme seen in Victoria and Albert Museum).
    Edward Crankshaw's translation was published in *Seven Plays* (London, The Bodley Head, 1935 and New York, 1936. Spalek 120 & 121) under the title *Mary Baker Eddy.*
40. Harold Conway. 2.10.'34. Periodical not known. Press cutting seen in V & A.
41. Anon. Periodical not known. Press cutting in V & A.
42. Programme seen in V & A. Even so, the Lord Chamberlain would not licence for public performance *any* play about Mary Baker Eddy, though several were written, and no less an actress than Sybil Thorndike wanted to appear in one. (Same press cutting as N. 41).
43. f. t. g. *loc cit.*
    . . . es ist ein Stück, das aufklären will, das heilen will, heilen von diesen sonderbaren dunklen irrationalen Bewegungen, die heute die Menschen heftig und rätselhaft ergreifen. Heilen von Heilslehren, die keine sind und die die Menschen von dem wirklichen Segen und Heil, nämlich einer vernünftigen Ordnung des materiellen Lebens, abtreiben, um sie mit Illusionen zu verwirren.
44. Originally the *Oxford Group,* founded by the American Frank Buchman (1878–1961) in the early 1930s. Re-founded by him as *Moral Re-armament* in 1939. His followers were also known as Buchmanites. The present writer, then in his teens, was temporarily seduced by this movement!
45. In *Volksblatt-Illustrierte. Wochenbeilage für die Leser des Sächsischen Volksblatts.* 6. Jahrgang. Zwickau den 13. Juni 1930. Nr. 24. pp. 2–3.

Press cutting seen in the Fritz Hüser Institut, Dortmund. (Not in Spalek)

46. cf. Genesis III 6–7: And when the woman saw that the tree was good for food, and that it was pleasant to the eyes, and a tree to be desired to make one wise, she took of the fruit thereof, and did eat, and gave also unto her husband with her; and he did eat. And the eyes of them both were opened, and they knew that they were naked; . . .
47. "Als er ganz vage zu irrlichtieren schien, kam ihm Hitler zu Hilfe, gab ihm einen neuen Feind, eine Arena". Emil Ludwig, *Radionachricht von Ernst Tollers Tod* in *Das neue Tagebuch,* 10 June 1939. Quoted by Richard Dove in *Fenner Brockway and Ernst Toller: Document and Drama* in *BERLIN – LETZTE AUSGABE!* in *GERMAN LIFE AND LETTERS* 38: 1 October 1984, p. 54.
48. *Giftmordprozeß Riedel-Guala* in *Die Weltbühne* XXVII Pt. 2. No. 41 Oct. 13 1931; pp. 552–554. Spalek 468. Reprinted in GW1 pp. 107–111.
49. It did not appear again in German until 1959 when Kiepenheuer produced a duplicated acting version, virtually identical with the 1st Ed. and not for sale. Remarkably, Frühwald and Spalek chose to omit this play (as well as *Die Rache des verhöhnten Liebhabers* and, understandably, *Wunder in Amerika,*) from their 'Collected works'. This 'painful renunciation' (schmerzlicher Verzicht), as they describe it, was made for economic reasons, but more than any other of their omissions it distorts any overall view of Toller the dramatist as derived from the *Gesammelte Werke.*
50. Even in *Feuer aus den Kesseln* a few such stylisations were still used, notably the use of identical sequences of 'choric' voices of members of the Reichstag to open and to end Sc. III.
51. Examples of the last are the legal speeches in court (Act II Sc. I) and the Wardress's language in the Women's Prison (Act III Sc. I).
52. Ein dramatisch vollendeter, lebensprühender erster Akt zeigt, wie die beiden, der Arzt und seine Geliebte, in der Fallgrube des Verdachtes stürzen.
    Felix Salten *Neue Freie Presse. Morgenblatt (Wien)* 1. Nov. 1932. Reprinted in part in *Fall* pp. 192 ff. Spalek 2271.
53. The basic traditionalism of the structure can be demonstrated by comparing it with that of John Galsworthy's *Justice* (1910). (*The Plays of John Galsworthy*. London 1929 pp. 217–274). In this 4–act

tragedy Act I shows how the crime is discovered (in *Justice* the 'victim' is in fact guilty). Act II is again the trial, and the evidence, as in *Die blinde Göttin,* provides the background and pre-history; Act III shows prison conditions; Act IV gives the catastrophe — for in this play there is no new evidence. Both plays are based on unhappy marriages and extra-marital love, and in both plays, though for very different reasons, the lovers become estranged in the last act.

54. *Die blinde Göttin* Berlin-Charlottenburg 1933. pp. 11–13.
55. Omitted in Edward Crankshaw's English translation in *Seven Plays,* possibly because it was thought to anticipate the conclusion too clearly. But Toller is not interested in a mere surprise curtain or thoughtless *coup-de-théâtre.*
56. This scene is very closely based on the Riedel/Guala case.
57. Is this to be thought of as the actual child of Färber or as a 'child actress' playing her part for the benefit of the court? Either answer raises questions in the mind of a student. Could a child be expected to re-enact such a scene in this way? Or how could a 'child actress' know what part to play? Toller doubtless relies on theatrical fluidity to avoid such questions arising in the mind of the audience, and he gets the child off-stage as quickly as possible, with only two lines to speak.
58. Von politischen Tendenzen jeglicher Art hält sich das Schauspiel Ernst Tollers diesmal vollständig frei. *"Die blinde Göttin",* das heißt Justicia, der eine Binde die Augen umhüllt, ist verhängnisvoll eben wegen ihrer Blindheit.
    Salten. *loc cit.*
59. Schieres Fleisch. Paar Herzen hast du!
60. cf. *Eine Jugend in Deutschland.* GW4 p. 209.
    . . . sie erbaten Liebespfänder, Locken schenkten sie sich, kleine Tücher, die sie nachts auf die Brust gepreßt hatten, Schamhaare. (They asked for love-pledges, gave each other locks of hair, little bits of cloth which they had pressed against their breast in the night, pubic hair).
    (NB: The English translation *I was a German* omits the pubic hair).
61. cf. The comments of anonymous figures and voices in the play *passim.*
62. The importance of this in Toller's mind is shown by the title of the radio play.
63. ANNA: . . . deine Schwäche mich tötete . . . du hättest dich ohne ihren Tod nicht entschieden . . . Du möchtest einen Menschen

besitzen, aber er soll nichts von dir wollen ... Ich glaube daß du niemand lieben kannst ... Warum bist du so geizig .... Wenn morgen jemand käme, der dich mißtrauisch machte gegen mich, du würdest mich verlassen.
FÄRBER: Diesen geizigen, schwächlichen Menschen liebst du?
ANNA: Ja, ich liebe ihn, trotzdem. Du, hörst du, ich liebe dich ... (Act I. p. 12)
ANNA: ... Your weakness was killing me ... You'ld never have decided if she'd lived ... You want to possess a woman, but she must want nothing from you ... I believe you can't love anyone ... Why are you so miserly? ... If someone came tomorrow, and made you mistrustful of me, you'ld leave me.
FÄRBER: This miserly, weakly man — you love him?
ANNA: Yes, I love him in spite of everything. You, — do you hear? — I love you.

64. Jetzt aber, nach dem Zuchthaus, nach dem Hohn des feierlichen Empfanges im Dorf, jetzt kann sie den Mann, um den sie gelitten, nicht mehr lieben, kann nicht wieder dort anfangen, wo sie früher mit ihm hielt, kann nicht weiter leben, als sei nichts geschehen, kann "nicht mehr bloß an sich denken".
Salten, *loc cit. Fall* p. 193.
65. ibid.
66. Riedel had shown himself a vacillating character.
67. Ich weiß, daß ich kein Recht mehr habe, zu leben wie früher, für mich, für dich, für die Sparkasse. (Act V).
68. Als du dann wirklich neben mir lagst, fror ich vor Widerwillen und Einsamkeit. (Act V).
69. Ich weiß jetzt, was ich nicht mehr tun kann. Was ich tun muß . . . ich werde es wissen. (Act V).
This aspect of the ending is not unlike that of Ibsen's *A Doll's House*. To some degree Anna has developed into a latter-day Nora.
70. Leb wohl, Franz. Ich habe dich sehr geliebt ... Ich habe dich so geliebt daß ich wirklich deine Frau hätte töten können. (Act V).
71. Act IV. See below in text for German.
72. cf. Matthew 5. 28.
73. Spalek p. 871.
74. Spalek p. 888.
75. Karl Lahm. 1.11.'32. Journal not known. Press cutting in Theatermuseum, Köln.
76. Salten *loc cit.* v. *Fall* 194.

77. Heinrich Eduard Jacob. 1.11.'32. Periodical not known. Press cutting in Theatermuseum, Köln.
78. Lahm *loc cit.*
79. F. Th. 1.11.'32. Periodical not known. Press cutting in Theatermuseum, Köln.
80. Lahm *loc cit*
81. Robert F. Arnold, *Das literarische Echo* 35. Jahrgang, 1932–33, Heft 4, Jan 1933 p. 220. Seen in Literaturarchiv, Marbach.
82. Jacob *loc cit*
83. Oskar Maurus Fontana, 2.11.1932. Periodical not known. Press cutting in Theatermuseum, Köln.
84. Spalek p. 872.
85. Spalek 89.
86. v. Spalek p. 871; 2290–2332 & 2272–2278.
87. Spalek 84.
88. Spalek 83 & 120.
89. Spalek p. 871.
90. Spalek 2274.
91. Spalek 2277 & 2278.
92. *Manchester Evening News*. Theatre advertisement, week beginning 3 June 1935.
93. Wardale. Taped interview.
94. *Manchester City News*. 29 June 1935.
95. *Manchester Guardian*, Tuesday 4 June 1935, p. 13.
96. ibid.
97. ibid.
98. ibid.
99. *Die blinde Göttin*. p. 30ff. *Seven Plays* p. 295ff.
The skill with which this is done is some measure of Toller's technical advance since *Hoppla, wir leben* Act IV Sc. iv, in which he first had a projector set up and later abandoned this device.
100. v. above in *The Defeat and Triumph of Justice*.
101. *Manchester Guardian loc cit.*
102. ibid.
103. ibid.
104. ibid.
105. "Labour well the Minute Particulars". William Blake, *Jerusalem*, f. 55 1.51.
106. 'right', that is, in M. C.'s opinion.
107. ibid.
108. ibid.

109. Wardale. Taped interview.
110. At the back-stage party held that night he actually told Enid Hewitt, "You are not right for the part, you are too cold, you are too cold". (Wardale). He evidently did not agree with the *Manchester Guardian's* praise of her "restraint".
111. The critic says that Toller was there on the *first* night, Monday, and that he "was very nice about the play". (*Manchester City News* Sat. 8 June 1935 p. 9).
112. ibid.
113. ibid.
114. ibid.
115. ibid.
116. ibid.
117. Did he know of the Welwyn Folk Players' production? The critic also says that the play is to have "an immediate London production". He does not say by whom: perhaps Toller himself had spoken optimistically. There was no London production. The same issue of the paper prints two prominent paragraphs at the beginning of "Watchman"'s *A Manchester Diary*, describing very vividly how Toller visited the Swiss prisons and shocked the Swiss public into abolishing the *Gatter* torture." Watchman" concludes, "It is always a delight to meet this vital figure, whose leonine head shouts distinction".

    (NOTE: Toller's article *Giftmordprozeß Riedel-Guala* in *Die Weltbühne* in XXVII, Pt. 2, No. 41 (13 Oct 1931) pp. 552–554 (Spalek 463) drew attention to a particularly barbarous punishment used in the Prison for Criminal Felons at Thorberg (where Riedel was imprisoned), namely *Das Gatter (The Gate)*. The prisoner could be confined in an unlighted, unheated, icy-cold, underground cell for up to three weeks. 'The Gate', which could be used for 24–hour periods to intensify the punishment, was an iron grid behind which the prisoner was confined to one corner of the blacked-out cell with only room to stand.

    As a result of Toller's exposure of it the torture was evidently stopped, and a statement of thanks to Toller published later in *Die Weltbühne* (9.2.1932) (Spalek 1440)).
118. *Manchester City News* 15 June 1935, p. 9.
119. ibid.
120. ibid.
121. *Manchester City News* Sat 29 June 1935.
122. *Manchester City News* 22 June 1935 p. 10.

123. As the play is omitted from GW and the adaptation evidently unpublished, a close comparison was not possible.
124. The present writer was there as an External Adviser to the Arts Council of Great Britain.
125. As no programme was available, details of direction, casting etc, cannot be given. A pleasing poster of the production, designed by David Venables, was on sale.
126. The present writer's words, written at the time.
127. Colin Bean The President of the Court; a Prisoner; an Official
Ken Binge Dr Franz Färber
Lindsay Blackwell Marie Hacker
Fred Denno Philipp Pflasterer; the Pathologist
Carol Holt Betty Färber; a Prisoner
Lesia Melnik Anna Gerst
Douglas Paul Max Franke
John Pickles The Defence Counsel; The Bandmaster
Martin Reeve Blasenkleffer (the Policeman); the Prosecuting Counsel
Joyce Wentworth The Gypsy; a Prisoner
Directed by Wilfred Harrison
Designed by Edward Furby
Lighting by William Roberts.
(Information from Programme)
128. i. *Complete Works of Oscar Wilde*. London & Glasgow 1948, Reprint 1977, pp. 843ff. e.g.
. . . I walked with other souls in pain
Within another ring . . .
. . . With slouch and swing around the ring
We trod the Fools' Parade . . .
. . . And crooked shapes of Terror crouched,
In the corners where we lay . . .
ii. Eric de Maré *The London Doré Saw*, London 1973, p. 159.
iii. GW2 p. 87ff & 99ff.
129. GW2 p. 88.
130. Information from theatre programme.

Nie wieder Friede

1. Fall p. 210, 211.
2. Ibid p. 195.
For a full and authoritative account of Toller's life in exile, see:

Richard Dove: *He was a German: a biography of Ernst Toller*. London 1990. Chaps XIII–XVIII.

3. *Eine Jugend in Deutschland* 1933; English Translation *I Was a German* Feb. 1934. *Briefe aus dem Gefängnis*. 1935; English Translation *Letters from Prison*, April 1936. It is relevant to note that the critical acclaim accorded to *Eine Jugend in Deutschland* in the German 'exile' press was weak, but that the critical response in the English press to *I Was a German* was astonishingly strong. (Fall p. 197)
4. *Nie wieder Friede* has no roots in time or place. *Pastor Hall* betrays Toller's lack of direct personal experience of Germany under the Nazis.
5. Spalek 47.
6. ibid.
7. GW3 pp. 185ff. Why Frühwald and Spalek printed this inferior play in preference to *Die blinde Göttin* is open to conjecture. Perhaps the temptation of a 'first edition' was irresistible.
8. *No More Peace, A Thoughtful Comedy by Ernst Toller.* London 1937.
9. Spalek 47. GW3 p. 185.
10. Malcolm Pittock *Ernst Toller* Boston 1979, p. 200 N. 34.
11. Spalek p. 887, & information from Victoria & Albert Museum.
12. *Evening Standard* 12.6.'36.
13. ibid. & H. H. 21.6.'36. Periodical not known.
14. *Times* 12.6.'36 & H. H. *loc cit.*
15. *Times loc cit;* H. H. *loc cit.*
16. *Times loc cit; Times loc cit;* periodical not known; *Sunday Times* n. d.; H. H. *loc cit.*
17. H. H. *loc cit.*
18. *Evening Standard loc cit.*
    None of these reviews is recorded by Spalek. He does, however, record the *New York Times* (3469) which quotes the *London Times*, and *The Stage* (3472), as well as two English reviews of the published book: Harold Brighouse *Manchester Guardian* 1.10.'37, and J. P. Fletcher *The Friend* 3.12.'37. Spalek 3479 & 3490.
19. *Sunday Times* 21.6.'36.
20. 4 productions add up to 22 performances. The number of performances of the 5th production is not recorded. Spalek pp. 887, 888.
21. Spalek p. 888.
22. Malcolm Pittock op cit. v. N. 10 above.
23. *No More Peace* London 1937, p. 3.

24. ibid p. 103.
25. ibid.
26. In Sc. 1 alone there are 18 additions to or expansions of the text as well as several other changes and a partial re-writing of the close of the scene.
27. ibid pp. 67–71.
28. Scene II. GW3 pp. 196 & 205. English: pp. 14 & 30. Scene II GW3 p. 211 & Scene VI GW3 p. 240. English: pp. 40 & 98.
29. GW3 p225. Parisian wings. Small. Elegant. Pleated. With gold embroidery in the middle.
30. Not 2 acts, as in the English version.
31. GW3 p. 218. I'm so young; it's so dreadful to die so young.
32. GW3 p. 13 . . . . that only looks so bad, when you're still young.
33. GW3 p. 207. I'm liable for military service . . I must report to the Legation.
34. John XX. 17.
35. GW3 p. 218. Why have I not put my faith in stones, in animals, in flowers? It's beautiful to love flowers. They are what they seem; they seem what they are. In the morning when they awake and the silent dew falls on the velvet chalices; in the evening when they sleep in the fading light. Only men disturb their peace.
36. GW3 p. 220. Is it not lovelier to die than to kill?
37. GW2 p. 45. Gekreuzigt wolln wir uns erlösen / Zu höher Freiheit auferstehen. (Crucified, we will redeem ourselves / Rise again to higher freedom).
    GW2 p. 110. Nur selbst sich opfern darf der Täter. / Höre: kein Mensch darf Menschen Töten / Um einer Sache willen.
    (He who acts may sacrifice only himself. / Listen: no one may kill people / For the sake of a cause).
38. GW3 p. 220. It was dark, and because it was dark you were afraid, and you thought I was the executioner. You were afraid, Jakobo. I am lucky that you were afraid. Do not be afraid of your fear; is it not human to be afraid?
39. GW3 p. 224. Sie haben Sokrates zuerst ins Gefängnis, dann ins Irrenhaus gesteckt. (They put Socrates first in prison, then in a madhouse). Toller had experienced both.
40. GW3 p. 222. For some it rains manna in peace-time, for some in wartime. The some and the some are mostly the some. (i.e. the ones and the others are mostly the same).
41. GW3 p. 223. The wisdom of this world / Does not dwell on the stars, / The wisdom of this world / You must learn.

42. This is Socrates' only scene and carries great weight for this reason. In the English version two more were added, one on Olympus (II. 3. p. 67f) and one in Dunkelstein (II. 4. p. 80f). Both merely detract from the impact of Socrates in his original scene.
43. The telegram as *casus belli* may have been suggested by the celebrated Ems Telegram that ultimately made the Franco-Prussian War of 1870 inevitable.
44. Dunkelstein=Dark Stone. Liechtenstein suggests Light Stone.
45. That phrase was in fact first used by Mussolini in Milan on 1.11.1936. (J. Bithell *Companion to German Studies* 5th edtn, London 1955, p. 181).
46. Even the White and Red Ants in Čapek's *The Insect Play* (1921) fought over the space between two blades of grass. Toller's play in this respect might have been more relevant to, say, the Falklands War and the extraordinary *volte face* of the Labour leader, Michael Foot in the House of Commons as soon as that war had been declared, than to the war-threat of the 1930s.
47. In Sc. III Franziskus and Napoleon simplistically equate hero-worship and Fascism. GW3 p. 215.
48. In the English version Napoleon *also* says he did not like the book, which makes the whole passage of dialogue pointless.
49. 1st Performance 1928, (Pittock op cit p. 200).
50. Pittock *op. cit.* p137.
51. GW3 p. 195. Fate has given to each one his gifts,/Laid down in Mrs Mama's bed./He who has nothing is supposed to have nothing,/He who has much has justly earned it.
52. GW3 p. 195. Because man is descended from the apes/Man does not want to be equal./Because man has a soul/Man also wants to be rich.
53. GW3 p. 195/6. When men at one time lived in forests, naked and bare on the trees . . . They also killed their neighbour with these clubs . . . Not until 2000 years after Christ did man become a pacifist . . . and humanity lives in good humour, for war is abolished.
54. See Appendix for examples.
55. See Appendix.
56. cf the use of Brazil in *Der entfesselte Wotan*.
57. Toller gives Laban an unbiblical wife, Eva, in the list of persons, simply called Frau Laban in the text (omitted from the English version), and Rahel (English, Rachel) an unbiblical nanny, Male (Sarah in the English version). Otherwise, with the exception of

Noah, no other characters are given Old Testament names. In the English version, however, Emil becomes, rather too obviously, Cain; James becomes Samuel; Tomas becomes David; and Robert becomes Lot. Nothing seems to be gained from these changes.

58. GW3 p. 200. Eine Dunkelsteinerin heiratet keinen Ausländer.
59. The Fat One, the Thin One, the Little One. Is "Der Dicke" an allusion to Hermann Goering, who bore this nickname? If so, no further use is made of it.
60. GW3 p. 203. You must do the right thing at the right time.
61. The rhythms of the closing lines are reminiscent of part of *Der Kanonen Song* in the *Dreigroschenoper*:
    Denn der Schnee schneit, wenn es kalt ist,
    Und die Rosen bluhn im Mai etc. [Toller]
    cf.:
    Soldaten wohnen,
    Auf den Kanonen
    Vom Kap bis Couch Behar.
    (Brecht. *Gesammelte Gedichte*. Bd. 4 p. 1099)
62. GW3 p. 203/4. Italy invaded Abyssinia on 2 Oct 1935. On 7 Oct the Council of the League of Nations declared Italy the aggressor. On 19 Oct the League imposed Sanctions against Italy. Whatever the failures and shortcomings of the League of Nations may have been, they were subtler and profounder than is implied in this speech.
63. GW3 p. 204. What does the content matter? Only the form is crucial. The form is what is eternal.
    Toller here seems to be using the Marxist-Leninist idea of 'formalism' to attack 'pure art'.
64. Here Toller is faintly echoing material from *Die Wandlung* and *Hinkemann*.
65. GW3 p. 210. The scene was, of course, emasculated in the English version on account of censorship.
66. GW3 p. 212. Rachel, marry me! / A kneeling Dictator. How absurd!
67. Anticipating "scorched earth" policies.
68. The alleged spy is only Noah.
69. In the English version the Angel has a telephone conversation with Laban and all theatrical subtlety is lost. pp70/71, & 78.
70. GW3 p. 212
71. GW3 p. 226. Das Spionenlied.
72. GW3 p. 230. Nieder mit den Ausländern.

73. GW3 p. 230. Better to be burnt by your own bombs than by the enemy's.
74. GW3 p. 232. Abandon all war operations. War a misunderstanding. Peace on Earth.
75. GW3 p. 234. No More Peace! I am allowing you three minutes to think about it. If you deny the state your help I will put you in prison.
76. There seems to be a half-hearted attempt at symbolism in naming the dog, a poodle, Napoleon. In Goethe's *Faust I* Mephistopheles first appears to Faust in the form of a poodle. Franziskus, regards dogs as "good, affectionate animals", though he himself would rather have his name applied to donkeys, "these gentle, modest beings with the most beautiful eyes in the world". (GW3 p. 217). The historical Francis of Assisi referred to the physical body as "Brother Ass".
77. GW3 p. 238/9.
When the day passes (dies)/All sorrow ends,/And the poor heart/Rests in serenity/ . . . The ocean has its bounds,/And the world is small,/Only man's stupidity/Has no limits!
78. The literary source for such a *Prologue in Heaven* is to be found of course in Goethe's *Faust* and in its model in the *Book of Job* Ch. I. v. 6ff.
79. GW3 p. 242/3. One day the dream will be fulfilled. Love will be stronger than hate, truth stronger than lies, and men will see and know themselves, and there will be peace on earth./When will this day be?/When the clever are silent. When the fools act.
80. Engl. edtn. p. 103.
81. Gerard Manley Hopkins *Poems* 4th Edition. London 1967 p. 100.
82. Thus though the play must be accounted a failure it is not merely "the sort of antiwar comedy that could have been written by a member of the Peace Pledge Union who happened to be a gifted dramatist" (Pittock *op. cit.* p. 137)
With all its shortcomings it is still the expression of Toller's personal struggle, *Das Ringen eines Menschen,* as he subtitled *Die Wandlung,* believing that 'only those who struggle are alive'. (*Nur die Ringenden sind die Lebenden).*

Pastor Hall

1. v. Spalek & Frühwald, *Ernst Tollers amerikanische Vortragsreise*

1936/7 in *Literaturwissenschaftliches Jahrbuch*, Neue Folge / Sechster Band. Duncker & Humboldt Berlin 1965 pp. 267–311.

2. v. *Am Sender von Madrid*. GW1 pp. 209ff.
3. 26.1.'39 Franco's troops take Barcelona, with Italian aid.
   27.2.'39 Britain and France recognise Franco's government.
   28.3.'39 Madrid's surrender to Franco ends civil war.
   1.4.'39 USA recognises Franco's government.
   19.5.'39 Franco's Victory Parade in Madrid.
   22.5.'39 Toller's suicide.
4. In *Das Wort* (Moscow) III No. 6 (June 1938) p. 35/36.
5. *Lola Montez* and *Der Weg nach Indien*. Only the former was completed, June 1937. Fall p. 23.
6. Fall p. 217.
7. GW3 p. 246.
8. Fall p. 23.
9. GW1 p. 209.
10. Fall p. 24.
11. Harold Hurwitz *Opfer oder Held* in *Dramaturgische Blätter* Jg. 1 Nr2 Berlin Mai 1947.
12. Hurwitz (*loc cit*) says that Toller wrote the play during the Autumn of 1938. But despite his close association with Toller, Hurwitz is not reliable on the dates of this period. e.g. Hurwitz says Toller was in France when the Munich Agreement was signed, which transferred Sudetenland to Germany, but this agreement was signed on 29 September 1938 and on that very day Toller delivered an impassioned denunciation of the Agreement at the Conway Hall, London. (Published 13.10.'38 in *Die neue Weltbühne*. Spalek 381. English version in *The Tribune* (London) 14.10.'38. Spalek 579).
    The Munich Agreement greatly intensified Toller's inner stress. . . . when the Munich Agreement was signed . . he realised that the end of democracy in Spain and Europe was drawing ever nearer. In these terrible times Toller felt the approach of a serious illness. (Hurwitz. *loc cit*).
    The tension of that period for pacifists was intense. The present writer remembers how, having welcomed the Agreement as avoiding war, he had his eyes opened through a passionate attack upon the Agreement delivered shortly afterwards at 6 Endsleigh St WC1, the headquarters of the Peace Pledge Union, by that undaunted pacifist, Max Plowman.
13. v. GW3 pp. 330/331. The first version as issued by Hurwitz (*loc*

cit) varies from this in its wording.

14. Hurwitz, *loc cit*.
15. GW3 pp. 313/316. The version printed by Hurwitz (*loc cit*) varies in its wording from this and is slightly longer.
16. Fall p. 218.
17. GW3 p. 330.
18. He separated from Christiane in July 1938.
19. Willibrand p. 111.
20. Rothe pp. 114/115.
21. *äußerlich betrachtet*. "W. E". Periodical and date not known, but reference is to the first post-war production of 1947. Press cutting in Theatermuseum, Köln.
22. Mario Thomas, *Telegraf* 26.1.'47: Die Vokabeln der Gaskammer und des Massenmordes fehlen dabei.
    Gerhard Grindel *Der Abend* 25.1.'47. Der Atomkern, der vernichtend verfiel, ist geistig noch nicht aufgespalten.
    (Press cuttings, Theatermuseum Köln).
    GW1 p. 216: . . . die Nazis noch weitere barbarische Akte vorbereiten; einer dieser Akte ist ein Judenpogrom.
23. Friedrich Luft, n. d. , periodical not known. Press cutting, Theatermuseum, Köln.
24. Pittock p. 139.
25. Rothe p. 115.
26. GW1 p. 207.
27. GW2 p. 110 . . . kein Mensch darf Menschen töten/Um einer Sache willen.
28. Fall p. 219.
29. GW3 p. 290. It has sometimes been said that Hall is based upon the celebrated anti-Nazi Pastor, Martin Niemöller, one of whose sayings is quoted by Paul von Grotjahn in the play (GW3 p. 226). This is firmly denied by Willibrand (*op. cit.* p. 111):
    "Pastor Niemöller is *not* the model for the hero.
    There are [i.e. in 1940, CWD] many pastors in German concentration camps and Hans Borchardt, from whom Toller purchased material for this play, knew about one of them."
30. GW3 pp. 279ff.
31. *I Was A German*, London 1934 pp. 2/4.
32. ibid p. 14.
33. Friedrich, in *Die Wandlung*, was a sculptor.
34. Written 1953. Fall p. 226.
35. ibid.

36. GW3 p. 280. I didn't feel at home in France.
37. Hurwitz *loc cit.*
38. GW3 p. 315. You didn't keep silent. That's the advantage we have over the Jews, you see: they have no choice. We can make a decision.
39. e.g. GW1 p. 82: I was a convinced pacifist, but reality set me right.
40. Fall p. 219.
41. GW3 p. 289. Der Geist war willig, aber das Fleisch schwach . . . Die Freiheit haben wir eine kleinbürgerliche Phrase geheißen, so wenig wußten wir, was Sklaverei ist.
42. GW3 p. 289. Würden Sie, wenn Sie die Macht hätten, sich rächen und Ihre Feinde martern und quälen?/
Töten, wenns sein muß, ja . . . Schinden, ne.
So in this version, simply and effectively. Spender's version , quoted by Pittock (op cit p. 143) reads; "When we are in power things will be different. I reject whippings, concentration camps, condemnations without a trial, secret beatings to death and all the rest of it. Our enemies will be brought before a people's tribunal, tried, and, if necessary, shot".
This, Pittock says "only sounds humane because the Nazis are worse". (ibid).
43. GW3 p. 290. Ich glaube heute nur an den Weg des Verstehens und der Liebe. Es gibt keine Frage auf Erden, die nicht gewaltlos gelöst werden könnte, und sei sie noch so verschlungen und verworren.
44. GW3 p. 290. Der Mut zu sterben ist billig geworden, so billig, daß ich mich oft frage, ob er nicht eine Flucht vor dem Leben ist.
45. GW3 p. 290. Es kommt darauf an, wofür man lebt und wie man stirbt.
46. *loc cit.* Erich Mühsam, one of Toller's colleagues in the Munich Soviet Republic, was put up against a wall before a firing squad and threatened with death if he did not sing the Horst Wessel Song. Instead he sang the Internationale. Later he was beaten to death. His body was hanged and it was claimed he had committed suicide. That was Mühsam, who said: "Anyone who beats his children, misuses his bodily superiority to create a relationship based on power and thereby confirms the power and authority of state and capital, through knocking into his child the madness of power." (Quoted in *Weimarer Republik* p. 161).
47. The parallel between Hall's death by heart-failure and Toller's suicide was seen by Harold Hurwitz as early as 1947:

Der Märtyrer stirbt, ohne durch die Erfüllung dessen, wofür er als Idealist kämpfte, sein Opfer gerechtfertigt zu sehen. Dadurch steht der Tod aus Schwäche des Pastor Hall mit dem Selbstmord Tollers in Beziehung (Hurwitz *loc cit*).
(The martyr dies, without seeing his sacrifice justified through the fulfilment of what he fought for as an idealist. Because of that, Pastor Hall's death through weakness has a relationship with Toller's suicide).

48. Pittock (pp. 141/142) understands that Toller himself felt unable to rise to the heroic heights of Mühsam, but draws the unwarrantable conclusion that the play is 'dishonest', while the present writer's argument is that it is almost unbearably honest in Toller's recognition of his own fatally divided soul. Pittock's principal quotation in support of his charges of 'dishonesty' and 'evasiveness' is the Pastor's speech before he leaves for the church at the end of the play. He quotes this in Spender's version:

"I will live. It will be like a conflagration which no worldly power can extinguish. The oppressed will pass it on to one another and will take new heart. One will say to another that Antichrist reigns, the adversary of mankind, and they will pool their strength and follow my example".
(Pittock 142)
In the German of GW3 p. 316 this reads:
"Ich werde trotzdem leben. Es wird wie ein Feuer sein, keine Macht wird es ersticken, die Ängstlichen werden Mut fassen, einer wird es dem andern sagen, daß der Antichrist regiert, der Verderber, der Feind des Menschen . . . [sic] und sie werden Stärke finden und werden meinem Beispiel folgen".

The differences, though small, are fundamental.

"I will live *nevertheless*. It will be a fire [NOT *a conflagration*]; no power [NOT *no worldly power*] will [NOT *can*] smother it; the timid [NOT *the oppressed*] will [NOT *pass it on to one another*, but] take heart [NOT *new* heart]. One will say to another that Antichrist reigns, the Corrupter [omitted in Spender], the Enemy of Man . . . and they will find strength [NOT *pool their strength*] and will follow my example".
In this version Hall's example will be to individuals; individuals will respond. They will not *pool their strength* (which seems to

allude to the League of Nations' concept of 'Collective Security'), but find strength — to do what? — to follow his example: to become martyrs.

49. In *Neuer Vorwärts* 21.5.'54. Press cutting seen in Fritz-Hüser Institut, Dortmund.
50. HALL: Hat Christus nachgegeben? GW3 p. 315.
51. GW3 p. 243. Wenn die Klugen schweigen. Wenn die Toren handeln.
52. GW3 p. 315. Isn't that really unreasonable, Friedrich?/(smiles) Was it reasonable of you just to throw Gerte out?
53. über die Hintertreppe. GW3 p. 315.
54. GW3 p. 331 C. (leise): Was bleibt uns?/I. (leise): Ein Grab./C. (stark): Ein Beispiel.
55. Pittock p. 144
56. Thom Gunn *Claus von Stauffenberg (of the bomb-plot on Hitler, 1944).* In *Selected Poems,* Thom Gunn & Ted Hughes, Faber, London 1962, p. 30.
57. "God who created iron, does not want any slaves". Originally Toller used a poem of the same period by Max von Schenkendorf, *Freiheit, die ich meine* (v. Pittock p. 145). A vestige of this remains in the text when General von Grotjahn says: . . . die Spieluhr . . . weigert sich, ein Lied zu spielen, in dem das Wort Freiheit vorkommt. (GW3 p. 274). The actual word *Freiheit (Freedom)* does not in fact occur in the Arndt song.
58. v. Martini, *Deutsche Literaturgeschichte,* Stuttgart 1965 p. 338.
59. William I of Prussia was proclaimed German Emperor at Versailles, 18 Jan 1871.
60. GW3 p. 281f. Johann Gottfried Herder, 1744–1803, was a famous 18th Century German man of letters. v. Martini op cit p. 218/9.
61. Willibrand p. 112.
62. Willibrand p. 112, quoting *New York Times* 24 Jan, 1937, x, 1: 5.
63. GW3 p. 276 . . . . in der Bruderschaft Gottes zu leben, in der alle Menschen gleich sind, und der Liebe und Erlösung bedürftig, Treue, Redlichkeit und ein offenes Herz zeigen, Vertrauen einflößen und des Vertrauens würdig sein, und sich der Wiesen und Wolken, der Tiere und Blumen und des Lichts zu freuen.
64. e.g.
Sol ich mein letztes End/und ersten Anfang finden/
So muß ich mich in Gott/und Gott in mir ergründen.
Und werden daß was Er: Jch muß ein Schein im Schein:
Jch muß ein Wort im Wort: ein Gott im Gotte sein.

Ich bin wie Gott/und Gott wie ich.
Jch bin so groß als Gott: Er ist als ich so klein:
Er kan nicht über mich/ich unter Jhm nicht seyn.
(*Epochen der deutschen Lyrik 1600–1700*. dtv München, 2nd edn. 1976, pp. 219 &220.

65. ter Haar p. 194.
66. ibid p. 195.
67. GW5 p. 67. Ich entdecke konservative Elemente in mir. Man könnte vielleicht sagen, daß der Revolutionär nur aus Liebe zu einem utopischen Konservativismus revolutionär wird.
68. ter Haar *loc cit*. Er besteigt die Kanzel, um seiner Gemeinde den Weg zur Menschlichkeit zu verkünden und zu zeigen.
69. ibid. Sein Leben und sein Tod werden zu einer Demonstration für den Menschen.
70. GW3 p. 283.
71. GW3 p. 299.

. . .
Doch fur uns gibt es kein Klagen,
Ewig kann nicht Winter sein,
Einmal werden froh wir sagen:
"Heimat Du bist wieder mein".
Dann ziehn wir Moorsoldaten
Nicht mehr mit den Spaten
ins Moor, dann ziehn wir Moorsoldaten
Nicht mehr mit den Spaten ins Moor!

(But we are not complaining; winter cannot last forever; one day we'll say happily: "Homeland, you are mine again".
Then we soldiers of the Marsh will *not* march with spades into the Marsh any more (bis)).

72. Paul Rilla. Press cutting in Theatermuseum, Köln. Date and Periodical not known.
73. Willibrand p. 111.
74. GW2 p. 54ff.
75. Altenhofer p. 312f.
76. Altenhofer among others points out (p. 318) parallels between *Pastor Hall* and Friedrich Wolf's *Professor Mamlock* (1935).
77. I am indebted to Stephen Wardale for first putting me on the track of this, when he said almost in parenthesis during the taped interview of 11.5.1984 already quoted: "and then in the first winter of the war they did *Pastor Hall*". For all further information about this production I am indebted to Manchester Central

Reference Library and its helpful staff.
Spalek records a puppet performance of Act II at Buenos Aires in July 1939, Direction, Alfredo Hermitte; Music, Daniel Devoto. Spalek p. 888.

78. 14.10.'39 *George and Margaret* (G. Savory): 23.10.'39. *Third Party Rich* (Lennox & Ashley); 30.10.'39 *The Middle Watch* (Ian Hay & Stephen King-Hall); 6.11.'39 *Fresh Fields* (Ivor Novello).
79. *Manchester Evening News* 20 Nov '39. p. 2. Toller's play was competing with:
Quiet Wedding at the Opera House,
C. B. Cochran's *Lights Up* at the Palace,
Tea for Two at the Manchester Hippodrome, and
All at Sea at the Hulme Hippodrome.
80. *Pastor Hall*. Programme pp. 3, 4, 5. In Arts Library, Manchester Central Reference Library.
81. An all-night raid on London, 23.8.'40, marked its beginning.
82. Programme p. 12.
83. Complete cast and credits (from Programme):

Ida Hall	Patricia Jessel
Julie	Eileen Ashe
Fritz Gerte	Charles Lamb
Friedrich Hall	Rafe Thomson
Traugott Pipermann	T. Leslie Jackson
General Paul von Grotjahn	Noel Morris
Christine Hall	Anne Brooke
Dr. Werner von Grotjahn	James Bould
1st Gestapo Officer	Ian Stuart-Black
2nd Gestapo Officer	Dan Killip
Egon Freundlich	Arthur C. Goff
August Karsch	T. Leslie Jackson
Hermann Stettler	Harry Hillyard
Johann Herder	Carter Livesey
Peter Hofer	Fred Granville
Karl Mueller	Henry H. Wood
Corporal Luedeke	Morton Wing
Heinrich Degen	Ian Stuart-Black

Prisoners: Dan Killip, Thomas Marsh, Thomas Kelly, Joseph McCarthy, Walter Burton.
The Play Designed and Produced by James Bould.
The Settings designed by James Bould, built by Charles Cottriall, painted by Hugh Freemantle. Chief Electrician, Frank Jones; Stage

Director, T. Leslie Jackson; Stage Manager, Elisabeth Kirby; Assistant Stage Manager, Evelyne Ward. Music under the direction of Mr Frederick J. Burns.

84. *Manchester Guardian* Tuesday 21 November, 1939 p. 8.
Note: A. S. Wallace, the reviewer, had also reviewed the book publication of *Pastor Hall* favourably in the *Manchester Guardian* 18.7.'39. Spalek 3558.
85. ibid.
86. ibid.
87. ibid.
88. ibid.
89. ibid.
90. *Variety* (Hollywood) 1940. Spalek 3542.
91. *New Statesman & Nation* XIX No 484 (June 1st, 1940), 700. Spalek 3537.
92. *Denver Post* 10.9.1940. Spalek 3530.
93. Other cast:

Werner von Grotjahn	Brian North
Pippermann (sic, in Spalek)	Eliot Makeham
Erwin Kohn	Peter Cotes
Freundlich	Edmund Willard

(Ida Hall does not appear in Spalek's cast list, and there are two new characters, Herr Veit and Lina Veit, played by Percy Walsh and Lina Barrie. Photography: Cecil Cooney. Camera, Mutz Greenbaum).
94. Spalek 3560, 3561.
95. Spalek 3554.
96. Spalek 3514 etc.
97. Spalek 3516.
98. Spalek 3517.
99. ibid.
100. Spalek 3521, 3523 etc.
101. Spalek 3543.
102. Spalek 3556.
103. Spalek 3555.
104. Spalek 3542. An interesting echo of Barrett H. Clark's reasons for rejecting the English translation of the play in December 1938: Fall pp217/8.
105. GW3 p246. Gewidmet dem Tag, an dem dieses Drama in Deutschland gespielt werden darf.
106. Spalek p. 888. There were 33 performances.

Cast:

Pastor Hall	Ernst Sattler
	"sympathisch, offen und klar".
Ida Hall	Käthe Haack
General von Grotjahn	Eduard von Winterstein
	"vortrefflich"
Pipermann	Max Gülstorff
	"hart auf die Grenze zwischen Ernst und Komik"
Fritz Gerte	Gerhard Haselbach
Hofer	Gerhard Bienert
	"überzeugend und echt."
Lüdecke	Erich Dunskus
	"eine vorzügliche Type"
Jule	Angelika Hurwicz
Prisoner	Friedrich Mauer

Other members of the cast were: Liselotte Reimann (presumably playing Christine), Alfred Cogho, Peer Schmidt, Horst Drinda, Harry Hindemith, Carl Jönsson.

(Information for this cast list derived from: Review of the production (Not in Spalek) signed "R. M"., in *Der Sozialdemokrat 23*, 28.1.'47. (Press cutting seen in Fritz Hüser Institut, Dortmund and *25 Jahre Theater in Berlin. Premieren 1945–1970. Vorwort Friedrich Luft. Berlin 1972, p. 117*).

107. e.g. In *25 Jahre Theater in Berlin* (quoted above); GW3 p. 331; Fall p. 217, 236; Spalek p. 888; Pittock p. 139, 200.
108. Spalek 1608, 1609, 3510.
109. Spalek 48.
110. Harold Hurwicz *loc cit.* But a copy of the Henschel duplicated typescript in the Deutsches Literaturarchiv at Marbach which has the later ending, has the year 1946 written in.
111. Hurwicz *loc cit.*
112. das Herzstück des Dramas. Dr Wolfgang Schimming, *Suddeutsche Zeitung* 11.2.'47. Press Cutting at Köln, Spalek 3511.
113. unheimliches Bühnenbild. Paul Rilla. *Berliner Zeitung* 26.1.'47. Press cutting, Fritz Hüser Institut, Dortmund, Spalek 3510.
114. R. M. in *Der Sozialdemokrat* 23, 28.1.'47. Press cutting in Fritz Hüser Institut, Dortmund. Not in Spalek.
115. Paul Wiegler. *Nacht Express: die Illustrierte Abendzeitung*, Sonnabend, 25.1.'47. Press Cutting, Theatermuseum, Köln. Not

in Spalek. Wiegler adds: this is the day to which the play was dedicated.

116. Mario Thomas. *Telegraf.* 26.1.'47. Press cutting, Theatermuseum, Köln. Not in Spalek.
117. e.g. Friedrich Luft: . . . es . . . sprachlich seltsam farblos ist. Press cutting in Fritz Hüser Inst. Dortmund. Spalek 3508.
118. Schimming *loc. cit.*
119. W. E. Press cutting in Theatermuseum, Köln. Periodical and date not known. Not in Spalek.
120. Luft *loc. cit.* . . . das aus der Ferne oft unklargefügte Milieu.
121. The vocabulary of the gas-chamber and mass-death is lacking. Thomas *loc. cit.*
122. Rilla *loc. cit.*
123. Wiegler *loc. cit.*
124. Wolfgang Harich, *Tägl. Rundschau,* 26.1.'47. Harich, too, felt that Toller might have actually experienced the concentration camp, as all the subtly differing attitudes of the weak and strong are shown.
125. Press cutting in Theatermuseum, Köln, 2.2.'47. Periodical not known. Not in Spalek.
126. Spalek 3508.
127. Rilla *loc. cit.*
128. Werner Fiedler. *Neue Zeit* 21.1.'47. Press cutting in Theatermuseum, Köln. Not in Spalek.
129. Paul Rilla *Berliner Zeitung.* 21.1.'47.
130. *Das Herz im Stacheldraht.* Press cuttings, 26.1.'47 in Theatermuseum, Köln, and Akademie der Künste, Berlin. Periodical not known. Not in Spalek.
131. Spalek p. 888.
132. See *Almanach der Thüringer Theaterschau 1947.* Spalek 3499, and *Thüringer Volk* 14 June 1947 or *Die Bühnenkritik* Sept. 1947. Spalek 3502. It was thought, wrongly, that this was the first time the revised ending had been used. (It had, of course, been used in Manchester).
133. A review by "Idm" appeared in *Die Union* 7.2.1948 of a production directed by Herbert Roehmelt who is criticised for doing the 1st and 3rd acts 'like an Ibsen society piece'. The reviewer, however, says that the play is "activist theatre, such as we need," adding, "Toller's accusation will be heard, must be heard". Press cutting in the Akademie der Künste, Berlin. No other reference to this production found.

134. Peter Engels, *Münstersche Zeitung* 16.5.'83. Press cutting in Akademie der Künste, Berlin.
135. H. H. in *Kieler Nachrichten*. 18.5.'83. Press cutting in Akademie der Künste, Berlin.
136. anon. *Berliner Zeitung* 11.5.'83. Press cutting in Akademie der Künste, Berlin.
137. Werner Schulze-Reimpell, *Nürnberger Nachrichten*. 17.5.'83. Press cutting in Akademie der Künste, Berlin.
138. e.g. his early use of 'montage' and of documentary techniques.
139. *General Anzeiger* Bonn, 31.5.'83.
140. ibid.
141. ibid.
142. ibid.
143. ibid. Was einer werden kann, das ist er schon.

V CONCLUSION

1. The rift in the age went right through the middle of his heart. Walter Mehring: *Die verlorene Bibliothek. Autobiographie einer Kultur*. Hamburg 1952, p155. Quoted by Rothe in *Toller* Reinbek 1983, p. 10.
2. GW2 p95. cf. *Tag des Proletariats*, p. 16: Masse wird Gemeinschaft (Masses become Community).
3. *Feuer aus den Kesseln*, moreover, is not only a play about the 1917 mutiny, nor only about injustice, but, as Frühwald and Spalek point out, it "Also applies to current events; it is evidence for the final liquidation of the revolution and of the republican spirit in Germany". (es ist Zeugnis für die endgültige Liquidierung der Revolution und des republikanischen Geistes in Deutschland). (GW1 p. 17)
4. GW2 p253
5. GW2 p271.
   Piscator: *Sturmflut* (Paquet), February 1926.
   Brecht: *Die Dreigroschenoper*. August 1928.
6. 1. Wotan mistakes a jazz-band for the music of the spheres, the angelic orchestra. (GW2 p. 281).
   2. A hurdy-gurdy plays familiar tunes and military pot-pourris during the interval. (ibid).

3. A flourish of trumpets followed by Luther's hymn *Ein' feste Burg* precede Wotan's disastrous appearance on the balcony. (GW2 p. 298).
4. The scenes are given musical headings:
Wotanisches Impromptu; Allegro; Andante;
Scherzo Furioso-Rondo, Finale.

7. Wenn er Größe besaß, so ist sie möglicherweise nicht einmal primär in seinem gedruckten oeuvre zu suchen . . (Rothe op cit p. 7)

8. . . in fast jeder Hinsicht ein Amateur, wenn nicht Dilettant war . . (Rothe op cit p. 7).
And cf: Seine Konkurrenten . . . . besaßen schärfere, eindeutigere Konturen. (ibid).

BIBLIOGRAPHY

Editions of Toller's Works Consulted

Aufrüttelung in *Der Freihafen, Blätter der Hamburger Kammerspiele.* Ed. Erich Ziegel. 3. Jg., Heft 1 p. 4. n.d. but probably 1920.

"Berlin — letzte Ausgabe!" [1930] in *Frühe Sozialistische Hörspiele* ed S. B. Würfel Frankfurt/M 1982.

Brief an Gustav Landauer [1917] in *Der Freihafen, Blätter der Hamburger Kammerspiele,* ed. Erich Ziegel. 3. Jg., Heft 1. pp. 5–7. n. d. but probably 1920.

Deutsche Revolution. Anhang I to Hans Marnette *Untersuchungen zum Inhalt-Form-Problem in Ernst Toller's Dramen.* Q. V. (Thesis).

Feuer aus den Kesseln. Berlin 1930.

Die Feuer-Kantate in *Das Wort* Jg. 3 Nr 6. Moscow, June 1928.

Gesammelte Werke in 5 Vols. Ed. John M. Spalek and Wolfgang Frühwald. Hanser Verlag, München, Wien, 1978.
(Abbreviated in text to GW1, GW2 etc).

Hinkemann Kiepenheuer, Potsdam 1924; Leipzig and Weimar 1979.

I Was a German (authorised English translation by Edward Crankshaw of *Eine Jugend in Deutschland*). London 1934.

Justiz: Erlebnisse. E. Laubsche, Berlin 1927.

Die Maschinenstürmer. 2nd Edition (Spalek 34), Leipzig, Wien, Zürich, 1922.

Masse Mensch. Stuttgart, Reclam, 1979.

Masses and Man (translated by Vera Mendel) London 1923.

Masses and Man: The Problem of non-violence and peace. London, Friends Book Centre 1934.

New Statesman and Nation.
Articles:
British Free People's Theatre 12.9.'36.
Madrid-Washington 8.10.'38.
Note upon Freedom in Russia 3.11.'34.
Promenade in Seville 4.4.'34.
Story
Grabbed by the Tail, a Story 17.8.'35.

No More Peace. A Thoughtful Comedy (Edward Crankshaw's translation of *Nie wieder Friede,* with Lyrics adapted by W. H. Auden). London 1937.

Prosa, Briefe, Dramen, Gedichte (Vorwort: Kurt Hiller). Reinbek bei Hamburg 1961. (Abbreviated in text to: PBDG).

Quer Durch. Kiepenheuer, Berlin 1930.

Die Rache des verhöhnten Liebhabers in *Die Weissen Blätter,* Jg. 7, Heft 11, Nov. 1920.

Die Rache des verhöhnten Liebhabers, Berlin 1925.

Die Rache des verhöhnten Liebhabers, Kiepenheuer Verlag, 1962 (Duplicated. Not for Sale).

Das Schwalbenbuch, Potsdam, Kiepenheuer, 1924.

Seven Plays, The Bodley Head 1935.

Szene aus dem unveröffentlichten Drama "Eugen Hinkemann" in *Blätter des Deutschen Theaters. Ausgabe für das Große Schauspielhaus.* Jg. 8, 1921–22, Heft 7. pp. 182–183.

Tag des Proletariats. Potsdam, Kiepenheuer, 1920.

Vormorgen, Potsdam, Kiepenheuer, 1924.

Weltliche Passion in *Internationale Literatur,* Nr. 4, 1934. Internationale Vereinigung Revolutionärer Schriftsteller. Zürich, Paris, Amsterdam, & Copenhagen. (Spalek 328 gives place of publication as Moscow)

With Alfred Mühr:

Nationalsozialismus. Eine Diskussion über den Kulturbankrott des Bürgertums zwischen Ernst Toller und Alfred Mühr, Redakteur der Deutschen Zeitung. Berlin 1930.

Secondary and Related Literature: Printed Books

AESCHYLI. *Septem Quae Supersunt Tragoedias.* ed. Denys Page. Oxford 1972.

AESCHYLUS. *The Oresteian Trilogy.* Trans. P. Vellacott, Harmondsworth. Penguin Books. 1956.

Almanach der Thüringer Theaterschau 1947. Ergebnisse und Folgerungen. Im Auftrag des Ministeriums für Volksbildung herausgegeben von Otto Fritz Gaillard. Weimar n. d. (?1948).

AUDEN, W. H. *Collected Shorter Poems 1930–1944.* London 1950. 2nd

Imp. 1953.

BAB, JULIUS. *Über den Tag hinaus.* Darmstadt 1960.

BECKETT, SAMUEL. *Waiting for Godot*. London, Faber, 1956.

BENSON, RENATE *German Expressionist Drama, Ernst Toller and Georg Kaiser*, London 1984.

BENTLEY, ERIC. *The Modern Theatre*. London, Robert Hale, 1948. 2nd imp. 1950. (1st pub. in US as *The Playwright as Thinker*).

Berlin, 25 Jahre Theater in. Theaterpremieren 1945–1970. Herausgegeben im Auftrag des Senats von Berlin. Berlin, Heinz Spitzing Verlag 1972.

BIELENBERG, C. *The Past is Myself.* p. b. edtn. Dublin 1982.

BITHELL, J. *Companion to German Studies.* 5th ed. London 1955.

BODE, DIETRICH [ed.]. *Gedichte des Expressionismus*. Stuttgart, Reclam 1976.

BOEHN, MAX von. *Puppen und Puppenspiele. Vol II: Puppenspiele*. Munich 1929.

BRAULICH, HEINRICH. *Die Volksbühne. Theater und Politik in der Deutschen Volksbühnen-Bewegung*. Berlin Henschel Verlag 1976.

BRECHT, BERTOLT. *Anmerkungen zur Oper Aufstieg und Fall der Stadt Mahagonny* [1930] in: *Aufstieg und Fall der Stadt Mahagonny*. Berlin, Suhrkamp 1963 [Text of 1955].

BRECHT, BERTOLT. *Gedichte und Lieder aus Stücken*. Frankfurt/Main. 1963.

BRECHT, BERTOLT. *Gesammelte Gedichte*. Frankfurt/Main. Suhrkamp 1967.

BRECHT, BERTOLT. *Mutter Courage und ihre Kinder*. Berlin 1974.

BROCKWAY, FENNER. *Inside the Left: Thirty Years of Platform, Press, Prison and Parliament*. London, 2nd Imp. 1947 (Post War Ed) [1st pub. 1942].

BRODBECK, A. *Handbuch der Deutschen Volksbühnen-Bewegung* Berlin 1930.

BÜCHNER, GEORG. *Gesammelte Werke*. Munich, Wilhelm Goldman Verlag 1958.

CRAIG, EDWARD GORDON. *On the Art of the Theatre.* 5th. imp. London 1957.

DAVIES, CECIL W. *Theatre for the People: The Story of the Volksbühne.* Manchester 1977.

DORST, TANKRED (ed). *Die Münchner Räterepublik. Zeugnisse und Kommentar.* Frankfurt/M 1966.

DORST, TANKRED. *Toller*. Frankfurt/M 1968.

DORST, TANKRED. *Toller*. Programme of the British Premiere. Workshop Theatre, School of English, University of Leeds. Dec. 1984.

DOVE, RICHARD. *Revolutionary Socialism in the Work of Ernst Toller.* Utah Studies in Literature and Linguistics. Vol 26. Peter Lang, New York, Berne, Frankfurt and Main, 1986.

DOVE, RICHARD. *He was a German: a biography of Ernst Toller.* London, 1990.

DROOP, FRITZ. *Ernst Toller und seine Bühnenwerke. Eine Einführung.* Schneider Bühnenführer. Berlin and Leipzig 1922.

DURZAK, MANFRED. *Das expressionistische Drama. Ernst Barlach. Ernst Toller. Fritz von Unruh.* Munich, Nymphenburger Verlagshandlung 1979.

ENGELS, F. *The Condition of the Working-Class in England in 1844.* Trans F. K. Wischnewetsky. London 1892.

ETTINGER, ELZBIETA [ed. & Trans]. *Comrade and Lover: Rosa Luxemburg's Letters to Leo Jogiches.* Cambridge, Mass., & London 1979.

ETTINGER, ELZBIETA. *Rosa Luxemburg, A Life.* London 1987.

EXPRESSIONISM IN GERMAN LITERATURE — WORD, PICTURE & STAGECRAFT 1910–1920. Descriptive Catalogue of: An Exhibition arranged by the Institut für Auslandsbeziehungen. Stuttgart n. d.

EXPRESSIONIST THEATER. [Descriptive Catalogue of] An Exhibition by the Goethe-Institut. Compiled & Commentated: Dr Eckehart Nölle. Munich 1977.

FRÜHWALD, W. &. SPALEK, JOHN M. *Der Fall Toller: Kommentar und Materialien.* Munich. Carl Hanser Verlag. 1979.

FURNESS, RAYMOND. *Wagner & Literature.* Manchester 1982.

GARDNER, B. [ed]. *Up the Line to Death.* London, Methuen, Rev. Ed. 1976, 3rd printing 1980.

GOETHE, J. W. *Faust.* Herausgegeben und Kommentiert von Erich Trunz. Munich, C. H. Beck 1974.

GOETHE, J. W. *Gesamtausgabe.* [Bd 8 mit einem Nachwort von Andreas B. Wachsmuth]. Munich DTV 1962.

GRAF, OSKAR MARIA. *Wir sind Gefangene.* Munich, Süddeutscher Verlag, 1978.

GRISAR, ERICH. *Opferung.* Dortmund 1927.

HAAR, CAREL ter. *Ernst Toller, Appell oder Resignation?* tuduv-Studien, Reihe Sprach- und Literaturwissenschaft, Band 7. Munich, tuduv-Verlagsgesellschaft 1977.

HAERTLE-DEDLER, CLEMENS. *Rochus Dedler, der Komponist der Passionsmusik zu Oberammergau. Festschrift zum 200. Geburtstag des Kompomisten, 15. Januar 1979.* Herausgeber: Gemeinde Oberam-

mergau. n. d. [1979].
HAFFNER, SEBASTIAN. *Die verratene Revolution. Deutschland 1918/1919*. Sherz Verlag. Bern, München, Wien, 1969.
HAMMER, A. E. *German Grammar and Usage*. London 1971.
HARSH, P. W. *A Handbook of Classical Drama*. Stanford 1944–67.
HASENCLEVER, WALTER. *Gedichte, Dramen, Prosa*. Intr. by Kurt Pinthus. Reinbek bei Hamburg, 1963.
HAUPTMANN, GERHART. *Fuhrmann Henschel*. In *Das dramatische Werk. I. Bd*. Frankfurt/M 1974.
HÄUSSERMANN, ULRICH. *Hölderlin*. rororo Bildmonograph, Rowohlt. Reinbek bei Hamburg. 1961–80.
HEINTZ, GÜNTER [ed]. *Deutsche Arbeiterdichtung 1910–1933*. Stuttgart 1974.
HERMAND, JOST [ed]. *Zu Ernst Toller, Drama und Engagement*. Stuttgart 1981.
HILL, CLAUDE & LEY, RALPH. *The Drama of German Expressionism. A German-English Bibliography*. University of North Carolina Studies in the Germanic Languages and Literatures. No. 28. University of North Carolina Press, Chapel Hill, North Carolina 1960.
HÖLDERLIN, FRIEDRICH. *Gedichte*. Ed. J. Schmidt. Insel Taschenbuch. Frankfurt/M, 1984.
HÖLDERLIN, FRIEDRICH. *Hyperion*. Stuttgart 1983.
HOFFMAN, E. T. A. *Werke*. Insel Verlag. Frankfurt/M 1967.
HOFFMANN, L. & HOFFMANN-OSWALD, D. H. *Deutsches Arbeitertheater 1918–1933. Eine Dokumentation*. Henschel Verlag. Berlin 1961.
IHERING, HERBERT. *Der Volksbühnenverrat*. Berlin-Zahlendorf. n. d. [16pp].
INNES, C. D. *Erwin Piscator's Political Theatre. The Development of Modern German Drama*. Cambridge 1972.
KESSLER, HARRY GRAF. *Walther Rathenau, sein Leben und sein Werk*. Wiesbaden 1962. [1st ed. Berlin 1928].
KESTING, MARIANNE. *Brecht*. Rowohlt, Reinbek bei Hamburg 1959.
KILLY, WALTHER [ed]. *Epochen der Deutschen Lyrik*. (9 vols). Munich 1974.
KITTO, H. D. F. *Greek Tragedy*. Methuen, London, 3rd ed., reprint 1968.
KLEIST, HEINRICH von. *Erzählungen*. DTV Munich 1964–74.
KLEIST, HEINRICH von. *Sämtliche Werke und Briefe*. 2. Bd. 4th Rev. ed. Munich 1965.
KLINGER, F. M. *Ausgewählte Werke Bd. I*. Stuttgart 1878.
KNILLI, F. & MÜNCHOW U. *Frühes Deutsches Arbeitertheater 1847–*

1918. Eine Dokumentation. Henschelverlag, Berlin 1961.
KOBBÉ, GUSTAV. *Wagner's Music Dramas Analysed.* New York, 1923.
LANDAUER, GUSTAV. *Aufruf zum Sozialismus.* Berlin 1911.
LANDAUER, GUSTAV. *Friedrich Hölderlin in seinen Gedichten.* Potsdam 1922.
LEEPER, JANET. *Edward Gordon Craig.* Harmondsworth 1948.
LENZ, J. M. R. *Werke und Schriften.* Stuttgart 1966.
LEYDA, JAY [ed]. *Eisenstein, Three Films.* London 1974.
MACGOWAN, K. & JONES, R. E. *Continental Stagecraft.* New York 1922.
MANN, KLAUS. *Mephisto.* Reinbek bei Hamburg. 1981.
MANN, THOMAS, *Der Tod in Venedig,* ed. T. J. Reed. Oxford 1971.
MARÉ, ERIC de. *The London Doré Saw.* London 1963.
MARTINI, FRITZ. *Deutsche Literaturgeschichte.* A. Kröner Verlag. Stuttgart, 1965.
MARX, KARL. *Capital.* Trans. E & C Paul. London 1930.
Marxist Philosophy, A Textbook of. Gollancz. London, n. d. [c. 1935].
MARX / ENGELS. *Manifesto of the Communist Party [Communist Manfesto].* Text of the English Edition of 1888, London 1983.
MENNEMEIER, FRANZ NORBERT. *Modernes Deutsches Drama, Kritiken und Charakteristiken. Bd. I. 1910–1933.* Wilhelm Fink Verlag, Munich 1973.
MEYER, C. F. *Die Versuchung des Pescara.* ed. W. D. Williams, Blackwell, Oxford, 1958.
MOLO, WALTER von. *So wunderbar ist das Leben. Erinnerungen und Begegnungen.* Stuttgart 1957.
MORENZ, LUDWIG & MÜNZ, ERWIN [eds]. *Revolution und Räteherrschaft in München. Aus der Stadtchronik 1918–1919.* Neue Schriftenreihe des Stadtarchivs München. Band Nr. 29. Albert Langen. Georg Müller Verlag, Munich-Vienna 1968.
MORTIMER, JOHN. *Clinging to the Wreckage.* Weidenfeld & Nicholson, & Penguin, 1982.
NESTRIEPKE, SIEGFRIED. *Neues Beginnen, die Geschichte der Freien Volksbühne Berlin 1946 bis 1955.* Berlin 1956.
Neue Sachlichkeit and German Realism of the Twenties. Arts Council of Great Britain, 1972.
OGLETREE, T. W. *The 'Death of God' Controversy.* SCM, London 1966.
OSSAR, MICHAEL. *Anarchism in the Dramas of Ernst Toller.* State University of New York Press, Albany, 1980.
PASCAL, ROY. *From Naturalism to Expressionism. German Literature and*

Society 1880–1918. Weidenfeld & Nicholson, London 1973.
Passionsspiele Oberammergau. 1634–1984. Textbuch. Oberammergau, 1984.
PATTERSON, M. *The Revolution in German Theatre 1900–1933.* London & Boston 1981.
PFÜTZNER, KLAUS. *Die Massenfestspiele der Arbeiter in Leipzig [1920–1924]*. Leipzig 1960.
PISCATOR, ERWIN. *Das politische Theater*. Reinbek bei Hamburg 1963. [orig. pub. Berlin 1929].
PISCATOR, ERWIN. *The Political Theatre.* Trans. Hugh Rorrison. London 1980.
PISCATOR, ERWIN. *Schriften 2*. Berlin 1968.
PITTOCK, MALCOLM. *Ernst Toller.* Twayne Publishers. Boston 1979.
PLIEVIER, THEODOR. *Des Kaisers Kulis.* DTV Munich 1984.
RATHENAU, WALTHER. *Gesammelte Schriften*. Berlin 1918.
RENKER, FELIX. *Am Webstuhl der Zeit.* Leipzig n. d.
RICHARD, LIONEL [ed]. *The Concise Encyclopaedia of Expressionism.* Trans. Stephen Tint. Omega Books, Ware, 1984.
RITCHIE, J. M. [ed]. *Vision and Aftermath. Four Expressionist War Plays.* London 1969.
ROBERTS, MICHAEL. *The Faber Book of Modern Verse.* London 1936. 15th imp. 1948.
ROTHE, WOLFGANG. *Ernst Toller.* Reinbek bei Hamburg 1983.
RÜHLE, GÜNTHER. *Theater für die Republik.* Frankfurt/M 1967.
RÜHLE, GÜNTHER. *Theater in unserer Zeit.* Suhrkamp. Frankfurt/M 1976.
RÜHLE, GÜNTHER. *Zeit und Theater, vom Kaiserreich zur Republik 1913–1925*. Propyläen Verlag. Berlin 1973.
RUSSELL, BERTRAND. *History of Western Philosophy.* London 1954.
SCHILLER, FRIEDRICH. *Sämtliche Werke.* Hanser Verlag, Munich, 1967.
SCHÖNLANK, BRUNO. *Erlösung.* Berlin 1924.
SCHÖNLANK, BRUNO. *Ein Frühlings Mysterium.* Berlin, 1925.
SCHWEITZER, ALBERT. *Civilization and Ethics.* Trans. C. T. Campion. Rev. by Mrs C. E. B. Russell. Unwin Books & A. C. Black. London 1961.
SHIRER, W. L. *The Rise and Fall of the Third Reich.* Book Club Associates Edition 1973.
SIDNEY, Sir P. *Apologie for Poetrie.* ed. J. Churton Collins. Oxford, Clarendon Press. 1907 (impression of 1947).
SIEPMANN, ECKHARD. *Montage: John Heartfield.* 3rd rev'd edtn. Berlin [West] 1977.
SIMONSON, LEE. *The Art of Scenic Design.* New York 1950.

SMOLJAN, OLGA. *Friedrich Maximilian Klinger, Leben und Werk.* Beiträge zur Deutschen Klassik. Herausgegeben von Helmut Holtzhauer und Karl-Heinz Klingenberg. Trans. from Russian by Ernst Moritz Arndt. Weimar 1962.

SOPHOCLES. ed. Jebb. Cambridge 1906.

SOPHOCLES. *The Theban Plays.* Trans. Watling. Harmondsworth 1947.

SPALEK, JOHN M. *Ernst Toller and his Critics. A Bibliography.* University of Virginia 1968. Reprinted by Haskell House Publishers Ltd., New York, 1973.

STRAMBOWSKI, ANTON. *Bund der Theatergemeinden.* Düsseldorf 1978.

STRANDMANN, von [ed]. *Walther Rathenau, Industrialist, Banker, Intellectual and Politician, Notes and Diaries 1907–1922.* Trans. Pinder-Cracraft. Oxford, 1985.

STRESEMANN, GUSTAV. *Schriften.* Berlin 1976.

STRINDBERG, AUGUST. *Six Plays.* Trans. E. Sprigge. Doubleday, New York, 1955.

STRINDBERG, AUGUST. *The Road to Damascus: A Trilogy.* English Version by Graham Rawson. London 1939.

TAYLOR, SIMON. *Germany 1918–1933.* London 1983.

THOMAS, EDWARD. *Collected Poems.* Faber. London 1936.

TILLYARD, E. M. W. *Shakespeare's History Plays.* Harmondsworth 1962. [1st ed. Chatto & Windus 1944].

TRAKL, GEORG. *Das Dichterische Werk.* 3. Auflage. DTV Munich 1974.

TRESSELL, ROBERT. *The Ragged Trousered Philanthropists.* Panther Books. London 1965. Reprint 1985.

TREWIN, J. C. *Sybil Thorndike.* London 1955.

TRIBÜNE, DIE. The First Programme. Berlin n. d.

VIVIANI, ANNALISA. *Das Drama des Expressionismus. Kommentar zu einer Epoche.* Munich 1970.

VOGT, PAUL. *Expressionism, German Painting between 1905 and 1920.* Cologne. 1979.

WARD, R. H. *Faust in Hell.* 2nd Edition. London 1945.

WEDEKIND, FRANK. *Frühlings Erwachen.* Reclam. Stuttgart, 1971.

Weimarer Republik. Kunstamt Kreuzberg, Berlin & Institut für Theaterwissenschaft der Universität Köln. Elefanten Press, Berlin. 1977.

WEISS, PETER. *Die Verfolgung und Ermordung Jean Paul Marats dargestellt durch die Schauspielgruppe des Hospizes zu Charenton unter Anleitung des Herrn de Sade.* Suhrkamp. Frankfurt/M 1973.

WILLETT, JOHN. *The New Sobriety. Art and Politics in the Weimar Period 1917–1933.* Thames & Hudson 1978.

WILLETT, JOHN. *The Theatre of Erwin Piscator.* London 1978.

WILLIAMS, RAYMOND. *Drama from Ibsen to Eliot*. Chatto & Windus 1952. Rev'd Edtn Peregrine Books 1964. 2nd Edtn, Rev'd: *Drama from Ibsen to Brecht*. Chatto & Windus 1968.

WILLIBRAND, WILLIAM ANTHONY. *Ernst Toller and his Ideology*. Univ. of Iowa Humanistic Studies, Vol VII. Iowa City 1945.

ZAREK, OTTO. *German Odyssey*. London 1941.

Articles

BAB, JULIUS. *Das Erstlingswerk des Dramatikers*. In *Der Freihafen*: Blätter der Hamburger Kammerspiele. Ed. Erich Ziegel. 3. Jg. Heft 1. pp. 8–13. n. d., (probably 1920).

BATAILLON, MICHEL. *Die Wandlung de Toller. Un exemple de StationenDrama*.
In: *L'expressionisme dans le Théatre Européen*. Editions du Centre National de la Recherche Scientifique. Paris 1971.

DAVIES, CECIL W. *Working-Class Theatre in the Weimar Republic 1919–1933*. In *Theatre Quarterly*,
Pt I in Vol X No 38, 1980.
Pt II in Vol X No 39, 1981.

DOVE, RICHARD. *Fenner Brockway and Ernst Toller. Document and Drama in Berlin-letzte Ausgabe*. In *German Life and Letters 38. 1, Oct. 1984 pp. 45–56.*

DOVE, RICHARD. *The Place of Toller in English Socialist Theatre 1924–1939*. In *German Life and Letters 38. 2, January 1985 p. 125.*

FEHLING, JÜRGEN. *Note on the Production of 'Masses and Man'*. In: Toller, *Masses and Man*, Trans. Mendel. London 1923.

FREYDANK, RUTH. *Briefe Ernst Tollers aus dem Zuchthaus*. In *Jahrbuch des Märkischen Museums, — Kulturhistorisches Museum der Hauptstadt der DDR, Berlin*. II/1976 pp. 59–64.

GROSSMANN, STEFAN. *Der Hochverräter Ernst Toller. Die Geschichte eines Prozesses*. Rowohlt Berlin 1919. Reprinted in *Ernst Toller: Prosa, Briefe, Dramen, Gedichte*. Rowohlt 1961.

HARBECK, HANS. *Ernst Toller*. In *Der Freihafen*. Blätter der Hamburger Kammerspiele. ed. Erich Ziegel. 3. Jg. Heft 1. pp. 1–3. n. d. probably 1920.

HAMBURGER, MICHAEL. *Die erhabene Kunst. Milton und Hölderlin*. In *Vernunft und Rebellion. Aufsätze zur Gesellschaftskritik in der deutschen Literatur*. Hanser. Munich 1968.

HEBBEL, FRIEDRICH. *Mein Wort über das Drama*. In *Sämtliche Werke* in 12 Vols. Hesse und Becker Verlag, Leipzig n. d., but *Vorwort* by

Emil Kuh is dated Oct. 1867.

HENSEL, GEORGE. *Nachwort*. In Wedekind, *Frühlings Erwachen*. Reclam, Stuttgart 1971.

HURWITZ, HAROLD. *Opfer oder Held*. In *Dramaturgische Blätter*, Jg. 1. Nr. 2. Berlin, May 1947

LAMB, STEPHEN. *Ernst Toller and the Weimar Republic*. In: Bullivant, Keith [ed], *Culture and Society in the Weimar Republic*. Manchester 1977.

MILLER, ARTHUR. *On Social Plays*. In *A View from the Bridge*. London 1957.

OSCHILEWSKI, WALTER G. *Geleitwort*. In: *Ernst Toller: Verbrüderung. Ausgewählte Dichtungen*. Berlin 1930.

OSTERWALDER, FRITZ. *Die Überwindung des Sturm und Drang im Werk Friedrich Maximilian Klingers. Die Entwicklung der republikanischen Dichtung in der Zeit der Französischen Revolution*. In: *Philologische Studien und Quellen*. Herausgegeben von Wolfgang Binder und Hugo Moser. Heft 96. Berlin 1979.

PETERSEN, CAROL. *Ernst Toller*. In: *Expressionismus als Literatur. Gesammelte Studien*. Ed. Wolfgang Rothe, Bern, 1969.

ROTHE, WOLFGANG. *Expressionism in Literature*. In: *German Art in the Twentieth Century*. R. A. A. & Prestel Verlag. London 1985.

SCHÜRER, ERNST. *Literarisches Engagement und politische Praxis: Das Vorbild Ernst Toller*. In: Papenfuss, Dietrich, & Söring, Jürgen [eds]: *Rezeption der deutschen Gegenwartsliteratur im Ausland. Internationale Forschungen zu neuen deutschen Literatur*. Stuttgart, Berlin, Köln, Mainz. 1976. pp. 353–366.

SPALEK, JOHN M. & FRÜHWALD, WOLFGANG: *Ernst Tollers Amerikanische Vortragsreise 1936/7*. In: *Literaturwissenschaftliches Jahrbuch. Neue Folge/Sechster Band*. Berlin 1965.

SPALEK, JOHN M. *Ernst Toller: The Need for a New Estimate*. In: *The German Quarterly* XXXIX, No. 4. Nov. 1966 pp. 581–598.

VOLLMOELLER, CARL. *Zur Entwicklungsgeschichte des Großen Hauses*. In: *Das Große Schauspielhaus. Zur Eröffnung des Hauses. Herausgegeben vom Deutschen Theater zu Berlin*. Im Verlage der Bücher des Deutschen Theaters. Redaktion: Heinz Herald. Berlin 1920.

Unpublished Dissertations Read in Typescript or on Microfilm

ALTENHOFER, ROSEMARIE A. J. *Tollers Politische Dramatik*. PhD Thesis. Washington University Department of Germanic Languages and Literature. 1976.

CAFFERTY H. L. *George Büchner's Influence on Ernst Toller*. PhD Dissertation. Michigan 1976.

ELSASSER, ROBERT BRUCE. *Ernst Toller and German Society: The Role of the Intellectual as Critic, 1914–1939*. PhD Thesis. Rutgers University, the State University of New Jersey. 1973.

HAJAN, RAINER. *Das politische Theater in Deutschland zwischen 1918 und 1933*. Doctoral Dissertation, Ludwig-Maximilian Universität, Munich. 1958.

KLEIN, DOROTHEA. *Der Wandel der dramatischen Darstellungsform im Werk Ernst Tollers [1919–1930]*. PhD Thesis, Bochum, 1968.

MARNETTE, HANS. *Untersuchungen zum Inhalt-Form-Problem in Ernst Tollers Dramen*. PhD Thesis, Paedagogische Hochschule, Potsdam, 1963.

PARK, WILLIAM MACFARLANE. *Ernst Toller: The European Exile Years 1933–1936*. PhD Thesis. University of Colorado 1976

REIMER, ROBERT C. *The Tragedy of the Revolutionary. A Study of the Dramas of Revolution of Ernst Toller, Friedrich Wolf and Bertolt Brecht*. Thesis, Kansas, 1971.

RESO, MARTIN. *Der gesellschaftliche-ethische Protest im dichterischen Werk Ernst Tollers*. PhD Thesis, University of Jena 1957.

ROGER, J. H. *Ernst Toller's Prose Writings*. PhD Thesis, Yale University, 1972.

SCHORLIES, WALTER-JÜRGEN. *Der Schauspieler, Regisseur, szenische Bühnenbauer und Theaterleiter, Karl-Heinz Martin. Versuch einer Biographie*. PhD Dissertation, Köln, 1971.

Audio Tape Recordings Used

1. GERDA REDLICH interviewed by the present writer on her involvement in and memories of Piscator's production of *Hoppla, wir leben!* and on the relationship between Toller and Piscator. (Date of Interview: 10. 5. 1974).

2. *Gespräch zwischen Ernst Toller und Alfred Mühr, 1930.*
An extract from the live broadcast discussion (1930) between Ernst Toller and Alfred Mühr on *Nationalsozialismus*: v. Bibliography for full published version. The extract formed part of a gramophone record, *Sprechstunden Deutscher Geschichte II 1918–1930*, issued promotionally to German medical practitioners. The tape was kindly given by Professor Wolfgang Frühwald.

3. STEPHEN WARDALE, formerly of the Rusholme Repertory Theatre, interviewed by the present writer on his personal experience of Toller's production in Manchester of *Draw the Fires*, with some reference also to the premiere of *Pastor Hall* at the same theatre. (Date of Interview: 11. 5. 1984)

Archives Consulted

In Germany

1. *Akademie der Künste, Berlin*
   Hanseatenweg 10, 1000 Berlin 21.
   Leiter des Archivs und der Bibliothek: Prof. Dr. Walter Huder.

   Sammlung Ernst Toller.
   Erwin-Piscator-Center

   Date of study-visit: 5–11 October 1985.

2. *Fritz-Hüser-Institut für deutsche und ausländische Arbeiterliteratur.*
   Ostenheilweg 56–58, Stadt Dortmund.
   Sacharbeiter: Dr Noltenius.

   Toller Collection.

   Date of study-visit: 3 & 4 October 1985.

3. *Institut für Deutsche Philologie, Universität München.*
   Prof. Wolfgang Frühwald.

   Toller Collection.

   Date of study-visit: November 1979. One week.

4. *Theatermuseum des Instituts für Theaterwissenschaft der Universität Köln.*
   Schloß Wahn, 5000 Köln 90.
   Dr. Roswitha Flatz.

   Toller Collection (particularly rich in newspaper cuttings). Also: valuable material on Karl-Heinz Martin; the Großes Schauspielhaus; Social-democratic workers' theatre; Alfred Jahn Verlag, Leipzig; Arbeiter-

Theater-Bund-Deutschlands; Oskar Maria Graf; Verband zur Förderung deutscher Theaterkultur, etc.

Date of study-visit: Nov–Dec 1979. 3 weeks.

5. *Schiller-Nationalmuseum Deutsches Literaturarchiv*
   D-7142 Marbach am Neckar.
   Dr Werner Volke.
   Handschriftenabteilung: Margit Berger.

   Toller Collection: valuable printed and handwritten material.

   Date of study-visit: 12–17 October 1985.

In England

1. *Theatre Museum, Victoria and Albert Museum.* Leela Meinertas.

   Programmes and reviews of 8 English productions between 1923 and 1953.

   Date of visit: 15 May 1985.

2. *Central Reference Library, City of Manchester.*

   Microfilm files of MANCHESTER GUARDIAN, MANCHESTER EVENING NEWS, and MANCHESTER CITY NEWS. Manchester Theatres Programme Collection.

APPENDICES

A MATTEO BANDELLO (1485–1561)

LE NOVELLE

La Prima Parte

NOVELLA 3

Beffa d'una donna ad un gentiluomo
edil cambio che egli le ne rende in doppio

[TRANSLATED BY W.I. HYSLOP]

The jest of a lady to a gentleman
and the way he turns the tables on her

Not so many years ago, there was in a city of Lombardy a respected gentlewoman, very richly married, the which was of a more capricious and wayward nature than became a woman of gravity.

She used to amuse herself marvellously by teasing everyone and often ridiculing them, and then in the company of other ladies deriding one or another, in a way that no one would have dared to make love to her or domesticate her, so that being as she was haughty and having cut, indeed ruptured, the rules of etiquette, she was wont to say everything that came into her mind providing that to whomsoever it was said someone would be stung. And because in truth it is not well for gentlemen to dispute with ladies or wish to question their words, which ought to be respected and honoured by them, nearly everyone used to flee who came into conversation with her, as it was known by all how much she was unrestrained and biting of tongue, and bore no respect for anyone.

She was then beautiful beyond measure, and in all the parts which make a beautiful lady so well formed, and with so much loveliness and gracefulness, that she made everything, each thing, each deed, each sign and each movement appear in her enhanced, so that, with such beauty, she was without equal in the whole of Lombardy. There were those who, not entirely knowing the character of the lady, set themselves to woo her and make love to her, the which she, since she had a sufficiency of sweet glances, with one or other jest would upset them, so that the incautious lovers remained miserably scorned. And although she was, as I have explained, disagreeable, nonetheless it pleased her to be courted, and often the better to lure the suitors she would pretend to wish such an approach and be scintillating to this or that one, but in the end, as the whim changed, it appeared that nobody had yet learned to know her.

Then it happened that a rich young nobleman of that city heard tell of the many sorts of jests of the lady and understood her circumstances, discovering her beautiful and charming, found himself so fiercely enamoured of her that he was not able to turn his mind or his thoughts elsewhere, and knew that he was of more influence than others of the same mind, whilst more were of the belief that such was not becoming to her, or her charms, which appeared more angelic than mortal.

And so her new lover turned over such matters as this in his mind, and all the accounts of her he had been told, pondering in joy or sadness according to whether he hoped or despaired, he decided to attain her love by any way which would be possible. Wherefore he arranged to pass often along the street where she resided, and always when he discovered her at the door he bowed most affectionately and then, whether on foot or horseback he would halt and engage in discussion with her. And although he would not dare to disclose his feelings to her, the eyes and passionate sighs spoke for him. She, who was perceptive and malicious and as not particularly amused to be courted, was perhaps more affected by his making eyes every time he was looking, and resorted little by little to showing him that she was displeased with him.

The young man had a sister who lived close by the house of his beloved. And because it is not for me to tell, out of proper respect, their true names, and having also gained the silence of the town, let us call the sister of the young man Barbara, and the other let us call Eleanor. It was Barbara who lived as a widow and brought up a tiny son, which since the death of her husband was alone very rich, while she remained absolute mistress, and the young man, who will be called Pompeio, going to his sister's house, was forced to pass in front of Eleanor's residence.

This Pompeio was looked upon with the greatest favour, the more so that his sister was more domesticated than Eleanor with whom she associated.

Now there was a day when he dared to show all his love to his inamorata, begging that she should show pity and accept his service, and saying many things such as is the way of those in love. The lady, who did not take heed of any man in the world, but did not judge to taunt Pompeio as he was among the first citizens in the town, made clear to him that another lady should be sought, and more in this vein should not be said to her.

The young man, not discouraged by this, still continued to follow her, and on all occasions that arose, to go on as before. But she showed herself always more and more hard and withdrawn to him. For his part, he found himself half desperate.

Whilst matters were in this state, it happened one day that Pompeio understood by chance how Eleanor's husband had gone to his country house, being towards the end of June. Perhaps it occurred to him to go and speak with the lady and to seek to render her pliant to his amorous protestation. Without thinking too much about it, he would mount his mule, which his servants would bring to her house, send them with the mule to await him at the house of his sister, enter the house at the hour of nine and make love boldly and in security.

He was fairly fortunate because the lady, who since midday had not been sleeping, was in a ground-floor room, as it happened, by a door which entered upon the main hall, where indeed she was then engaged with her silken needlework. He, entering the house and meeting nobody, went directly to the hall, and here saw the lady before he was seen by her, and entered in her direction. She raised her head, saw the young man and was completely dismayed, because she was alone and all the house slept. Whereupon, before he could speak, she said: "Oh, Pompeio, what has brought you alone at this time?" He, making a deep bow, replied to her that having learned that her husband had gone to the country house, had wished to visit her and to hold discourse with her for a while, and that without being seen he had sent his attendants to his sister's house, and had entered in. When he wished to start upon the story of his love, she, interrupting him, said: "Oh! to what danger you put your life and mine! and in what balance do you weigh my honour at this moment? Because my husband has not gone away from the town, and will not be long in returning, since he has gone on a certain errand and must now be on his way back. Oh, pray, Pompeio, if you care for me, if you love my honour at all, leave here. Otherwise my heart trembles in my breast at the thought of seeing my husband at any moment." She had only just said this when her husband was heard speaking in the street, in a voice she recognised and so did Pompeio. The lady was trembling with fear, and Pompeio also trembled not knowing what to do. Before dismounting from his horse, the husband remained outside the door in discussion with someone. In this situation, at her helpful advice, he made up a hiding-place in a great chest in the self-same room where Pompeio had found her, and with some clothing which was there they covered him so well that no one was able to notice him, and she commanded him not to move away on any account.

She then awoke one of her maids who was sleeping in a little ante-room.

Having dismounted, her husband entered the hall. Eleanor, making a good countenance, said with a firm voice: "Who is that? Who comes?" The husband replied, and having done so entered the chamber and seated himself on the bed, saying meanwhile "My dear, I have bought a thin-bladed sword from a poor countryman, the best and the finest in this city, and perhaps another such could not be found for many miles. I thought to have it a little better tempered, then to make for it a fine scabbard of velvet and then give it to our friend Captain Brusco, which would certainly make a man such as he better armed than ever. And saying these things as if to make her remember, and showing it to his wife he said: "Here it is; look if you have ever seen the like of it". The lady replied, smiling jokingly: 'I have not thought much about such matters, which are not a woman's trade, nor do I intend them to be so, and so I would not know how to tell you of their quality, except that from reputation and adornment it seems to me fine. But I do not know what you wish to do with so much arms and equipment, so much of which you have in your room, and yet not be able to cut a cream-cheese with three strokes of your swords or scimitars. It would be better to buy other things and spend your money on things of greater profit."

"Quite so," he replied, "I will buy the bonnets and all those other gew-gaws which you must have every day; new styles of hat, new collars, and new covers fringed with gold on the carriage, with four fine steeds from the Kingdom of Naples or four incomparably decorated Frisian horses."

"Yes, yes," added the lady, "you men always say evil things of the ladies and contradict them. These little things suit us and are of our quality. If we adorn ourselves in a slip-shod way, without art helping natural beauty, you others will make jokes at our expense and say that we are unwashed, dressed like peasants or for the kitchen. Then when you see someone better adorned, even were she not beautiful and even with a painted face, you all run after her like billy-goats. You will know that I know you. But in matters of arms what do you ever do? It seems from the weapons you have you should be imperial captain, yet I have already said that you could not slice a cream-cheese."

"So let it be," the husband said, "I must have arms of wax or be frozen rigid. In heaven's name, I would cut a horse in two pieces with one blow of this blade, it is so keen and well made!" At this the wife smiled, rose to her feet, and betook herself close to where Pompeio was concealed, and laying her hand on top of one of her dresses of crimson velvet under which the lover was hidden, said to the husband: "I would like to wager with you any nice thing that you will not cut this garment in two strokes where I now have my hand," — and she had her hand over the legs of Pompeio. It was thus in this moment that it entered the lady's imagination to give the lover a grave fright, and it was to this end that she was inviting her husband to cut the garment, and not heeding the consequences. You will, however, imagine what must have passed through the mind of Pompeio, hearing what the lady was saying, and feeling more dead than alive, and was near to jumping out and revealing himself. But finding himself alone and not having a weapon with which to defend himself, and hearing that the husband was in the room with the servants and had the sword in hand, all he could do was stay there unhappily, for it appeared to him that his head was on the chopping-block and there was a ruffian with a chopper above him.

Turning over these various things in mind, and thinking also that he had so much clothing over him that it did not seem possible to be cut in two at once, he remained with trembling heart, awaiting the outcome of these whims of Eleanor in an icy-cold sweat. Then however he heard the lady say to her husband, what would he wish to wager that he would not sever the garments. The husband said to her, "Wife, I do not know how I profit either you or me by wreaking destruction on your dresses, for they would all be damaged. So let us make the test in some other way, as you would like me to cut with whatever sword what not even a razor would cut."

"Let us wager, let us wager," replied the lady, "on this dress, that if you cut it, I will have made for you a gown of golden brocade, richer than riches, and if you are not able to cut it you will have made for me a dress of white satin."

She had herself some income of her own, by an inheritance which had been left by an aunt and from which no small profit derived; with this she could wager freely with her husband. He, believing simply that his lady planned to see the proof of the much-praised sword, then put aside any argument, rose from his seat, raised his arm and said, "Tell me, lady, where do you want me to strike and cut?" She had, as this was said, her hand on the dress directly by his legs, and she now lifted its position against Pompeio's thighs, and said, "Cut here, if you have the will to succeed with honour."

"You are judging me or teasing me — as for my will I am going to satisfy that desire at once."

"Then I am obliged to say it is from better judgement than I would have for me," she added, "but perhaps it could be too easily cut there, but not perhaps here," — and she placed her hand over the chest of the concealed lover, and then from the chest put it on the middle of the neck and said: "Come now! cut here, where there is the yellow ribbon." Nevertheless she kept her hand there. The husband then being himself in a state ready to strike, said to her: "Move over there, if you want me to show you what the sword can do, and you will see a real blow for once."

There were other robes above and below Pompeio. Regarding these, smiling, she said to him, "In good faith, I believe your eagerness is so great that you would ruin all these dresses. Come, come! When you have done that, I do not know if I would have any others. I don't want the strength of your arm to be demonstrated just now on all my dresses." And with these and other words she guided her husband out of the room, and he mounted his horse and went off to the city in search of pleasure.

She, having sent her ladies away from the house on various errands, entered the chamber and uncovered the poor lover, who was more dead than alive, and she unburdened herself of her condemnations a thousand times over. And then, he being uncovered, she smiled at him and said, "Now be on your way and see to your own affairs, and do not molest me any more in the cause of love, because every time you come to this house to woo me in this way I will pay you in the same coin, or worse."

Pompeio recovered some spirit. "My lady," he replied, "do not blame a man for too much love: I have been driven to this." And not wishing to provoke her to further words, he parted in a conflict of love and disdain.

Thinking in what way he could possess her love and be revenged of the lady, a strange idea came into his mind, and not waiting on events, he greeted and followed the lady as before, and she, when she saw him, was moved to laugh, remembering how she had treated him.

Not long after, it came about that Eleanor's husband left Lombardy and went to Rome, where Pompeio knew he would stay for a few months and not leave, so Pompeio feigned to be ill, and let it be known around the city that his illness was grave. Thus he remained closed up in his room having a solemn doctor in attendance who did whatever Pompeio wished. He also took the precaution of advising his sister, the lady Barbara. She one day invited Eleanor to dine with her, and the latter accepted willingly, because they were on close terms.

Whilst they were dining and discussing Pompeio's illness, a servant came in and addressed her in these terms:

"Signora, a strange accident has just befallen your brother — he has lost the gift of speech."

"Alas," she replied, "have the coach made ready."

Lady Eleanor comforted her and offered to go with her, so leaving the other ladies to dine at the house, they both mounted the carriage, and sinking into its seats they went in haste to Pompeio's house.

He was in bed in a very dark room. Entering the room the two ladies approached the bed and the sister said to him, "Brother, be of good cheer, here is the lady Eleanora come to visit you." He, with the faintest of voices, uttered a few broken phrases which were meaningless and showed him to be very ill indeed. The servants, as they had been told, left the two ladies with their master; the lady Barbara, not appearing to know what she was doing, cleverly slipped through the door and closed it. When the cunning young man confirmed that he had trapped his cruel beloved, he leaped from the bed and throwing his arms around her neck, said to her: "You are my prisoner." She wished to escape his grasp, but she struggled in vain. He, holding her firmly opened a window. The lady was weeping knowing that he would not let her call out and hotly blamed the lady Barbara, calling her disloyal and treacherous. The young man comforted her as best he could with amorous words, telling her to set her mind at rest because it was his intention that they should lie together, and that she would never escape from his hands until he had his wish and had been avenged of the harsh and terrifying joke which she had played on him against all conventions of society. But now things would be different, of this he was resolved. She by no means wished to concede submission, and being, as she was, proud, stubborn and strong, she flew into a rage full of scorn and anger, and would not yield at all. Then unrestrainedly weeping, and without help or succour against her vengeful lover, she wished to escape.

Pompeio, when in due course she gave up her weeping and wild lamentation, and in spite of her, took her into his arms and kissed her many times on the lips and breast, and began once again to remind her of his protestation, saying: "You know for how long I have been your slave, and that there is nothing in the whole world be it however difficult, I would not have done for your love. You looked favourably upon me and showed that it was pleasant to you that I should serve you. And because it seemed that there was never the right time or the right means to manifest to you my most fervent adoration, and because of you I was deprived of all peace and repose, having lost the need for food or even sleep, I resolved to sieze upon whatever opportunity arose when I was told that your consort had gone away to his villa. Thus trembling and burning with desire I came to find you. You must remember the manner in which you treated me, and that which you did against all customs. And if by chance you can imagine the extreme anguish your haughtiness and pride caused, you must believe that I have not forgotten it, indeed on the contrary it is written on my heart, and I remember all the time that you, without my having deserved it, punished me at the risk of my life. You should not have used such methods towards me, but realised as I realised that I was in love with you, and if my love did not please you, you could have given me the decent leave that I should turn my mind elsewhere. So I intended to take that revenge which appeals to me. And knowing that you would not have come from your house to mine, I devised a plan to have you brought here by a trick, and now, being here, do me the great favour and tell me that you cannot turn me away."

Finally, after many arguments, she was persuaded to undress and enter the bed with her lover, where their arguments were love-play and each touch a discovery. Thus Pompeio was satisfied that the love-making had pleased her just as he had desired. Finally, after these amorous preliminaries, Pompeio opened one of the doors of the chamber and caused the lady to enter into another room, most richly appointed, in the middle of which there was a bed worthy of any great gentleman. There were four mattresses of down with the finest of sheets all embroidered with silk and gold. The coverlet was of crimson satin decorated with golden thread, with fringes of crimson silk richly interwoven with golden thread. There were four beautifully worked pillow-cases. Curtains of cloth-of-gold with crimson stripes encircled the rich bed. The room, hung with crimson velvet and marvellously richly appointed, contained a tasteful table covered with a silk cloth. There could be seen eight beautifully inlaid chests positioned around the room. There were also four armchairs covered in crimson velvet and some marvellously framed pictures from the hand of Leonardo da Vinci.

Into this room the lady Barbara had arranged for about twenty-five of the leading young men of the town to come. Knowing this, Pompeio, who had already laid the lady in the bed and covered her face with a rich veil, and perfumed the shining wood of the room with tamarisk, hyacinth and other odours, drew back the curtains, telling the lady not to make the slightest movement whatever she should hear.

This being done, he, elegantly attired and of completely cheerful countenance, entered the drawing-room and gracefully welcomed the assembled gentlemen. They all marvelled at how he was, he whom they had taken to be gravely ill. Possibly he could very easily recognise their wonder and spoke to them in this manner:

"Gentlemen and friends, I believe that all of you must be amazed that I, whom only a short time ago you believed to be gravely ill, should show such health. It is true that I have been very sick and in peril of my life; but today I took a salutary medicine which has, as you see, cured me. And perhaps so that all of you can take displeasure at my sickness, I wished to gladden you with my presence. I should like all of you to see that salutary medicine which has restored me to health, in which connection I would like you to pledge me your trust so that you will not be disturbed at anything I may do."

With this he introduced them into the chamber. It seemed to them that they had entered into a paradise, so beautiful was the place and so sweet the scent which was disseminated. The lady, who had heard the people and perhaps even knew the voice of a relative or one of her household, remained utterly trembling, not knowing what Pompeio wanted to do. As soon as all had praised the arrangements and wanted to see who should be lying in the bed, Pompeio said:

"In this bed, sirs, is the precious and salubrious medicine which has today cured me, and which I intend to show you — but little by little."

This said, avoiding the disclosure of the countenance, he, with the help of his servant, lifted away carefully the coverlet from the bed, so that the lady remained covered only by an extremely thin sheet which scarcely concealed any part of the delicate and feminine form. Pompeio then lifted the sheet a little disclosing two small, very white and well-proportioned feet, with the ivory toes showing long and smooth and the nails resembling pearls. Nor did he linger in showing most of the legs. The lady being stretched out, at the appearance of the delicate legs and limbs, the onlookers thought to awaken her as she slept. Pompeio asked them what they thought of this medicine. Each one totally commended it and wanted to taste it. In respect of which he, with part of the sheet, hiding that which dwelt between her legs, revealed all the breast as far as the throat, the which to the onlookers was miraculously delightful, because being of a most beautifully formed body, the breasts were beautiful beyond belief. Everybody gazed with incredulous delight at the raised and shining white breasts, with the round, firm nipples, which appeared to be formed of alabaster — with no less delight because, as she was trembling, they showed a certain undulation. They were all waiting to see the angelic face, when Pompeio suddenly replaced the covering over the exposed limbs and led the gentlemen into the drawing room where the lady Barbara had arranged to have prepared some fruit of the season, sweetmeats and the finest of wines. After eating and drinking and talking of various matters they left one by one. Whilst the sweetmeats were being eaten, the lady Barbara entered where the lady Eleanor was still lying in bed, and said to her:

"My lady, is my brother still to be scorned?" Then she, crying, begged her to let her take the blame for the deception which she greatly regretted. Pompeio appeared, saluted her and said: "My lady, we are about even. In any case reason argues that yours is the blame" — and then he soothed her with many words. And having already enjoyed the embraces of her lover and found them more delicious than those of her husband, she let the anger pass away and behaved in such a manner that they enjoyed their love for a long time, and she, playing no more practical jokes on anyone, became pleasant and extremely courteous.

And so, my dear ladies, learn not to play jokes on others, if you do not wish them to be returned perhaps twofold.

[Note: A translation of Toller's play by Alexander Henderson appeared in *8 New One-Act Plays of 1935* Ed. John Bourne. London, 1935.]

B THE SECOND EDITION OF *DIE MASCHINENSTÜRMER*

(Spalek 34)

(I am grateful to the Librarian of the University of Birmingham for allowing his library's copy to be made available for me in Manchester).

The book does not announce itself as the second edition, but simply as fifth to tenth thousand. The first edition was of 1,000 copies, and the second impression, 3,000 copies, was also published before the first production (1). The text of the play in the two impressions is identical (2). The next 6,000, however, present "a thoroughly revised version of the play", (3) which incorporates, as Spalek rather non-commitally expresses it, "changes which are most probably the results of the staging of the play" (4). In the Bibliography Spalek refers to "numerous deletions, additions, and rearrangements, all of them designed to make the language of the play less rhetorical and descriptive and more dramatic" (5). I fail to see upon what evidence Spalek bases this comment. His account of specific changes is so shockingly inaccurate that one is bound to speculate whether this normally meticulous scholar did not entrust the reading of this edition to an unreliable assistant. On the basis of what he calls "the improvements", he says that "the second edition must be considered the authoritative edition of the play" (6). He must have modified this opinion later, for GW, edited by himself and Wolfgang Frühwald, uses the text of the first edition — rightly, it will be argued here.

The major changes are:

1. Act III Sc. 1 of 1st Edition has been moved to form Sc. 1 of Act V (7).
2. The Overseer in the final scene is Henry Cobbett. The crude brutality of the Overseer is clearly out of character for Henry.
3. Many of the *First Woman's* lines have been given to Margaret. As a consequence the wife / mother figure of the 1st Edition becomes the "robust rabble-rousing woman" described by Max Osborn (8).
4. Albert, whose mental instability has been carefully prepared (especially when Act III Sc. 3 was in its original position), does not go mad: his madness is given to the Engineer, who has been presented as a rational technician. A certain facile and melodramatic symbolic effect may be gained by this, but character and dramatic logic have been destroyed (9).
5. The touches of ritualism, antiphony and religious symbolism have

been enlarged:

a) In Act I, seven extra speeches have been added to the *Litany*.
b) The Weavers' Song, which originally appeared only in Act I [3 verses] and Act III Sc. 4 [1 verse], now occurs also in Act II Sc. 2, Act III Sc. 4 [of 1st Edition: now Sc. 3], and on the exeunt of the weavers in the final scene of the play.
c) The latter part of Act V Sc. 1 [now Act V Sc. 2] is expanded and re-written with additional imagery: the Beggar weaves a crown of straw and places it on Jimmy's head — a piece of 'Christ' symbolism less subtle than what is found in the first edition.

6. Klaus Pringsheim's music for the Weavers' Song, as used in the production, is printed in the first act where the song first occurs. The new stanza which appears in the 1st Edition in Act III Sc. 4, and which does not exactly fit the music, has been replaced by the first stanza in Act I. The second stanza in Act I has also been re-written.
7. Jimmy's speech in Act III Sc. 2 (GW 147) which calls for picketing at the factory gate, and thus relates to the Trades Union theme in the play, is replaced by one which presents Jimmy as a tactical revolutionary:

> Es wundert dich, daß ich mit Ure verhandeln will? Laß dir den Grund sagen. Wir müssen heute dem Entscheidungskampf ausweichen. Trieben wir es heute zum entscheidenden Kampf, die Niederlage wäre gewiß. Sie schwächte unsere Kraft. Der Entscheidungskampf kommt, wenn das Volk in England bereit ist. Dann, Kamerad, verhandeln wir nicht mehr! (10).
>
> (It surprises you that I will negotiate with Ure? Tell yourself why: today we must avoid the decisive struggle. If we carried it today as far as the decisive struggle, defeat would be certain. It would weaken our strength. The decisive struggle is coming, when the people of England are ready. Then, comrade, we won't negotiate any more!)
>
> And further on in the scene these two lines are introduced:
> WIBLE: So willst du Maschinenknechtschaft?
> JIMMY: Ich will die Revolution! (11)
> (WIBLE: So you want slavery to the machine?
> JIMMY: I want the revolution!)

There are also many minor changes. Most of these are of the kind that might occur during rehearsals. Some simplify or clarify the language, some are neutral — things that could just have happened in one particular production but need not be permanently incorporated in the text. Some changes in stage directions clearly refer to production: e.g. when *BLACKOUT* becomes *CURTAIN*.

The examination of the critiques and programmes which we undertake in the main text of this chapter shows, (1) that some of the changes are definitely derived from the production, and (2) that not all changes made in production were incorporated in the text. Notably the big 'operatic-chorus' entrance immediately before the machine wrecking scene and described by Michel is not incorporated.

I believe it is safe to conclude that ALL the changes in the 2nd edition text are derived from the production. If Toller himself was indeed able to supervise the revision from prison (which cannot be proved) it is surprising that he admitted so many changes that blurred or distorted his original intention — especially as they are derived from a production he had not seen and could not see.

In an undated letter to Elsbeth B., probably written in July 1923, Toller wrote:

> Sie sprechen von den "Maschinenstürmern". Ich bin für Verschandelungen, melodramatische Versüßlichungen, Regie-Rotstifte nicht verantwortlich und habe, solange ich hier gefangen sitze, keinen Einfluß auf die Art der Darstellung (12).
> (You speak of the Machine Wreckers. I am not responsible for ruination, melodramatic sugariness or Directors' red-pencils, and I have, so long as I'm imprisoned here, no influence over the kind of presentation).

Although it is not certain to which production Toller is referring the probability is that it is to Karl-Heinz Martin's (13). If Toller so disliked what he understood to have been done to his play by Martin, it is highly improbable that he would have incorporated Martin's alterations in a definitive text. The conclusion is that the text of the First Edition must be therefore be regarded as authoritative.

NOTES

1. Spalek p. 39.
2. ibid p. 40.
3. ibid p. 41.
4. ibid p. 39.

5. ibid p. 41.
6. ibid p. 42.
7. Spalek (p 41) wrongly says it is deleted and a new scene written for Act V Sc. 1.
8. Berliner Morgenpost 13.7.22, and Rühle p.387.
9. Spalek incorrectly, and indeed absurdly, says:"the logic of the arguments in Act V has been significantly improved by assigning some of Albert's speeches in behalf of the machine to the Engineer" (p. 42).
10. 2nd Edition p. 54.
11. ibid. p 55.
12. GW5, p. 159.
13. By July 1923 the play had been produced in Erfurt (October 1922), Moscow (November 1922) and London (May 1923); but the most recent and accessible production — and thus the one most likely to have been seen by Toller's correspondent — was Karl-Heinz Martin's revival of his original production in Vienna in June 1923.

C TOLLER'S CONTRIBUTIONS TO THE *LEIPZIGER MASSENFESTSPIELE*

In the early years of the Weimar Republic the working-class socialists of Leipzig regarded the five annual *Massenfestspiele (Mass Festival Plays)* as being numbered among their greatest experiences, and this opinion is shared even by a Marxist commentator highly critical of their ideologies (1). Three of the *Massenfestspiele* were based on outlines provided by Toller from prison, but, as Toller's own scripts do not survive it is inappropriate to deal with these works in the body of this book: we can no longer determine the degree of his responsibility for the actual performances.

From as early as 1879 the Leipzig *Arbeiter-Verein* (leader Friedrich Bosse) had developed cultural and educational activities (libraries, choirs, sport-and theatre-groups) among the working class, culminating in the founding of a theatre audience organisation on the model of the Berlin *Volksbühne,* in December 1899. This soon developed, especially after the founding in April 1907 of the Workers' Educational Institute (*Arbeiter-Bildungs-Institut: ABI*), into one of the strongest Volksbühne organisations in Germany, while the ABI itself was able to carry through cultural and educational work as a whole on a significantly broader basis (2).

These movements were primarily led and supported by non-Marxist socialists of the kind who broke away from the Social Democratic Party (SPD) after the Erfurt conference of 1891 to form the short-lived *Verein unabhängiger Sozialisten (League of Independent Socialists)*, the forerunner of the *Unabhänginge Sozialdemokratische Partei Deutschlands (German Independent Social Democratic Party: USPD)* founded in April 1917, which Toller supported.

To appreciate the nature of Toller's three contributions to the *Massenfestspiele* some knowledge of the first two is necessary.

1. *Spartakus* 1920

Produced on the Cottaweg Cycle-racing Track (64,000m^2) for the Trades Union Festival on 1.8.1920. Repeated by popular demand on 2.8.1920. Conceived and directed by Joseph von Fielitz (actor and director, Leipzig Schauspielhaus). Cast of 900+. Audience of 50,000.
The whole area was used for the performance, plus:

1. A platform 20m × 10m, 3/4m high, with 3 steps on longer side, set in the middle of the grassed area.
2. Opposite the main grandstand, a giant stairway, 40m broad at its foot and narrowing to 25m broad above. Platforms at the sides and in the middle. The stairway began at the inner edge of the concrete race-track and ended on the upper edge of the audience-embankment. The stairway represented the way "to Rome".

The play portrayed through mass-movement and spectacle a simplified history of the slaves' revolt under Spartacus in 73 B.C. The topical significance and the parallel with the defeat of the "Spartacists" under the leadership of Rosa Luxemburg and Karl Liebknecht in January of the previous year, were, of course, obvious. There were four scenes:

1. Twilight. Messengers of victory; solemn sacrifices; procession of triumphant army and captive slaves. Slave market.
2. Patrician Victory Festival; procession of Bacchantes; slaves at labour, whipped and kicked. Exeunt patricians, drunk; slaves threaten, try to follow; collapse. Song of revenge, individual speakers call for revolt.
3. Roman Citizens' Festival; dance of priests and priestesses; gladiatorial contest to be held on centre platform. Slaves refuse to fight each other. Revolt; many patricians and others killed. Slaves advance "to Rome". Fire. Legionaries defeat slaves. Slave leaders captured.

4. Long procession of priests, legionaries, patricians, senate, citizens. Rebels in the midst, carrying their crosses. Crosses erected on embankment; slaves bound to them: Spartacus centre on largest cross. The citizens go. Slaves throw themselves down before the crosses. A powerful song of revenge ends the play.

The play was almost entirely visual, apart from the songs and the speeches of rebel leaders; and the visual aspect consisted primarily of the movements of masses of people, not of individuals. This was an effective means of communication in the circumstances of a mass audience in the open air.

2. *Der Arme Konrad (Poor Conrad)* 1921
Subtitled: Ein Volksspiel in Vier Bildern (A Folk-play in Four Scenes)

Produced on the Cottaweg Cycle-Racing Track for the Trades Union Festival 14.8.1921. (Because of heavy rain a performance without costumes etc was given on the day of the festival, and a full-dress performance the following day).
Artistic Direction: Josef von Fielitz, assisted by Emma Grondona, Herbert vom Hau and Werner Ladwig.
Music Composed by Werner Ladwig.
Gustav-Schütze Orchestra conducted by Werner Ladwig.
Costumes: Dresden Landstheater and Leipzig Schauspielhaus.
Properties: Leipzig Stadttheater.
Setting: Giant stairway, as for *Spartakus,* about 50m broad, backed by a "city wall" with 4 Gothic "gateways" with black masks behind them. 3 of the 4 gateways had figures over them representing the 3 exploiting classes of the Middle Ages: the Knights, the Clerics and the Lords of the Manor. The 4th gateway was the gate of the "Lord over All" — Death. 5m in front of the stairway was a stage 50cm high.
Lighting: white, green and red floodlights.
Cast of 1,800 +.

This play of the Peasants' Revolt, like *Spartakus,* strongly suggested contemporary parallels. It had a Prologue and four scenes:

PROLOGUE
THE DANCE OF DEATH
With appropriate music this scene presented just what its title suggests: a Dance of Death involving all states and conditions of people.

1. THE COUNCIL OF THE ESTATES
A grand festival of the high ranks; strife between towns-people and peasants; humiliating comic punishment (duelling with broom-sticks.)

2. POOR CONRAD
The peasants go in and out of the three gates of the exploiters, finally going through Death's Gate, worn out. Agitators rouse the crowd. The *Bundschuh,* symbol of revolt, is raised. They storm the walls and tear down the 3 figures over the 3 gates. But Death still looks on.

3. THE EMPEROR'S POWER
The Emperor, surrounded by nobility etc. Peasant deputation carry in the flag of 'Poor Conrad'. At the Chancellor's command the soldiers drive them back. The Peasant Army attacks the soldiers, but the soldiers have the victory.

4. THE "BLOODY ASSIZES"
The Emperor's power holds judgement over the rebels. They are punished in various barbarous ways. The remaining peasants still smoulder with revolt. Death enters and leads *everyone* — the Emperor last of all — through Death's Gate.

The show was most impressive. Impressive above all was the skill with which Fielitz and his colleagues "fused the huge mass of 1,800 into a single organic body" (3); but the fatalism of the conclusion and the triumph of Death, however true to a sixteenth century *Weltanschauung,* was felt by the same critic to contradict the revolutionary hopes of the workers. Revolution and the Dance of Death were incompatible.

From these two *Massenspiele* two things had been clearly demonstrated for future productions: 1) that such a show must be primarily visual, with broad effects, mass choreography, brilliant but simple lighting , music and only occasional spoken words, 2) that despite the parallelisms of *Spartakus* and *Der arme Konrad* with contemporary events, the ideal material for a mass play in this context had yet to be found.

It was at this point that Toller, close to the organisers ideologically, but cut off in prison from any opportunity for experiencing the practical working of a *Massenfestspiel,* and himself primarily an artist in language, was brought in. His three *Massenspiele* must be examined both individually and as a sequence.

1.
Bilder Aus Der Grossen Französischen Revolution (Scenes from the Great French Revolution) 1922
Subtitle: Historische Folge in Fünfzehn Bilder (Historical Sequence in fifteen scenes)

(Note that Toller uses the word *Bild* (literally: *Picture*), rather than *Szene*. This strongly suggests that he set out with the intention of working through visual means, though of course it is not unusual to use the word *Bild* to mean *Scene*.)
The work is described as *entworfen (sketched out)* by Toller.
Overall Artistic Direction: Dr. Kronacher, Intendant of the Leipzig Schauspielhaus, who also edited the text.
Artistic Direction: Dr Winds
Gustav Schütze directed the music, with his own orchestra.
Dances arranged by Emma Grondona.
Costumes and Properties kindly lent by the Leipzig Schauspielhaus and Städtisches Theater.

In providing even an outline for a proletarian mass-play, Toller, whose plays and poetry until now (including his latest play, *Die Maschinenstürmer*) had been dominated thematically by conflicts within revolutionary movements and by his own closely related subjective problems, faced a completely new challenge. Neither his private voice nor his private problems could contribute to this new work, which demanded his public voice in treating of public questions and which must be designed to inspire and encourage a mass working-class audience.

In *Die Maschinenstürmer* he had for the first time chosen to create a play out of historical material. In doing so he had quite consciously followed the example and tradition of Schiller in freely altering historical fact in order the more effectively to make his point.

Wisely, and in this respect following not only his personal line of development as a playwright, but also the examples of *Spartakus* and *Der arme Konrad*, he chose historical material for his first mass-play. In choosing the use material from the *French* revolution he was also following the example of Büchner who in *Dantons Tod* (1835) wrote about the French Revolution with German problems in mind. He was probably also influenced in his choice by what he must have read about Reinhardt's magnificently staged production of Romain Rolland's revolutionary *Danton* at the Großes Schauspielhaus in February 1920. Indeed, the *Massenspiele* themselves were firmly rooted in contemporary fashion, their style and staging owing much both to Reinhardt and to Expressionism, as well as to the interest of the amateur movement in older and simpler forms of theatre (4).

Toller's scenario covered the first period of the French Revolution, from the summoning of the States General on 5 May 1789 until the execution of the King on 21 January 1793. This period was obviously chosen because during that period the divisions on the revolutionary side were not yet apparent: the straightforward development of the revolution to the point of initial success — the proclamation of the Republic — was most suitable for the occasion. A play about the later period, with the clashes between the Girondists and Jacobins, or a new 'Danton' play, would have re-embodied the themes already treated in *Masse Mensch* and *Die Maschinenstürmer*, would have been more complex to portray through the *Massenspiel* medium, and above all, would have lacked the rather simple inspirational quality which the Festival required.

The message of the mass-play, as expressed in the programme / brochure, was:

> Unüberwindlich ist die Kraft der Masse, wenn sie von elementarer Begeisterung, unerschütterlichem Kampfeswillen und aufopferungsvoller Hingabe an das Gemeinwohl getragen wird (5).
> (The power of the masses, when it is sustained by elemental enthusiasm, unshakeable will to struggle and self-sacrificial devotion to the common good, is invincible).

This being the aim it was reasonable to depict the French Revolution as having been a proletarian revolution instead of what it was historically, viz. a bourgeois revolution carried out with proletarian support. As in *Die Maschinenstürmer* Toller was prepared to present history anachronistically for the sake of his immediate theatrical aim — in this case, inspiration.

In the very first scene, in which the class-situation of the period is symbolically expounded, the bourgeoisie is equated with the nobility and the clergy, the three being represented as three horsemen of the

Apocalypse against whom the people (*Volk*) struggle. The leaders of the people tear the masks from the faces of the horsemen with cries of, "Liberty, Equality, Fraternity!" The horsemen raise their knouts against the people, who are thus seen as carrying through the revolution against the bourgeoisie, nobility and clergy — a twentieth century image, if one allows that nobility and clergy still exercised considerable power in a Germany of bourgeois capitalism.

Marxist criticism has inevitably interpreted Toller's unhistoricity in a far more sinister way: because the French Revolution was historically a bourgeois revolution leading to a bourgeois republic, the bourgeois republic was propagated in the play as a goal worthy to be striven for by the proletarian movement. This, argues the Marxist critic, corresponded with the theory and practice of the SPD leadership, who wanted the Weimar Republic (regarded by the Communist Party as rightist and bourgeois) to be seen as the sole heir of the November Revolution and as <u>the</u> appropriate state for the workers (6).

To impute such a motive to Toller is, of course, ludicrous, and Pfützner avoids making the direct imputation by claiming that we cannot know today (writing in 1960) whether the unhistoricity was by design or ignorance (!), nor how to apportion responsibility between the committee of the ABI, the Trades Unions and Toller himself (7).

As with *Sprechchöre*, so with *Massenspiele*, the Marxist demands instruction rather than inspiration as the aim, and so this mass-play is criticised for being what it intends to be, and not something else: it was a question of presenting "Pictures" of the popular movement of the period (albeit false pictures) rather than conveying certain political insights to the onlookers through historical examples (8).

Like its two predecessors this mass-play operated primarily through mass visual effects (this time with no fewer than 3,000 actors, dancers and singers) though it was inevitable that the involvement of the poet Toller would lead to the spoken word's having greater importance. Even so, language was sparingly used and only at important nodal-points in the action or for brief agitational speeches. Even these, however, were barely intelligible, and it is very interesting that the critic of the Leipzig newspaper, anticipating the later practice of Brecht and Piscator, suggested the use of the written, rather than the spoken word in future mass-plays.

> So wie es im Kino geschieht. Eine weiße Wand, an die während der Pausen der Scheinwerfer in großen Lettern die Worte

> wirft, die im folgenden Bild vorkommen (9).
> (Just as is done in the cinema. [This was still the period of the silent film. CWD]. A white screen, upon which, during the intervals the spotlight throws in large letters the words which occur in the next scene.)

Unfortunately, as we shall see, neither Toller nor his collaborators took this advice.

The actual performance was given at the Probstheida Messegelände (Exhibition Area) and was staged similarly to the first two mass-plays, but this time the huge open-air stone stairway (60m wide and 20m deep: even larger than those built at the Cycle-racing Track) was already available on the eastern side of the Exhibition Area. Costumes and scenery were more lavish than ever, and at every phase of the play the appeal was to the eye of the audience both in variety of detail and in broad mass movements. Symbolism alternated with naturalism, mass-mime with scraps of dialogue and *Sprechchöre*. An account of some of the scenes will illustrate these points.

SCENE 1. Symbolic. See above.

SCENE 2. A sumptuous gala festival of Marie Antoinette with music and dancing. The common people are cowering below in the arena. Necker joins the festival. The people demand liberty and bread. Necker promises these.

SCENE 3. The Summoning of the States General. The Three Estates enter in a long procession, take their places according to an established ceremonial and await the king. The Third Estate, historically the Bourgeoisie, is here represented as being the People (*Volk*). This 'Third Estate' takes the first revolutionary step: after the king has been greeted with bared heads, the Third Estate put their hats on again.

SCENE 4. Broadsheet sellers inform the people of the progress of the National Assembly (10).

SCENE 5. The meeting having been broken up by royal

	troops, the National Assembly has to meet in the indoor tennis-court. Members swear to use all their powers to establish a republican constitution (11).
SCENE 6.	When the king sends troops a second time to break up the National Assembly, the people take up arms. "Desmoulins stands on a raised place in the arena, rousing the people in a powerful speech . . . Erupting with elemental force, the people storm out of the arena in order to storm the arsenals — not visible, but assumed to be behind the scenes — and, above all, the Bastille. The arena remains empty. A red, fiery glow, gunshots, canon-shots and the sound of bells indicate the off-stage fight between the armed people and the royalists . . . Jubilant cries of victory give the certainty that the people have conquered and that power is in their hands" (12).
SCENE 7.	Celebration of victory over the monarchy: predominantly dancing and music.
CLOSING SCENE	This represented the king's flight, capture and execution in symbolic form. "The stage is darkened (13). Suddenly the guillotine is seen in the background, in a red glow, with Death alongside as Executioner, a Jacobin cap on his skull, holding up the king's head in his raised hand. The stage becomes light. The vision disappears. The Convention members rise and cry solemnly, 'Long live the Republic!' . . . the assembled people join in the cry, 'Long live the Republic' (14).

As the overall plan and original text were by Toller, it is plain that he was able at this date to detach himself from his personal plight in prison and project his imagination into the most public of dramatic forms — the open-air mass-play. This was the period when he was preoccupied by the swallows in his cell and when his letters to Tessa are exceptionally personal and emotional (15). In this period of 'transition' from primarily subjective to primarily objective dramatic creation, Toller's creative powers were at a peak (16). Even though we cannot now know precisely what Toller set down for this play, the evidence available is enough to prove its power — politically, imaginatively and theatrically.

In the use of naturalistic and symbolic (Expressionist-style) scenes, in the development of grand visual effects from historical data, in his ability, isolated in a prison cell, to conceive a scenario for a cast of 3,000, he showed that he was able to deploy his artistic skills in very unfavourable circumstances, in a quite remarkable way.

2.
Krieg und Frieden
(War and Peace) 1923

Less information is available about this (which bears no relation to Tolstoy's novel) than about any of the other *Massenfestspiele*. There is one review and a few surviving pictures.

Performed 12 August 1923, again using the open-air stairway of the *Messengelände*.

Music by Didam.

Setting: five flagpoles bearing the flags of France, Russia, England, Austria and Germany. Exactly how these were arranged is in doubt (17). The seating was placed nearer to the open-air stage than the previous year, and the whole production was on a smaller scale.

THE ACTION

At each flag was a group representing the "masses" or the "army" of that nation. Apparently the leaders of each nation stood on the steps and the people below.

The five groups — which at the outbreak of war were deployed as armies — retained their separate identities until the end of the play, when they came together after the revolution in a festival of Joy and Fraternity.

The revolution — which was seen in the play as taking place simultaneously in all five countries — was brought about by agitators within each group. The five groups then stormed the "seat" of the military and civil leaders (presumably on the great stairs), and erected A Statue of Liberty around which was held the Festival.

We also learn that speech played an important part, the problem of audibility being partly overcome by the position of the seating and the smaller scale of the production. Toller's poetry is mentioned: and in the photographs some figures have typically rhetorical poses. Much use was made of blackouts:

> Darkness is a splendid member of the cast: it continually destroys pictures and begets new ones (18).

The music is said to have been a means of unification and intensification.

> As the reviewer justly remarks:
>
> It is not the end which the World War actually had, but it is the end that wars must have in the will and longing of proletarian people (19).

It was a conclusion of wishful thinking. The reviewer pointed out that "Toller's whole thought is rooted in the events of the World War" (20). Indeed, this play represents a retreat to the simple optimism of the conclusion of *Die Wandlung* and is evidently lacking even the tensions and struggles of that play's protagonist. It is as if Toller had forgotten Munich and wiped *Masse Mensch* and *Die Maschinenstürmer* out of his consciousness. Yet, strangely enough, *Krieg und Frieden,* which must have been shorter than the other mass-plays, was preceded by a scene (unfortunately we do not know which) from *Masse Mensch.*

3.
Erwachen
(Awakening) 1924

Described as being based on "motifs" by Toller, the surviving text must be considered to be by Dr Adolf Winds, Principal Director of the Magdeburg Municipal theatre, who had also directed Toller's first mass-play. The evidence for this is that the *Leipziger Volkszeitung* reviewer regretted that nothing of Toller's style survived.

The production on 3 August 1924 was intended as a high point in the first *Workers' Week of Culture* from 2 to 6 August, organised by the Workers Educational Institute. It was performed on and by the

Auensee (Lake Auen). In addition to a cast of 1,000 players the Leipzig Aquatic Sports organisations and Workers' Choir took part.

Toller, who had been released from Niederschönenfeld on 15 July, attended the Cultural Week and took part in putting the show on: how great a part it is impossible to know.

The multiple setting consisted of a wooden raft anchored in the lake, and two acting areas on the far side of the lake away from the audience. The raft was some 150m from the spectators and the areas on the lakeside a further 150m beyond. The raft represented an island rich in oil resources inhabited by savages and their Chiefs. The acting area to the left, as seen by the audience, was *Westreich (Western Empire)* and that to the right, *Ostreich (Eastern Empire).*

Like *Krieg und Frieden* this was primarily an anti-war, rather than a specifically socialist play. The action was thus:

Ostreich sent a fleet to the island offering only civilisation and culture in exchange for the oil. The natives declined the offer and the fleet returned home without having achieved anything. Westreich on the other hand offered schnaps and gold and soon came to an agreement, so that the island came into the possession of Westreich. Consequently the government of Ostreich declared war on Westreich. The two navies met, shot at each other and sank each other until only two boats survived. The crews of both boats then fraternised and raised the Red Flag. On land, too, a group of Reds incited the people against the government. When the two governments wanted to send troops against the rebels, the ships ran into port. The people drove out the governments, proposed a toast to Peace and set up a Palace of Peace on the oil-rich island. Ships and small boats with coloured lanterns paraded past the island. Formation swimmers with torches swam in patterns of figures and stars. The finale was a firework display.

The play was a complete flop. In spite of the huge distance between audience and players, it was made more dependent on the spoken word than any of its predecessors. Thousands of spectators, unable to hear a word and therefore unable to understand what the play was about, left early. Nor was the lighting powerful enough, and so, as the reviewer remarked, "we remained in the dark in every respect" (21).

Even had it been intelligible, however, this play lacked any real substance, having even less historical basis than *Krieg und Frieden*. In addition, the relationships between capitalism, colonialism, war and revolution were left unexplained and confused. It has been not unfairly described by two East German scholars as having degenerated into 'a mere aquatic spectacle' (22).

The sequence of three mass-plays, the latter two each bearing less relevance to reality than its forerunner, displays, in contrast with his principal, more wholly language-based works of the period (23), a decline in creative power and a retreat towards the over-facile optimism that preceded his Munich experiences, as well as towards the abstraction, generalisation, rhetoric and symbolism into which Expressionism had tended to fall.

After finding in the French Revolution material appropriate for the purposes of the Leipzig festival and fitting in with his own state of creative development, and after gaining strength, firmness and vitality in thus having to work from an historical basis, however freely treated (as he had also done in *Die Maschinenstürmer*) Toller allowed himself in the other two mass-plays, to evade the uncomfortable challenge of the facts of history and the other challenge of his own growing pessimism both as to the potential solubility of the most acute problems of the human condition, and as to the political future of Europe, and instead fell back, as it were, on the all-too-simple vision of Friedrich at the end of *Die Wandlung*.

In *Bilder aus der Großen Französischen Revolution* Toller found an outlet for what we are calling his 'public voice' just when he was about to produce the greatest work of his 'private voice', *Das Schwalbenbuch*. It would seem that he was able to bring his creative imagination, shown at its strongest in the highly personal sequence of poems, to bear on the requirements of a highly public dramatic form. But in *Krieg und Frieden* and *Erwachen* he permitted the supposed requirements of the workers' festival to stifle his imagination to such an extent that on the one hand he avoided posing the very moral and political questions which most deeply stimulated him as a writer, and on the other hand lost his imaginative grip upon the actual physical circumstances in which the plays were going to be performed.

Toller's *Massenfestspiele*, considered as a series, thus form a counterpoint to, or mirror-image of his progress as a theatre-dramatist and poet during the years when they were written.

Erwachen was the last of the Leipzig *Massenfestspiele*. They had lost their artistic strength and their hold upon the audience, but their demise may well have been in part for political rather than artistic reasons. The Workers' Educational Institute, which had been primarily influenced by the Independent Socialist Party, became in 1922 an institution of the SPD and then lost interest in the *Massenfestspiele.*

NOTES

1. Klaus Pfützner, *Die Massenfestspiele der Arbeiter in Leipzig (1920–1924)*, Leipzig, 1960, p. 5.
2. ibid. p. 7. But a somewhat different account is given in: A. Brodbeck, *Handbuch der Deutschen Volksbühnen-Bewegung*, Berlin, 1930, p. 296: In Leipzig nimmt das Arbeiter-Bildungs-Institut seit Jahren für seine zahlreiche Mitgliedschaft in den städtischen Theatern planmäßig Vorstellungen ab. Einige andere Leipziger Organisationen geben ebenfalls geschlossene Vorstellungen. 1926 wurde in Leipzig eine "Freie Volksbühne" gegrundet, die sich allerdings nicht entsprechend der Größe der Stadt entwickeln konnte. Verhandlungen mit dem Ziel, das Arbeiter-Bildungs-Institut umzuwandeln und das Institut dem Verband anzugliedern, konnten seither nicht zu einem positiven Ergebnis geführt werden, trotzdem die Leitung des Arbeiter-Bildungs-Institut dem Volksbühnengedanken durchaus freundlich gegenübersteht. Die Freie Volksbühne Leipzig gehört seit Frühjahr 1930 dem Verbande an.

   (For many years the Workers' Educational Institute in Leipzig has bought up scheduled performances in the municipal theatres for its numerous membership. Some other Leipzig organisations likewise give closed performances. In 1926 a "Freie Volksbühne" was founded in Liepzig, which, however, could not grow in proportion to the size of the city. Negotiations with the aim of changing the nature of the Workers' Educational Institute and affiliating it to the Association [i.e. of the Volksbühne movement. CWD] have not since that date been able to be led to a positive outcome, even though the leadership of the Workers' Educational Institute has taken an entirely favourable attitude to the Volksbühne concept. The Leipzig Freie Volksbühne has belonged to the Association since Spring 1930.)
3. *Leipziger Volkszeitung 16.8.1921.*
4. v. Cecil W. Davies *Working-Class Theatre in the Weimar Republic, 1929–1933: Part I.* In *Theatre Quarterly* No. 38. p. 80.
5. Quoted in Pfützner *op.cit.* p. 24.
6. ibid. p. 22.

7. ibid. pp. 21 & 22.
8. ibid p. 24.
9. ibid p. 24.
10. Formed by the Third Estate 17.6.1789 to frame a constitution. It existed until 30.9.1791.
11. Historically 20.6.1789.
12. Desmoulins steht in der Arena auf einer erhöhten Stelle, in mächtiger Rede das Volk aufpeitschend . . . Das Volk stürmt, elementar ausbrechend, aus der Arena, die hinter ihr angenommen, aber nicht mehr sichtbaren Waffendepots und vor allem die Bastille zu stürmen. Die Arena bleibt leer. Roter Feuerschein, Schüsse, Kanonenschüsse und Glockenläuten lassen den hinter der Szene sich abspielenden Kampf des bewaffneten Volkes mit den Royalisten ahnen . . . Brausendes Siegesgeschrei gibt die Gewißheit, daß das Volk gesiegt hat und die Macht in seinen Händen ist. (Programmzettel zu *Bilder aus der Großen Französischen Revolution,* p. 3, quoted by Pfützner, op. cit. p. 23).
    Historically the date represented is 14.7.'89.
13. Like the earlier mass-plays, this one evidently began at dusk.
14. Die Bühne verdunkelt sich, im Hintergrund sieht man plötzlich im roten Schein die Guillotine, daneben den Tod als Henker, auf dem Schädel die Jaconbinermütze, in hochgehaltener Hand den Kopf des Königs. Die Bühne wird hell, die Vision verschwindet. Der Konvent erhebt sich und ruft feierlich: 'Es lebe die Republik!' . . . Das versammelte Volk stimmt ein in den Ruf: 'Es lebe die Republik!'. (Programmzettel, q. by Pfützner *op. cit.* p.22. Historical date of the king's execution: 21.1.1793.)
15. v.GW5 p. 106 etc.
16. cf. D. Klein, *Der Wandel der dramatischen Darstellungsform im Werk Ernst Tollers (1919–1930)* Ph.D Thesis, Ruhr-Universität Bochum, 1968, pp. 85ff and passim.
17. Pfützner *(op. cit.* p. 26) describes a picture of the setting: Around flag-poles, from each of which the national colours of the five countries were flown, army camps were pitched. One flag-pole was on the upper plinth of the steps, the other four left and right of the open-air stairway, on the arena.
    The review in the *Leipziger Volkszeitung,* also quoted by Pfützner *(loc. cit.),* however, says:
    The 'Leaders' of the states had their places on the steps, which were divided among them, and the 'Masses' were grouped around

the flag-poles in the open space in front of them.
Pfützner could not resolve this contradiction even when he discussed the problem with people who had taken part (*loc. cit.*).

18. Ein prachtvoller Mitspieler ist die Dunkelheit, die unaufhörlich Bilder vernichtet und neue erzeugt. (*loc. cit.*)
19. Es ist nicht das Ende, das der Weltkrieg in Wirklichkeit genommen hat, aber es ist das Ende, das die Kriege in dem Willen und der Sehnsucht der proletarischen Menschen nehmen müssen. (Q. Pfützner *op. cit.* p. 25).
20. Tollers ganzes Denken wurzelt in den Ereignissen des Weltkrieges. (*loc. cit.*)
21. . . . und man blieb so in jeder Beziehung im Dunkeln. (*op. cit.* p. 27)
22. Ludwig Hoffmann/Daniel Hoffman-Ostwald, *Deutsches Arbeitertheater 1918–1933*, Berlin, (DDR) 1961, p. 87.
23. I am thinking particularly of *Hinkemann, Das Schwalbenbuch, & Der entfesselte Wotan.*

D A *HINKEMANN* CHRONOLOGY

26.3.'21	*Deutsche Revolution* in *Das Tagebuch.*
22.5.'21	Letter to Puttkammer re *Fra Dolcino.*
2.2.'22	Letter to Tessa re *Fra Dolcino.*
Jan/Feb '22	Act II Sc 1 of *Die Hinkemanns* in *Volksbühne.* With *'Widmung'.*
1922	Droop sees MS of *Eugen Hinkemann.*
1922	Act III Sc 2 of *Eugen Hinkemann* in *Blätter des Deutschen Theaters (1921/22).* (Not in Spalek. Seen at Marbach.)
1923	Act III Sc 2 of *Der deutsche Hinkemann* in *Die neue Dichtung.* (Publication of book announced as forthcoming.)
13.6.'23	Letter to Stefan Zweig on *Hinkemann.*
Late 1923	1st Edition, *Der deutsche Hinkemann.* (One copy exists with cover only changed to *Hinkemann.*)

19.9.'23	1st production *Der deutsche Hinkemann*. Leipzig.
18.10.'23	Letter to Valtin Hartig. Consternation at pictures of production.
Autumn 1923	Moscow production. Russian translation.
29.11.'23	*Der deutsche Hinkemann* produced at Altenburg Landestheater. About 5 performances.
7.12.'23	*Der deutsche Hinkemann* produced at Karlsruhe, Konzerthaus. 2 performances.
Autumn '23	*Der deutsche Hinkemann* produced at Glauchau.
15.12.'23	*Eugen neschastnyi (Eugen Hinkemann)* produced at Leningrad.
17.1.'24	*Der deutsche Hinkemann* at Dresden. 1 performance.
Early 1924	Cover and title page of remaining copies of 1st edition probably changed to *Hinkemann*.
1924	Letter (n.d. but apparently 1924) to Director of Deutsches Theater, Berlin, asking for title *Hinkemann* to be used. Printed among letters of 1923 in *Briefe aus dem Gefängnis* (GW5 p. 152), but must be later than 17.1.'24, the date of the Dresden scandal.

Further Productions 1924

10.2.'24	*Hinkemann*. Vienna. 1 performance.
9.4.'24	*Hinkemann*. Delitzsch. 1 performance.
11.4.'24	*Hinkemann*. Berlin. Closed performance.
14.4.'24	*Hinkemann*. Berlin. Open performance.
15.7.'24	Toller released from prison.
18.7.'24	Toller attends *Hinkemann* in Berlin.
Spring 1924	*Der blutiker gelekhter (Bloody Laughter)*. Yiddish. New York.
1924	Between April & July. *Der blutiker gelekhter*. Paris.

22.5.'24	*Hinkemann.* Magdeburg. About 6 performances.
15.7.'24	*Hinkemann.* Hamburg. About 40 performances.
1.9.'24	*Hinkemann.* Frankfurt/M. About 30 performances. Co-directed by Toller.
26.12.'24	*Eugen neschastyi.* Moscow.
1924	*Hinkemann.* Cracow.
1924	*Hinkemanis.* Moscow. Latvian Theatre.

(For subsequent productions see Spalek p. 876ff.)

Further Editions 1924

1924	*Hinkemann.* 2nd Edition. (Probably 4–8 thousand). Important changes.
1924	*Hinkemann.* 2nd edition, 2nd impression (Further changes).
1924	*Hinkemann.* 2nd edition, 3rd impression (Some small changes). 14–23 thousand!

(NOTE: Altogether 20,000 copies printed in 1924.)

(For later editions, see Spalek.)

E VARIANT READINGS OF HINKEMANN'S SPEECH IN THE LAST SCENE.

1) GW: which usually follows 1st edtn.
   p. 225.
   "... Alles Sehen wird mir Wissen, alles Wissen Leid. *Ich will nicht mehr.*"
2) Kiepenheuer, Leipzig und Weimar 1979.
   p. 72–73.
   "... Alles Sehen wird mir Wissen, alles Wissen Leid.
   Menschen, die alles Leid leben und dennoch wollen ... i c h w i l l n i c h t m e h r."
3) 2nd Edtn (Spalek 24).
   p. 59.
   As (2).

4) 2nd Edtn, 2nd Impression (Spalek 25).
   p. 59.
   "Alles Sehen wird mir Wissen, alles Wissen Leid . . . Einst wurde mir alles Leid: Wille . . . I c h w i l l n i c h t m e h r."
5) 2nd Edtn, 4th Impression (Spalek 27).
   p. 59.
   "Alles Sehen wird mir Wissen, alles Wissen Leid . . . Alles Leid leben und dennoch wollen . . . I c h w i l l n i c h t m e h r."
6) PBDG
   p. 433 (as 2nd ed. 2nd Imp).
   "Alles Sehen wird mir Wissen, alles Wissen Leid . . . Einst Wurde mir alles Leid: Wille . . . *Ich will nicht mehr.*"

F INTERVIEW WITH STEPHEN WARDALE

Partial Transcription

. . . the old Rusholme Repertory Theatre on Wilmslow Road. Closed as a theatre in 1940. Now a second-hand car salesroom.

The production [of *Draw the Fires*] was by the Manager, Dominic Roche. Two weeks' rehearsal: that was lucky! Opened very well. Packed out for a fortnight. But it was one of those plays that emptied the theatre for the next few weeks, because I think it depressed people a bit. Trouble with Germany then — depressing effect.

Toller tried to copy other producers — Reinhardt, Piscator. [Discussion of his best known plays]
When he was on this Manchester thing, I think he was on the down-grade then.
He never seemed to do anything in England.
We took *Draw the Fires* to the Grand Theatre, Oldham, which is no more, for a week; did fairly well there. Twice nightly, there!
And then we took it to the Arts Theatre, the Cambridge Theatre (London) for a Sunday performance. So it has been performed there, but of course . . . . .
that was a disgraceful performance — we had a stage manager called Arthur Johnson, he'll be dead, so we can use his name, and he always used to think, you know, this German, ordering me, telling me what to do; y'know it was like that. A blazing row at the dress-rehearsal in

London. And Johnson got the sack for his part in it. The Director sacked him for being in a row with the producer — an international producer — they sacked him: but it was disgraceful, it was a disgraceful thing; and I remember, he sent the curtain up on the last scene: with being on that execution scene, and Arthur Johnson sent the curtain up — we'd gone up to change and go down into the boilers; the curtain went up with about two men in the boiler-room.
CWD: You were acting in it, were you?
Yes, yes, I was in this, I played — I was in the boiler-room. One boiler's blown up and a man shouts out, "Minna, Minna"' — he's a bit of a sick man, well, he's blown up and they carry him out dead; we, of course, stayed in the boiler-room, but Toller wanted us to clean up the boiler. We used to say to him, "Now, Toller, if this boiler's been blown up and a man's been killed, these men would not be *able* to get up, it would kill everybody." Eventually what he had done was — when the blow-up, he had a sort of slide come across, the lights went out and a slide came across as though, and a painted scene, as though it was ruined, you know; they only brought one man out screaming about 'Minna, Minna', and then . . .
[Some irrelevant material]

I said to Wilfred Harrison, he seemed to be on the downward grade.
[CWD refers to revival of interest in Toller]
CWD: But in this version they cut all the scenes in the Reichstag, did they?
Yes, there were no Reichstag scenes.
CWD: And otherwise was it fairly realistically staged?
Yes, it was. When it opened, we opened the doors — and we had a sort of ballet when we opened the doors — impressionistic — open the door, one man shovelled coal into the fire, straight off, another shovelled the coal to the other man, there was no coal there, but it was sort of . . .
CWD: You mean imaginary coal?
Yes, but they had the fires there, y'know [CWD: Had a glow]
Yes. But it brought the place down when it came up. Every night it brought the place down — that thing did, you know.
CWD: The actual stoking, you mean?
Yes, yes.
[Discussion of the Reichstag scenes. CWD: less interest to English audiences?]

[Wardale looks at new edition and pictures]
Funny, fifty years since I've seen this.
[Reference to English translation]
Crankshaw we did.

What he did in Manchester. He came up to do *The Blind Goddess*, well, he didn't do it; first night *Manchester Guardian* gave *The Blind Goddess* and Toller a great build-up, everything, on the third night, Toller from London. He didn't like the way the first three scenes were produced, but he liked the rest of it after that. Well, it was a silly thing for an author to say. The *Manchester Guardian* gave us a good crit . , the *Evening News*, but there was a magazine in those days, a paper called *The City News*. So of course the *City News* get this; they're there that night, and of course they start pulling the production to pieces — Dominic Roche has produced it, so of course it looks as though they took Toller's word; you know what journalists are; they don't know whether a play's produced well or not, but they got hold of that, so it caused a sort of row in the press, this lot. Dominic Roche wrote to the *City News*; he didn't quite agree with what Mr Toller had said; he thought it was impudence after giving this play, and it became sort of — a sort of feud.
[CWD: Do you think Toller was being a bit too honest in giving his opinion, he ought really to have said something a bit smooth?]
– He shouldn't have said anything!
Then he said to the girl who played — the woman, he said to her at the party that night, "You are not right for the part, you are too cold, you are too cold."
You know, well, it's hardly a thing to say — because it was very undiplomatic; and he treated poor Hanns Eisler — Y'know the Manchester Playgoers' Club, he was going to address them, he said to him, "You go down and play the piano for them." Y'know there was a lot like that about him. A lot of people . . . . But he was a Bavarian.
[CWD interrupts. Not a Bavarian etc]
He was president of Bavaria for a few days.
[Lots of CWD]
I went into Germany, I went . . . [? to Stuttgart]
I lived at [uncertain, perhaps Sindelfingen], they had a beautiful library there. [He probably means in Stuttgart]
— Kaiser, people like that. I could not read them, but I'd have looked — not one — not one of his!
[CWD on editions of Toller]

He looked an intense man, though, didn't he?
[CWD Auden wrote a poem about him just after his death and referred to him as one who was 'egotistical and brave'.]
That's what he was, egotistical, that's it.
[Conversation on Toller's being an egotist.]
But I know Hanns Eisler did this music for us — and you see all that sort of stuff's forgotten. I wonder what's happened to this music.
[CWD. I don't know, that would be interesting. *Note, 1987: It is at Yale University. See Spalek 88*]
Eisler went back to East Germany. Worked with Brecht.
[Conversation on Brecht]
Hanns Eisler conducted the orchestra, but — the Repertory Theatre Orchestra — an overture to it "Going to Sea" and . . .
He was going to give a lecture in Dublin just after he left Manchester; de Valera said if he set foot in Dublin he'd send him back to Germany — of course that would have been death.
[Conversation on Ireland's neutrality in war etc]
Then I tell you we took it to London and we took it to the Cambridge Theatre on a Sunday — and it must have been in May or June 1935, 'cos it was the week after King George and Queen Mary's 25th Anniversary
[Conversation on Toller's marriage in May to Christiane Grautoff]
When we were going home that night (we'd got to get back to Manchester actually on the Sunday night train) everybody said, "It's all right for Ernst Toller: he's in bed with Christina." [*Note: Wardale consistently referred to Christiane as Christina or Christine*].
10th February. There must be other people living who were in it, but I said to what-y'call [meaning Wilfred Harrison] I must be the only person living; I don't know why I said that when I wrote to him. But I can remember it clearly.
I can remember a lot of things back there clearly.
[Conversation on Gerda Redlich and Toller]
[Some reference to Toller's temper]
He always used to [word not clear] me and he'd tell me something and I didn't know what he's said; when he lost his temper he suddenly said [inaudible], and then he used to come and talk to me.
But Christina [sic] would hold your hand (she was about my age — she'd be about 70 now)
Probably she hadn't had a happy time with him. [CWD: No, I imagine not].
She was a proper German type of girl though, I've seen plenty like her;

her father was a member of the Anglo-British [obviously meaning Anglo-German] Friendship Society.
[More conversation on Christiane and on Toller's liking good hotels etc.]
He stayed at the Midland [i.e. in Manchester]
[Conversation on Spanish Relief etc]
He took everything so much to heart, though, didn't he? You can tell with those eyes, can't you? Other people have had those sort of things; I never knew why, why he was in so much despair with the state the world had got into. He could have done with Buddhism, couldn't he? He wasn't diplomatic. I don't think he'd got great knowledge of production.
[CWD: No, he hadn't. He'd had no means of acquiring it etc]
Now, of course, this is language — when he wanted lighting he didn't know whether front battens or back battens; he didn't know. When someone said "Front batten" then he would echo it, "Front batten."
[CWD: What was his command of English like?]
Fairly good, fairly good.

There was a boy playing with us, I've never seen him since, he'd been to Reinhardt's School in Salzburg, called Tony Allingham, and because Tony Allingham had been to Reinhardt's School he made a bit of a fuss of Tony Allingham; and Tony Allingham, they kicked him out of the Rep. — And when he got to London Tony Allingham wrote him and Toller let him play a sailor. Is it one of the men's mother's who's ... — a sailor comes to see his mother and tell her about the son dying. [CWD: He brings the letter, doesn't he?] — he brings the letter, that letter, well, another boy had been given this, but when he got there he said, "I don't want you to play that." Manchester Rep were bringing it down — he shouldn't have altered the cast. But you see, things like that. And then he got Christine to rehearse him — he was married then. And he said, this chap said, he was expecting a big lot of people there tonight and was expecting a big lot of productions — and he never heard of it again, you see.

He's never been done much in this country, [Conversation on English productions of Toller: *Machine Wreckers* at Half Moon; *Machine Wreckers* in general; and *Blind Goddess*].
Blind Goddess was done after *Draw the Fires* — and then in the first winter of the war they did *Pastor Hall*.
[Neither of these Manchester productions is recorded by Spalek].
They made a film of that. Wilfrid Lawson played it.

[More conversation on his marriage, intensity and suicide].
[CWD (concluding an account of his death): . . . . he d hanged himself].
Yes, he *would* do that, no consideration for anybody else but himself. No, that's just it. I think you've got him there. No consideration. That's it. All his ideas — they're very subjective characters. Thinking of his own . . . — thinking of what-d'y'call-it. He would never think of the woman's coming up. There was no mercy there, was there? There was no kindness there. All this what-d'y'call-it about loving kindness, never thinking about his secretary having to find him.
[CWD on Arthur Sharp's suicide]
Toller had to be dramatic, though, didn't he?
Someone said to me when they'd read that book *I was a German*, "He's a publicist, a self-publicist."
[CWD . . . . no private life]
There was the actor *in* him.
[CWD on dramatisation in the autobiography.]
Then he once went on starvation for so many days.
[Conversation on prison life, on *Seven Plays*, on the autobiography; on Wardale's life after leaving the theatre; on Frank Sladen-Smith; on how people get forgotten, e.g. young theatre people who have not heard of Martin-Harvey.
Reinhardt. Decision to let Wardale hear the tape of Toller's voice. This tape ends abruptly.]

[This interview took place on Friday 11 May 1984 at 68 Banks Court, Ridgeway Park, Timperley].

G *NIE WIEDER FRIEDE*

Examples of W.H. Auden's Lyrics

FINANCIER'S SONG

When it's time for saving hold, but do not spare your neighbour's gold
When it's time for hunting yield to impulse in your neighbour's field
When it's time for war rejoice, but say it was your neighbour's choice
When peace comes, though it's a farce, bear it with patience; it will pass

Chorus:

For snow falls in December,
And roses bloom in May
And vows will break, remember,
And love is for a day.
"The proper thing at the proper season"
Is the golden rule of reason;
So be clever, then, and never
Give yourself away

etc

(English Edition p. 25)

SPY SONG

Spies in the bedroom, spies on the roof,
Spies in the bathroom, we've got proof
Spies on the lawn where the shadows harden,
Spies behind the gooseberries in the kitchen garden,
Spies at the front door, spies at the back,
And hiding in the coat-stand underneath a mac.
Spies in the cupboard under the stairs,
Spies in the cellar, they've been there for years.

Take care, take care!
Beware, beware!
You never know,
You never know.
Eena, meena, mina mo,
You're a spy, so out you go.

etc

(English Edition p. 73)

Examples of Herbert Murrill's Settings

PEACE SONG

(English Edition p. 14)

NOAH'S SONG

(English Edition p. 58)

SPY SONG

(English Edition pp. 72/73)

INDEX

A Note

ä, ö, ü are indexed as a, o, u.

The Definite Article is usually ignored in the alphabetical arrangement.

Toller's works etc are listed under his name in the Index of Persons and not in the General Index.

GENERAL INDEX

INDEX OF PERSONS

Works

Contemporary Theatre Studies title list continued.

Volume 10
The Plays of Ernst Toller: A Revaluation
Cecil Davies

Volume 11
Edward Bond Letters: Volume II
Selected and edited by Ian Stuart

Volume 12
Theatre and Change in South Africa
Edited by Geoffrey V. Davis and Anne Fuchs

Volume 13
Anthropocosmic Theatre
Nicolás Núñez, translated by Ronan Fitzsimons, and edited, with a foreword by Deborah Middleton

Volume 14
Edward Bond Letters: Volume III
Selected and edited by Ian Stuart

Volume 15
Pulp and Other Plays by Tasha Fairbanks
Edited by Gabriele Griffin and Elaine Aston

Volume 16
Art into Theatre: Performance Interviews and Documents
Nick Kaye

Volume 17
Feminist Stages: Interviews with Women in Contemporary British Theatre
Lizbeth Goodman. Research Assistant Jane de Gay

For Product Safety Concerns and Information please contact our EU representative GPSR@taylorandfrancis.com Taylor & Francis Verlag GmbH, Kaufingerstraße 24, 80331 München, Germany

T - #0060 - 090625 - C0 - 246/174/38 - PB - 9783718656158 - Gloss Lamination